Colonial Survey and Native Landscapes in Rural South Africa, 1850–1913

African Social Studies Series

VOLUME 33

The titles published in this series are listed at *brill.com/afss*

Colonial Survey and Native Landscapes in Rural South Africa, 1850–1913

The Politics of Divided Space in the Cape and Transvaal

By

Lindsay Frederick Braun

BRILL

LEIDEN | BOSTON

Cover image: Surveyor E. G. Hall's official photograph of 'Gingqi' trigonometrical beacon, Idutywa district, 1909. A local assistant is shielding the objective lens of the elevated survey instrument (theodolite) from sun glare, creating the impression of standing before an altar to technical precision. Source: H3/1/10, Chief Directorate: National Geo-spatial Information, Department of Rural Development and Land Reform, Mowbray. RSA State Copyright.

Library of Congress Cataloging-in-Publication Data

Braun, Lindsay Frederick.
Colonial survey and native landscapes in rural South Africa, 1850-1913 : the politics of divided space in the Cape and Transvaal / by Lindsay Frederick Braun.
pages cm. -- (African social studies series ; v. 33)
Includes bibliographical references and index.
ISBN 978-90-04-27233-0 (pbk. : alk. paper) 1. Blacks--Land tenure--South Africa. 2. Real property--South Africa. 3. Land tenure--South Africa. 4. South Africa--Politics and government--1836-1909. 5. South Africa--Politics and government--1909-1948. 6. South Africa--Race relations--History--19th century. I. Title. II. Series: African social studies series ; v. 33.
DT1760.B73 2014
333.3096809034--dc23

2014031166

This publication has been typeset in the multilingual "Brill" typeface. With over 5,100 characters covering Latin, IPA, Greek, and Cyrillic, this typeface is especially suitable for use in the humanities. For more information, please see www.brill.com/brill-typeface.

ISSN 1568-1203
ISBN 978-90-04-27233-0 (paperback)
ISBN 978-90-04-28229-2 (e-book)

This book is printed on acid-free paper.

MIX
Paper from responsible sources
FSC® C109576
FSC
www.fsc.org

Printed by Printforce, the Netherlands

Contents

Acknowledgements

This book has taken a long time to research, and nearly as long to write and refine. It takes its shape from the struggles of the past, but it also implicitly concerns investigative journeys through the largely unplumbed (and sometimes arcane) depths of South Africa's mapping and surveying archives in the present. Like most journeys into such historical and personal *terrae incognitae*, mine were not possible without the knowledge, guidance, and kindness of those who know portions of the route and have inspired me to travel it. This is true not least because of the sheer volume of records concerning surveying and land in various South African public and institutional archives, which I feel I barely know even after a decade of research trips and tens of thousands of documents. Accordingly, I owe many debts across three continents and many years for inspiration and tireless efforts on my behalf. The geographical organization of the acknowledgements that follow is for clarity's sake, and is not meant to imply a hierarchy of importance.

Here in the United States, where all of my journeys began, my thanks run the widest gamut. Foremost, I owe an incalculable debt to my colleagues in History at the University of Oregon, where I joined the faculty in 2009. For a supportive and friendly environment, I could not have hoped for better. In particular, Andrew Goble, David Luebke, Glenn May, John McCole, Jim Mohr, Jeff Ostler, Daniel Pope, and Marsha Weisiger have offered supportive comments in various discussions about our respective work that helped me refine and clarify my own thinking. From advice on managing my work and writing style to sage advice about the publishing world, however, virtually every member of our department had some hand in this process. The extraordinary generosity and support of the Brush and Endeavour Faculty Fellowships through the Department of History, as well as additional junior faculty grants from the College of Arts and Sciences here at Oregon, permitted me to conduct several additional seasons of research that have reshaped the entire project for the better. Beyond the confines of History, my friends and compatriots in African Studies across the university have been energetic and encouraging in both word and example, especially Alfredo Burlando, Stephen Dueppen, Daphne Gallagher, Lisa Gilman, Melissa Graboyes, Doris Payne, Janis Weeks, Stephen Wooten, and our recent past librarian for History and Africana, John Russell.

My network of academic support in North America, however, extends far beyond Eugene. Matthew Edney, curator of the Osher Map Library at the University of Southern Maine and now also Director of the History of Cartography Project at the University of Wisconsin-Madison, commented on early papers, asked provocative questions, and provided me pre-publication copies of his own work. Tom Bassett of the University of Illinois likewise sent me English versions of his essays from foreign-language publications. Allen Howard at Rutgers University not only provided crucial insight into concepts of African spatial history, but read chapter drafts and helped me refine my presentation of complex ideas. Michael Adas and Julie Livingston at Rutgers raised my awareness of gaps in my analysis, particularly where African voices were concerned. Graham Burnett at Princeton University helped me to think about research and writing as more of an aesthetic process and less like producing an outsized lab report, and Jim Webb at Colby College convinced me even to enjoy the process through encouragement and example.

At Eastern Michigan University, my *alma mater*, Roger Long has been a mentor, a colleague, and a friend throughout the past two decades. Beyond sharing more good professional advice and editorial commentary on chapters than any student has a right to expect, Roger has provided me with the proverbial kick in the pants more than once. Joseph Engwenyu, who first taught me African history, shaped my path towards thinking about colonial processes as African ones. Twenty years later both scholars retain influences upon this former student's intellectual journey. The late Dick Goff, also from Eastern, provided another indispensable spark on this long journey through his uncompromising standards for research and writing and his inexhaustible supply of patience and goodwill. Dick's students were like family and remained in his thoughts far beyond graduation, and he would have been pleased to see this volume in print. I am proud to count myself among his creations.

There is an aphorism that "South Africa is a small town," and nowhere does it ring more true than in the academic and surveying communities there. In Pretoria, and in South Africa more generally, nobody has done more for me than Elri Liebenberg, Professor Emeritus of Geography at the University of South Africa (UNISA). She kindly made contacts among her vast network for me, provided recommendations, made myriad comments and corrections, and even emailed photographs of documents I'd missed. Her thesis and various papers set me on this road, and she has been immensely supportive of my work for nearly fifteen years now, so it is fitting that I mention my debt to her first. Jane Carruthers, Greg Cuthbertson, and John Lambert created a collegial atmosphere at UNISA during my year in residence (2002–2003), which the US and South African Fulbright Commissions made possible. At the National Archives in Pretoria, the staff was always helpful and patient. I had a number of enlightening conversations with Iain R. Smith, Elizabeth van Heyningen, and Lufuno Mulaudzi while there, which helped to direct my research inquiries. Andy Tladi and André Loubser gave me pointers to enormously useful documents on land restitution and historical memoirs respectively, and I had the good fortune to spend a bit of time with Dr. Mphaya Henry Nemudzivhadi, whose deep knowledge of the history of Ha Ramabulana's great houses cleared up a tremendous number of questions for me. I also benefited from the insights and assistance of Lize Kriel and Johan Bergh at the University of Pretoria. At the Office of the Surveyor-General in Pretoria, Silence Phalanndwa, Derrick de Nysschen (now Surveyor-General in Polokwane), Julian Williamson, and the late Chris van Dyk all assured that I had complete access to the plans and records in their care.

In Cape Town, a variety of offices and archives welcomed me. My very first contacts came from the Chief Directorate: National Geo-spatial Information in the suburb of Mowbray. Richard Wonnacott, then Director of Surveys, not only allowed me to consult the archives, but suffered my constant sharing of new discoveries there and let me arrange and catalog the manuscripts. Linda Fedder and Steven Jansen at NGI have also been great and supportive friends, and have helped me obtain many documents and maps from across the Atlantic. At the Office of the Surveyor-General on Plein Street, my unfettered access to the riches there resulted from the hard work and kindness of many people: Solomon Ross, Sylvia Schuller, and Ncediswa Pepese in the registry, and Surveyor-General John Obree with assistant Surveyors-General Tony Wynne (now retired) and Hendrik van Zyl in administration. Surveyor Chris Esterhuizen patiently explained the logistical vagaries of working in the Transkei, and the deep knowledge of the late Rupert Hurly, who was an active surveyor for most of the twentieth century, helped to acquaint me with the profession as a social entity. Professors Brian Warner, Nigel Worden, and Roger Fisher at the University of Cape Town provided insight, collegiality, and logistical help at various times. At the old Cape Observatory (SAAO) I benefited from the knowledge of astronomer Ian Glass and librarian Shireen Davis. The conscientious staff of the Cape Archives on Roeland Street also kept me well supplied with documents. Jaco van der Merwe was of particularly great assistance when I needed to photograph large maps or find obscure items, and Erika le Roux cleared the path for me to work quickly in my later visits. Further east, Alan Kirkaldy and Jeff Peires at Rhodes University in Grahamstown shared their interest and knowledge during my all-too-brief visit.

In England, I enjoyed the support of many archivists and map historians, catalyzed through the welcome support of the J.B. Harley Fellowships and continuing ever since. My conversations with Christopher Board, Catherine Delano Smith, and Ian Mumford illuminated the metropolitan side of the British cartographic archive for me. At the British Library the Map Librarians, Tony Campbell (now retired), Peter Barber, and Andrew Cook (of the Oriental and India Office Library), provided invaluable support and an on-the-job education. At the Royal Geographical Society, Francis Herbert and Andrew Tatham handled my innumerable questions with clarity and grace. The staffs of the Cambridge University Library, the British Library, and the National Archives also efficiently fulfilled even the oddest requests. James R. Smith, Professor Emeritus at the University of Portsmouth and peripatetic historian of surveying and geodesy, advised me in South Africa and the United Kingdom both. Beyond British shores, the editors at Brill in The Netherlands, particularly Franca de Kort and Joed Elich, have been diligent yet patient with this first-time author. My gratitude extends to the series editors as well as the anonymous reviewers and my copy editor, Tamara Holloway, whose helpful advice I hope I have done justice. Although I have refined my ideas and hunted down my errors assiduously, any shortcomings in the text that follows are mine alone.

Finally, beyond the purely academic journey, my small but supportive circle of family and loved ones has also been essential to my spiritual and emotional well-being in this entire process. In Oregon, my partner Larissa Ennis has done more than anyone to keep us both sane despite my tendency to work in unpredictable bursts, and I am endlessly grateful for her affection but also for her forbearance and her endurance in the face of an often nerve-wracking intellectual process. My sister Lisa, brother-in-law Joe, and my niece and nephew Sarah and Daniel are all vital anchors to the world outside my office. Finally, I owe the greatest debt to my mother, Thayer, who is still very close to my heart even though she was unable to see the completion of this project. She, too, extolled the freedom of discovery and the value of knowledge, and in so doing sent a son into the world to seek knowledge and to return both smarter and wiser. That journey can never be quite complete, but it is to her memory and ongoing example that I dedicate this work.

A few passages from Chapters 1 and 5–7 have appeared in prior publications, but in radically different forms. Those publications are "Dividing Native Lands on the Cape and Transvaal Frontiers, ca. 1864–1900," in *The History of Surveying and Land Tenure Collected Papers Volume 2*, ed. R.C. Fisher (Cape Town: Institute of Professional Land Surveyors, 2004), 93–126; "Spatial Institutionalisation and the Settler State: Survey and Mapping in the Eastern Transvaal, 1852–1905," *South African Historical Journal* 53 (2005): 146–178; and "The Returns of the King: The Case of Mphephu and Western Venda, 1899–1904," *Journal of Southern African Studies* 39, no. 2 (2013): 271–291. The editors have kindly permitted my use of that material in this volume. Copyrights for the images reproduced in this volume remain with the originating agencies or current repositories that have generously permitted their reproduction, as indicated in the captions.

Notes on Terminology and Usage

Questions of orthography and ontology are difficult ones in the context of colonial Africa generally and South Africa specifically, so any author must make careful choices. Generalization and universalization in the name of concision or consistency are potentially occlusive, especially when applied to groups of people or corporate entities. I therefore seek to employ identic terms with care so not to diminish the importance of kinship and patronage networks in particular circumstances, including the flexible, cross-cutting relationships and lines of authority at varying levels, even between individuals from very distinct groups. Outside of quotations, I primarily employ present-day academic spellings of proper nouns for social or political groups, but for Bantu names I use only the roots (e.g., "Sotho strategies," "Xhosa-speakers," or "Venda territories"). Because the meanings and extents of these labels were neither fixed nor absolute between categories of speakers, I explain the differences where necessary. The one major exception is the specific case of Fingoes, or Mfengu, who are partially defined by their position relative to colonial patronage. There, I have opted to use the term 'Fingo'—still used in English—in preference to the more modern Xhosa back-formation.[1] Several quotations and office titles include language that is quite offensive today, but I have tried to minimize that occurrence. Finally, the adjective 'colonial' includes the South African Republic (Transvaal) and Orange Free State, as well as the self-governing British colonies, because it accurately reflects the nature of those settler states and their relationship to the land regardless.[2]

In other matters, I err on the side of contemporary usage. I use colonial parlance and spelling (e.g., 'Tembuland') where it appropriately reflects colonial perception and division, especially with features of administrative geography like town or district names. For the same reason I employ the old geographical term 'Transvaal' where the shorthand is relevant. I carry this philosophy over to the use of those contemporary spellings and names on certain key maps. When dealing with personal names and office titles, I also prefer

1 Alan Webster, "Unmasking the Fingo: The War of 1835 Revisited," in *The Mfecane Aftermath: Reconstructive Debates in Southern African History*, ed. Carolyn Hamilton (Johannesburg: University of Witwatersrand Press, 1995), 241–276, esp. 241 n. 1; Timothy Stapleton, "The Expansion of a Pseudo-Ethnicity on the Eastern Cape: Reconsidering the Fingo 'Exodus' of 1865," *International Journal of African Historical Studies* 29 (1996): 235.

2 On definitions, see Jürgen Osterhammel, *Colonialism: A Theoretical Overview*, trans. S. Frisch (Princeton: Markus Wiener, 2005), 11–12.

contemporary spellings when no significant variation exists. In the case of personal names, offices, and place names assigned in Bantu languages, textual variations could be vast in the era under study, so I generally employ the spellings used by historians today (e.g., for Mphephu, who was variously M'pefu, Mpefu, Piffaw, Impepu, and Mphefu in documents). Patents of nobility appear in cases where contemporaries knew the individual in question under that name (e.g., Lord Selbourne), but I avoid primarily honorific titles such as knighthoods ('Sir') and orders (such as K.C.M.G.) wherever possible otherwise. In the interests of readability, parenthetical birth and death dates for individuals (when known) are restricted to picture captions or the index.

Finally, two climatic notes are in order. Readers north of the equator should keep in mind that the seasonal references I make are local to South Africa; that is, the seasons are reversed (summer in January, winter in July). Second, summer is the primary season for rainfall everywhere except the southwestern Cape Colony, not winter as is the case there and in other temperate climes. These facts affect discussions of land clearance, planting, and harvest that figure into land inspection and survey differently in the two main areas under study.

List of Illustrations

Maps

Photographs

List of Abbreviations

(For descriptions of manuscript record classes, please see the bibliography.)

ASG	Assistant Surveyor-General
AYB	*Archives Year Book for South African History*
BNA	UK National Archives, Kew
BPP	Command Papers, House of Commons, UK
CPP	Cape Parliamentary Papers (Official Publications)
CUL	Cambridge University Library, UK
F.A.M.P.	Frontier Armed and Mounted Police, Cape Colony
KAB	Cape Archives Depot, Cape Town
LMG	*Landmeter Generaal* (Surveyor-General), South African Republic
NGI	Chief Directorate: National Geospatial Information, Mowbray, SA
RA-PTA	Registrar of Deeds, Pretoria
RDLR	Department of Rural Development and Land Reform, SA
RE	Royal Engineers
SAAO	South African Astronomical Observatory, Cape Town
SAB	National Archvies Depot, Pretoria
SANAC	South African Native Affairs Commission (1903–1905)
SG	Surveyor-General
SGO-Cape	Office of the Surveyor-General, Cape Town
SGO-PKW	Office of the Surveyor-General, Polokwane
SGO-PTA	Office of the Surveyor-General, Pretoria
SPP	Union of South Africa Parliamentary Papers (Official Publications)
TAB	Transvaal Archives Depot, Pretoria
TKP	Transvaal Colony Publications (Official Publications)
URB	*Uitvoerende Raadsbesluit* (Resolution of the Executive Council, ZAR)
VOC	*Vereenigde Oostindische Compagnie* (Dutch East India Company)
VRB	*Volksraadsbesluit* (Resolution of the Legislature, ZAR)
ZAR	*Zuid-Afrikaansche Republiek* (South African Republic)
ZPP	ZAR Official Publication

CHAPTER 1

Introduction

The Construction of Colonial Territory

> I may here note that I have searched in vain through our colonial South African codes of law, without discovering any recognition of *native* land tenures, other than those invented for the natives by their European rulers and legislators. Had any such really aboriginal land tenures been found existing, with recognized force among the native tribes subdued by, or annexed to, the Colony, they could hardly fail to have been mentioned in codes...
>
> H.B.E. FRERE, 1883[1]

Between the 1850s, when Britain first acceded to limited local governance in the Cape Colony and withdrew from the Boer republics of the South African Highveld, and the advent of the Natives Land Act (No. 27) of 1913, surveyors and cartographers constructed the geographical basis of the modern South African state. During that period agents of the various governments of the region divided, labeled, charted, and numeralized most of the space within its present-day borders. During that same era white settlers and colonial officials claimed enormous swathes of land, progressively restricted black landholders' ownership and free occupancy rights to a tiny fraction of the country, and incorporated the landed and landless alike into an economy dominated by settler and mining capital. These processes were inextricably connected, but they were not linear or even unilateral. The colonial system of territorial demarcation and geographical knowledge encoded the extent, ownership, use, and sometimes meaning of land, but it could and did have to take the demands of other groups and individuals into account. Survey and mapping in South Africa

1 H. Bartle Frere, "On Systems of Land Tenure among Aboriginal Tribes in South Africa," *Journal of the Anthropological Institute of Great Britain and Ireland* 12 (1883): 262. Frere was Governor and High Commissioner in Cape Town from 1877 to 1880, and while there championed comprehensive systems of survey and land tenure on European models; see "Copy of Memorandum on South African Surveys," 15 Feb 1879, pp. 163–165, RGO 15/98, Royal Greenwich Observatory Archives, Cambridge University Library (CUL). For an early differing view on African land tenures in this era, see Elizabeth Colson, "The Impact of the Colonial Period on the Definition of Land Rights," in *Colonialism in Africa 1870–1960*, ed. Victor Turner (Cambridge: Cambridge University Press, 1971), 3:193.

 | DOI 10.1163/9789004282292_002

themselves have attracted sporadic scholarly attention in brief critical discussions, popular accounts, or technical summaries, but the central question remains: How did this landscape of plots and boundaries come into existence, and what did the acts of depicting and dividing land mean to the various people involved?

Colonial Survey and Native Landscapes in Rural South Africa is my attempt to address this persistent question during a critical period in its evolution. This book explores the establishment of fixed boundaries and new models of proprietorship across rural South African landscapes prior to the 1913 Land Act, and the ways that people interacted with this new language and logic of spatial order. The argument I present here is twofold. First, colonial survey and the creation of boundaries involved a far greater amount of negotiation and subjectivity relative to local landscapes and communities than its presentation or its practitioners admitted. Second, the landscape of properties and boundaries that resulted—a cadastral landscape—increasingly became the new frame of reference for action, whether people on the land saw them as tools or treated them as obstacles; they were arguably hegemonic in form but not in meaning. These two arguments are particularly relevant for so-called native landscapes, to use a deliberately anachronistic term that reflects predominant views of African social practices and spatial organization as retrograde relative to their settler counterparts. Native landscapes included not only titled farms with nonwhite owners or tenants and smallholder lots where European forms of land tenure obtained, but also the lands that various governments held out as reserves for 'communal tenure' and 'traditional authority,' which were neither.[2] It was an evolutionary process, rife with hybrid and incomplete knowledge about what these new spaces meant. Although the transformation of societies and changes in ideas about landscape certainly did not cease in 1913, the tremendous shocks of later state interventions (such as forced removals or the policies of Betterment and Rehabilitation from 1939 onward) started from the same basic framework of spaces, as do efforts at redress today.

The new landscapes that surveyors, inspectors, administrators, and magistrates presented, as well as their manners of representation, therefore determined the basis for later contests over ground between the state, white settlers, and extant African societies. Whether an act of land division served to atomize African social networks, overwrote their presence, or simply set them apart from the settler-dominated colonial landscape, earlier patterns of habitation

2 Ben Cousins, "More than Socially Embedded: The Distinctive Character of 'Communal Tenure' Regimes and its Implications for Land Policy," *Journal of Agrarian Change* 7, no. 3 (2007): 282–283.

and local circumstances were normally left so transparent on survey documents that a distant administrator like Frere could earnestly believe them to be ephemeral or irrelevant. It was a fundamental irony of imperial cartography that the equations describing spaces, and the panoptic of maps and plans imagining the colonial landscape, were never meant for the people they most affected.[3]

This irony certainly holds true for South Africa, and in fact it may be doubly ironic because the Land Act, and the cadastral spaces set down mostly before its passage, form chronological, physical, and legal boundaries for land restitution claims today. But the converse was also true before 1913: African subjects did not ascribe the same level of constraining power or the same intention to the surveyor's output that the state machinery of native administration did, even though people recognized its existence and operated within its bounds to varying degrees. Surveyors and cartographers in the employ of successive governments evaluated claims and balanced directives while creating precise title diagrams, plans, and maps. But that textual output, now part of the archives and registries of the state, has flattened the discourse that created it in favor of a single, unitary vision of landscape.[4] In turn these documents define a high modernist legal and conceptual framework that persisted throughout the intervening eras and still subtly inform every discussion about land in South Africa today. The technicians and informants have become invisible, and their work has taken on its own life and authority.[5] If we render the contemporary exchanges and contests around the technical agents of the state visible, however, the constraints and contingencies that attended their activities become clear.

A more nuanced history of land division has importance not only within South Africa, but through much of the former colonial world. The negotiation and conflict over boundaries and land that were inherent to territorial delineation in the colonies and republics of southern Africa, where settlers of European descent were a minority from the 1840s onward, invite comparison to other settler societies and colonial regimes that share one or another of its features.[6] Settler societies in the Americas, across Africa, and in the

3 Matthew H. Edney, "The Irony of Imperial Mapping," in *The Imperial Map: Cartography and the Mastery of Empire*, ed. James R. Akerman (Chicago: University of Chicago Press, 2009), 32–41.

4 David McDermott Hughes, *From Enslavement to Environmentalism: Politics on a South African Frontier* (Seattle: University of Washington Press, 2006), 9.

5 Raymond B. Craib, "The Archive in the Field: Document, Discourse, and Space in Mexico's Agrarian Reform," *Journal of Historical Geography* 36 (2010): 418.

6 On geography and comparability, see Lorenzo Veracini, "The Imagined Geographies of Settler Colonialism," in *Making Settler Colonial Space: Perspectives on Race, Place, and Identity*, ed.

Pacific, among other regions, universally sought to determine what, if any, 'native title' existed on the land before their arrival; by extinguishing, dismissing, or otherwise reorganizing it, they laid the foundation for the legitimacy of their own legal and spatial orders.[7] Land alienation combined with colonial subjugation not only created unrest at the time, but later led to such anticolonial movements as the Land and Freedom Army movement (colloquially 'Mau Mau') in Kenya, rural struggle and civil war in Algeria, Namibia, Mozambique, and elsewhere, and later confrontations such as the politically-fraught Fast Track land reform program after 2000 in Zimbabwe.[8] Earlier struggles are still written on the landscape, and in former settler colonies around the world the issues of land ownership and distribution remains a central—if not *the* central—focus for measures of justice and redress of grievances against the historical state.[9] Through the ongoing presumption of scientific objectivity in survey and mapping, the labels and lines set down by these colonial technicians have enjoyed "remarkable persistence."[10] People on the most fractured settler-colonial landscapes have incorporated these parcels into an emergent cadastral politics that today places greater value on measures of land and less on relationships of clientage.[11]

This volume approaches the creation and negotiation geographical knowledge in South Africa through the relationships between surveys, mapping, native policy, and land tenure before 1913 (and occasionally a bit later) in two distinctly different areas (see Map 1.1). The first area includes the Kei river valley, particularly the four districts grouped together in 1878 as 'Fingoland and the Idutywa Reserve,' which experienced a colonial project of social engineering and

---

Tracey Banivanua Mar and Penelope Edmonds (New York: Palgrave Macmillan, 2010), 180–181.

7 Michael P. Adas, "From Settler Colony to Global Hegemon: Integrating the Exceptionalist Narrative of the American Experience in World History," *American Historical Review* 106, no. 5 (2001): 1704–1720; John C. Weaver, *The Great Land Rush and the Making of the Modern World, 1650–1900* (Kingston, ON: McGill-Queen's University Press, 2003), 11–45, 133–177.

8 See D. Anderson and D. Throup, "The Agrarian Economy of Central Province, Kenya, 1918 to 1939," in *The Economies of Africa and Asia in the Inter-War Depression*, ed. Ian Brown (New York: Routledge, 1989), 8–28; H. Bernstein, "Land Reform in Southern Africa in World-Historical Perspective," *Review of African Political Economy* 96 (2003): 203–226; Tapiwa Zimudzi, "Power Syndrome: Robert Mugabe and the Land Reform and Governance Crisis in Zimbabwe," *South African Historical Journal* 47 (2002): 213–228; Sam Moyo, "Three Decades of Agrarian Reform in Zimbabwe," *Journal of Peasant Studies* 38 (2011): 493–531.

9 See Karin Lehmann, "Aboriginal Title, Indigenous Rights, and the Right to Culture," *South African Journal of Human Rights* 20 (2004): 86–118.

10 Hughes, *From Enslavement to Environmentalism*, 49; A.J. Christopher, *The British Empire at its Zenith* (London: Croom Helm, 1988), 198.

11 Hughes, *From Enslavement to Environmentalism*, 45–46.

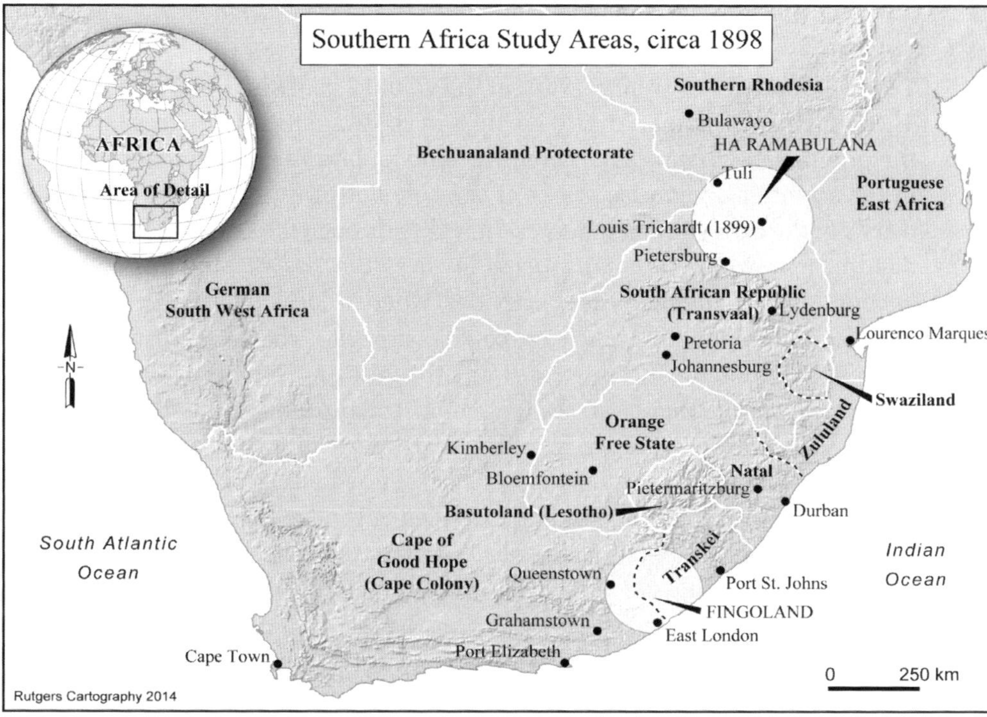

MAP 1.1 *Main areas of study.*

atomization that involved relatively direct interaction. The second region includes the powerful kingdoms of the former northeastern Transvaal, particularly the Venda kingdom of Ha Ramabulana. That kingdom retained its *de facto* independent authority over extensive lands until its military subjugation in 1898, but maintained unexpected territorial potency afterward. These areas' distinct histories—the former a territory of people supposedly 'without chiefs' and the latter a region of well-defined kingdoms—show that differences in backgrounds, interactions between evolving social and cultural ideas in settler and African societies, and varying relationships with colonial administrations produced distinct native landscapes within the colony. These clusters of spaces existed between the extremes of dispossession and autonomy, and offered different venues for action. The variable arrangements of space and authority in each colony after the South African War (1899–1902) brought forth complications that fed into the 1913 Natives Land Act. The Act in turn was an important step towards the later elevation of spatial and cultural segregation to an official policy goal.[12]

12 Saul Dubow, *Racial Segregaion and the Origins of Apartheid in South Africa* (London: Macmillan, 1989), 21–50; Phyllis Lewsen, "Liberals in Politics and Administration,

Conceptual Frameworks and Geographical Knowledge

Two major processes were at work in the colonial geography of South Africa. The first was the state's drive to create and control territorial spaces through the production of knowledge about the land and its inhabitants, culminating in the scientifically precise assays of the colonial surveyor and the universal claims of the cartographer to represent reality through the selective use of that data on maps.[13] The second process involves the less visible cross-cultural encounters that attended these activities, wherein local actors with differing agendas and competing knowledge could complicate, change, and sometimes entirely confound the first process. Both processes involved the deployment of diverse *metageographies*—a "set of spatial structures through which people order their knowledge of the world"—that informed identities and actions across the colony and, through experience, defined places of meaning within broader conceptual landscapes and extended beyond what was visible.[14] Both processes also proved to be a great deal thornier than any of the parties imagined at the outset, and did not involve simple binaries of domination and resistance but a broader constellation of forces that affected the process of spatial reorganization in unexpected ways. Local parties could oppose, ignore, or co-opt surveyors and their work, and colonial administrators sometimes also saw greater benefits in leaving certain ambiguities intact for the cartographer to paper over. These balances changed over time, as we shall see.

In theory, the surveyor was a perfect observer of a neutral landscape who commanded sophisticated instrumentation and measurement technologies, usually a theodolite, standard chains or alloy tapes for measurement, trigonometrical tables, and a variety of other optical and computational equipment. With such vestments of science, he could divine an accurate and precise

---

1936–1948," in *Democratic Liberalism in South Africa: Its History and Prospect*, ed. Jeffrey Butler, Richard Elphick, and David Welsh (Cape Town: David Philip, 1987), 98–100.

13 On the positivism of scientific cartography, see the 1989 essay "Deconstructing the Map" in J.B. Harley, *The New Nature of Maps: Essays in the History of Cartography*, ed. Paul Laxton (Baltimore: Johns Hopkins University Press, 2001), 153–158.

14 Martin Lewis and Kären Wigen, *The Myth of Continents: A Critique of Metageography* (Berkeley: University of California Press, 1997), ix; John McAleer, *Representing Africa: Landscape, Exploration, and Empire in Southern Africa, 1780–1870* (Manchester: Manchester University Press, 2010), 15–17; Allen M. Howard, "Nodes, Networks, Landscapes, and Regions: Reading the Social History of Tropical Africa 1700s–1920," in *The Spatial Factor in African History: The Relationship of the Social, Material, and Perceptual*, ed. Allen M. Howard and Richard M. Shain (Leiden: Brill, 2005), 26–27, 30–31, 73–74. For reasons of simplicity, I prefer 'geographies' to 'metageographies.'

geographical fix for lots and boundaries that the cartographer or compiler—who was sometimes the surveyor himself—could arrange according to logical precepts. In reality, surveyors were often unreliable even by the standards of their own profession, leading to wild variations in quality and reliability of even basic measurements into the twentieth century. Surveyors, cartographers, inspectors, magistrates, and other colonial authorities correspondingly corrected colonial surveys and maps subjectively, although they may have differed in how to deal with spaces of uncertainty.[15] Surveys and maps were tactically significant acts, conceived and executed in particular colonial contexts that extended beyond physical geography into social and cultural realms.

Those acts, however, were neither the simple transposition of a far-away ethos of imperial control nor objective acts of scientific divination, and their proliferation particularly in the British empire as a basis for control seems at odds with how unreliably those surveys represented the land.[16] Survey and mapping never faced basic philosophical scrutiny as a form of knowledge, and colonial logic attributed all failings to the vagaries of political economy, insufficient clarity of purpose, or the personal limitations of surveyor and surveyed.[17] Geographical knowledge embodied progress to the colonial state, even though that knowledge was itself an illusion of order.

In order to maintain this illusion, the geographical and legal bodies of the state needed to seem complete if nothing else. The aggregation of observations, surveys, plans, and maps formed a crucial piece of the archives that governments used to devise or analyze policy. This 'geographical archive,' as described by map historian Matthew Edney, is the official body of knowledge that enabled the reconstruction of territory for myriad exploitative purposes, be they pragmatic (settlement, taxation, mining) or vain (personal or imperial glory)—in short, the "territorial imperatives of a particular political system."[18]

15 On surveyors' omissions versus cartographers' commissions, see D. Graham Burnett, *Masters of All They Surveyed: Exploration, Geography, and a British El Dorado* (Chicago: University of Chicago Press, 2000), 10–12.

16 Edward Said, *Culture and Imperialism* (New York: Vintage Books, 1994), 7; Patricia Seed, *Ceremonies of Possession in Europe's Conquest of the New World* (Cambridge: Cambridge University Press, 1995), 146.

17 Clare Kelso, "Ideology of Mapping in Apartheid South Africa," *South African Geographical Journal* 81, no. 1 (1999): 15.

18 Matthew Edney, *Mapping an Empire: The Geographical Construction of British India, 1765–1843* (Chicago: University of Chicago, 1997), 39–41; Christopher, *British Empire*, 195; J.B. Harley, "Maps, Knowledge, and Power," in *The Iconography of Landscape*, ed. Denis Cosgrove and Stephen Daniels (Cambridge: Cambridge University Press, 1988), 279. Giselle Byrnes applies a similar concept to the graphical and textual discourses of

In the context of the colony, this archive rendered space knowable and governable, and by extension exposed it to further rational, logical reorganization (or 'rationalization') by state agents. Europeans conflated the accuracy of this geographical archive, like other forms of colonial knowledge, with the strength of its scientific precision. This acceptance of the authority of that archive and its adjudicators, even though it was often wildly inaccurate or misrepresentative, had troubling implications. Europeans might summarily dismiss any data the technicians of empire did *not* explicitly record or that did not fit into their framework of knowledge, as with the indigenous land tenures in Frere's account. Rural inhabitants' ideas of landscape and ownership, and their historical interactions with the archive of the state and its scientific practitioners, however, had an effect on the creation of that knowledge which still resonates.[19] This book employs that same problematic archive, but evaluates its contents in a critical way to draw out the conditions of its production.

The broader colonial drive to reorganize spaces on a small scale and simplify complex structures, the better to control human and material resources, also figures prominently in encounters between various state agents of spatial and social rationalization and non-state actors. Political scientist James Scott employs the useful Foucauldian concept of 'legibility' to describe the state's effort to collect knowledge and produce recognizable and controllable spatial and social order, through processes that historian Bernard Cohn terms 'modalities,' including enumeration, survey, observation, and surveillance.[20] Such measures included not only the construction of the geographical archive, but also the creation and deployment of criminal and civil legal codes, the collection of demographic information through censuses, and the reorganization of systems of authority. Although Scott's view tends to efface

surveying in New Zealand, which she terms the "survey archive." See Giselle Byrnes, *Boundary Markers: Land Surveying and the Colonisation of New Zealand* (Wellington: Bridget William Books, 2001), 10.

19 Craib, "The Archive in the Field," 420. Like most geographical archives, the South African one is 'living,' meaning that its territorial files are still at government institutions that consult or amend them as needed.

20 James C. Scott, *Seeing Like a State: How Certain Schemes to Improve the Human Condition Have Failed* (New Haven: Yale University Press, 1998), 5, 80, 89, 223; Bernard S. Cohn, *Colonialism and its Forms of Knowledge: The British in India* (Princeton: Princeton University Press, 1996), 6–8, 10–11. See also Roger J.P. Kain and Elizabeth Baigent, *The Cadastral Map in the Service of the State* (Chicago: University of Chicago Press, 1992), 328–329; Thomas Richards, *The Imperial Archive: Knowledge and the Fantasy of Empire* (London: Verso, 1993), 5–9.

individual interactions and motives in the creation of this order, it is an effective description of broad state aspirations to control through information.

The informational functions of the state were the province of colonial experts, who determined what knowledge mattered and how properly to present it to the colonial archive. The figure of the expert tended to mute the voices of other intellectual actors within the colony, white and nonwhite alike. Even when they directly mediated the knowledge of colonial subjects or synthesized new understandings using it, experts in law, linguistics, medicine, ethnography, religion, and (of course) geography expressed their ideas using language and formats that colonial governments accepted as legitimate and authoritative.[21] Legibility was therefore an important goal of the state, but status determined what could be read and who could read it. However, the colonial state did not possess a monopoly on relevant spatial information, nor did it produce it in a vacuum. One implicit argument in this book is that a different kind of legibility was also important for local people, who exchanged knowledge with state actors and one another in ways that historian of science Kapil Raj describes as "reciprocal, albeit asymmetric, processes of circulation and negotiation."[22]

Beyond local interactions, the late nineteenth and early twentieth centuries also witnessed dramatic changes in the material and social relationships between map, survey, and landscape within the colonial empires more widely. The massive expansion in cartographic production, and mass consumption, allowed a broader European public to share the totalizing gaze of kings and minsters, and so make empires conceptually their own.[23] Yet this crucial transformative era remains one of the most poorly understood in the history of colonial surveying and cartography. Histories of exploratory enterprises flourish, as do discussions of European literature in creating the conceptual space

21 Dmitri van den Bersselaar, "Acknowledging Knowledge: Dissemination and Reception of Expertise in Colonial Africa," *History in Africa* 33 (2006): 390; Matthew G. Hannah, *Governmentality and the Mastery of Territory in Nineteenth-Century America* (Cambridge: Cambridge University Press, 2000), 114–117. Hannah also makes an explicit analytical link between Scott and Cohn, although some of Scott's critics find his approach to be itself reductive and essentialist; see Frederick Cooper, *Colonialism in Question: Theory, Knowledge, History* (Berkeley: University of California Press, 2005), 141.

22 Kapil Raj, *Relocating Modern Science: Circulation and the Construction of Knowledge in South Asia and Europe, 1650–1900* (New York: Palgrave Macmillan, 2007), 13.

23 Christian Jacob, *The Sovereign Map: Theoretical Approaches in Cartography throughout History*, ed. Ed Dahl, trans. Tom Conley (Chicago: University of Chicago Press, 2006), 325–327.

of the colony that sometimes extend to cartographic themes.[24] Critical studies of colonial cartography and surveying during the late 1800s only began to appear around 2000, despite a much older chorus of historians and geographers who saw the link between maps and empire during this era.[25] Nevertheless, historians remain comparatively reticent to engage late-nineteenth-century colonial geography for a variety of reasons, among them the map-trade bias in favor of earlier maps, the great epistolary messiness of the period, the silence of many surveyors while in the field (South Africa, for example, did not require detailed reporting until 1929), and the sheer confusion attendant upon the introduction of cheap lithography and pulp paper by the middle of the nineteenth century that radically expanded cartographic output.[26]

The result of this reticence is that discussions of mapping in colonial Africa generally follow a variant of the positivist, triumphal narrative of Western scientific progress and technological achievement so persistent in historical overviews of state surveying and cartography.[27] In that narrative, Africa has no

24 Burnett, *Masters of All They Surveyed*; Felix Driver, *Geography Militant: Cultures of Exploration and Empire* (London: Blackwell, 2001), 39–40; Mary Louise Pratt, *Imperial Eyes: Travel Writing and Transculturation* (London: Routledge, 1992), esp. 201–227; Itala Vivan, "Geography, Literature, and the African Territory: Some Observations on the Western Map and the Representation of Territory in the South African Literary Imagination," *Research in African Literatures* 31 (2000): 49–69; Michelle Adler, "'Skirting the Edges of Civilization': Two Victorian Women Travelers and 'Colonial Spaces' in South Africa," in *Text, Theory, Space: Land, Literature and History in South Africa and Australia*, ed. Kate Darian-Smith, Liz Gunner, and Sarah Nuttall (London: Routledge, 1996), 83–98; Zbignew Białas, *Mapping Wild Gardens: The Symbolic Conquest of South Africa* (Essen: Die Blaue Eule, 1997).

25 Cole Harris, *Making Native Space: Colonialism, Resistance, and Reserves in British Columbia* (Vancouver: UBC Press, 2002); Ian J. Barrow, *Making History, Drawing Territory: British Mapping in India, c.1763–1905* (Oxford: Oxford University Press, 2003); Raymond B. Craib, *Cartographic Mexico: A History of State Fixations and Fugitive Landscapes* (Durham: Duke University Press, 2004); James Akerman, ed., *The Imperial Map: Cartography and the Mastery of Empire* (Chicago: University of Chicago Press, 2009); Alan Lester, "Introduction: Historical Geographies of Southern Africa," *Journal of Southern African Studies* 29, no. 3 (2003): 596.

26 On the privileging of earlier maps, see Jeffrey C. Stone, *A Short History of the Cartography of Africa* (Lewiston: Edwin Mellen, 1995), 47–48; on the effect of lithography, see Ian Mumford, "Milestones in Nineteenth-Century Lithography" (PhD diss., University of Reading, 1999). In the monumental Wisconsin *History of Cartography* project, the nineteenth century volume (v. 5) was the last to get underway, and the only one of the six to commence out of chronological order.

27 John Pickles, *A History of Spaces: Cartographic Reason, Mapping, and the Geo-Coded World* (New York: Routledge, 2004), 61; R.S. Rose-Redwood, "The Surveyor's Model of the

maps or geographical awareness until Europeans arrive, map the coast, and incorporate information solicited from informants and explorers into crude interior maps. Those become the basis for territorial claims until ever more precise triangulations and mapping operations produce authoritative, planimetrically accurate maps of Africa that eventually link local colonial orders to a broader European global order. This narrative of progress and discovery is so transparent that few articulated its broad structure before geographer Jeffrey Stone divided the process into overlapping stages in 1995.[28] But even in more critical discussions of the place of survey and mapping within the imperial project, the agency remains European. Such studies keep mapping squarely in the realm of settler history and European science, even though African knowledge visibly influenced exploration, boundary commissions, and the cartography that emerged from those activities.[29]

African understandings of space, however, usually figure only insofar as Europeans directly confirm their existence and contribution, because there is little independent textual evidence of nonliterate Africans' geographical awareness and their effect on map output. The critical conceptual point for the history of cartography is that African maps, and by extension claims on the territory, are somehow *absent*. By demanding that only a direct analogue of the European map can be considered as evidence of sophisticated geographies among Africans, that knowledge is given a solely European origin in contrast to the distinct and usually retrograde knowledge of Africans, in a model that scientific historian Helen Tilley calls "epistemic pluralism."[30] This tendency to focus on the European side of the encounter between cosmographical models in Africa may not be intentional, but it reflects a Europe-centered institutional

World: The Uses and Abuses of History in Introductory Surveying Textbooks," *Cartographica* 39, no. 4 (2004): 45–54.

28 Stone, *Short History*, 109–136.

29 Paul Nugent, "Arbitrary Lines and the People's Minds: A Dissenting View on Colonial Boundaries in West Africa," in *African Boundaries: Barriers, Conduits, and Opportunities*, ed. A.J. Asiwaju and Paul Nugent (New York: Pinter, 1996), 41–46; Thomas J. Bassett, "Cartography and Empire Building in Nineteenth-Century West Africa," *Geographical Review* 84 (1994): 316–335; Thomas J. Bassett, "African Influences on European Mapping of Africa in the 19th and Early 20th Centuries," English manuscript version of chapter in *Culture dell'Alterità: il territorio africano e le sue rappresentazioni*, ed. E.C. Moreschi (Milan: UNICOPLI, 1998), 359–371; Howard, "Nodes, Networks, Landscapes, and Regions," 78. Ironically, contemporary reports often acknowledged debts to African informants.

30 Helen Tilley, *Africa as a Living Laboratory: Empire, Development, and the Problem of Scientific Knowledge, 1870–1950* (Chicago: University of Chicago Press, 2011), 328–332.

and archival inertia that still affects the study of scientific history.[31] The evidence that historians of geography want is sometimes quite different from the evidence that actually exists, although a number of scholars have called attention to this African input from time to time.[32]

The privileging of literacy and exact sciences during the colonial era tended to further remove African knowledge from the realm of colonial rationality. However, oral and sometimes graphical systems of geographical knowledge involving time, space, and power already existed across West Africa and permitted the administration of bureaucratically complex states.[33] Complex geographies also produced undeniably cartographic representations in literate areas of the Horn of Africa, the Swahili Coast, and the Sahel.[34] None of these systems or maps corresponded exactly to the totalizing and ostensibly precise geographic pretensions of scientific Europe at the time, a fact that prolongs the condition of colonial myopia about geography. But if we consider social, spiritual, or cultural meanings that were not normally, or at least openly, incorporated into the body of European geographical science in the nineteenth and early twentieth centuries, the realm of geographical and cartographic discourse grows immensely. Pictorial and discursive expressions further enhance

31 See J.M. Blaut, *The Colonizer's Model of the World: Geographical Diffusionism and Eurocentric History* (New York: Guilford Press, 1993), 108–119.

32 Jeffrey C. Stone, "Pioneer Geodesy: The Arc of the 30th Meridian in Former Northern Rhodesia," *Cartographic Journal* 13 (1976): 122–128; Charles G. Hunt, "Some Notes on Indigenous Map-Making in Africa," in *Maps and Africa*, ed. Jeffrey C. Stone (Aberdeen: University of Aberdeen, 1993), 32–35; Stone, *Short History*, Chapters 5–9; Thomas J. Bassett, "Indigenous Mapmaking in Intertropical Africa," in *Cartography in the Traditional Africa, American, Arctic, Australian, and Pacific Societies*, book 3, vol. 2 of *The History of Cartography*, ed. David Woodward and G. Malcolm Lewis (Chicago: University of Chicago Press, 1998), 24–48; Isabel Voigt and Kathrin Fritsch, "Transcultural Aspects of Exploring and Mapping South West Africa Between 1850 and 1914," *Journal of Namibian Studies* 9, no. 1 (2011): 61–83; Adam Jones and Isabel Voigt, "'Just a First Sketchy Makeshift': German Travellers and their Cartographic Encounters in Africa, 1850–1914," *History in Africa* 39, no. 2 (2012): 9–39.

33 Howard, "Nodes, Networks, Landscapes, and Regions," 21–140 but esp. 21–36, 74–87, 92–103, 106–112; Christopher Gray, "The Disappearing District? Territorial Transformation in Southern Gabon 1850–1950," in *The Spatial Factor in African History*, ed. A. Howard and R. Shain (Leiden: Brill, 2005), 221–244; for an early exploration of this theme see Ivor Wilks, "On Mentally Mapping Greater Asante: A Study in Time and Motion," *Journal of African History* 33, no. 2 (1992): 175–190.

34 Jeffrey Herbst, *States and Power in Africa: Comparative Lessons in Authority and Control* (Princeton: Princeton University Press, 2000), 35–61; Howard, "Nodes, Networks, Landscapes, and Regions," 79, 107.

our understanding of geography as culturally and socially embedded.[35] Instead of asking why there are few (or no) African maps, we could instead consider the broader question of how changing African ideas about land and locality interacted with colonial applications of geography to create or modify spatial order. The result is an understanding of geography that involves negotiation and co-production instead of mere imposition.

The elusiveness of direct African contributions to the technical work of survey and mapping made it all the easier to dismiss their roles within the production of geographical knowledge. The assumption of African unsuitability or incapacity for precise survey was almost a truism across the continent in the period before the First World War, despite the compelling precedent of highly competent Indian survey technicians.[36] Thomas Holdich, long-time surveyor in India and future president of the Royal Geographical Society in London, expressed his frustration with this attitude in 1901 through blunt statements that unless the colonies engaged "native agency" to carry out basic survey work, the task of mapping Africa could never be achieved, and that there was no good reason to presume that Africans could not learn the necessary skills.[37] Holdich's argument landed with a dull thud in the settler colonies of eastern and southern Africa, despite significant support in London and the emergence of the first trained African surveyors in Southern Nigeria and the Gold Coast within just a few years.[38] The idea's weak reception was second only to geographers' transparent silence on the idea that women from any background could undertake survey fieldwork or contribute to scientific ideas about land use and planning.[39] The colonial geographical archive therefore remained predominantly European and male, and that fact served as an additional filter on the information that could enter it.[40]

---

35 Lewis and Wigen, *Myth of Continents*, 202.

36 Michael P. Adas, *Machines as the Measure of Men: Science, Technology, and Ideologies of Western Dominance* (Ithaca: Cornell University Press, 1989), 259–265.

37 T.H. Holdich, "How Are We to Get Maps of Africa?" *Geographical Journal* 18 (1901): 591, 599–601.

38 Colonial Survey Committee, The Surveys and Explorations of British Africa (Colonial No. 500), 1906, Cd. 2684-46 at 6–7; Olayinka Y. Balogun, "The Training of Nigerian Surveyors in the Colonial Era," *Surveying and Mapping* 45, no. 2 (1985): 159–160. These surveyors however tended to come from the mission-educated colonial elite.

39 Clara Greed, *Surveying Sisters: Women in a Traditional Male Profession* (London: Routledge, 1991), 52–55, 59–62. Inertia has assured that the surveying profession in South Africa today remains predominantly white and male.

40 Byrnes, *Boundary Markers*, 8–9. Women worked as mathematical computers for the Surveyors-General in later years, but their names were never connected to the specific data they produced.

From that body of data, survey authorities generated the structured archive of intertwined plans, diagrams, deeds, and a bevy of words and numbers that depended upon and in turn supported the instrumental knowledge that other experts produced about people and places in the colony.[41] The geographical archive therefore included knowledge from other European male figures of authority, especially magistrates and missionaries, as the primary conduits for any African knowledge that the colonial state might deign to incorporate. But in terms of geography, such sources took priority only in spaces or at times that surveyors did not or could not work. Sometimes colonial administrations preferred to leave matters that way, in deliberate acts of *not* surveying that also said a great deal about power relations within areas of contested authority and the meaning of survey to colonial subjects.

Such substitutions for scientific geography usually began as colonial expedients, not solutions. The geographical archive allowed administrators to code small territories or social units as knowable, taxable commodities, so precision was desirable where possible.[42] Surveyors' small-scale property diagrams (cadasters) within the state's geographical archive therefore had a special immediacy to the project of colonial rationalization, as maps of the most fundamental and utilitarian sort.[43] Colonial regimes appropriated, altered, and even experimented outright with African social and spatial order in their belief that existing land use was an impediment to development and, where possible, they dispatched surveyors to implement their prescriptions and to return with usable data.[44] Governments extended at least the spatial concern to white settlement as well, with progressively greater worry over the definition of settler properties. In both cases, another key element was 'addressing,' usually numerically, to assign labels to farms or lots that treated them as commodities but also as pieces in the larger machinery of state.[45] All South African systems of geographical delineation,

41 Edney, "Irony of Imperial Mapping," 31.

42 Pickles, *History of Spaces*, 116.

43 Scott, *Seeing Like a State*, 44–52.

44 Colson, "The Impact of the Colonial Period," 196–199; Thomas J. Bassett, "Introduction: The Land Question and Agricultural Transformation in South Africa," in *Land in African Agrarian Systems*, ed. Thomas J. Bassett and Donald E. Crummey (Madison: University of Wisconsin Press, 1993), 4–8.

45 The nascent literature on addressing tends to focus on the production of space in urban environments, but many of the same principles could function in less congested rural ones. See R.S. Rose-Redwood, "Indexing the Great Ledger of the Community: Urban House Numbering, City Directories, and the Production of Spatial Legibility," *Journal of Human Geography* 34 (2008): 286–310.

however rudimentary, included registry numbers and files that are traceable to the parcel in the government archive even today.

In keeping with the anticipation of an increasingly legible future built upon cadastral blocks, these states peremptorily and prematurely declared ownership of all land inside their claimed boundaries unless specifically granted or sold—*Crown Lands* in the British colonies, and *Gouvernements Gronden* in the Boer republics.[46] That the archive's technical content was entirely European corresponded neatly with its pretension to universal logic and its privileging of scientific literacy and numeracy, not to mention its positivist view that colonial territory was perfectly knowable given sufficient scientific control and correction of those documents. Cartographers duly smoothed out the source material of the archive in a way that aided this fiction through the production of maps that pretended more complete knowledge or, at the very least, showed where the colony needed it. Governments in the British colonies and the Boer republics of South Africa shared a common fixation of colonial regimes with the legal and scientific partition of lands, whether to situate new settlers or to control indigenous land tenures.[47]

But this body of geographical knowledge was not solely a European creation, and it included more than cadasters. The colonial bureaucracy was rarely of one mind and prevaricated about administrative priorities. The South African geographical archive bears corresponding traces of local practices and alternate geographies that co-produced its colonial knowledge.[48] The topological organization of missionaries' maps in spaces of limited geographical knowledge, for example, merged with more systematic data to create hybrid maps that included signs of African networks and nodes across South Africa. Chiefs, headmen, or other leaders could mobilize communities or the legal machinery of the state itself to alter the recorded boundaries around or within their lands, and limit the extent of colonial control over spaces to benefit their networks' own positions. The variation of interactions in the Kei watershed and around western Venda points to different initial conditions of social and spatial order in each society, but their experiences also expose different limits to the power and legal writ of the colonial state.

---

46 Özlem Ülgen, "Developing the Doctrine of Aboriginal Title in South Africa: Source and Content," *Journal of African Law* 46, no. 2 (2002): 133–135; Bassett, "The Land Question," 7.

47 Christopher, *British Empire*, 159–188; Steven Pierce, *Farmers and the State in Colonial Kano: Land Tenure and the Legal Imagination* (Bloomington: Indiana University Press, 2005), 46–48.

48 Raj, *Relocating Modern Science*, 60–65; Raymond B. Craib, "Relocating Cartography," *Postcolonial Studies* 12, no. 4 (2009): 485–487.

The colony's legal machinery was itself important. The delineation of land and the creation of spatial order had a powerful traveling companion in colonial law. Colonial legal codes constituted a technological framework that prescribed social interactions and land tenure, among other things, and manufactured official legitimacy in so doing. Law and geography intersected repeatedly in the creation of colonial space, just as they did in other modernist state systems, whether by making local ('traditional') legal practices legible or furthering some end of social engineering for the state.[49] Like colonial law elsewhere in Africa, land law in South Africa sought to divine local realities and articulate models of land tenure that reflected or, more often, contributed to changes in society at large.[50] As a system of archived knowledge, law in fact shares a great deal with geography, although its practitioners were more acutely aware of its artificiality as they altered the legal relationship between people and the landscape through fees, inheritance laws, and other codifications. These measures functioned only sporadically, in part because of limits on the ability of the state to enforce them, but also because rural African social networks retained greater flexibility that confounded administrative fashions and fixations.[51] The increasingly prescriptive and restrictive land regulations, influx controls, and conservation measures of South African regimes between 1913 and 1990 might appear in this light as a continuation of the earlier push to give force to an idealized order drawn from colonial maps and archives.[52] The corresponding shifts in the philosophy behind state policy and an increased ability to intervene did not, however, signal any improvement in competency.

Rural African societies before the late nineteenth century constituted space and social meaning, as well as their visions of landscape, on a number of scales and at a number of levels that did not square with the forms of the colonial archive. One useful concept is what spatial historian Allen Howard refers to 'nodality,' or the existence of centers of social activity (nodes) within broader networks and regional systems. The existence of dynamic connection and

49 Clifton C. Crais, *The Politics of Evil: Magic, State Power, and the Political Imagination in South Africa* (Cambridge: Cambridge University Press, 2002), 84–87; Martin Chanock, *The Making of South African Legal Culture* (Cambridge: Cambridge University Press, 2001), 243–272.

50 Pierce, *Farmers and the State*, 79–110.

51 Clifton C. Crais, *Poverty, War, and Violence in South Africa* (Cambridge: Cambridge University Press, 2011), 136–141; Howard, "Nodes, Networks, Landscapes, and Regions," 106–109.

52 Kelso, "Ideology of Mapping," 17–18; Mahmood Mamdani, *Citizen and Subject: Contemporary Africa and the Legacy of Late Colonialism* (Princeton: Princeton University Press, 1996), 138–145.

meaning within particular places and institutions on a broad landscape stands in opposition to the static, neutral, and isolated spaces depicted on colonial maps. Precolonial systems of organization and landholding continued into the colonial era and adapted to exploit new opportunities or mitigate new restrictions.[53] The robustness of African networks across regions in part explains the frustration colonialists expressed, and the force they sometimes applied, when they considered African claims on land and landscape or discharged those places' meanings in favor of their own understandings.[54] These spatial links between nodes were also temporal ones, linking past and present, and incorporating spiritual and seasonal aspects into broader local and regional landscapes. Politics did not organize by territory specifically but by social connections to other nodes and networks, which meant African identities and affiliations were complex, contingent, and adaptable across a potentially vast area before the expropriation of land for the nodes and networks of white settlement in the nineteenth century.[55]

Colonial regimes after the 1850s had to face these incongruent social orders as they incorporated growing (and in the case of South Africa, majority) non-European populations, albeit ones they sought to exclude from the body politic and deny its entitlements, including land.[56] Those populations represented a significant complication for settler colonialism, because they potentially challenged the legal precepts of *terra nullius* or *vacuum domicilium* (empty land) that were so crucial to expropriation in North and South America, New Zealand, Australia, and even the southwestern Cape Colony.[57] Although the popular means of circumventing the issue for settlers involved the creation of primacy and right through historical mythology and an exclusive claim to civilization, the technical issues were a bit more tenacious.[58] Highly formulaic

53 Howard, "Nodes, Networks, Landscapes, and Regions," 35–36, 112.

54 Ibid., 104–106.

55 Paul Landau, *Popular Politics in the History of South Africa, 1400–1948* (Cambridge: Cambridge University Press, 2011), 42–74, 108.

56 Jacob Metzer and Stanley Engerman, "Some Considerations of Ethno-Nationality (and Other Distinctions), Property Rights in Land, and Territorial Sovereignty," in *Land Rights, Ethno-Nationality, and Sovereignty in History*, ed. Jacob Metzer and Stanley L. Engerman (London: Routledge, 2004), 14–15.

57 Anders Stefansson, *Manifest Destiny: American Expansion and the Empire of Right* (New York: Hill & Wang, 1995), 24–26; Robert Ross, *The Borders of Race in Colonial South Africa: The Kat River Settlement, 1829–1856* (Cambridge: Cambridge University Press, 2014), 7; see also Weaver, *The Great Land Rush*, 90, 171–176.

58 Clifton C. Crais, "The Vacant Land: The Mythology of British Expansion in the Eastern Cape, South Africa," *Journal of Social History* 25, no. 2 (1991): 255–275.

rural survey measures, like the grid system of the Northwest Land Ordinance of 1785 and the Rectangular Survey that followed in the United States, were difficult to carry out wherever people already lived on the land in great numbers.[59] The demographic complication made prescriptive mapping harder, but it did not stop acquisitive land claims, and it had an important corollary for the extraction of labor. The labor needs of settler agriculture, mining, and other industries did not square with African self-sufficiency or African market competition through their continued control of productive territory. Administrators in the nineteenth century therefore required a body of knowledge regarding who occupied the land and where they were, before dealing with the much more difficult questions of how to define their presence on the land and how to circumscribe it. Colonial geography in southern Africa shifted its weight from descriptive exploration to prescriptive domination accordingly in the last few decades of the nineteenth century, much as it had in other colonial dependencies, but it was still subject to the varied conditions of its production.[60]

That shift to an increasingly regimented state model of scientific geography raises another piece of settler colonialism's historical baggage, in the form of the frontier narrative. General histories of South Africa in the late nineteenth and early twentieth centuries followed a geographical trajectory similar to contemporary writing in other colonies of settlement, whether in English, Dutch, or Afrikaans. South African examples, especially those surrounding the inland migration of the Boers, may place a stronger emphasis on conquest and struggle than one finds in the analogous words of Frederick Jackson Turner regarding the American West, but they are very similar overall.[61] The vision of an empty land awaiting the hardy settler informed a settler archive of knowledge that included the colonial geographical archive wherever the latter conferred legitimacy upon it.[62] Indeed, nascent colonial identities placed particular importance on dominion over land and people through rational enumeration and the control of knowledge, even on a conceptually empty

59 Bill Hubbard Jr., *American Boundaries: The Nation, the States, and the Rectangular Survey* (Chicago: University of Chicago Press, 2009), 181–214; Kain and Baigent, *Cadastral Map*, 289–297; Scott, *Seeing Like a State*, 49–51.

60 Driver, *Geography Militant*, 21–22.

61 Stefansson, *Manifest Destiny*, 74–75; Frederick Jackson Turner, "The Significance of the Frontier in American History," *Annual Report of the American Historical Association* 4 (1893): 199–227.

62 Lorenzo Veracini, "Colonial Genocides: Notes for the Analysis of a Settler Archive," in *Empire, Colony, Genocide: Conquest, Occupation, and Subaltern Resistance in World History*, ed. A. Dirk Moses (New York: Berghahn, 2010), 149.

land.[63] Colonists in southern Africa, just as in the Americas and Oceana, cast themselves as pioneers either taming an empty wilderness (provided by God, as He provided Eden) or conquering it (by the same proviso, only recalling Israel). The Boers produced a similar narrative of civilization and Christianity replacing savagery on a distinct frontier.[64] Whether promoting European settlement or reorganizing African lands on the basis of disuse, misuse, or forfeiture, such settlers selected or constructed maps and testimonies that underscored their preferred beliefs.[65]

Geographically, the South African case (and, I would argue, all cases of colonial frontiers) shares a great deal with the concept of borderlands that originated in US history but now enjoys wider application. Other scholars of South African history have observed that the concept of borderlands is more appropriate historically and stronger analytically, although some seem reticent to jettison the notion of the frontier and its terminology entirely and there is not universal agreement on the applicability or meaning of each.[66] But borderlands too are not perfect, because the diffuse edges of colonial settlement comprise a region of shifting accommodation and exchange between distinct parties—not always states—that emphatically must come to terms with one another's changing worldviews.[67] Divisions between states are usually less important than shared experience and horizontal movement, especially

---

63 Benedict Anderson, *Imagined Communities* rev. ed. (London: Verso, 2006), 163–164, 173.

64 F.A. van Jaarsveld, *The Afrikaner's Interpretation of South African History* (Cape Town: Simondium, 1964), 9–14, 58–60; Nigel Penn, *The Forgotten Frontier: Colonist & Khoisan on the Cape's Northern Frontier in the Eighteenth Century* (Athens: Ohio University Press, 2005), 10; Paul Carter, *The Road to Botany Bay* (London: Faber and Faber, 1987), 159–161. Carter in particular expresses skepticism with the classic concept of the frontier.

65 Norman Etherington, "A False Emptiness: How Historians May Have Been Misled by Early Nineteenth Century Maps of South-Eastern Africa," *Imago Mundi* 56, no. 1 (2004): 72, 82–83; Norman Etherington, "A Tempest in a Teapot? Nineteenth-Century Contests for Land in South Africa's Caledon Valley and the Invention of the *mfecane*," *Journal of African History* 45 (2004): 203–219; Carter, *Road to Botany Bay*, 160.

66 Landau, *Popular Politics*, 2–3; Laura J. Mitchell, "Global Context, Local Objects, and Cultural Frontiers: Unsettling South Africa's National History in Four Moves," *Settler Colonial Studies* 4, no. 2 (2014): 162–170. Landau consciously employs 'borderlands' where earlier studies used 'frontier' for the southwestern Highveld, but in explaining his choice he does not discuss the latter term; Mitchell recasts the concept itself expansively, noting its unsettled and "elastic" character. For the earlier prevailing definition of the term, see Leonard Thompson and Howard Lamar, "Comparative Frontier History," in *The Frontier in History: North America and Southern Africa Compared*, ed. Leonard Thompson and Howard Lamar (New Haven: Yale University Press, 1981), 7–13.

67 Lewis and Wigen, *Myth of Continents*, 150–152.

among laborers and other circulating or itinerant agents of culture in an era of social and economic incorporation, and borders between colonies rarely stopped this horizontal movement. The Transvaal Labour Commission of 1903, to cite just one example, deliberated at length over possible sources of labor from throughout Africa—not just the British Empire—and included labor from outside Africa as well.[68] People in fact circulated widely, and large numbers of Africans lived on cadastrally 'white' farms into the apartheid era despite efforts to regulate or remove them by changing the legal landscape.[69] The language of frontiers, whereby they open and close depending on the absence or presence of an overriding and unitary political order, leaves little room for cross-cultural interaction about spaces, places, and landscapes that extend beyond the passage of political boundaries. If we use a regional, cultural frame, we leave room for multiple levels of networking, ongoing processes of negotiation and change, the exercise of political power across borders, and local African communities' use of boundaries for their own purposes.[70]

Surveys, Cartography, and Colonialism

The social and cultural interactions that historians attributed to a frontier did not cease once a colonial government drew lines on paper or issued titles to land. Nonetheless, the title deeds that described geographical spaces between lines on paper had and still have real power. The ownership and conditions of those spaces may be under discussion and revision now, but not the basic structure, and we have barely pulled apart the presumptive knowledge that created them. Territorial delineation underscores virtually all aspects of rural history yet slips through the gaps between political, economic, social, and even

68 Transvaal Colony Publication (hereafter TKP) (unnumbered), *Report of the Transvaal Labour Commission: Together with Minority Report, Minutes of Proceedings and Evidence* (Johannesburg, 1903), xvii–xxv.

69 Francis Wilson, "Farming, 1866–1966," in *The Oxford History of South Africa*, ed. M. Wilson and L.M. Thompson (Oxford: Oxford University Press, 1971), 2:145–147; A.H. Jeeves and J. Crush, ed., *Black Farms White Labor: The State and Agrarian Change in South Africa, 1910–1950* (Portsmouth, NH: Heinemann, 1997); Charles van Onselen, *The Seed Is Mine: The Life of Kas Maine, a South African Sharecropper* (New York: Hill & Wang, 1996), 5–8.

70 Howard, "Nodes, Networks, Landscapes and Regions," 32–34; Fred Morton, "Chiefs and Ethnic Unity in Two Colonial Worlds: The BaKgatla baga Kgafela of the Bechuanaland Protectorate and the Transvaal, 1872–1966," in *Partitioned Africans: Ethnic Relations Across Africa's International Boundaries, 1884–1984*, ed. A.J. Asiwaju (New York: St. Martin's, 1985), 127–153; Nugent, "Arbitrary Lines and the People's Minds," 48–55.

cultural history.[71] Unexamined, these representations of space have become universal and real. Beneath the history of contested landscapes, the history of colonial surveying and cartography as a vehicle for creating them has vanished into transparency, or worse, hagiography.[72] The subjective details regarding the creation and recording of boundaries, routes of travel, and even geographical features, are now figuratively buried beneath twelve feet of technical soil at an intersection between disciplines and forgotten in discussions about land, yet they are crucial to understanding colonial encounters over territory.[73] Through this technical transparency, the characterizations and divisions laid upon territory escape the scrutiny of their origins and the specific mechanics of their creation.

Compared to explorers, missionaries, and other agents of cultural transfer and colonial authority such as magistrates, the land surveyor receives little attention and even less understanding in critical histories of colonialism. The use of knowledge collection for purposes of imperial aggrandizement is especially evident in the work of itinerant geographers from across Europe and North America, who often rewrote and recapitulated the archive in order to deploy their own contributions, and in the process legitimated imperial expansion and ideas of European superiority.[74] By contrast, the surveyors and other expert observers who generated data for maps and plans were paid agents between the colonial apparatus and the people on the land, and governments expected them to create knowable, ordered spaces prefatory to effective colonization and control.[75] Theirs was a less romantic and generally less verbose occupation. Land surveyors ranged across wide swathes of territory, interacted sporadically with local people, stayed only briefly in any particular locale, and produced more mathematical or computational records than narrative or qualitative ones. Routine does not, however, render surveyors and cartographers unimportant. Their work usually did not create sharply contentious

---

71 T.R.H. Davenport and K.S. Hunt, "Introduction," in *The Right to the Land*, ed. T.R.H. Davenport and K.S. Hunt (Johannesburg: David Philip, 1974), vi.

72 The most recent case of this technological triumphalism relative to South Africa is Andrew Duminy, *Mapping South Africa: A Historical Survey of South African Maps and Charts* (Pretoria: Jacana, 2011).

73 Jacob, *The Sovereign Map*, 28–33.

74 See, respectively, Burnett, *Masters of All They Surveyed*, 37–46; Anne Godlewska, "Napoleon's Geographers (1797–1815): Imperialists and Soldiers of Modernity," in Godlewska and Smith, *Geography and Empire*, 31–53; Bassett, "Cartography and Empire Building," 316–335; Richards, *Imperial Archive*, 13–22.

75 Kain and Baigent, *Cadastral Map*, 329.

discourses, but like other expressions of geographical science, its transparency indicates just how close it was to the heart of the informational matrix that supported British colonial rule.[76]

The surveyor's work in fact represented a direct encounter between metropolitan science and the social spaces of the colony.[77] Every question about land returned to the collection of knowledge in the colonial state's geographical archive, and so granted surveyors a more powerful claim to spatial authority than inspectors and magistrates had. The diagrams and plans of surveyors were both a reflection of and a prescription for the colonial environment, as were the larger general plans and maps that various cartographers compiled from them. Confidence in the results related directly to the perceived level of technical precision and consistency in surveys and maps. The varying levels of precision and planimetric accuracy arose directly from the neglect of other kinds of survey operations, especially triangulation and topographical survey, which theoretically offered some kind of control above the level of the boundary and property surveys that this book considers most closely. Just as a struggle existed between description and prescription among surveyors and colonial authorities, another existed between the far-reaching aims of imperial geographers (including astronomers and cartographers stationed in South Africa itself, and even a few colonial government leaders) and the immediate needs of economy-minded colonial administrations. The colonial surveyor existed between the frustrating yet 'adequate' imprecision of magistrates or agents and the fetish of exactitude in European metropoles.

Levels of precision and cost could vary widely, especially depending on the type of survey. Imperial geographers and colonial survey officials championed high-level frameworks of triangulation, ideally extrapolated from a *geodetic* survey—one of such mathematical precision and extensive astronomical correction that its fixed stations could describe the size and shape of the Earth. Taken alone, a geodetic survey was primarily an esoteric scientific exercise, useful only for isolated measures of position. Its triangles could be fifty kilometers or more on a side, and wide spaces existed where none of its large fixed beacons were visible to land surveyors who might want to use them to position their own work. The geodetic survey required further chains of primary triangulation to extend the area it covered and, ultimately, smaller triangles of secondary and tertiary triangulation to define additional points within a shorter distance of one another for the small instruments and limited computational

76 C.A. Bayly, *Information and Empire: Intelligence Gathering and Social Communication in India, 1780–1870* (Cambridge: Cambridge University Press, 1996), 300.

77 See Edney, *Mapping an Empire*, 32.

abilities of land surveyors.[78] At the same time, triangulation defined fixed points for the charting of landforms and human geography through topographical survey, and the resulting topocadastral maps would combine all of these elements into a planimetrically accurate representation of whatever information a mapmaker sought to portray.

But geodetic surveys and broad systems of precise triangulation were also exceptionally expensive correctives, owing to the extended programs of observation necessary, the extremely sensitive instrumentation involved, the periodic baseline measurements necessary to determine the length of triangular sides, and the large parties of specialized technicians who came from Europe to carry out these tasks. Despite proponents' constant repetition of evidence that trigonometrical surveys slashed the cost of resurveys and the number of land disputes in the long run, and provided the only reliable control for precise topographical mapping, the immediate cost meant that the imperial treasury would not fund such work in the colonies unless it served some broader geopolitical concern. Although there was no shortage of ambitious schemes, colonial governments also rarely committed money to such large survey operations unless revenue collection, resource control, or military security indicated an immediate need—and ideally partial funding from Europe. This triage-based philosophy of management was widespreadeven in wealthier colonies like India in the late 1800s, even though a geodetic framework already existed there.[79]

Solutions that were less expensive in the short term therefore held a great deal of attraction for colonial administrations. Their surveys tended to work backwards, from small-scale piecework to larger compilations that multiplied any errors, and results varied depending on the perceived need for planimetric accuracy and precision. Initially a trained surveyor was a pure luxury for settlers, who used an exceptionally vague system of inspection and claim until that became untenable. The survey of specific parcels or blocks that slowly supplanted inspection systems remained the normal mode of land survey (at least across rural South Africa) into the twentieth century. These isolated surveys usually had only tenuous links with other surveyed areas, because no useful broader framework for measurement existed without a larger triangulation network. Small-scale surveys, such as the laying out of town lots or surveys for mines and railroad lines, involved tightly limited areas or claims with higher values where tight precision and even local triangulation were desirable and profitable.

78 On the forms of trigonometrical surveys, see also Edney, *Mapping an Empire*, 16–30.

79 Deepak Kumar, *Science and the Raj, 1857–1905* (Delhi: Oxford University Press, 1997), 75–76.

Geological and magnetic surveys were much more stochastic in their sampling, but those dealt with ways of making the natural world and the body of the earth legible in terms of invisible inner structures, and so they had an additional but more indirect effect on the human geography that concerned colonial land surveyors during this period.[80]

Later surveys of single farms or large blocks were more deliberate about describing sides and angles numerically and depicting basic topography, but without a framework for determining absolute position, increasing efforts to include absolute measures like latitude and longitude on a title diagram were almost cosmetic. As a result, the survey officers charged with examining the correctness of diagrams could only really adjudge consistency, not accuracy, and diagrams included only an official statement that the figure was 'reasonably' consistent. By the late 1880s, survey officials across the governments of South Africa required that surveys of individual properties as well as blocks of farms involve some kind of local triangulation to determine relative positions and perhaps permit their adjustment into existing or future networks of high-level trigonometrical survey. But those measures merely assured a broader degree of planimetric consistency in the illusion of knowledge. Varying levels of disconnection between property surveys and South Africa's eventual trigonometrical framework persisted deep into the twentieth century, and later governments removed many native landscapes from the attention of land surveys—but not topographical survey, then possible by aerial photography at large scales—after the philosophy of internally colonial rule through state-recognized chiefs or headmen gained ascendancy.[81]

Studies of survey operations published in the last fifteen years have begun to consider the link between colonial geography, survey, and mapping more critically. Recent studies on India, the US-Mexico border, and Guiana, for example, follow particular survey processes from their inception through the eventual map (and text) production in trigonometrical surveys, boundary

80 See Bruce Braun, "Producing Vertical Territory: Geology and Governmentality in Late Victorian Canada," *Ecumene* 7, no. 1 (2000): 7–46. Geological surveying, particularly connected to mining, grew in importance during the 1870s and had an indirect effect on African societies through labor, land speculation, and the purchase of mining concessions. The magnetic survey, under J.C. Beattie after 1901, served to correct navigation and set the basis for further geological exploration.

81 On the development of topographical mapping in South Africa and the major historical developments in its large-scale mapping, see E.C. Liebenberg, "Die Topografiese Kartering van Suid-Afrika, 1879–1972" (master's thesis, UNISA, 1973).

commissions, and traverse surveys respectively.[82] These studies focus primarily on European surveyors or travelers and geographies of state; the multitudes who inhabit the colony or exist at its margins correspondingly form an elusive presence that rarely exerts direct agency. That focus permits a closely-detailed examination of the creation of colonial space through geographic performance and production, and offers a number of illuminating perspectives on the metropolitan discourse over colonized space and its relationship to colonialism.[83] But it does not allow for much negotiation by non-European agents and therefore gives us only a partial impression of the overall process of landscape colonization. The absence of those agents arises from the cultural embedding of history within language which pairs it, by extension, with the colonizer's organization of knowledge, so that they appear only relative to normative European geographers' scientific practices.[84] Indigenous knowledge and practice that did not approximate the literacy and numeracy that defined European rationality consequently became illegitimate (or nonexistent) logics, as we have already seen.

Highly precise scientific practices and mathematical operations are also rooted within language and the grammar of ideas, words, and signs that technicians carried and used to produce the appearance of order in a way that was accessible only to administrators and the favored settlers on the land.[85] Their claim to universal, natural logic for their graphical and numerical representations is powerful and persistent, and it closed off any other articulation of logic as the flawed thinking of rural Africans who were not, after all, trained experts.[86] The later panacea of precise triangulation as a control on

---

82 Edney, *Mapping an Empire*; Paula Rebert, *La Gran Línea: Mapping the United States-Mexico Boundary, 1849–1857* (Austin: University of Texas Press, 2001); Burnett, *Masters of All They Surveyed.*

83 Burnett places his focus on traverse specifically in opposition to Edney's goals in *Mapping an Empire*. Burnett highlights the traveling explorer-surveyor's solitary gaze, whereas Edney's work deals with the organizational structure and "governmentality" of a large, formal survey operation as different practices in the production of colonial space; see Burnett, *Masters of All They Surveyed,* 9–10; D. Graham Burnett, "Hydrographic Discipline Among the Navigators: Charting an 'Empire of Commerce and Science' in the Nineteenth-Century Pacific," in *The Imperial Map: Cartography and the Mastery of Empire*, ed. James R. Akerman (Chicago: University of Chicago Press, 2009), 216–217.

84 Carter, *Road to Botany Bay*, xxii, 325–327.

85 Jennifer Beningfield, *The Frightened Land: Land, Landscape, and Politics in South Africa in the Twentieth Century* (New York: Routledge, 2006), 112.

86 Helen Verran, *Science and an African Logic* (Chicago: University of Chicago Press, 2001), 150–152, 205, 237.

land surveys simply lent more potency to this claim. The articulation of non-European geographies was thus only directly visible where it became overt resistance. Competing voices received little credit on the portrayed reality of the map, but the incongruency between local landscapes and the map only became visible when governments tried to employ that knowledge for policy ends.[87] If we see European ways of ordering, measuring, and representing the world as culturally and socially contingent, and recognize the potency of African physical, social, and spiritual geographies, the uneven experiences of people over issues affecting the landscape make more sense.[88]

To understand survey and mapping as social and cultural acts, historians need to broaden the range of influences they include in the processes of representation and spatial reorganization that we usually ascribe solely to survey and mapping. This process potentially includes the actions, ideas, and voices of all groups and individuals affected by colonial survey and mapping, even those not normally in direct dialogue with one another. The colonial archive and the status of science still puts surveyors and cartographers at the forefront in the state's pursuit of legibility through survey, enumeration, and eventually surveillance, but a wider field can address anyone who circulated between worlds, such as missionaries, magistrates, traders, and travelers or migrants, all of whom catalyzed other, broader colonial encounters and exchanges of culture outside the narrow confines of official colonial knowledge.[89] The visible discourse is uneven, particularly with African voices. The power and status of an individual relative to state recognition determined the attention their ideas and activities received from its agents, but the voices of headmen and chiefs were not alone. African households and homesteads of all ranks sought the most efficient generation of wealth and security as they defined those things, and worked within social networks to sustain the legibility of their own worlds. These matters dictated the acceptance, rejection, modification, or

87 Edney, *Mapping an Empire*, 331–332; Pierce, *Farmers and the State*, 189–210.

88 Paul Carter has termed this approach spatial history, as opposed to imperial histories that treat space as a neutral physical constant. See also Greg Dening, *Islands and Beaches: Discourse on a Silent Land: Marquesas 1774–1880* (Chicago: Dorsey, 1980), 1–6; Thongchai Winichakul, *Siam Mapped: A History of the Geo-Body of a Nation* (Honolulu: University of Hawai'i Press, 1997); Craib, *Cartographic Mexico*, esp. 165–171.

89 Leroy Vail, "Introduction: Ethnicity in Southern African History," in *The Creation of Tribalism in Southern Africa*, ed. Leroy Vail (Berkeley: University of California Press, 1989): 1–19; Cohn, *Colonialism and its Forms of Knowledge*, 10–11; M. Foucault, "Questions on Geography," in *Power/Knowledge: Selected Interviews and Other Writings, 1972–1977* ed. and trans. Colin Gordon (New York: Pantheon, 1980), 74–76. In considering modes of control, Foucault notes that "surveillance" and "survey" share a root word.

simple disregard of colonial schemes for spatial reconstruction. Questions of continuity and change in local spatial orders worried colonial administrators and survey officials who did not understand these processes beyond their deviation from state prescriptions, but knowledge and control were never complete or static. The South African government is still trying to perfect its knowledge of and control over territory today, though the image-conscious ANC that succeeded the apartheid state would be loath to describe it in such undemocratic terms, and most people in rural and urban areas alike continue to pursue their own particular interests without too much empathy for the state's geographical fixations.

The Landscape of South African History

Up to this point I have treated landscape and survey across a variety of settings, with limited attention to the specific literature on politics, society, and culture in colonial South Africa. There are two main reasons for this approach. The first reflects my feeling that the South African experience can, through its shared and particular features alike, help us think about settler colonialism more generally—a point Margaret Jacobs has made recently about the historiography of the US West which, like that of South Africa, has often suffered from introversion.[90] The second, related reason is that the history of survey, title, and mapping in colonial South Africa touches on many specific debates over the development of state and society, each of which has a voluminous literature and contains various threads of criticism that could fill their own books. My intent is not to diminish the value of South Africa's historiography or the painstaking research of those scholars, nor to suggest a reductionist thesis around the subjects of surveying and landscape change. Rather, I wish to situate this book in its own context without restricting it to a particular set of exchanges.

One of the key debates that the history of surveying and landscape addresses concerns the role of African resilience, invention, and adaptation. That view of

90 Margaret D. Jacobs, "Parallel or Intersecting Tracks? The History of the US West and Comparative Settler Colonialism," *Settler Colonial Studies* 4, no. 2 (2014): 155–161. South African history is less introverted today than it tended to be before the 1990s, and a few scholars have actively engaged in transnational, comparative study relative to settler colonialism and landscape in particular. See Howard Lamar and Leonard Thompson, ed., *The Frontier in History: North America and Southern Africa Compared* (New Haven: Yale University Press, 1981); William Beinart and Peter Coates, *Environment and History: The Taming of Nature in the usa and South Africa* (New York: Routledge, 1995).

South African history from the vantage of colonized people or others 'from below,' notable in the presentation of Davenport and Hunt's 1974 document collection *The Right to the Land*, gained particular traction after the Soweto rising in 1976.[91] It complicated the ascendant, more rigidly structuralist analyses of political economy (often labeled 'radical' and drawing heavily from Marxian analysis) that emphasized capitalist penetration and progressive proletarianization that dispossessed and subordinated nonwhite South Africans. The challenge was not a total paradigm shift, but a more subtle move that ascribed greater importance to African societies and state interventions as key influences in the development of the racial and class structure peculiar to the country. The groups of writers involved on both sides were similar enough in their methodological language that, as social historian Timothy Keegan noted, an uninitiated reader might be hard pressed to tell them apart.[92]

In this new wave of historical investigation, a number of researchers approached rural African societies before and during colonization, stressing their experiences and the "scope for defensive responses," although they tended to present African landscapes, livelihoods, and adaptive strategies in relation to the same socioeconomic structures of industrializing South Africa as before.[93] The emergent History Workshop at the University of the Witwatersrand was especially active, and produced several volumes of essays from this new generation of scholars. The monographs that followed approached particular African social and political organizations or looked at patterns of socioeconomic stratification across broader regions of South Africa.[94] These studies elaborated on the capacity of African producers

91 Davenport and Hunt, ed., *The Right to the Land.*

92 T.J. Keegan, "The Origins of Agrarian Capitalism: A Reply," *Journal of Southern African Studies* 15, no. 4 (1989): 666.

93 William Beinart and Peter Delius, "Introduction: Approaches to South African Agrarian History," in *Putting a Plough to the Ground: Accumulation and Dispossession in Rural South Africa 1850–1930*, ed. W. Beinart, P. Delius, and S. Trapido (Johannesburg: Ravan, 1986), 49; Clifton C. Crais, *White Supremacy and Black Resistance in Pre-industrial South Africa: The Making of the Colonial Order on the Eastern Cape, 1770–1865* (Cambridge: Cambridge University Press, 1992), 2.

94 Peter Delius, *The Land Belongs to Us: The Pedi Polity, the Boers, and the British in the Nineteenth Century Transvaal* (Johannesburg: Ravan, 1983); Jonathan Crush, *The Struggle for Swazi Labour, 1890–1920* (Kingston, ON: McGill-Queen's University Press, 1987); Philip D. Bonner, *Kings, Commoners, and Concessionaires: The Evolution and Dissolution of the Nineteenth Century Swazi State* (Johannesburg: Ravan, 1983); Kevin Shillington, *The Colonisation of the Southern Tswana, 1870–1900* (Johannesburg: Ravan, 1985); Colin Murray, *Black Mountain: Land, Class and Power in the Eastern Orange Free State* (Washington, DC:

to navigate changing political, social, and economic conditions, whether by ameliorating loss or exploiting situations of relative advantage. Colin Bundy's *Rise and Fall of the South African Peasantry* was the single most prominent of these, as well as one of the first, and it remains an important point of reference for critical studies of rural society in the late nineteenth century. Bundy took the broad position that African agricultural producers initially exploited the growth of colonial economies effectively until state interventions near the end of the nineteenth century altered the rules—including land law and tenancy restrictions—to favor settler agrarian capitalism and industrial demand for labor, which dictated the strangulation of this emergent black peasant class.[95]

Surveyors (or inspectors) were instruments of the colonial state in the context of these new readings of rural history, bringing technological interventions that augured the dispossession and destitution of Africans. Although the new historical turn said little about the critical meaning of those technical acts or their execution, their emphasis on local actors, rural class formation and social differentiation, and African strategies in the colonial encounter recast the struggle for the land as a process that altered African rural societies in different ways depending on their particular circumstances.[96] The mosaic of spaces and boundaries that arose in the colonial era did reflect the interests of an emerging agrarian and industrial capitalist order, but they could not dictate meaning, and their ability to engineer social and cultural changes was another matter entirely.

At the same time that these new social histories emerged, some researchers opened another avenue of inquiry into the relationship between race and class

---

Smithsonian Institution, 1992); William Beinart and Colin Bundy, *Hidden Struggles in Rural South Africa* (Johannesburg: Ravan, 1987); William Beinart, *The Political Economy of Pondoland 1860–1930* (Cambridge: Cambridge University Press, 1982); T.J. Keegan, *Rural Transformations in Industrializing South Africa: The Southern Highveld to 1914* (London: Macmillan, 1987); Jeremy Krikler, *Revolution from above, Rebellion from Below: The Agrarian Transvaal at the Turn of the Century* (Oxford: Clarendon Press, 1993); John Lambert, *Betrayed Trust: Africans and the State in Colonial Natal* (Pietermaritzburg: University of Natal Press, 1995).

95 Colin Bundy, *The Rise and Fall of the South African Peasantry* (Berkeley: University of California Press, 1979). See also the revised edition that includes reflections on the debates that followed; Colin Bundy, *The Rise and Fall of the South African Peasantry* 2nd ed. (Cape Town: David Philip, 1988). I have simplified his argument in the interests of brevity.

96 The work of Peter Delius on the Pedi polity represents an important exception to the first point, and his discussion of the fictions involved in inspection and title in the South African Republic (or 'notionality') inspired the extended research into that system for Chapters 5 and 6. See Delius, *The Land Belongs to Us*, 126–136.

on the land by delving specifically into the pre-industrial roots of the South African racial order. The single most important work in this wave of early colonial histories was Richard Elphick and Hermann Giliomee's 1980 edited volume *The Shaping of South African Society 1652–1820*.[97] Most of that volume's contributors agreed that nascent forms of racial distinction and stratification existed in the colonial era, but they varied in their conclusions regarding where, when, and precisely how it manifested. Their work provoked enough new research and discussion to warrant a revised edition (extended to 1840) at the end of the decade, a volume that remains a fundamental historiographical touchstone for social and cultural histories of that era a quarter century later.[98]

A second strand of this search for origins involved the system of locations, native law, and government chiefs that arguably prefigured apartheid-era separate development and homelands policy. That literature sought to divine the roots of a wider philosophy of indirect rule in South Africa (or even colonial Africa more generally) through the life and work of Theophilus Shepstone as Secretary for Native Affairs in the Natal Colony between the 1840s and 1870s.[99] More recent histories by Thomas McClendon and Jeff Guy, however, point out that the negotiations and accommodations involved in Shepstone's policies—if indeed they can even rightly be called his—greatly complicate any genealogy of territorial segregation or African social change that might be rooted there.[100] Johan Bergh's essays on the location system in the South African Republic and its successor states further attest to the evolutionary complexity of the issue, as does the present study.[101]

---

97 Richard Elphick and Hermann Giliomee, ed., *The Shaping of South African Society 1652–1820* (London: Longman, 1980).

98 Richard Elphick and Hermann Giliomee, ed., *The Shaping of South African Society 1652–1840* (Middletown, CT: Wesleyan University Press, 1989).

99 David Welsh, *The Roots of Segregation: Native Policy in Colonial Natal* (Cape Town: Oxford University Press, 1971); Norman Etherington, "The 'Shepstone System' in the Colony of Natal and Beyond the Borders," in *Natal and Zululand from Earliest Times to 1910*, ed. Andrew Duminy and Bill Guest (Pietermaritzburg: Shuter and Shooter, 1989), 170–192; Mamdani, *Citizen and Subject*, 62–108.

100 Thomas V. McClendon, *White Chief, Black Lords: Shepstone and the Colonial State in Natal, South Africa 1845–1878* (Rochester: University of Rochester Press, 2010) and Jeff Guy, *Theophilus Shepstone and the Forging of Natal* (Pietermaitzburg: University of KwaZulu-Natal Press, 2013).

101 See Johan Bergh, "Grondverdeeling tussen Blank en Swart in Suid-Afrika: 'n 19de-Eeuse Transvaalse Perspektief," *J.B.M. Hertzoggedenklesing* XXXIV (2005): 20–22; Johan Bergh, "'(To) Reserve to the Native Tribes Such Locations as They May Be Fairly and Equitably Entitled To': The Transvaal Location Commission (1881–1899)," *South African Historical Journal* 54 (2005): 14–15.

The broad discussion over colonial origins continued into the 1990s, but it progressively shifted towards cultural history and away from the structural focus of earlier debates, in keeping with the sudden prominence of post-structural, postcolonial, and postmodern approaches to historical writing generally as the end of apartheid became imminent.[102] The effect was significant, although perhaps muted in comparison to other parts of the globe. Clifton Crais was among the first to employ this toolkit extensively, in his 1992 study of the rural Eastern Cape before 1865. That book approached the racial order as a product of interaction and confrontation between groups of people with different worldviews and systems of knowledge, in tandem with material factors but not subordinate to them.[103] Tim Keegan conversely retained a focus on structural elements in his wide-ranging 1996 study of the colonial origins of racial policy in the pre-industrial era, but he nevertheless presented race as 'an autonomous variable' that evolved together with relations of production, economic class, and social order.[104] Both gave significant weight to land issues relative to social change, but Crais ascribed especial power to shifting and selectively imperfect cultural ideas about landscape, territory, and spatiality in the evolution of group identities and the emergence of the racial order.[105]

Crais in particular has continued to engage the shifting perceptions of landscape during the process of colonization and control. His insights about the role of the territorial imagination and colonial scientism on the emergence of state power in South Africa developed powerfully in subsequent works, notably his 2002 and 2003 chapters on mapping, counting, and classification in the colonial Transkei that directly touch upon the subjects of this book but do not duplicate them.[106] We share some analytical framing and concur about the general aims and ideals of the state, but this study approaches colonial geography in detail as the result of a co-productive process involving homesteaders,

---

102 See Colin Bundy, "New Nation, New History? Constructing the Past in Post-apartheid South Africa," in *History Making and Present Day Politics*, ed. Hans Erik Stolten (Uppsala: Nordiska Afrikainstitutet, 2007), 78–79.

103 Crais, *White Supremacy and Black Resistance.*

104 T.J. Keegan, *Colonial South Africa and the Origins of the Racial Order* (Cape Town; David Philip, 1996), 13.

105 Crais, *White Supremacy and Black Resistance*, 11.

106 Crais, *Politics of Evil*, 71–95; Clifton C. Crais, "Conquest, State Formation, and the Subaltern Imagination in Rural South Africa" in *The Culture of Power in Southern Africa: Essays on State Formation and the Political Imagination*, ed. Clifton C. Crais (Portsmouth, NH: Heinemann, 2003): 27–48.

surveyors, settlers, and administrators, each of whom had their own ideas and agendas, often separate from the legal solemnization and enduring legacy of the results.[107] Cadastral frameworks reflected unclear ideas about race and land alike in the colonial era, but they provided furrows that channeled later rural interventions and contests. By reconsidering the machinery of survey, mapping, and title this way, I take heed of Crais's own recent call for the renewed critical study of topics "that may seem, to those in the cultural turn, to be decidedly old hat and uninteresting—topics such as warfare, crop history, and colonial policy—but hopefully…in unexpected ways."[108]

To a great extent, the boom since the mid-1990s in literature on South African environmental history and the creation of knowledge prefigured this call (as Crais himself notes) by employing precepts of cultural history in tandem with social history and political economy.[109] Scientific and environmental or ecological subjects, after all, have direct links to material conditions on the land, whether they concern the development of inequality through environmental power, the emergence of ideologies of conservation and degradation, the development of scientific orthodoxies, or conceptions of the natural and human worlds. In recent years this loosely-defined corpus has tended to include the study of local exchanges of knowledge and information as a corollary to an earlier focus on conflict between systems of knowledge about medicine, landscape, and ecology.[110] The position of technicians and scientists in South Africa

---

107 This concept involves disaggregation, particularly on the part of state actors. See William Beinart, "Soil Erosion, Conservation and Ideas about Development: A Southern African Exploration, 1900–1960," *Journal of Southern African Studies* 11, no. 1 (1984): 53.

108 Crais, *Poverty, War, and Violence*, 8. Land, authority, and the transformation of rural society naturally remain at the heart of that book as well, although his thematic focus on violence engages them differently.

109 See Crais, *Poverty, War, and Violence*, 7–8; William Beinart, *The Rise of Conservation in South Africa: Settlers, Livestock, and the Environment, 1770–1950* (Oxford: Oxford University Press, 2003), xv.

110 See *inter alia* Beinart and Coates, *Environment and History*; Jane Carruthers, *The Kruger National Park: A Social and Political History* (Pietermaritzburg: University of Natal Press, 1995); Beinart, *Rise of Conservation*; Nancy Jacobs, *Environment, Power, and Injustice: A South African History* (Cambridge: Cambridge University Press, 2003); Alan Kirkaldy, *Capturing the Soul: the Vhavenda and the Missionaries 1870–1900* (Pretoria: Protea, 2005); Jacob Tropp, *Natures of Colonial Change: Environmental Relations in the Making of the Transkei* (Athens: Ohio University Press, 2006); Patrick Harries, *Butterflies and Barbarians: Swiss Missionaries and Systems of Knowledge in South-East Africa* (Oxford: James Currey, 2007); William Beinart and Karen Brown, *African Local Knowledge & Livestock Health: Diseases & Treatments in South Africa* (Athens: Ohio University Press, 2013); Ross, *Borders of Race*, 12–69.

has accordingly come in for re-evaluation in the last few years, in keeping with broader movements in African history. William Beinart, Karen Brown, and Daniel Gilfoyle have recently noted the independent and responsive nature of these individuals in adapting new knowledge and ideas, even when they did not accord with the ostensible aims of the state or when the results were less than salubrious.[111] Although their essay mostly concerned exchanges of ecological and medical knowledge, their observations apply to other sorts of technicians who interacted with local communities such as surveyors and inspectors. This volume follows those strands of technical autonomy and information transfer to tell a new story of the creation of native landscapes in South African history, without losing sight of the material factors that constrained or catalyzed particular actions.

Stories of communication, confrontation, incorporation, rationalization, and negotiation thus dictate the structure of this book. I have divided this volume into two major sections relating to the Eastern Cape and Fingoland (Chapters 2–4) and the Transvaal and Ha Ramabulana (Chapters 5–7) respectively. Africans, and some white settlers, sought to manage the autonomy of their societies as the colonial state became more pervasive. In both regions, they negotiated and modified the spatial prerogatives of colonial rule in ways that were specific to their circumstances. Each colony or republic differed in its composition, goals, and ultimately its geographical acts. The roles and activities of the agents of colonial geography, particularly land surveyors and cartographers, also resist generalization. The broad political, social, technical, and cultural background of each case therefore appears in the first chapter of the corresponding section.

Part I, covering the northeastern banks of the Kei and centering on the many Xhosa-speaking communities and sub-groups in the area between the Kei and Mbashe rivers, focuses on successive, progressively more invasive phases of colonial survey and mapping. Chapter 2 considers the makeup of the Cape Colony's survey machinery and its relationship to independent Xhosa societies that faced expulsion, erasure, and spatial engineering. Chapter 3 discusses the development of Fingoland and the Cape government's shift towards a more invasive ideal of individual tenure on small surveyed and titled lots that failed to produce the order colonial surveyors and administrators prescribed, whether through local circumvention or simple refusal. Finally, Chapter 4 treats the most invasive phase of the surveyor's employment on the Eastern Cape: the recasting of individual tenure and

111 William Beinart, Karen Brown, and Daniel Gilfoyle, "Experts and Expertise in Colonial Africa Reconsidered: Science and the Interpenetration of Knowledge," *African Affairs* 108, no. 432 (2009): 424–425.

governance in line with the Glen Grey Act of 1894. The Glen Grey system sought nothing less than a full-scale reorganization and proletarianization of African society under the guise of improvement and assimilation. Surveys in the division of Glen Grey disregarded local patterns of occupation and so generated a great deal of discontent. Thereafter, as surveys extended to districts in Fingoland, surveyors increasingly modified their instructions based on their own encounters and local negotiations, to the annoyance of the state. The extension of the Glen Grey system ceased shortly after 1916 in the face of concerns over the costs and benefits of carrying out careful surveys and the skepticism of the so-called traditional authorities and homesteaders who still held sway far to the northeast of the Kei.

The three chapters comprising Part II treat the Transvaal, called variously the South African Republic (ZAR), Transvaal Colony, and a number of other names depending on the dates. In Chapter 5, I deal with the inaccurate inspection systems of the Boers who first began squatting on the central Highveld. The vast gap between their settler-driven geographical archive's pretensions and the existing landscape figure prominently, as well as the odd usefulness—even necessity—of that gap for the purposes of the state. The difficulty of reforming that system by employing precise survey and mapping directly relates to the unwillingness and inability of the ZAR to press its absolute claims against powerful African kingdoms as well as settler and state desires to erase existing landscapes. Chapter 6 describes the longest-running adversarial encounter within the nineteenth century Transvaal: the standoff between the ZAR and the western Venda kingdom of Ha Ramabulana. Surveyors and land inspectors were not such invasive figures there as in the reserves near the Kei, but their activities (and, at times, personal agendas) still figured into contests over the land that culminated in the military destruction of the state in 1898. As the final chapter in Part II attests, however, the ZAR's defeat of the Venda king Mphephu in 1898 did not end Ramabulana power. With the South African War (1899–1902) and British annexation of the Transvaal, the king returned, and employed a variety of territorial interventions to restore his authority underneath the cadastral framework that the colony progressively extended over his former lands. The British administration and the provincial government that followed made significant concessions to gain his acquiescence to their rule, concessions that permitted him to regain his *de facto* primacy over Venda chiefs and people in the region before his death at the beginning of 1925.

I conclude in chapter 8 by examining a number of developments after the South African War that indicated a growing centralization of colonial power over land and the concomitant universalization of strategies to countermand it. The 1903–1905 Lagden Commission (formally the South African Native Affairs Commission, or SANAC) took evidence from witnesses all over the region on matters of land and administration, and brought together various colonial and African ideas on native landholding and survey for the first time, albeit with some telling lacunae in the conversation. The subsequent 1905 judgment in *ex parte Tsewu*, in favor of African title to land without restriction, threatened to extend the Cape's potentially permissive and assimilative land policy to the rest of South Africa.

Ironically, the Tsewu victory moved the state and its survey officials towards a cadastrally-defined segregationist model for African ownership. Both study areas theoretically came under a single unified system of governance within the Union of South Africa in 1910, but the variations in power and the terms of land settlement were great enough that no single solution could address them all. The result of this impasse was the Natives Land Act of 1913, which aspired to institute a legal cordon between 'white' and 'black' lands based on the lines of demarcation within the geographical archive. Later policies moved the cordon or reorganized space within the confines of that older elemental structure, but the framework the surveyors laid down still resonates in the form of cadastral politics today.

PART 1

Imagining Lands without Chiefs

CHAPTER 2

Redefining Land and Location in the Eastern Cape

In January 1932, the 67-year-old Presbyterian missionary Tiyo Burnside Soga tendered a plea to the office of the South African Prime Minister, J.B.M. Hertzog, regarding a parcel of well-watered land then located in the district of Stutterheim just to the west of the Kei River. Soga, a nephew of the Anglican convert and missionary Tiyo Soga and the grandson of the Ngqika councilor Old Soga who had long served the chiefs Ngqika, Tyhali, and Sandile, requested compensation for unfair confiscation of land following the War of Ngcayecibi in 1877–1878.[1] T.B. Soga wrote that his grandfather was, before that war,

> in occupation of certain land in the Gaika [Ngqika] Territory in the District of King-Williamstown, Records and evidence can prove that he took no part in the rebellion but nevertheless after it was over his land was taken from him and sold without compensation.
>
> The property in question was sold as Lot No. 4060 situate in the Division of Kingwilliamstown and in the late Gaika Territory called "SOGA" measuring seven hundred and ninety five morgen, three hundred and eighty seven square roods [about 1,650 acres].
>
> Amongst the Gaika Community this piece of land is still referred to as the "Soga's" farm, and in view of the refusal of my grandfather to join in the rebellion his dispossession can only be regarded as a hasty war measure which cannot be held justifiable when regarded from an unbiased standpoint after the feeling in existence at the time has subsided.[2]

1 Many Cape officials had viewed Soga with particular favor for his early adoption of European farming methods, although Soga's lack of a spiritual conversion to accompany the technological one left missionaries suspicious. See J.B. Peires, *The House of Phalo: A History of the Xhosa People in the Days of Their Independence* (Berkeley: University of California, 1982), 108; Colin Bundy, *The Rise and Fall of the South African Peasantry* 2nd ed. (Cape Town: David Philip, 1988), 45–46; Les Switzer, *Power & Resistance in an African Society: The Ciskei Xhosa and the Making of South Africa* (Madison: University of Wisconsin Press, 1993), 120–121; Richard Price, *Making Empire: Colonial Encounters and the Creation of Imperial Rule in Nineteenth-Century Africa* (Cambridge: Cambridge University Press, 2008), 117–119. Tiyo Burnside Soga was the son of Zaze, Tiyo Soga's half-brother.

2 T.B. Soga to J.B.M. Hertzog, 12 Jan 1932, File Stut.5, Office of the Surveyor-General, Cape Town (hereafter SGO-Cape).

 | DOI 10.1163/9789004282292_003

To investigate the matter, the Prime Minister's office forwarded his letter to the Native Affairs Department, which in turn forwarded it to the Surveyor-General of the Cape Province in February 1932. In response, the Deputy Surveyor-General, J.H. Holland, transcribed excerpts from a group of records dealing with the confiscation and survey of Ngqika lands in general and forwarded them to Native Affairs. Holland asserted that he "cannot confirm or disprove that the farm 'Soga' is the piece of land which the original Soga was in occupation of, but the point is not material inasmuch as it was definitely the policy of the Government of that day to entirely clear the Gaikas from that territory and people it with Europeans."[3] Furthermore, the case must have been "duly considered at that time" and any applicable compensation offered in Gcalekaland (Kentani district in particular; see Chapter 3), where the Colony relocated loyal Ngqika on far smaller and less arable plots of land in 1878 after the defeat and death of Sandile.[4] The land had never been surveyed or granted by the Cape government for Soga's grandfather, whose claim to land existed only at the pleasure of Sandile and vanished with the dispossession of that chief. By invoking the destruction of the conceptual place, the Deputy Surveyor-General obviated any question of the identity of the parcel in Stutterheim bearing the Soga family name; by setting forth the chronology of survey, he eradicated any claim pertaining to that particular cadaster.

Reverend Soga clearly devised some sections of his plea with rhetorical position in mind. Soga characterizes himself as "a native Missionary" resident in the district of Matatiele, Griqualand East, accepting for the purpose of the letter the subordinate position assigned to Xhosa (and indeed all Africans) within the racial hierarchy of Hertzog's South Africa.[5] He emphasizes the loyalty of his grandfather to the colony and appeals to a sense of justice for redress, and concedes that "the land cannot now be returned," but the moral injustice of taking the land required suitable redress. The loyalty of Old Soga was admittedly not absolute, but he had given up the struggle against the colony and retired to his home village before its African levies killed him in 1878, and

---

3 J.H. Holland to Secretary of Native Affairs, 13 Feb 1932, File Stut.5, SGO-Cape. Some wealthy Africans also bought a few of these farms; see Bundy, *Rise and Fall*, 88, and the names of owners on J. Newey, "Gaika Location, Containing Portions of the Divisions of Cathcart, Stutterheim, and Komgha" (1889), Maps 2/1892, KAB. 'Soga' (No. 144) was however owned at that time by a J.E. Broneman.

4 Ibid. The lots envisaged in Kentani were only about ten acres each; see Chapter 3.

5 Harvey Feinberg, "The Natives Land Act of 1913 in South Africa: Politics, Race and Segregation in the Early 20th Century," *International Journal of African Historical Studies* 26, no. 1 (1993): 65–109.

Hertzog never bothered to ask about it.[6] What is interesting geographically is that the younger Soga identifies the land by indicating its concordance with a place that persisted in the memories and landscapes of individual Ngqika, while providing identifiable cadastral information (name of parcel, area in morgen, and number of sale) that links an older landscape to the engineered, legible ideals of successive governments in Cape Town and Pretoria.[7]

This hybrid of cadastral information and landscape memory authenticated Soga's specific details and situated them within an administrative and territorial landscape the officials of the Union could recognize. However, the claim also exposes the flattening of official discourse over territory by the 1930s. The data with Soga's claim were based upon a fiction, one that the colonial government had promoted through its structures of knowledge: that the farm called 'Soga' correlated in some necessary way to the land previously occupied in location and extent, and that title in 1932 had the same implications as occupancy in 1877. Soga's invocation further confers representational authority upon the cadaster, and recognizes its correlation with an actual landscape—a concordance that itself was clearly fictional. Soga mentions the sale and quitrent values of the land as well as an indeterminate 'true' value, which melds the idea of land as a flexible, community resource within a social landscape with the idea of land as an alienable commodity with an assessable monetary value, but also recognizes that the landscape that produced its true value is not recoverable. The appeal also raises the marks of legibility the state prized: revenue, legality, and absolute position.

We do not know anything else about the genesis or the ultimate outcome of Reverend Soga's appeal for compensation, except that no land changed hands. We also cannot say much more about the place that Old Soga occupied before 1878, and the farm 'Soga' that may or may not have overlapped it, except that the cadastral definition of the farm in 1878 followed instructions to survey farms of about 1,500 acres each for European occupation.[8] We only know

6 Timothy Stapleton, "'Valuable, Gallant and Faithful Assistants': The Fingo (or Mfengu) as Colonial Military Allies during the Cape-Xhosa Wars, 1835–1881," in *Soldiers and Settlers in Africa, 1850–1918*, ed. Stephen Miller (Leiden: Brill, 2009), 43.

7 The standardized morgen unit of area is peculiar to South Africa, and represents 2.116539816 English acres (rounded to 0.8567 hectares, 0.008565 km^2, or 0.003307 mi^2). See D.R. Hendrikz, *South African Units of Length and Area*, Special Publication No. 2 (Pretoria: Department of Lands, 1944).

8 "Instructions to a Commission Appointed by H.E. the Governor…," 4 Sep 1878, 2, S.10819 (vol. 829C), SGO-Cape. The use of acres instead of morgen catered to the expected abilities of the surveyor, a Scottish immigrant named Donald Macdonald.

T.B. Soga's request from its referral to the Surveyor-General and the accompanying discussion of property, ownership, and provenance, with references to the radical reorganization and redistribution of land that took place in the Kei valley between 1850 and 1913. The spatial reorganization of the areas abutting the Kei looked absolute enough that Soga presumed the authority of its visual structures and landmarks, despite having grown up during the period of uncertain colonial power when much of that framework came into existence. Just as the missionaries augured the application of European social and cultural structures to non-European societies, the surveyor and the cartographer progressively imparted a European model of spatial order through the creation of legible territories, followed by their atomization into units and repurposing into farms, reserves, townships, outspans, and locations. But like the missionaries, colonial surveyors and cartographers worked on—and over—a contested landscape.[9]

Surveyors possessed great power as extensions of the colonial apparatus, and on the Eastern Cape after 1850 they divided lands as quickly as possible to ensure speedy European occupation and prevent untrammeled African reoccupation. Colonial surveyors divided Sandile's pre-1878 lands into 237 large farms, two township commonages, and several reserves for European immigrants by the end of 1879, not only providing revenue to the colonial government and rendering ex-rebel and refugee Ngqika landless, but also adding crucial data to the colonial geographical archive and appendages to the body of the state in the form of diagrams and titles.[10] The surveyors who divided and defined those lands re-drew the landscape, changing it from a dark patch of chaos outside direct state authority into a legible, rational, modern space, although that was only possible by uprooting the Ngqika sources of landscape memory who might challenge it effectively.[11] Beyond their centrality to delimitation,

9 See Elizabeth Elbourne, *Blood Ground: Colonialism, Missions, and the Contest for Christianity in the Cape Colony and Britain, 1799–1853* (Kingston, ON: McGill-Queens University Press, 2002), 7–22.

10 Cape Parliamentary Paper (hereafter CPP) G.33-'80, *Report of the Surveyor-General for the Year 1879*, 11. The orders to begin advertising farms began in January 1879; see J. Laing (Commissioner of Crown Lands & Public Works) to A. de Smidt (Surveyor-General), 20 Jan 1879, S.10819, vol. 829C, SGO-Cape. Memorials requesting grants of land in the Location had already begun arriving in 1878, see Memorial of W.P. Ferriera, [n.d.] 1878, [F40], CO 4198, Cape Archives Depot, Cape Town (hereafter KAB).

11 James C. Scott, *Seeing Like a State: How Certain Schemes to Improve the Human Condition Have Failed* (Yale: Yale University Press, 1998), 37–39; Raymond B. Craib, *Cartographic Mexico: A History of State Fixations and Fugitive Landscapes* (Durham: Duke University Press, 2004), 164–168.

surveyors also determined the value of lands surveyed, and ascribed official names to the land being divided—even going so far as appropriating (in the case of Soga) the names of the very families being driven from the land, creating the combined illusion of authenticity and legitimacy. Holland's words in response to the Soga claim—and the inclusion of transcriptions of the surveyor's instructions from 1878—further show that it was only the act of the land surveyor that created the formal space in contention, regardless of any other legal issues surrounding the expulsion of the Ngqika from the western banks of the Kei. The activities of surveyors on the ground, both as agents and as mediators, thus were the immediate loci of discourse between colony, settler, and colonized about land ever eastward.

Most of the colonizing processes that intersected with survey and mapping were not unique to the Colony of the Cape of Good Hope, but had global scope. These processes included increasing settler hunger for land with its concomitant demand for labor, and the extension of colonial rule, law, and economy over previously-independent polities. In turn, these processes entailed the reorganization, rationalization, and simplification of political and social economies to facilitate rule as well as the extraction of labor, land, and resources.[12] Surveyors were first and foremost technicians, so their work addressed specific tasks or problems in the mechanics of the colonial land system, using scientific knowledge and practices fundamental to European ideas of territory and ownership in ways that presumed their universality. When land policy at the Colony of the Cape of Good Hope initially came into contact with Xhosa-speaking polities, the surveyors correspondingly gave these apparent anomalies a wide berth until colonial power could dictate the reorganization of those landscapes, or local people themselves acquiesced to the act.

Spatial Order and Early Colonial Encounters

The story of land alienation and dispossession is a familiar part of histories of South Africa, but there is less discussion of what order existed on the land before or how the encounter affected the knowledge that entered the geographic archive. Despite the complexity of the subject, we still must somehow

12 See John C. Weaver, *The Great Land Rush and the Making of the Modern World, 1650–1900* (Kingston, ON: McGill-Queen's University Press, 2003), esp. chs. 4–8. On far-reaching rural "simplification" and resource management see Scott, *Seeing Like a State*, 225–229; Jacob A. Tropp, *Natures of Colonial Change: Environmental Relations in the Making of the Transkei* (Athens: Ohio University Press, 2006), 31–88.

characterize the composition, history, and evolution of the spatial universes that informed cross-cultural interactions in the Colony of the Cape of Good Hope. Every part of colonial South Africa had its own specific constellations of power and practice, but we can make a few useful generalizations through the early history of contacts between Europeans and Africans in the Eastern Cape region. I do not mean to suggest that these societies were internally uniform or in some kind of primordial, unchanging equilibrium beforehand, and I am aware of the additional perils of neo-tribalization in ascribing identifications to precolonial South African groups.[13] This means that we can identify some general spatial patterns in African agripastoral societies and their European-derived counterparts in southern Africa, but that we must be careful to qualify these descriptions once we approach specific cases.

In African history generally, low population densities meant that arable land was a widespread resource, and networks of kin and bonds of personal loyalty meant that individuals rarely sought to exercise permanent rights to a particular extent of land. The power of the individual over the land could vary so greatly by society and generation as to sometimes allow the effective sale of land through barter or its transfer as bridewealth.[14] That abundance of land, however, meant that wealth in people or animals was far more important and exit was a viable alternative to conflict, a point relevant to understanding slavery as a socially-embedded source of wealth and control in some parts of Africa.[15] In southern Africa, enslavement was less common even with the rise of colonialism, but absorption and hierarchical systems of clientage were no less widespread.[16]

This dynamic allowed Bantu-speaking agripastoralists to absorb and incorporate Khoesan-speaking hunters or herders, and the evident unevenness of

---

13 John K. Wright, "Sonqua, Bosjesmans, Bushmen, and abaThwa: Comments and Queries on Pre-Modern Identification," *South African Historical Journal* 35, no. 2 (1996): 16–29; Paul S. Landau, *Popular Politics in the History of South Africa, 1400–1948* (Cambridge: Cambridge University Press, 2010), 246–250.

14 John Iliffe, *Africans: The History of a Continent* new ed. (Cambridge: Cambridge University Press, 2007), 1–2, 100–130; Herbst, *States and Power in Africa*, 37–40; Michael J. Watts, "Idioms of Land and Labor: Producing Politics and Rice in Senegambia," in *Land in African Agrarian Systems*, ed. Thomas Bassett and Donald Crummey (Madison: University of Wisconsin Press, 1993), 159.

15 John K. Thornton, *Africa and Africans in the Making of the Atlantic World* 2nd ed. (Cambridge: Cambridge University Press, 1998), 87–90.

16 Barry Morton, "Servitude, Slave Trading, and Slavery in the Kalahari," in *Slavery in South Africa: Captive Labor on the Dutch Frontier*, ed. E. Eldredge and F. Morton (Boulder: Westview Press, 1994), 215–217.

the synthesis between the two owes to the larger populations of Bantu-speaking societies, whose systems of clientage enjoyed a cyclical relationship with the accumulation of vast herds of cattle, and whose models of land use and seasonal management could support more people.[17] Their population advantages were all the greater south of the Limpopo (or Vhembe) river where the incidence of trypanosomiasis (tsetse) and malaria falls off dramatically. Just as wealth in labor and livestock flourished on the Highveld and the well-watered coastal strips further south, so too did large wild game, allowing not only Bantu-speakers but also Khoesan herders and hunters to prosper, specialize, and interact in the transfer of people, goods, and knowledge.[18] Although many groups remained within decentralized networks or small chiefdoms, centers of trade and authority developed periodically wherever clear advantages existed.[19] A side effect of this wealth accumulation was social stratification and conflict over resources, notably water.

The system of land occupation under coastal Bantu-speaking societies shared certain common elements in the eighteenth century, including clan structures, kin and client networks with widely-distributed connections, and the vital importance of cattle as a measure of wealth. Spatially, these features manifested themselves in the institution of the homestead (*umzi* in Xhosa), which contained varying numbers of households that were not always directly related. Cattle byres tended to rest close to homestead dwellings, which in turn adjoined cultivated lands that could shift seasonally. Such complexes (*imizi*) were of variable size depending on personal patronage, and formed extended domestic spaces that were both secure and socially cohesive.[20] These homesteads were not egalitarian, but were complicated networks of obligation and authority where the 'head man' might control a great many cattle and have many wives, while the majority

17 Ben Maclennan, *A Proper Degree of Terror: John Graham and the Cape's Eastern Frontier* (Johannesburg: Ravan, 1986), 43–44; Pieter Jolly, "Interaction between South-Eastern San and Southern Nguni and Sotho Communities, c.1400 to c.1880," *South African Historical Journal* 35, no. 1 (1996): 30–61.

18 Martin Hall, *The Changing Past: Farmers, Kings, and Traders in Southern Africa, 200–1860* (Cape Town: David Philip, 1987), 43–73.

19 Innocent Pikirayi, *The Zimbabwe Culture: Origins and Decline of Southern Zambesian States* (Walnut Creek, CA: AltaMira, 2001), 152–153.

20 For highly simplified schematics of southern Nguni settlement circa 1800, see the diagrams in R. Derricourt, "Settlement in the Transkei and Ciskei before the Mfecane," in *Beyond the Cape Frontier: Studies in the History of the Transkei and Ciskei*, ed. C.C. Saunders and R. Derricourt (London: Longman, 1974), 66–68. Derricourt's spatial model is useful, but the primacy of social change via fission and 'tribal clustering' does not recognize the dynamic accretion and circulation of clients within and between these societies.

of households were monogamous and had fewer animals, and a variety of junior kin or clients exchanged labor for patronage.[21] On the land, the homestead might take the form of clustered dwellings or separate household enclosures depending on the physical character of the land, with cultivation situated in the most advantageous positions nearby and grazing reserved for less arable lands further afield.[22] Homesteads also did not exist in isolation, but operated within networks of exchange and patronage under at least nominal leadership.[23]

Clusters of such units, connected by fealty and kinship, formed networks of settlement across the land. In smaller areas, headmen and chiefs could parcel out land and resources to clients and kin in the area who would provide labor and food, but central authority fell off rapidly with distance and the reach of a chief or king could vary greatly.[24] Larger political units under chiefs or kings thus tended to be flexible, and the primacy of exit worked with the availability of open land against centralization.[25] Communities might move and generate new social formations entirely, or link with other networks if land proved to be unproductive, environmental conditions changed, conflict threatened, or people wished to colonize a promising area and start a new settlement.[26] These polities changed dynamically, meaning that not only their *arrangement* but also their *composition* could change markedly over time, and the cultivation of particular lands was impermanent and contingent upon short-term assessments of arability. Khoe pastoralists in the far southwest had sparser populations than Bantu-speakers, but the dynamism was perhaps even more important as a result.

The Dutch East India Company (VOC) in Cape Town and, later, British colonial authorities found such flexibility to be supremely illegible and frustrating, despite strenuous efforts at divination.[27] Their confusion shows. Maps of the period display multiple names that almost certainly refer to the same groups

---

21 Jack Lewis, "The Rise and Fall of the South African Peasantry: A Critique and Reassessment," *Journal of Southern African Studies* 11, no. 1 (1984): 4–6.

22 Derricourt, "Settlement in the Transkei and Ciskei before the Mfecane," 65–70.

23 On self-sufficiency and exchange in related homestead systems further east, see John Lambert, *Betrayed Trust: Africans and the State in Colonial Natal* (Pietermaritzburg: University of Natal Press, 1995), 8–12.

24 Clifton C. Crais, "Custom and the Politics of Sovereignty in South Africa," *Journal of Social History* 39, no. 3 (2006): 725.

25 Iliffe, *Africans*, 118–120; Herbst, *States and Power in Africa*, 39–40.

26 Allen M. Howard, "Nodes, Networks, Landscapes, and Regions: Reading the Social History of Tropical Africa 1700s–1920," in *The Spatial Factor in African History: The Relationship of the Social, Material, and Perceptual*, ed. Allen M. Howard and Richard M. Shain (Leiden: Brill, 2005), 93.

27 Crais, "Custom and the Politics of Sovereignty," 725.

of people, depending on which traveler had asked whom for information, and what other authorities a cartographer integrated with their work. The precise location of any group of people could be uncertain anyhow owing to African transhumance and European topographical ignorance, thus leading to a scheme of depiction that conveyed only a vague sense of occupation. As a result, broad areas 'lost' their inhabitants and became available for settler appropriation, even though it was rare that they were truly unoccupied.[28] From the beginning of European settler expansion into the lands of Khoesan-speakers outside Cape Town, they recast such unexpected occupants as illegal tenants, invaders, or potential sources of labor.

The Dutch, French, and other settlers from Europe who took up freehold and leasehold farms from 1657 onward, in contrast to their African counterparts, understood land as a scarce commodity that was secure only through title issued by the governing (and taxing) state.[29] The promise of obtaining land easily without fear of persecution lured a significant number of people to the Cape of Good Hope and other settler colonies. In the eighteenth century Cape Colony, a landless European immigrant farmer (known by the Dutch term *boer*) might obtain a grant of up to 6,000 acres on perpetual leasehold, and could expect similar grants for male children.[30] These loan farms required no survey, only registration with the local sheriff-magistrate (*landdrost*) and notation in Cape Town, although some of the more itinerant, outward-migrating farmers (*trekboers*) did not even comply with that and effectively squatted across the landscape.[31] Over time these rural farmers stopped seeing the

28 Norman Etherington, "A False Emptiness: How Historians May Have Been Misled by Early Nineteenth Century Maps of South-eastern Africa," *Imago Mundi* 56, no. 1 (2004): 67–86.

29 J.P. Kain and Elizabeth Baigent, *The Cadastral Map in the Service of the State* (Chicago: University of Chicago Press, 1992), 9–46; Leonard Guelke, "Land Tenure and Settlement at the Cape 1652–1812," in *The History of Surveying and Land Tenure Volume 1*, ed. C.G.C. Martin and K.J. Friedlaender (Cape Town: University of Cape Town, 1984), 9; Leonard Guelke, "Freehold Farmers and Frontier Settlers, 1652–1780," in *The Shaping of South African Society, 1652–1840*, ed. R. Elphick and H. Giliomee (Middletown, CT: Wesleyan University Press, 1989), 84–100.

30 John C. Weaver, "The Dismal Science, Land Reform, and the Cape Boers, 1805–1822," *Journal of Imperial and Commonwealth History* 29, no. 3 (2001): 8. Although some freehold and fifteen-year quitrent grant existed in the VOC era, they were a tiny minority relative to loan farms.

31 Leslie Clement Duly, *British Land Policy at the Cape, 1795–1844: A Study of Administrative Procedures in the Empire* (Durham: Duke University Press, 1968), 15; Maclennan, *A Proper Degree of Terror*, 57, 142–143.

provision of vast quantities of land to grantees under relatively loose governance as a stroke of good fortune, but rather as a right. Land was something that could be taken freely and then recognized by the authorities later, even though it came at the expense of the seasonal range of the transhumant Khoesan groups who, if they could, moved away from the acquisitive new migrants from Cape Town.[32] Trekboers expected their model of birthright expansion to continue even when their assumption of land began to cross over the edge of Bantu-speaking Africans' settlements in the Zuurveld region between the Fish and Sundays rivers.

At first, the Boers who settled with their slaves and laborers among interspersed African and mixed Khoe societies in the late eighteenth century did not create alarm. The Europeans did not utilize excessive amounts of land, and African communities did not pay much attention to claims to exclusive ownership at that point because they had little visible effect on the landscape. The Boers were powerful, but few compared to the populations of Xhosa-speaking agripastoral homesteads, and the latter may have expected to absorb the former through intermarriage and clientage, much like various Khoesan societies throughout the colonization of the South African subcontinent from the north.[33] Indeed the relationship between the two populations was initially symbiotic and even amicable, but the two groups had very different ideas about social position and incorporation, as well as the meaning of claims to land and resources.[34] These differences eventually escalated to cattle theft and open violence by 1779, despite the prior existence of beneficial exchange between the parties involved.

The outbreak of open warfare introduced a new and chaotic opacity to the edge of colonial rule, and highlighted the illegibility of the entire situation to the Company. The VOC in fact charged its company surveyors to compile more detailed topographical maps and define the eastern boundary of the colony in the 1700s, and although they could graft together the former in a way that created symbolic knowledge and an illusion of control, none of them evidently felt comfortable defining the latter beyond the occasional river.[35] Any line on a

---

32 Maclennan, *A Proper Degree of Terror*, 26.

33 J.B. Peires, *The House of Phalo: A History of the Xhosa People in the Days of Their Independence* (Berkeley: University of California Press, 1981), 53–54.

34 Hermann Giliomee, "The Eastern Frontier, 1770–1812," in *The Shaping of South African Society, 1652–1840*, ed. R. Elphick and H. Giliomee (Middletown, CT: Wesleyan, 1989), 432–433; Maclennan, *A Proper Degree of Terror*, 45–47.

35 Siegfried Huigen, *Knowledge and Colonialism: Eighteenth Century Travellers in South Africa* (Leiden: Brill, 2009), 219–220.

map was only as effective as the ability to police it, and neither the titular Xhosa authorities nor the Company whose fractious colonists were moving away from its control had that capacity in the eighteenth century.

With growing competition over rural land, and the illegibility of both the landscape and the people living upon it, the British who took over the Cape settlement during the Napoleonic Wars faced the task of understanding the dispositions of various South African societies—all of which required travel, inquiry, survey, and description, including the production of books and maps. One of the very first tasks at the Cape after the British first landed in late 1796 was to send a diplomatic agent, John Barrow, to undertake traverse surveys and journeys meant to produce a map of the territory and a substantive evaluation of its inhabitants.[36] The written accounts Barrow produced became the basis for marking difference among the 'natives' (in this instance, Khoesan) and the Boers at the same time that it reduced both to "traces on the landscape," while Barrow's maps effaced them almost completely.[37] After British occupation effectively became permanent in 1806 (though not legally until 1814) and especially when new English-speaking settlers arrived after 1820, competition between the forces of spatial control and local desires for colonial expansion became more complex and widespread, leading to concerted colonial military efforts to expel Bantu-speakers and control their interactions with the colonial population through the 1830s.[38] It would be an evolutionary process, but the preferred colonial remedy to encounters with African communities through the early 1860s remained to push or cajole them eastward into spaces where colonial military action had created some sort of temporary opening, and then survey the vacated land further west for sale to white settlers.

The 1830s however also witnessed the incorporation of Xhosa-speaking 'people without chiefs' into the colony for the first time, in the form of the

36 Nigel Penn, "Mapping the Cape: John Barrow and the First British Occupation of the Colony, 1795–1803," in *Maps and Africa*, ed. Jeffrey C. Stone (Aberdeen: University of Aberdeen, 1993), 108–127. The British erroneously believed the VOC had not charted the interior at all, but in fact the maps had been sent back to the Netherlands and were not rediscovered until 1950. See C. Koeman, ed., *Tabvlae Geographicae Qvibvs Colonia Bonae Spei Antiqva Depingitvr* (Amsterdam: NVHA Uitgevers Maatschappij, 1952), 1–4.

37 Mary Louise Pratt, *Imperial Eyes: Travel Writing and Transculturation* (London: Routledge, 1992), 59. Siegfried Huigen disagrees with the level of diminution Pratt ascribes to Barrow's textual treatment of human geography while admitting Barrow's fixation on the physical landscape outside of humans and his use of hierarchical classifications of people by physical and material traits; Huigen, *Knowledge and Colonialism*, 154–159.

38 Alan Lester, "Cultural Construction and Spatial Strategy on the Eastern Cape Frontier, 1806–c.1838," *South African Geographical Journal* 78, no. 2 (1996): 98–107.

'Fingoes' (Mfengu). Their conditional admission to the colony starting in 1835 marked a change in the older pattern, but the colonial government effectively took on the role of patron, and expected them to provide military service on its borders and contract labor for its farmers, in an arrangement of locations positioned for the benefit of European settlers.[39] Although this was the first incorporation of people from beyond the colonial boundary, it was not the first effort to engineer a settlement of nonwhites in volatile areas of the Eastern Cape. That distinction belongs to the Kat River Settlement, which the colonial government formed in 1829 as an area for Khoe farmers to take up smallholdings on European tenure—and which became a battleground for colonial ideas about race and civilization that the arrival of Xhosa-speakers certainly complicated.[40]

The communities that crossed west into the Cape Colony came from a variety of backgrounds before accepting or acquiring the Fingo metonym, but one thing they shared was relatively devolved authority which presumably eased their transition to the client role relative to the colonial state.[41] The affiliation and its social networks were attractive enough to Xhosa-speakers that people continued to cross into the colony and simply assume Fingo identity—or accept its ascription—with all the benefits and liabilities that carried, while Europeans avoided directly acknowledging the flexibility of Fingo identity to preserve their own benefits and sense of control.[42]

With the creation of the separate colony of British Kaffraria in 1847 and the Cape Colony's incorporation of several districts to the north in the early 1850s, colonial rule reached the Kei, and African communities under established chiefdoms entered the sphere of colonial governance. These chiefdoms controlled land and networks that did not see the colony as their primary referent, and so represented a major administrative problem for colonial pretensions of control. African social and cultural bodies embodied an order that was only legible to the colonial state through its belief in the total power of chiefs over land, labor, and livelihoods, and the ability of a British resident agent to meld various

39 Petrus van Biljon, *Grensbakens tussen Blank en Swart in Suid-Afrika* (Cape Town: Juta, 1947), 140–142.

40 Robert Ross, *The Borders of Race in Colonial South Africa: The Kat River Settlement, 1829–1856* (Cambridge: Cambridge University Press, 2014), 7–11.

41 Alan Webster, "Unmasking the Fingo: The War of 1835 Revisited," in *The Mfecane Aftermath: Reconstructive Debates in South African History*, ed. Carolyn Hamilton (Johannesburg: Witwatersrand University Press, 1995), 241–242, 255–261.

42 Timothy Stapleton, "The Expansion of a Pseudo-Ethnicity on the Eastern Cape: Reconsidering the Fingo 'Exodus' of 1865," *International Journal of African Historical Studies* 29 (1996): 233–250.

African practices and British principles in a hybrid that ironically helped to concentrate more power in chiefly authority.[43] In these areas, European geographical knowledge was even spottier than it was in the colony at large.

Institutionalizing Survey at the Cape of Good Hope

The early survey profession at the Cape of Good Hope was far from a uniform institution. Under the rule of the VOC and through the Napoleonic Wars, there was only one Company or government surveyor at a time, charged with supervising fortifications as well as the laying out of *erven* (lots) in towns and the assay of public works in the Colony. It is not recorded how many, if any, other surveyors resided in the Colony during the VOC period, though the number could not have been great as there was little demand for expensive scientific surveys and the registration of loan farms—each literally a 'place' (*plaats*, or *plaas* in Afrikaans today)—did not legally require them. After the second British conquest of the Cape of Good Hope in 1806, the office soon merged with others and enjoyed the support of a small battery of sworn surveyors. These sworn surveyors, whose credentials consisted of little more than an oath until 1835, drew no salary, and initially only performed private survey work in their locales. But under the Cradock land grant system of 1813 that opened Crown lands on perpetual quitrent tenure and permitted the conversion of existing lands to quitrent, the government intended that sworn surveyors inspect all new farms on government pay as one member of a local land commission, with the ambitious goal of regularizing revenue and fostering productivity.[44] That requirement expanded the scope of government employment for the surveyor's eye, but it also multiplied requests for land grants that piled up in the hundreds, leading government officials to presume rather than assure the responsible conduct of surveyors' work.[45]

---

43 Price, *Making Empire*, 205–210. The Cape governor in 1846 characterized the chiefs so incorporated as Fingoes by dint of colonial clientage, although they did not accept that ascription; see Stapleton, "Valuable, Gallant and Faithful Assistants," 24.

44 Duly, *British Land Policy*, 52–53; Weaver, "Dismal Science," 3–4, 14–26. The land commission system involved a local *landdrost* or magistrate, the surveyor, and a third person meant to be drawn from the local governing body (*heemraad*). This of course did not prevent settlers occupying territory well before any grant, which was a common tactic throughout southern Africa.

45 Maclennan, *A Proper Degree of Terror*, 149.

The growing density of farm settlement at the Cape led a Board of Commissioners to prescribe the creation of a centralized post of Surveyor-General in 1826. This officer would superintend and regulate of surveys within the colony, promote a trigonometrical survey, and produce a map of the Colony.[46] Charles Cornwallis Michell, an energetic colonel of the Royal Engineers with a penchant for sketch and watercolor, accepted the post in 1828 and quickly set about these tasks when he arrived at the beginning of 1829.[47] The limitations of colonial knowledge, a shortage of funds, and a simple lack of colonial will to pursue triangulation and mapping stopped Michell cold. An enormous backlog of farm and town plot diagrams awaiting approval and, after 1834, the added duty to administer titles for land, made the workload impossible for the two or three people in the Office of the Surveyor-General.[48] The resulting frustration over slow land registration in the eastern districts, including some cases of outright fraud, may have contributed to the departure of *voortrekker* parties for the interior in the following years.[49]

Changes aimed at standardization and control produced some results, such as the examination of diagrams before the payment of survey fees and an examination for surveyors who sought government work. A Board of Enquiry in 1827 suggested a two-level survey for prospective surveyors, but the Astronomer Royal at the Cape Observatory, Fearon Fallows, believed that none of the practicing land surveyors had the education or ability to pass the upper level of examination, which involved the mathematics necessary to correct the surveys of the lower level.[50] In 1834 Michell set forth a new, more basic model for the examination of land surveyors in the Colony who wished to perform government work, and in 1836 he extended the requirement to surveyors admitted before the regulation.[51] This examination contained sections on

---

46 "Report of the Commission," in G.M. Theal, *Records of the Cape Colony* vol. 27 (Cape Town: Saul Solomon, 1897), 493–502.

47 On Michell generally, see Gordon Richings, *The Life and Work of Charles Michell* (Simon's Town: Fernwood Press, 2006).

48 P.J. Venter, "Government Departments of the Cape of Good Hope 1806–1910" (unpublished manuscript, Cape Town, 1933), 79. The Surveyor-General was also Commissioner of Public Works in this early period.

49 Timothy Keegan, *Colonial South Africa and the Origins of the Racial Order* (Cape Town: David Philip, 1996), 187. Keegan suggests that corruption and incompetence were routine for surveyors, but the evidence implies that the inadequate administrative machinery and low survey tariffs were far greater issues.

50 Fisher, "Emergence and Education," 41–42.

51 J.G. Obree, L.F. Braun, and R.C. Fisher, "Land Policy at the Cape and the Office of the Surveyor-General, 1813–1912," in *The History of Surveying and Land Tenure Collected Papers*

drafting and topographical drawing, mathematics including plane trigonometry, and a practicum in the use of instruments including theodolites or a sextant (circle) and azimuth, which assured a basic standardization of the tools and skills of the trade but effectively wrote off the prospect of planimetrically accurate and mathematically precise cartography. After the exam, the candidate provided surety bonds for £400 against the cost of resurveys and could employ the title of 'Government Land Surveyor.'[52] In theory, exams and bonds improved the accuracy, efficiency, and responsibility of land surveyors, but in practice it was the opening volley in a struggle for autonomy and authority between governments and surveyors that continued until the Survey Act (No. 9) of 1927 took full effect in 1929.

The demand for inspection and survey also created enormous growth within the ranks of the Government Land Surveyors in the century before Union. Beyond Cradock's proclamation, survey was also required for land transfers, which ideally would lead to a fully surveyed colonial landscape in time.[53] In 1818, the Cape Almanac listed 17 'sworn surveyors' residing in the Colony. By 1860, a total of 102 had been admitted to practice as Government Land Surveyors, 31 of them between 1855 and 1859 alone. Between 1860 and 1913, 365 more surveyors joined their ranks, though the rate of new admissions stabilized after about 1880.[54] At the time of the statutory incorporation of a mandatory Cape Surveyors' Institute in 1904, 113 surveyors (both active and retired) received information.[55] The growth in absolute numbers, however, still represented a surprisingly small total for a profession charged with the delineation and remediation of territorial spaces across more than half a million square kilometers.

This community of land surveyors shared some key characteristics. All were white and male, as was true of most colonial technicians during the nineteenth century, and all were literate. European administrators deemed Africans to be incapable of undertaking the work, and considered women to be unsuited in temperament, education, and physical capacity—assumptions that the

---

Volume 2: Surveying and Land Tenure at the Cape, 1813–1912, ed. R.C. Fisher (Cape Town: IPLSWC, 2004), 16.

52 R.C. Fisher, "The Emergence and Education of the Land Surveying Profession 1813–1912," in *The History of Surveying and Land Tenure Collected Papers Volume 2: Surveying and Land Tenure at the Cape, 1813–1912*, ed. R.C. Fisher (Cape Town: IPLSWC, 2004), 42–43; Obree, Braun, and Fisher, "Land Policy at the Cape," 16 n. 23. The surety requirement ended in 1890, replaced by a standard insurance bond.

53 Duly, *British Land Policy*, 183–184.

54 Compiled from Surveyors' Oaths, File S.8710, volumes 739A-739E, SGO-Cape.

55 Fisher, "Emergence and Education," 41.

surveyors shared and reinforced in their interactions with rural people.[56] These assumptions were hardly unique to land surveying, and were systemic enough in settler society that no female or nonwhite applicants even attempted to enter the Cape surveying profession between 1860 and 1913. Most land surveyors also came from middle-class backgrounds, which privileged both the technical content of the surveyor's work as well as the image of masculine physical prowess deemed necessary for fieldwork. A majority of the land surveyors active before 1900 were born in Europe, primarily in Great Britain and Germany, and often received their educations in Europe (including in surveying, which only gained a local curriculum at the Cape in 1874). These immigrants came to the Cape with the intent of taking up the profession as their means of support despite a relatively low tariff and no occupational security. The percentage of Cape land surveyors born in Europe exceeded the average of 6.8% (1865) to 4.3% (1891) European-born rural whites and very likely the higher Colony-wide percentage (about 15%) as well.[57] There were a few established and well-connected multi-generational surveying families such as the Melvills, Greatheads, and Watermeyers, who usually set up practices in the districts nearest to Cape Town. New arrivals therefore tended to settle in more remote districts or take up apprenticeships, given that senior surveyors in a particular area usually had priority in obtaining government work. That practice reflected a desire to limit delay and travel expenses, but it also expressed a desire to avoid conflict between surveyors in the field and a belief that a surveyor's familiarity with a locale and its people was conducive to a competent and careful survey.

As professionals, land surveyors tended to work alone or with one apprentice; they were certainly paid as individuals and all correspondence originates from the surveyor of record in that person's hand, although in the case of triangulation or other precise operations surveyors sometimes found it beneficial to work together.[58] Other people were always involved, however. Generally

56 On the differentiation of genders in fieldwork, see Alison Blunt, *Travel, Gender, and Imperialism: Mary Kingsley and West Africa* (New York: Guilford Press, 1994), 65–71; on the debate over African capacity and advancement with regard to science in the late 19th century, see Saul Dubow, *A Commonwealth of Knowledge: Science, Sensibility, and White South Africa, 1820–2000* (Oxford: Oxford University Press, 2006), 109–117.

57 A.J. Christopher, *The Crown Lands of British South Africa, 1853–1914* (Kingston, ON: Limestone Press, 1984), 4.

58 The position of the surveyor as an autonomous professional is further confirmed by F.H.S. Orpen, who discovered, while conducting trial observations for a primary triangulation, that "I had been proposing to myself to do what appears to be quite beyond the power of a solitary Surveyor who has to live by his work" and that he needed a second trained person to hold a heliostat for distant observations. See Orpen to Maclear, 3 Apr 1871,

these people were unskilled Africans hired locally to build stone beacons to mark corners or survey points, perform general labor, or interpret for the surveyor. But without any legal obligation to produce a daily record of activity before the Survey Act of 1927, our knowledge of their operations is fragmentary, and surveyors only reported disruptions that radically changed their plans. This relative silence (outside of fairly mechanical correspondence about logistics and pay) represents a discursive effacement of the surveyor as well as the displacement of any African adjuncts or inhabitants.[59] The invisibility of surveyors on the landscapes, beyond a signature denoting their authority as observers and experts, was itself a necessary element of the objective pretense of scientific geography.[60] That tendency for effacement also explains comments in Cape Town regarding whether an individual was "well fitted both by professional ability and tact to deal with the natives," as the Surveyor-General described one long-time location surveyor in 1876, although that vague statement suggests that the Surveyor-General did not know much more about local interactions than we do.[61]

It is ironic, then, that many surveyors displayed rather poor knowledge of the non-European landscapes where they lived and worked, and sometimes even of other white rural residents. For example, language skills beyond English were not a prerequisite for admission to practice in the Cape during the colonial era. The graphical and numerical cadaster was the only communication required of a specialist, and the intrusion of extraneous information about the land could only harm that. Surprisingly few surveyors had fluency in languages other than English, even in the case of Dutch or its local dialects. Still fewer surveyors appear to have known more than a few words of Xhosa or other Bantu languages, relying instead upon interpreters or local magistrates, which increased the perceptual distance between the positivism of the land surveyor and the people actually living on the land and also fostered distrust.[62] Contrary

---

pp. 69–70, RGO 15/66, Royal Greenwich Observatory Archives, Cambridge University Library (CUL).

59 The combination of effacement and displacement usually figures into discussion of travel writing, but it works in this more rigidly scientific venue as well. See Mary Louise Pratt, "Scratches on the Face of the Country; or, What Mr. Barrow Saw in the Land of the Bushmen," *Critical Inquiry* 12, no. 1 (1985): 127–128.

60 Matthew Edney, *Mapping an Empire: The Geographical Construction of British India, 1765–1843* (Chicago: University of Chicago Press, 1997), 74.

61 CPP G.33-'77, *Report of the Surveyor-General* [for the Year 1876], 8.

62 For example, the surveyor in charge of location surveys between 1900 and 1920, E. Gilbert Hall, still required an interpreter in 1916 despite over thirty years' residence in the European settlement at Cala in the Transkei; at the same time, Hall decried the lack of

to the supposition that surveyors' presence near the forefront of colonization led many to become magistrates in the new districts northeast of the Kei after 1860, there were very few appointments of that sort; even then military experience was their qualification, not their knowledge of surveying.[63] Surveyor-magistrates like Joseph Millerd Orpen and Charles Lennox Stretch were thus unusual and rarely stayed very long in a field office. Many land surveyors did qualify as justices of the peace (the better to settle land disputes and perhaps earn additional fees), and some, including Orpen and his older brother F.H.S. Orpen, became prominent in the inner circles of colonial governments. Land surveyor John X. Merriman, who became the last Prime Minister of the Cape Colony before Union (1908–1910), was perhaps the most prominent example of this pattern that existed in the Transvaal as well.[64]

The number of surveyors who headed magistracies in the Transkei pales in particular comparison to the number of missionaries' offspring who took up those posts. That latter group often enjoyed an advantage in straddling worlds, as part of the political and social economy of the areas where they resided. Many grew up among Xhosa-speakers, were known to the people and nominally respected the chiefs, and became fluent (or very nearly so) in Xhosa dialects, which aided their prospects for entry if not safety. The killing of the magistrate Hamilton Hope and his party on the orders of the Mpondomise chief Mlhontlo at the outset of the Transkeian Rebellion of 1880–1881 illustrates this point. In that episode, Hope's clerk, the brother of a missionary, was the only European spared because the missionaries and traders were individuals within local social landscapes and not mere functionaries of a distant power.[65] Land surveyors did not possess this indispensable, though complicating, advantage unless they were also missionaries or the children of missionaries. The well-known connections between Victorian geographical science and African missionaries such as David Livingstone and Mary Slessor

surveyors who understood the "Natives & their Ways." See G.R. Hughes (Secretary of Lands) to A.H. Cornish-Bowden (Surveyor-General), 13 Sep 1916; Hall to Bowden, 23 Mar 1916; both S.8676, SGO-Cape.

63 Clifton C. Crais, *The Politics of Evil: Magic, State Power, and the Political Imagination in South Africa* (Cambridge: Cambridge University Press, 2002), 74.

64 J.M. Orpen, *Reminiscences of Life in South Africa from 1846 to the Present Day* (Cape Town: Struik, 1964 [1908]), 33. Merriman's opposite number in the Transvaal, the surveyor J.F.B. Rissik, was Minister for Lands and Native Affairs from 1907 to 1910, and the first administrator of the Transvaal Province under Union.

65 Sean Redding, *Sorcery and Sovereignty: Taxation, Power, and Rebellion in South Africa, 1880–1963* (Athens: Ohio University Press, 2006), 32.

notwithstanding, the number of missionaries and magistrates who in turn possessed the scientific training and equipment to survey colonial land for title was also exceedingly small, although a number of them produced traverse maps and sketches of their own volition that had value for basic administrative needs or compilation mapping.[66] Surveyors on the Eastern Cape were therefore not cross-cultural agents in quite the same way that missionaries, magistrates, and settlers in the zone of interaction tended to be, but in translating a system of measurement and representation created in Europe across evidently unmarked yet clearly productive land in Africa, they struck just as deep a nerve.

The Surveyor-General and other proponents of rational government obsessed over matters of precision and accuracy and believed in their absolute importance, just as those matters occupied other fields of scientific endeavor during the nineteenth century.[67] Within the surveying profession, technical ability could vary widely, as did the amount of trust survey authorities would put in the scientific precision of a surveyor's work. The class of work that Government Land Surveyors performed most—cadastral surveys for purposes of title—was not especially rigorous in terms of precision even on farms of five or six thousand acres. Provided that surveys of farms and blocks had numerical consistency, and after 1879 that some kind of documented rough triangulation served as a check on truly gross errors, the work was adequate for basic administration.[68] The highly precise trigonometrical surveying necessary to fix absolute points

66 L.F. Braun, "Missionary Cartography in Colonial Africa: Cases from South Africa," in *History of Cartography: International Symposium of the ICA Commission, 2010*, ed. E.C. Liebenberg and I.J. Demhardt (Berlin: Springer, 2012), 249–257; Matthew Edney, "The Irony of Imperial Mapping," in *The Imperial Map: Cartography and the Mastery of Empire*, ed. James R. Akerman (Chicago: University of Chicago Press, 2009), 31. On Livingstone and Slessor, see Felix Driver, *Geography Militant: Cultures of Exploration and Empire* (London: Blackwell, 2001), ch. 4 *passim*; Cheryl McEwan, "'The Mother of the Peoples': Geographical Knowledge and the Empowering of Mary Slessor," in *Geography and Imperialism 1820–1940*, ed. John M. MacKenzie (Manchester: Manchester University Press, 1995): 125–150.

67 See Michael P. Adas, *Machines as the Measure of Men: Science, Technology, and Ideologies of Western Dominance* (Cornell: Cornell University Press, 1989), 259–265; Simon Schaffer, "Exact Measurement is an English Science," in *The Values of Precision*, ed. M. Norton Wise (Princeton: Princeton University Press, 1995), 135–172; for a South African application, see Deborah Posel, "A Mania for Measurement: Statistics and Statecraft in the Transition to Apartheid," in *Science and Society in Southern Africa*, ed. Saul Dubow (Manchester: Manchester University Press, 2000), 116–125.

68 See Cape Proclamation No. 229 of 26 Feb 1879.

on the earth's surface, and construct a framework for consistent if not accurate mapping, conversely represented a stratospheric level of complexity in terms of mathematical rigor and astronomical work—skills that few land surveyors possessed before the opening of the surveying program at the South African College in 1874. The two drives worked at cross purposes, even after geodetic operations on the coast up to the Kei from 1859 to 1862 ('Bailey's Survey') and from the Cape Colony to Natal between 1883 and 1892 (the Geodetic Survey of South Africa) promised more consistency in such individual surveys.

Regulations, examinations, and bonds could not, after all, automatically transform the land surveyor into a precise instrument. They simply encouraged him to hide his shortcomings, which was an easy task on a landscape that the colonial archive considered to be blank. Surveyors continued to make gross mathematical errors in their individual and block surveys after 1835, occasionally creating disputes between surveyors in neighboring areas or committing outright fraud through fabrication that went undiscovered for years or decades.[69] 'Cooking' diagrams' data to ensure mathematical consistency, rather than returning to the field to track down errors, was another common practice among Cape land surveyors before the 1880s.[70] Accuracy was a major goal, but speed was also a major concern for any surveyor who sought to earn a living. Low survey tariffs that paid by area, not *per diem*, also encouraged surveyors to work quickly and expend the minimum effort required to avoid a corrective resurvey, and little incentive existed to catalogue features beyond basic topography, forests, and water sources other than a surveyor's own predilection. In areas of recent conflict, the safety attendant on speed won out. This partial disincentive to detail created a fictional landscape of vacancy, which conveniently reinforced the disconnect between land and people among the administrators and magistrates in the eastern Cape Colony. For African households far to the north and east of Cape Town, this effacement of their landscapes on diagrams and charts was almost universal, but few of them ever saw the representations that entered the archive unchallenged.

---

69 Keegan, *Colonial South Africa*, 187; Duly, *British Land Policy*, 184. For two signal examples, see CPP (unnumbered), *Proceedings of the Committee of the Legislative Council appointed to Examine and Report on the Papers Laid by His Excellency the Governor upon the Council Table Relative to the 120 Diagrams* (Cape Town, 1856); CPP G.37-'56, *Correspondence with the Deputy Surveyor-General, Mr. Robinson, on the Subject of the Report of the Special Commissioner, Major Hope, upon the Granting and Occupation of Farms in the Divisions of Victoria and Queen's Town.*

70 Obree, Braun, and Fisher, "Land Policy at the Cape," 25–26.

Problems and Solutions for Cartographic Construction in the Eastern Cape

Nowhere was the potential for geographical confusion and unreliable surveying so great as it was in the heavily populated and contentious areas near the Kei river. Geographical knowledge regarding the Kei and its tributaries was poor before the 1860s, and most cartographers showed only vague data north and east of Grahamstown if they included features or information at all. What little information they included came primarily from an 1833 map by John James Centlivres Chase, often through the medium of a large manuscript plan drawn originally in 1830 by L. Hebert for the Colonial Office in London that was updated subsequently as new data—including Chase's map—arrived there.[71] Textual notes about the people and character of the ground, gleaned from the travelogues that existed at the time, stood in for topographical detail and created a landscape filled with imaginary places and people on a map that was still so large in scale to be almost useless beyond the abstract imperial gaze. The Astronomer Royal at the Cape of Good Hope in 1857, the Irish-born Thomas Maclear, stated simply that any maps of southern Africa at the Colonial Office were clearly misleading and "unworthy of confidence."[72]

The practical obstacle to correcting the mythical landscape of southern Africa was the demand from London that the colonies support themselves. In the struggle for scarce financial resources, long-term cartographic investment lost to short-term expediency at the Cape just as it did in wealthier India.[73] Independent efforts by the Royal Engineer detachment at the Cape to conduct a military topographical and trigonometrical survey of the immediate environs of Cape Town in the mid-1820s ran afoul of this poverty, as the Imperial treasury objected to non-military uses of its resources and the Cape was unable to reimburse the Treasury.[74] The ambitious trigonometrical survey and broader mapping operation Michell devised in accordance with his instructions as

---

71 The large plan was updated at least until the 1840s. E.C. Liebenberg, "Mapping South Africa in the Mid-19th Century: The Cartography of James Centlivres Chase," *Historia* 52, no. 2 (2007): 1–18; L. Hebert, Sr., "Map of South Africa" [1830], CO 700/Cape of Good Hope 12, National Archives, London (hereafter BNA).

72 CPP G.17-'57, *Memoir on Geography and Topography of the Cape of Good Hope, by Thomas Maclear, Esq., F.R.S., Her Majesty's Astronomer*, 5. Maclear had been at the Cape since 1834, following the death of Fallows in 1831.

73 Edney, *Mapping an Empire*, 29.

74 Colonial Office to R. Bourke (Governor), 24 Jun 1826, 97, CO 49/19, BNA; R. Bourke to Colonial Office, 10 Jun 1827, 89, CO 48/149, BNA; R.W. Hay (Colonial Secretary) to W. Hill (Treasury Secretary), 3 Jun 1826, 270–271, CO 49/18, BNA.

Surveyor-General also perished for want of funds and trained personnel to carry it out.[75] Maclear carried out a sparse geodetic triangulation around Cape Town between 1837 and 1841, with the partial assistance of his friend and collaborator John Herschel, but they were not addressing a question of land survey.[76] Scientific questions of interest to the British Admiralty, which paid Maclear's salary, determined the scope and purpose of their work, and that institution gladly reaped the international prestige.[77] The geodetic chains that a party of Royal Engineers under Captain William Bailey measured eastward from Cape Town along the coast up to the Kei between 1859 and 1862, long after Michell's 1848 retirement, were more useful. However, Bailey's survey served the pragmatic purpose of safe navigation after a number of wrecks, including the loss of the transport *HMS Birkenhead* in 1852. Bailey's 1863 report clearly laid out its value for the rational administration of land and mapmaking in the borderlands and so promoted its future extension, albeit with no results before the 1880s.[78]

The only detailed maps of the Cape's western districts for many years were therefore *ad hoc* cadastral compilations, with the topography drawn from diagrams and route sketches instead of systematic survey; most eastern districts did not even have that. These maps quilted the legal diagrams of individual plots of land together, combined and corroborated with whatever topographical sketches or localized road surveys existed. Though the Surveyor-General kept many of these plans in the Cape Town office, a few originated with the Deputy Surveyors-General of the Eastern Province (1847–1867) and British Kaffraria (1855–1867), whose mere existence spoke to the desire for more responsive and reliable work in those localities far from Cape Town.[79] These compilation maps were usually the work of private individuals (or at least surveyors in their capacity as private individuals), and involved the payment of a

75 Colonial Office to G. Lowry Cole (Governor), 19 Jul 1833, No. 1370, GH 1/93, KAB.

76 Thomas Maclear, *Verification and Extension of La Caille's Arc of Meridian at the Cape of Good Hope* vol. 1 (London: HMSO, 1866).

77 Steven Ruskin, *John Herschel's Cape Voyage: Private Science, Public Imagination and the Ambitions of Empire* (Burlington, Vt.: Ashgate, 2004), 37–73.

78 Abraham de Smidt, *A Brief History of the Surveys and Cartography of the Colony of the Cape of Good Hope: Read Before the International Geographical Congress (London, July, 1895)*, Brighton: T.G. Bishop, 1895; CPP G.26-'63, *Report on the Trigonometrical Survey of a Portion of the Colony and British Kaffraria by Captain W. Bailey, R.E.*, 4, 34–35 ("Notes on National Surveys").

79 The Deputy Surveyor-General of British Kaffraria, in King William's Town, was elevated to Surveyor-General between 1860 and 1865 while the colony was a separate dependency. Both offices were re-absorbed by Cape Town.

gratuity based on the apparent quality of the work. The process of compilation was more of an art than a science, as the surveyors' skills and equipment varied so greatly that the pieces rarely fit. It was generally left to the cartographer, who usually had no acquaintance at all with the territory, to reconcile the diagrams with the vague and occasionally unintelligible sketches that travelers and military personnel tendered to the office. The resulting maps were skewed and unreliable, and uneven from one district to the next in style and substance alike.[80]

The assay of the state of compilation cartography in the Cape Colony that Charles Davidson Bell, Michell's successor as Surveyor-General in Cape Town, delivered to the colonial government in 1860 is instructive. Bell's overview showed that these district maps were the work of different surveyors or draftsmen (cartographers) with highly variable standards. Some of these maps were built from contiguous surveys, but many were compilations of disparate diagrams within the survey office that exercised great artistic license, and one map of Namaqualand was only a rough topographical sketch with a few natural and human features.[81] While Bell was sympathetic to the aesthetics involved, as a talented painter himself, it was an administratively chaotic situation.[82] The Cape government approved the hire of a dedicated compiler of maps in short order, although an official map of the entire Colony for commercial reproduction languished because the time, money, and personnel that would be needed to fit together the disparate sketch and compilation maps and account for the gaps was prohibitive.[83] The Cape government therefore permitted draftsman Henry Hall to use the maps and plans in the possession of the Surveyor-General to compile and correct editions of his own large-scale maps of South Africa during the 1850s, which carried over into his revised productions through the mid-1870s.[84] That same officer did not consider Hall's

80 E.C. Liebenberg, "The Role of the Compilation Map in British South Africa," *The Globe* 46 (1998): 44–46.

81 C.D. Bell (Surveyor-General) to R.W. Rawson (Colonial Secretary), 11 Aug 1860, No. 189, CO 769, KAB; The heterogeneity of surveyors' maps and the consequent inability to construct a map of the colony had been a complaint at least since Michell's early days; see Michell to Colonial Secretary, 6 Dec 1832, SG 2/1/1/1, KAB.

82 For an overview of Bell's large body of work, see Phillida Brooke Simons, *The Life and Work of Charles Bell* (Vlaeberg: Fernwood Press, 1998).

83 C.N. Thomas, "The Distant Past," *South Africa,* 5 Oct 1923, 30. Thomas served as compiler from 1861 to 1900, and drew or supervised virtually every major compilation map produced by the Surveyor-General during that era.

84 E.C. Liebenberg, "'Providing a Tolerably Correct Map of South Africa': The Cartography of Henry Hall," in *Proceedings of the International Symposium of the ica Working Group on the*

work, however artistically meritorious, to be really useful for colonial knowledge and refused to underwrite it directly.[85]

The Office of the Surveyor-General only began compiling its own official map of the colony in 1875 with the advantages of slightly fresher data and its official imprimatur, which created authenticity but not accuracy. This map, like Hall's maps, sought to create a colonial landscape that formed a natural whole, topographically and politically, and proclaimed its possession and mastery to Europeans and white South Africans.[86] Compiling the diverse and unreliable sources for the areas around the Kei and to its east into an extension map was, however, a more difficult process that required two more years of work, and even then it omitted detail for large areas that no surveyors had crossed even within the colony.[87] Only vague sketch maps existed for regions nearer the Kei and the lands across it, until circumstances allowed British and colonial military forces to jettison the inhabitants, efface their landscapes, and appropriate the space as a landscape of European settlers and suitably pliant African clients. Even in fully surveyed districts, however, the compound error was tremendously troublesome, and the Surveyor General put a report to government in 1876 that proposed a general survey with a basis in first- and second-order triangulation to correct grossly erroneous property surveys and control the proliferation of new ones that extension of colonial rule seemed sure to bring.[88] The Survey Commission of 1878, which included a number of surveyors who had risen to government posts and the legislature, specifically concurred with this proposal.[89]

History of Colonial Cartography in the 19th and 20th Centuries, ed. P. van der Krogt, E.C. Liebenberg, and I.J. Demhardt (Pretoria: ICA, 2007), ch. 8.

85 In regard to Hall's request for a subsidy to create a new version of his map in 1873, the Surveyor-General commented that "it is not in the power of any one to publish a correct Map of this Colony in the present state of things, and that new Editions, however neatly got up, not only perpetuated existing errors, but tended to mislead the Public, and stand in the way of a Parliamentary Grant for compiling a really reliable and useful map." See H. Barkly (Governor) to Lord Kimberley (Colonial Office), 11 Jun 1873, Cape No. 56, p. 164, GH 23/32, KAB.

86 Edney, "Irony of Imperial Mapping," 18–20. The map itself only appeared in 1878, despite an 1876 pressmark. See Liebenberg, "Cartography of Henry Hall," 21.

87 CPP G.38-'78, *Report of the Surveyor-General for the Year 1877*, 46. A copy of this map is at M4/65, KAB.

88 CPP G.30-76, *Report of the Surveyor-General on the Tenure of Land, on the Land Laws and Their Results, and on the Topography of the Colony*, 101–111, 119–124.

89 CPP (unnumbered), *Report of the Commission Appointed by His Excellency the Governor to Make a Full Investigation into, and Report Upon, a More Adequate Means of Testing the Accuracy of Land Surveys in this Colony*… (Cape Town, 1878), xiii–xiv.

Among its proposals, the 1876 report and the Surveyor-General's testimony in 1878 suggested that principal triangulation employ the same scientifically-trained *imperial* military personnel who had conducted broad topographical sketching of conflict areas or precise geodetic work before.[90] Most notable among these personnel were members of the Royal Engineers (RES), who also planned fortifications and finely arrayed patterns of military settlement.[91] That imperial exactitude found a unified apex in the military establishment exposes the close relationship between science and domination in the colonial context. Metropolitan military officers and the (usually expatriate) scientists and technicians who consulted with them in the colony possessed the combination of education, instrumentation, political weight, and financial support necessary to promote complex survey operations across a wide area—including, in rare circumstances, geodetic surveys.

Imperial survey personnel were, however, very expensive to retain, and although the War Office in London was willing to pay for the topographical sketching that attended military operations, they refused to fund surveys for purposes of colonial administration. RES and other officers consequently only took up surveys either when British forces were in the field or when colonial and imperial treasuries agreed to share the work and the costs. The general division of labor thus engendered—less precise cadastral work by Government Land Surveyors and both high-level trigonometrical surveying as well as topographical sketching by RES—remained the rule even after the grant of 'responsible government' to the Cape Colony in 1872 shifted more policy decisions to Cape Town. Local survey education produced some highly trained individuals within South Africa in the following decades, especially with the incorporation of a dedicated survey education program at the University of the Cape of Good Hope in 1873, but the preference for RE parties in high-level geodetic work remained until Union in 1910.[92]

Native Lands, Colonial Landscapes

With each extension of colonial rule, Government Land Surveyors crossed increasingly larger pieces of occupied but unsurveyed territory that government

90 Ibid., 125.

91 D.A. Webb, "Lords of All They Surveyed? The Royal Engineers, Surveying, Mapping and Development in South Africa's Eastern Cape," *African Historical Review* 45, no. 1 (2013): 22–45. Van Biljon (*Grensbakens*, 304) raises this point but incorrectly implies that the RES themselves expropriated the land.

92 Fisher, "Emergence and Education," 57–59.

labeled as waste. For large block surveys, land surveyors reluctantly covered hundreds or thousands of square kilometers of territory with networks of extremely rough triangulation on the instructions of the Surveyor-General, meant to provide some kind of basic control of new property boundaries. A rough estimate of latitude and longitude gave heft to qualitative statements about wood, water, land quality, and sale or lease value on the printed inspection forms the Surveyor-General required after 1868. The surveyors, however, had little concern for precise measurement of topographical or human features on the land; their task was to define discrete parcels for public sales. Ideally, their work ensured that the boundaries on the ground reasonably matched those on the diagram, because once an erroneous figure was incorporated into a title it *became* the land in a legal sense.[93] After the Land Beacons Act (No. 10) of 1859, and with increasing emphasis in later amendments, surveyors provided relative coordinates for the corners of farms via triangulation ideally to permit their reconstitution even without standing monuments. Such a transcendentally mathematical prescription acknowledged the possibility that neighbors or, more worrisome, the land's other occupants might move or destroy a beacon. Through science and the archive, the colony's landscape could effectively transcend the physical disposition of the ground it claimed, just as diagrams and titles conceptually separated the African population from the colonial landscape.

The 1859 Beacons Act and its amendments, the massive growth of large-scale survey operations, and the Surveyor-General's attempts to catalogue compilation maps of the colony coincided with other developments, including the Crown Lands Act (No. 2 of 1860) and the Crown Lands Leasing Act (No. 19 of 1864) that sped the sale and lease of supposed waste lands, a push to standardize units of measure in Cape Town, and the Royal Engineers' geodetic survey near the coast.[94] That confluence was no accident, nor was the fact that

93 This was evident in the "Red Line" system that existed from 1879 to 1929, whereby the legally-binding information was recorded in black and the corrected boundary data in red, thus creating a duality that separated the legal territory from the spatial one. See Obree, Braun, and Fisher, "Land Policy at the Cape," 27; G.H. Maasdorp, "Correspondence: The Red Line System," *South African Survey Journal* 1 (1925): 334–335; "Annual Report [of the Surveyor-General] 1913," §1, pp. 4–5, SG 6/9, KAB.

94 Scott, *Seeing Like a State*, 30–33; CPP G.1-'59, *Report of the Commissioners Appointed by His Excellency the Governor for the Purpose of Determining the Unit of Land Measure Within the Colony, and of Providing for its Uniform Adoption in Future*, following on Act No. 11 of 1858; T. Zakiewicz, "Units of Length Measure and Geodetic Standards at the Cape, 1813–1912," in *The History of Surveying and Land Tenure Collected Papers Volume 2*, ed. R.C. Fisher (Cape Town: IPLSWC, 2004), 188–194; Christopher, *Crown Lands*, 44–54. The timing is also

they all happened in tandem with a massive reconfiguration of African lands in the area around the Kei that began around 1857 and continued for over a half century. These measures were at heart reflections of colonial anxiety about enumeration and surveillance in Cape Town that fueled a progressive drive for knowledge after 1850.[95] But the guiding philosophy at the Cape changed at the same time from the cordoning of lands and the expulsion of Africans towards increasingly insistent efforts to engineer a colonized African landscape on an ever more intrusive scale.

One way of colonizing the landscape involved awarding lands, or permitting their sale, to individual non-whites of particular merit within the colonial cadastral framework in order to create a privileged subclass of African landholders.[96] These in practice tended to be 'school people'—mission-educated, Christian Africans, often Fingoes, who had the resources and knowledge to make use of a piece of land hundreds of acres or more in extent. The Cape Colony started allowing Fingoes in the colony to lease land from the 1840s onward, and in 1858 then-Cape governor and High Commissioner, George Grey, opened the sale of Crown land in the heavily Xhosa-populated eastern districts in 1858 to anyone who could pay the rather exorbitant sum of £1 per acre for survey and title, although many paid less.[97] In 1865, for example, the Reverend Davis of Peddie testified that some thirty Fingoes had farms in his district, all with brick houses, and many of those were built by white laborers.[98] These farmers, who enjoyed relative prosperity for decades, represented a small but important stratum of society that successfully navigated the colonial market economy, although many others prospered in the period before 1900 through the formal and sometimes informal hire of surveyed land.[99] In noting the confusion over the precise disposition of land, the 1865 Commission on Native Affairs specifically prorogued the land question in its report, and

---

interesting comparatively; the Crown Lands Act of 1860, for example, has some points of contact with the Homestead Act of 1861 in the United States in promoting the expansive grant of unallocated lands. See L.G. Robson, "The Royal Engineers and Settlement Planning in the Cape Colony, 1806–1872" (PhD diss., University of Pretoria, 2011), 147–148.

95 Dawn Nell, "'For the Public Benefit': Livestock Statistics and Expertise in the Late Nineteenth-Century Cape Colony, 1850–1900," in *Science and Society in Southern Africa*, ed. Saul Dubow (Manchester: Manchester University Press, 2000), 104–105.

96 Clifton C. Crais, *Poverty, War, and Violence in South Africa* (Cambridge: Cambridge University Press, 2011), 102–108.

97 Bundy, *Rise and Fall*, 52.

98 CPP (unnumbered), *Proceedings of, and Evidence Taken by, the Commission on Native Affairs* (Cape Town, 1865), 23.

99 See Bundy, *Rise and Fall*, 54.

later commissions would find the matter no easier to tackle.[100] This self-sufficient subclass of unseen tenants lent an element of uncertainty to the drive for colonial knowledge, one that South African governments sought to stamp out over the next century by applying the legal machinery of state to the spaces in the archive.

Another option, in cases where chiefs came under colonial rule, was to exchange their authority over land and people for the grant of a farm in perpetuity. This model co-existed with the creation of grants for meritorious and 'progressive' Africans across the eastern districts in the Tambookie Location, which became known in the 1870s as Glen Grey as part of an incremental process that spread the names of prominent colonialists across the Transkei.[101] After a largely failed emigration scheme to push Thembu chiefs and people out of the Location in 1865, government offered quitrent grants to chiefs who were willing to toe the colonial line while simultaneously declaring their powers extinguished. At the same time, the colony awarded farms on quitrent to particular Africans—many Christian Fingoes or other non-Thembu, often from the same family—as progressive and reliably pro-government farmers or new headmen.[102] This scheme by which grantees created new fiefdoms did not pass without challenge. Nonesi, the powerful Thembu matriarch and regent, had people chase off a land surveyor marking such a grant in 1868 on the grounds that government was paramount, but within the Location the land was hers alone to apportion.[103] It is no coincidence that the government found a pretense for expelling her to Pondoland the following year.

Between 1870 and 1873 the Surveyor-General sought to eliminate the illegible spaces in the Tambookie Location by having the entire area surveyed into medium-sized farms, spaces that could theoretically be known and governed under a more

100 CPP (unnumbered), *Proceedings of, and Evidence Taken by, the Commission on Native Affairs* (Cape Town, 1865), xxiii–xxiv.

101 Governors Grey, Wodehouse, Barkly, Frere, and even one Astronomer Royal (Maclear) became spaces in the colonial landscape this way, as did at least one missionary family prominent in "native affairs" (the Ayliffs).

102 E.A. Judge and J. Ayliff [with J.H.O. Southey], "Report of the Commission," 16 Jul 1870, p. 32, S.140/26, SGO-Cape.; E.J.C. Wagenaar, "A History of the Thembu and Their Relationship with the Cape Colony, 1850–1900" (PhD diss., Rhodes University, 1990), 216; Richard Bouch, "Glen Grey before Cecil Rhodes: How a Crisis of Local Colonial Authority Led to the Glen Grey Act of 1894," *Canadian Journal of African Studies* 27, no. 1 (1993): 4, 11–12.

103 Wagenaar, "A History of the Thembu," 107.

rational system of paid headmen with discrete territorial boundaries.[104] The scheme anticipated the progressive clearance of Thembu farmers from its rich black soils in favor of white cultivators, but despite the neat erasure of Thembu occupation from every single general plan and diagram that emerged from the survey, the people remained (see Map 2.1). Thembu communities in Glen Grey continued to occupy a "peculiar and inconvenient" position, in the words of Governor Grey's successor Philip Wodehouse, being within the legal space of the colony but still not quite beholden to its laws or an approved hierarchy of headmen.[105] The precedent of chiefly co-optation through farm grants, on

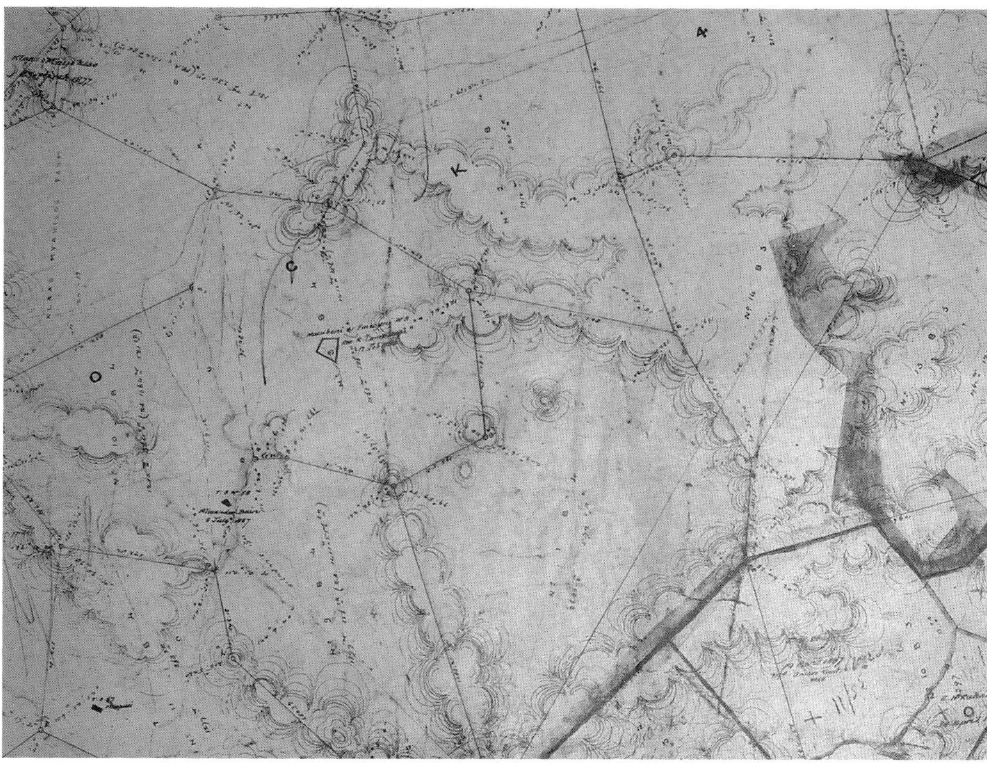

MAP 2.1 *Detail from a general plan of blocks 3 and 4 of the Tambookie Location (1870), showing long lines of triangulation and numerical data for farm boundaries that stand in contrast to the rough topography. The only buildings it shows are European trading posts and mission stations despite the presence of hundreds of homesteads in this area.*

SOURCE: TSKEI PLAN PLAN 6918, OFFICE OF THE SURVEYOR-GENERAL, CAPE TOWN. RSA STATE COPYRIGHT.

104 Scott, *Seeing Like a State*, 36; Bouch, "Glen Grey before Cecil Rhodes," 10.

105 Wodehouse to Cardwell, 11 Oct 1865, No. 99, p. 68, GH 23/30, KAB.

the other hand, reappeared in other localities, and in a few places chiefs or consortia officially bought or hired land as well.[106] But these cases all implicitly accepted survey and colonial law, just as smaller purchases by prosperous Africans had.

The few other places where the mosaic of surveyed territories in the geographical archive had to contend with lands specifically reserved to non-whites were extensive locations generally under Fingo stewardship. These locations were not prone to expulsion or expropriation, but their populations grew so rapidly in size through the apparent arrival of many people who took on the label that the colonial government created a legal system of 'certificates of citizenship' for Fingoes to rein in population expansion through registration in 1857, and tried to replace these with more descriptive forms and annual renewals in 1864 owing to circumvention.[107] Surveyors only defined the locations' lands subtractively after 1850 by parceling away farms around their territories instead of actually marking off Fingo ground itself, primarily because there was no budget for the latter work. This approach created problems later. The Civil Commissioner of the Queenstown division, for example, discovered while researching a boundary dispute in 1867 that geographical data did not exist for the major Oxkraal and Kamastone Fingo locations.[108] Sometimes the surveyor's work also appropriated landscapes where Fingoes had settled or expanded in the years between the vague award of location lands and the acceleration of European settlement in the 1850s. In those cases, the surveyors seemed to chase Fingo communities from place to place, destroying the spaces they possessed and threatening existential destruction, leaving only unsurveyed ground as a place of safety.[109]

Other Xhosa communities in British Kaffraria and the new Cape divisions to the north were also aware of the surveyors' work, even if they did not encounter the technicians themselves or suffer the immediate dismemberment of their network of places and people. The surveyor's red flags, generally tacked to rot-resistant sneezewood posts prefatory to the erection of more permanent stone beacons, were powerful touchpoints for Xhosa descriptions of the changing landscape as the first clear signs of impending loss.[110] By enclosing, and later subdividing, the spatial extents of African communities' lands, the excluded

106 Bundy, *Rise and Fall*, 70, 98.

107 Stapleton, "Expansion of a Pseudo-Ethnicity," 238–243, 241.

108 C.D. Griffith (Civil Commissioner, Queenstown) to Bell, 7 Dec 1867, SG 1/1/1/15, KAB.

109 Testimony of headman Kaulela (Peddie), 25 Sep 1881, in CPP G. 4-'83, *Report and Proceedings with Appendices of the Government Commission on Native Laws and Customs*, 2:171.

110 See Peires, *House of Phalo*, 167.

ground and its population entered the colonial landscape, and only the preservation of toponyms and family connections among laborers hinted at the earlier order. The existence of some farm leases near the Kei under non-whites' stewardship was a significant but temporary wrinkle in this trajectory, but even there property lines and the machinery of colonial law changed the reach and depth of patron-client relations. The colonial state as a whole neither desired nor encouraged security of tenure for Africans away from whatever locations might exist. Native locations and chiefdoms were null-spaces in colonial geography, even when they were subject to its laws. Surveyors and their diagrams for title ignored the presence of Africans just as they ignored most buildings, signs of cultivation, and other temporary or transitory features that were out of place on their idealized blank landscape.

Those erasures, however, had significant ramifications for the landscape that emerged, particularly in the lands around the Kei River where the fluidity of landscapes and identities arguably provoked the strongest colonial effort to rationalize spaces and populations into a legible whole. The incorporation of the lands around the Kei into the colonial geographical archive fits roughly into three phases, proceeding from large to small, with each increasing in precision and progressively atomizing the land while altering people's relationship to it. In the first phase, missionaries, military personnel, or other travelers conducted rapid surveys or sketch traverses that filled a need for basic charts depending on the immediate situation. Second, the colony subdivided authority territorially, whether by reckoning or through the work of a surveyor, and intervened spatially to co-opt or supplant existing structures of authority. Finally, a third phase of land surveys created new spatial orders within areas remaining in non-European hands, usually through individual tenure on the basis of 'one man, one lot.' This rough process, however, did not dictate the content or the outcome of the encounters that necessarily followed.

Cartographic Erasure and the Genesis of Fingoland

The Kei River is significant to historians for a number of reasons. The Kei formed a useful boundary for colonial writ in the mid-1800s, and afterward it became another kind of boundary between the Colony proper and an unfurling Territory that included divergent legal and social environments.[111] Furthermore, when taken with the point of European entry—the sub-metropole of

111 William Beinart and Colin Bundy, *Hidden Struggles in Rural South Africa* (Johannesburg: Ravan, 1987), 5–6.

Cape Town—the Kei also became a territorial designator, separating 'Ciskei' (*cis*, same side) and 'Transkei' (*trans*, other side) in a geography of colonial expansion that retains a peculiar staying power in South Africa.[112] The river, however, also represented the center of a borderland, with many migratory and commercial crossings at its various drifts. Before the arrival of European settlers in the vicinity, the Kei formed a divide between the authority of the two sons of the Xhosa chief Phalo, Gcaleka and Rharhabe, and thus marked the primary division among seaward Xhosa as of the 1820s.[113] But to the colony by the 1840s it was an edge and a marker that separated a space of order, however much a work in progress, from a space of ongoing chaos that hearkened back to the 'disturbances' of the 1820s and 1830s that later acquired the label *mfecane*.[114] Throughout this borderland, the provision of land and the means of livelihood usually vested in social structures—patrons, elders, kin, and clients—and not in particular defined and deeded pieces of land. Such spaces had meanings as places within the landscape, but only as constituted in these social and cultural contexts.

Today, a visitor traveling from East London to Mthatha (Umtata) will notice the presence of low scrub and the occasional invasive stand of Australian wattle on the uncultivated riverbanks and steep ravines and hillsides near the Kei, extending some distance from the river network itself. On the hilltops, small houses and shacks occupy small, partially-fenced lots in clusters, and a few hundred feet from the N2 highway bridge across the Kei, an iron bridge dating to 1879 still carries some traffic. At greater distances from these Kei bridges a rough plateau covers the districts that were once collectively known in one breath as Fingoland and the Idutywa Reserve—Gcuwa, Ngqamakhwe, Tsomo, and Dutywa today. There the land undulates more softly, with copses of trees

112 That model also applies to the Gariep (Orange) and Vaal Rivers where similar abrupt disjoints in the colonial structure existed. It is worth noting that other rivers that more temporarily served as colonial boundaries, such as the Great Fish River and the Keiskamma River, rarely receive this treatment. In the histories of other settler societies, this river convention appears only occasionally, such as the Mississippi in the US.

113 Alan Lester, *Imperial Networks: Creating Identities in Nineteenth-Century South Africa and Britain* (London: Routledge, 2001), 11–12. Gcaleka however remained the titular ruler of the Xhosa, and he passed that ceremonial standing to his grandson, Sarhili.

114 Regarding the *mfecane*, see John K. Wright, "Turbulent Times: Political Transformations in the North and East, 1760s–1830s," in *The Cambridge History of South Africa* v. 1, ed. C. Hamilton, B. Mbenga, and R. Ross (Cambridge: Cambridge University Press, 2010), 211–252; Norman Etherington, "A Tempest in a Teapot? Nineteenth-Century Contests for Land in South Africa's Caledon Valley and the Invention of the *mfecane*," *Journal of African History* 45 (2004): 203–211.

in some low-lying areas, clusters of residences aligned in ridgetop villages, and treeless hillocks covered in earthen or stone contour banks intended to prevent the erosion of soil. Today's human geography is an artifact of radical state conservation campaigns and economic transformation after 1939, but those efforts built on much earlier interventions upon the native landscape.

Before then, and even more so before 1913, those hillsides along the Kei included a patchwork of farmland dotted with homesteads, the villages were few, and the forests were still limited but had less of the pernicious black and silver wattle. In 1891, land surveyor H.C. Schunke described the Transkei generally as the best-watered and most reliably drained land on the subcontinent, with a surfeit of the sweet grass that nurtured healthy herds of cattle and flocks of sheep.[115] To him, the two seaward 'tiers' of his tripartite division of the Transkei by elevation were rich in the necessities of life, if not always suited to the open-field agriculture of the South African Highveld. The first Chief Magistrate of the Transkei, Matthew Smith Blyth, called the whole "a fine and fertile country," where the higher elevations fostered healthy livestock and the seaward reaches produced bountiful harvests of corn and wheat even in years of poor rainfall.[116] Caesar Henkel, Chief Conservator of Forests in the Transkei until 1898, noted the region's "abundance" in normal years despite the difficulty of irrigation.[117] The observations of Schunke, Blyth, and even Henkel, however, predated the subdivision of land and the immobilization and compression of people beyond its capacity, with all the managerial hand-wringing that ensued.

Itinerant European travelers in the area from the 1600s onward noted this abundance too, and carefully described the people and places they encountered there. Sometimes they even sketched meaningful scenes and described their contexts, which makes the later colonial sketch maps of those landscapes all the more remarkable because they efface almost every such sign.[118] But that silence also owes to the usual conditions and purposes of their production, because military maps of discrete pieces of land are meant primarily to depict its rise and fall as well as important barriers to travel and major landmarks. Thus such maps naturally depicted rivers, mountains, roads, and

115 H.C. Schunke, "The Transkeian Territories: Their Physical Geography and Ethnology," *Transactions of the South African Philosophical Society* 8, no. 1 (1890–1891): 3, 7.

116 "Report on the Social and Political Condition of the Transkei for the year 1878," CPP G.33-'79, *Blue Book on Native Affairs, 1879*, 95.

117 C.C. Henkel, *The Native- or Transkeian Territories: The Country between Cape Colony and Natal* (Hamburg: V & D Actien-Gesellschaft, 1903), 16–18.

118 Robin Derricourt, "Early European Travelers in the Transkei and Ciskei," *African Studies* 35, no. 3–4 (1976): 273–291.

colonial enclaves. They also noted points where the colony prevailed in combat or captured African capitals—'Great Places'—but omitted the more mundane places of evacuated human landscapes that might soon be forfeit anyhow. The retention of toponyms hinted at another geography, but the act of recording in text what had before often existed only in oral transmission and memory also served to appropriate it for the new claimants of the landscape. The colonial map recognized the existence of the earlier landscape only at points where they could appropriate or subjugate it. The absence of human geography is not entirely surprising, given that riding with armed parties around the countryside was likely to put homesteads to flight, but it is telling that their absence was necessary to carry out wide-ranging survey and mapping at all. That too was an important element of the landscape, because in omitting people, the representation portrayed it as a geographically discrete and uniform space devoid of any active claims and thus ready for inscription.[119] Conquest, appropriation, and selective erasure worked together.

The military surveys of 1858–1862 in the lands between the Kei and Mbashe (Bashee) rivers following a brief punitive campaign against the Gcaleka king Sarhili fit this pattern of appropriation and erasure well. In the wake of the devastating Cattle-Killing movement of 1856–1857, the expansionist Governor Grey sent colonial forces eastward across the Kei to expel Sarhili for ostensibly masterminding it.[120] Sarhili had promoted the millenarian prophecies, which promised that the destruction of existing polluted cattle and crops would bring about the rebirth of the land with 'new people,' full grain-pits, and new, healthy cattle on an anointed day. Xhosa believers, chiefs and commoners alike, had already witnessed evidence of this pollution in the form of the horrifying cattle lungsickness (bovine pleuropneumonia) epizootic in 1855, and slaughtered around half a million cattle in anticipation.[121] The result of the prophecies' repeated failure was famine, dislocation, and forced migration across Xhosaland, which Grey claimed was a plot to incite starving Xhosa to rise up and attack the colonies starting with British Kaffraria on the southwestern banks of the Kei.[122] British Kaffraria, the construct animated in 1847 as a space

---

119 Matthew Edney, "Irony of Imperial Mapping," 18–19.

120 E.J.C. Wagenaar, "A Forgotten Frontier Zone: Settlements and Reactions in the Stormberg Area between 1820–1860," *Archives Year Book for South African History* (hereafter AYB) 45, no. 2 (1984): 187–188.

121 Peires, *The Dead Will Arise: Nongqawuse and the Great Xhosa Cattle-Killing Movement of 1856–1857* (Johannesberg: Ravan, 1989), 295–296; Switzer, *Power & Resistance*, 66–67.

122 According to Alan Lester, the Xhosa population of British Kaffraria fell by 65% (105,000 to 37,000), and the overall number of displaced people in the region was about 150,000. See Lester, *Imperial Networks*, 183.

to contain chiefs and people who had accepted British rule, was certainly unpopular with those Xhosa households that felt the weight of Grey's ambitions.[123] The governor already had demonstrated his gift for seeing opportunity in misfortune when he sought to destroy the power of independent Xhosa society and authority through high-minded but naïve efforts at social engineering after the epizootic of 1855, so it is hard to know whether he really believed Sarhili was responsible.[124] Nevertheless, Grey's pronouncement of guilt was the motive force behind what followed.

Grey also had a generally acquisitive mien when it came to land and the colony, and in the wake of the Cattle-Killing he ordered the seizure and sale of land that corresponded to Gqunukhwebe, Ndlambe, and Ngqika chiefs (among others) who believed in the prophecies even if the people had not taken part.[125] The unbelievers among those communities either ended up in abbreviated reserves or suffered displacement and a search for new social networks. Both categories faced a new policy of villagization and the exchange of chiefly privilege for grants of land, which was part of a process of 'Fingoization' that Grey pushed upon chiefs and locations in order to obtain more land and labor for white settlers.[126] If they did not wish to live in these impoverished villages, Xhosa had to depend upon forbearance and employment from the Europeans who occupied their lands with the legal sanction of a surveyor's diagram and a colonial title.[127] Although objections and obstruction abounded, not even the staunchest allies of government had the power to prevent this reorganization entirely.

---

123 For an evocative description of the Xhosa experience of British Kaffraria, see Peires, *House of Phalo*, 169.

124 Clifton C. Crais, *White Supremacy and Black Resistance in Pre-Industrial South Africa: The Making of the Colonial Order in the Eastern Cape, 1770–1865* (Cambridge: Cambridge University Press, 1992), 195–196. Grey used the damaging of patronage systems through the loss of cattle to try and attenuate chiefs' power by placing magistrates with them and imposing the colonial monetary system of exchange, but the chiefs often used Grey's model for their own ends. See Timothy Stapleton, *Maqoma: Xhosa Resistance to Colonial Advance* (Johannesburg: Jonathan Ball, 1994), 190–192; Price, *Making Empire*, 272–274, 277–284.

125 Lester puts the number of 1,500-acre farms so created at about 300. See Lester, *Imperial Networks*, 184.

126 Peires, *The Dead Will Arise*, 291–297. The term 'Fingoization' for the process of colonial patronage, incorporation, and villagization is Timothy Stapleton's coinage; see Stapleton, *Maqoma*, 201.

127 Webster, "Unmasking the Fingo," 241–242, 255–261; Stapleton, "Expansion of a Pseudo-Ethnicity," 233–250.

The colonial assault across the Kei in autumn 1858 was almost perfunctory in such conditions. Sarhili and the depleted population between the Kei and Mbashe rivers had no hope of mounting any kind of resistance to trained British horsemen and Fingo levies, and they fled with their remaining cattle across the Mbashe so quickly that the military could barely capture enough animals to support themselves.[128] To forestall any immediate occupation of the eastern bank of the Kei, a number of Fingo soldiers and their families moved permanently in August 1858 from British Kaffraria to a spot between the Dutywa and Mbashe Rivers, and there settled in eight villages where relocating Ndlambe chiefs later joined them.[129] Governor Grey and his superiors at the Colonial Office in London considered this 'Idutywa Reserve' to be a precursor to the permanent occupation of the region with "Europeans and friendly Natives."[130] Very little detailed information, however, existed about the geography of the land between the Kei and Mbashe rivers, and the few route maps available from missionaries were of little use away from the main roads. Military officers in the area therefore gathered information on the physical character of the land, any crops found growing there, and the potential of various sections for European colonization.[131]

One of the officers in the campaign against Sarhili was Captain George Pomeroy Colley, who already had general orders to "make a rough survey of the country, and report on its capabilities for agriculture, sheep farming, &c., the direction in which roads should be made, and whether any of the mouths of the rivers could be made into harbours."[132] Colley was not a Royal Engineer, but he had attended the Royal Military Academy at Sandhurst and thus had the education in military sketching and traverse survey expected of a nineteenth-century military officer.[133] Colley had already produced a number of local

---

128 Walter Currie (Commander, Frontier Armed and Mounted Police) to J. Maclean, 1 March 1858, 1–2, BK 78, KAB.

129 Switzer, *Power & Resistance*, 72–73; C.C. Saunders, "The Annexation of the Transkeian Territories," *AYB* 39 (1976): 11–12; A.E. Du Toit, "The Cape Frontier: A Study of Native Policy with Special Reference to the Years 1847 to 1866," *AYB* 17, no. 1 (1954): 179; Gawler to Maclean, 31 Aug 1858, BK 79, KAB.

130 Wynyard to Newcastle, No. 45, 12 Mar 1860, GH 23/28, KAB; Newcastle to Grey, Cape No. 115, 23 Apr 1860, CO 49/55, BNA; Newcastle (Colonial Secretary) to Grey, Cape No. 139, 18 May 1860, GH 1/277, KAB.

131 See, for example, Gawler to Maclean, 31 Aug 1858, BK 79, KAB.

132 G.P. Colley to "his brother," [n.d.] Feb 1858, cited in W.F. Butler, *The Life of Sir George Pomeroy-Colley* (London: John Murray, 1899), 41.

133 Matthew Edney, "British Military Education, Mapmaking, and Military 'Map-Mindedness' in the Later Enlightenment," *Cartographic Journal* 31, no. 1 (1994): 14–20.

topographical sketches of strategic points that he sent to the Chief Commissioner of the colony of British Kaffraria, John Maclean.[134] The flight of organized opposition across the Mbashe in early 1858 opened a field for survey operations on the eastern bank of the Kei, so Colley promoted a wide-ranging reconnaissance of the area. Grey's own career had begun with exploration and surveying in Australia, so he was well aware of the value of survey and mapping for establishing colonial power and readily approved of Colley's request, just as he did the Royal Engineers' geodetic coastal survey later that same year.[135] Maclean also approved, reflecting his own administrative fixation with codifying and classifying African social order, and he also collected expert knowledge from missionaries and their progeny among colonial agents to form his long-lived 1858 *Compendium of Kafir Laws and Customs*.[136]

Governor Grey and Commissioner Maclean, however, did not wait for Colley, and went to work devising new landscapes upon even the roughest of drawings in order to embrace and dominate the territory immediately. One small color tracing map, probably drawn during 1858, built on early reports about the terrain and divided the territory by suitability for Europeans and 'Natives' as well as particular areas thought "good for sheep" and showed some areas already inhabited (see Map 2.2).[137] Those who had actually seen the land conversely saw folly in the sweeping characterizations of armchair

---

134 See Gawler to Maclean, 17 Mar 1858, BK 78, KAB; for sketches, see Colley, "Memo. on the Country along the River Bashee (to accompany sketch)," 27 Aug 1858, BK 79, KAB; Colley, "Sketch of the Country Around Butterworth," 10 Sep 1858, BK 79, KAB. Colley also produced topographical sketches of the strategic villages he laid out, which he sent to the Deputy Surveyor-General in King William's Town.

135 Butler, *Life of Sir George Pomeroy-Colley*, 25; James M.R. Cameron, "Agents and Agencies in Geography and Empire: The Case of George Grey," in *Geography and Imperialism 1820–1940*, ed. M. Bell, R. Butlin, and M. Heffernan (Manchester: Manchester University Press, 1995), 13–35.

136 J. Maclean, ed. and comp., *A Compendium of Kafir Laws and Customs* (Mount Coke: Wesleyan Mission Press [for the Government of British Kaffraria], 1858). The *Compendium* bears no foreword that indicates this purpose, but its timing and content are indicative. It was reprinted twice in South Africa, in 1866 and 1906, and retained an advisory role until the Native Administration Act in 1927. Ironically the book does not contain a geographical map, although genealogical and ethnographic maps designed to make networks of heredity legible pervade it.

137 "Between Kei & Bashee, Police Stations &c" [Apr 1858?], DSGBK 56, KAB. A modified print version of this map appeared in papers relative to the European settlement scheme in 1861; see C.N. Thomas, "Sketch Referred to in Sir Walter Currie's Report [1861]," MPG 1/936/3-4, BNA; CPP A.102-'61, *Further Papers on the Subject of the Occupation of the Transkeian Territory*, appendix.

MAP 2.2 *Sketch of the Transkeian Territory with Occupation Notes [1858–1859]. The lack of any clear "up" orientation is unusual; I arbitrarily chose the key.*
SOURCE: DSGBK 56, CAPE ARCHIVES DEPOT, WESTERN CAPE ARCHIVES AND RECORDS SERVICE, CAPE TOWN. RSA STATE COPYRIGHT.

geographers and policymakers. Colley himself raised significant professional objections in late 1858 to the labeling of certain lands as "Adapted for Europeans" on the basis that large arable farms could not be assembled there and only "the native" could be satisfied with farming irregular lots on rocky ground.[138] He backtracked somewhat in 1859 and suggested instead that the distribution would depend "solely on the system to be adopted in the admixture of the two populations" and opined that blocks of white farms and grants to discharged soldiers surrounding police posts would be an effective start.[139]

---

138 Butler, *Life of Sir George Pomeroy-Colley*, 45.

139 Colley to Maclean, 8 Jul 1859, BK 79, KAB; Colley to Maclean, 22 Oct 1859, 1/IDW/Add./1/1/1, KAB.

Better surveys were clearly necessary to make the ground meaningfully legible to the state, and the topographical reconnaissance Colley began in 1858 represented an important step forward for realizing colonial control of the lands northeast of the Kei. Unfortunately he only had one full season in the field before taking the role of military governor in the area under the title of Transkeian Magistrate, a posting that prevented his return to the field until the first few months of 1861. Colley sensed that some kind of impending settlement might interfere with his open field of work, so he enlisted a new assistant, Lieutenant James Murray Grant of the Frontier Armed and Mounted Police (F.A.M.P.).[140] Grant took over the survey when Colley left for England to seek promotion in December 1861, but he quit in November 1862 owing to the low pay he received as a colonial officer.[141] He handed his sketches and notes over to the Deputy Surveyor-General in King William's Town, along with notes intended to facilitate a resumption of the work at some later date under a less miserly regime, but kept returning to take copies of the map or suggest the resumption of survey at various times.[142]

A great deal of the topography between the Kei boundary and the colony of Natal thus remained uncertain, if not unknown, until the twentieth century. Cartographers only had the military plan that Colley drew at the end of 1861 to embody all of his work to that point (see Map 2.3), a few drawings of mission lands and trade roads, and Grant's revised sketches for compiling maps.[143] The legacy of this early conceptual labor was a rotation about thirty or forty degrees clockwise that put the Indian Ocean coast parallel to the bottom of the sheet that framed most Anglophone maps of the Transkei or its subsections for a half century.[144] This rotation was economical in framing the image as a rectangle,

140 Colley to Maclean, 22 Mar 1861, BK 78, KAB; Colley to Maclean, 9 Jul 1861, BK 78, KAB.

141 Colley to Maclean, 2 Dec 1861, BK 78, KAB.

142 See Grant to Brownlow, 30 Jun 1862, BK 79, KAB; Grant to Brownlow, 16 Jul 1862, BK 79, KAB; Grant to Brownlow, 30 Oct 1862, BK 79, KAB; Grant to Brownlow, 17 Nov 1862, BK 79, KAB; Grant to R. Southey (Colonial Secretary), 14 Jul 1867, No. 140, CO 4146, KAB; Grant to R. Southey, 27 Nov 1867, No. 170, CO 4142, KAB; L.F. Braun, "The Colonial Archive and Maps of the Western Transkei, 1857–1898," in *Proceedings of the Symposium of the Commission on the History of Cartography in the 19th and 20th Centuries*, ed. E.C. Liebenberg, Peter Collier, and Imre Josef Demhardt (Pretoria: ICA, 2009), 11.

143 Colley to Maclean, 1 Jan 1862, BK 79, KAB; Copy of G.P. Colley, "Outline Map of the Country Between the Kei and Bashee Commonly Known as the Transkeian Territory," Plan 5614, SGO-Cape. Colley's plan of the Butterworth mission grounds' topography dated 10 Sep 1858 is present in BK 79, KAB.

144 For example, the map of the entire Transkei that accompanied surveyor H.C. Schunke's 1885 article in *Petermanns Geographische Mittheilungen* is oriented northward. That map, however, was not entirely Schunke's own work and carried many erroneous place names. See H.C. Schunke, "Kaffraria und die östlichen Grenz-Distrikte der Kaap-Kolonie," *Petermanns Geographische Mittheilungen* 31 (1885): 161–171, 201–209.

MAP 2.3 *Traced reproduction of Colley's rough 1861 sketch map. The dots (red on the original) show the initial villages in the Idutywa Reserve, while wash colors distinguish areas of Gcalekaland, Idutywa, and a section ceded to Thembu occupation as of 1864 from the remainder.*

SOURCE: TSKEI PLAN 5614, OFFICE OF THE SURVEYOR-GENERAL, CAPE TOWN. RSA STATE COPYRIGHT.

but it also generated a legible image of the territory whereby a map reader or colonial official could truly 'read' the Transkei as a narrative text from left to right, progressing in both time and space. Indeed this orientation of the Transkei whenever it appeared in isolation predominated until after the First World War. The major exception was one "tolerably correct" north-oriented compilation Grant himself drew in 1872 to depict the boundaries of kingdoms and chiefdoms between the Kei and Natal as described textually by a special commission that included Grant himself.[145] The highly stylized and geometrically suspect version of Grant and Colley's work published by the imperial government in 1875 returned to the tilted axis, and the Surveyor-General's ten-sheet 1912 Map of the Transkeian Territories tilts it *left*, putting the Indian Ocean on the right margin.[146] Few printed maps broke up the region and instead hewed to sheetlines in depicting a single unified territory that was nonetheless dismembered from the colony, in testament to the power of state geography to mark such problematic lands and its persistence in doing so.

If the archive considered the territory between the Kei and the Mbashe blank following Sarhili's expulsion, the land itself was certainly not. The military contingent available to patrol it was small enough that people who moved frequently could live by hunting, fishing, and grazing while maintaining a link to permanent communities beyond the Mbashe.[147] Whether or not households continued to make proscribed land their home, people from a variety of origins took the opportunity to use it or simply did not know it was forbidden to them.[148] Reports of grazing and hunting on the land multiplied,

145 The map is in fact a compilation of Grant and Colley's map with route maps by earlier missionaries, and Grant did no further surveying to compile it. J.M. Grant, "Sketch Map of Kaffraria" (1872), MPG 1/943/2, BNA; CPP A.12-'73, *Report of Select Committee on Native Affairs*, 109. The Surveyor-General's 1878 "Map of the Eastern Border Districts of the Cape Colony" (which extended to the Mbashe but left blank space to its northeast) and the 1877 "Sketch Map of Kafraria, Basutoland, and the Eastern Frontier of the Cape Colony" by the Intelligence Branch in London derive heavily from Grant's extension and modification of his 1872 map that appeared in the Blue Book on Native Affairs for 1875 (CPP G.21-'75), and which includes Lesotho and several of the intervening districts as well.

146 Office of the Quartermaster General, "Military Sketch of the Transkeian Territory" (1875), Maps 3/32, KAB.

147 The F.A.M.P. reported such establishments as early as September 1858. Colley to Maclean, 29 Sep 1858, 1/IDW/Add./1/1/1, KAB.

148 See, for example, the case of a man hunting within boundaries that were "never defined" and whose dog the F.A.M.P. shot, in Colley to Sub-Inspector Jekisch, 14 Jan 1859, 1/IDW/Add./1/1/1, KAB. Only the shooting of the dog led to the report, suggesting that many unreported cases existed.

as did complaints that people were simply returning and dispersing into the eclectic Xhosa populations around Idutywa and Butterworth that the colony actively sought to Fingoize.[149] New villages and locations soon emerged near these and other colonial foci such as the new (1855) Anglican mission station at St. Marks.[150] The colonial government progressively ceded more and more land between 1860 and 1864 to various African authority figures as an alternative to their ineffectual policing.[151] The Thembu regent Joyi occupied a section of the northern third of the area on the recommendation of the colony's Tambookie Agent, the missionary Joseph Cox Warner, who was fighting his own battles with Thembu authority in the nearby Tambookie Location (Glen Grey) and may have sensed in him an ally.[152] Sarhili reoccupied the southern third of his former lands in 1864, after protesting in 1862 that a colonial land grant further east would place him among his enemies and that government stubbornness to permit his return to the land was a further personal affront.[153] He wasted no time trying to place additional headmen in lands beyond his own, without success.[154] On the colonial side, the autocratic Philip Wodehouse had succeeded Grey as Governor and High Commissioner in 1862, and ordered the Royal Engineers to stop their geodetic survey at the Kei pending the determination of the future disposition of the Transkei.[155] Colonial ambitions to settle Europeans across the Kei, however, ran afoul of high quitrents and survey fees combined with small lots and a three-year occupation requirement,

149 Stapleton, "Expansion of a Pseudo-Ethnicity," 247; W.G.B. Shepstone (acting Transkeian Magistrate) to Maclean, 16 Jun 1860, 1/IDW/Add./1/1/1, KAB.

150 Copy of H. Tempest Waters (missionary, St. Mark's) to W.B. Chalmers (Transkeian Magistrate), 3 Oct 1861, BK 78, KAB.

151 Chalmers to G. Brownlow (Secretary to Lt. Gov., British Kaffraria). 28 Sep 1862, BK 79, KAB; Charles Cobbe (Fingo Agent) to J.C. Warner (British Resident, Transkei), 20 Dec 1865, in CPP, A.14-'67, *Correspondence with Reference to the Principles, Conditions, and Detailed Arrangements on which the Fingo Exodus has Been Carried Out*, 10; Colley to Maclean, 8 Jul 1859, BK 79, KAB.

152 J.C. Warner to R. Southey (Secretary to Chief Commissioner), 16 Mar 1858, BK 79, KAB. See also Chapter 2.

153 "Statement made by Kreli," trans. W.B. Chalmers, 4 Apr 1862, BK 79, KAB. In this transcription of a translation, Sarhili refers to the land as "unoccupied," but elsewhere he seems to define occupation as the presence of a chief or king specifically.

154 Transkeian Magistrate, Diary Entry for 26 Dec 1864, p. 7, 1/IDW/Add./1/1/2, KAB.

155 Lord Newcastle (Colonial Office) to P.E. Wodehouse (Governor, Cape Colony), 3 Oct 1862, pp. 105–106, GH 1/292, KAB. Wodehouse proposed restarting the survey in 1865, but the cost estimate was too high for the budget. See Cardwell (Undersecretary, Colonial Office) to Wodehouse, 7 Dec 1865, p. 110, GH 1/310, KAB.

terms that were too expensive for poor settlers and too onerous ("a swindle") for richer ones.[156] No farm surveys took place, and the government canceled all preliminary grants.

The fear that any cost contingent on defending a Transkeian salient would fall on the imperial treasury led the Colonial Office in London to dictate a retreat of the colonial boundary itself to the Kei in August 1864.[157] This order shifted the colonial focus toward inducing people with chiefs to cross the Kei and ideally freeing land for white settlement, but few chiefs were eager to move. In 1865, Wodehouse offered the remaining central portion of the Transkei to Fingoes from locations in the Cape Colony and British Kaffraria, although that solution opened less land for Europeans.[158] The Fingoes who moved had little reason for attachment to the crowded reserves and labor demands of the colonies, which had created increasing friction between settlers and Fingoes in the seven years following the devastation of other Xhosa communities within British Kaffraria.[159] They also may have been selective about their destinations, given that sheep farming had grown dramatically in some Fingo reserves and the lands between the Kei and Mbashe were better suited for wool than lands within British Kaffraria.[160] Surveyors also divided most of the Fingo reserves in the districts of Peddie, Victoria East, and Fort Beaufort for individual titles in the late 1850s and early 1860s, a fact that implies a potent role for questions of authority over land in decisions to cross the

---

156 Before the publication of terms, some 600 applications arrived seeking land; after their publication, virtually none did. See British Kaffraria, Government Notice No. 21 of 1864, p. 351, BK 109, KAB; Applications for Farms in Transkei, 1858–1864, BK 417, KAB; Saunders, "Annexation," 12; John Shedden Dobie, *South African Journal 1862–1866*, ed. Alan F. Hattersley (Cape Town: Van Riebeeck Society, 1945), 161 (entry for 19 Apr 1864).

157 Cardwell to Wodehouse, Cape No. 784, 5 Aug 1864, p. 101, GH 1/304, KAB.

158 Cardwell to Wodehouse, 3 Dec 1865, Cape No. 959, p. 58, GH 1/310, KAB; Bundy, *Rise and Fall*, 14–15; Du Toit, "The Cape Frontier," 212–213; R. Southey to J.C. Warner, 20 Jan 1866, in CPP, A.14-'67, *Correspondence with Reference to the Principles, Conditions, and Detailed Arrangements on which the Fingo Exodus has Been Carried Out*, 8–9. Stapleton points out that the classic narrative whereby *no* Fingo land in the colony passed into settler hands is incorrect; see Stapleton, "Expansion of a Pseudo-Ethnicity," 248. The idea of giving the land to Fingo headmen may have come from the Fingoes themselves, given that the headman Sobekwa of Oxkraal, in Queenstown, requested land across the Kei in autumn of 1864 and crossed the river in 1866. See E.J. Warner, 21 May 1864, "Daily Journal of the Proceedings & Observations of the Superintendent of Fingoes," INQ 1/1, KAB.

159 Stapleton, "Expansion of a Pseudo-Ethnicity," 243–244.

160 Richard Bouch, "The Colonization of Queenstown (Eastern Cape) and Its Hinterland, 1852–1886" (PhD diss., University of London, 1992), 184.

Kei.[161] Junior headmen with smaller networks of patronage or occupying less productive land than established chiefs or headmen were receptive to opportunity (as well as coercion) in making the decision to leave the colonial reserves and take up new lands and grow their communities across the Kei.[162] In any case, crossing the Kei promised Africans of various social standings a remedy to issues of autonomy and landlessness alike. Colonial governments used these promises to sell the idea of emigration when it wished, and white settlers cleaved as much land from the reserves as they could in its wake. In any case, the impending annexation of British Kaffraria to the Cape Colony in 1865 created even more discontent, and people trickled as nodal networks—homesteads under headmen of varying power, households, and individuals alike—across the river to a landscape that soon entered the colonial archive as 'Fingoland.'[163]

161 "Surveyor-General's Report," in CPP G.4-'83, *Report and Proceedings with Appendices of the Government Commission on Native Laws and Customs*, 2:369–370.

162 Stapleton, "Expansion of a Pseudo-Ethnicity," 245–246.

163 The movement of people in small groups without chiefs and headmen was widespread enough to engender complaints in British Kaffraria. See C.S. Manona, "Captain Matthew Smith Blyth's work in South Africa, 1869–1889" (M.A. thesis, UNISA, 1973), 10.

CHAPTER 3

"Cut Into Little Bits": Engineering Social Order

> If the country is cut into little bits we should die of starvation. We are headmen for Government, and what should we have to look after if the country were cut into little bits. Individual tenure is like a man with one wife; when his solitary wife dies, what is the good of him.
>
> TETYANA, 1881[1]

In spaces where the Cape Colony expected to absorb African communities under chiefs or headmen, survey abetted a peculiar kind of spatial and social atomization. Transplantation had not been enough to create legibility. Colonial action uprooted existing social and spatial formations and moved other people onto that landscape under the illusion that the new order would be pliant. Once emplaced, these new societies constituted their own landscapes and networks, indifferent to the desires of the colonial state and its legal and technical agents. In turn, they devised ever more radical formulas for re-engineering African social and spatial landscapes. Such endeavors to create and modify African social formations on new landscapes are peculiar within South Africa to the Eastern Cape and the so-called Transkeian Territories. They were, at heart, signs of the collapse of faith in the idea of co-existence and civilization through missionary work and education and the rise of a settler-driven philosophy of uneven amalgamation based on the destruction of African social, political, economic, and intellectual autonomy.[2] The survey and division of land struck all of these points.

Social engineering also spoke directly to the intrusive geographical science of the surveyor and the evolving ethnographic fixations of magistrates, who worked with missionaries and headmen alike to realize schemes for managing these areas' administration in the name of progress and industry as well as economy. Mission stations, schools, and magistracies shaped social and cultural

---

1 Testimony of headman Telgana [*sic;* Tetyana] of Idutywa, 2 Nov 1881, in CPP G.4-'83, *Report and Proceedings with Appendices of the Government Commission on Native Laws and Customs*, §8197, 1:467.

2 Andrew Bank, "Losing Faith in the Civilizing Mission: The Premature Decline of Humanitarian Liberalism at the Cape, 1840–1860," in *Empire and Others: British Encounters with Indigenous Peoples, 1600–1850*, ed. M. Daunton and R. Halpern (Philadelphia: University of Pennsylvania, 1999), 376–380; Alan Lester, "Humanitarians and White Settlers in the Nineteenth Century," in *Missions and Empire*, ed. Norman Etherington (Oxford: Oxford University Press, 2005), 83.

 | DOI 10.1163/9789004282292_004

practices in these new spaces, and played early roles in this spatial imposition. The colonial state itself used these agents' scientific knowledge to invent knowable legal quasi-sovereignties during the period of initial settlement under chiefs or headmen, using its own understanding of authority and law (whether 'native' or 'colonial' in name) to bind them within its landscapes.[3] The Cape government's fixation with prescriptive legibility culminated in a push to survey communally-managed areas into small (usually eight to ten acres) freehold agricultural and building lots for approved candidates who could pay the expenses—a system of survey and titling that its proponents called individual tenure.[4] Colonial dissatisfaction with the limited order possible in native locations and other semi-autonomous territories led ultimately, between 1878 and 1884, to abortive pushes for survey and subdivision in newly annexed territories to the northeast of the Kei. These pushes never turned out the way the Cape government anticipated, whether local people fended off pressure for survey and title entirely, reluctantly acquiesced, or simply disregarded the matter.

Order, Organization, and Inoculation in Fingoland

Although the surveys of Colley and Grant brought a limited and selective legibility to the land east of the Kei, the Fingoes' acquisition and use of that land in some ways made it *less* legible in the eyes of the colonial state. The government in Cape Town considered Fingoland to be a sort of colonial satellite and buffer zone, but the people living there had their own goals and ideas regarding their land. In fact, the colonial government understood little about who the inhabitants of Fingoland were in 1865, and a census quickly ensued that produced numbers to suggest that the headmen quickly absorbed thousands of Xhosa and others (including some Khoesan-speakers) into a broader Fingo network, if not identity.[5] Fingoland's external and internal boundaries themselves were entirely textual in nature and depended on topography that few

3 Clifton C. Crais, "Custom and the Politics of Sovereignty in South Africa," *Journal of Social History* 39, no. 3 (2006): 730.

4 R.T. Ally, "The Development of the System of Individual Tenure for Africans, with special reference to the Glen Grey Act, c.1894–1922" (master's thesis, Rhodes University, 1985), 62–63; B.M. Jones, "The Apportionment, Tenure, Registration, and Survey of Land in Southern Africa and Proposals for the Establishment of a Cadastral System for the Bantu Areas of South Africa" (PhD diss., University of Natal, 1964), 24.

5 Timothy Stapleton, "The Expansion of a Pseudo-Ethnicity on the Eastern Cape: Reconsidering the Fingo 'Exodus' of 1865," *International Journal of African Historical Studies* 29 (1996): 246–247. The numbers of Fingoes emigrating and the number of people on the land is still uncertain,

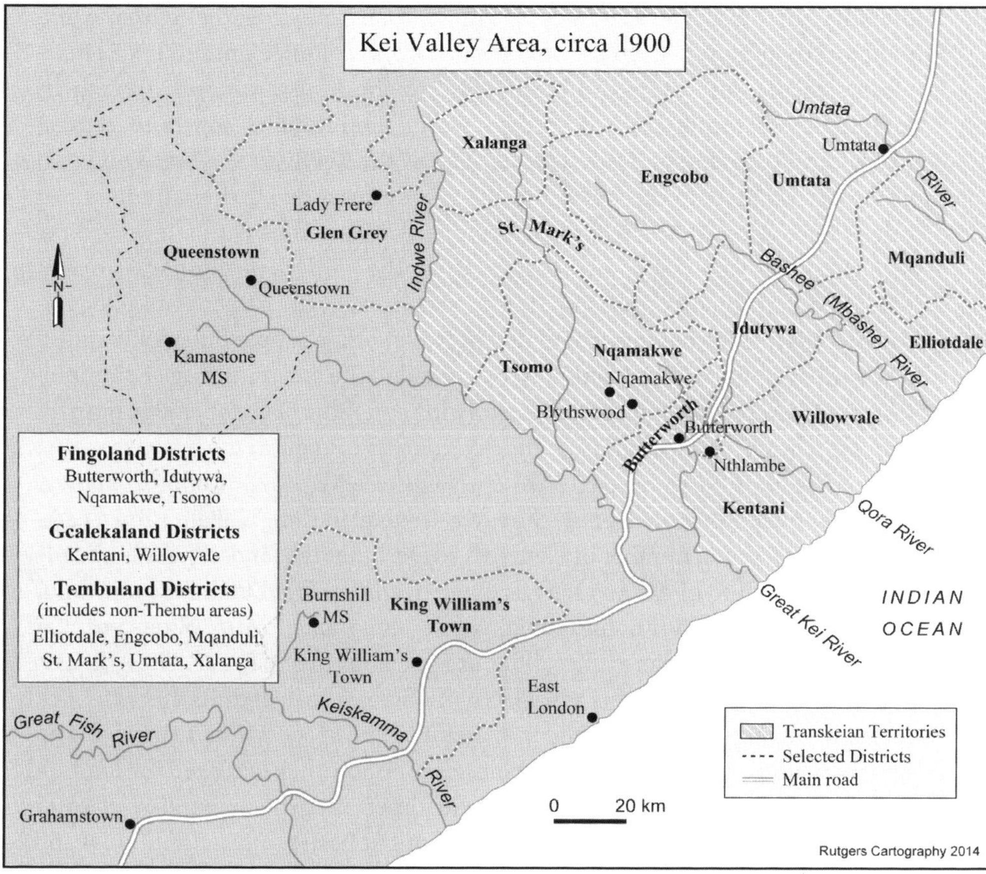

MAP 3.1 *Colonial Magisterial Districts and Divisions around the Kei.*

even among the Fingoes initially knew very well, despite some having resided in the area before.[6]

Colley had already run into frustration when trying to define the extent of land the titular Xhosa paramount Sarhili forfeited in 1858 because he could not find anyone who could indicate its boundaries precisely. To Colley, that

---

despite Stapleton's effort to clarify them. According to the register of the F.A.M.P. officer charged with locating them, around 17,240 men made the journey. The number of women and children, as well as the method of determining these figures, remains unknown. See "List of the Fingoe Chiefs with Their Locations," FA 8/2, KAB.

6 David Blair Hook, *With Sword and Statute on the Cape of Good Hope Frontier* (Cape Town: Juta, 1907), 147. Hook, who was a veteran of the campaign against Sarhili and Acting Chief Magistrate from March 1883 to October 1884, states that some Fingoes clamored for particular areas based on prior knowledge as servile people there.

inability arose from the vagueness of chiefs' boundaries, together with the tendency of their people to cross into new areas and colonize unused lands, making a straight line "utterly unintelligible" to the Xhosa mindset, though he might just as easily have described white land-hunters by those terms.[7] Externally Fingoland had the clear borders of the Kei River westward and part of the Gcuwa River to the south, but the colony described the remainder along ridges separating watersheds and periodic river crossings with a few cardinal directions thrown in for good measure. To say the border's position was unclear would be flattering its precision, but at least it used the same terminology as the boundaries the colony articulated between other people outside its rule.

Charles Cobbe, the Resident newly assigned to the emigrant Fingo communities, produced the first map of the territory in September or October 1865 from his own sketches. The uncertainty of the boundary is evident in the broad arcs that appear between the numbered river crossings (see Map 3.2).[8] Cobbe's map was valuable enough that the Deputy Surveyor-General in King William's Town carefully copied it, but a number of elements suggest that the landscape was already becoming a hybrid of old and new as Fingo headmen fused their new networks. In particular, many river names remained the same, albeit with Cobbe's peculiar transliterations, but other names differ or appear for the first time. The map also depicts many smaller streams as well as paths across the river drifts that extended through the territory and marked it as an inhabited space without conveying an understanding of who those inhabitants were or how they occupied the land.

As a colonial creation under pliant headmen in a space emptied of prior claims, Fingoland and the Idutywa Reserve might have promised a rational and governable order. In reality, control of space and authority were fluid and accumulated in the hands of the headmen the colony recognized, not just those it appointed. Matthew Smith Blyth recalled in 1882 that the F.A.M.P. under Walter Currie had arranged the arriving people into 105 locations of 2,000 to 10,000 acres each, with boundaries to circumscribe the reach of individual headmen.[9] The creation of these areas, however, could not have been simultaneous, given that colonial administrators were sending new headmen into the area in 1866.[10] These areas also did not appear on any map, and seem to have

---

7 Colley to Maclean, 15 Oct 1858, 1/IDW/Add.1/1/1, KAB.

8 W.P. Oak, 9 Nov 1865 copy of Chas. Cobbe, "Map of Fingoe Land," DSGBK 56, KAB. Cobbe's map is unusual in that it does not appear to derive from Grant and Colley.

9 Information of M.S. Blyth (Chief Magistrate, Transkei), 22 Sep 1878, in CPP G.4-'83, *Report and Proceedings with Appendices of the Government Commission on Native Laws and Customs*, 2:267.

10 Entry for 5 Apr 1866, Daily Journal, FA 1/1/1/1, KAB.

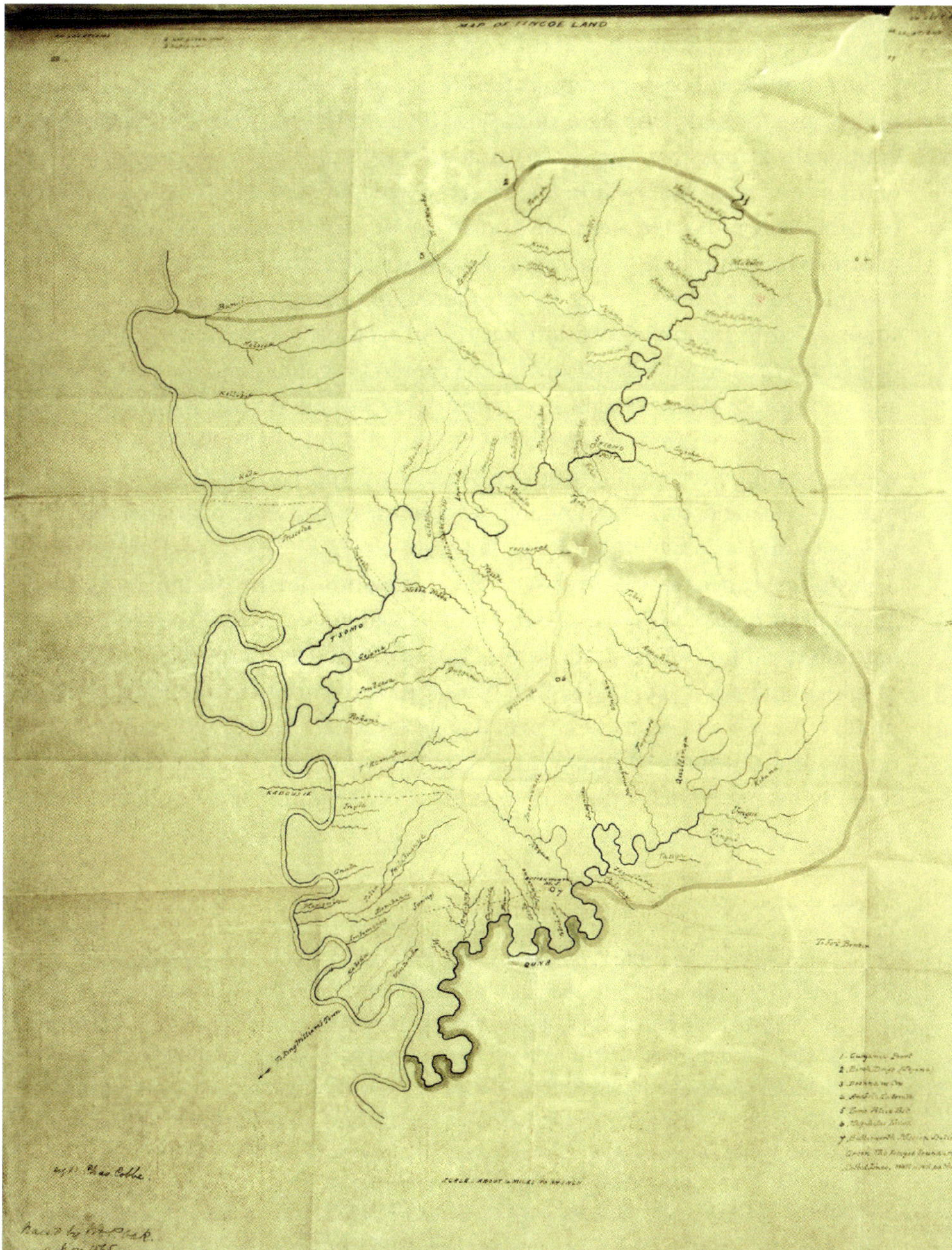

MAP 3.2 *Charles Cobbe's 1865 "Map of Fingoe Land," as traced by W.P. Oak of the Deputy Surveyor-General's Office, King William's Town, November 1865.*

SOURCE: DSGBK 56, CAPE ARCHIVES DEPOT, WESTERN CAPE ARCHIVES AND RECORDS SERVICE, CAPE TOWN. RSA STATE COPYRIGHT.

depended on a series of small unrecorded beacons, the memories of the individual headmen involved, and the pages of a single handwritten record book Cobbe and his successors kept at the Residency.[11] The book was, however, of limited use for boundary determination. Its descriptions were sometimes geographically impossible, subject to unrecorded alterations, or had never aligned with the beacons at all.[12] Until an intractable dispute arose between communities, this fact remained invisible and irrelevant to headmen, cultivators, and grazers who ignored the disparities and observed whatever boundary was most advantageous or useful for local people. Sometimes that informal boundary superseded the book, depending on the officials and claimants in question. Even after the formal extension of Cape rule to Fingoland and Idutywa in 1879, adjudication was uneven and required local support. Within the locations headmen retained their discretion over land allocation and internal disputes, which usually reached Blyth only when it involved two headmen. Land disputes between headmen and people were rarer, and often appeared in requests to leave Fingoland which agents usually denied.[13]

Amongst those uncertain spaces, then, the domineering Cobbe had to create *one* rational space for himself. There is evidence he tried to do so on the land reserved for the Resident, which Cobbe named 'Namaqua' in a fit of geographical malapropism (given that Namaqualand was nearly a thousand kilometers distant). He set aside a special page for it in his book, with columns for names and numbers of huts, but also with conditions that anyone residing there would serve as a pool of workers, police, and special constables for

11 This volume survives as FA 8/2, KAB. The number of actual headmen was 104; the 105th location became Cobbe's reserve. The register also contains an abortive list of hired police (five, through April 1866), licensed traders, livestock impoundments, and licenses to cut wood. It remained in reference use there in Nqamakwe until at least 1900. J.M. Grant did try to chart the location of particular headmen and the limits of their lands in the mid-1870s but his boundaries were partial and sometimes even absent; see J.M. Grant, "Outline Map of the Transkeian Territory…Seat of the Frontier War, Cape of Good Hope," M2/439, KAB. On the creation and various editions of that map, see L.F. Braun, "The Colonial Archive and Maps of the Western Transkei, 1857–1898," in *Proceedings of the Symposium of the Commission on the History of Cartography in the 19th and 20th Centuries*, ed. E.C. Liebenberg, Peter Collier, and Imre Josef Demhardt (Pretoria: ICA, 2009), 11–12.

12 Minutes of Enquiry into Dispute between Headman Maduma of Nqamakwe and Matthew Headman of Tsomo, 6 May 1898, facing p. 21, FA 8/2, KAB; Note on Dispute between Maduma and Lambata, 5 Apr 1899, facing p. 25, FA 8/2, KAB.

13 See, for example, C.J. Levey, entry for 30 Jun 1874 ("Mafuta of Kwekwezis"), FA 1/1/3, KAB.

Cobbe ("at a fair rate of pay"), carry government messages free, and acknowledge the magistrate (presumably the Resident) as their only chief. He added one further condition that residents keep their cattle properly herded, in stockades and with close supervision on pasturage, presumably including the livestock that would be impounded there for sale in Queenstown later.[14] The lack of even one name on the page suggests how unappealing the price of tenancy was.

Cobbe himself was a stern and controlling figure, and his employment of corporal punishment would not have endeared potential tenants. He constructed himself as the center of rational civilization, a task that later magistrates carried on after the name of the place had become the more Xhosa-sounding 'Nqamakwe' in the 1870s. One visitor in the late 1870s noted that Cobbe had built in the style of an "Indian bungalow, having a garden falling away from it arranged in terraces" and took this sign of orderly management as a natural companion of Fingo progress.[15] The colonial house (with a veranda on all sides) was Cobbe's, but the gardens and orchards were the creation of later colonial agents, each of whom added his own piece. The colonial magistrate there in the late 1890s, William Charles Scully, proudly boasted of his own creation of a massive new English garden and orchards.[16] No town existed near the Residency until surveyors laid one out in 1898, which suggests that this odd colonial microcosm was not the center of Fingo landscapes, however much they might interact with its directives.[17] The same was true of the later Chief Magistracy that resided close to the Butterworth mission after 1878, and which remained relatively untraveled despite its location near the major roads through the region.[18] There was no real incentive for local people to build their understandings of place around such points of colonial oversight.

Nominally, people across the Kei were not the direct responsibility of the Cape Colony or the British until annexation took effect in 1879. This was true of

14 "Names of Men permitted to locate on the Magistrate ground at Namaqua" and "Regulations for the Impounding Horses, Cattle, &c," FA 8/2, KAB. The seizure of livestock took place, but it is unclear who monitored them. We do not know if anyone took up residence around 1866, but by 1872 eleven men (and presumably their households) resided on that government reserve under M.S. Blyth with the same general conditions; see "Residents on Government Reserve," FA 1/1/3, KAB.

15 George St. Vincent Cripps, "Highlands and Lowlands of Kafirland," *Cape Monthly Magazine*, n.s., 14 (1877): 340–341.

16 William Charles Scully, *Further Reminiscences of a South African Pioneer* (London: T.F. Unwin, 1913), 295.

17 "Survey of Nqamakwe Township" [1898], File L.11141, LND 1/703, KAB.

18 Hook, *With Sword and Statute*, 312.

the Fingoes and the people of the Idutywa Reserve who still enjoyed the *de facto* patronage of the colony without paying tax or falling under its laws.[19] Agents like Cobbe, who were purportedly under the authority of Joseph Cox Warner as the general 'Transkeian Resident' from 1865 to 1869, were to advise local authorities with their backing in a way conducive to colonial interests. But Warner, Cobbe, and other agents composed themselves more like magistrates in settling disputes over land and cattle without enlisting the chiefs or headmen—a tendency that on at least one occasion in 1868 brought the men of an entire location out under arms to protest Cobbe's presumption of authority over a question of bridewealth.[20] The Resident in fact had no independent authority whatsoever, so any action Cobbe took on his own indelicate initiative was overreaching, despite regulations written in the colony but ostensibly passed by the Fingoes to empower his office.[21] He had almost no real leverage over the headmen, given that barely a quarter of them drew pay from government, and even that was a small sum.[22] This fact quickly became clear to the Fingoes, and Governor Wodehouse withdrew Cobbe in May 1869 for his indiscretions. Only the end of the residency system and the appointment of Matthew Smith Blyth as Fingo Agent in November 1869 drew back the capricious exercise of dubious judicial power. Blyth's greater respect for the need to work within the social order, his limited judicial power over colonial subjects, and his clearer connection to the Department of Native Affairs after its creation in 1872 did not directly change the local landscape, but it aided the push for rationalization.

Aside from village areas at the mission stations, the organization of locations remained entirely within the province of their headmen. As Fingo Agent, Blyth enjoyed little direct power to impose whatever vision of order he had for Fingoland. The result was a more active advisory role during his time as Agent,

19 The position between colonial dependency and true autonomy remained vague between the various parties, and was useful whether or not it was deliberate. C.C. Saunders, "The Annexation of the Transkeian Territories," *AYB* 39 (1976): 15, 41–42; "Memorandum by Mr. Orpen laid before the Select Committee on Native Affairs, 27th May 1873," in CPP A.12-'73, *Report of Select Committee on Native Affairs*, 1–3.

20 Waldemar B. Campbell, "The South African Frontier, 1865–1885: A Study in Expansion," *AYB* 22, no. 1 (1960): 80–83.

21 Memorandum of Sir Walter Currie, 21 Aug 1865, in CPP A.12-'73, *Report of Select Committee on Native Affairs*, 178–179. These closely match the regulations listed in FA 1/1/3, KAB, down to their deference to Commissioner Maclean's 1858 *Compendium of Kaffir Law and Custom* in judicial matters.

22 27 of 97 recorded headmen drew pay in 1872. See "Headmen in Receipt of Pay," FA 1/1/3, KAB.

one of mediation and facilitation through the headmen. But Blyth's presence was also one that also represented an anachronistically liberal version of the Cape's colonial mind that still aimed at assimilative incorporation on some distant day. For the Fingoes' part, they saw someone who would serve their goals of securing the land to them and promoting access to commerce without foisting onerous burdens upon them. The only restraint, such as it was, on Fingo alteration of the landscape was Walter Currie's vague initial 1865 reservation of all forests to government for use "as his Excellency may think fit."[23] The effectiveness of forestry licensing was uncertain. By July 1873 Blyth and his young subordinate, Charles Joseph Levey, were issuing licenses to sawyers, but they also granted simple permission to some who sought to collect wood for personal use.[24] There were many possible rationales for honoring a system of licensing and approval, but commercial advantage and Blyth's status as a patron may have played roles.

Blyth himself hoped that education and industry would serve as an inducement for the separate locations to organize themselves. Experiments with cotton cultivation were unsuccessful, but sheep farming proved to be highly efficient and profitable given the recurrence of cattle lungsickness.[25] Even with worsening early-season drought during the 1870s and the imposition of the first hut tax payments in 1874, Fingo cultivators were able to sell excess produce and purchase ploughs and carts.[26] Prominent residents of Fingoland likewise built a consultative partnership with Blyth for co-funding key projects that provided market access and future security, including the establishment of trade schools and the improvement of roads that culminated in their heavy subscription towards construction of a bridge over the Kei between 1877 and 1879.[27] Such growth and construction did not benefit all people equally, and headmen did particularly well, but Blyth only issued around 1,600 passes to Fingoes seeking work in the colony in 1872 (about 15% of the adult male population) and even fewer in the hard year of 1874, despite recurring appeals from labor agents which suggested a fairly broad base of community

23 Currie to Southey (Colonial Secretary, Cape Town), 25 Aug 1865, in CPP A.12-'73, *Report of Select Committee on Native Affairs*, 177.

24 M.S. Blyth, entries for 8 Jul 1873 and 4 Jul 1873, FA 1/1/3, KAB.

25 CPP G.34-'73, *Reports on the Social and Political Condition of Natives in the Transkeian Territory, 1872*, 4.

26 Bundy, *Rise and Fall*, 71.

27 CPP G.41-'72, *Reports on the Social and Political Condition of the Natives in the Transkeian Territory*, 2. Blyth had reported the great interest in funding the bridge as early as 1871.

prosperity.[28] The Agent did not interfere directly in the control of headmen over land allocation and organization, although he adjudicated boundaries between headmen and so sought to bring their reach in line with territorial demarcations as far as the latter could be determined.

In the neighboring Idutywa Reserve, where the Ndlambe chief Smith Mhala, the Gcaleka chief Sigidi, and their clients resided together with Fingoes and other incorporated Xhosa in a system of villages, matters were a bit different. The two chiefs in particular had complained almost immediately in 1864 to the acting special magistrate, H.B. Warner, that the system of "being huddled together" in villages created sickness and social disorder ("other evils"), which drew the response that Warner would not oppose changes to the village system or interfere with chiefs' power to settle petty suits. The chiefs emphasized the difference in their claims on the government from the Fingoes as chiefs who moved voluntarily, and they expected that their positions and lands would be protected and preserved in Idutywa or given back their old lands west of the Kei.[29] Sigidi took this one step further and complained the next day about his people's location on the Mbashe, where they reputedly came into contact with Sarhili's people once that chief had returned to lands south of the Reserve, and requested a new location further from the river. Although his stated reason had to do with avoiding accusations of treachery for the unavoidable communication his clients would have with Sarhili's headmen and people, he likely worried much more about the threat to his own authority and power. At the same time, Smith Mhala worried about being left to the mercy of Sarhili if government withdrew. He had reportedly also sought to bring his father Mhala across the Kei to bolster his own standing, until that potential presence became a liability when Smith's younger brother took up residence near Sarhili.[30]

By 1866 the hated villages had dispersed into homesteads under headmen across the rural landscape, and a few years later Sigidi sought to hire cattle pasturage near his pre-1858 lands, where many of his clients probably still lived.[31] In 1874 the two chiefs petitioned the Cape Parliament for surveyed farms to no avail, presumably in response to news of impending annexation

28 "About a third" of 4,828 passes issued in 1872, versus 1,326 for laborers and government work in 1874. CPP G.34-'73, *Reports on the Social and Political Condition of the Natives in the Transkeian Territory*, 4; CPP G.21-'75, *Blue Book on Native Affairs, 1875*, 32.

29 Transkeian Magistrate, Diary Entry for 4 Nov 1864, p. 2, 1/IDW/Add./1/1/2, KAB.

30 Transkeian Magistrate, Diary Entry for 5 Nov 1864, pp. 2–3, 1/IDW/Add./1/1/2, KAB; H.B. Warner to J.C. Warner, p. 20, 1/IDW/Add./1/1/2, KAB.

31 J.A. Cummings (Superintendent of Idutywa Reserve) to Blyth, 29 Jan 1871, p. 38, 1/IDW/Add./1/1/2, KAB.

and a desire to obtain the leverage of special grants.[32] Their spatial concerns, however, clearly revolved around the preservation of chiefly power and the networks it depended upon, which required control over the composition and physical position of people on the land but also encouraged reaches beyond colonial borders. They still defended their spaces within the district, and in 1879 Sigidi openly challenged the claim of the magistrate, Thomas Merriman, to adjudicate boundaries between the headmen under him.[33] By 1881 the boundary disputes had become so widespread that the new magistrate, Thomas Pattle, sought to retain a surveyor to mark the boundaries and create a district map of the district, but his estimate of the cost (£100) was one-twelfth of the conservative estimate of the surveyor, so the disputes continued.[34] It is quite possible that these disputes were conflicts between the client networks of the location—the Fingo headmen and those of the chiefs—that sought to employ the magistrate. But even with surveyed farms, chiefs had no reason to expect their actual power to stop at those boundaries.

The headmen of Fingoland proper, however, obtained a special guarantee of their right to occupy and govern their land that the chiefs and headmen at Idutywa did not. Several prominent headmen had sent a petition to Governor Wodehouse in 1866 requesting a formal assurance covering the whole territory, which Wodehouse's successor Henry Barkly provided in 1871. The origins of the request, and the discourse around its fulfillment, almost certainly involved Blyth given that he championed the same solution for other unsurveyed areas as Chief Magistrate in 1887 and 1888.[35] This guarantee became known as the Fingo Title, which Barkly issued on 17 August to confirm the possession of Fingoland in the hands of its collective headmen. The Colonial Secretary duly forwarded a copy to the Surveyor-General.[36] The 'title' itself was one sentence long, beyond which it simply repeated the original textual boundaries of 1865. The accompanying printed map was a purpose-made 1871 compilation from

---

32 Garner (Superintendent of Idutywa Reserve) to C.P. Brownlee, 8 Jun 1875, No. 481/75, 1/IDW/6/1/1/1, KAB.

33 T.R. Merriman to Ayliff, 19 Jun 1879, No. 28a, CMT 2/22, KAB.

34 Blyth to Ayliff, 18 Mar 1881; Blyth to Ayliff, 4 May 1881; Blyth to Sauer, 14 Jun 1881 (with enclosures), all NA 4, KAB.

35 CPP G.12-'87, *Blue Book on Native Affairs, 1887*, 64–65; CPP G.6-'88, *Blue Book on Native Affairs, 1888*, 33–34.

36 Colonial Office to Bell (SG), 22 Aug 1871, p. 342 (with map enclosure), SG 1/1/3/46, KAB. Bell set aside the Title copy and map as "extra Colonial" but was adamant that it not "be lost sight of." This advice seems to have been in vain, because the Surveyor-General requested a new copy in 1883. See de Smidt (SG) to Hook (Acting Chief Magistrate, Transkei), 3 Jul 1884, CMT 2/13, KAB.

the Surveyor-General's Office that originated in the plans of Grant and Colley, but which included printed boundary lines for Fingoland that the office further highlighted in red (see Map 3.3). Although it did not follow the normal form of a colonial title to land, the Fingo Title included all the prerequisites of an entry in the colony's territorial archive. A textual description, a 'diagram' based on the only survey data in existence, and the imprimatur of the Governor all served as marks of colonial guarantee and presumably a semi-incorporated protection.[37] Indeed, Blyth himself announced the award to a general meeting at Nqamakwe by holding up the "Title Deeds" marked with "the Government seal," that would remain in his office as its representative.[38]

Whether or not that conformity mattered to Fingo headmen, the title may have brought an expectation of greater local self-government among them. The single most prominent headman in the region, Veldtman Bikitsha, responded to the announcement of hut taxes in August 1873 with a request that such money be kept in Fingoland and representatives from among the headmen travel to Cape Town to consult with the Governor.[39] In response, Blyth invited Bikitsha to serve on an advisory board to oversee the local use of those funds, which enhanced his prestige. The existence of the Title proved to be a powerful touchstone after the colonial government formally annexed Fingoland and the Idutywa Reserve and sought to end its spatial fluidity through the extension of individual tenure across the Kei. It retained its imaginative power even after the colonial government adjudged that the Fingo Title had no real legal force when investigating their power to designate lands for traders and other purposes in 1905.[40]

The Cape government resolved to annex Fingoland and the Idutywa reserve in 1875, although the legislature did not act on it until 1877 (Act No. 38) and the annexation only became effective by proclamation (No. 110) in 1879.[41] In the

37 The surveyor Joseph Millerd Orpen, acting as a member of the Legislative Assembly (Parliament) in Cape Town, certainly read the Fingo Title as a *de facto* claim of ownership and colonial registration. See "Memorandum by Mr. Orpen laid before the Select Committee on Native Affairs, 27th May 1873," CPP A.12-'73, *Report of Select Committee on Native Affairs*, 2.

38 "Meeting of the Transkei Fingoes," *The Kaffir Express*, 1 Oct 1871, 4.

39 M.S. Blyth, entry for 12 Aug 1873, FA 1/1/3, KAB. The request had no immediate effect, but ten years later Bikitsha had in fact gained entry to the administrative loop. For one of the few known photos of Bikitsha, see Pic 3,030, Cory Library, Grahamstown.

40 See memorandum dated 22 Feb 1909, S.622, SGO-Cape; W.G. Cumming (Secretary, Native Affairs) to Colonial Office, 22 Jul 1905, file B.2368, NA 652, KAB.

41 Frank Brownlee, comp., *The Transkeian Native Territories: Historical Records* (Lovedale: Lovedale Institution Press, 1923), 10.

MAP 3.3 *C.N. Thomas's lithographed compilation of the Transkeian Territories, marked for the purposes of the Fingo Title, 1871. See also Map 2.3 (its main source).*

SOURCE: SG 1/1/3/46, CAPE ARCHIVES DEPOT, WESTERN CAPE ARCHIVES AND RECORDS SERVICE, CAPE TOWN. RSA STATE COPYRIGHT.

interim, severe drought had created enormous tensions in the region, matters not helped by Sarhili taking in as many clients as possible on his abbreviated lands and working to prevent outward migration that might sap his authority. When a fight broke out between Gcaleka and Fingoes at a wedding party in Fingoland, it escalated into a general military conflict in the Kei Valley—the War of Ngcayecibi—that included the rising of Ngqika under Sandile that cost him his life and his people their lands, just as it cost Old Soga.[42]

At the end of the conflict, in June 1878, Sarhili was again across the Mbashe, a number of rebellious colonial chiefs were in custody, and the colony appropriated their lands for a new round of spatial engineering. Those sent off of the land did not go quietly, and widespread fires in Gcalekaland at the beginning of winter (June 1878) probably marked an effort to deny any precipitous expansion of Fingo pasturage.[43] The instructions the Colonial Office gave to Blyth, who became the first Chief Magistrate of the Transkei in 1878, were quite clear about the direction this endeavor would go in Fingoland and the Idutywa Reserve: closer authority over headmen and individual tenure over land. The newly empowered Chief Magistrate was to "inform the natives in those districts that it is the intention of Government to have the country laid out in locations, and surveyed. A plot of ground of about ten acres is to be assigned to each head of family, for which an individual title is to be issued, and a sufficient extent of commonage will be alloted [*sic*] to each location."[44] The fraught history of this system, and the way it would play out in Gcalekaland, should have given its proponents greater pause even in lands across the Kei where the Governor could rule by proclamation and the application of colonial law was malleable.[45]

The Promises and Practices of Individual Tenure

In theory, individual tenure improved the sustainability and productivity of African agriculture, acclimated people to European ideas of ownership, and

42 M.W. Spicer, "The War of Ngcayecibi, 1877–1878" (master's thesis, Rhodes University, 1978), 24–25.

43 John Eustace (Magistrate, Idutywa and Gcalekaland) to Charles Pacalt Brownlee (Superintendent of Native Affairs), 12 Jun 1878, p. 180, NA 1, KAB.

44 Colonial Secretary (J. Gordon Sprigg) to Blyth, 11 Sep 1878, CMT 2/10, KAB.

45 The text of Act 38 of 1877 allowed the Cape legislature to countermand proclamations later, but the Governor's power to put them into force with the "advice" from the Executive Council is clear. Furthermore, no new Acts applied across the Kei unless specifically stipulated in the Act text.

granted them membership in the colonial state under a system of direct rule by government headmen.[46] Colonial military and civilian administrators alike also believed that giving men precisely surveyed titles to land would dismantle the retrograde social networks and the power of independent chiefs and headmen upon which successive Cape governors placed so much blame for instability, and substitute loyalty and tranquility among title holders.[47] A rational system of land management would in their reckoning induce 'idle' men to leave the location grounds, and take part in the colonial economy as wage laborers. Individual title further offered a semblance of legal security against the rapacity of white settlers and speculators who constantly sought new lands.

The practical effects of individual tenure looked very different in comparison. Removing the power of allocation from chiefs and headmen altered systems of clientage, inheritance, and accumulation within African societies, and added to the symbolic power of magistrates and surveyors. Individual tenure furthermore required registration, survey, and eventually transfer, all of which necessitated documentation, entailed significant expense (payment of survey costs were required to take up title), and asked headmen and people to acquiesce consciously to colonial reorganization of their homes and livelihoods. A quitrent title represented a particularly potent surrender to the power of the colony over the local landscape, and the acceptance of an ongoing financial and legal relationship that required the landholder or a headman to repeat that surrender regularly to a magistrate or other colonial authority in much the same way that tax collection via headmen and chiefs had begun the ritualization of rule.[48] Individual tenure furthermore limited the number of cultivators and the extent of their lands (usually to ten or twelve acres, plus an allowance for commonage), and those landholders tended to be a small stratum of those with some wealth and at times political clout. To the extent that it worked, the effect was to increase class stratification and push more and more people out into the labor market. As the modernist drive of the colonial state for legibility reached further, these supposedly

---

46 Although colonial histories often draw distinctions between 'direct' and 'indirect' models of administration depending upon the attitude towards precolonial authority, the reality was much more fluid and contingent. See Jeffrey Herbst, *States and Power in Africa: Comparative Lessons in Authority and Control* (Princeton: Princeton University Press, 2000), 81–87; Mahmood Mamdani, *Citizen and Subject: Contemporary Africa and the Legacy of Late Colonialism* (Princeton: Princeton University Press, 1996), 16–18.

47 Bank, "Losing Faith," 380; Ally, "Development of the System of Individual Tenure," 64.

48 Sean Redding, *Sorcery and Sovereignty: Taxation, Power, and Rebellion in South Africa, 1880–1963* (Athens: Ohio University Press, 2006), 13–16.

freehold titles also offered progressively less freedom and carried conditions of loyalty, restrictions on sale and transfer, and prohibitions on acquiring multiple lots that attacked any effort at accumulation or adaptation.

The spatial element of these schemes prescribed even greater shifts. The lots that surveyors laid out for individual tenure did not simply mark off land in perpetuity, but determined their purpose to be agricultural or residential. The undivided remainder in a location was commonage for grazing animals unless surveyed for other approved uses or transformed into prohibited spaces. Such restricted and prohibited spaces usually related to community resources and the ecology of the location, and constituted another direct colonial affront to the appropriative power of local headmen and chiefs as well as a threat to self-sufficiency.[49] Management schemes for forests, pastures, water, and even market access closed off avenues for individual advancement, and recast the reserve as a machine that would produce human wealth in the form of migrant labor by those without land. Surveyors had the legal power to inscribe such forbidden or controlled spaces into the state's institutional memory, and they did so in the areas where they carried out surveys for individual tenure.[50] These lots also became male spaces, whether for agriculture or building, because the colonial state and its male technicians expected to see male proprietorship and wished in this era to control male labor. The state focused on men even though women generally controlled agricultural output in this era and their presence in household compounds directly related to levels of payable hut tax.[51] When women received titles, it depended on their relationship to men, particularly if the grantee was a widow. Women certainly administered titles and paid quitrent for men who were away laboring or otherwise absent, but surveyors and magistrates usually only saw men on titles. At least one scheme considered adding acreage for women in polygynous households under the husbands' names to reflect the existing practice of specific plots for wives, but rapidly reversed course in view of legal complications and the belief that it would promote multiple marriage.[52]

---

49 Jacob A. Tropp, *Natures of Colonial Change: Environmental Relations in the Making of the Transkei* (Athens: Ohio University Press, 2006), 40–41.

50 The demarcation of those areas preceded survey, but survey was not necessary for policing; see Tropp, *Natures of Colonial Change*, 45–52. For the role of forest management in state legibility, see James C. Scott, *Seeing Like a State: How Certain Schemes to Improve the Human Condition Have Failed* (New Haven: Yale University Press, 1998), 11–22.

51 Redding, *Sorcery and Sovereignty*, 38.

52 H.E. Richard Bright (Under-Secretary for Native Affairs) to Blyth, 24 Jan 1880, CMT 2/2, KAB. Such a plan only reappeared in the surveyed districts of the Transkei after 1936,

Individual tenure also envisioned clustered building lots in an idealized village system away from orderly agricultural lands in order to exert maximum administrative efficacy and control, but that system ran contrary to rural logic, which saw groups of homesteads within landscapes of flexible authority and spatial order. Such socially-contingent and shifting politics and geographies seemed irrational to the British, who sought to divine, define, and control, or if necessary supplant, the extant centers of authority. But fixing the spatial arrangement of a community promised to isolate and identify political authorities. The broad idea that particular 'tribes' under singular 'chiefs' held definable lands on communal tenure, subject to certain practices or native laws, held out the prospect of legibility and hegemony if only those values were known to government.[53] Determining the extent of any given territory, its pre-existing conditions of ownership (its 'native title'), and the holder of that prior ownership were crucial steps towards changing or stripping away those things in part or in whole, and colonial rule was good at replacing flexibility with invented sovereignty to achieve that goal.[54] Such methods of reformulating space and society through the collection and deployment of colonial knowledge were, after all, not unique to South Africa.[55]

Colonial fantasies about tribalism and progress therefore abetted processes of dispossession and immobilization. Without surveyed allotments, colonial authorities could only determine occupation of a given area based on 'tickets of occupation,' hut-tax registers, or inhabitants' recognition by headmen or chiefs who oversaw communal tenure. Without a finite cap on legal occupation through a system of survey and title, people could subsist on marginal scraps of land rather than obtaining disadvantageous terms as labor tenants on settler-owned farms or later as migrant laborers in the hazardous mines of Kimberley and the Witwatersrand.[56] More to the point, their social networks

---

whereas the allotment system of unsurveyed districts already accounted for these households through headmen. The potential disincentive to Christian marriage in surveyed districts was one objection. See "Land Allotments, Forfeiture and Re-Allotment," File 15/B, Umtata Archives, Mthatha, South Africa.

53 Richard Roberts and Kristin Mann, "Law in Colonial Africa," in *Law in Colonial Africa*, ed. Kristin Mann and Richard Roberts (London: James Currey, 1991), 3–5, 19–27; Crawford Young, *The African Colonial State in Comparative Perspective* (New Haven: Yale University Press, 1994), 114–117.

54 John C. Weaver, *The Great Land Rush and the Making of the Modern World, 1650–1900* (Kingston, ON: McGill-Queen's, 2003), 133–177; Crais, "Custom and the Politics of Sovereignty," 723–730.

55 Scott, *Seeing Like a State*, 33–39; Mamdani, *Citizen and Subject*, 138–141.

56 Prospective migrants carefully considered whether the benefit-to-risk ratio of mine labor outweighed the profit of working land, especially where (and when, such as during

would certainly insulate them. European settler agriculture and industry thus deeply influenced the survey of land for individual tenure, even though most requests for survey and title were ostensibly democratic requests from 'advanced' people who had the most to gain by excluding others.[57] The presence of surveyors promised to expedite a shift from an African agrarian system whose logic evaded officials to one that embodied the rational perfection of European land tenures—but only to a point.

Persuasion, Imposition, and Escape

In the colonial mind, the annexation of Fingoland and the conquest of Gcalekaland provided an ideal opportunity to sell or impose individual tenure on a large scale. The reason was to be found in the colonial discourse that grew up around the Fingoes themselves and their relative success in navigating changing conditions of land and market access. This discourse of improvement turned heavily on the conceptual link between government, mission stations, and schools. Mission-educated Fingo Christians—'school people,' as opposed to purportedly unenlightened and tradition-bound 'red people'—enjoyed the relative favor of the colonial regime and had greater access to social networks as well as the legal and financial tools necessary to obtain colonial titles to land in freehold or leasehold.[58] The mission station was in many ways the colony writ small, an exemplary institution that combined spatial and ideological influence. It provided access and acclimatization to the knowledge of the colonizer from an initially empowering humanitarian viewpoint that later would challenge European settler capitalists' narrower vision of

---

drought or war) the land could not provide a useful return. See Nancy Jacobs, *Environment, Power, and Injustice: A South African History* (Cambridge: University of Cambridge Press, 2003), 94.

57 Martin Chanock identifies this dialogic divination of "customary rights" and the corresponding promotion of European forms of tenure as progressively civilized as a common theme of the early colonial period. See M. Chanock, "Paradigms, Policies, and Property: A Review of the Customary Law of Land Tenure," in *Law in Colonial Africa*, ed. Kristin Mann and Richard Roberts (London: James Currey, 1991), 62–63.

58 For two views of the contours and exceptionality of Fingo prosperity within this framework see Bundy, *Rise and Fall*, 52–54; Richard Bouch, "The Mfengu Revisited: The 19th Century Experience of One Mfengu Community through the Eyes of Historians and Contemporaries," *Institute of Commonwealth Studies Collected Seminar Papers: Societies of Southern Africa in the 19th and 20th Centuries* 42 (1992): 81–89.

unequal incorporation.[59] Most missionaries nevertheless approved of separate spaces for nonwhite habitation and subsistence with the influence of a strong Christian presence that could promote European cultural, social, and commercial values, stripping the chiefs of their uneven and capricious legal power over time and consigning the 'red people' to history.[60] After 1847, successive governors in Cape Town expressed increasingly expansive views of the need to bring rational order to native reserves through survey and title, and they approached Fingo areas first in this context.[61]

Surveys of such reserves west of the Kei had already expanded as part of a broader push for legibility within the colony during the 1850s and 1860s, as the philosophy of civilization and uplift gave way to the extractive settler paternalism of the late nineteenth century. On the Eastern Cape some people voted with their feet and crossed the Kei, or invoked particular understandings of the landscape in opposition. The Burnshill Presbyterian mission station and village near Rabula, which originated in a grant from Sandile in 1831, passed into the sphere of colonial authority after 1852 and was surveyed for title at the behest of its resident missionary in the late 1860s. Xhosa in the mission village, probably mindful that the final resting place of Ngqika himself (Sandile's father) was close by, felt that only an Ngqika chief could grant the land and so refused to participate in the granting of titles.[62] Some Fingo households agreed to receive titles, but others objected to the limitation on the number of landholders and the designation of land use, and emigrated across the Kei to join the Fingo headmen and communities residing since 1865 on formerly Xhosa land between the Kei and Mbashe rivers. Even after survey, government could not compel people to live in the village, and they continued to build homesteads

59 Crais, *White Supremacy and Black Resistance*, 100–105; On categories of colonialism as seen from the mission, see John L. Comaroff, "Images of Empire, Contests of Conscience," in *Tensions of Empire: Colonial Cultures in a Bourgeois World*, ed. Frederick Cooper and Ann Stoler (Berkeley: University of California, 1997), 179–181.

60 Richard Elphick and V.C. Malherbe, "The Khoisan to 1828," in *The Shaping of South African Society 1652–1840*, ed. R. Elphick and H. Giliomee (Middletown, Conn.: Wesleyan University Press, 1989), 48; John Barker, "Where the Missionary Frontier Ran Ahead of Empire," in *Missions and Empire*, ed. Norman Etherington (Oxford: Oxford University Press, 2005), 101.

61 Ally, "Development of the System of Individual Tenure," 69–72; Richard Bouch, "The Colonization of Queenstown (Eastern Cape) and its Hinterland, 1852–1886" (PhD diss., University of London, 1992), 175–176.

62 Robin M. Derricourt, *Prehistoric Man in the Ciskei and Transkei* (Cape Town: Struik, 1977), 162; M.E. Elton Mills and M. Wilson, *Keiskammahoek Rural Survey* vol. 4 (Pietermaritzburg: Shuter and Shooter, 1952), 69.

near lands and pasture until the 1930s and 1940s, when new state conservation policies forced them to relocate.[63]

Although there are few such specific complaints from Fingo and Xhosa farmers in the archive, misgivings about cost, meaning, and simple acceptability of the surveyed lots clearly existed. The presumed objectivity of law and science combined with a lack of specialized instructions for surveys of native lands to produce an outwardly rational yet sometimes nonsensical system. For example, the titles to these ten-acre lots cost the full survey tariff normally intended to apply to farms of thousands of acres. The Cape government upheld this principle in early 1859, while the model in British Kaffraria, where the government employed a greater degree of coercion to introduce villages and titles after the Cattle Killing, left the surveyor himself to negotiate the fees with the grantees and collect them.[64] As a result many titles went unclaimed, about 10% at Burnshill but nearly 50% overall by 1881, and the Surveyor-General had received only £8,915 15s. of the £21,823 10s. due by 1880.[65] The problems of cost and consultation were evident enough that the Cape Government ordered a halt to the survey of reserve lands in Victoria East at the end of 1861, pending special arrangements regarding the cost of survey and a clear indication of agreement.[66] An *ad hoc* system of experimentation with costs continued until 1879 when the colonial treasury agreed to pay half the cost of location surveys, but weak consultation between the surveyors and people living on the land continued to complicate surveys and helped to assure the impermanence of title schemes.[67]

Surveys for individual tenure continued into the 1870s west of the Kei, but the surveyors still showed only cursory regard for the order on the ground or the wishes and practices of the people. The commissioners in divisions with great numbers of African inhabitants, such as James Rose Innes in King

63 Mills and Wilson, *Keiskammahoek Rural Survey*, 4:69–70.

64 "Surveyor-General's Report," in CPP G.4-'83, *Report and Proceedings with Appendices of the Government Commission on Native Laws and Customs*, 2:375; J.B. Peires, *The Dead Will Arise: Nongqawuse and the Great Xhosa Cattle-Killing Movement of 1856–1857* (Johannesburg: Ravan, 1989), 290–293.

65 "Surveyor-General's Report," in CPP G.4-'83, *Report and Proceedings with Appendices of the Government Commission on Native Laws and Customs*, 2:371–373. The number of titles "not taken up" represented 4,984 of 10,046, though 3,087 of those titles were cancelled altogether, mostly due to unsuitability of the ground.

66 Colonial Office to C.D. Bell (Surveyor-General), 31 Dec 1861, CO No. 3821, SG 1/1/3/1/2, KAB.

67 Les Switzer, *Power & Resistance in an African Society: The Ciskei Xhosa and the Making of South Africa* (Madison: Univeristy of Wisconsin Press, 1993), 89. The standardization of cost-sharing was part of the Native Location Lands and Commonage Act (No. 40), 1879.

William's Town, nevertheless became aggressive in their promotion of individual tenure by 1876 as the only way to encourage "improvement in our native population" regardless of its execution.[68] The Surveyor-General from 1872 to 1889, Abraham de Smidt, likewise considered his official duty with regard to individual tenure to be "one of primary consequence," and surveyors openly employed fear as a tool for manufacturing consent.[69] In 1876, surveyor Alfred Everitt Murray visited the Newlands Location in the division of King William's Town in response to the resident missionary's interest in survey and title as a means of alleviating a sense of insecurity among the people. Murray used this as a weapon, in a remarkable speech that characterized the Fingoes in the colony as occupants on government land who could "be sent away at a word from the Government" and whom only the power of survey and title could save:

> ...the world is going forward, and you Kaffirs must go forward with it or you will surely be left behind in the race. Look at that iron-road at which so many of you are making fortunes, or would be but for the curse of drink. To what does it point? It points to this, that a new era has dawned upon the country, that the past state of things can never come back, and wise men will go onward with the stream. ...I must tell you, that thousands of white men are coming to this country, and the value of land will increase very much; when fortunate will be those people who can say: "Here is our land which no one can take from us."[70]

The explicit threat underlining Murray's back-handed moralizing was that without survey and title, the land could and would be lost—not possibly lost, at some future date, but definitely lost and in a very short time. The promise of security and the protection of law required Africans' acceptance of a particular position within the state, the payment of regular fees, loyalty, and beneficial occupation, all under adjudication of the colonial authorities.[71] The people at Newlands evidently decided that the conditions and costs of title were unacceptable, because no survey took place until September 1906.[72] We have no

68 CPP G.12-'77, *Blue Book on Native Affairs, 1876*, 113.

69 CPP G.33-'77, *Report of the Surveyor-General* [for the Year 1876], 8, 10–12. For Abraham de Smidt in general, see Marjorie Bull, *Abraham de Smidt: Artist and Surveyor-General of the Cape Colony* (Cape Town: Printpak, 1981).

70 CPP G.33-'77, *Report of the Surveyor-General* [for the Year 1876], 10–12.

71 Weaver, *Great Land Rush*, 135.

72 CPP G.29-1907, *Report of the Surveyor-General for the Year Ended 31st December 1906*, 5.

record of Newlands residents' thoughts about Murray, who would go on to refine his pitch for another two decades.

The senior land surveyors who claimed priority on such long-term government projects had neither a special technical acumen for it, nor were they attentive to conditions on-site, and consequently they had little success in restricting agriculture to defined plots or, more importantly, obtaining revenue for themselves or the state.[73] Without constant supervision, people vacated villages in favor of residences near their lands, shifted cultivation, accumulated or subdivided land without formal legal transfer, and plowed commonage intended for grazing. These cultivators disregarded the cadastral diagram's spatial limitations and viewed titles as legal guarantees of occupancy but not as territorially restrictive documents under colonial control.[74] The lot corners described areas that did not necessarily represent the most efficient spots for cultivation in any given year, and a three-field rotation within an area smaller than twenty acres was far less productive than the earlier model of shifting agriculture. The intentions of the land surveyor and the colonial magistrate clearly did not match the priorities of the people living on the land.

The Civil Commissioner of the division of Victoria East, Alex Stewart, put a finger on the long-term results of the breakdown between colonial logic and African knowledge. There, the Cape government surveyed several Fingo locations for title between 1855 and 1861. In 1881, Stewart discovered that some titles were twenty years in arrears on quitrent payments, and in seeking to collect on these debts he discovered "a state of almost inextricable confusion."[75] Almost nobody working the land could show a legal right of occupation, much less a title, and the lot beacons were long gone, with the result that homesteads and cultivated lands could be found in a variety of places. The independent social and economic landscape had prevailed in the Fingo locations of Victoria East, albeit in a condensed fashion thanks to the increasing population in the reserve and the settler occupation of bordering lands. The people worked with one another through their own social networks rather than the machinery of the colonial state. They resided near their agricultural land and livestock instead of moving to designated building lots on the colonial village model,

73 Ally, "Development of the System of Individual Tenure," 74–76; Switzer, *Power & Resistance*, 89.

74 See South African Parliamentary Paper (hereafter SPP) U.G.42-'22, *Report on Native Location Surveys*, 1–5.

75 A. Stewart (Civil Commissioner, Victoria East) to H.H. McNaughton (Assistant Commissioner of Crown Lands), 29 Apr 1882, appended to "Surveyor-General's Report," in CPP G.4-'83, *Report and Proceedings with Appendices of the Government Commission on Native Laws and Customs*, 2:379–380.

and many people erected additional structures for family needs that the colony defined as extralegal but could not stop. Capitalizing land tended to increase inequality between landed and landless people, which meant that few people saw a benefit in adhering to a costly and limiting system of situating, transferring, and inheriting land.[76] Whether those decisions reverted to headmen under the colonial magistrate or represented a more autochthonous process at the household or community level is unclear, but Stewart made no mention of headmen in his report to the Commissioner for Crown Lands in 1882, which suggests that any arrangement was local or familial.[77]

In the 1870s, some communities sought to create a third option–group title–within the legal environment of the colony, as a way of obtaining the security of title but retaining ownership in common. It is tempting to link this development to the influence of missionaries who promoted secure title, or to credit the precedent of the Fingo Title directly, but we have no clear evidence of the idea's origin. For example, men at the Kamastone Mission between 1870 and 1874 consistently and with near-unanimity sought a title in common trust instead of restrictive individual titles to six-acre lots as government proposed. Edmund C. Jeffrey, the superintendent of the Oxkraal and Kamastone locations in Queenstown division, held numerous meetings in an effort to sell individual tenure, including some where the Superintendent of Native Affairs was present. No matter the composition, the disapproval remained the same. The proposed allotments of six acres, the householders maintained, would undercut their commercial income from selling a great deal of surplus grain to nearby white farmers, reduce some of them to poverty, and do nothing to secure their costly buildings, water furrows, and other improvements; they wanted a title to the land "*in one piece*" that colonial law would recognize.[78] Jeffrey continued trying to make the case to them, but encountered so much disapproval and skepticism of the motives of government that he scribbled his frustrations on the back of a June 1873 report to the Surveyor-General with the statement that "[t]he people of Kamastone are a nuisance—a bad lot."[79] Kamastone residents also clearly considered their lots to be fairly bad, in all senses of the term.

76 Mills and Wilson, *Keiskammahoek Rural Survey*, 4:6; Ally, "Development of the System of Individual Tenure," 81–82.

77 "Surveyor-General's Report," in CPP G.4-'83, *Report and Proceedings with Appendices of the Government Commission on Native Laws and Customs*, 2:380.

78 Memorial of the Kamastone Village to the Resident Magistrate, n.d. [1872] and Memorial of the Kamastone Village to the Resident Magistrate, Queenstown, dated Feb 1873, S.2150 (vol. 289), SGO-Cape. The quoted section is emphasized in the original.

79 Report of E.C. Jeffrey, n.d. [Jun/Jul 1873], S.2150 (vol. 289), SGO-Cape.

The machinery of Cape land policy countenanced no middle ground; no Fingo Title could exist for locations within the colony. Only one model of secure title existed, and that was based on the survey of individual allotments.[80] Kamastone only accepted the principle of title if the lands could be situated where they already cultivated, append allotments for male children, and make better allotments to those who built improvements—conditions that the Surveyor-General and the local authorities promised to incorporate if only to manufacture a compliant majority.[81] The colonial intent to locate people in villages and take future questions of allotment away from headmen and elders did not change. In the Oxkraal and Kamastone locations more generally, the general machinery of survey only moved forward with a July 1875 petition that did not directly approve individual tenure itself, but only the locations' division into nominal farms under particular headmen where people would obtain land, a process of incremental partition with only one possible end.[82] The colonial government used this vague expression, together with a colonial subsidy of survey fees, to push through a broad survey in 1875 and individual survey for titles in 1876. Eventually the entire area complied, likely out of fear as much as opportunity.

Surveyor-General de Smidt was aware that problems existed with the implementation of individual tenure. But he was a principled paternalist who believed in the clear and unimpeachable benefits of individual tenure on competently-surveyed lots, so the problem had to rest with some factor that elicited a grantee's fundamental irrationality. In his 1881 report to the Commission on Native Laws and Customs (the Barry Commission), de Smidt settled on cost as the likely culprit. He suggested that government should attach a greater sense of legal ritual to the delivery and administration of title, but that survey expenses should be lowered or at least amortized over a longer period for the applicants, in view of the benefits that government derived from regular revenue as well as knowledge of "the topographical facts registered by the survey" for more abstract mapping purposes. But de Smidt also recognized a problem in the surveyor's efforts to *pre*scribe rather than *de*scribe patterns of occupation—a small glimmer of understanding that unfortunately did not translate well into colonial policy.[83]

80 C.P. Brownlee to de Smidt, 9 May 1874, S.2150 (vol. 289), SGO-Cape.

81 Jeffrey to E.A. Judge (Civil Commissioner & Resident Magistrate, Queestown), 13 Jul 1874, S.2150 (vol. 289), SGO-Cape. In practice, variances were small and limited in number.

82 John Frost to C.P. Brownlee, 10 Jul 1875, p. 2, S.2150 (vol. 289), SGO-Cape.

83 "Surveyor-General's Report," in CPP G.4-'83, *Report and Proceedings with Appendices of the Government Commission on Native Laws and Customs*, 2:373–375.

The case of Oxkraal and Kamastone is instructive of just how badly the colonial model did translate. At the time of their survey, de Smidt held up those locations as a sign of things to come, with reduced fees and a more conscientious regime of survey, including additional lot surveys later. By 1908, however, disregard for the strictures of individual title was so evident that the Native Affairs Department retained the services of a full-time "Government Surveyor in Native Locations" specifically for resurveys west of the Transkei, a position they extended indefinitely the following year.[84] The first destination for this surveyor, L.M. Walton, was Oxkraal and Kamastone.[85] Walton discovered that many allotments had been transferred or inherited without approval or payment of transfer fees, squatters had taken up some lots, and lost stone beacons and encroachments were rife, but his instructions prohibited him even from issuing warnings to errant landholders.[86] Indeed there was suspicion regarding his arrival at Oxkraal and Kamastone, because among the local residents "the feeling was that Government had not been asked to send a Surveyor," they did not want one, and that they simply could not afford a full resurvey.[87] It is much more likely that the transfer and succession of occupancy had shifted to the headmen, and people preferred a more informal community model of consultation that predated the costly and unfeeling machinery of rule unless they had the resources to employ that legal leverage. Walton replaced some of the physical marks of the survey and reported conditions in a process that lasted over eight years, but the matter continued to deteriorate from the colonial ideal, and his work did nothing to stop continuing local circumvention and informal allotment practices even among administrators.[88] In 1922 M.C. Vos,

84 D.A. Bremner (Assistant Surveyor-General) to L.M. Walton, 23 Sep 1908, S.2150 (vol. 291), SGO-Cape; E. Dower (Secretary to the Native Affairs Department) to Cornish-Bowden, 1 Sep 1909, S.2150 (vol. 291), SGO-Cape. Walton's remit did not extend east of the Kei until much later.

85 A.H. Cornish-Bowden (Surveyor-General) to Civil Commissioner, Queenstown, 17 Oct 1908, S.2150 (vol. 291), SGO-Cape. Walton's original destination was to be Glen Grey, which had similar but less pressing issues.

86 Civil Commissioner, Queenstown to Cornish-Bowden, 31 Oct 1908, S.2150 (vol. 291), SGO-Cape; Cornish-Bowden to Walton, 23 Sep 1908, S.2150 (vol. 291), SGO-Cape. For the registry of lost beacons, many hundreds of entries long, see "Register of Beacons Replaced by Native Location Surveyor (Mr Walton) 1909 [-1913]," INQ 2/4/1, KAB.

87 Inspector of Native Locations to Civil Commissioner, Queenstown, 24 Oct 1908 and 26 Oct 1908, S.2150 (vol. 291), SGO-Cape.

88 Cornish-Bowden to F.J. Phillips (Native Location Surveyor), 6 May 1916, S.2150 (vol. 293), SGO-Cape; L.M. Walton to F.F. Elliott (Surveyor-General), 14 Dec 1936, S.2150 (vol. 293), SGO-Cape.

a land surveyor and briefly Secretary for Native Affairs in the Union, found that only 626 out of 1,864 agricultural lots were occupied by their registered owners, and that many continued to shun village lots in favor of unapproved residency closer to grazing areas on the commonage.[89] But in 1878, such inconvenient discoveries remained for the future.

The Surveyor's Eye and the Lost Archive of Gcalekaland

1879 seemed auspicious to surveyors and social engineers alike. The newly-installed Astronomer Royal in Cape Town, a Scottish-born, mechanically gifted watchmaker's son named David Gill, promoted a renewed and expanded geodetic survey that he envisioned would not only improve the consistency of survey within southern Africa, but would eventually carry a precise triangulation all the way to Cairo in true imperial style.[90] Henry Bartle Edward Frere, the technocratic Governor and High Commissioner since March 1877, had been convinced from the beginning that the future wealth of South Africa depended on precise survey in a trigonometrical framework, and set out a memorandum on surveys even before he took office.[91] Gill's plans thus gained Frere's quick support, as did the idea of applying individual tenure to the newly-acquired lands around the Kei. Gill's new triangulation between the Cape and Natal was not complete until 1892, but the initial reorganization of Fingoland and Gcalekaland could link to Bailey's survey chain. The colonial government broke Fingoland into the magistracies of Butterworth, Nqamakwe, and Tsomo in 1878 on the principle of roughly equal population, while Idutywa remained its own district and Gcalekaland became Kentani and Willowvale districts in 1878 and 1879 respectively.[92] Fingoland thus persisted as a conceptual category for the people there just as it did for the magistrates appointed to it, but Gcalekaland appeared to be a completely blank territory available for redesign.

Whether as a postscript to the War of Ngcayecibi or a narrative element of the dispossession of African chiefs and agriculturalists, almost every historian

---

89 SPP U.G.42-'22, *Report on Native Location Surveys*, 3.

90 CPP A.104-'80, *Despatches, Correspondence and Papers &c Relative to Proposed Continuation of the Trigonometrical Survey of the Cape Colony in Connection with the Adjacent Territories*, 4–8. The chain in question, the Arc of the 30th Meridian, eventually took 75 years to complete.

91 "Copy of Memorandum on on South African Surveys," 15 Feb 1879, pp. 163–165, RGO 15/98, Royal Greenwich Observatory Archives, Cambridge University Library (CUL).

92 For the rationale in dividing Fingoland, see Blyth to Ayliff, 4 Nov 1878, NA 1, KAB.

of the Eastern Cape dealing with this period mentions a survey of Gcalekaland into locations and lots on individual tenure. But they do so from the viewpoint of a *fait accompli*, using the official knowledge production of the colonial state that prescribed and anticipated the creation of such an order so long as things went according to plan. The few histories that reference the scheme seem unaware that it failed miserably in the face of persistent social order and patterns of land use on the landscapes where people rebuilt their communities, and that it was never even finished.[93] The surveyors, magistrates, and local communities were all on completely different pages. The result was suspension of the surveys in 1881 and their abandonment between 1883 and 1889. Individual tenure never took root in the districts of Gcalekaland, a point that was so embarrassing to colonial technocrats that they virtually wrote it out of the history of their work. Even the government institutions charged with the initial task lost the memory of its failure more than once, but its traces remain scattered throughout the geographical archive.

As Gcalekaland was a conquered territory, the new Secretary for Native Affairs, William Ayliff—himself the son of a Transkeian missionary—could simply move forward with recommendations to government for its disposal. Ayliff's predecessor and advisor, Charles Pacalt Brownlee, noted the failure of efforts to induce Gcaleka leaders to surrender using promises of a return to a portion of their land in May 1878, and suggested that the offer be withdrawn after watiting a few more months and the land then be given to other people from the Colony or some agreeable neutral party.[94] Ayliff's plan followed this model in cutting Gcalekaland into a series of block locations for various relocated groups, including those Ngqika who had supported the colony, under direct colonial rule and a system of individual titling. Every step involved precise survey, from the creation of locations and blocks of agricultural allotments to the layout of central villages where paid government headmen would exert maximum influence.[95] Together with the application of the Colony's various Native Location Acts for the collection of taxes and local supervision, Ayliff believed this fracturing would weaken the power of any chiefs or hereditary headmen. Although Ayliff only spelled out his intent in November 1878, the relocation had already begun. The two major relocated Ngqika parties (formerly under

93 Saunders, "Annexation," 62–65, 84; Bundy, *Rise and Fall*, 97. Only George McCall Theal mentions any part of the scheme's outcome; G.M. Theal, *History of South Africa* vol. 10 (London: George Allen & Unwin, 1919), 73, 137–139.

94 C.P. Brownlee, "Memo on Letter of Chief Magistrate Fingoland regarding Occupation of Galekaland," 31 May 1878, NA 1, KAB.

95 "Memo regarding future settlement of Kafirland," 14 Nov 1878, CO 3299, KAB.

Sandile and Anta, totaling around 7,500 people with well over 10,000 animals), reached the western (Kentani district) locations on 19 and 22 September 1878 after a ten-day journey under an armed escort and imperfect efforts to clear the old human landscape from the former Ngqika lands west of the Kei.[96] It is not surprising that the officers in charge of this forced emigration registered and tallied their charges, human and animal alike.

The Gcalekaland planning commissioners, however, were barely ahead of these Ngqika parties, and the surveyors were not far behind. The new spatial order in Gcalekaland was to revolve around ten 20,000-acre locations in two clusters (optimistically meant to support 15,000 people per cluster), situated on open ground away from defensible terrain or valuable forests, and allotted on the basis of individual tenure. These two clusters were not only separate from one another, but were also separated from territories outside Gcalekaland by bands of large farms intended for white ownership, and monitored through "military posts to be permanently held" at strategic points (see Map 3.4).[97] Governor Frere hoped that such security would also allow the state to prohibit moral perils by excluding canteens and policing traders from the time of establishment, despite a lack of any legal authority without annexation.[98] All of these plans required new surveys, and initially they required armed protection and rations for resettled people as well, especially after lungsickness and "change in grass" reportedly cut herds by more than half by the end of 1878 and the population neared 9,000.[99]

Those surveys were to be based upon a trigonometrical extension from Bailey's existing geodetic stations west of the Kei River, a task the Surveyor-General entrusted to Scottish-born Donald Macdonald. Macdonald's recent service on the flagship individual tenure surveys of Oxkraal and Kamastone made him a natural

96 CPP G.33-'79, "Blue Book on Native Affairs" (1879), 110–111; W. Wright (special magistrate) to Sprigg (Colonial Secretary), 28 Sep 1878, NA 1, KAB. Former rebels and people without land remained landless in the colony itself.

97 J. Gordon Sprigg (Premier and Colonial Secretary), "Instructions to Commissioners for Laying out the Country between the Kei and the Bashee Rivers for the settlement of Europeans and Natives," copy in S.5237/8 (unbound folder), SGO-Cape. These instructions also appear in CPP G.29-'79, *Report of the Surveyor-General for the Year 1878*, 15.

98 Frere to M. Hicks Beach (Secretary of State for the Colonies), 10 Jan 1879, in British Parliamentary Papers (hereafter BPP), Further Correspondence Respecting the Affairs of South Africa, 1879, C.2252, 35–36; Frere to Hicks Beach, 19 May 1879, No. 152, GH 23/35, KAB.

99 CPP G.33-'79, *Blue Book on Native Affairs, 1879*, 115–117. Given that B.J. Liefeldt, the same inspector who compiled those figures, did not even mention an outbreak of sickness but reported that people were "well satisfied" and that many had money to spend on seed and grain, it is quite possible that some animals were sold and reported to Liefeldt as dead to avoid any possible complications or taxes.

MAP 3.4 *Tracing of J.M. Grant's sketch map of Gcalekaland, 1878, showing notional occupation designations prior to the subdivision of European farms.*
SOURCE: S.5237/8 (VOL. 463F), OFFICE OF THE SURVEYOR-GENERAL, CAPE TOWN. RSA STATE COPYRIGHT.

choice. He very quickly discovered that the position of Bailey's closest station was in error and that several reference stations required rebuilding, forcing him into the unenviable position of second-guessing a geodetic survey. Macdonald had to work carefully as, in the words of the exacting Assistant Surveyor-General and Examiner of Diagrams, Leopold Marquard, "your triangulation is an extension of Capt. Bailey's Trigonometrical Survey, and must therefore be regarded as a work of much professional importance."[100] That work was also important for fixing the beacons of the new farms and allotments mathematically to defy any intent by residents to violate their boundaries or, in the case of small plots, change position. Triangulation however only began in May 1879, contemporary to the local surveying of farm beacons—in effect, working in reverse order.[101]

100 Marquard to MacDonald (draft), 10 Oct 1879, H4/1/16, NGI.

101 The trigonometrical work took about four months. See Macdonald to de Smidt, 29 Apr and 19 Sep 1879, both S.5237/8, (vol. 463F), SGO-Cape. General plans show that Macdonald's trigonometrical stations were reckoned only from a few of the closest farm beacons,

The reason for this oddity was colonial unction, as problems with implementing Ayliff and Frere's system of spatial control arose almost immediately. The Land Board charged with setting the general parameters for the location boundaries complained in their report of 2 October 1878 that "the prompt coming of the Gaikas [in September 1878] made necessary" certain inaccuracies in the prescribed size of the locations for the sake of beaconing them, lest the incoming Ngqika arrive to find surveyors in the field and raise a protest.[102] The Commissioner for Crown Lands and Public Works (the office over the Surveyor-General until 1892) expressed a similar concern several months earlier as well, asking that no surveyors be in the field until the Ngqika were relocated, but simultaneously urging that they retain enough surveyors to "perform the necessary work with the requisite despatch."[103]

The government's desire for speedy work was in earnest. The commission appointed in August 1878 to inspect the land for European settlement commented, when sending their description of the first 76 European farms to the Secretary for Native Affairs and the Surveyor-General, that hundreds of Ngqika families were cultivating lands and cutting wood miles outside the supposed location boundaries, and Fingo homesteads and thousands of their cattle had crossed from the north.[104] The surveyor who replaced J.M. Grant and handled land inspection as part of the official Land Commission was Robert Jukes Hughes, a Royal Navy officer only admitted to practice as a land surveyor in the Colony a few months prior.[105] Hughes had little familiarity with local patterns of land use, but he was not oblivious to the reality of the situation. The commission recommended the sale of grazing licenses in accommodation of such *de facto*

---

attesting to their lateness. See, for example, the bottom center of Hughes's plan of farms in Willowvale from 1879, Tskei Plan 6930, SGO-Cape.

102 "Report of No. 1 Kentani Division, Western Gcalekaland," in CPP G.33-'79, *Blue Book on Native Affairs, 1879*, 111; Report of Gcalekaland Land Board (Eustace, Sansom, and Grant) dated 2 Oct 1878, S.5237/8 (vol. 463F), SGO-Cape. The first Gcalekaland Commission report also suggested that European settlement be encouraged on small lots around each military post in order to create secure towns and spread influence "as amongst the Barbarians in the Roman Empire." Clearly the Commissioners did not fully appreciate the implications of their analogy.

103 C.R. Elliot (Assistant Commissioner, Crown Lands) to de Smidt, 13 Aug 1878, S.10819 (vol. 829c), SGO-Cape; A.E. Baker, "Historical Notes on Land Surveying and the Surveyor-General's Office (Cape) 1652–1950," (unpublished mss., NGI Library, 1958), 19.

104 Report of Gcalekaland Land Commission (Eustace, Sansom, and Hughes) dated 28 Dec 1878, S.5237/8 (vol. 463F), SGO-Cape.

105 Oath of Robert Jukes Hughes, Survey Registration 159, 30 Sep 1878, S.8710, SGO-Cape. Grant likely was called away on military service as an officer of the Cape Mounted Rifles (the successor to the F.A.M.P.).

usufruct as opposed to confrontation at a time of unrest over the expansion of colonial rule. Blyth, however, tended to deny permission to those who wished to graze cattle outside the locations based on his belief that the locations had ample pasture built in, which encouraged simple defiance.[106] At the same time, Hughes quietly created the basis for future management measures and revenue streams encumbering the resources Africans had hitherto used freely by marking all forests larger than five acres as Crown reserves.[107]

Hughes and the commission, however, did not even sketch out the area around the Manubie Forest on the Qora and Qaninga rivers, between the districts of Kentani and Willowvale, because it could not be reliably sketched in the short time available. They defused its potential as a space without purpose by recommending it all as a forest reserve to government, but it was never fully bounded by the surveyors.[108] In survey compilations and general plans it remained conspicuous as a blank spot of data too unreliable for inclusion until the compilation of new topographical sketch maps in 1912. Indeed, the only official general plan of the area, which compiler C.N. Thomas drew at the Office of the Surveyor-General in 1892, left the gap rather than patch in radically less precise information (see Map 3.5).

The commission beaconed off ground for 161 2,000-acre farms for white ownership, and returned general observations about water, wood, and topography to Cape Town about each potential farm for advertisement. The three-person party situated farms on the perimeters of each district, which coincided with the best supplies of indigenous timber and water, usually along the major rivers themselves (for example, 52 of the 85 inspected between the Qora and Mbashe rivers).[109] It was up to the surveyors to verify this rough inspection with mathematical precision between 1878 and 1881. But the colonial government was so eager to put Europeans on the land—the Prime Minister and Colonial Secretary at the time, J. Gordon Sprigg, called it the "first object" for Gcalekaland—that they advertised the farms widely among prospective white settlers even before the work of surveying

106 Blyth to M.B. Shaw (Resident Magistrate, Kentani), 19 Dec 1879, 1/KNT/4/1/7/1, KAB. On the one hand, Blyth took the word of the Land Board and the Land Commission as mechanically true; on the other, pastoralists in Kentani may have preferred to avoid denuding their own land while richer pasturage was available.

107 Report of Gcalekaland Land Commission dated 28 Dec 1878, S.5237/8 (vol. 463F), SGO-Cape. For acceptance of this demarcation, see Crown Lands to de Smidt, 20 Jan 1879, S.5237/8, (vol. 463F), SGO-Cape.

108 CPP G.29-'79, *Report of the Surveyor-General for the Year 1878*, 15–16.

109 CPP G.33-'80, *Report of the Surveyor-General for the Year 1879*, 11, 16–17.

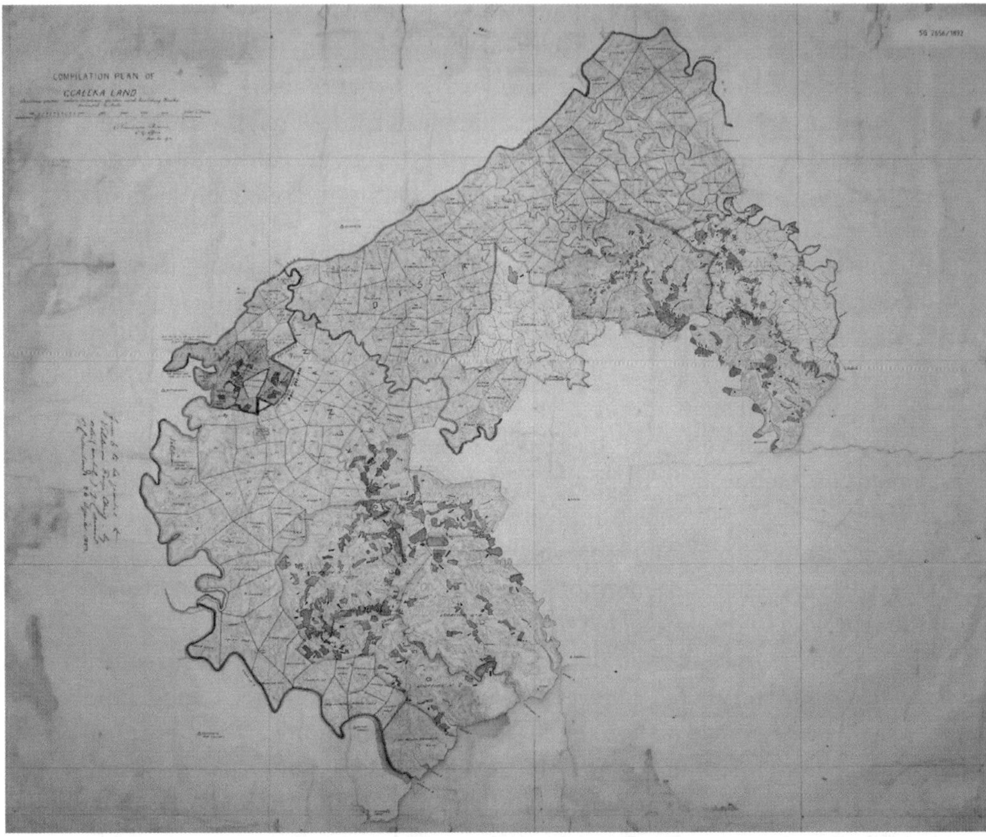

MAP 3.5 *C.N. Thomas's compilation plan of Gcalekaland, 1892, showing all surveyed farms and location blocks, with incomplete central section where land-based surveys stopped.*

SOURCE: TSKEI PLAN 5678, OFFICE OF THE SURVEYOR-GENERAL, CAPE TOWN. RSA STATE COPYRIGHT.

was underway, and included conditions of personal occupation by the buyers that betrayed the surveillance aspects of the scheme.[110] At the end of January 1879, Surveyor-General de Smidt contracted surveyors Gert Greeff and Otto Mehliss to verify the angles and areas of the beaconed farms, and they began this work in mid-April 1879 as soon as Hughes was available to point out the beacons.[111] The surveyors tendered their plans of these farms by

110 J.G. Sprigg, "Memorandum on Gcalekaland Farms," 20 Feb 1879, Notices 218 and 267 of 1879 dated 24 Feb and 6 Mar 1879, and Notice 81 of 1879 dated 23 Jan 1879, copies in S.5237/8 (vol. 463F), SGO-Cape; Crown Lands to de Smidt, 20 Jan 1879, S.5237/8, (vol. 463F), SGO-Cape.

111 De Smidt to Macdonald, 22 Mar 1879, S.5237/8, (vol. 463F), SGO-Cape.

early 1880, not as separate diagrams, but as general plans of entire sections with the intent that the chief compiler, C.N. Thomas, would frame individual farm diagrams for title in Cape Town; according to Macdonald, who superintended the farm surveys, the work was completed early in 1880.[112] But the Commissioner of Crown Lands on 27 March 1879 postponed the proposed sale of the farms until further notice, citing a delay in the formal annexation of Gcalekaland that was linked to other political questions in Cape Town.[113] Meanwhile, people continued to organize themselves with little regard for boundary markers that the magistrates themselves could not police, and the magistrates in turn presumed they could simply fix the matter by wedging people into the locations under a system of government headmen or inspectors after any given harvest.[114]

The Commissioner of Crown Lands therefore pressed de Smidt to arrange for the definition and subdivision of the Native Location clusters for individual tenure while the surveyors were still there.[115] The technicians and administrators knew little about the actual conditions within the delimited location areas, though Macdonald confidently stated to the Surveyor-General in September 1879 that the good agricultural land was almost exclusively in the area laid out for white farms, not the locations.[116] In response, de Smidt only could make the statement that blocks of ten-acre lots within the locations would be situated according to the desires of local cultivators and not be imposed by the surveyors, though he made clear that the surveyors found the residents' selection of land to be "as unfavorable for surveying purposes as it possibly can be, and the work of laying it out laborious and tedious."[117] Although sneezewood posts and six-foot-long trenches dug six inches deep in the turf along the boundary were to mark the corners and directions to the adjoining beacons of irregularly-shaped lots, Macdonald lamented that the ongoing destruction of such markers and the guesswork of survey where people did not express clear preferences would lead to "disputes, confusion, and

112 Two of these general plans and the Commission's first rough sketch have survived at the Office of the Surveyor-General as Tskei Plans 5604, 6929, and 6930, SGO-Cape; CPP G.53-'81, *Report of the Surveyor-General for the Year 1880*, 10–11.

113 John Laing (Commissioner of Crown Lands) to de Smidt, 27 Mar 1879, S.5278/8, (vol. 463F), SGO-Cape; Saunders, "Annexation," 74–76; Campbell, "The South African Frontier, 1865–1885," 143; H.B.E. Frere (Governor and High Commissioner) to Colonial Office (London), 19 May 1879, No. 152, GH 23/35, KAB.

114 See Shaw to Blyth, 29 Apr 1880, CMT 2/27, KAB.

115 Laing to de Smidt, 29 Apr 1879, S.5237/8, (vol. 463F), SGO-Cape.

116 Macdonald to de Smidt, 19 Sep 1879, S.5237/8, (vol. 463F), SGO-Cape.

117 CPP G.33-'80, *Report of the Surveyor-General for the Year 1879*, 13.

discontent."[118] Furthermore, Macdonald made clear that the technique was not very practical for agricultural lots where people actually cultivated, in ravines or hillsides, and his only solution was to leave a four-foot pole and flag at every corner point at significant cost.[119] Gert Greeff had the opposite problem to the east, and did not trench building lots because the ground was hard and rocky. The solution offered from Cape Town was to follow instructions literally where possible but otherwise to try to achieve goals of visibility and durability that were already difficult.[120]

M.B. Shaw, the magistrate at Kentani, only began taking over location lot beacons in mid-1880, a year after Macdonald finished his work. Shaw felt that the prior headmen were useless and should be replaced by "intelligent and educated natives acting as sub-Inspectors," although he primarily wanted to keep the peace until matters settled, which led him to place only willing people onto allotments, which meant that only five agricultural lots out of over 500 had occupants by July 1880.[121] Given that the district appeared to have no water shortage, he hoped that prosperity under government would help ease the headmen out, but in fact they retained their positions. At the same time, more Ngqika from the colony sought to re-establish their social nodes within Kentani, which already had more households than allotments would cover.[122] Drought and crowding, however, became cover for continuing the self-organization of the districts in 1880 and 1881. The plowing of new grounds, Shaw stated, had been impossible in 1880, bouts of heavy rain in the late summer prevented the allocation of many village and garden lots in both years, and the loss of his Xhosa-speaking clerk (to whom Shaw improperly delegated the task) was to blame for a lack of progress in the winter of 1881.[123]

At the end of November 1881, an exasperated Blyth requested that Shaw simply carve most of the district into locations—farms and all—and in January 1883 he could only declare that "The ten acre lots have not been taken up…they [Ngqika] decidedly object to being placed in villages, and they have plenty of

118 Ibid., 21. The trenching is an interesting practice and implies that without the trench, the wrong post might easily be taken to define the lot.

119 Macdonald to Marquard (Acting Surveyor-General), 26 Sep 1879, S.5237/8 (vol. 463F), SGO-Cape.

120 Gert Greeff to de Smidt (with marginalia from Marquard), 12 Aug 1880, SG 1/1/2/19, KAB.

121 CPP G.33-'79, *Blue Book on Native Affairs, 1879*, 114–115; Shaw to Ayliff, 15 Jul 1880, CMT 2/27, KAB.

122 CPP G.13-'80, *Blue Book on Native Affairs, 1880*, 157.

123 Shaw to Blyth, 8 Mar 1881 and 19 Jul 1881, both CMT 2/28, KAB; J. Rose Innes (Under-Secretary for Native Affairs) to Blyth, 22 Jun 1881, CMT 2/3. The clerk, Alwin Rein, made no comment on the charge.

land to cultivate."[124] Shaw had expressed a sense in the interim that Ngqika communities and headmen were settled enough that there was no reasonable objection to the settlement of further Ngqika households who wished to reside among 'friends' in Kentani.[125] He, however, complained just a few months later of severe overcrowding in the arable portions of the district and the cultivation of supposed grazing land, but the initial advice he received in response was that he should scold the offenders into leaving.[126] When Shaw's successor, William Girdwood, expressed understandable confusion about the difference between the plans in his office and the actual situation in the district in late 1883, the Native Affairs Department had folded its final fate into the simultaneous push for survey in Fingoland and Idutywa, by which time the location areas had expanded by over 50%.[127]

In the portion of Gcalekaland east of the Qora River (Willowvale district), the occupants in late 1878 were an impoverished mix of colonial Xhosa, Fingoes, and a few loyalist Gcaleka who had availed themselves of the conditions of return. Starting in June 1879, the colonial government reluctantly accepted the return of some Gcaleka headmen there, including Sarhili's brother Lindinxiwa, but they never agreed on terms for Sarhili himself to return, and the Secretary for Native Affairs expressed constant disapproval of Gcaleka resettlement.[128] But the ongoing influx delayed surveys. The first colonial magistrate in Willowvale, Frank Streatfeild, indicated that people only came to the locations in small parties "of a dozen or so," totaling around 2,500 by the end of 1879; Macdonald reported that four of the six Willowvale locations were still officially empty in January 1880 and so had not yet been surveyed at all, but that he planned to carry the work forward and admonish the surveyors to exercise "due regard" for "native requirements," which in practice leaned toward ease of survey.[129] That work only began in June 1880, but increasingly unsettled conditions during the rebellions and wars of 1880 and 1881 limited the amount of

124 Blyth to Shaw, 11 Apr 1882, 1/KNT/4/1/7/1, KAB; Blyth to J.W. Sauer (Secretary for Native Affairs), 5 Jan 1883, p. 11, NA 6, KAB. The 30 Nov letter (No. 759) from Blyth has not been found.

125 Copy of Shaw to Blyth, 5 Apr 1882, pp. 220–221, 1/KNT/4/1/7/1, KAB.

126 Hook to Shaw, 22 Mar 1883, 1/KNT/4/1/7/1, KAB. In a later letter (3 Jul 1883), Hook stipulates only that the area of the district abutting Butterworth and Idutywa need be left clear.

127 J.R. Rose Innes to Hook, 17 Dec 1883, NA 6, KAB.

128 Ayliff to Blyth, 12 Jun 1880, No. 2/835, CMT 2/2, KAB; Ayliff to Blyth, 10 Sep 1881, No. 2/474, CMT 2/3, KAB.

129 G.13-'80, "Blue Book on Native Affairs" (1880), 160–161; F.N. Streatfeild, *Reminiscences of an Old 'Un* (London: Eveleigh Nash, 1911), 194; CPP G.33-'80, *Report of the Surveyor-General for the Year 1879*, 20.

time surveyors were in the field, lest their work contribute to a general rising.[130] The technical boundaries that emerged from such work exasperated Streatfeild, who found that descriptions of precise measure were "totally incomprehensible to the Natives and in some instances to myself" compared to visible features or lines drawn on topographical sketches.[131]

What had been small bands of people crossing into the district also turned into a flood in 1881. Streatfeild and his lone clerk could barely track, much less stop, the influx, and he stated at the end of 1882 that the location areas were "now full."[132] In a moment of great candor a few months later, Streatfeild defended the headmen who did not know the government's rules and could not stop the movement of individuals and families across the Mbashe, so that the only way to get any kind of census was to spend several months in the field and take it himself.[133] Even then, he could only say that there were "about four thousand Gcaleka families" all over the district, but his official published reports did not even venture that level of precision.[134] By that time the matter had become untenable, and Blyth himself was suggesting the release of the white farms along the Mbashe to Fingo headmen as a cordon against inward migration but also as a way of allowing a Gcaleka society to consolidate within the district.[135]

The rebellion of Griqualand East in 1878 and the broader Transkeian Rebellions including the Sotho Gun War in 1880–1881 probably did a great deal to put an end to systematic schemes for extending individual tenure for Africans east of the Kei, if not the establishment of white quitrent farms as well.[136] As a very visible activity that exacerbated Africans' concern about an

130 Streatfeild seems to have suggested the prudence of suspending the survey. G. Greeff to de Smidt, 5 Nov 1880, SG 1/1/2/29, KAB.

131 Streatfeild to Blyth, 18 Mar 1881, 1/WVE/4/1/1/2/1, KAB.

132 G.8-'83, "Blue Book on Native Affairs" (1883), 152.

133 Streatfeild to Blyth, 6 Apr 1883, CMT 2/40, KAB. The headmen also had little incentive to stop the flow of people, if the new arrivals were potential clients and not people with additional headmen.

134 Streatfeild to Hook, 12 Jul 1883, CMT 2/40, KAB.

135 Memorandum of M.S. Blyth, 31 May 1883, in J. Rose Innes to Hook, 17 May 1883, CMT 2/5, KAB.

136 It is no coincidence that a great deal of activity between 1874 and 1878, when Griqualand East was only a nebulous protectorate, was expended on surveys and a brisk trade in titles developed. That alienation of land certainly contributed to discontent. See Robert Ross, *Adam Kok's Griquas: A Study in the Development of Stratification in South Africa* (Cambridge: Cambridge Univeristy Press, 1976), 129–130. One major imposed spatial reorganization did generate a system of rough titles and surveys in the district of Xalanga (Xhalanga)

evident colonial assault on their livelihoods, land division on such an intimate scale could not be imposed without repercussions. Citing unrest over surveys in the eastern district of Maclear (formerly Gatberg, where a number of Fingoes and various others had settled), the Commissioner for Crown Lands ordered a halt to all surveys "having for their object the granting of Titles to Natives, on the individual tenure" in June 1881, presumably pending the outcome of the Commission on Native Laws and Customs then collecting evidence.[137] A second note sent in July asked the Surveyor-General to terminate all surveys of all types east of the Kei unless specifically told by his superior; de Smidt in turn issued the surveyors instructions to "stop all these surveys so far as any further field work is concerned."[138] Although the farms as well as the four locations in Kentani were surveyed, only three and a half of the six Willowvale locations were charted, and in the last (No. 5) the surveyors had finished barely two dozen garden lots. Only a small amount of preliminary location took place in Kentani and no actual grants took place anywhere, yet Shaw confidently described its inevitable success to the Commission on Native Laws and Customs in 1881. Streatfeild was more circumspect.[139] Only a few numerical entries in appendices to later reports of the Surveyor-General attest to the failure of the scheme: hundreds of lots surveyed, but no titles issued or taken up.[140]

This unexpected population boom showed how woefully inadequate the originally-proposed native locations and systems of inspectors were for a combined population that grew to well over twice the anticipated size within twenty years with no concomitant increase in administrative resources.[141]

---

in Emigrant Tembuland in 1883, but that was a specific outgrowth of those rebellions that accomplished the same task of diminishing independent chiefly power. See Lungisile Ntsebeza, *Democracy Compromised: Chiefs and the Politics of the Land in South Africa* (Leiden: Brill, 2005), 55–63.

137 H.H. McNaughton (Assistant Commissioner for Crown Lands) to de Smidt, 13 Jun 1881, S.5237/8, (vol. 463F), SGO-Cape.

138 McNaughton to de Smidt, 19 Jul 1881, and de Smidt's undated comments thereupon, S.5237/8, (vol. 463F), SGO-Cape.

139 CPP G.4-'83, *Report and Proceedings with Appendices of the Government Commission on Native Laws and Customs*, 2:275, 2:277. Both maintained a façade of magisterial control in their reports, a far cry from their communications with the Chief Magistrate.

140 See G.10*-1904, *Report of the Acting Surveyor-General for the Half Year ended 30th June 1904*, 43–44.

141 See Reports of N.O. Thompson (Resident Magistrate, Kentani) and M.W. Liefeldt (Resident Magistrate, Willowvale), enclosures E-F in Report of H.G. Elliot (Chief Magistrate, Tembuland and Transkei), 2 Jan 1897, in CPP G.19-'97, *Blue Book on Native Affairs, 1897*, 95–99.

According to the recollections of former magistrate M.W. Liefeldt in 1923, "the want of transport facilities and the fact that each European settler would require about 6 policemen to protect his property from marauding natives," together with the return of Gcaleka communities and the belief in Cape Town that hut-tax receipts from communal areas would exceed any quitrent payments from individual titles and new settler farms, caused the settlement scheme's abandonment.[142] Some remaining cleared areas were given to Fingo occupation, including several small groups arriving from Izeli near King William's Town, the provision of a large farm for Veldtman Bikitsha in Kentani, and the placement of other Fingoes in Willowvale. Bikitsha's family even petitioned for a 'tribal title' for the latter Fingo lands in 1890, but to no avail.[143] The abandonment of the European farm scheme only became official in 1889, and the government transferred a small section of Kentani where they had granted five farms and a few Fingo areas in 1891–1892 to the district of Butterworth in 1893.[144] By then, the carefully laid plans for individual tenure and white settlement in Gcalekaland were already long gone.

Unlike the land scheme itself, Gcalekaland's record in the geographical archive still holds the pieces of this lost history of state fixation and failure. The surveyed general plans and location surveys contributed to compilation maps insofar (and only so far) as they were completed, leaving both the meaningless locations and farm blocks as well as the empty space around the Qora river in district maps of Kentani and Willowvale around 1900 (see Map 3.6). In 1937 the Surveyor-General's office 'rediscovered' these charts as primary sources for the assay of territory under the Natives Trust and Land Act (No. 18) of 1936 and the ecologically harsher regimes of Betterment and land rehabilitation that continued as late as the 1980s.[145] In Willowvale, for example, planners' prescriptions for land management in the 1970s and 1980s employed charts that did not involve any new reconnaissance of the land, and assigned arable

142 M.W. Liefeldt to A.H. Cornish-Bowden (Surveyor-General, Cape Province), 26 Apr 1923, S.1429, SGO-Cape.

143 Statement of J. Bikitsha, "Minutes of Meeting Held at Idutywa on the 29th September 1890 with Chiefs and Headmen of the Willowvale District," NA 453, 1–2.

144 Colonial Secretary to de Smidt, 13 Nov 1889, SG 1/1/3/94, KAB; marginalia on C.N. Thomas, "Compilation plan of Gcalekaland," 30 Nov 1892, Transkei Plan 5678, SGO-Cape.

145 See, in particular, C.N. Thomas, "Compilation plan of Gcalekaland," which served as the region's only base map for 20 years until the compilation of a 1912 ten-sheet "Map of the Transkeian Territories," despite being very incomplete; see office memoranda of E. Mabin and R.M. Du Toit, 31 Aug and 9 Sep 1937, S.1429, SGO-Cape.

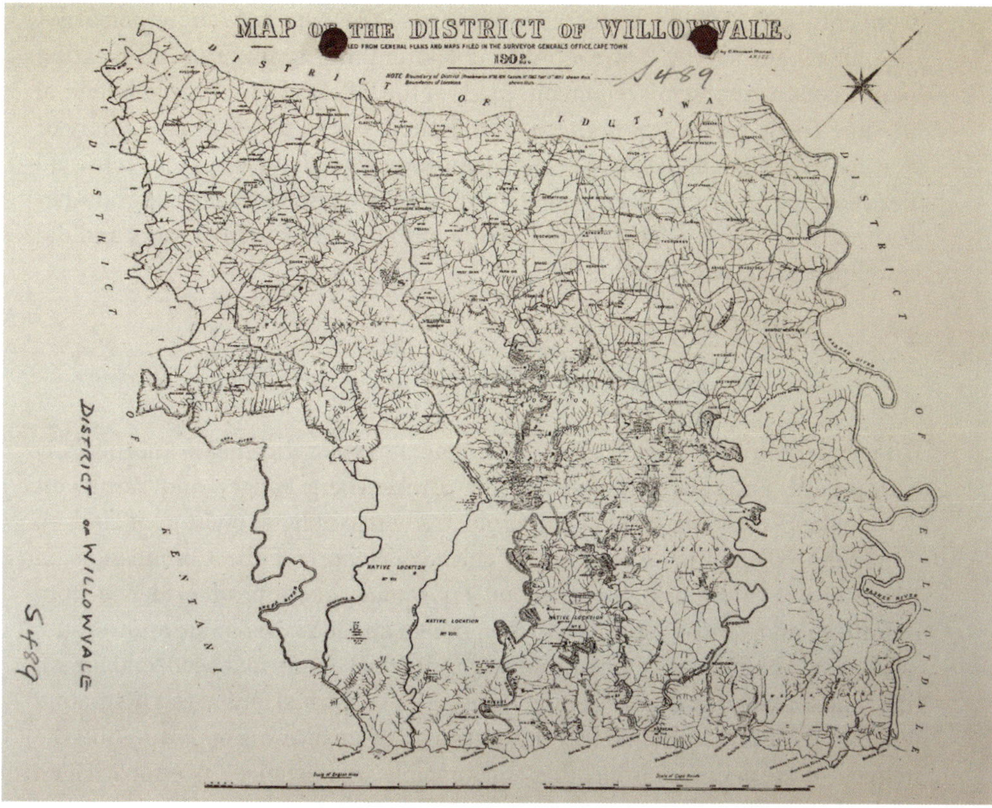

MAP 3.6 *Willowvale District Map by C.N. Thomas for the Surveyor-General's Office, 1902. Note the incomplete location sections, as well as the persistence of farm boundaries that had long ceased to have any meaning. Labels would persist on later maps.*

SOURCE: S.489, WILLOWVALE MAIN FILE, OFFICE OF THE SURVEYOR-GENERAL, CAPE TOWN. RSA STATE COPYRIGHT.

allotment fields that were too small and ill-situated—as one might expect if they based any of their knowledge of land quality on these century-old plans.[146]

Tenancy in Kentani and Willowvale therefore remained on a system of tickets of occupation and communal allotment whereby legality of residency could still be controlled, though not with the same spatial rigor as precise survey, and it left a great deal of power with the headmen of the various wards. The presence of mission stations and schools increased with time, and regulations governing the use of forest resources, pasturage, and cattle vaccination

146 Patrick McAllister, "Resistance to 'Betterment' in the Transkei: A Case Study from Willowvale District," *Journal of Southern African Studies* 15, no. 2 (1989): 361–362.

were enforced with increasing effectiveness as the state grew more pervasive. The allotment survey, however, was not attempted again. The old location plans remain among miscellaneous plans at the Office of the Surveyor-General in Cape Town, with a few perhaps finding their way to the National Library of South Africa just a few blocks away.[147] Land surveyors themselves only returned between 2007 and 2010 to complete the district-wide fixing of general boundaries, but they did not share the atomizing intent of their predecessors and did not repeat their work.[148]

The Barry Commission and the Failure of the Fingoland Survey

The experience of Gcalekaland and points further northeast (particularly Griqualand East and the foot of the Drakensberg range) and northwest (Griqualand West) suggested great problems with a general division of lands to European colonial specifications.[149] The 1883 Report of the Commission on Native Laws and Customs, based on enormous amounts of evidence from European and African informants taken in 1881 and 1882 over a vast array of subjects, stated bluntly that efforts to impose individual tenure had been "embarrassing," and that a general survey of the Transkei for individual tenure was premature but that government should take advantage of "every favoring opportunity at the request of the people or from other encouraging circumstances" to establish it on a small scale.[150] In short, the commission believed that a plan would work only if the inhabitants recognized its benefits from an aspirant European point of view and produced a strong majority in favor of accepting survey and title. Such a belief was probably correct mechanically, but it was utterly flawed in its implicit expectation that Africans yearned to become Europeans by way of advancement to a colonial ideal that whites did not really observe themselves. The commission in fact applied this kind of logic beyond systems of landholding, and engaged in a great deal of investigation around gender relations and

147 Clifton C. Crais, *The Politics of Evil: Magic, State Power, and the Political Imagination in South Africa* (Cambridge: Cambridge University Press, 2002), 77 fig. 5. Crais presents such an image (Macdonald's chart of 'Native Location No. 3, Gcalekaland') as a typical location map, but does not note the failure and abandonment of the scheme it represents.

148 J.G. Obree (Surveyor-General, Cape Town), personal communication, 17 Dec 2012.

149 Kevin Shillington, *The Colonisation of the Southern Tswana, 1870–1900* (Johannesburg: Ravan, 1985), 61–120.

150 "Report of the Commission," in CPP G.4-'83, *Report and Proceedings with Appendices of the Government Commission on Native Laws and Customs*, §109, 1:40.

social institutions that also normalized a white, Christian, patriarchal ideal, but in this they also failed to understand the nature of practices like circumcision and bridewealth they attacked as being retrograde.[151]

In evidence before the commission, retired Gcaleka agent William Fynn, who had attended Sarhili as part of the colony's *ad hoc* native administration machinery for nearly 30 years before 1878, intoned strongly against pushing individual tenure east of the Kei and against the creation of large central villages. Fynn suggested that any villages should be "not more than twenty families, and each kraal a hundred yards from any other" and two or three miles at least between villages, hardly the centralized European village model of hundreds that other magistrates lauded as the best means of "sufficient supervision."[152] In Fynn's own words, communal titles to large locations were preferable to attempts at close subdivision, so as to "let them [Africans] feel that they are secure against the Government, because it is the Government that they do not trust" and to allow local communities to adjudicate disputes over land through existing authorities and not the enumerative machinery of colonial survey.[153] Fynn faulted the creation of small fixed lots and large central villages for being fundamentally anathema to African agripastoralism, but he did not blame the surveyors, expressing a fundamental trust in the technicians even while challenging their task.[154]

Such testimony about the failure of small-holding tenure schemes recurred throughout the commission's evidence, with witnesses offering a number of possible solutions, but most put the blame for those failures squarely on African social and agricultural practices. There was certainly no shortage of suggestions from magistrates and missionaries about the best way to rearrange African space, and the European fixation tended to revolve around questions of control and efficiency from their point of view. John Liefeldt, the former British Resident with the Ngqika chief Anta, even sketched out his ideal community order (see Map 3.7), which would see "communities of

151 Natasha Erlank, "Gendering Commonality: African Men and the 1883 Commission on Native Law and Custom," *Journal of Southern African Studies* 29, no. 4 (2003): 937–953.

152 Testimony of William Fynn, 10 Oct 1881, in CPP G.4-'83, *Report and Proceedings with Appendices of the Government Commission on Native Laws and Customs*, §5078-§5094 *passim*, 1:277–278; Testimony of W.B. Chalmers (Civil Commissioner and Magistrate, King William's Town), 6 Oct 1881, in CPP G.4-'83, "Commission on Native Law and Custom," §4947, 1:268.

153 Testimony of William Fynn, 10 Oct 1881, in CPP G.4-'83, *Report and Proceedings with Appendices of the Government Commission on Native Laws and Customs*, §5084–§5087, 1:278.

154 Ibid., §5079, 1:277.

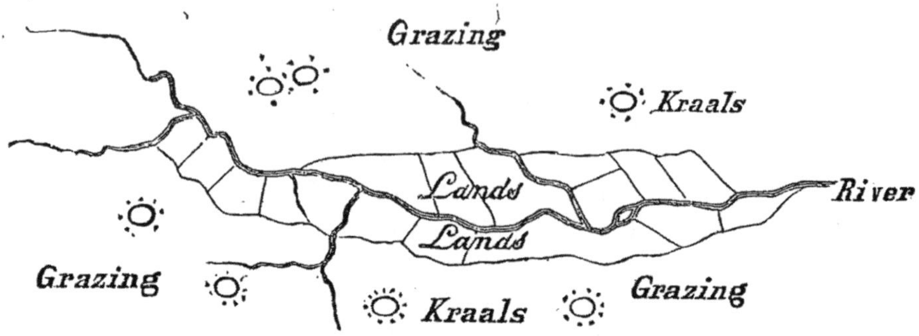

MAP 3.7 *Former British Resident John Liefeldt's idealized organizational scheme for locations, whether or not under individual tenure.*
SOURCE: CPP G.4-'83, *COMMISSION ON NATIVE LAWS AND CUSTOMS*, 2:132.

sub-locations" in a loose cluster around a block of lands through which "[s]upervisions would be much facilitated."[155]

African witnesses, on the other hand, tended to link the subdivision of land to more important matters of social and political hierarchy. Some headmen of the Idutywa reserve, including Tetyana, who equated fixed title to enforced monogamy at the beginning of this chapter, recognized the impingement upon the their positions and powers that arose from missionary prescriptions and land survey alike. Tetyana's comment goes further still, linking the division of the land directly with the destruction of the existing social order. Mission-educated 'school people' who had quitrent farms, like Sam Sigenu in Glen Grey, recognized that many of the non-mission-educated Africans generally "do not care for individual tenure, which binds them down more" but at the same time the 'school people' drew a careful link between willingness to accept individual tenure, being "more advanced," and having the capacity to take a leadership role in broader society as per their own examples.[156]

Some communities still sought a middle way between atomization by survey and insecure communalism. A deputation of twelve Fingo headmen and other representatives from Nqamakwe expressed jointly before the commission at Butterworth that "industrious" people who had built improvements should be able to obtain secure title to "their own cultivated lands," but others should equally

155 Appendix C in CPP G.4-'83, *Report and Proceedings with Appendices of the Government Commission on Native Laws and Customs*, 2:132.

156 Testimony of Sam Sigenu, 19 Oct 1881, in CPP G.4-'83, *Report and Proceedings with Appendices of the Government Commission on Native Laws and Customs*, §6129–6130, 1:343.

be able to continue holding land in common.[157] Indeed the local magistrate had noted in 1879 that a constituency of prosperous individuals was anxious for the survey.[158] It is however telling that the Nqamakwe delegation offered no formula for the size of the titled holdings, merely basing it on what they cultivated at the time. We have no record of the extent of the land cultivated by these twelve witnesses, but their standing as headmen or otherwise prominent individuals would suggest the possession of comparatively large holdings. Given that people in Fingoland were already alert to the prospect of individual tenure, their testimony may also represent an effort to assure that the format of any survey would allow them to maintain or improve their positions with colonial sanction.

Though self-interest may partially explain such testimony, the health and welfare of broader communities certainly figured as well. One member of the deputation from Nqamakwe, Tanga, made it clear that dividing up the land entirely would leave some owners of small flocks of sheep or a few cattle with "nothing to live upon" in support of his deputation's suggestion that communal tenure be continued for those not wishing title.[159] Veldtman Bikitsha, as the most prominent Fingo headman, of course offered his own opinions regarding colonial schemes for individual tenure and the creation of villages:

> 8450. Are you, Veldtman, expressing the opinion of all your people in asking for title to your lands?—Veldtman: Yes.
> (One man says):—What will the poor people do?
> Almost all agree that Veldtman has expressed their wish.
> Sanga [*sic*] says: We have no objection that a man should receive title to the ground he actually cultivates, provided he has right to common grazing ground.
> 8451. Do any of you like to live in villages?—None of us. A man likes his own home, he has lived there possibly for years. Why should he be removed then, like a rebel, and brought into a village against his will. When we live in villages we quarrel continually; your children run into your neighbour's hut, and squabbling results.[160]

---

157 Testimony of "Zalala, Tanga, George, and nine other natives and headmen from the Nqamakwe District, Transkei," 4 Nov 1881, in CPP G.4-'83, *Report and Proceedings with Appendices of the Government Commission on Native Laws and Customs*, §8496, 1:484.

158 F.P. Gladwin (Resident Magistrate, Nqamakwe) to Blyth, 5 Jul 1879, CMT 2/32, KAB.

159 Testimony of Tanga, 4 Nov 1881, in CPP G.4-'83, *Report and Proceedings with Appendices of the Government Commission on Native Laws and Customs*, §8496, 1:484.

160 Testimony of Veldtman, and Fingoes of Transkei [*sic*], 3 Nov 1881, in CPP G.4-'83, *Report and Proceedings with Appendices of the Government Commission on Native Laws and Customs*, §8450–§8451, 1:481.

In articulating the desire for individual title within the colonial state, then, a complex web of personal and common interests was clearly at work. The central point Bikitsha and others expressed was that people should determine their own arrangements within landscapes they defined, although the headmen expected to wield outsized influence and felt title was a way of securing their existing privilege, as Tanga's invocation of "the ground he actually cultivates" makes clear. Bikitsha stated later in this testimony that only Fingoes—that is, people within the existing social structure—should receive title in Fingoland. But the lone, unnamed voice asking about the poor expresses the clear knowledge that title would increase inequality and also damage society. Bikitsha also pointed to a peculiar dynamic in invoking the specter of children—junior kin—running into a neighbor's hut, suggesting that the breakdown attendant on spatial compression would involve the destruction of authority at the household level. The colonial state expected more well-to-do African headmen and cultivators to push the eventual decision in favor of survey and title, but any willing parties had their own interests as well as broader demands for stability from the people under them. Without evidence of a broad desire for survey and individual title or clear evidence of its success, the Barry Commission recommended a system of group titles in trust for the short term in its December 1882 report with individual tenure as a more distant aspiration—a recommendation that the government quietly disregarded.[161]

Indeed, when the Transkeian headmen went before the Barry Commission, Frere and the colonial government in Cape Town had already made their wishes clear to the Fingoes and the people at Idutywa. Blyth and Ayliff convened several public meetings in September and October 1878 to announce the appointment of magistrates, the surrender of firearms, the prohibition of certain dances and circumcision rites, and the intended survey of lands.[162] In one particular meeting at Nqamakwe on 3 October 1878, Blyth characterized all of these things as an end to caprice, uncertainty, and conflict. Government, he said, would give them individual "parchment titles" to their homes and "say ten acres" of land, not just then but in a matter of time. The Fingo headmen who spoke in response made laudatory statements on most matters, but found ten acres too small and bristled at the idea of taking all cases to new magistrates instead

161 "Report of the Commission," in CPP G.4-'83, *Report and Proceedings with Appendices of the Government Commission on Native Laws and Customs*, 1:40–41 (§110). Even James Ayliff, who differed with his colleagues enough to produce a written dissent, propounded the value of common title and its security as a stopgap. See §80–82 of his minority report.

162 CPP G.33-'79, *Blue Book on Native Affairs, 1879*, 97–98.

of headmen.[163] The responses suggest that these headmen, like the administrators, did not know at that early date exactly how effective the enforcement of any changes would be, but Veldtman Bikitsha in particular took the opportunity of a visit from Ayliff to suggest that all headmen enter the government payroll and, in any allotment scheme, receive larger lots than ordinary households.[164]

Blyth's announcement anticipated Frere's proclamation on 15 September 1879 that ordered headmen to tender lists of people suitable for allotments of land to the Chief Magistrate and vested all power to allot land in the Governor as per the new Native Location Lands and Commonage Act (No. 40) of 1879.[165] Frere made no specific mention of survey or title, however, so any colonial designs on the landscape of Fingoland remained in limbo. No serious proposal to carry out a survey even existed until May 1883, timing that may owe to an improved harvest after a season of drought in 1882 but that may also reflect opposition from Matthew Smith Blyth himself.[166] Blyth had expressed concerns to the Barry Commission in 1881 that Fingoes might not be ready for the political participation that could ensue from titles, but he felt that the land question had been settled by the Fingo Title, and individual titles could be created without a survey if people desired them.[167]

This was not a solution that appealed to colonial technocracy. In March 1883 he was transferred to Basutoland and the Acting Chief Magistrate, David Blair Hook, did not possess Blyth's stature, presence, or force of will. Hook also did not have the political acumen of Veldtman Bikitsha, although the two had been friendly since the campaign against Sarhili in 1858.[168] It was Bikitsha, then, who worked out the principles of a "Settlement of Fingoland" in direct consultations with Abraham de Smidt, J.W. Sauer (the new Secretary for Native Affairs) and surveyor John X. Merriman (then Commissioner for Crown

163 "Report of a Meeting held at Nqamakwe Fingoland on 3rd October 1878," pp. 9–10, 22–23, CO 3299, KAB.

164 CPP G.33'-79, *Blue Book on Native Affairs, 1879*, 97.

165 A.N. Macfayden, *Statutes, Proclamations, and Government Notices in Force in the Native Territories of the Cape of Good Hope on the 30th June 1907* (Cape Town: Cape Times, Ltd., 1907), §40–44, 15. There is no evidence that anyone actually compiled such lists.

166 See, e.g., CPP G.8-'83, *Blue Book on Native Affairs, 1883*, 130, about the passage of good rains; CPP G.3-'84, *Blue Book on Native Affairs, 1884*, 100 regarding a "lavish harvest" the prior year.

167 Testimony of M.S. Blyth, 4 Nov 1881, in CPP G.4-'83, *Report and Proceedings with Appendices of the Government Commission on Native Laws and Customs*, §8495, 2:484; Appendix C in CPP G.4-'83, *Report and Proceedings with Appendices of the Government Commission on Native Laws and Customs*, 2:47; CPP G.8-'83, *Blue Book on Native Affairs, 1883*, 129.

168 M.S. Blyth, entry for 6 Sep 1883, CMT 2/112, KAB. The grant itself is dated 20 Jul 1883 and was in motion by June; see notes on R.J. Hughes, "General Plan of No. 1 Section Gcalekaland Farms," Tskei Plan 6930, SGO-Cape; Hook, *With Sword and Statute*, 147, 312.

Lands).[169] De Smidt and Bikitsha certainly shared a deep desire to promote individual tenure far and wide. Their reasons, on the other hand, likely drew upon different agendas and assumptions about the meaning of those titles.

At around the same time, the insecurity that grew out of the events of the 1880–1881 wars and rebellions across the subcontinent led some in Gcalekaland and elsewhere to embrace the idea behind the Fingo Title, which Blyth championed and the Barry Commission had supported in its formal report. In Kentani, for example, M.B. Shaw announced his conversion to the idea that the district should be reserved for Ngqika alone in 1882, and the chiefs and headmen there resolved to request a 'tribal title' in March 1883 in part to prevent Bikitsha and other Fingoes from receiving land within the district, though government did not grant their request.[170] Sigidi and Smith Mhala (through Zenzile, his grandson and successor) in Idutywa, insofar as they articulated any firm claim to the land, considered it theirs by right of exchange.[171] Sigidi, at least, also continued to complain about the theft of chiefly authority through the appointment of government headmen.[172]

But even in Fingoland itself, the plan that Bikitsha devised with the Native Affairs and survey machinery of the colonial state faced an uneasy constituency. He assured de Smidt and the others that Fingoes would soon clamor for individual title to land for security amidst a rapidly growing population, as well as the property qualification for the Cape voting franchise it brought. The assumption that an individual tenure system could rapidly become one where the educated and wealthy class of increasingly Christian Fingoes and headmen were the bulk of title holders, and who certainly would be the majority of those who erected improvements valuable enough to actually meet the asset test, was implied throughout. People who "have enclosed and otherwise improved their lands" were to receive title, not others, and the grantees would pay the cost of their own surveys while a general rate would underwrite the comprehensive topographical survey and mapping of Fingoland. There was no condition of relocation into villages, and lots would be larger that in previous

169 Minute of the Commissioner of Crown Lands, 4 May 1883, in Sauer to Hook, 21 May 1883, CMT 2/5, KAB.

170 CPP G.8-'83, *Blue Book on Native Affairs, 1883*, 151; CPP G.3-'84, *Blue Book on Native Affairs, 1884*, 108; CPP A.51-'83, *Petition of the Gaikas in Gcalekaland against the Locating of the Izeli Fingoes…*; J. Rose Innes to Blyth, 10 May 1884, 1/KNT/4/1/7/1, KAB.

171 "Statement made by Sigidi before RM Idutywa 7th August 1893," in W.T. Brownlee (Resident Magistrate) to H.G. Elliot (Chief Magistrate, Tembuland and Transkei), 30 May 1894, CMT 3/98, KAB.

172 William Beinart and Colin Bundy, *Hidden Struggles in Rural South Africa* (Johannesburg: Ravan, 1987), 81–82.

schemes, up to thirty acres. Hook aired this proposal at a meeting of magistrates and prominent headmen at his office on 5 June 1883, and Bikitsha set the tone as the first respondent by declaring that "as regards country & ground for the Fingoes, it is the greatest thing [we] expected," as well it should have been because it embodied his own views.[173]

The existence of the Fingo Title made the Surveyor-General and the Department of Native Affairs wary of employing too heavy a hand in manufacturing consent. Therefore, despite the legal ability to unilaterally declare a survey and subdivision under the Location Act of 1879, the Chief Magistrate asked that the district magistrates ascertain clear approval before taking any steps.[174] What constituted clear approval was left for them to decide, as with so much else northeast of the Kei. But they were confident enough that surveyor Hughes was back in the area in October, to subdivide lands around the Chief Magistrate's new residency at Nthlambe, near Butterworth, and a handful of small abutting farms for Scottish immigrants in Kentani, and would be ready to expand his work when approval came.[175] Indeed Hughes noted that some interested African purchasers approached him during his work, believing that he was subdividing a far greater area.[176]

The discussions that ensued, however, exposed fissures in the communities of the region, and a variety of reasons for approval or rejection (and shades in between) existed. The records of the magistrates are fragmentary and depended heavily on the individual magistrates' personalities for their coverage, but the survey occasioned heated discussion across the three districts of Fingoland and in the Idutywa Reserve that revolved around whether to survey the territorial boundaries, individual location boundaries, or individual garden lots for title. Not a single commentator raised a concern about district boundaries, which were effectively meaningless on the landscape, and every commentator focused on boundaries and not topography, ecology, or any other question of the survey. All expressed concern about the broader implications of a survey's alteration of social landscapes, but the fact that every commentator was male exposed the diminution of women's vital productive

173 "Meeting of Magistrates and People at Enthlambe on the 5th June 1883," enclosure in Hook to Sauer, 14 Jun 1883, pp. 81–82, NA 6, KAB.

174 Sauer to Blyth, 21 May 1883, NA 5, KAB. For a copy of the instructions as issued, see Circular No. 29, 7 Jun 1883, 1/BUT/5/1/2, KAB. The circulated instructions omit any mention of Bikitsha's role in the process.

175 CPP G.32-'84, *Report of the Surveyor-General for the Year 1883*, 17; Hook to Girdwood, 15 Feb 1884, 1/KNT/4/1/7/1, KAB. The Surveyor-General's instructions were dated 13 Sep 1883.

176 Hughes to A.E. Murray, 23 Jan 1884, enclosure in Murray to de Smidt, 29 Jan 1884, SG 1/1/2/36, KAB.

roles on that land—itself a crucial change in social power that the transparent assumption of a 'one man, one lot' system reflected.

The Native Affairs Department therefore only expressed worry regarding the possible appearance of impropriety favoring the class of headmen, which might derail popular approval. In reality, the Department was happy to engage in the act of favoritism itself. A confidential circular urged the magistrates to assure the headmen individually that the government would see to any exceptional grants, instead of having it come up at general public meetings.[177] Bikitsha himself received title to a large farm surrounding the house he had constructed just across the Gcuwa River in Kentani district in 1880. He built there with the sanction of then-magistrate Thomas Merriman, but the approval of his 4,000-acre farm grant ('Nkondwane') only in April 1883 suggests a connection with his prominence among headmen in the push for survey.[178] However, in Idutywa, the chiefs Sigidi and Zenzile, along with the headmen, expressed such immediate opposition to survey that the irritable Resident Magistrate, C.G.H. Bell, briefly proposed leaving the matter until Fingoland proper moved on it.[179] Many Gcaleka, Fingo, and Ndlambe headmen of Idutywa favored survey, but the two chiefs opposed it, and so long as they remained unmoving, most of the headmen would not break with them openly. Sigidi was particularly emphatic: "The survey stabs us. Smith and myself would have asked for a survey and not the Headmen who have been put over us."[180] In October, Sigidi spelled it out even more clearly: he felt a survey would generate separation and sectionalism among the headmen and people in place of deference to the chiefs who felt the land was theirs. Bell, in trying to smooth the matter over, suggested that Hook should resurrect the chiefs' 1874 request for a farm to take their opposition out of the equation, while promising somehow to preserve their primacy and thus the balance of power

177 Hook to T.R. Merriman (Resident Magistrate, Butterworth), Confidential, 8 Jun 1883, 1/BUT/5/1/2, KAB.

178 The title itself bore the date 20 Jul 1883. Macdonald to Blyth, 19 May 1880, CMT 2/13, KAB; D.B. Hook, entry for 6 Sep 1883, CMT 2/112, KAB; Quitrent Grant TR Q. 4.25, 20 Jul 1883, S.6864, SGO-Cape.

179 C.G.H. Bell (Resident Magistrate, Idutywa) to Hook, 9 Jun 1883, CMT 2/24, KAB. Bell was an avowed enemy of chiefly prerogative, and observed: "I am not surprised at this decision on the part of the Chiefs and Headmen; it is generally their custom to look upon a surveyor with superstitious horror and to imagine him to be a man who has come to take their land from them, and cut it up for the benefit of the people." See also Beinart and Bundy, *Hidden Struggles*, 82.

180 "Minutes of meeting of Chiefs, Headmen and people at the Idutywa Reserve held at Idutywa on Thursday 14th of June 1883," in C.G.H. Bell to Hook, 21 Jun 1883, CMT 2/24, KAB.

between Fingoes and the two chiefs in the reserve.[181] Sigidi was not convinced that the magistrate could back up such a guarantee, and remained opposed.

Thomas King, the magistrate at Nqamakwe, held his first meeting at the Residency there on 13 June 1883, barely a week after hearing of the scheme and asking the headmen to gauge opinion. King himself had questionable ethics; he employed convicts for his personal use and treated them with such severe brutality that several reputedly died, but the investigation that only followed in August 1884 did not remove him from office.[182] Nevertheless, King diligently and carefully recorded these proceedings, which provide a microcosm of concerns and personal agendas. As was common in such meetings, the most prominent headman, John Mazamisa, spoke first. Mazamisa favored survey on standard lots and claimed to have a majority in favor, but conveyed the concern of some prosperous families that additional wives should occasion larger allotments to reflect the common practice of wives cultivating separate plots. Sobekwa, who had come from Oxkraal and Kamastone (Queenstown) purportedly to avoid survey there, complained that his people had so many cattle that they had to graze in areas belonging to other headmen, and asked for more land while simultaneously opposing any survey whatsoever that might stunt his ambition. Other headmen also conveyed general opposition to individual and regional surveys alike, but most noted that one or two people might be interested in a title if they had built houses, including some of the headmen themselves. The most interesting expatiations came from headmen Inbulawa and Dingiswayo. In the case of Inbulawa, the men at his general meeting expressed that "they had to leave the colony because they had had their ground surveyed, as they found they could not live well and they do not like it," besides which any additional taxes would be an impossible burden given the bad harvest of that year. Dingiswayo drew the distinction between 'school' and 'red' people, placing the former with the headmen personally in favor and the latter mostly in opposition. None of the headmen could say unambiguously that people favored survey, although in at least one case a headman claimed that people would fall in line behind him.[183]

---

181 C.G.H. Bell to Hook, 13 Oct 1883 (with enclosure, 3 Oct 1883), 1/IDW/6/1/2/2, KAB.

182 CPP A.14-'85, *Return of Papers Regarding the Use of Convicts by Mr. King, Magistrate of Nqamakwe, for Private Use, his Suspension from Office, and Investigation of his Conduct.*

183 "Meeting of Fingo Headmen and people in re the Surveying of Fingoland, held at Nqamakwe, on Wednesday the 13th June 1883," enclosure in King to Hook, 19 Jul 1883, CMT 2/33, KAB. Sobekwa was probably exaggerating his reasons, having come across in 1866, but the granting of farms around his area in Queenstown had in fact cut off pastures, and he complained about crowding before his emigration; see chapter 2 (81n158), and Bouch, "Colonization of Queenstown," 177–178, 184.

Faced with this nearly universal rejection, King went about lobbying for the scheme, and held another meeting on 4 July 1883 where all but one of the headmen present agreed to the general survey of Fingoland, though not to a system of survey and title for individual tenure. The reasoning had to do with local opposition to the scheme, and came through in the qualified approval they gave to the general survey. They agreed to the general survey, King relayed, "providing such survey did not in any way interfere with the present existing system of grazing, and water rights which they desire to be kept free as heretofore," though he did not put the conditional clause anywhere in his official report and Hook took it as encouraging.[184] The concern of households for access to needed resources and pasturage is clear despite the good harvest of 1883 (or perhaps because of it), in light of reports of unprecedented diversity and extent of cultivation in both Butterworth and Nqamakwe districts at the start of 1884.[185]

The meeting of headmen at Tsomo on 6 July 1883 produced an even more concise report of rejection from magistrate M.W. Liefeldt, without even the qualified acquiescence of Nqamakwe. No survey was necessary, the headmen said, because they knew the location boundaries and "the country they occupy belonged to them by virtue of a title granted to them by Sir H. Barkly," so other evidence of ownership or any intrusion into the organization of land was unnecessary.[186] The Fingo Title logically had created a landscape subject primarily to arrangements that were acceptable to the headmen of the district and, to a lesser extent, the people. Beyond the recognition of colonial rule, the people on the land were remarkably reluctant to change it.

In Butterworth, the magistrate—Thomas Merriman, who had moved from Kentani—only held a meeting on 6 August to discuss the proposal. It had already leaked out piecemeal owing to prior meetings in the other districts and two delays before a quorum of headmen could arrive, but some two hundred men (including nineteen of twenty-four headmen) turned up to address the question. After two hours of deliberation among themselves, only four headmen favored individual tenure, while four others agreed to have the location boundaries surveyed, and eleven stated that only a "direct and distinct" order from government would induce them to accept survey at all. Some fifty people spoke, and almost all opposed their titular headmen, whether they were smallholders who opposed survey because they were not part of the headman's family and rightly feared favoritism, or who favored survey in opposition to their headman for the same reason. Merriman reported this outcome with little

184 King to Hook, 19 Jul 1883, CMT 2/33, KAB; CPP G.3-'84, *Blue Book on Native Affairs, 1884*, 111.

185 CPP G.3-'84, *Blue Book on Native Affairs, 1884*, 100, 112.

186 Liefeldt to Hook, 12 Jul 1883, CMT 2/36, KAB.

detail but with an expectant tone, and concluded with the observation that "I do not think the Fingoes as a nation are sufficiently advanced to enjoy the benefits of individual tenure."[187]

The widespread rejection of survey at any level came as a surprise to Hook, who was sure it would be a simple matter. In August, Hook asked the Secretary for Native Affairs "whether these replies from the people should be accepted as final" or whether he himself should go out and try to reverse that decision through "proper persuasion."[188] Hook did not wait to begin this campaign, but had already started it at the end of July 1883 and visited each of the six districts under his purview. In Idutywa, Hook oddly characterized Sigidi and Zenzile as simply two headmen in opposition, and his promise to forward the resolutions of earlier meetings clearly meant different things in his mind than it did in the chiefs'.[189] Kentani and Willowvale headmen concerned themselves with the extent of communal lands, not questions of individual title.

Hook held two particularly enlightening meetings within days of one another in August. At a meeting in Butterworth on 20 August, Veldtman Bikitsha tried mightily to set a tone of acceptance at the outset to counter Hook's expression of disappointment, but that only served to sharpen the critiques. Headman Faleni stated a common feeling that survey and title threatened a total breakdown of social order and the destruction of headmen: "We don't want it because we are in distress. We know what surveying is. If the land is surveyed, every one is Chief and we shall eat each other up." Gcilitshani, who was not a headman and lived near the Butterworth mission, conversely spoke for his elder brother—and with the benefit of that senior authority—in saying that his brother would surely want survey "if he were a big Headman," but that it had no benefit for those who were not wealthy. Several others stated that a survey would scatter (or destroy) the people—especially the children—because there were more people than land, and that it was already happening elsewhere. Even those who lauded government guidance and declared their loyalty generally ended with disapproval of the survey, and only Bikitsha and three others were clearly in favor. Two of those claimed to possess titles to small lots in the colony, which raises the question of why they were living in Fingoland at all. Hook was exasperated, and ended with a paternal lecture about the government's care for their interest, and that "civilization is coming

187 Merriman to Hook, 7 Aug 1883, CMT 2/19, KAB.

188 Hook to Sauer, 10 Aug 1883, pp. 56–60, NA 6, KAB.

189 "Minutes of Meeting held at Idutywa Magistracy on July 27th 1883," enclosure in Hook to Sauer, 13 Sep 1883, pp. 180–185, NA 6, KAB.

on & cannot be stopped," a clear warning of dispossession.[190] Two days later, at Nqamakwe, Hook repeated the ritual, but there only John Mazamisa claimed to have a constituency that approved of individual tenure. Other headmen who supported it noted that many of their people did not, and a few thought it would be the ruin of all headmen. One headman changed his mind at the meeting to oppose survey for title, while still approving of a general survey of Fingoland's boundaries and those of the various locations in light of increasing disputes over uncertain borders. Headman John Adam was clear that he personally favored a survey but that his people felt it was not necessary precisely *because* of the existence of the Fingo Title. Hook suggested in response that the Fingo Title was not secure like an individual title, but even he seemed unconvinced.[191]

With such reports, it was clear that no agreement existed on the level or extent of survey among the headmen of Fingoland, much less among the people they spoke for. After conferring with the Commissioner of Crown Lands, the Under-Secretary for Native Affairs informed Hook at the beginning of November that any survey required "practical unanimity" and the differences in degree of acceptance, as well as the simple refusal of many, meant the survey would be held in abeyance indefinitely.[192] That decision brought great displeasure from Thomas King at Nqamakwe, who pleaded in his official report to the Secretary for Native Affairs with professions of belief in the survey's civilizing potential, in contrast to his earlier attitudes.[193] M.W. Liefeldt in Tsomo claimed that people simply hadn't really understood the meaning of survey and were very sad at its suspension, but he offered no evidence of how they expressed this sentiment.[194] The suspension also meant the end of any attempt to restart the Kentani and Willowvale allotment and village systems.[195] The first detailed map of the lands from the Kei to Natal, which C.N. Thomas compiled as a truly massive, roller-mounted manuscript noting plan in 1883, replicated this state

190 "Minutes of Meeting held at Butterworth Magistracy on August 20th 1883," enclosure in Hook to Sauer, 13 Sep 1883, pp. 195–203, NA 6, KAB.

191 "Minutes of Meeting held at Nqamakwe Magistracy on August 22nd 1883," enclosure in Hook to Sauer, 13 Sep 1883, pp. 186–194, NA 6, KAB.

192 J. Rose Innes to Hook, 2 Nov 1883, CMT 2/5, KAB.

193 Report of Resident Magistrate, Nqamakwe, 2 Jan 1884, in CPP G.3-'84, *Blue Book on Native Affairs, 1884*, 111–112.

194 Liefeldt to Hook, 1 Dec 1883, CMT 2/36, KAB.

195 Sauer to Hook, 17 Dec 1883, enclosure in Hook to Girdwood, 31 Dec 1883, 1/KNT/4/1/7/1, KAB.

MAP 3.8 *Detail of the departmental noting copy of the 1884 "Map of the Territories Formerly Known as Kaffraria Proper" published by the Surveyor-General in Cape Town. The printed map reflects the stoppage of colonial survey, with blank spaces in a unitary Gcalekaland as well as a lack of any newer location data or even district boundaries within Fingoland and the Idutywa Reserve.*

SOURCE: MISC PLAN 505, OFFICE OF THE SURVEYOR-GENERAL, CAPE TOWN. RSA STATE COPYRIGHT.

of knowledge, complete with the gaps in Gcalekaland and the twenty-year-old rough topography of Fingoland. That plan was a literal checklist for data collection for a quarter century, but the reduced version that Abraham de Smidt had published in 1884 for public sale reproduces its limitations (see Map 3.8).[196]

Like the failure of survey and title in Gcalekaland, the foundering of the proposed survey of Fingoland attested to the continuing independence of the social order that arose on those purportedly manufactured landscapes, and its resilience in the face of colonial efforts to render it somehow legible. In Gcalekaland, people simply disregarded boundaries and the colonial government tended to look the other way rather than generate conflict. In Fingoland, some headmen and householders saw benefit or even advantage in fixing their lands by title, particularly those who were wealthy, but even the well-off detected a significant element of dislocation inherent in the proposals. All of these African landscapes may have existed within a broader Cape colonial landscape of settlement, conquest, and administration, but they were still under the individual determination of local authority structures that retained enormous influence and connective power. The extracolonial nodes and networks of the people in Fingoland, Idutywa, and Gcalekaland were slow to weaken, and their strength manifested itself in community resistance to survey. In Fingoland, at least, the colonial state would eventually try again under a new legal and spatial regime that would occasion its own controversy.

---

196 The original roller map is C.N. Thomas, "Plan of the Territories Formerly Known as Kaffraria Proper…" [1883?] M4/211, KAB; CPP G.17-'85, *Report of the Surveyor-General for the Year 1884*, 25, xliv.

CHAPTER 4

Survey and Mediation in Fingoland

The dismal failure to impose individual landholding on the eastern banks of the Kei before 1884, even in places where the survey work took place, did not alter the convictions of survey authorities or the colonial officers who employed them. Spatial interventions, particularly individual tenure and the bounding of spaces on the basis of 'one man, one lot,' remained central to colonial efforts to render African societies legible in order to uproot their labor and diminish competitive potential.[1] This effort resumed in earnest with the Glen Grey Act (No. 25) of 1894, which was the brainchild of Cape Prime Minister and mining magnate Cecil John Rhodes. That Act, named after the first district to face its application, was a union of colonial legal, financial, and spatial prescriptions that attacked extended social networks by yoking survey and quitrent title to systems of separate local governance (location boards and councils) and by taxing landless men who did not labor outside the district.[2] At the same time, the Act hobbled any potential benefits to ownership of titles through legal conditions of use, restrictions on transfer, and their disqualification as assets towards the property test for voting, which transformed those costly titles into little more than glorified tickets of occupation.[3] Regimented surveys under teams of government land surveyors were central to delimitation and control in this invasive new iteration of individual tenure, because it involved the detailed subdivision and reorganization of entire districts at a time. But surveyors also became agents of active mediation as their contact with African households and landscapes became more sustained under this new regime, as we shall see.

---

1 See J. Robinson, "'A Perfect System of Control'? State Power and 'Native Locations' in South Africa," *Environment and Planning D: Society and Space* 8 (1990): 145–146; Clifton C. Crais, *The Politics of Evil: Magic, State Power, and the Political Imagination in South Africa* (Cambridge: Cambridge University Press, 2003), 101; James C. Scott, *Seeing Like a State: How Certain Schemes to Improve the Human Condition Have Failed* (New Haven: Yale University Press, 1998), 51–52.

2 Alan Lester, *From Colonization to Democracy: A New Historical Geography of South Africa* (London: I.B. Tauris, 1996), 57. For a discussion of the component elements, see Les Switzer, *Power & Resistance in an African Society: The Ciskei Xhosa and the Making of South Africa* (Madison: University of Wisconsin Press, 1993), 101–106.

3 Fred Hendricks and Lungisile Ntsebeza, "Chiefs and Rural Government in Post-Apartheid South Africa," *African Journal of Political Science* 4, no. 1 (1999): 102.

 | DOI 10.1163/9789004282292_005

In the Act's text, the first three parts deal with issues related to survey and land tenure, reflecting their centrality within the larger Glen Grey system. The first stipulates the creation of locations within the unalienated land of the district, and removes the headmen's powers to allot land. In their place, the colonial state would survey blocks of small household agricultural allotments of about four morgen (8.5 acres) each, with a certain subjective allowance for common grazing land around the blocks. Married men, and young men about to marry, could apply for allotments prior to survey if they were taxpayers, but grantees had to pay survey and title expenses (£3 10s in Glen Grey, plus a 5s stamp) as well as a quitrent of 15 shillings or more annually.[4] Rebellion, criminal conviction, a failure to cultivate, or a failure to pay costs and quitrent would lead to forfeiture. The locations' common resources were to be under control of an appointed location board on the model of colonial village management boards, although there was no requirement that grantees move into villages.

Part II of the Act placed severe restrictions on transfer, and built upon decades of precedent by prohibiting sale without government approval, the accumulation of multiple lots, and any kind of subdivision or mortgage.[5] Attorney General James Rose Innes (Junior), whose father had been the Under-Secretary for Native Affairs since 1881, characterized the condition in paternalistic terms in 1893: by forcing government approval of transfer, Rose Innes maintained, Africans would be safe from rapacious speculation and their own poor judgment, and the colony would retain a reliable labor reservoir in the locations.[6] Some Thembu also saw danger in titles that were too freely transferable, but they did not care for the colonial solution, particularly at the five mission stations in Glen Grey that were surveyed in advance of the Act. An 1892 meeting of male householders at Agnes Mission Station in Glen Grey, for example, agreed that titles should require consent before transfer, but from the local community members, not government—a request that fell on deaf ears.[7] The second portion of the Act also established male primogeniture as the means of inheritance, with contingencies falling on a broader hierarchy as

4 The inclusion of men who were soon to marry was an expedient in the field aimed at quelling dissent. See R.T. Ally, "The Development of the System of Individual Tenure for Africans, with Special Reference to the Glen Grey Act, c. 1894–1927" (master's thesis, Rhodes University, 1985), 148–149.

5 D.J. van der Post, "Land Law and Registration in Some of the Black Rural Areas of Southern Africa," *Acta Juridica* (1985): 217–218.

6 J. Rose Innes (Jr.) to F.C. Mackarness, 9 Dec 1893, in *Sir James Rose Innes: Selected Correspondence 1884–1902*, ed. H.M. Wright (Cape Town: Van Riebeeck Society, 1972), 130.

7 "A Meeting of Natives of Glen Grey District, held at Agnes," 29 Jun 1892, NA 215, KAB.

colonial administrators distilled it, but which rarely ended up functioning properly. Women, however, could only receive proceeds of sale and property in absence of any male heir, and could not inherit allotments in their own names, in keeping with the tendency of colonial law to simplify local practice in a way that disregarded women's economic and social power.[8]

The third part of the Act was Rhodes's solution to the concerns of nervous white settlers on the Eastern Cape. Relative prosperity caused more Africans to meet the property test for voting in the 1880s, and the advent of parliamentary representation for the Transkei in 1887 augured further expansion. The colonial response was the Parliamentary Voter Registration Act (No. 14) of 1887, which disqualified land held on communal tenure from the calculation of property values, and sparked a great deal of organized protest by those it directly and indirectly affected.[9] Organized registration efforts in its wake helped the numbers of African voters recover within a few years, which prompted the 1892 Franchise and Ballot Act (No. 9) that tripled the property qualification to £75 and instituted a literacy test that cut the African and Coloured electorates by 15%.[10] With individual title and a few improvements on the land, whole districts of allotment holders might soon qualify to vote anyway. Accordingly, Part III of the Glen Grey Act stated that allotments would be considered communal property and would not count towards the property qualification for the franchise—a measure that applied retroactively to other surveyed areas later.[11]

Glen Grey, however, contained insufficient land for every resident man to receive a lot, and there was no guarantee that it would become the idyllic landscape of subsistence farmers and migrant workers that the social

8 See Clifton Crais, *Poverty, War, and Violence in South Africa* (Cambridge: Cambridge University Press, 2011), 137–139.

9 André Odendaal, *The Founders: The Origins of the ANC and the Struggle for Democracy in South Africa* (Johannesburg: Jacana, 2012), 112–128.

10 Ruth Edgecombe, "The Glen Grey Act: Local Origins of an Abortive 'Bill for Africa'," in *Studies in Local History: Essays in Honour of Professor Winifred Maxwell*, ed. J.A. Benyon *et al.* (London: Oxford University Press, 1976), 92–94; Les Switzer, "The Beginnings of African Protest Journalism at the Cape," in *South Africa's Alternative Press: Voices of Protest and Resistance, 1880–1960*, ed. Les Switzer (Cambridge: Cambridge University Press, 1997), 63.

11 George M. Fredrickson, *White Supremacy: A Comparative Study in American & South African History* (Oxford: Oxford University Press, 1981), 183–185; T.R.H. Davenport, "The Cape Liberal Tradition to 1910," in *Democratic Liberalism in South Africa: Its History and Prospect*, ed. Jeffrey Butler, Richard Elphick, and David Welsh (Cape Town: David Philip, 1987), 32.

engineers imagined. The remaining four parts of the Glen Grey Act therefore sought to prevent circumventions that the government in Cape Town believed might compromise the allotment system or prevent labor migration. Part IV abandoned subtlety with a tax of 10s on men who did not labor on contract for at least three months out of the prior year, which became the most direct source of complaint in the early days of the Act's operation. That stipulation reflected not only the colonial desire for the registration of migrant workers who sought to avoid the tax, but also an increasingly widespread settler belief that flexible land tenure produced idleness, and that individual title was an unacceptably slow corrective.[12] Indeed those who cultivated land or otherwise worked for themselves were not exempt from the labor tax because, Rhodes believed, they received commensurately greater benefit from the proceeds of those taxes.[13] In monetary terms, the Act created a potential tax liability of thirty shillings where before it had been ten or fewer, and imposed further costs if title to land was involved, making opposition almost certain. Part V therefore theoretically redirected any complaints or political aspirations into separate District Councils that handled local expenditures and improvements. These fed later into a Transkeian Territories General Council in Umtata (Mthatha).

Finally, the Act reserved certain matters to colonial paternalism. One restricted liquor licensing, in a nod to theories of moral degeneracy among Africans (Part VI), and Part VII permitted the Governor a wide berth to modify the Act as necessary by proclamation, without the input of local people. That last part allowed the modification of the Act and its extension to new areas, although the formality of local acceptance remained as important as it had been since the Barry Commission in 1883.[14] The fourth and fifth parts of the Act had stripped away any incidental benefits that African title-holders might gain in this drive for spatial legibility, but the seventh made provision for adaptation or, if necessary, imposition. The Act was a legal framework that made the social and economic status quo even more precarious—a fact that was not lost

12 Ally, "Development," 107–115; R.J. Thompson, "Cecil Rhodes, the Glen Grey Act, and the Labour Question in the Politics of the Cape Colony" (master's thesis, Rhodes University, 1991), 81–82; Petition of the Lady Frere Village Management Board, 30 Apr 1894, NA 225, KAB.

13 CPP A.16-'95, *Return in Reply to a Resolution... For Copies of all Petitions, Reports, and Communications Having Reference to Proclamation No. 352...*, 21–22.

14 "Report of Commission," in CPP G.4-'83, *Report and Proceedings with Appendices of the Government Commission on Native Laws and Customs*, §110 sub. 9, 1: 40.

on its targets, who had suffered blows to their individual productivity and market access by road and rail even before 1894.[15]

Surveyors and administrators, however, shared great confidence in their ability to apply such a high-modernist order for the Cape Colony's native districts by the 1890s. The Glen Grey Act was evolutionary in each of its parts, but as an integrated system towards a regimented legal and spatial order in South Africa, it was a novel step. The Act's architect, Cecil Rhodes, in fact saw it as a whole and complete 'Bill for Africa' that could apply broadly to Britain's African colonies, with each provision necessary for the others in some way.[16] In this breadth of ambition, and likely without realizing it, Rhodes and his confederates were part of a global phenomenon. The Act's universalization of a particular regime of subdivision and control was in line with the contemporary broadening of titling schemes worldwide, notably the General Allotment (Dawes) Act of 1887 in the United States that shared much of its basic individual tenure model (there called 'title in severality'), its evolution from limited precursors, its restrictive conditions, its paternalist ideology, and its connections to settler land hunger.[17] But historians rarely link the Glen Grey and Dawes Acts, even when they consider processes of spatial rationalization and titling in settler colonies generally.[18] Both were, however, starkly rational systems for the organization and control of territory, and depended on the same kinds of colonial confidence in

15 Eduard Fagan, "Roman-Dutch Law in Its South African Historical Context," in *Southern Cross: Civil Law & Common Law in South Africa*, ed. R. Zimmerman and D. Visser (Oxford: Oxford University Press, 1996), 58–59; John W. Cell, *The Highest Stage of White Supremacy: The Origins of Segregation in South Africa and the American South* (Cambridge: Cambridge University Press, 1982), 78.

16 Robert I. Rotberg, *The Founder: Cecil Rhodes and the Pursuit of Power* (Oxford: Oxford University Press, 1988), 468–469; see R.J. Thompson and B.M. Nicholls, "The Glen Grey Act: Forgotten Dimensions on an Old Theme," *South African Journal of Economic History* 8 (1993): 58 no. 1, for the original source of the term. In his own drive for control as Prime Minister, Rhodes took the additional portfolio of Native Affairs for himself after 1893.

17 On the Dawes Act, see D.S. Otis, *The Dawes Act and the Allotment of Indian Lands*, ed. F.P. Prucha (Norman: University of Oklahoma Press, 1973 [1934]); Frederick C. Hoxie, *A Final Promise: The Campaign to Assimilate the Indians, 1880–1920* new ed. (Omaha: University of Nebraska Press, 2001), 70–81, 147–187.

18 See, e.g., John C. Weaver, *The Great Land Rush and the Making of the Modern World, 1650–1900* (Kingston, ON: Queens-McGill University Press, 2003), 329–336. Even works that mention both Acts do not link them, save in footnotes; see C.C. Saunders, "Political Processes in the Southern African Frontier Zone," in *The Frontier in History: North America and Southern Africa Compared*, ed. H. Lamar and L. Thompson (New Haven: Yale University Press, 1981), 168, no. 66.

administrative legibility on the ground. The reorganization of land tenure on a surveyed landscape was central to that legibility, and formed an important part of the extension of the Act's provisions by proclamation across the Kei.

In creating individual tenure on the Glen Grey model, the surveyor would ideally draw up a new spatial order through consultation with local people, headmen, and magistrates, along with his own judgment regarding spatial logic and long-term viability. Through the Act, colonial law and local jurisprudence would then guide people into accepting this natural dispensation. This broader and more integrated scope was an important evolution of the concept of responsible survey that Abraham de Smidt raised before the Barry Commission in the early 1880s. De Smidt retired as Surveyor-General in 1889, and the highly technocratic Leopold Marquard, now Assistant Secretary for Crown Lands and Mines, took over until the elevation of Assistant Surveyor-General John Templer Horne to the post in 1892. Horne's assumption of the post was part of a new dispensation that placed the office of the Surveyor-General under a new Department of Agriculture, which in turn assigned that office the sole responsibility for collecting fees, receiving quitrents, and ordering titles in the Colony and the Territories (as the Transkei became known).[19] The surveyors correspondingly also became even more closely yoked to the legal and financial imperatives of colonial rule, and thus central to the implementation of the Glen Grey system.

Critical studies of the Glen Grey Act have tended to focus on the councils and the labor tax (and primarily in Glen Grey itself), while the reorganization of space and ownership has usually been subordinate to those political and pecuniary concerns.[20] These concentrations are understandable historiographically,

19 John Obree, L.F. Braun, and R.C. Fisher, "Land Policy at the Cape and the Office of the Surveyor-General, 1813–1912," in *The History of Surveying and Land Tenure Collected Papers Volume 2*, ed. R.C. Fisher (Cape Town: IPLSWC, 2004), 30.

20 The major exceptions are Richard Bouch, "Glen Grey before Cecil Rhodes: How a Crisis of Local Colonial Authority Led to the Glen Grey Act," *Canadian Journal of African Studies* 27, no. 1 (1993): 1–24; Crais, *Poverty, War, and Violence*, 110–118. On the historiography of the Act's tenure provisions, see Ally, "Development," 21–47; for historians' general treatment of the Act, see R.J. Thompson, "Cecil Rhodes, the Glen Grey Act, and the Labour Question in the Politics of the Cape Colony" (master's thesis, Rhodes University, 1991), 5–44. See also Edgecombe, "The Glen Grey Act: Local Origins," 89–98; William Beinart and Colin Bundy, *Hidden Struggles in Rural South Africa* (Johannesburg: Ravan, 1987), 138–165; Colin Bundy, *The Rise and Fall of the South African Peasantry* 2nd ed. (Cape Town: David Philip, 1988), 133, 135–136; Thompson and Nicholls, "Forgotten Dimensions," 58–70; Crais, *Politics of Evil*, 19–20; Sean Redding, *Sorcery and Sovereignty: Taxation, Power, and Rebellion in South Africa 1880–1963* (Athens: Ohio University Press, 2006), 71–73.

because they speak directly to the proletarianization of rural people and processes of social change. They are also understandable in terms of prominence, because the labor tax provoked a great deal of direct protest and noncompliance before its 1905 repeal, and general objections to the Act were strongest where and when they came into force first. By contrast, survey provisions of the Act extended only to a handful of districts before their abandonment in the 1920s. Although survey and title did not provoke such sharp engagements when they passed on to Fingoland and the Idutywa Reserve, the creation and allotment of surveyed lands faced a number of local challenges. The orderly colonial landscape that planimetric drawings and legal regimes represented was ultimately at odds with local reality and the limits of state power, but certain social strata found its elements useful for their own reasons.

There is a certain irony for the colonial state in such an outcome. Rhodes and like-minded Cape administrators and magistrates championed their massive effort at social engineering in places where communities had the longest experience with colonial rule. Glen Grey and Fingoland seemed like ideal canvases from that perspective. Presumably many people in such areas were already disposed to think of ownership in European terms. Glen Grey had faced active efforts to institute colonial law, control the appointment of local headmen, and break the power of local chiefs since the 1860s. After a generation of headmen who served at the approval of the government, Fingoes presumably also had less independent civil societies than did people under chiefly lineages further east.[21] Indeed, W.T. Brownlee, magistrate at Butterworth, stated in 1898 that that "the Fingoes as a tribe [*sic*] have been broken up and dispersed and have not the cohesion or feeling of patriotism that animates almost all the other tribes. They are not the sons of the soil."[22] Thus the residents of Glen Grey and Fingoland were mere supplicants subject to government dictates, and at the same time they lacked a primordial 'tribal' association to a particular territory that colonial administrators believed could prevent their embrace of a modern system of survey and land titling. This view was fundamentally flawed in light of the simple fact that people made these landscapes their own, but it explains why those areas were the early focus of colonial spatial engineering under the Glen Grey Act.

21 William Beinart, *The Political Economy of Pondoland, 1860–1930* (Johannesburg: Ravan, 1982), 3–5; Bundy, "Mr Rhodes and the Poisoned Goods," 141. See also Scott, *Seeing Like a State*, 49, on the relationship between the state imposition of cadastral (property) surveys and the cohesion of civil society.

22 CPP G.42-'98, *Blue Book on Native Affairs, 1898*, 81.

The possibility that the people being surveyed might redirect or selectively oppose colonial survey efforts for their own reasons escaped the colony's engineers, and in part explains the four-year gap between the extension of the governing provisions of the Act to Fingoland and the Idutywa Reserve in October 1894 and the extension of the tenure provisions to the first district there (Butterworth) in August 1898.[23] Dividing land and demanding payment on that basis (survey fees, quitrents, or labor taxes) had an immediacy for homesteads and households that the creation of local governance did not. The technicians who implemented that division became central to delimitation and disagreement alike.

These disagreements crystallized in the actual survey of Glen Grey. That survey took place in several phases under the superintendence of senior surveyor Alfred Everitt Murray, who had corresponded directly with Rhodes about land tenure before the Act's passage and so was the clear choice to supervise.[24] In the first phase, Murray and the former magistrate, H.A. Jenner, held a preliminary series of meetings with headmen and conducted land reconnaissance to frame lists of claimants to certain extents of land in each amalgamated location. The second task was to decide where blocks of agricultural holdings should be, so as to keep agricultural lands together and provide a relatively unified block of land for shared grazing commonage. That process prioritized the survey's instructions to lay out rectangular farm blocks, with numbered lots for ease of administration, in low-lying areas and to eliminate isolated groups or clusters. Finally, a battery of surveyors themselves arranged the lots' corner beacons in each amalgamated location—conceptually revised from 43 headmen's separate areas into 18 locations, with an eye to the distribution of 'clans' as Jenner understood them—and surveyed the relative positions of those corner points and boundaries for well over seven thousand lots by 1899.[25] Each surveyor tendered location plans that in turn defined the property diagrams on the individual titles. As a purely technical matter, the survey was quite smooth, with only a few disruptions from smoke or fog.

As a matter of social and spatial engineering, however, the survey resulted in confusion and discontent. By consulting the headmen alone and placing an emphasis on speed, the grantee lists were incomplete and many qualified claimants were left out. In addition, no general triangulation existed to control the individual location surveys, creating uncertainty about their accuracy and

---

23 Proclamation 352 of 4 Oct 1894 and Proclamation 227 of 12 Aug 1898 respectively.

24 Murray to Rhodes, 7 Feb 1894, NA 225, KAB.

25 CPP G.6-'95, *Report of the Surveyor-General for the Year 1894*, 4–8; CPP G.13-'99, *Report of the Surveyor-General for the Year 1898*, 12. No headmen were removed or positions eliminated in the process.

eliminating any usefulness beyond Glen Grey itself.[26] Widespread Thembu anger over forced relocation from fertile kloofs (steep highland valleys) with good water to long, narrow blocks on less-productive low ground, which sometimes entailed the loss of access to adequate pasture and leased lands that some herds depended upon, worried local administrators more directly. Murray and Surveyor-General Horne anticipated some of these issues and admonished the surveyors that "patience and firmness" would be enough to forestall complaints.[27] When the individual surveyors began to plot out allotments and more people saw how much land the surveyors assigned and where they situated it, complaints nevertheless multiplied rapidly and people approached the individual surveyors for redress.[28] Murray was unsure of how to deal with the problem, and he urgently telegraphed the Surveyor-General in January 1895 about his daily receipt of petitions, including many with the support of the individual surveyors, and his lack of authority to make any decisions.[29] The Resident Magistrate also reported a significant number of complaints from men who were away laboring when the lists were compiled or who felt the extents given them were too small or unsuitably situated.[30] Horne soon had volumes of correspondence and notes on particular cases to forward to the Secretary for Agriculture.[31]

The inflexibility of surveyors' instructions was embarrassing, because it exposed the surveyors who defined lands to Thembu cultivators as people without the power commensurate with such an activity, which in turn created significant suspicion among the people of the district. Furthermore, it annoyed the surveyors, who received pay per lot surveyed and felt that dealing with disputes during the survey itself was unacceptably frustrating and time-consuming even for experienced location surveyors.[32] For the grantees it was far more alarming, with belated discoveries that their land was awarded to others, sudden demands to relocate, and a lack of provision for more extensive cultivation or the needs of male children and widows. Existing occupation took a back seat to an administratively more legible and easier to survey system of blocks and locations (see map 4.1). The result of the many petitions

26 Murray to Horne, 10 Jun 1895, 3–4, S.8168 (vol. 665), SGO-Cape. Some of the surveyors nevertheless did connect to beacons of the Geodetic Survey when they were visible.

27 See C.H.L.M. Jurisch (Assistant Surveyor-General) to F. Skead, 24 Sep 1894, S.8168 (vol. 665A), SGO-Cape.

28 See Murray to Horne, 28 Feb 1895, S.8168 (vol. 665), SGO-Cape; A.D. Tudhope to Murray, 17 Feb 1895, S.8168 (vol. 665), SGO-Cape.

29 Murray to Horne, 26 Jan 1895, telegram 6494, S.8168 (vol. 665), SGO-Cape.

30 Sweeney to Milton, 28 Jan 1895, NA 225, KAB.

31 Horne to Secretary for Agriculture, 7 Feb 1895, S.8168 (vol. 665), SGO-Cape.

32 See *inter alia* E.D. Barker (surveyor) to C.J. Sweeney (Resident Magistrate, Glen Grey), 16 May 1895, 1/LDF/4/1/8/11, KAB.

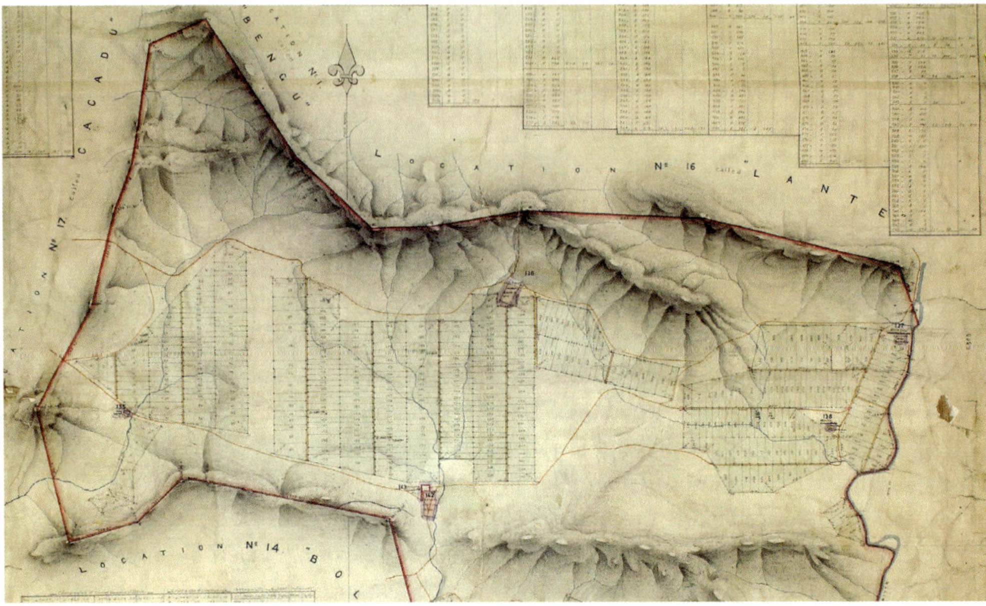

MAP 4.1 *Detail of the general plan of Mbinzana Location (No. 15), Glen Grey, surveyed by Charles Marais in 1895. Note the rectangular blocks, with judiciously spaced schools and mission out-stations. This idealized plan removed cultivators from the fertile kloofs, one of which is visible at the top of this excerpt.*

SOURCE: TSKEI PLAN 6990, OFFICE OF THE SURVEYOR-GENERAL, CAPE TOWN. RSA STATE COPYRIGHT.

against aspects of survey and allotment was a series of inquests, starting with a Select Committee in July 1895 while the survey was still underway.

The report of that committee included a number of recommendations that identified the excessive ambition of the Act's goal of spatial reorganization and recognized the admissions of its defenders and the complaints of its detractors. Upon their observation that surveyed lands often fell miles away from an existing homestead, and that headmen sometimes received large allotments that displaced other people who had been working the land, they resolved that lands should be assured in their existing locations, and if not, that an unspecified "compensating advantage" should be given to relocated people. The committee recommended further that an independent officer "who has not been connected with the allocation of the land" should serve to convey grievances to government "before the matters complained about are placed beyond the possibility of appeal by the general issue of titles." Other observations concerned the issues of tax and exemptions for labor, the inclusion of omitted names, the importance of respecting the extent of land previously cultivated, and the issue of inheritance that the committee thought was unsatisfactory for excluding widows with children in particular.[33]

The completion and aftermath of the survey did not produce the neat social revolution that the Act's architects envisioned. Sweeney allowed at the beginning of 1896 that the survey was "from the first a difficult task" but still blustered that they had treated Thembu claimants fairly and that the Glen Grey system of survey and title was "one of the best enactments bearing on native policy ever passed, both for the native and the country."[34] Murray disingenuously declared in 1895 that he had encountered fewer problems than expected even though the survey was behind schedule and impeding cultivation.[35] Fieldwork only ended in winter 1896, two years after it began, and Murray tendered his last plans that October.[36] By the end of 1897, however, local officials had recovered only half of the survey costs from grantees.[37]

Further deposits and quitrent payments came in even more slowly, especially with the arrival of the deadly *rinderpest* epizootic in May 1897. *Rinderpest*, an extremely virulent viral infection that was fatal to the vast majority of ruminants that contracted it, attacked the center of rural African measures of wealth, cattle, and spread through the very acts of exchange that gave the animals their social value. Although *rinderpest* did not turn heavily on residence patterns once people knew of its approach and Thembu householders learned countermeasures, it accompanied several years of inadequate rainfall, and the combination devastated rural wealth.[38] The survey's movement of agricultural lots away from the water-collecting kloofs directly exacerbated the effects of drought, and harvests suffered enormously. Indeed, the local council only characterized three crops between 1895 and 1903 as good.[39] The land confiscation and re-allocation machinery of the Act operated regardless of such strokes of misfortune, a point that even magistrate Sweeney conceded was unfair.[40] If the system were to be extended, as its proponents expected, it would have to become more flexible about the use and maintenance of land and more trusting of those who worked it.

---

33 CPP A.19-'95, *Report of the Select Committee on Glen Grey Allotments*, iii–vi. The basic principle of patriarchy remained unchallenged.

34 CPP G.47-'96, *Reports on the Working of the Glen Grey Act, 1894, in the Division of Glen Grey, and of Proclamation 352 in Fingoland and the Idutywa Reserve*, 2–3.

35 CPP G.8-'96, *Report of the Surveyor-General for the Year 1895*, 11–12.

36 Murray to Horne, 24 Oct 1896, S.8168 (vol. 665A), SGO-Cape.

37 CPP G.15-'98, *Report of the Surveyor-General for the Year 1897*, 4.

38 S. Cowper (Secretary to Prime Minister) to Sweeney, 28 May 1897, NA 225, KAB.

39 E.J.C. Wagenaar, "A History of the Thembu and Their Relationship with the Cape Colony, 1850–1900" (PhD diss., Rhodes University, 1990), 322–323.

40 CPP G.42-'98, *Blue Book on Native Affairs, 1898*, 27.

The lots themselves were also not sacrosanct. Owing to the destruction of many beacons and widespread cases of encroachment on grazing lands and adjoining lots, the beacons erected during the survey required redefiniton between 1914 and 1917.[41] Investigation between 1919 and 1922 further found that the occupants of nearly 40% of the allotments were not the registered holders of title, and nearly 4,000 married men and their households were living on the commonage and paying hut taxes without owning any land at all, but aside from land shortage, the likely social and economic reasons behind these irregularities went unrecorded.[42] Some of the landless households were cultivating small unsurveyed plots on the commonage in contravention of law, which land surveyor and former Minister of Native Affairs M.C. Vos characterized in his 1923 report as "a peach tree or a bit of tobacco" that actually had a beneficial effect on the land.[43] Clearly people in Glen Grey who lacked the means of headmen or other elites found other ways around the title system and its expenses when they could, and they did so within their familial and social networks. The magistrate found virtually all of the legal holders of the titles within a year and recorded their approval of others working the land, and no title cancellations resulted from this initial discovery even though the deed holder was not in actual occupation.[44] The conditions of the impoverished and landless were generally beyond Vos's territorial vision.

Proclamation and Protest in Fingoland

Even before the Act's passage and the extension of its administrative framework in October 1894, it was clear that the colonial government intended to press for surveys for individual title in Fingoland and the Idutywa Reserve on the heels of a presumed success in Glen Grey. The magistrate in Idutywa, C.G.H. Bell, stated in January 1893 that no system "either in the division of land for cultivation or building purposes" existed, leading to disputes involving individuals and headmen alike, which in his opinion soon would require a regime for "locating the people in such a manner as to keep the commonage, garden lands, and villages distinct from each other."[45] When the Chief Magistrate of Tembuland and Transkei, H.G. Elliot, asked Bell to suggest ways to accomplish

41 L.M. Walton (Native Location Surveyor) to A.H. Cornish-Bowden (Surveyor-General), 5 Sep 1914, and section 2, 3-201 *passim*; S.8168 (vol. 665D), SGO-Cape.

42 SPP U.G.42-'22, *Report on Native Location Surveys*, 5–6.

43 H.G. Turner (Magistrate, Lady Frere) to Cornish-Bowden, 11 Aug 1916, S.8168 (vol. 665D), SGO-Cape.

44 SPP U.G.42-'22, *Report on Native Location Surveys*, 5.

45 CPP G.4-'93, *Blue Book on Native Affairs, 1893*, 49.

this division, he advised against creating any standard rules for land occupation. Instead, magistrates needed to encourage headmen to reorganize their own locations into orderly blocks of lots and villages, and only then could formal survey bring "a more correct and uniform system" into being.[46] The rightful landscape of Fingoland was one of order, but it had to be generated from within Fingo society. Veldtman Bikitsha echoed this in a general meeting on 29 September 1894, where he stated that the people were not yet ready for survey, but that when it came it needed to take a form that the people—in practical terms, meaning the headmen—approved of.[47] In Bikitsha's mind, however, the problem was not survey itself, but the sheer scope of the changes the Glen Grey Act prescribed simultaneously that would make the task of reshaping them far more difficult. He accordingly propounded his opinion that changes should come one or two steps at a time and be considered individually, to permit their mediation by headmen and other elites.[48]

Such assessments did not please Elliot, who maintained at the end of January 1896 that there was no rational order in Fingoland at all. In his view, the land was "dotted all over with huts, kraals, and garden lands in the most confused and chaotic manner imaginable," homesteads' locations depended on a combination of indolence and mere fancy, and the individual household itself was legally impossible for him to discern.[49] The reality that these patterns depended upon local relationships, soil conditions, and even internal conflict over land within particular locations, was invisible to him. Elliot therefore approved of the Act's promise to create spatial efficiency, and he envisioned a system of adjoining lands on slopes that backed up to homesteads on the high, dry ridges as a healthy and productive model—the antithesis of Glen Grey's agricultural blocks in elevation but not in intent.[50] When the

46 C.G.H. Bell (Resident Magistrate, Idutywa) to H.G. Elliot (Chief Magistrate, Tembuland and Transkei), 10 Feb 1893, CMT 3/98, KAB. The offices of Chief Magistrate in Tembuland and Transkei merged under Elliot, who had been Chief Magistrate of Tembuland, in September 1891. See P.J. Venter, "Government Departments of the Cape of Good Hope 1806–1910" (unpublished manuscript, Cape Town, 1933), 132c.

47 CPP A.16-'95, *Return in Reply to a Resolution... For Copies of all Petitions, Reports, and Communications having reference to Proclamation No. 352...*, 6.

48 "Transkeian Local Government," *Imvo Zabantsundu*, 17 Oct 1894, 3.

49 CPP G.47-'96, *Reports on the Working of the Glen Grey Act, 1894, in the Division of Glen Grey, and of Proclamation 352 in Fingoland and the Idutywa Reserve*, 9; CPP G.9-'94, *Blue Book on Native Affairs, 1894*, 49–50.

50 CPP G.47-'96, *Reports on the Working of the Glen Grey Act, 1894, in the Division of Glen Grey, and of Proclamation 352 in Fingoland and the Idutywa Reserve*, 9–10. See also the draft report from H.G. Elliot, 31 Jan 1896, PMO 145b, KAB.

administrative and tax provisions of the Glen Grey Act extended to Fingoland and the Idutywa Reserve on 4 October 1894 under Proclamation 352, one-man, one-lot survey therefore appeared to be close behind. However, Cecil Rhodes and J. Gordon Sprigg, now his Treasurer, had already instructed Elliot to assure the meeting of Fingo men on 29 September that the government would not take any steps regarding land without local approval.[51] That statement proved to be a wise caveat, given the position that Bikitsha conveyed at that meeting and the vociferous objection to the Act's other provisions that followed in subsequent weeks.

The council system and the general rate (ten shillings or more per adult) exposed deepening fissures between the headmen and the people under their authority. The councils initially incorporated unelected headmen, which stood in contrast to the more inclusive and collaborative efforts of earlier years that ironically had led Rhodes and Elliot to expect a smooth extension of the system. In Idutywa the new magistrate, W.T. Brownlee, presciently warned against the extension of the Act in late August 1894, and his subordinate noted broad popular discontent following Proclamation 352 in October.[52] Indeed, even the magistrates were surprised by the speed of events, and received only two days' official notice.[53] In Tsomo the next February the magistrate reported secret meetings without headmen but cutting across all sections of society, "the educated, the Christian or civilized, and the red."[54] In October 1894 and again at the end of 1895, Brownlee specifically cited the lack of elected representation as a major grievance about the extension of tax provisions and the council system (which other magistrates identified as well), and Idutywa headman Enoch Mamba made a direct complaint in February 1896 that the laws had never been clearly communicated to the people.[55] Indeed, some groups of

51 CPP A.16-'95, *Return in Reply to a Resolution... For Copies of all Petitions, Reports, and Communications having reference to Proclamation No. 352...*, 4–5.

52 Brownlee to Elliot, 22 Aug 1894, CMT 3/98, KAB; CPP A.16-'95, *Return in Reply to a Resolution... For Copies of all Petitions, Reports, and Communications Having Reference to Proclamation No. 352...*, 10.

53 Milton (Secretary to the Prime Minister) to R.W. Stanford (Resident Magistrate, Butterworth), 2 Oct 1894, 1/BUT/5/1/11, KAB. The enclosure was a copy of the instructions given to Elliot (see note 5).

54 "Confidential Report of Resident Magistrate, Tsomo," n.d. [Feb 1895], CMT 3/164, KAB.

55 Brownlee to Elliot, 24 Oct 1894, CMT 3/99, KAB; CPP G.47-'96 *Reports on the Working of the Glen Grey Act, 1894, in the Division of Glen Grey, and of Proclamation 352 in Fingoland and the Idutywa Reserve*, 11, 14; "Enquiry regarding certain complaints made against Mr. W.T. Brownlee, Resident Magistrate of Idutywa," 3 Feb 1896, p. 27, NA 449, KAB.

householders in Fingoland sent petitions directly to Rhodes complaining that they had never been consulted and already faced hardship.[56]

Although some more prosperous individuals could afford the new levy, Fingoland had become crowded enough, with enough marginal harvests, that protest quickly arose from subsistence farmers and landless people as well as a few more prominent, mission-educated voices.[57] Some of the same figures who worked against the Parliamentary Voter Registration Act of 1887 arranged meetings and drew up petitions against the council system in the name of a Committee of the Fingo Nation.[58] A broad undercurrent of non-compliance thus developed in 1894 and 1895 that was openly hostile to headmen who accepted the councils and promoted the Act's provisions.[59] Even the formidable Veldtman Bikitsha could not bend this public dismay. At a general meeting at Butterworth in January 1895, Bikitsha was badly outvoted in his attempt to preserve the general rate for male payers from a broad popular proposal to petition against it.[60] Widespread unofficial meetings, which alarmed the headmen and magistrates alike, were even more condemnatory and initially resolved to oppose the new rates.[61] The headmen were keenly aware that their support of the Act made them ever more reliant on magistrates and government, even as it increased their power and privilege over the people under them.

On the other hand, no real division existed between headmen and people regarding the onerousness of the labor tax, even though the headmen claimed to support the entirety of the Glen Grey Act. Official meetings across the four districts in October 1894 brought condemnation against the extension of general rates and possibly labor taxes to women and young men, who had no independent income or labored for their families in some way invisible to the colonial state.[62] Although most people in the four districts grudgingly paid most of the general rate once it became clear that it worked at the household

56 See Petition of William Nojiwa and others, n.d. [1895], PMO 256, KAB.

57 Beinart and Bundy, *Hidden Struggles*, 141-44; Odendaal, *Founders*, 132–133.

58 The most prominent of these was the energetic, mission-educated Campbell Kupe. Odendaal, *Founders*, 132–133; CPP A.16-'95, *Return in Reply to a Resolution... For Copies of all Petitions, Reports, and Communications having reference to Proclamation No. 352...*, 33–36.

59 Beinart and Bundy, *Hidden Struggles*, 145.

60 Bikitsha's amendment drew less than 25% in support. CPP A.16-'95, *Return in Reply to a Resolution... For Copies of all Petitions, Reports, and Communications having reference to Proclamation No. 352...*, 23.

61 Beinart and Bundy, *Hidden Struggles*, 144–146.

62 In published minutes this objection came from headmen and chiefs, and most often took the patriarchal form of fathers paying rates for unmarried sons, sons laboring for fathers,

level, they defied the labor tax without opposition from the headmen. For example, magistrate R.W. Stanford in Butterworth reported at the end of 1895 that he had registered the men of each area and determined exemptions through the testimony of witnesses, but those he determined to be liable almost never appeared to pay the tax because, Stanford believed, it was "tantamount to an admission that [the payer] is an idler."[63] Veldtman Bikitsha, who accepted nomination to the district council three weeks after the proclamation, was a firm opponent of the labor tax from the very beginning and proposed a delegation to see Rhodes personally about the matter.[64]

Rhodes instead came to a general Fingoland meeting in March 1895, and Bikitsha told him directly on behalf of the Butterworth people that they were not happy with the new taxes, and that they were worried about having to leave the land to obtain money. The headmen and some commoners from other districts openly backed Bikitsha with a frankness that led Rhodes to scold them with a reminder that "they are talking to Govt," but he did not change his stance in any meaningful way and admonished them to obey the law.[65] An even franker set of statements later that day in Idutywa (including the simple declaration that people would not pay) may have moderated Rhodes's response, and he simply implored them to "try the law" and tell him afterwards if they still found it harsh.[66] Nevertheless Rhodes and James Rose Innes, still his Under-Secretary for Native Affairs, invited Bikitsha to Cape Town to discuss matters privately in late June 1895.[67] In practice, however, headmen took their own initiative and played an actively obstructive role, increasingly shielding claimants by supporting their claims to exemption from the labor tax and simply not reporting liability, with the result that receipts of labor tax fell dramatically. In Tsomo, the tax liability fell by over 75% between 1895 and 1897, and eligibility was impossible to police.[68] William Charles Scully, magistrate at

---

or widows. See CPP A.16-'95, *Return in Reply to a Resolution... For Copies of all Petitions, Reports, and Communications having reference to Proclamation No. 352...,"* 8–12.

63 CPP G.47-'96 *Reports on the Working of the Glen Grey Act, 1894, in the Division of Glen Grey, and of Proclamation 352 in Fingoland and the Idutywa Reserve*, 11.

64 R.W. Stanford (Resident Magistrate, Butterworth) to Elliot, 24 Oct 1894 and 23 Jan 1895, both CMT 3/58, KAB.

65 "Meeting with Fingoes by Right Hon C.J. Rhodes at Nqamakwe on Saturday 25 March 1895," CMT 3/520, KAB.

66 "Meeting with Premier, & Idutywa Natives. Idutywa, 25.iii.95," CMT 3/520, KAB.

67 See "The Week," *Imvo Zabantsundu*, 4 Jul 1895, 3. The same paper mentions the departure of its editor, J.T. Jabavu, with a deputation of Fingoes to meet with Rhodes as well, but the minutes of those meetings have not been found.

68 W.J. Thomson (Resident Magistrate, Tsomo) to Elliot, 12 Mar 1898, CMT 3/165, KAB.

Nqamakwe, confidentially complained that the use of testimony as a basis for exemption placed a premium on deception and the headmen "almost invariably endorsed whatever story was told."[69] The magistrates universally found it a pure liability, and redundant in its goal of inducing wage labor when taken together with the general rate.[70] By 1898, John Tengo Jabavu, the influential editor of *Imvo Zabantsundu* (*Native Opinion*), could rightly describe the labor tax as inoperative, and Elliot himself could remain a great booster of the Act while simultaneously stating that the labor tax was "absolutely without any benefit whatever."[71]

The general rate and the council system evoked suspicion and division, and the labor tax brought more united opposition and circumvention, but the survey and titling of lands was potentially the most fundamental change of all. In the wake of protests over the allotment system in Glen Grey itself, skeptical Fingo homesteaders and headmen were informed and wary. In fact a few people made the link between the impositions of regulations by proclamation and the threat of a general survey of lands. James Ntongana of Nqamakwe sent one such letter to the Chief Magistracy on behalf of unnamed Fingoes at the end of December 1895 to ask after their petitions against the taxes, but he also mentioned general annoyance at rule by proclamation and the fear that the government would use headmen to impose an undesired allotment survey as well.[72] But the situation of Fingoland had changed dramatically in the half-generation since the failed push of 1883, and a variety of pressures worked to produce a different outcome.

Changing Conditions and the Selling of the Survey

The extension of the Glen Grey system of survey and title to Fingoland carried a veneer of routine that barely hid colonial anxiety over the embarrassing execution of the first survey and the discontent of the Act's other provisions in Fingoland itself. Ideally, the legal provisions of the Glen Grey Act would clear the ground for a more rational order of producers and laborers. The process of consultation, grant, survey, and title under the Act was a machine that employed a relatively constant corps of surveyors from district to district.

---

69 Scully to Elliot (Confidential), 9 Apr 1896, CMT 3/196a, KAB.

70 Redding, *Sorcery and Sovereignty*, 72.

71 CPP A.33-'98, *Report of the Select Committee on the Glen Grey Act*, 13 §87, 24 §184–185.

72 James Ntongana to Elliot, 31 Dec 1895, CMT 3/192, KAB. Ntongana was an educated Christian but not evidently a headman himself, and he sent the letter through a legal agent.

The process overlapped in a way that suited the colonial government and kept it in motion without the problems attendant on a shortage of survey technicians and office personnel in Cape Town: as people in one district received titles, another would be under survey, and preliminary consultations would be underway in a third district. If this was not the original plan, it soon became a point in favor of extending survey in the eyes of the local magistrates and the Native Affairs Department, though the surveyors were wary of pressing forward without completing existing work.[73] In a pragmatic sense, this also kept a critical mass of surveyors available for these activities and familiar with the process. But in response to local objections and interests, each of these activities underwent modification. Some modifications were intended to mollify the recipients of title, while the purpose of others was to improve the quality of the geographical fix and maintain the primacy of colonial knowledge. If the survey was a machine that produced rational spaces, it was a badly calibrated and unreliable one.

This is not to say that nobody saw an opportunity in the possibility of legitimation through survey. Veldtman Bikitsha, for one, carefully studied the implementation of the Glen Grey Act and, in a general meeting with H.G. Elliot in August 1896, made clear that "certain clauses" were unlikely to be acceptable without alteration. Bikitsha expressed his certainty that survey was coming, and optimistically predicted that there would be no widespread opposition to the principle as there had been in 1883; the "Fingoes consider [the] time arrived to settle [the] land question." Furthermore, Bikitsha revived his 1883 strategy for how the survey should be carried out, and its conditions: first, location boundaries should be surveyed, then commons and allotments, based on all the land a claimant cultivated at that time so as to reward industry without destroying the old lot. The titles should be inalienable, not liable for debt or mortgage, and heritable only by males. In this, Bikitsha fused the recommendations of the committee on allotments in Glen Grey and his own thoughts from thirteen years prior into a format that fit government objectives, with a peppering of flattery that found a receptive target in Elliot.[74]

But just two days later at a meeting in Tsomo, headman Matanga reported widespread complaints about the prospect of a survey there. Elliot professed ignorance of any such plans, but still described what was happening in Glen Grey in glowing terms. Matanga's response was that they were not part of

---

73 See Brownlee to Elliot, 24 Aug 1899, p. 641, 1/BUT/6/1/1/15, KAB; Brownlee to Elliot, 18 Jun 1901, p. 64, 1/BUT/6/1/1/18, KAB; E.G. Hall to C.H.L.M. Jurisch (Surveyor-General), 15 Oct 1903, S.183 (vol. 76), SGO-Cape.

74 Minutes of Meeting at Butterworth (fieldbook notes), 11 Aug 1896, CMT 3/520, KAB.

Glen Grey, and were not rebels deserving of scattering, but they understood that "letters had passed with Veldtman" and survey was coming. Elliot could only ask that they discuss it and decide among themselves, to which others at the meeting professed relief because, as one resident put it, "all the kraals of Fingoland are crying out because of the expense in connection with the Survey—& the children would be scattered—No one here is in favour of the Survey."[75] Fear of generational scattering through landlessness and worry over the growth of inequality were deep and widespread across Tsomo. But Bikitsha had already been in the district in June 1896, holding meetings himself to promote surveys and individual tenure. The resident magistrate had been alarmed enough at complaints he received about the meetings to consult the Chief Magistrate about their legality, but Elliot dismissed such worries at the August meeting by stating that "there was no reason why he or anyone else should not call a meeting, if Veldtman wishes you to discuss land matters or dip sheep you may go if you like."[76]

The optimism and initiative of Bikitsha clearly enjoyed official support in 1896, but it stood in opposition to a number of ongoing grievances about the Act, while ecological and legal developments complicated the whole matter. Drought, locusts, and smallpox created a sense of unease, and concerns about the balance of environmental and social health even led some people to disregard locust-eradication campaigns to the detriment of grain and forage.[77] However, Glen Grey surveyor Alf Tudhope, who crossed the Transkei in late 1896 to scout potential rail routes, spoke highly of the potential of the entire Transkei to supply Kimberley and Johannesburg with food, based on the quality of the land and the scale of trade to the affected areas from other, easterly Transkeian districts.[78] The lack of actual railway construction at that moment meant it was not a factor in local unrest, but Tudhope clearly saw promise in its potential to colonize local landscapes even further.

---

75 "[Minutes of meeting] 13 Aug 96, Major H.G. Elliot CM, H.H. Bauer RM, 20 Headmen and about 100 Fingoes Tsomo," CMT 3/520, KAB.

76 Bauer (Resident Magistrate, Tsomo) to Elliot, 27 Jun 1896, CMT 3/164, KAB; "[Minutes of meeting] 13 Aug 96, Major H.G. Elliot CM, H.H Bauer RM, 20 Headmen and about 100 Fingoes Tsomo," CMT 3/520, KAB.

77 Jacob Tropp, "Locust Invasions and Tensions over Environmental and Bodily Health in the Colonial Transkei," in *Indigenous Knowledge and the Environment in Africa and North America*, ed. David Gordon and Shepard Krech III (Athens: Ohio University Press, 2012), 119–123.

78 CPP G.58-'97, *Report on Preliminary Examination of Transkeian Territories by A.D. Tudhope, 1897, and Survey of Indwe to Natal Border by the Late P. Fletcher, 1896, with a View to the Construction of a Line of Railway*, 2.

The demarcation and reservation of forests also had an especially threatening character in this light, not only because it denied communities free access to forest resources, but also because it impinged on the customary rights of headmen. An 1891 attempt to designate forests and extend regulations in Tsomo aggrieved the headmen and soon fell into abeyance for lack of fencing and policing, and by the late 1890s Elliot and his counterparts at the Forest Department were wary of surveying and fencing the few forests in Fingoland without local consultation and legal opinions.[79] For their part, the headmen told Elliot that the forests were theirs to control under the 1871 Fingo Title.[80] The details of the reliance of Fingo headmen and nearby homesteads on income from woodcutting are not clear, but the local forest officer in Butterworth reported in 1894 that it was "by no means small revenue," perhaps hundreds of pounds sterling each year.[81] But the early implementation of forest regulations deeply threatened local economies of ecological control elsewhere across the Transkei, and resistance in those cases certainly did not commend a tighter regime of control in Fingoland.[82]

The few forestry officials in Fingoland in fact endured a total lack of recognition, much less cooperation, from the magistrates and headmen in policing forests in those districts before 1900. Even with the arrival of survey, the magistrate in Butterworth strongly advised that the matter be imposed or left for the location boards under the Glen Grey Act, and not put to the headmen or people at large.[83] In the end, the demarcation of forests of Butterworth only took place after the survey was finished and the surveyors had left the district; in the case of Tsomo, surveyed in 1906 and 1907, the Forestry Department decided that the forests were "so badly cut out" that they could not justify the cost of a precise survey.[84] Forest regulations did not command much more respect

79 CPP G.23-'92, *Reports of the Conservators of Forests and District Forest Officers for the Year 1891*, 70; CPP G.4-'93, *Blue Book on Native Affairs, 1893*, 57; CPP G.9-'94, *Blue Book on Native Affairs, 1894*, 60; Elliot to W.G. Cumming (Secretary to the Native Affairs Department), 5 Dec 1900; Cumming to Elliot, 21 Jun 1901; both A.1204, NA 570, KAB.

80 Elliot to W.E. Stanford (Superintendent of Native Affairs), 23 Mar 1898, A.1204, NA 570, KAB.

81 M. Krausz (District Forest Officer, Butterworth) to C.C. Henkel (Conservator of Forests, Transkei), 13 Mar 1894, 1/BUT/5/1/11, KAB.

82 Jacob Tropp, *Natures of Colonial Change: Environmental Relations in the Making of the Transkei* (Athens: Ohio University Press, 2006), 40–52.

83 Brownlee to Elliot, 19 Jun 1901, pp. 66–67, 1/BUT/6/1/1/18, KAB.

84 Hall to Jurisch (Surveyor-General), 27 Apr 1904, S.183 (vol. 76), SGO-Cape; J.G.B. Clayton (for Acting Chief Conservator of Forests) to Cornish-Bowden, 7 Aug 1906, S.64 (vol. 26), SGO-Cape.

locally for those who collected customary fees or the increasingly impoverished households who needed timber.

These changes added up to broad concerns about survey that proponents would need to allay. Bikitsha followed up the August meetings in Tsomo with a confidential letter to Elliot in November to coincide with the expected visit and meetings of J. Gordon Sprigg, who succeeded Rhodes as Prime Minister. In it, Bikitsha stated that "the principal fingoes [*sic*] have a great wish to have the Fingoland Surveyed now" and he included three petitions signed by a few dozen men and addressed to Sprigg. The opposition in Tsomo came from young and inexperienced headmen, according to Bikitsha, and he recommended that the departing magistrate there be replaced with an experienced person who can "get these people in the line of Government."[85] The petitions were identically revised versions of the Glen Grey title conditions, and clearly indicated their purpose as negotiations over a regime of survey. They hearkened back to the 1871 Fingo Title as a governing document to which all individual titles must answer, and proposed that titles should only be transferable within the same location, to people conveniently under the existing headmen. All of them proposed quitrents only a quarter of those stipulated in the Act, and were adamant that people should receive the lands they actually cultivated, with preference to those who had built European-style houses and other improvements, with a three-year period before default and forfeiture only for rebellion. Reallocation, the petitions maintained, should keep the lot within the same family, and male primogeniture should not be applied to inheritance in polygamous households.[86] These proposals embodied a combination of headmen's worries about the Glen Grey titles, Bikitsha's vision, and the local concern for the cost of surveyed lots and inheritance. The petitions and the sense of division between headmen and people made the need to modify conditions of title and adapt the survey process clear to Elliot, the individual magistrates, and by extension the Surveyor-General and the Prime Minister. Nevertheless W.T. Brownlee, now magistrate in Butterworth, felt he could safely declare that his new district had voted irrevocably in favor of survey and title in his report for 1896.[87]

The continued weight of new taxation, combined with the ecological factors, however, meant that by March 1897, significant anxiety existed in Fingoland regarding the prospect of survey and title. Elliot was worried enough to request confidential reports from the magistrates and ask that they work

85 Bikitsha to Elliot, 4 Nov 1896, NA 571, KAB.

86 Enclosures in Bikitsha to Elliot, 4 Nov 1896, A.1218, NA 571, KAB.

87 CPP G.19-'97, *Blue Book on Native Affairs, 1897*, 87.

quietly to make the case for survey and dispel rumors.[88] One group of headmen in Nqamakwe in particular had organized meetings and reached out across district lines to build opposition, and they found it across several locations in Butterworth. The headman Hlanga Magadla was particularly responsive, perhaps because he lost a significant piece of his own location to a neighboring headman the prior year and did not wish to see that situation made permanent or even worsened.[89] The response of Magadla and men of his location included sending a messenger and contributing to a collection to retain legal counsel, which drew Brownlee's attention.

Although he was unable to find out the identities of the contributors to this fund, Brownlee enlisted Bikitsha to conduct a meeting with Magadla and his people to determine what their objections were, and to warn them about the danger of opposing government wishes on the matter. Brownlee recorded objections about the possibility that people might not receive the land they cultivated, and that no allowances existed for polygamous households, which Brownlee identified as matters covered by the petitions Bikitsha tendered in November 1896, although not so explicitly.[90] The magistrate directly disavowed any idea that the survey would result in the expropriation of any land for Europeans. But other objections connected to patterns of land use and distribution, including a cap in the future number of landholders, and the possibility that new models of market-oriented food production—wheat and oats—might destroy the custom of grazing cattle on fallow during winter, went without a direct answer beyond a promise that people would be satisfied with title. Bikitsha declared that such clandestine opposition was "only embarrassing those who had already approached the Government in a constitutional manner and applied that the survey might be brought about in such a manner as to cause the least possible dissatisfaction to the people," but rumors aired at the meeting alleged that Bikitsha had by himself brought on the survey and, according to one man, intended to buy up all the land in the district while avoiding survey in his own location.[91] These apprehensions embodied headmen's fear of losing control (whether to Bikitsha or the colony directly) as well as homesteads' concerns about losing land entirely and their reluctance to alter functioning patterns of occupation.

---

88 See Tsomo copy of Chief Magistrate's circular G.12, 4 Mar 1897, 1/TSM/5/1/7/8, KAB; Elliot to Sprigg, 24 Mar 1897, A.1218, NA 571, KAB.

89 R.W. Stanford (Resident Magistrate, Butterworth) to Elliot, 7 Feb 1896, CMT 3/59, KAB.

90 W.T. Brownlee (Resident Magistrate, Butterworth) to Elliot, 17 Mar 1897, CMT 3/59, KAB.

91 Ibid. Brownlee indicated that such rumors placing survey and title at Bikitsha's feet were widespread.

Such individual meetings led the three Fingoland magistrates—Brownlee, W.C. Scully of Nqamakwe, and the acting Resident Magistrate in Tsomo, C.J. Levey—to convene a joint meeting on 20 March. This meeting involved the three magistrates and around thirty men, most of whom were avowed and known opponents of survey. Some attendees brought petitions of their own protesting against survey, including one signed by the elder Nqamakwe headman Sobekwa (formerly of Oxkraal) that reiterated his unconditional rejection from 1883.[92] Other invitees had strong and clear objections, including many that Brownlee had encountered in Butterworth. The magistrates' recommendations to Elliot represented an effort to square colonial aims with local concerns, in order to produce a regime that they could apply without difficulty to the entire Transkei.[93] In many cases these solutions developed around the suggestions that Bikitsha and his select petitioners had made earlier. Although Bikitsha was not noted as being present at this meeting, a copy of his modified conditions for individual title, in his own handwriting, was among the magistrates' enclosures to Elliot.[94]

The recommendations the three magistrates embraced started with the recognition that the brand of Glen Grey was by itself poisonous, and that otherwise amenable people would oppose survey and title if the Glen Grey precedent stood. As a general rule they recommended the recognition of existing social relations and the need for familial security, but they accepted changes that would show effects generationally. For example, polygamous households were a major sticking point, and the idea that all right to land would vest in one man, one wife, and one heir was something that the magistrates recognized as a legitimate grievance. Going forward, the magistrates therefore recommended that all new grants recognize a one-spouse model, but that the initial survey should consider each wife and heir separately. The magistrates also held that survey and title must cover the extents and locations of land that grantees cultivated at that time, even if it was in more than one piece, but they did not consider the practice of shifting occupation in response to environmental pressures. The Fingo men at the meeting, however, pressed the matter of cattle grazing freely on farmland after harvest, and the magistrates agreed that the

92 "Resolutions Passed at a Meeting of the Fingo People at Manyibashe [*sic*] Fingoland on Wednesday the 17th day of March 1897," enclosure to Scully, Brownlee, and Levey to Elliot, 20 Mar 1897, CMT 3/148, KAB. On Sobekwa in 1883, see page 131.

93 Scully, Brownlee, and Levey to Elliot, 20 Mar 1897, CMT 3/148, KAB.

94 "Re-Survey of Land in Fingoland," enclosure to Scully, Brownlee, and Levey to Elliot, 20 Mar 1897, CMT 3/148, KAB.

impounding of trespassing stock in winter was unrealistic, even though they tacitly undercut the eventual goal of fencing allotment blocks by saying so.[95]

The cost of the Glen Grey model was another major concern for local households. The magistrates suggested that a superficial survey of location and allotment boundaries in order to provide basic certificates of occupation would be adequate and cost two-thirds less. This model existed in the African section of Xalanga district to the north after 1883, although the Tembuland Commission that recommended it had only intended the certificates to be a stopgap until a regular survey could take place.[96] In fact, the primary land surveyor there, Edwin Gilbert Hall, complained in 1896 that people on those "*roughly* surveyed" lots were enclosing and cultivating commonage.[97] The magistrate in Xalanga at that time was the same C.J. Levey who administered Tsomo district in 1897 and who had worked under Blyth decades prior, and his response indicated an awareness of irregular cultivation patterns. None of the landholders had complained to him, however, so he firmly believed this "evil" would cure itself with time.[98] For Levey, the benefits of economy far outweighed the costs of imprecision, and he believed the system there was a success. The quitrent under the Glen Grey Act was also too high for the magistrates' liking, and they recommended a 10s quitrent up to four morgen and 2s 6d for each morgen above four, which fell almost exactly halfway between the Glen Grey schedule and Bikitsha's lower figures. Confiscation for arrears and criminal conviction were as draconian to the magistrates as they were for Bikitsha, and they endorsed the idea that only rebellion or extensive arrears (five years, longer than Bikitsha's suggested three) should forfeit titles.[99] No disagreement existed on the point that the lots should be under perpetual quitrent and never actually convert to freehold, indicating a limit on the security they wanted titles to possess.

Finally, Brownlee and Levey disagreed with Scully in recommending that headmen who had arrived in the territory in the 1860s should receive special grants of up to twenty morgen, and all other headmen should receive ten. Scully was an opponent of the persistence of headmanship entirely as a "relic of the days which it should be our business to make the Natives forget as soon as possible," and he had expressed a hope in an 1894 lecture at the mission

95 Scully, Brownlee, and Levey to Elliot, 20 Mar 1897, CMT 3/148, KAB.

96 Lungisile Ntsebeza, *Democracy Compromised: Chiefs and the Politics of the Land in South Africa* (Leiden: Brill, 2005), 63.

97 Hall to Horne, 30 Apr 1896, SG 1/1/2/56, KAB.

98 Response of C.J. Levey (Resident Magistrate, Xalanga), 8 Jul 1896, in Hall to Horne, 30 Apr 1896, SG 1/1/2/56, KAB.

99 Scully, Brownlee, and Levey to Elliot, 20 Mar 1897, CMT 3/148, KAB.

school at Lovedale that European inspectors would replace headmen in any areas surveyed for individual title.[100] Correspondingly, Scully felt that large grants to headmen would entrench hereditary advantage, and suggested instead a temporary 'headman's glebe' for the office-holder in a particular area. At the same time he agreed with the others that larger grants based on merit or industry by European standards were acceptable. In order to obtain a level of legibility that might persist, the magistrates were prepared to compromise with local concerns over the depth of the social and spatial engineering the proponents of the Glen Grey Act desired, but only to a point.[101]

Elliot duly forwarded the magistrates' recommendations to the Native Affairs Department, and the Prime Minister responded that the government had no desire to force the intended survey without a clear majority expressing approval, besides which Alfred Murray was still busy with matters connected to the survey in Glen Grey.[102] In the month that followed the magistrates' report, opponents of survey continued to organize to retain legal counsel and send a deputation to Cape Town to appeal directly, but the campaigning of headmen like Bikitsha, the magistrates, and others in favor of survey left opponents unable to collect the necessary funds.[103] The Chief Magistrate eagerly looked forward to the movement against survey going out "like a damp squib" through its proponents' relentless promotion based on the terms laid out in the magistrates' report.[104] Prime Minister Sprigg had hoped to begin the survey in late 1897, and the new Transkeian General Council assembled under Proclamation 352 had already retained its own surveyor for roads, bridges, and other projects under its local purview.[105]

The arrival of *rinderpest* in Nqamakwe district during June 1897 and its subsequent spread across the region, however, changed the entire calculus of negotiation. Elliot had raised the specter of the disease as a side note in

---

100 Scully was magistrate in Peddie district at this time. W.C. Scully, "The Native Question: A Lecture Delivered before the Lovedale Literary Society on February 23rd, 1894," *Christian Express*, 1 Mar 1894, 35. Part of this paper in fact reached the Surveyor-General and figured into deliberations over the Glen Grey Act; see S.8168 (vol. 665), SGO-Cape. Scully himself later characterized his statements as "ill-advised" for their effects more than their content; see W.C. Scully, *Further Reminiscences of a South African Pioneer* (London: Unwin, 1913), 242.

101 "Minority Report," in Scully, Brownlee, and Levey to Elliot, 20 Mar 1897, CMT 3/148, KAB.

102 See Elliot to Brownlee, 22 Mar 1897, 1/BUT/5/1/1/1, KAB; Sprigg to Elliot, 5 Apr 1897, enclosure in Elliot to Brownlee, 14 Apr 1897, 1/BUT/5/1/13, KAB.

103 Brownlee to Elliot, 8 Apr 1897, CMT 3/59, KAB.

104 Elliot to Brownlee, 15 Apr 1897, 1/BUT/5/1/13, KAB.

105 This surveyor was William Henry Biggs, who was not a Government Land Surveyor. See notice in Brownlee to Scully, 15 Jan 1897, 1/TSM/5/1/6/7, KAB.

meetings as early as winter 1896, after a harvest that was poor in aggregate but did not fail evenly within the districts.[106] By April 1897 the approach of the disease was certain, but even so W.C. Scully in Nqamakwe recalled a certain shared surprise when it actually showed up unannounced in the middle of his district, and a period of severe anxiety and unrest followed as animals began dying and veterinarians tried to devise and implement some means of inoculating animals.[107] The regular traffic in cattle, local resistance to colonial efforts to interfere with livestock, and a universally poor understanding of the etiology of the disease and its transmission, worked together to assure a mortality rate around 40% among inoculated cattle and more than 90% among those not inoculated.[108] Among those who resisted inoculation were some extremely prominent headmen, including John Mazamisa of Nqamakwe, whose supporters maintained that inoculation was part of a plot to poison cattle to destroy their wealth and so actively discouraged it.[109] The survey question did not figure into inoculation opponents' statements but it was in their minds, and it became a factor in the aftermath.

At once, this episode of mass death made survey and title more likely and less practical. Brownlee felt in October 1897 that the time was right to introduce survey and title, starting in Butterworth, but subject to the conditions the three magistrates laid down in March for less costly and more responsive survey "or some similar basis."[110] Levey and Scully expressed the same sentiment.[111] Brownlee in particular felt that losses due to resistance against inoculation of cattle left people "now in that frame of mind in which they will readily acquiesce in almost any measure which the govt might wish them to accept," and that survey would have a reassuring effect, provided that the deadlines for payment of fees were extended in light of local homesteads' distress.[112]

---

106 Usually this mention came near the end of meetings, as a warning of a then-distant possibility, but it was not a universal point of discussion at that time. See Elliot's fieldbook notes of meetings in various districts, CMT 3/520, KAB; CPP G.19-'97, *Blue Book for Native Affairs, 1897*, 30–31.

107 Scully, *Further Reminiscences*, 315–316; CPP G.42-'98, *Blue Book on Native Affairs, 1898*, 75–78.

108 See, *inter alia*, figures for Butterworth in CPP G.42-'98, *Blue Book on Native Affairs, 1898*, 81.

109 Scully, "Changes in the personnel of Headmen: Recommending." 21 Oct 1897, CMT 3/196a, KAB.

110 Brownlee to Elliot, 11 Oct 1897, CMT 3/59, KAB; Brownlee to Elliot, 25 Oct 1897, 1/BUT/6/1/1/13, KAB.

111 See Levey to Elliot (Confidential), 20 Oct 1897, CMT 3/165, KAB; Scully to Elliot, 15 Oct 1897, A.1218, NA 571, KAB.

112 Brownlee to Elliot, 11 Oct 1897, CMT 3/59, KAB.

Chief Magistrate Elliot agreed that the losses of cattle to *rinderpest* would reduce resistance to the introduction of individual title, and he reported these opinions to W.E. Stanford, the Superintendent of Native Affairs, a few weeks later.[113] This movement of opinion had effects on the ground, where the disease was popularly known as the "great equalizer" and threatened the standing of people who had been wealthy in cattle and, by association, were well positioned on the land.[114] Survey became a potentially attractive vehicle for buttressing the existing social order. One nervous headman in Nqamakwe even fenced part of his area's commons with the apparent intent of claiming it during the anticipated survey despite apparently not using it at the time.[115]

Stanford and the Prime Minister, however, kept at the forefront the ultimate goal of territorial legibility that was the foundation of the Glen Grey Act. The magistrates' suggestion to use less costly certificates of occupation was an early casualty. The Surveyor-General noted that the certificate quitrent titles in Xalanga district were neither uniform nor precise, and the attached diagrams were "useless for the purposes of Land Registry when Certificates are to be exchanged for quitrent titles, and in cases of boundary disputes the diagrams are of little or no value to settle them satisfactorily."[116] To Horne, surveyed quitrent titles remained the only unimpeachable way to assure the equality of proprietors of land before the law. The Department of Agriculture supported this view, with the additional observation that the Glen Grey Act as a whole might make quitrent titles likely to persist in a way they did not in the Colony itself.[117] Stanford and Sprigg agreed, in February 1898, that a system of certificates and rough survey was unacceptable, and that a delay of the work until local grantees could pay the higher costs of a 'final' settlement was preferable to a less thorough survey.[118] This recommendation apparently only reached the headmen and households when Elliot held a public meeting at Butterworth on 4 March.

Nonetheless, Elliot reported to Stanford by wire that same day to say the meeting produced an almost unanimous consent in favor of survey when Veldtman

113 Elliot to W.E. Stanford, 4 Nov 1897, File A.1218, NA 571, KAB. No office of the Secretary for Native Affairs existed from 1893 to 1899, so the acting Under-Secretary used the title of Superintendent at this time. Stanford would become fully Secretary in 1899.

114 Pule Phoofolo, "Zafa! Kwahlwa! Kwasa!: African Responses to the Rinderpest Epizootic in the Transkeian Territories, 1897–8," *Kronos* 30 (2004): 99, 103.

115 Scully to Elliot, 31 Dec 1897, CMT 3/148, KAB.

116 Report of Surveyor-General, 21 Dec 1897, A.1218, NA 571, KAB.

117 See Hammond-Tooke (Under-Secretary for Agriculture) to W.E. Stanford, 18 Jan 1898, A.1218, NA 571, KAB.

118 See comment by J. Gordon Sprigg (Prime Minister) on schedule of papers, 4 Feb 1898, A.1218, NA 571, KAB.

Bikitsha raised the issue.[119] The headmen and prominent householders remained concerned about issues of forfeiture and succession, matters that directly affected social order and familial wealth, but Elliot believed that these were minor points that could be decided between the time of survey and the issue of title.[120] Nobody asked after the interests of the landless. In his commentary in April 1898 on the points Bikitsha raised in November 1896, Acting Chief Magistrate A.H.B. Stanford noted that the points at issue unsurprisingly showed the stamp of headmen's interests, but he agreed with the need for a more dynamic allotment system that did not create uniformity at the expense of fairness.[121] It would be up to the surveyors in practice to work out what this meant on the ground, person to person. But no matter how responsive the system, it involved a level of invasive presence that changed the landscape from one of flexible households (*imizi*) to one of numbered 'pegs' (*izikhonkwane*)—a Xhosa term for titled allotments that encompassed not only the posts holding surveyors' flags and the steel pegs that later followed, but the sense of being fastened to one piece of ground.[122]

Triangulating the Machinery of Allotment

Extension of individual tenure on the Glen Grey model to Fingoland officially began with Proclamation 227 of 1898, which applied it specifically to Butterworth.[123] From the beginning, the planners of the Act's extension gathered any lessons available from the experience of Glen Grey, for in the words of the Fingoland magistrates, "any attempt to impose, unmodified, the conditions of the title deed under the Glen Grey Act upon the local Natives would evoke the most general and serious opposition from all ranks," even those in favor of the principle of survey and title.[124] The Chief Magistrate suggested allowing women to inherit land, larger allotments in general, and no special consideration for headmen. The Civil Commissioner of Glen Grey, in relating his fraught experience, suggested that the extension of survey and title should include a thorough and consultative inspection process, with power for the magistrate and surveyor-in-charge (if not the surveyors as a whole) to settle all

119 Copy of Elliot to W.E. Stanford, 4 Mar 1898, A.1218, NA 571, KAB.

120 Elliot to W.E. Stanford, 7 Mar 1898, A.1218, NA 571, KAB.

121 A.H.B. Stanford, "Survey of Fingoland," 13 Apr 1898, A.1218, NA 571, KAB.

122 See Brownlee to Elliot, 11 Feb 1899, p. 131, 1/BUT/6/1/1/15, KAB.

123 Proclamation 227 of 1898, *Cape of Good Hope Government Gazette* 8049 (12 Aug 1898): 1781–86.

124 Scully, Brownlee, and Levey to Elliot, 20 Mar 1897, 1, A.1218, NA 571, KAB.

disputes on-site.[125] These matters, however, affected the success of the survey as an administrative device, not its execution as a technical one.

Compared to Glen Grey, the demand for precise data did not lose out to urgency, in keeping with the deliberate choice against a model of rough survey and tickets of occupation as well as the belief that objective scientific precision would assure the success of the system. The Surveyor-General in fact went further and lobbied to control these surveys with a precise triangulation extension from the Geodetic Survey of South Africa. Horne and his assistant, Max Jurisch, began to cultivate E. Gilbert Hall as a likely candidate for the work in August 1897 when they sent a copy of the published report of the Geodetic Survey of South Africa to his home in Cala.[126] In February 1897, Hall met with the Surveyor-General in Cape Town, and the following month he tendered a basic plan that would connect several dozen secondary triangulation points in Fingoland to the Geodetic Survey, dense enough to provide terrestrial coordinates for every beacon and peg in the allotment scheme.[127] Horne and Jurisch promoted Hall's plan as necessary for success, and invoked the specter of Glen Grey, where the chance for precision was "unfortunately lost" owing to haste.[128] Problems in Glen Grey in fact had little to do with matters of survey precision, but having a high-order trigonometrical framework promised to free the survey from the rectangular blocks that created discontent in Glen Grey, and might in theory cut down on resurveys and head off disputes over boundaries and shifted beacons. The fact that it served the abstract purpose of extending the modernist fetish of precise triangulation in areas of territorial opacity was just as important in creating a sense of urgency.[129]

Although money for the allotment survey of Butterworth was slow in coming, Horne successfully impressed on his superiors at the Department of Agriculture the need for triangulation to precede location surveys despite the significant added cost.[130] The Surveyor-General received approval to dispatch Hall on 21 September 1898, the same day that the Agriculture Department authorized the chief location surveyor, A.E. Murray, to proceed to Butterworth

---

125 Elliot to W.E. Stanford, 13 Apr 1898, B.1218, NA 571, KAB; Sweeney to W.E. Stanford, 14 Mar 1898, A.1218, NA 571, KAB.

126 See Hall to Horne, 10 Aug 1897, SG 1/1/2/56, KAB.

127 Hall to Jurisch, 10 Mar 1898, H2/330, Chief Directorate of National Geospatial Information, Mowbray (hereafter NGI); CPP G.10-1904, *Report of the Surveyor-General for the Year 1903*, 8.

128 Jurisch to Charles Currey (Under-Secretary for Agriculture), 31 Mar 1898, H2/330, NGI.

129 On the perceived value of triangulation for modern precision and as a palliative for uncertainty, see Matthew Edney, *Mapping an Empire: The Geographical Construction of British India, 1765–1843* (Chicago: University of Chicago Press, 1997), 236–237.

130 The estimated cost of this work was £600. Jurisch to Currey, 16 Sep 1898, H2/330, NGI.

for his preliminary tour.[131] Horne and Murray, however, hobbled Hall by agreeing that any preliminary reconnaissance survey would cause delays, and that simple enlargements of the sketches G.P. Colley and J.M. Grant made in the 1860s would "be sufficient for the purpose of all preliminary duties" connected to the allotment survey.[132] This reliance on inaccurate topography would prove to be troublesome and costly to Hall later, besides creating disputes over location and lot boundaries during the survey itself.

The Examiner of Diagrams at the Surveyor-General's Office, J.J. Bosman, devised the official specifications for the trigonometrical survey, including its beacons, its level of precision, and the format for its data, in a 21-page handwritten document that went to Hall at the end of September 1898.[133] The Surveyor-General intended Hall to be the vehicle through whom the roughly four thousand square kilometers of Fingoland would be absolutely and perfectly incorporated into the scientific landscape of the general triangulation of the Cape Colony.[134] As the conveyor of a very abstract spatial rationality, Hall would appropriate and alter the landscape in order to obtain the numerical values that represented it—but these alterations and appropriations had careful boundaries of their own, and assured that Hall would be more instrument than agent. Indeed, Hall expressed annoyance at the very particular directions about where to measure a baseline to check his work, what mathematical computations to perform, and where to situate many of his stations, which differed from his own judgment, and he wryly remarked that "in face however of the 21 pages of instructions I felt bound to abide by the arrangement as planned by you in the office."[135] The goal of those instructions, however, was both regularity and permanence, and the most visible manifestations of this aim were the beacons, physical landmarks that sat atop the points of the survey.

These cairns atop the iron pins that marked the trigonometrical stations were monumental in every sense of the word. Made of flat stones (mostly dolemite) and seven feet in height, tapering from five feet across at the base to about three feet at head level, these beacons stood atop hills and ridges as passive reminders of colonial survey that were visible to the homesteads around them.[136] Beyond

131 Currey to Horne, 21 Sep 1898, H2/330, NGI; Currey to Horne, 21 Sep 1898, S.8140 (vol. 661), SGO-Cape.

132 Horne to J. Gordon Sprigg (Prime Minister), 20 Sep 1898, S.8140 (vol. 661), SGO-Cape.

133 J.J. Bosman, "Specifications and Instructions Relating to the Secondary Triangulation of Fingoland," 28 Sep 1898, H2/1/3, NGI.

134 Horne to Hall, 29 Sep 1898, H2/1/3, NGI.

135 Hall to Horne, 26 Jun 1900, H2/1/3, NGI.

136 J.J. Bosman, "Specifications and Instructions relating to the secondary Triangulation of Fingoland," 28 Sep 1898, pp. 4–5, H2/1/3, NGI.

simply devising durable markers, Bosman's instructions transformed the beacons into individuals themselves. Not only did they acquire unique names, either the local name for the hill where it stood but sometimes the name of a community or headman, but each bore a white cross about twelve inches below the top of the pile for purposes of visibility.[137] There is no record of what anyone in nearby homesteads thought about these remarkable pieces of colonial statuary. Large carins or *izivivane* were well known throughout the Eastern Cape, and they marked graves, served as landmarks, and even became local places where the addition of a stone could bring good luck, but those cairns tended to be flatter, broader, and looser.[138] The possibility that Hall's beacons would have been seen in the same way is small, although they had their own arcane purpose and arguably religious symbolism, and their visibility surely provided a target for those who opposed survey regardless of their motivation.

Although preliminary work compiling lists of grantees only affected Butterworth in 1898, Hall (presumably through his locally-hired beacon builders) erected around forty of these seven-foot stone giants across the region. Even if the technical details of Hall's presence and the intent of his monuments were not clear to local people, they correctly identified it as a step in the chain leading towards survey and individual title. Horne and Hall had considered the possible effects of the triangulation on local opinion at the outset. Hall believed that any suspicion would be minimal because he would be confined entirely to the hills and that local people would only care if a surveyor "starts walking through their gardens, or lands & planting flags," but that Elliot should explain Hall's presence to the headmen as only for mapping purposes.[139] Nonetheless, within a few months of starting work, people tampered with two of the beacons and, despite Hall's complaint, they destroyed several others in early 1899. The unknown assailants removed large stones that caused two to collapse entirely, and in a third case they utterly destroyed a beacon of the Geodetic Survey except for the central iron pole found "twenty yards away, with iron wire guys, & sheet iron discs torn off."[140] Hall suggested erecting costly concrete beacons, but Horne and Jurisch preferred the more economical yet ineffective model of legal threats. That approach only changed in 1908, when renewed destruction of trigonometrical beacons in Idutywa gave Hall

137 Ibid., pp. 6-7.

138 Don MacLennan, "The Stone Cairns of Southern Africa," *The Digging Stick* 17, no. 1 (2000): 7–10.

139 Hall to Jurisch, 10 Mar 1898, H2/330, NGI. The Assistant Surveyor-General concurred, but there is no evidence that Elliot actually carried this request out.

140 Jurisch to Currey, 31 Dec 1898, H2/1/3, NGI; Hall to Horne, 23 Mar 1899, H2/1/3, NGI.

and Bosman fresh evidence to convince a new Surveyor-General of the need for this physical strengthening.[141]

These issues surrounding beacon damage—whether by humans or animals—together with difficult terrain, grass burning by Fingo cultivators during the planting season, Hall's complaints about inadequate pay, and the outbreak of the South African War in 1899, transformed an anticipated three months of work into a two-year odyssey.[142] Hall only provided about a third of the finished results by November 1899, seven months after a disappointed scolding from Horne, and the remainder of the work dragged on until May 1900 for Fingoland proper, whereas the fieldwork in the Idutywa Reserve did not begin until 1908.[143] By that time, Bosman agreed with Hall that the beacons required expensive masonry and concrete construction up to four feet in height, with an iron pole extending above that, because they were still at that time "continually tampered with," so daunting monumentality was no guarantee of durability.[144] The refined instructions Bosman provided for Idutywa also required a photographic record of Hall's beacons, which he duly provided, using his local assistants (and possibly his interpreter) as scale models to site his whitewashed monuments in a colonized African landscape (see Photo 4.1 as well as the cover image). For Butterworth, Nqamakwe, and Tsomo, triangulation ended with Hall's tender of plans in 1901, and allotment surveys went ahead even though Hall continued to discover significant, usually deliberate damage to his triangulation piles.[145]

Surveyor and Surveyed in Butterworth

The Surveyor-General appointed A.E. Murray to superintend the survey of Butterworth, in a reprise of his role in Glen Grey. However, Murray and the Resident Magistrate, W.T. Brownlee, adjudged claims with far greater care than in Glen Grey. Instead of calling meetings, interrogating headmen, and using old tax registers, they collected names and then visited each claimant to verify the individual allotment size and location before survey, and head off as many complaints as possible at the outset.[146] Murray commented that

141 Bosman to A.H. Cornish-Bowden (Surveyor-General), 22 Apr 1908, S.3505 (vol. 365), SGO-Cape.

142 Hall to Horne, 9 Feb 1900, H2/1/3, NGI; Hall to Horne, 23 Jun 1900, H2/1/3, NGI.

143 Hall to Horne, 2 Nov 1899, H2/1/3, NGI; Horne to Hall, 6 Apr 1899, H2/1/3, NGI; Hall to Horne, 23 May 1900, H2/1/3, NGI; Bosman to Hall, 17 Nov 1908, H3/1/10, NGI.

144 Bosman to A.H. Cornish-Bowden (Surveyor-General), 22 Apr 1908, H3/1/10, NGI.

145 See Hall to Jurisch, 18 Apr 1904, S.183 (vol. 77), SGO-Cape.

146 Brownlee to Elliot, 29 Oct 1898, p. 575, 1/BUT/6/1/1/14, KAB.

PHOTO 4.1 *E. G. Hall's Gxara* [sic] *secondary triangulation beacon in Idutywa district with camp assistant for scale, 1909. This modified form (with the metal flag and partial use of concrete) deviated from the instructions for earlier Fingoland triangulation beacons, in part to improve their survival rate. Those beacons were taller, made entirely of stone, and whitewashed all the way to the top, but no photographs are extant.*
SOURCE: H3/1/10, CHIEF DIRECTORATE: NATIONAL GEO-SPATIAL INFORMATION, DEPARTMENT OF RURAL DEVELOPMENT AND LAND REFORM, MOWBRAY.
RSA STATE COPYRIGHT.

> [t]his process is necessarily slow, but is thorough and the only way it can be done, to avoid trouble during the survey—all disputes are settled on the spot—taking the opinion of the headman & of any others that may be interested the Magistrate, comes to a decision & the people appear to be satisfied...we insure each man getting his own land sometimes a little less but it is all thoroughly well defined.[147]

Indeed the pace was far slower than it had been in Glen Grey, and not only because of the more rugged terrain. The work in Butterworth ultimately required 264 days in the field between October 1898 and August 1899, whereas the entire preliminary survey of Glen Grey took place between September and November 1894 (no more than 90 days) despite the latter district covering over two and a half times the area.[148] This evaluation of the process expresses concern not only for the grantee and the magistrate, but also the continuing need to mollify the headmen and secure their cooperation even where favorable opinions were strongest. Other parties, including traders and the missionaries of the Free Church of Scotland at Toleni, sought to assure their inclusion in any new cadastral landscape on the basis that the Fingo Title had allowed headmen to grant sites for churches and schools, which in turn they felt a truly descriptive survey should confirm.[149] W.T. Brownlee, however, opposed asking the headmen or people for written confirmation, for fear it would sow doubt about the motives and rights of government.[150]

In carrying out the preliminary assay of land, it was perhaps natural that the people under Veltdman Bikitsha should be the first whom Murray and Brownlee visited on 20 October 1898.[151] As the most vocal proponent of survey, and in many ways its architect, Bikitsha needed to accept the survey first to dispel lingering rumors about his motivations and ambitions, and he would provide the friendliest possible launching point for the introduction of individual title in Fingoland. They approved—and duly numbered—147 applicants under Bikitsha out of 582 in the general area they called 'Gcuwa' after the

---

147 Murray to Horne, 25 Oct 1898, S.8140 (vol. 661), SGO-Cape.

148 For the total number of days Brownlee was out of the magisterial office, see undated [30 Aug 1899] memorandum, p. 648, 1/BUT/6/1/1/15, KAB; on Glen Grey, see H.A. Jenner (former magistrate, Glen Grey) to Hammond-Tooke, 1 Dec 1894, S.8168 (vol. 665), SGO-Cape. As computed in 1906, Butterworth district covered 311 square miles (805 km^2), while Glen Grey extended 878 (2274 km^2); see *Statistical Register of the Cape of Good Hope for 1906* (Cape Town: Cape Times, 1907), 10.

149 Rev. B. Ross to Brownlee, 25 Mar 1898, 1/BUT/5/1/14, KAB.

150 Brownlee to Elliot, 19 Jun 1901, pp. 66-67, 1/BUT/6/1/1/18, KAB.

151 Murray to Horne, 18 Nov 1898, S.8140 (vol. 661), SGO-Cape.

nearby river, and they assured that the headmen received particularly generous allotments even if, as in Bikitsha's case, they had other lands elsewhere.[152] But among Bikitsha's people there was a wrinkle: just as his own personal farm was technically in the district of Kentani to the south, the expansion of the Butterworth town commonage had relocated some of the people under him into Kentani as well. The survey did not disturb their presence there, and they would not be subject to its strictures until such a time as that district was resurveyed. Bikitsha therefore retained some of his own power to arbitrate land matters, at least in the vicinity of his farm Nkondwane, although there is no evidence he intended or expected that result.[153]

Murray reported that most cultivators among the first five headmen were eager to obtain title, and only a few refused to take part. A few people cultivating very small extents close to one another had to agree to move, and in other cases polygynous households and others who cultivated land in several parts required cajoling to accept any consolidation, but the matters usually resolved themselves by consensus, and only occasionally did Brownlee impose his will.[154] Still, some people were skeptical, and rumors spread that failure to cultivate or pay quitrent on time would lead government to seize the land for white settlement. With that in mind, Brownlee sought to leave the most likely sources of resistance for last.[155]

In fact, summer 1899 saw a small resurgence in opposition to survey in Fingoland. The appearance of Hall and Murray in the field created a "recrudescence" of opposition among people in Nqamakwe that involved clandestine meetings and the circulation of petitions in January 1899.[156] Elliot passed the matter on to Cape Town in February, characterizing the familiar grievances as being of little importance but likely a sign that headmen were worried about the loss of arbitrary power over the land.[157] The Prime Minister, the Superintendent of Native Affairs, and the Chief Magistrate called a joint

152 "Butterworth List of Applicants for Land. Location No. 1, Gcuwa,..." n.d. (Oct 1899), S.8140 (vol 661), SGO-Cape.

153 W.E. Stanford (as Secretary for Native Affairs) to Elliot, 2 Jun 1899, enclosure to Elliot to Brownlee, 7 Jun 1899, 1/BUT/5/1/15, KAB. Brownlee forwarded this note directly to Bikitsha in reference to a conference the two had some time earlier on the subject of title for Butterworth Fingoes in Kentani.

154 Brownlee to Elliot, 29 Oct 1898, p. 575, 1/BUT/6/1/1/14, KAB; Brownlee to Elliot, 7 Nov 1898, pp. 591–592, 1/BUT/6/1/1/14, KAB; Brownlee to Elliot, 3 Dec 1898, pp. 726–727, 1/BUT/6/1/1/14, KAB.

155 Brownlee to Elliot, 21 Dec 1898, p. 575, 1/BUT/6/1/1/14, KAB.

156 Scully to Elliot (Confidential), 1 Feb 1899, CMT 3/196a, KAB.

157 Elliot to W.E. Stanford, 18 Feb 1899, CMT 3/281, KAB.

meeting in Nqamakwe in early March, where they shared the signatories' names in response to a demand from people in favor of survey. Although the headmen maintained that some of the signatories were dead or had left the region, many other people on the list claimed actually to be in favor of survey and the hapless victims of forgery.[158] The truth of the matter consequently became irrelevant to the question of survey, but in some cases opposition did not rest solely on paper.

In Butterworth, people voiced objections directly to Murray and Brownlee when they visited certain headmen's areas in January and February 1899. Whether the timing was connected to matters in Nqamakwe is unclear, but at a meeting on 23 January 1899, a large but unspecified number of men in Ndaba Nqenqa's location declared a refusal to take survey on the grounds that the land was theirs already, and that surveyed lots would impose new limits and restrictions related to inheritance and conditions of forfeiture.[159] In the first week of February, a meeting at Mqambili's location produced similar questions about government interference with land disposal. Opponents of survey in Butterworth mobilized the language of the Fingo Title as a guarantee of their control over the land, and survey as an act of deprivation that should only be visited upon enemies of the state.[160] Surprisingly, cost did not enter into the recorded slate of objections, although a number of false rumors about the government's intent to take the land or settle Europeans there did.

Although Brownlee and Murray made efforts to explain the benefits of survey and title as they saw them, their method of doing so exposed the same kind of appeal to fear and authority that had animated Murray in his 'advice' to the Newlands people twenty years prior. There was no requirement that people accept title, said Brownlee, but government had already decided to survey the land, and those opposed could go somewhere unsurveyed and so free up lots for willing applicants in the crowded locations. After the 23 January meeting, a number of opponents climbed down from their opposition when it failed to halt the survey, and in February the people still disliked the survey but most accepted it because the government had decided the matter. The opponents who refused were not openly included in the preliminary survey, but their homesteads often were included in the provisioning, in the expectation that the reality of being cut out of the land would bring opponents around through

158 "Meeting of Fingoes of Dist. B'Worth Nqamakwe & Tsomo with Prime Minister also SNA & CM," 9 Mar 1899, CMT 3/520, KAB.

159 Brownlee to Elliot, 2 Feb 1899, pp. 97-100, 1/BUT/6/1/1/15, KAB.

160 Brownlee to Elliot, 11 Feb 1899, pp. 131-135, 1/BUT/6/1/1/15, KAB.

pressure from their dependents and elders who sought the relative security of the 'peg' at a time of great social dislocation.[161]

A few weeks later a number of petitions against the survey came forward purporting to be from six locations, including the two difficult cases of February as well as four others that had not produced objections to survey before.[162] According to Brownlee, many of the names on the petitions belonged to people who were away laboring, too young or junior to claim land, or otherwise could not have signed or did not reside in the locations. When Brownlee summoned the petitioners from five of the locations, only about ten per cent of the signatories—a total of 141 men—turned up.[163] The magistrate believed that the people who framed the petitions simply attached lists of males in each location without discrimination, and that there was no real worry of active opposition. Brownlee felt that no change in the pace of the work he and Murray carried out was necessary. In his words, "any vacillation or hesitation now would be regarded as a sign of fear which I think would be fatal to the interests of the survey when it comes to be extended to the neighbouring districts," by making it look like a matter of consent and discussion instead of the settled matter of policy that Murray and Brownlee preferred to present.[164] The magistrate's bluff was effective. The meeting in Nqamakwe convinced Elliot and Sprigg that the decision in favor of survey was certain, and that in Butterworth at least it was final.[165] When matters resumed in August at the location of Hlanga Magadla—who had so openly entertained opposition in 1897—the preliminary survey encountered questions about forfeiture and the prospect of Europeans moving in, but there was no open opposition at all.[166] Brownlee also tried to forestall objections by seeking to secure widows on allotments, awarding extents that were actually under cultivation, making provision for empty lots in case of expanded grant lists, and keeping the very unpopular practice of forcing cultivators to give up lands to a minimum.[167]

By that time, however, Murray was no longer entirely in charge of the survey. He had suffered a mild heart attack in April 1899, and nominated E. Gilbert

161 Brownlee to Elliot, 11 Feb 1899, p. 134, 1/BUT/6/1/1/15, KAB; Brownlee to Elliot, 2 Feb 1899, p. 100, 1/BUT/6/1/1/15, KAB.

162 Enclosures in Brownlee to Elliot, 6 Mar 1899, CMT 3/61, KAB.

163 Brownlee to Elliot, 6 Mar 1899, pp. 205–207, 1/BUT/6/1/1/15, KAB.

164 Brownlee to Elliot, 6 Mar 1899, p. 207, 1/BUT/6/1/1/15, KAB.

165 Copy of Stanford (Secretary for Native Affairs) to Elliot, 11 May 1899, in Elliot to Brownlee, 17 May 1899, 1/BUT/1/15, KAB.

166 Brownlee to Elliot, 7 Aug 1899, pp. 606–607, 1/BUT/6/1/1/15, KAB.

167 Brownlee to Elliot, 30 Aug 1899, pp. 650–652, 1/BUT/6/1/1/15, KAB.

Hall—the triangulator—to take over his tour of the district.[168] Hall replaced the ailing Murray as superintendent permanently in early 1901, despite his inexperience with office supervision and unease with the responsibility.[169] However, the basic design of the stamped iron pins used at the lot corners was Hall's, and he was at least familiar enough with the geography of the whole district to make informed recommendations about fixing boundaries with durable markers.[170] This experience was all the more important in light of the absence of a reconnaissance survey before the preliminary tour, so the district plan Murray framed in 1899 to guide surveyors in the locations was an odd mix of gross inaccuracies and small-scale angular precision (see map 4.2).[171]

Horne retained Hall, Murray, and four other surveyors to carry out the work and frame diagrams for title in May 1899, but suspended the project indefinitely on 17 October in light of the impending outbreak of war up-country.[172] Only in August 1900 did matters permit the survey to continue, though organizing the work plan afresh delayed its start until late November.[173] This timing was fortunate because a lack of rain had prevented planting, which eliminated worries about the survey interfering with maturing crops. By the time the surveyors arrived, rains had begun in earnest, allowing cultivation to begin and changing the mood of areas that had faced possible famine in August. Ironically, that peril and short-term hunger also helped to mitigate damage from locusts that visited the region during the spring of 1900, and further improved local dispositions.[174] The initial task of Brownlee and Murray that November was to introduce each surveyor at a meeting of the people whose lands he would survey, in the interests of marking the beginning of the survey and creating a clear chain of consultation and appeal that would smooth operations.

168 Murray to Horne, 17 Apr 1899, S.8140 (vol. 661), SGO-Cape; Horne to Hall, 25 Apr 1899, S.8140 (vol. 661), SGO-Cape.

169 Murray to Horne, 23 Jan 1901, S.8140 (vol. 661), SGO-Cape; Horne to Hall, 18 Feb 1901, S.8140 (vol. 661), SGO-Cape; Hall to Horne, 26 Feb 1901, S.8140 (vol. 661), SGO-Cape. Murray and his partner, W.G. Atherstone, nevertheless surveyed a section in Butterworth, and later took up a section of the Nqamakwe Survey in 1904. See Murray to Jurisch, 12 Feb 1904, S.183 (vol. 76), SGO-Cape. Murray died in April 1909.

170 See Hall to Murray, 3 Aug 1899, S.8140 (vol. 661), SGO-Cape.

171 A.E. Murray, "District of Butterworth, Shewing Agricultural Land Coloured Green Proposed to be Granted to Natives on Individual Titles," 27 Sep 1899, Tskei Plan 6999, SGO-Cape.

172 Horne to Murray, 19 Sep 1900, S.8140 (vol. 661), SGO-Cape. Wilson Greathead, E.D. Barker, D.W. Ballot, and Arthur Goodger were the other four surveyors. Walter Atherstone eventually took over for Greathead.

173 Murray to Horne, 12 Nov 1900, S.8140 (vol. 661), SGO-Cape; Brownlee to Elliot, 23 Nov 1900, pp. 309–310, 1/BUT/6/1/1/17, KAB.

174 CPP G.52-1901, *Blue Book on Native Affairs, 1901*, 37–38.

MAP 4.2 *A. E. Murray, preliminary sketch of Butterworth allotments and rough location boundaries, 1899. This plan was based on his preliminary tour and reflects a marriage of poor topographical knowledge with Murray's charge to reconcile the needs of the state for regularity with existing patterns of occupation.*

SOURCE: TSKEI PLAN 6999, OFFICE OF THE SURVEYOR-GENERAL, CAPE TOWN. RSA STATE COPYRIGHT.

Of course, the local landscape was not static in the year or more that passed between the preliminary survey and the arrival of the surveyors to solemnize the lots. Brownlee fielded a number of complaints about interference with allotments in 1900, which often turned on a grantee's right to have a nominee from his (or rarely her) family plow the ground or an absent grantee's belated discovery that part of his gardens were in another lot. Many of these concerns arose in August, as people prepared to sow early crops, and reflected a fear that the season might be lost otherwise. The method of inspection tended to limit the amount of displacement of patterns of occupation, but it did not wholly end confusion and disputes, particularly when people stridently asserted claims to ownership in a particular place or control over their relationship to the land. In several cases, the written appeals arrived from legal agents John Henley and Alexander Kemlo in the names of people who admitted opposing the preliminary survey, but only one involved the non-receipt of ground.

Problems of multiple claims and the exercise of authority were the most evident. In several instances Murray and Brownlee assigned the headman to point out new lots when grantees or new claimants did not already cultivate somewhere, which led in June 1899 to an odd complaint in Nakanye Khamba's location whereby three people began building cattle byres and homesteads alongside the same plot of arable land—a matter that created confusion because the headman had pointed out the rough area to all three, and the main complainant had three other family members with lots in the vicinity.[175] For those added as new landholders later, this was also a problem, with one Rayi of Ndaba Nqenqa's location complaining that the headman was ignoring Brownlee's order to mark out ground for him and another in time to plow for 1900.[176] In other cases the matter involved designated cultivators, whereby a nearby homestead prevented a claimant's wife or brother from plowing in his absence in order to claim those lands as derelict.

Such claims mobilized the language of ownership to supersede any community positioning, and these complaints were most numerous in August and September 1900. Claims for land promised in certain locales comprised another issue, including provision for the eldest right-hand son of a homestead, and the simple desire to obtain the land closest to structures already in existence.[177] Such complaints did not mention what the lists of grantees and the location plans show: these cases often involved the positions of allotments held by members of the same family, or anticipatory claims of land for unmarried men. These matters were easy to address before the advent of fixed lot sizes and geometries, but even the preliminary survey created a new set of potential conflicts among homesteads. The three-person management boards for each new amalgamated location area (six in Butterworth, split into twelve in 1904 plus the Butterworth mission to address headmen's grievances about representation) included headmen almost exclusively. That fact did not portend much real change in local governance.

As a technical exercise, the survey of Butterworth locations—nearly 4,000 lots—went fairly smoothly on the ground from late 1900 into 1901. The preliminary survey had already worked against the continuing colonial desire to see regular blocks of allotments, and the surveyors duly measured household lots

175 John Henley *pro* Qawa [Qhawe Gomba] to Brownlee, 23 Jun 1899, 1/BUT/5/1/15, KAB.

176 Alexander Kemlo *pro* Rayi to Brownlee, 27 Aug 1900, 1/BUT/5/1/15, KAB.

177 See Alexander Kemlo *pro* Mko Mbani, 30 Aug 1900, 1/BUT/5/1/15, KAB; Alexander Kemlo *pro* Ngebulana Xeke, 27 Aug 1900, 1/BUT/5/1/15, KAB. In the case of Mko Mbani, the holder of the land he desired had no nearby roots and was willing to exchange it for good land elsewhere after harvest.

MAP 4.3 *Detail of lots in location Ndabakazi A/B, Butterworth, 1901, surveyed by D. W. Ballot. Note the highly variable shapes and placements of the lots. This plan includes additional lots surveyed later, around 1910, as well as lot alterations that arose from the creation of a railway south of the Toleni River. The radical difference from the philosophy of Glen Grey (Map 4.1) is clearly evident.*
SOURCE: TSKEI PLAN 7004, OFFICE OF THE SURVEYOR-GENERAL, CAPE TOWN. RSA STATE COPYRIGHT.

that were scattered throughout the kloofs and valleys, with some entirely isolated (see map 4.3).[178] As with Murray's initial tour, the first area completed included the people under Veldtman Bikitsha, although Hall carried out the work. However, Bikitsha soon began to seek additional security for the wealthy and educated households of his area by clamoring for the survey of additional building lots for some 20 applicants who had erected substantial houses and

178 See especially E.D. Barker, "General Plan of Toleni," Tskei Plan 4155, SGO-Cape.

small gardens. Bikitsha not only arranged to meet directly with Hall and the acting magistrate (Brownlee being absent), but he also sent a letter directly to the Chief Magistrate claiming that Matthew Blyth had promised to give title to those sites.[179] These houses were far from the agricultural allotments of the dwellers and "dotted about the commonage" on gardens larger than the one acre that Proclamation 227 stipulated, but Hall recommended accommodating them up to twice that amount. Despite the Surveyor-General's emphatic reminder about the one-acre limit, many of the lots Hall surveyed ended up being quite a bit larger.[180] Bikitsha himself obtained a building lot of inordinate size just before his death in July 1910, to go along with his fifteen-morgen agricultural lot and his quitrent farm Nkondwane nearby in Kentani.[181]

Reports of unhappy grantees and protests about the granting of allotments were few, in part because dispute resolution had devolved locally to the point that major inquests were unnecessary. Brownlee was, however, quick to tell new petitioners for land, usually through Kemlo and Henley, that the award of a grant in the first place remained outside the power of the surveyors or headmen to determine and rested solely in the hands of government by way of the magistrates.[182] But surveyors also took the initiative to move location boundary markers when they might cut off portions of agricultural lots, and otherwise lay out vacant lots in logical areas near occupied plots.[183] The surveyors treated every boundary as recent and flexible because the magistrates themselves could not be certain of their position. Indeed Scully's replacement as magistrate in Nqamakwe, C.J. Warner, could only adjudicate location boundary disputes in 1900 by trying to divine the principles at work in Charles Cobbe's old location book and take local testimony because the boundaries were "very vaguely described."[184] So far as the surveyors were concerned, vagueness created flexibility, which ironically helped them eradicate that same flexibility without provoking resistance.

However, some grantees did employ the survey guidelines to gain familial advantage, or applied for land that appeared open. In one case in Gcuwa location, E.G. Hall tried to enlarge an isolated plot to nine morgen for Roqo Ngabu; instead, Ngabu requested no more than five, and Hall created another

179 Hall to Horne, 1 Apr 1901, S.8140 (v.661), SGO-Cape.

180 Horne to Hall, 10 Apr 1901, S.8140 (v.661), SGO-Cape; E. Gilbert Hall, "Section Plan No. 4 of Location No. 1 called Gcuwa, District of Butterworth," Jan 1902, Tskei Plan 7492, SGO-Cape.

181 On Bikitsha's death and family, see MOOC 6/9/648 No. 1957, KAB; on Nkondwane, see S.6864, SGO-Cape.

182 Brownlee to Kemlo *pro* Barnes, 6 Mar 1901, p. 562, 1/BUT/6/1/1/17, KAB.

183 See Murray to Horne, 24 Jan 1901, S.8140 (vol. 661), SGO-Cape.

184 Warner to Elliot, 26 Jun 1900, CMT 3/149, KAB.

allotment from the remainder for which the first grantee's family members immediately applied.[185] Ngabu's own allotment was legally indivisible and so would have been a greater burden at the largest size, but two smaller lots held within a family permitted more flexibility within the law in addition to any extralegal sharing of lands. But the government requested that the applications piling up in Brownlee's office wait until after the completion of the entire survey and an assay of remaining lots and lands.[186] The eventuality of such applicants was no surprise to Elliot, Brownlee, Murray, or Hall, but the difficulty in keeping track of such things exasperated Brownlee and inspired an unsuccessful plea for a clerk to perform that duty in June 1901.[187]

Hall's ascent to leadership over the surveys in 1901 may nevertheless have materially affected the liberalization of negotiability in the terms of the survey. Horne considered Hall to be qualified because "he knows the Native mind and, I believe, speaks the language fairly well having resided in Tembuland for many years," though the question of language is open given that Hall demanded and received leave to hire an interpreter in Nqamakwe in 1902 and still had one in Engcobo district in 1916.[188] There is little doubt, however, that Hall was more conciliatory and popular than his predecessor. Under Hall, the surveyors deviated ever further from the allotment grants carefully determined and approved through Brownlee and Murray. Hall readily admitted that the surveyors acted precipitously specifically to forestall complaints, even though following standard rules on area and geometry would have been "much nicer" from the surveyor's point of view.[189] Despite such apparent insubordination, the Secretary for Agriculture supported the surveyors, and informed the new Secretary for Native Affairs that

> [t]he Surveyor has made it a practice to survey the area actually in occupation and under cultivation by the respective natives instead of adhering to the areas recommended in the approved lists, which have already received the sanction of His Excellency the Governor. In a number of cases this has resulted in a very appreciable increase of the areas approved

185 Hall to Murray, 1 Feb 1901, S.8140 (vol. 661), SGO-Cape.

186 W.E. Stanford to Elliot, 21 Nov 1900, enclosure in Elliot to Brownlee, 26 Nov 1900, 1/BUT/5/1/15, KAB.

187 Brownlee to Elliot, 20 Jun 1901, p. 69, 1/BUT/6/1/1/18, KAB.

188 Horne to Hammond Tooke, 5 Feb 1901, SG 2/1/2/93, KAB; A.H.B. Stanford (Assistant Chief Magistrate, Transkei) to Warner, 11 Sep 1902, 1/NKE/5/1/2/6, KAB; Currey (Agriculture) to Horne, 2 Jun 1902, S.183 (vol. 76), SGO-Cape; G.R. Hughes (Lands) to Cornish-Bowden, 13 Sep 1916, 3, S.8676 (vol. 711), SGO-Cape.

189 Hall to Jurisch (as Surveyor-General), 5 Jun 1903, L.11097, LND 1/701, KAB; *South African Native Affairs Commission 1903–5*, vol. II (Cape Town: Cape Times, 1904), §13,011, 931.

> of—in some instances the areas have been almost doubled. ...It should be noted that if the extents as surveyed by the Surveyor are not approved of the greater part of the survey will be upset.[190]

The Native Affairs Department heeded this advice and approved the surveyors' decisions. The Secretary, W.G. Cumming, embraced the principle of following existing patterns of occupation, and acknowledged that "[t]o disregard it would simply mean that the Natives generally would strenuously oppose the introduction of the system of individual tenure," a point solemnized in a February 1902 proclamation that cultivated and improved areas would be respected, even if it warranted a larger grant.[191] Clearly both practitioners and policy had moved towards favoring the wishes of people on the spot, but this same trajectory ironically made precise survey more costly and rendered its results less useful for social engineering.

Extension and Collapse of the Survey Machine

In Nqamakwe, the example of survey in Butterworth as well as its lessons worked to assure a lower level of resistance to survey when the magistrate, C.J. Warner, informed a meeting on 4 November 1901 that government had approved survey there. Old worries about inheritance, conditions of forfeiture, the prospect of Europeans moving in, the security of existing farmland and improvements, and villagization arose, usually with the pejorative invocation of the Glen Grey Act. These inquiries were answered not by Warner but by W.T. Brownlee, who attended the meeting for exactly that purpose. With varying levels of veracity, Brownlee implied that forfeited lands might stay in the same family, assured people that widows with families would have grants, that people would get the land they had improved, and that partial cultivation or conviction for petty crimes would not lead to the loss of land. Brownlee also made clear that the commons and the lots would not be released to Europeans, and that "the Government had no intention of interfering with the Fingoland

190 W.W. Thompson (for Acting Under Secretary for Agriculture) to W.G. Cumming (Secretary for Native Affairs), 12 Jun 1903, L.11097, LND 1/701, KAB.

191 Cumming to Thompson, 15 Jun 1903, L.11097, LND 1/701, KAB; "No. 30, 1902" in *Proclamations and Government Notices Relating to The Establishment of Councils for the Administrationof Local Affairs and the Granting of Allotments in the Transkeian Territories* (Cape Town: Cape Times, 1903), 56. This proclamation directly altered the content of Proclamation 227 of 1898, and therefore extended to every future district.

title or making the people live in villages," but he did not comment on the restrictions against accumulation and transfer that did exist.[192] By the following April, Warner reported that people were anxious for survey to begin, but instructions for Hall and Warner to conduct the initial assay waited until July owing to office work in Butterworth.[193] Hall hoped that he could simultaneously supervise the last few location surveys in the prior district and work in Nqamakwe, which he felt would need six to eight months' work to situate the roughly 7,000 ratepayers in the district.[194]

The survey certainly was a welcome development to some. In one case, older men of Xume had complained to Warner in April 1901 that their new headman was deliberately and illegally allotting lands in such a way as to deprive their cattle of water and pasture. This, they maintained, was a way to force them to move their homesteads away in favor of new people who offered stronger allegiance and, presumably, hoped to claim their fields in perpetuity.[195] The charge was troublesome, but sometimes Warner did not even know who these headmen were. When the magistrate finally investigated the matter in April 1902, he reported that several headmen had been receiving cash subsidies in the names of their (literal) predecessors for over a quarter century.[196] As in Butterworth, however, the Native Affairs Department made clear that the clustering of headmen into a smaller number of 'official' locations for survey would not cost any of them their standing or their subsidies, but it would ideally recast them into more reliable government functionaries with less independent power over people.[197]

The preliminary survey of Nqamakwe was less eventful than its predecessor. Unlike Brownlee in Butterworth, Warner made reports every week or two as he and Hall moved through the district. They encountered questions about provision for widows and polygynous households, with the responses that the former would be recommended for allotment and the latter would receive grants according to their actual cultivation. In the third procedural report, Warner noted no objections but complained about the difficulty of explaining boundary alterations to "raw and uncivilized" people (some of whom were not Fingoes) in some locations, which they read as a measure of civilization

192 Warner and Brownlee to Elliot, 4 Nov 1901, CMT 3/149, KAB.

193 Warner to Elliot, 19 Apr 1902, CMT 3/149, KAB; Warner to Elliot, 9 Jul 1902, CMT 3/150, KAB.

194 Warner to Elliot, 19 Apr 1902, CMT 3/149, KAB; Hall to Horne, 11 Sep 1901, S.183 (vol. 76), SGO-Cape.

195 Petition of the Men of Xeke, 2 Apr 1901, CMT 3/149, KAB.

196 "List of Headmen in the Nqamakwe District who draw subsidies in names other than their own," 1 Apr 1902, CMT 3/149, KAB.

197 W.G. Cumming (Secretary, Native Affairs) to Warner, 14 Jul 1902, 1/NKE/5/1/2/6, KAB.

compared to more educated people, and not as one of skepticism from people with less affinity and patience for colonial administration.[198]

Nevertheless Hall and Warner laid out allotments where people occupied ground even where location boundaries were still in dispute, preferring the order on the ground to the impressionistic boundaries and qualitative silence of Cobbe's register. In some fertile areas people sought areas smaller than four morgen, in part to remain in the best areas, and the Department of Agriculture approved those grants wherever Warner and Hall considered them necessary.[199] In the valley location of Skelewu Mbeki (the grandfather of future South African president Thabo Mbeki), Hall and Warner thus laid out a number of lots smaller than four morgen at grantees' requests.[200] At the same time, however, they discovered that Mbeki had appropriated the lands of at least seven people who departed the area, and had accumulated some thirty morgen without any approval from the magistrates.[201] Although Mbeki's family apparently cultivated the numerous patches of land involved, Warner cut it by around half, and persuaded Elliot not to levy fines or sanctions against the headman because he had been otherwise reliable.[202] At the same time, Warner and Hall induced people to move away from forested areas to some of those lots, with an eye to later reservation and fencing of the remaining wooded areas.[203] In general, the survey adopted a stance of accepting claims to smaller lots in the interest of meeting the immediate claims of households, but they encountered delays in many cases where families cultivated multiple small lots and needed mediation to "effect exchanges and arrangements" to consolidate lots.[204] In 24 cases where people resided on the government reserve around the old Residency at Nqamakwe, the government also agreed

198 Warner to W.E. Stanford (Chief Magistrate, Transkei), 1 Sep 1902, CMT 3/150, KAB. Stanford took up the office on 24 Jul 1902, following Elliot's retirement. He later resumed his prior office as Secretary for Native Affairs (1904) without relinquishing the Chief Magistracy until his retirement in 1907. See J.W. MacQuarrie, ed., *The Reminiscences of Sir Walter Stanford*, vol. 2 (Cape Town: Van Riebeeck Society, 1962), 228–229 ; *Dictionary of South African Biography*, ed. W.J. de Kock (Pretoria: Nasionale Boekhandel, 1968–81), s.v. "Stanford, Sir Walter Ernest Mortimer."

199 Hammond-Tooke (Agriculture) to Max Jurisch (Surveyor-General), 19 Feb 1903, S.183 (vol. 76), SGO-Cape.

200 On Skelewu Mbeki's line of descent, see Mark Gevisser, *A Legacy of Liberation: Thabo Mbeki and the Future of the South African Dream* (London: Macmillan, 2009), 15–17.

201 Warner to W.E. Stanford, 16 Feb 1903, CMT 3/150, KAB.

202 Warner to W.E. Stanford, 13 Mar 1903, CMT 3/150, KAB.

203 Warner to W.E. Stanford, 24 Dec 1902, CMT 3/150, KAB.

204 Warner to W.E. Stanford, 19 Mar 1903, CMT 3/150, KAB.

to defer to Hall and Warner in their desire to carve allotments out of it for those people or provide monetary compensation if they were uprooted.[205]

The local commission of two therefore rigorously maintained the consultative model in Nqamakwe, which papered over existing grievances, adapted the existing landscape to the form of the colony, and provided the appearance of equitable settlement and compliance with colonial dictates. But Hall made some changes. He sought some eight thousand wooden pegs to mark the lots he pointed out instead of using existing landmarks or nearby stones as in Butterworth, a request that the Assistant Surveyor-General, Henry van Renen, approved on the basis that "placing the pegs at once will prevent disputes and encroachments."[206] At the least, it created a sense of fixture among the *izikhonkwane* more quickly than in Butterworth. Hall also obtained a larger plan of Nqamakwe for the preliminary survey than for Butterworth, but asked that it show only the rivers, not roads, and that no names be written on it "as the spelling is generally incorrect."[207] While putting down pegs, Hall and his interpreter, E. Nogaga, would therefore be recording and appropriating topography and toponymy as well. The final report Hall tendered, summarizing the preliminary survey, expressed his diligence but also his barely subsumed frustration with considerations of local headmen's relative power to one another in the district councils and the inevitability of questions arising between cultivators and surveyors anyhow.[208] Hall did not assign a location survey to himself, but left the sixteen locations for eight surveyors who included many of the same technicians employed in the Butterworth survey, and many of whom would later continue to Tsomo. The Nqamakwe fieldwork required a little over two years to complete, ending in late 1906, but they did not encounter any intransigent objections to it.[209]

Hall's departure from fieldwork duties owed to the government's desire that the survey machine should roll forward without hindrance. The Resident Magistrate of Tsomo, Walter Thomson, was already lobbying Hall in October 1903 to begin preliminary survey there and even took some of "the more intelligent people of the district" to see Hall and Warner at work in the last week of October.[210] Hall did not like the idea, but forwarded a plan for balancing the superintendence of upcoming surveys of Nqamakwe with preliminary work in

205 H. van Renen (Assistant Surveyor-General) to Hall, 19 Jun 1902, S.183 (vol. 76), SGO-Cape.

206 Hall to Horne, 19 Jul 1902, and marginalia by H. van Renen, dd. 28 Jul 1902, S.183 (vol. 76), SGO-Cape.

207 Hall to Jurisch, 30 Apr 1903, S.183 (vol. 76), SGO-Cape.

208 Hall to Jurisch, 18 Apr 1904, S.183 (vol. 76), SGO-Cape.

209 CPP G.29-1907, *Report of the Surveyor-General for the Year Ended December 31st 1906*, 4.

210 Thomson to W.E. Stanford, 6 Oct 1903, CMT 3/167, KAB; Thomson to W.E. Stanford, 15 Oct 1903, CMT 3/167, KAB; Thomson to W.E. Stanford, 22 Oct 1903, CMT 3/264, KAB.

adjoining Tsomo to Max Jurisch,who was now Surveyor-General in Cape Town.[211] Hall expected to finish his preliminary work in Nqamakwe by February 1904, and for formal survey there to begin in April after the harvest, points that favored starting preliminary work in Tsomo around that time.[212] Thomson, however, died suddenly at the beginning of November 1903 and his temporary replacement was little more than a clerk, resulting in a delay until L.F.E. Farrant, the new magistrate, arrived in July 1904.[213] In the meantime, Hall discovered that he would have to correct gross errors in local topography himself because even the basic, unadjusted data of his triangulation disagreed with the position Colley and Grant had charted for the single most important feature of the district, the Tsomo River.[214]

In touring the district and arranging survey, several matters changed from Nqamakwe. Hall and Farrant noted an increase in fenced lands and cultivation immediately around homesteads, which they characterized as "recent."[215] Cultivators' expectation that such marks of use and ownership would assure their receipt of such land almost certainly drove short-term decisions, as did the fear that they might lose their claim on areas that included their fruit trees as well as any fallow. The Surveyor-General requested that Hall mark location boundaries with fewer and smaller beacons than in the past, because the cost of earlier beacons and their obtrusiveness outweighed any benefit of marking off headmen's areas from one another.[216] The work of consultation and preliminary beaconing took eight months, and Hall tendered his plans and reports in May.[217] Fieldwork extended from September 1906 to January 1908, but the location surveyors' instructions included for the first time an express warning against "the settlement of disputes between natives" or noting land claims, effectively returning them to positions of instrumentality and vesting

211 Hall to Jurisch, 15 Oct 1903, S.183 (vol. 76), SGO-Cape.

212 Hall to Jurisch, 21 Dec 1903, S.183 (vol. 76), SGO-Cape.

213 Lloyd (acting) to W.E. Stanford, Confidential 1/1903, 7 Nov 1903, CMT 3/167, KAB; Jurisch to Hall, 5 Jul 1904, S.183 (vol. 76), SGO-Cape. Initially the Native Affairs Department actually appointed Warner to accompany Hall into Tsomo, though the Surveyor-General objected; see Cumming to Warner, 24 Feb 1904, 1/NKE/5/1/2/6, KAB; A.H. Cornish-Bowden. (Assistant Surveyor-General) to Hammond-Tooke (Agriculture), 4 May 1904, S.183 (vol. 76), SGO-Cape.

214 Hall to Jurisch, 27 Jun 1904, S.64 (vol. 26), SGO-Cape.

215 L.F.E. Farrant, "Tsomo District Survey, Report No. 4," 18 Sep 1904, in S.64 (vol. 26), SGO-Cape.

216 H. van Renen (Acting Surveyor-General) to Hall, 23 Sep 1905, S.64 (vol. 26), SGO-Cape.

217 Hall to A.H. Cornish-Bowden (Surveyor-General), 11 Mar 1906 and 17 May 1906, S.64 (vol. 26), SGO-Cape.

adjudicative power in Hall and Farrant alone.[218] At the same time that the new Surveyor-General, A.H. Cornish-Bowden, notified the surveyors to begin work in Tsomo, he also notified Hall that he should begin the preliminary survey of Idutywa district.[219] W.E. Stanford, now both Chief Magistrate and Secretary for Native Affairs, had fought to protect funding for these activities from budget cuts in 1906, and his argument in favor of funding the Tsomo survey and Idutywa tour turned precisely upon a desire for continuity of policy.[220] Hall began his preliminary survey of Idutywa in November, following local meetings in October that approved the survey, but the government withdrew the funds and put the matter on hold for over five months.[221]

The machine's ideal pattern was however set: Hall would carry out a secondary triangulation and a preliminary consultative survey with the local magistrate; the team of surveyors would follow, solemnize the plots in each location, and send general plans to Hall; and office work in Cape Town would then produce titles upon grantees' payment of deposits. Each subsequent district occasioned a new round of struggle to keep the machine going, and cost shifted further towards the grantees. In Idutywa, Hall was furthermore requested to carry out the preliminary work with as little assistance from the magistrate as possible, again owing to cost, even though the chiefs Zenzile and Matumbu (the son of Sigidi, who died in 1897) would later cause issues in requiring larger areas for themselves at the expense of other claimants.[222] Those sorts of issues led to repeated requests for some simpler and potentially more flexible method of marking and registering land that edged ever further toward the model of tickets of occupation that Brownlee, Scully, and Levey had suggested at the outset, but Hall was insistent even as his role became more abstract and his preliminary surveys became less directly consultative. By the time the Idutywa survey was wrapping up, the headmen and chiefs had regained a prominent enough role that the Thembu king (and colonially-sanctioned paramount) Dalindyebo petitioned for the extension of individual tenure into Tembuland after his deputation to Hall reported favorably upon its execution.[223]

218 Cornish-Bowden to Boyes, 7 Sep 1906, S.64 (vol. 26), SGO-Cape.

219 Cornish-Bowden to Hall, 29 Aug 1906, S.64 (vol. 26), SGO-Cape.

220 W.E. Stanford to L.S. Jameson (Prime Minister), n.d. [25 Apr 1906], NA 1049, KAB.

221 John Page Cumming (Resident Magistrate, Idutywa) to W.E. Stanford, 29 Oct 1906, S.3505 (vol. 365), SGO-Cape; Cumming to W.E. Stanford, 25 Feb 1908, 1/IDW/6/1/2/11, KAB.

222 Cornish-Bowden to Hall, 3 Apr 1907, S.3505 (vol. 365), SGO-Cape; Cumming to A.H.B. Stanford (Chief Magistrate, Transkei), 2 Jul 1908 and 26 Jul 1909, 1/IDW/6/1/2/11, KAB.

223 "Report of the Surveyor General of the Cape Province [1910]," p. 6, SG 6/9, KAB. Survey eventually extended to Umtata and Engcobo districts.

As the overall superintendent of location surveys, Hall eventually kept the survey machine running by himself. He served as a member of the local Natives Land Committee charged with weighing in on the land provisions of the 1913 Natives Land Act in the Cape Province, despite its lack of legal force there—a committee that former Nqamakwe magistrate W.C. Scully himself chaired, and which adopted his viewpoint that the extended Glen Grey system was in perfect operation in Fingoland.[224] In fact, Hall was so central to official confidence in the scheme that his death in 1921 crystallized existing doubts about the future of individual title surveys then underway in the Engcobo district of Tembuland.[225] In 1923, the Surveyor-General judged Hall to have been "unnecessarily deliberate" in addressing local wishes and thus raising the cost of surveys, but he believed that Hall had been successful as a direct result.[226] If the landholders and headmen did not see themselves as under immediate assault, it was easier to marginalize the landless people or others who might raise complaints, although later investigators discovered rampant circumvention of the new legal landscape. Effectively the survey became a collaborative work of fiction between the headmen, the grantees, and the surveyors, with conflict and competition pushed to the margins or, more ominously, put off for the next generation.

But this co-production of a new landscape of allotments did not mean that associations of place followed suit. Corner beacons did not survive reliably, and people often encroached upon commonage land with or without them. The selling of this new landscape therefore required a certain sleight of hand relative to the state, and that involved turning a blind eye to its circumvention. The same 1922 report by M.C. Vos that found so much trouble in Glen Grey saw similar problems beginning in Tsomo just fourteen years after the issue of title; out of 6,473 garden lots, 1,244 were in one or another form of irregular occupation by people who did not hold title at that time.[227] Beyond that, many people lived only on smaller building lots without paying for title or squatted on pasturage and paid hut tax, which complicated occupation patterns in fact if not in law. Vos believed a system of inspectors could monitor the issue, together with the Chief Magistrate exercising control over title transfers, but he also suggested a return to the simplified pegging of whole blocks at a time, with less concern for locality, and the handling of a simpler title to the allottee.[228]

---

224 SPP U.G.8-'18, *Local Natives Land Committee, Cape Province, Report with Annexure, Being Schedule of Areas Recommended for Native Occupation*, 1–7, esp. §25.

225 A.H. Cornish-Bowden (Surveyor-General) to D.A. Bremner (surveyor), 12 Jul 1921, S.975/39 (vol. 200a), SGO-Cape.

226 Cornish-Bowden to the Secretary for Lands, 7 Mar 1923, 8–9, S.975/39, SGO-Cape.

227 SPP U.G.42-'22, *Report on Native Location Surveys*, 8.

228 SPP U.G.42-'22, *Report on Native Location Surveys*, 13–15.

This retrograde suggestion did not meet with the broad approval of the Surveyor-General, who still wanted numerical data and a careful preliminary inspection, and the matter was left in abeyance and eventually rendered moot.[229] The termination of new surveys in the Transkei had begun with the cancelation of preliminary survey in Mqanduli district in 1921, but they ceased entirely in 1923 in the face of broad rural recognition that it advantaged relatively few in densely-populated districts and effectively dispossessed some family lineages permanently over time, together with government recognition that circumvention was common and people exceeded their lots, transferred them without official sanction, subdivided them contrary to the conditions of title, or simply occupied unsanctioned lands.[230] Survey failed to produce the new model of modern agricultural smallholding its proponents promised because it could not simply override existing social landscapes or fight demographic trends, which emerged in the surveyed districts just as they did in the unsurveyed districts to the northeast where land division and allotment remained legally less formal.[231]

The administrative provisions modeled on the Glen Grey Act had a different trajectory. Those elements applied in most of the Transkei by 1926, and provoked little overt resistance because headmen and chiefs generally dominated the new councils.[232] Individual tenure under the Glen Grey regime arguably became a concession to these kinds of local interests, and it remained restricted to seven western districts: Glen Grey, the districts of Fingoland and Idutywa, and the Engcobo and Umtata (Mthatha) districts of Tembuland. In areas such as Bomvanaland, Pondoland, parts of Tembuland, and other areas that retained existing hierarchies of local authority throughout the period—in short, stronger and more independent civil societies—individual tenure never became a serious issue and government policy turned towards the idea of regulating allotment-holding under communal tenure systems.[233] The system of

229 A.H. Cornish-Bowden, "Report on Native Location Surveys by M.C. Vos," 7 Mar 1923, pp. 109–120, S.975/39, SGO-Cape.

230 Cornish-Bowden to Hughes, 27 Aug 1920; SGO-Cape, S.8676, Hall to Cornish-Bowden, 22 Sep 1920, S.308 (unnumbered folder), SGO-Cape; Hughes to Cornish-Bowden, 14 Mar 1921, S.308, SGO-Cape; Monica Wilson, "The Growth of Peasant Communities," in *The Oxford History of South Africa*, ed. M. Wilson and L. Thompson (Oxford: Oxford University Press, 1971), 2:60–61; Ally, "Development," 254–259.

231 Crais, *Poverty, War, and Violence*, 133, 136–139.

232 Gwendolen M. Carter, Thomas Karis, and Newell M. Stultz, *South Africa's Transkei: The Politics of Domestic Colonialism* (Evanston: Northwestern University Press, 1967), 88; W.D. Hammond-Tooke, *Command or Consensus: the Development of Transkeian Local Government* (Cape Town: David Philip, 1975), 187–194.

233 Beinart and Bundy, *Hidden Struggles*, 231–232.

spatial control even in surveyed districts became more indirect as succeeding segregationist and apartheid governments reversed course and empowered chiefs and headmen to be local agents of policy. The right to own and apportion land still remains a sore point between households, government ministries, and chiefs or other government-recognized traditional authorities.[234]

Individual tenure sought to create an atomized landscape of African farms on a 'modern' system of titling, and so convert their relationship to the land from an opaque system under the power of communities and headmen to a knowable and controllable one under the hand of government. The landscapes individual tenure systems created, however, were rational on the map and in the archive, but not on the ground. Expensive precise surveys and ever more active efforts to conciliate the claims of local people to land did not close the distance between the intent of the state and the eventual outcome, even if that care ameliorated the problem of immediate opposition to survey and title. The most the colonial survey apparatus could achieve was a fictional landscape of control and knowledge that never met the promises of its proponents.

By the time the push for individual tenure died out, the Natives Land Act of 1913 offered a more stridently segregationist model for territorial and administrative division in the Union of South Africa. Even though the Act did not initially apply in the Cape because of its interference with the property test for that province's small black electorate, the impulse transcended the technicality, and eventually the modernist system of land division and title faded into the background as a partial anomaly. In its stead, the state favored neo-traditionalism under the Native Administration Act of 1927 and later measures, but population pressures on the land continued to grow rapidly despite the release of additional land under the 1936 Natives Trust and Land Act.

Informed by their beliefs in the inferiority of African cultivation practices and a belief that ecological crisis was imminent, a new breed of state technicians devised so-called betterment and rehabilitation policies that forced Africans to cull stock, reorganize their land use patterns, reduce cultivation in many cases, and relocate their homes to central villages.[235] Those policies created a further powerful shock to the landscape and to people's livelihoods, but they involved the combination of a newer scientific discourse about erosion,

234 See Ntsebeza, *Democracy Compromised*, 131–253.

235 Nancy Jacobs, *Environment, Power, and Injustice: A South African History* (Cambridge: Cambridge University Press, 2003), 173; William Beinart, *The Rise of Conservation in South Africa: Settlers, Livestock, and the Environment 1770–1950* (Oxford: Oxford University Press, 2003), 356–357, 365; Joanne Yawitch, *Betterment and the Myth of Homeland Agriculture* (Johannesburg: SAIRR, 1981), 14–15.

degradation, and conservation in communication with the geographical frameworks already laid down long before, and their architects came armed with the enumerative tools they had refined over the prior century.[236] In theory, the assay of areas was supposed to begin with a new survey, but between issues of cost, availability, and local opposition, an even simpler model of pegging lands than Vos had suggested in 1922 prevailed, and planners leaned heavily on the geographical archive.[237] It is perhaps telling, then, that the first demonstrations of these newer, more robust conservation policies in 1939 took place in Butterworth, where the geographical archive could offer some of its most precisely detailed illusions of native landscapes to the new engineers.[238]

---

236 Crais, *Politics of Evil*, 159–160.

237 Ivan Evans, *Bureaucracy and Race: Native Administration in South Africa* (Berkeley: University of California Press, 1997), 202–203.

238 Beinart, *Rise of Conservation*, 359; William Beinart, "Soil Erosion, Conservation and Ideas about Development: A Southern African Exploration, 1900–1960," *Journal of Southern African Studies* 11, no. 1 (1984): 80.

PART 2

Locating the Enduring Kingdom

CHAPTER 5

The Notional Republic

On the large 1899 compilation map of the South African Republic (ZAR) produced by Fred and Charles Jeppe, or the similar maps of their associate Gustav Troye from 1892 and 1896, the single most striking feature is the network of red lines crisscrossing the entire body of the state, interspersed with names and numbers corresponding to the white, yellow, and green geometries between them.[1] These patterns represent construction as much as fragmentation; the various cartographers drew upon a geographical archive that reflected some sixty years of territorial arrogation, occupation, and contestation, but they spent years making the patchwork of incompatible cadasters fit. The maps reflect a recognizable, though unreliable, veneer of legibility that conceptually erased earlier occupation patterns and legitimized the various settler and colonial governments that claimed authority after 1850 in the area between the Vaal and Limpopo rivers that Europeans colloquially called 'the Transvaal.' The geographical processes that created this artificial landscape often deliberately excluded surveyors in its early phases and eschewed accuracy, in a mode of practice that Isabel Hofmeyr evocatively (and generously) described as "shambolic."[2] That archive and its notional contents nevertheless reflected local interactions and informed subsequent land and native policies, and in increasingly refined forms, they have underlain claims of ownership ever since.

The boundary lines connote divisions between town and country, mining and agriculture, and settler and 'native,' all initially based upon the territorial unit of the farm or, in the telling Dutch term brought from the Cape, *plaatsen* ('places').[3] Each *plaats* was (and still is) represented in government offices by a cadaster, in the form of a short description usually accompanied by a sketch or, in later years, a diagram drawn up by a professional surveyor. Legal ownership

1 Fred [Friedrich Heinrich] Jeppe and C. F. W. Jeppe, *Map of the Transvaal or S. A. Republic* 6 sheets (Winterthur: J. Schlumpf, 1899); G.A. Troye, *Troye's Map of the Transvaal* 6 sheets (London: Edward Stanford, 1892); G.A. Troye, *Troye's Map of the Transvaal* rev. ed. 6 sheets (London: Edward Stanford, 1896).

2 Isabel Hofmeyr, *'We Spend Our Years as a Tale That Is Told': Oral Historical Narrative in a South African Chiefdom* (Johannesburg: Witwatersrand University Press, 1993), 75.

3 In Afrikaans, the terms are *plaas* (s.) and *plase* (pl.); the overwhelming majority of contemporary sources, however, use the Dutch form. All translations of Dutch or Afrikaans terms and quotations are mine unless otherwise noted.

 | DOI 10.1163/9789004282292_006

of these farms accrued to a class of white landholders properly called *burghers* (citizens) but often, and especially to English-speakers, collectively known as Boers (farmers). In theory, the cadasters of Boer farms fell within a neatly interlocking grid of fairly regular polygons subtending the breadth of the state, forming a perfect representational mosaic of the settler state. The reality, however, varied substantially, and the lines on most title diagrams described land that did not actually conform to the sketch plan, if it existed at all.

To understand the nature of settler land policy and its interplay with African landscapes and ideas about territory, we must look at the basic principles of inspection, survey, and title the ZAR and the Transvaal Colony employed, and then consider a few examples of the intersection between these activities and African communities to highlight the clash of worldviews. The settler appropriation of Transvaal environments and the compilation of its geographical archive went through three phases, roughly sequential but all coexisting at various times. First, they used inspection systems that barely approximated territorial extents, distances, and features. Second, surveyor-assisted boundary determination sought to correct the grossest errors. Finally, the precise survey of land offered the greatest legibility to the state in matters of ownership, occupation, and taxation, but was far costlier. Each practice had its own potential for erasing African ownership or, after 1876, cordoning it off into distinct and enumerated 'native locations' (*locaties* in Dutch) as special pieces within the cadastral framework. The building blocks of the state were therefore often mere notions of future possession, if not outright fictions, as was the power of the state that made them.

The omission of African populations and polities in Europe's geographical knowledge of the Transvaal, however, long predated land registration there. Such pre-existing lacunae may be to blame for the myth of the empty land and the *mfecane* so long integral to South African history.[4] Norman Etherington has noted a wedge-shaped region of omission in early maps of southeastern Africa that includes the arc of independent chiefdoms in the eastern and northern Transvaal. Settlers and other new arrivals could not ignore this previously unrepresented land or its inhabitants when they moved into the region, but other omissions and obfuscations took its place, usually regarding the identity and land rights of the people in those missing or otherwise unlabeled spaces.[5]

4 Norman Etherington, "A False Emptiness: How Historians May Have Been Misled by Early Nineteenth Century Maps of South-eastern Africa," *Imago Mundi* 56, no. 1 (2004): 72, 82–83.

5 Norman Etherington, "Putting Tribes on Maps," in *Mapping Colonial Conquest: Australia and Southern Africa*, ed. Norman Etherington (Crawley: University of Western Australia, 2007), 86–92; see also Norman Etherington, "A Tempest in a Teapot? Nineteenth-Century Contests

Whether those ongoing omissions stemmed from expedience, ignorance, malice, or a combination of all three, they served the later purposes of the colonial state in claiming and then exerting power over territory and placing boundaries around and over 'native' landscapes.

The cadastral structure that compilation maps made so visible by the eve of the South African War in 1899 endured other disruptions and disputes as well. The term *Transvaal* itself, like Transkei, hearkens back to a colonial origin (Cape Town) and reflects an impression of territorial extension, and the organization of its geographical archive at first followed upon that presumption. Changes in government, most notably the first British colonial period in 1877 to 1881, brought shifts in bureaucracy and policy; the expansion of wealth, particularly the discovery of gold on the Witwatersrand in 1886, provided the resources necessary to translate such changes into action. Of the regions within the Transvaal, the contest between representation and reality was clearest in those furthest from settler power by dint of simple distance, defensible geography, or inclement biology. Those areas included a broad arc from the eastern Lowveld and through the Soutpansberg range in the far north (today eastern Mpumalanga and Limpopo provinces). Whether under the control of Boer settlers or British colonialists, successive governments respected the basic authority of legal ownership in that archive despite being fully aware of its nearly irredeemable flaws. Those flaws were all the greater in areas far from effective settler power, as was the temptation to gloss them over.

Historians and archaeologists have identified extended patterns of African occupation in the northeastern part of the Transvaal—the northern section of Etherington's 'wedge'—that not only put the lie to the myth of empty land, but also attest to extended networks of African commercial, social, and potentially political linkages in the eastern and northern Transvaal. One especially dense system of stone settlement is the Bokoni Complex in Mpumalanga near the Pedi heartland, which included extensively terraced agriculture and walled road systems for traffic control among homesteads in thickly populated areas.[6] That broad structure appears to have been absorbed into Pedi polities following the period of conflict in the 1820s and 1830s, and although many returned to their own areas, others became clients of other chiefs in more defensible

---

for Land in South Africa's Caledon Valley and the Invention of the *mfecane*," *Journal of African History* 45 (2004): 203–219.

6 Tim Maggs, "The Mpumalanga Escarpment Settlements: Some Answers, Many Questions," in *Five Hundred Years Rediscovered: Southern African Precedents and Prospects*, ed. N. Swanepoel, A. Esterhuysen, and P. Bonner (Johannesburg: Witwatersrand University Press, 2008), 171–176.

locations. These networks had not fully re-established themselves by the time the Boers of the future ZAR encountered their elements, which may explain the inconsistent level of notice they received and people's limited propounding of earlier affiliations.[7] Nevertheless, people did live in clusters of homesteads across the Highveld, particularly in areas like Bokoni or the Zoutpansberg where environmental variation provided for greater prosperity in difficult seasons. The material evidence is abundant, and some of this occupation pattern persisted well into the era of the Republic, forming flexible and mobile extensions of then-dominant centralized states that complicated efforts to expropriate land.

The convolutions and conditions of developments in survey and titling raise questions about the contingencies involved in collecting geographical information and defining boundaries. Though scientific narratives portray the development of surveying methods and cartographic output as inevitably progressive in retrospect, the imprecision and uncertainty of the earlier forms of cartographic representation were indicative of the spatial contestation in the colony between settlers, chiefs, bureaucrats, squatters, and speculators of all sorts. Indeed, accuracy and precision alike were sometimes the enemies of everyone involved in the expropriation and alienation of land in southern Africa, and the state's mapped landscape deviated far from the vision on the ground. Between the Vaal and Limpopo rivers, as in the Eastern Cape, the struggle involved a drive to transform the landscape to one built upon precisely defined spaces, but that survey modality ran afoul of a variety of fictional landscapes that had other functions and some unintended consequences for the state itself as well as the pre-existing kingdoms and communities within its ostensible boundaries.

Notional Territory: Inspection Systems in the Transvaal, 1840–1877

The arrival of large organized parties of European settlers north of the Vaal in the 1830s necessitated a system of identifying and registering lands granted to farmers or intended for town lands, whether or not prior inhabitants complicated the matter. Claims operated under a principle established by the Boer government of Natalia in 1840 that each male settler had the right to claim two

7 Peter Delius and Maria Schoeman, "Revisiting Bokoni: Populating the Stone Ruins of the Mpumalanga Escarpment," in *Five Hundred Years Rediscovered: Southern African Precedents and Prospects*, ed. N. Swanepoel, A. Esterhuysen, and P. Bonner (Johannesburg: Wits University Press, 2008), 154–155.

farms of roughly 3,000 morgen (6,350 acres) each, one on freehold and one on perpetual lease, intended to provide separate lands for sowing and grazing. Each burgher had the right to a township lot as well. This entitlement was commonly known as *burgherregt* or *burgherrecht*, but sometimes went by other names (*landsregt*, *grondregt*, *plaatsregt*, and so forth). Eventually this right extended to all white males who took up residence within the eventual boundaries of the South African Republic before the end of 1852, and in the attenuated form of one freehold farm and one lot for those who arrived before 1866.[8] The importance of farming and livestock to the livelihood of settler communities in the south central Transvaal, together with expectations of growth, explains the expansive grants that the state made as well as the low rents occupants paid—if they paid at all, or bothered to collect title.

The earliest burghers did not always pursue their entitlement immediately, and in some areas they simply could not. Those who took land could not necessarily occupy all the ground they claimed, a few fraudulently made more claims than the law allowed, and some people and companies simply accumulated land. After 1865 new claims required a certificate as well as a £500 bond against fraud, but government was still responding to fresh claims of *burgherregt* in the 1890s.[9] The poverty of many of these early farmers in the meantime assured the rise of a trade in the sale of poor Boers' *burgherregt*, the rental of ground to Africans and Europeans by investors and land companies, and owners' employment of black homesteaders or landless whites as labor tenants (*bywoners*). Speculators acquired large numbers of freehold farms from these holders of *burgherregt*, which further increased demand for title—and worries about speculation and "misuse by new immigrants" led to the termination of grants to those arriving after 26 October 1866.[10] As the amount of available

8 Alkis Doucakis, "The Origins of Doornfontein and its Adjoining Farms, Being the Earliest Histories of Johannesburg, Bedfordview, Edenvale, Sandton, Alberton, and Germiston, 1841–1853," *Historia* 42, no. 2 (1997): 8–9; ZAR Official Publication (hereafter ZPP) No. 1-1884, *Rapport van den Landmeter-Generaal, gevende een historisch overzicht van de wijze van de vervreemding en het inspecteeren van gronden, gelegen in de Zuid-Afrikaansche Republiek en van Landmeten in het Algemeen*, 5–6.

9 Petrus Naudé, "Boerdery in die Suid-Afrikaanse Republiek, 1858–1899," vol. 1 (D.Litt. diss., University of Pretoria, 1945), 69–72; ZPP No. 1-1884, *Rapport van den Landmeter-Generaal*, 6.

10 VRB Art. 566, 26 Oct 1866, in *SA Argiefstukke: Transvaal No. 6*, ed. J.H. Breytenbach (Cape Town: Staatsdrukker, 1957), 65. By VRB Art. 318, 26 Nov 1868, any claimaint to freehold (*eigendomsregt*) had one year to register with the local *landdrost* (magistrate), after which all new claims would be on costlier loan tenure, which could also be revoked more easily.

land in central areas diminished and hunting became unprofitable, poor Boers and speculators claimed ever remoter areas. It did not matter to claimants if these lands were already occupied or otherwise unsuitable as farms. The ZAR and its various sub-entities claimed legal authority over a huge area based variously on right of conquest over Mzilikazi's Kumalo Ndebele, an 1846 treaty with Mswati II, and a personal cession from the Pedi paramount Sekwati. But the state had little machinery to enforce its perception of ownership or demand tax and labor except the threat of the use of local militias (*commandos*), so its power was ephemeral where it existed at all.[11]

It is on those landscapes, far from Potchefstroom and Pretoria, that the idea of notionality becomes important. Peter Delius has given the term 'notional farms' to plots in those areas that were theoretically claimed by settlers, crossed by inspectors, awarded deeds, and traded as commodities by speculators, none of whom ever saw the land in question much less occupied it.[12] Delius further refers to the ZAR's claim to the right to dispose of land in the eastern Transvaal at all, based on the 1846 treaty with Mswati which that king certainly did not intend to confer permanent rights, as 'notional ownership' by the state.[13] It is, however, useful to extend this concept even further, to the ZAR itself as a 'notional republic' with a geographical and legal body built from fictions of power and space. On this imaginary landscape, lands lay open for the state's disposal, and extant occupation or land use rarely figured except as an onerous problem in need of resolution that appeared only in the names ascribed to the notional farms involved.[14] As Paul Carter notes for prescriptive surveys in Australia, inspections rendered space as "a conceivable object…that the mind could possess long before the lowing herds."[15] The difference in the Transvaal was that these conceivable objects often had very little concordance with anything on the ground. The mechanics of land claims and inspections from the

---

11 Johan Bergh, "Die Veranderende Grense van 'Transvaal' 1840–1994," *Historia* 41, no. 2 (1996): 11–13; D.J. Erasmus, "Re-thinking the Great Trek: A Study of the Nature and Development of the Boer Community in the Ohrigstad/Lydenburg Area, 1845–1877" (master's thesis, Rhodes University, 1995), 40, 90.

12 Peter Delius, *The Land Belongs to Us: The Pedi Polity, the Boers, and the British in the Nineteenth-Century Transvaal* (Johannesburg: Ravan, 1983), 133.

13 Delius, *The Land Belongs to Us*, 32, 130; for just such a historical justification, see J.C. Otto, "Die Regsgronde van die Grondbesit deur die Boere in Noordost Transvaal," *Historiese Studies* 1, no. 4 (1940): 46–59.

14 Johan Bergh, "Grondregte in Suid-Afrika: 'n 19de Eeuse Transvaalse Perspektief," *Historia* 40, no. 2 (1995): 39–41.

15 Paul Carter, *The Road to Botany Bay* (London: Faber & Faber, 1987), 113.

beginning of official inspections in 1851 to the mid-1880s show clearly how inspection became, through unavoidable negligence and inevitable malfeasance, an entirely corrupt practice.

The process itself was fairly straightforward in theory. First, in response to a request forwarded via an eligible claimant's local *veldcornet* (field cornet or sheriff), a *landdrost* (district magistrate) registered the claim in his *aanteekeningboek* [*sic*] or *landsboek*, and provided a paper copy of that entry called an *uittreksel* to the claimant, who then took up occupation. If the prospective farm proved inadequate for farming needs or was otherwise unsuitable, the holder of the *uittreksel* could cancel it and take out another. If the farm was suitable, the settler could request an inspection for purposes of obtaining title. After enough inspection requests came from a particular area, the government would approve an inspection of lands and send the local land commission (*landcommissie* or *inspectie commissie*), normally headed by the local *veldcornet* and two neutral burghers who served terms of up to five years.[16] That commission tried to inspect multiple farms at once for reasons of economy (pay depended on the number of inspections, with only a small allowance per diem) and the difficulty of holding a commission in the field. Instructions permitted the inspectors to collect fees from settlers but admonished them in block inspections to reserve at least one-tenth of the inspected farms for government, but the *veldcornet* alone was supposed to hold out land that African communities with identifiable chiefs occupied.[17]

The state expected inspectors to settle disputes in the course of their duties, and their instructions provided basic guidance in handling overlapping or disputed claims if neighbors saw the notice of the land commission and (rarely) turned out to evaluate the work. In the case of identifiable *uitvalgrond*

16 See Doucakis, "The Origins of Doornfontein," 9–10. The neutrality issue involved familial relations, and instructions disqualified any burgher within three degrees of legal or blood relation to a land claimant. The stipulation, however, rarely prevented such conflicts of interest, especially if the *veldcornet* was involved. See §4 of Gouvernments Berigt, 7 Dec 1859, in *De Locale Wetten der Zuid-Afrikaansche Republiek 1849–1885*, ed. and comp. F. Jeppe and J.G. Kotzé (Pretoria: J.F. Celliers, 1887), 124, and reiterations in §5 of "Wet No. 4, 1870" and "Wet No. 4, 1875," in Jeppe and Kotzé, *De Locale Wetten*, 369, 612.

17 Delius, *The Land Belongs to Us*, 130; *Bylaag* 1 (16 Oct 1857), Art. 238–239, in *SA Argiefstukke: Transvaal No. 3*, ed. J.H. Breytenbach (Cape Town: Staatsdrukker, 1951), 468–469; W.A. Stals, "Die Kwessie van Naturelle-eiendomsreg op Grond in Transvaal, 1838–1884," *AYB* 35, no. 1 (1972): 4–5. Just how large a settlement needed to be to qualify for reservation was never specified, and the inspection and reservation imperatives did not merge until after the survey law (No. 2) of 1884.

(excess ground, or gores) between farms, the inspectors divided it among the neighboring farmers or inspected it as a separate piece of government land depending on estimated size.[18] Following a further payment, a deed (*grondbrief*) would be drawn up to confer title upon the burgher, which placed a name on the plot and gave it a number in a registry—essential preconditions for administrative legibility. After a period of three months, during which neighboring burghers could lay protests if desired, the settler could pay a fee and take possession of the deed.[19] Inspected farms without burghers might be held for later claimants or for those who held titles to farms that could not be occupied, and a burgher could also lay claim to a piece of inspected but unclaimed ground and, after paying the inspection cost, apply for the deed. The books of inspection reports, which ideally included both textual descriptions of the parcels and sketch plans, then entered the geographical archive through the central *Registrateur van Akten* (Registrar of Deeds) after 1866.

As technical operations, these inspections were, however, barely cursory, and their imprecision helped to undermine them. Though several methods of marking rectilinear plots of land developed, they took time to settle into a single accepted system.[20] The most common method for individual inspections was *een uur gaans overkruis*, meaning up to four one-hour rides in two sections, at right angles from a central point (variously the *middelpunt*, *ordonnantie*, or *aanvraag*), and a beacon placed at each turn or stop. This method would ideally produce a square farm sixty minutes' ride on a side and containing about 3,000 morgen (about 6,350 acres or 25.7 square kilometers) of land, with up to 3,750 morgen permitted much later (1882) on the grounds that using the legal definition of the speed of a horse first set in 1859 would produce

18 Art. 12 of "Instructie voor de inspecteurs van plaatsen" (1853) in Jeppe and Kotzé, *De Locale Wetten*, 27. Later instructions removed the requirement to divide such plots.

19 VRB Art. 141–142, 29 Sep 1864, in *SA Argiefstukke: Transvaal No. 5*, ed. J.H. Breytenbach (Cape Town: Staatsdrukker, 1953), 54; "Wet No. 6, 1870," in Jeppe and Kotzé, *De Locale Wetten*, 375.

20 For general discussions of the inspection system and its irregularities, see Doucakis, "The Origins of Doornfontein"; W.M. Edwards, "Early Land Grants in South Africa," in Great Britain, Colonial Office, Colonial No. 70, *Conference of Empire Survey Officers 1931: Report of Proceedings* (London: HMSO, 1932), 250; F.A. van Jaarsveld, "Landmeting in die oue dae," *Historiese Studies* 8, no. 1 (1947): 45–53; F.A. van Jaarsveld, "Die Veldkornet en sy Aandeel in die Opbou van die Suid-Afrikaanse Republiek tot 1870," *AYB* 13 (1950): 243–252; F.J. Potgieter, "Die Vestiging van die Blanke in Transvaal (1837–1886)," *Archives Year Book for South African History* (hereafter *AYB*) 21, no. 2 (1958): 139–142; A. J. Christopher, "The European Concept of a Farm in Southern Africa," *Historia* 15, no. 2 (1970): 96; Gert van den Bergh, "Voortrekker plaasbesetting op die Transvaalse Hoëveld: 'n Versteurde Beeld," *South African Journal of Surveying and Mapping* 20, no. 7 (1990): 301–311.

that extent.[21] The earliest inspections, centered around the Vaal river drifts from 1839 into the 1840s, proved chaotic because the basic premise of rectilinear claims did not match the variable size and situation of individual farms, and multiple authorities sometimes registered the same grants.[22] Registration was also chaotic, and multiple methods remained in use even after the principle of *een uur gaans overkruis* emerged as the preferred one in 1841.[23] Furthermore, only cursory corner beacons made of the crudest material (bones, sticks, or even anthills), if even that, indicated the position of land claims, which meant that farm locations and boundaries were easy to lose.[24]

Because it was dependent on untrained practitioners and lacked meaningful accountability or standards, the inspection system was ripe for abuse. The potential was readily evident at the time, and the same 1869 inspection law that reiterated the primacy of *een uur gaans overkruis* stipulated that inspectors could not themselves be land agents.[25] Such restrictions did not prevent agents of government from obtaining title to vast lands anyhow. Sometimes officials gained land through awards in lieu of pay from the cash-strapped ZAR, but they also engaged in open speculation and used their position in the information chain to best advantage, especially at auctions of debtors' freehold farms.[26] Inspectors and surveyors also had better knowledge of the

---

21 §11 in Gouvernements Berigt, 7 Dec 1859, in Jeppe and Kotzé, *De Locale Wetten*, 125; M.W. Wedepohl, "Historical Review of Legislation Affecting Surveying and Registration of Land in the Transvaal," *South African Survey Journal* 9, no. 2 (1958): 10; URB Art. 251, 5 Jul 1882, pp. 230–232, UR 6, TAB; VRB Art. 744, 7–8 Jul 1882, in Jeppe and Kotzé, *De Locale Wetten*, 1126. The morgen used was the same as the Cape measure, that is, 1.167269756 ha, 2.116539816 acres, 0.008565 km^2, or 0.003307 mi^2. See D.R. Hendrikz, *South African Units of Length and Area*, Special Publication No. 2 (Pretoria: Department of Lands, 1944). The equivalence of ZAR and Cape measures was, however, only confirmed in law in 1874; see "Wet No. 2, 1874," §2, in Jeppe and Kotzé, *De Locale Wetten*, 561–562.

22 Van den Bergh, "Voortrekker plaasbesetting," 302–305; Inspection instructions from 1853 on (and embodied in Law No. 3, 1869) also stipulated that the longest distance from *aanvraag* to side could not exceed ¾ hour, and that the *uittreksel* need not dictate the *middelpunt* of the inspected farm—creating another potential source of confusion and error.

23 Doucakis, "The Origins of Doornfontein," 10–12; Van den Bergh, "Voortrekker plaasbesetting," 306.

24 Alkis Doucakis, "'Een uur gans overkruys': The Earliest Form of Land Survey North of the Vaal, 1841–1860s," in *A Century of Land Surveying in the Transvaal, 1903–2003*, ed. D.S. Pound *et al.* (Pretoria: Sereti Press, 2003), 67.

25 "Wet No. 3, 1869," §1, §18, in Jeppe and Kotzé, *De Locale Wetten*, 326–328.

26 Stanley Trapido, "Reflections on Land, Office, and Wealth in the South African Republic, 1850–1900," in *Economy and Society in Pre-Industrial South Africa*, ed. S. Marks and A. Atmore (New York: Longman, 1981), 355–358.

character of land they traversed beyond the simple description on the report, and they could seek the lease or purchase of ground with better foreknowledge. The problem did not diminish with time or technical precision. The land surveyor Anthony Lennox Devenish, for example, owned shares in up to twenty farms at one point, and in the late 1890s the Transvaal Land Exploration Company, chaired by Johann F.B. Rissik (then Surveyor-General of the ZAR), with J.C. Minnaar (the Registrar of Deeds) as a director, held the titles to over six hundred.[27]

Questionable ethics constituted only one potential difficulty. Self-interested inspectors at least tended to take care in their work, but many inspections were brazenly slapdash. The inspections of blocks of hundreds of *plaatsen* in response to growing claims of land and the state's own financial needs in the 1860s unsurprisingly introduced problems of disputed ownership and vague location through simple, undetailed sketches of square lots with sides measured in minutes (usually 60), and a failure to erect durable monuments on the ground as law increasingly required.[28] In keeping with the primacy of economy and enabled by legal language that only required that farms be a size consistent with the method of *een uur gaans overkruis*, inspectors by the late 1860s were riding in parallel passes through blocks and erecting at most a single corner beacon roughly every sixty minutes.[29] This meant that the outside boundary or boundaries of one farm conveniently became the inside boundaries of the adjoining ones in the same block, but there was no check on precision or accuracy. The effect compounded in block inspections: if each successive *plaats* was dependent upon the one before, settlers far from the initial corner point of the block could not be sure of the size and extent of a farm or indeed whether they were in the right place at all.[30] There was no assurance that an inspection commission did not simply ride around the whole block, visit a few burghers, and consider the matter finished, a practice that was not unknown but not sanctioned.[31]

Government in fact only required that the textual descriptions with these inspection plans note whether the land had water and wood, along with some

27 Erasmus, "Re-thinking the Great Trek," 62; Trapido, "Land, Office, and Wealth," 357.

28 J.W.N. Tempelhoff, "Die Okkupasiestelsel in die Distrik Soutpansberg, 1886–1899," *AYB* 60 (1997): 45.

29 "Wet No. 3, 1869," §1, in Jeppe and Kotzé, *De Locale Wetten*, 326.

30 Een Hollander [K.J. de Kok], *Toen en Thans: Mededeelingen en Beschouwingen omtrent de Twee Republieken in Zuid-Afrika* (Cape Town: Jacques Dusseau, 1898), 54–56. Although de Kok worked in the Orange Free State, the process he describes and its failings are identical to practices further north.

31 ZPP No. 1-1884, *Rapport van den Landmeter-Generaal*, 15–16.

indication of the general situation of the farm block based on the number of hours' ride to a town.[32] Whether by design or accident, sketch plans and reports also regularly failed to note the presence of African homesteads. Land commissions were not required to note existing occupation as part of their writ, because the *veldcornet* already had the responsibility to report the presence of major settlements in their wards.[33] In enormous block inspections or large northern districts even a well-meaning *veldcornet* could miss people—and in the case of potentially valuable farms, he might be encouraged to miss them on purpose. Some inspection sketches were quite detailed and specific despite their basic imprecision, even going so far as to note all built areas and who lived in each, but economy usually won out and erased that presence. In 1871, for example, the Transvaal Commission on Native Labor heard credible evidence that most African homesteads in the southern districts were spread across land that had become notionally the private farms of others.[34]

Prime examples of truly shoddy inspections, and the ones repeatedly invoked by those calling for the reform of inspection and survey regulations, were those carried out between 1869 and 1873 in the northern districts of Waterberg and Zoutpansberg. In one particularly egregious example, *veldcornet* Jan Anthonie Smit tendered reports for 577 *plaatsen* (14,826 square kilometers) ostensibly inspected between 4 October and 4 November 1869 in the Waterberg district—a pace of over 18 farm inspections per day, seven days a week.[35] Whether by *een uur gaans overkruis* or by riding one side of each farm in a block, an inspection required more than an hour's work per farm. Time to prepare reports, settle disputes, and erect markers preliminary to later, permanent monuments all added to the total, making such a pace of work clearly impossible. The likeliest explanation is that Smit's commission rode around a large area and divided it by reckoning, and then carried out only those few inspections where burghers were in occupation. The quality was not even uniformly bad, but bespoke overt favoritism. The farm that Smit's commission inspected for the influential Portuguese viscount Alfredo du Prat, for example, received a detailed topographical sketch that stands in sharp contrast to its

32 "Wet No. 3, 1869," §14–15, in Jeppe and Kotzé, *De Locale Wetten*, 327–328.

33 "Instructie voor de Veldcornetten [1858]," §59, in Jeppe and Kotzé, *De Locale Wetten*, 99.

34 Johan Bergh, "Grondverdeeling tussen Blank en Swart in Suid-Afrika: 'n 19de-Eeuse Transvaalse Perspektief," *J.B.M. Hertzoggedenklesing* XXXIV (2005): 10.

35 Inspectie Rapporten Waterberg (voorzitter J.A. Smit), RAK 2762, Transvaal Archives, Pretoria (hereafter TAB). The reports further omit the specific date of each inspection and the time required to complete it, despite an entry for those items on the form used.

neighbors.[36] In the case of farms for poor burghers or for sale and lease by the government, there was little incentive to be so diligent. There was also little fear of sanctions.

Smit's case was severe but hardly exceptional. He had already overseen 569 inspections over six weeks in February and March 1869, and 508 more between 22 March and 4 May 1869.[37] The 200 February and March 1869 inspection reports by C.G. Bodenstein (also in Waterberg) included 195 iterations of the same simple diagram at a rate of eight or more inspections per day, a pace that still stretches credulity.[38] Bodenstein and Smit maintained a virtual monopoly on block inspections in Waterberg, and although they were not fond of one another, they were of the same mind regarding the profitable business of block inspections. Increased scrutiny of this sinecure did not improve matters very much. Smit's re-inspection of Bodenstein's block between 29 March and 25 April 1873 displayed slightly more care, but the data remained sparse, with a maximum of one detail per farm quadrant and sometimes a notable feature of the farm edge or the *middelpunt* (see map 5.1). Those 1873 sketches also show where some beacons were erected, but because of the mode of inspection, each only shows a maximum of one beacon—and even then, very few have beacons at all.[39] Virtually all of the reports state that the inspectors spent only about an hour per farm inspection, if they make any statement at all, but the rate was a more modest seven farms per day.

The geographical fix therefore remained almost nonexistent, and locating any particular piece of land remained totally dependent on the *veldcornet*'s memory and propriety. The sole government surveyor in the district, Edwin Griffiths, minced no words about Smit and the merits of his work in 1874:

> I will say for instance Mr Jan Anthonie Smit, the Chief Inspector of the Waterberg, who though false, neglectful, and unprincipled, and by no means a desirable man to hold the important office of *Chief Inspector*, in whose hands lie to a very great extent the unchecked control of the very vitals of a new country—the *Land*!—is yet the only man who professes

36 Inspection report of farm 'Lisbon,' n.d., p. 36, RAK 2762, TAB.

37 Inspectie Rapporten Waterberg (voorzitter J.A. Smit), RAK 2760 and RAK 2761, TAB.

38 Inspectie Rapporten Waterberg (voorzitter C.G. Bodenstein), RAK 2673, TAB. Bodenstein carried out several other Waterberg inspections, to the point that Smit complained about his poaching of work; see R.A. van Nispen (*landdrost*, Nylstroom) to M.W. Pretorius (president), 23 May 1870, R/745/70, SS 124, TAB.

39 For one example of a sketch showing a beacon, see report for 'Leeuwkuil,' No. 35, 29 Mar 1873, Inspectie Rapporten Waterberg (voorzitter J.A. Smit), RAK 2766, TAB.

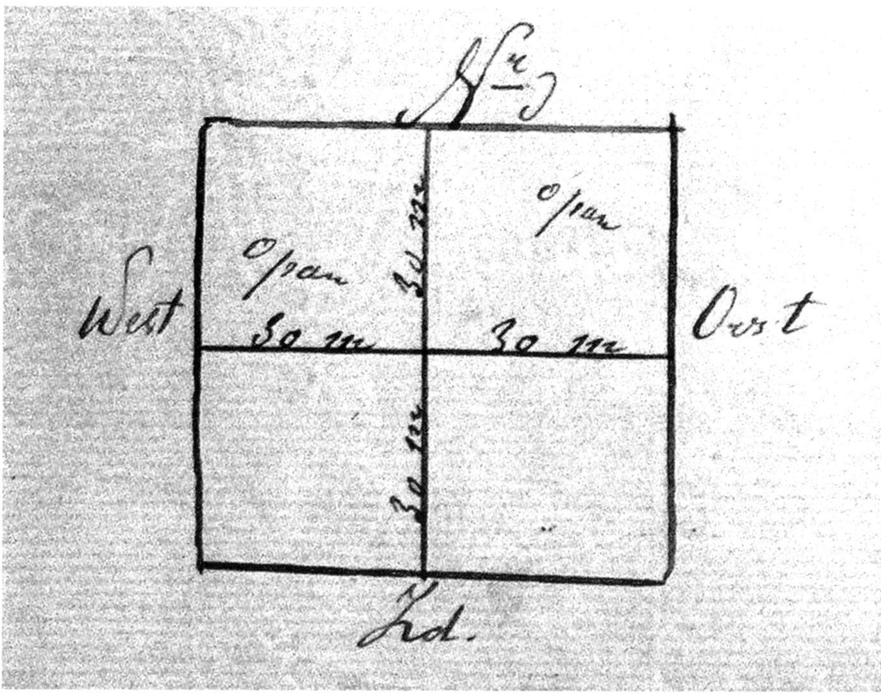

MAP 5.1 *Sketch map of 'Knopiesdoorn Boom,' inspected for B.G. Lindequé by the Waterberg land commission under J.A. Smit, 4 April 1873. Note the single details in the upper quadrants; the commission passed along the northern boundary although no corner beacon is indicated on this particular sketch. The cross is meant to suggest the use of the system of* een uur gaans overkruis, *although the claim of one hour per farm inspection on the form renders that impossible.*

SOURCE: REPORT NO. 36, RAK 2766, TRANSVAAL ARCHIVES DEPOT, NATIONAL ARCHIVES AND RECORDS SERVICE OF SOUTH AFRICA, PRETORIA. RSA STATE COPYRIGHT.

> to have any knowledge of the unoccupied farms in the District, and in case of this man's death the ownership of the Farms would at once come to a deadlock, and the Farms become virtually forfeited, unless a fresh Inspection were to be instituted…[40]

The shortcomings of his work continued to come to light for many years afterward. In 1885, nearly a hundred burghers in the south central Zoutpansberg district protested against one of Smit's inspections, because he had apparently included land that had been inspected before, had done so without actually

40 Griffiths to the *Uitvoerende Raad*, 12 Jan 1874, R54/74, pp. 95–96, SS 167, TAB. Smit's memory was somewhat legendary, or at least he made a good show of it; see G.G. Munnik, *Memoirs of Senator the Hon. G.G. Munnik* (Cape Town: Maskew Miller, 1933), 123.

visiting the ground in question, and besides that, he wasn't even supposed to be in their district.[41] Such massive overlap and poor documentation made the issue of valid titles difficult at best.

Beyond the local abuse and error involved in scaling up the system of inspection, it also potentially alienated huge amounts of land to speculators and denied that land and income to the state and its citizenry. The representative legislature of the ZAR, the *Volksraad*, thus resolved on 20 September 1871 to suspend the issue of new *uittreksels* and the tender of *grondbrieven* for any land then under inspection until they could determine whether the law had been followed.[42] The execution of existing inspection requests was a trickier matter. First, shortly after the resolution, the *Volksraad* set the cutoff at the end of 1868, but fifteen months after a general suspension in June 1873 they modified the date to be that of the first resolution in 1871.[43] The backlog meant that inspections did not stop, but the large block inspections on the old system dwindled and faced greater skepticism after 1873. Correcting bad inspections was complicated because inspectors often could not find their own beacons or identify boundaries, and in early 1877 the *Volksraad* simply suspended all efforts at correction until a general survey law existed to address it.[44] Unfortunately the moratorium on inspections and titles also meant that the holders of *uittreksels* were not liable for taxes and rents, a point that worked against the financial condition of the state.[45]

Basic concordance between the Republic's inspection diagrams and the ground they represented existed in the rare cases where truly distinctive features appeared, but for the most part, the geographical archive those sketches and reports composed was unwieldy and suspect. No requirements existed for what had to be shown, aside from the ride times on the boundaries, which were presumed all to have been conducted at the same speed; water would usually be noted, but beyond that, topography was unevenly portrayed and contour mapping was out of the question. The *veldcornet* rarely even had a compass for basic correction. The resulting documents had some use for administration and tracking claims, but they were virtually worthless for

41 "Memorie van J.H. du Preez, J.L. Grobler, & 34 Anderen" and "Memorie van G.J.L. Helberg, C. Platteau, & 60 Anderen," n.d. [Nov 1885], R6068/85, pp. 219–226, SS 1136, TAB.

42 VRB Art. 75, 20 Sept 1871, in Jeppe and Kotzé, *De Locale Wetten*, 421.

43 VRB Art. 151, 12 Oct 1871, in Jeppe and Kotzé, *De Locale Wetten*, 422; VRB Art. 146, 11 Jun 1873, in Jeppe and Kotzé, *De Locale Wetten*, 523; VRB Art. 10, 23–24 Sep 1874, in Jeppe and Kotzé, *De Locale Wetten*, 594.

44 Gouvernements Kennisgeving (Government Notice) 572, 16 Mar 1877, in Jeppe and Kotzé, *De Locale Wetten*, 685.

45 See minute by the Surveyor-General, 26 Jan 1879, pp. 8–9, LMG 82, TAB.

compiling reliable maps, and cartographers struggled in the gaps, as did some landowners.[46] Such imprecision could, however, keep the peace, because without precise boundaries, various burghers and Africans could occupy lands in defiance of the notional title.

The geographical archive of the state as created by the inspection reports thus displayed its idealized settler geography, which was an important but often unrealized source of revenue.[47] That body of information and its administration are important to understand relative to the Cape system because it sought a different sort of legibility. The inspection compilations and deed books either reflected white settlement already *in situ* or put a vague legal form to an existing claim, a practice different in order and accuracy from precise contemporary land surveys in the Cape Colony that prefigured sales and leases of Crown land. The variability between the two systems is not unique to South Africa; in North America, the Virginia (descriptive) and New England (prescriptive) systems of cadastral survey suffered many of the same problems as the ZAR and Cape systems respectively.[48] The search for efficacy in land policy was a common theme of colonial survey and registration, and suggests the struggle between the survey and enumerative modalities of the state.[49] In the South African Republic a highly imperfect enumerative model held sway because it was the only feasible option, but the proponents of precise survey were hardly quiet about the matter.

Parsimony, Territoriality, and Survey, 1864–1899

The most obvious palliative for the issues of imprecision and gross inaccuracy in titling was the employment of land surveyors, as in the Cape Colony.

46 Cartographer and periodic ZAR bureaucrat Friedrich Jeppe, for example, made note of the rough location of inspected farm blocks but did not try to show their theoretical boundaries until later re-inspection with surveyors. See Friedrich Jeppe, "Notes on Some of the Physical and Geological Features of the Transvaal, to Accompany His New Map of the Transvaal and Surrounding Territories," *Journal of the Royal Geographical Society of London* 47 (1877): 217–250 and map. Jeppe's map went through at least five editions between 1877 and 1881, but none changed that detail.

47 James C. Scott, *Seeing Like a State: How Certain Schemes to Improve the Human Condition Have Failed* (New Haven: Yale University Press, 1998), 33.

48 Roger J.P. Kain and Elizabeth Baigent, *The Cadastral Map in the Service of the State* (Chicago: University of Chicago Press, 1992), 269–288.

49 Bernard S. Cohn, *Colonialism and Its Forms of Knowledge: The British in India* (Princeton: Princeton University Press, 1996), 7–8.

In contrast to the uneven, imprecise sketches of inspectors, surveyors framed diagrams with mathematical data, with numerical angle and side measurement (in the latter case using either Cape or, before 1874, Rhenish measure). Ironically, the aesthetic qualities of the surveyors' diagrams were well developed because they lacked quantitative measurements of heights, features, roads, or the like. Artistic rendering, in watercolor or pen shading, was their only method of depicting occupation, foliage, cultivation, and so forth, though the choice of what to include and how to depict it was initially left to the individual surveyor. The resulting symbolic landscapes brought to mind a controlled and stable European countryside, or at least one that offered pleasing familiarity to settlers. Although an admitted surveyor was assumed to be competent and to represent the land faithfully, normal practice was for another surveyor to examine the diagram tendered to ensure its internal and external consistency and completeness. The surveyor was in this way held to a far higher standard of consistency than the inspector despite the abstraction common to both, and government expected the cadasters that survey professionals produced to be usable for the compilation of maps that could encompass far greater claims to territory. For the purposes of the state, then, the surveyor's work was far more useful than that of the inspector, but it was also far more expensive and required a great deal of time from a tiny number of qualified individuals.

For the preternaturally cash-strapped South African Republic, the major source of state wealth was the very land that needed measurement, creating an odd cycle wherein land alienation paid for state functions that included the assay of land for alienation. As a result, the ZAR sought to underwrite its activities with that asset from the 1850s on.[50] A national deeds registry, established in 1866, was critical to handling the increased demand for title and transfer that hitherto had been the province of each district's *landdrost* by centralizing all inspection reports and title deeds. But the only reliable way of guaranteeing the extent and value of the land represented by those deeds was with accurate diagrams, as opposed to the uneven and unreliable inspection reports. Only surveyors trained in European methods and instrumentation could perform this function for the state. That required recruitment outside the Republic, where there was no existing system for training surveyors. In their first attempt to invite a surveyor in 1854, the *Volksraad* in fact went all the way to The Netherlands.[51] Virtually every land surveyor admitted to practice in the ZAR

50 VRB Art. 5, 25 Sep 1857, in *SA Argiefstukke: Transvaal No. 3*, ed. J.H. Breytenbach (Cape Town: Staatsdrukker, 1951), 151.

51 This surveyor, Karel J. de Kok of Rotterdam, purportedly was needed to survey some land near Lydenburg; see Report of J. Stuart, [2] Jun 1855, in *SA Argiefstukke: Transvaal No.2*, ed.

through the South African War was an import, most often from the British Cape or Natal colonies.

In mid-1864, the *Volksraad* approved in principle the general survey of all government-owned lands, and in July and October of that year the *Uitvoerende Raad* (or Executive Council) admitted Robbert Bristow Tatham (from Natal) and Magnus Forssman (from Sweden) respectively as the first *gouvernements landmeters*, or state surveyors.[52] There was no examination standard, but Articles 216 and 217 of the 1858 *Grondwet* (Constitution) required each surveyor to provide evidence of his credentials and to take out a bond of £500 against costs incurred in correcting poor work. The failings of the inspection system were not yet fully evident to the *Volksraad* members, who apparently assumed that boundaries would be self-evident. It is also not clear that they quite understood the distinction between inspection and survey, because they sometimes used the Dutch term *opmeting* in reference to inspections as well as to surveys.

Tatham, as the first admitted surveyor, received the title *gouvernements generale landmeter* (used interchangeably with *landmeter-generaal* or Surveyor-General) on 12 October 1864. At the time no actual description of that office and its duties existed, and there is some evidence that his appointment came in response to his threat to abandon the Transvaal entirely.[53] In March 1865, Tatham nevertheless resigned his position amid a flurry of recriminations about his low pay and lack of work—or his inability to complete it.[54] President

---

J.H. Breytenbach (Cape Town: Staatsdrukker, 1950), 315; J.F.J. van Rensburg, "Die Opmeet en Toeken van Grond in die Oranje-Vrystaat tot 1902," vol. 1 (PhD diss., University of the Free State, 1990), 212–213. De Kok instead set up in the Orange Free State (see note 30) and did not conduct any recorded surveys in the ZAR; see "G.P. Index of Surveyors," unnumbered manuscript volume, Office of the Surveyor-General, Pretoria (hereafter SGO-PTA).

52 VRB Art. 142, 29 Sep 1864, in Breytenbach, *SA Argiefstukke: Transvaal No. 5*, 55; Gouvts. Kennisgeving No. 46, *Z.A.R. Staatscourant* 58, 19 Jul 1864, p. 1; Kennisgeving 99, *Z.A.R. Staatscourant* bijvoegsel, 1 Nov 1864. Tatham and Forssman had only arrived in the Republic earlier that year.

53 R.B. Tatham to *Volksraad*, 22 Aug 1864, R627/64, SS 58, TAB; Gouvts. Kennisgeving No. 88, *Z.A.R. Staatscourant* bijvoegsel, 1 Nov 1864, 1; Tatham to M.W. Pretorius, 20 Sep 1864, R824/64, SS 59, TAB. The equivalence is clear in the government response to his resignation on 15 Mar 1865; see Hendrik van der Linden (Staatsecretaris) to Tatham, 18 Mar 1865, BB730/65, SS 8615, TAB.

54 Tatham to Government, 15 Mar 1865, R302/65, SS 65, TAB. Tatham later begged for his position to be returned, but only his status as Government Surveyor was actually renewed; see Van der Linden to Tatham, 7 Apr 1865, BB863/65, SS 8615, TAB. Tatham returned to Natal sometime in 1865.

M.W. Pretorius personally proposed that the *Volksraad* appoint Forssman as Tatham's replacement in April 1866.[55] Forssman's candidacy benefited from his government connections as well as his personal wealth, which promised fewer complaints about the rate of pay; the only other applicants for the position were two Natal land surveyors who probably shared Tatham's financial concerns.[56]

Despite his inauspicious and brief tenure as Surveyor-General, Tatham did leave something behind. In 1864 he "assisted to draw up for the Volksraad a short Land Beacon's [*sic*] Act as used in the Cape Colony & Free State," partially in response to the destruction of his own markers, which entailed additional uncompensated work.[57] This evolved into the Beacons Law (No. 3 of 1864), given force in March 1866, which set standards for durable property markers, their protection, and the settlement of disputes between owners of properties where markers had been lost or had not actually been erected after inspection, as well as an improved standard tariff for land surveyors.[58] However, the inspection law of 1869 still allowed for beacons to be only approximately (*naar gissing* or literally 'by guess' in the law, a term it also applied to distances and areas) situated in cases where access was difficult, thus enshrining another source of error. Of course the law assumed that the inspection commissions would adhere to the law at all, which does not seem to be the case because it was necessary in 1866 and 1872 to restate the inspectors' responsibility for erecting beacons and pointing them out to landowners.[59] A requirement to erect beacons did not change the actual practice of inspection or the fact that inspectors were not technicians, and it certainly did not assure that the beacons would conform to the spirit of the law.

Law only defined the role, establishment, and duties of the Surveyor-General in 1870. So few sworn surveyors worked in the ZAR by that time—nine at most, including Forssman himself—that the officeholder was in practice first among equals.[60] This did not, of course, stop Forssman from revising instructions for

---

55 VRB Art. 733, 10 Apr 1866, in Breytenbach, *SA Argiefstukke: Transvaal No. 5*, 150. Over time, Forssman has come to be regarded as "the first Surveyor-General of the Transvaal" in a remarkable case of institutional amnesia.

56 R. Osborn to M.W. Pretorius, 26 Apr 1865, R496/65, SS 66, TAB; T.W. Fannin to M.W. Pretorius & *Uitvoerende Raad*, 26 May 1865, R614/65, SS 67, TAB.

57 Tatham to M.W. Pretorius, 20 Sep 1864, 2, R824/64, SS 59, TAB.

58 "Wet No. 3, 1864" in Jeppe and Kotzé, *De Locale Wetten*, 243–250.

59 VRB Arts. 503–507, 22 Mar 1866, in Breytenbach, *S.A. Argiefstukke: Transvaal No. 5*, 125–126; VRB Art. 80, 11–12 Jul 1872, in Jeppe and Kotzé, *De Locale Wetten*, 464.

60 As per *Index der Staatscouranten over de Jaren 1857 t/m 1870* (Pretoria: Staatsdrukkerij, 1897).

inspectors in an effort to alleviate his own headaches over their work. As a professional and a government official with personal connections to President Pretorius, he could be assured of some support in his efforts. With the legal definition of the Surveyor-General's duties in 1870 and the formulation of new instructions for surveyors between 1868 and their publication in 1871, Forssman gained some sway over their admission and their work. The Surveyor-General also acquired the responsibility to "look through and comment upon" inspection reports for the *Uitvoerende Raad*, although they rejected few if any out of hand.[61]

Flawed block inspections could, however, gain the attention of the executive council or the *Volksraad* as a whole later, and draw in the survey technicians. Landowners complained about C.G. Bodenstein's unreliability and overlaps in connection with his 1869 and 1870 inspections, and some were so bad that government demanded payment of his £500 bond and, as we have seen, actually turned to Smit in mid-1872 to retrace and correct all of Bodenstein's work.[62] Smit wisely asked for a surveyor to serve as the third member of his land commission, which was approved but not actually carried out, and in his general damnation of Smit's work in 1876, Forssman's successor in the office of Surveyor-General would include these re-inspections as well.[63] In the Zoutpansberg district, two separate commissions in 1869 and 1871—the latter including a surveyor—covered some of the same land. The result was a mess that in 1875 required a special commission involving three land surveyors and the Surveyor-General to sort out the facts and determine that most of the earlier inspection was so cursory as to have effectively not happened.[64] The only solution at that time, beyond the general postponement of most inspections, was to demand that inspectors retain complete documentation of all statements and activities—a condition that probably arose from the frustration over these very cases—but the basic flaws remained.[65]

---

61 "Wet No. 5, 1870," §4, in Jeppe and Kotzé, *De Locale Wetten*, 371–372.

62 S.P. van der Merwe to *Uitvoerende Raad*, 3 Nov 1869, R1228/69, SS 115, TAB; Petition of G.J. Erasmus and 5 others, 18 Jun 1870, R810/70, SS 124, TAB; VRB Art. 507 (13 Feb 1872), 418, A2075/1, TAB; URB Art. 103, 5 Jun 1872, p. 178, UR 4, TAB.

63 Smit to *Uitvoerende Raad*, 29 Apr 1872, R589/72, SS 143, TAB; URB Art. 56, 22 May 1872, pp. 156–157, UR 4, TAB; URB Art. 71, 2 Aug 1872, pp. 236–237, UR 4, TAB; S. Melvill (Surveyor-General) to N.J.R. Swart (Staatsecretaris), 18 Apr 1876, R820/76, pp. 189–190, SS 207, TAB.

64 "Rapport van de Commissie benoemd door Uitv. Raads Besluit d.d. Mei 10 1875, in Zake de Inspectie van Esterhuyse en Frank in Distrikt Zoutpansberg," 3 Jun 1875, R1239/75, RAK 2794, TAB. See chapter 6 for the specific context of these inspections.

65 URB Art. 122, esp. changes to §11 and 14, 22 May 1875, pp. 318–319, UR 5, TAB.

Those flaws could persist because no obligation existed for burghers to obtain a precise survey, or for government to provide one, whether the landholders occupied ground on freehold or loan tenure. By the 1866 tariff, survey costs for a farm of the standard 3,000 morgen were £19 4s beyond the simple inspection that cost around £1 10s. Given that the *grondbrief* cost a further £1 2s 6d, a proper survey was a luxury for most landholders, if they could even afford to collect their titles.[66] Surveys also had the potential to upset landowners considerably by altering their farms' notional boundaries and extents. A survey that revealed a farm's extent to be greater than the title indicated would entail additional cost and incur a greater tax as well, and some of these farms were found to be two or three times the size on the inspection report when surveyed years later.[67] If the extent were revealed to be smaller, or to exclude certain valuable ground, the value of the farm would diminish without any compensation to the owner—or, in some cases, survey might resolve overlapping claims that would dispossess someone entirely.[68] Beyond the precise survey of political boundaries or new township lots for government, only land companies and mining concerns therefore generated any demand for surveys before the 1880s. Forssman worked alone, and inspected a mere 53 farm diagrams by four surveyors from April 1866 to August 1867, including some that were at least two years old.[69]

Resistance to surveyors' activities on the ground could be a much more difficult matter. Forssman in particular encountered, or at least anticipated, non-mathematical problems. In 1865, 48 petitioners including the local *veldcornet* requested that the *Uitvoerende Raad* bar Forssman's passage "in our midst or over our farms."[70] Their reasoning was unclear, but probably reflected the suspicion that a survey, or perhaps even the surveyor's idle glance, would reveal the true extent of their lands and carry dire consequences. Such reactions were common enough that by the time Forssman met the explorer Thomas Baines a

66 The problem of uncollected titles was eventually bad enough to require a law enforcing their collection on pain of fine or forfeit in 1883; see "Wet No. 4, 1883," in Jeppe and Kotzé, *De Locale Wetten*, 1184–1185.

67 See for example "Case for the Opinion of the Honble the Attorney General," 15 Jul 1879, pp. 86–87, LMG 82, TAB.

68 Wedepohl, "Historical Review," 10.

69 Forssman to M.W. Pretorius, 21 Aug 1867, 1, R861/67, SS 90, TAB. That report also includes a précis of Forssman's work since 1864, which included nearly a thousand small town lots (*erven*) in existing and new towns.

70 F.A. van Jaarsveld, "Die Veldkornet en sy Aandeel," 250. Van Jaarsveld suggests the reason for the hostility to Forssman was affection for the older inspection system; if so, it was a venal one.

few years later, he traveled fairly well-armed.[71] Baines's description suggests that the landowners were the primary danger to the surveyor, reflecting the fact that surveyors most often operated on ground already inspected and occupied by white settlers, or at the very least not in areas of the state actively contested by forces outside the ambit of the ZAR. As so often the case with officials in the cash-strapped republic, Forssman often received payment in land, both for surveying and as Surveyor-General. Given his knowledge of the land, however, Forssman negotiated the maximum benefit from this arrangement by selecting lots with the best future potential, which could not have allayed burghers' suspicions of his motives.[72] During the 1870s A.L. Devenish encountered the same sorts of hostility when dealing with shifted beacons and encroachment, both on other private farms and (more often) on government land. When law required him to survey farms in order to reconcile deeds, Devenish faced accusations of self-interest or conspiracy with the government to defraud the owners.[73]

The expense of surveys alone meant that even land companies sought to avoid laying out too much capital until a return was assured. One strategy in particular was to have a very large block of ground surveyed—usually a company's whole concession—and then to have it inspected as farms by the old process within that discrete parcel. Such a process allowed the holding company some security in what they acquired, although the government included a stipulation for the eventual survey of any farms created in that block as early as 1864.[74] This strategy created areas that became known by their block names—Industria, Moodie's, Harmony, Alexandria, and so forth—under only a single vetted diagram that was not immune to internal disputes when owners subdivided the block later.[75] Nevertheless, the demand for land surveys

---

71 Jane Carruthers, "Cartographical Rivalries: Friedrich Jeppe and the Transvaal," in *Mapping Colonial Conquest: Australia and Southern Africa*, ed. Norman Etherington (Crawley: University of Western Australia, 2007), 113.

72 See, for example, *Bylaag* 74 and *Bylaag* 77 of 1865/66, 15 and 16 Mar 1866 in Breytenbach, *SA Argiefstukke: Transvaal No. 5*, 391–392, 393–394.

73 E.F. Short (Devenish), "Twenty Years in the Transvaal Republic," ed. A.D. Irvine, *Pretoriana* 107 (Nov. 1995): 13.

74 Art. 3 of concession agreement between Alexander McCorkindale (Proprietor, 'New Scotland') and ZAR, in *SA Argiefstukke: Transvaal No. 6*, ed. J.H. Breytenbach (Cape Town: Staatsdrukker, 1957), 254.

75 See, for example, the sale of 80 farms to the Glasgow Company out of the nominally 300-farm McCorkindale block of New Scotland south of Swaziland, which was still a matter of dispute in 1881 between company, estate, and squatters. See testimony of Morrison Barlow, 28 May 1881, in BPP, Transvaal Royal Commission, Report of the Commissioners… Part II, 1882, C.3219, at 57. The confusion created when inspection and block survey

increased throughout the 1870s as land speculation and its value increased in the Transvaal, as it had long before in the Free State, bringing with it an increase in the number and expertise of land surveyors.[76] Despite the absurdities of the inspection system, very little would change without institutional will or adequate funding. As early as 1873 the *Uitvoerende Raad* also reserved the right to demand that a surveyor accompany land commissions, although such employment was so irregular that they renewed the stipulation in government notices in 1875 and 1882.[77] This was poor enough medicine that one *Volksraad* member rose in June 1875 to declare that land commissions should simply be abolished in favor of land surveyors—even though the majority had just voted down a comprehensive survey law.[78]

In the meantime, Forssman had taken other steps to rein in the inspection system. He appointed outspoken surveyor Edwin Griffiths of Nylstroom, in the troublesome Waterberg district, as examiner for inspection plans and surveys on 14 March 1873.[79] Griffiths worked on the backlog of inspection reports, but by the end of the year he was so frustrated with their quality that he penned a long letter to the *Uitvoerende Raad* and the technical-minded new President, Thomas Francois Burgers. In it, Griffiths complained that inspectors did not point out beacons or demanded inordinate fees from landholders for doing so, and in his experience that meant no durable beacons were ever fixed on the majority of farms in the north. The result was that people did not know where their farms were relative to others, and so despite announcements could not attend inspections that might encroach on their land or overlap it entirely. He suggested as a solution that government should render all inspection plans void and require surveys of occupied farms within a certain time on pain of forfeiture. The end result would be growing chains of surveyed blocks based on inspected and occupied land, leaving out other land as open to new claimants.[80] Such a draconian proposal had no chance of becoming law, but it nicely expressed the frustration of state technicians with an illegible landscape and an uncooperative rural population.

---

collided in Waterberg was even worse; see S.B. Melvill (Surveyor-General) to N.J.R. Swart (Acting Colonial Secretary), No. 45 (with report), 26 Apr 1877, LMG 78, TAB.

76 On the explosion of speculation in the Free State, see T.J. Keegan, *Rural Transformations in Industrializing South Africa: The Southern Highveld to 1914* (London: Macmillan, 1987), 4–5. Keegan paints the Transvaal case as significantly different until much later, but survey and transfer records suggest a closer parallel.

77 VRB Art. 741, 7 Jul 1882, in Jeppe and Kotzé, *De Locale Wetten*, 1125.

78 "De Volksraad—Dingsdag, 1 Junij," *De Volksstem*, 26 Jun 1875 (bijvoegsel).

79 Forssman to Swart, 14 Mar 1873, R447/73, SS 155, TAB.

80 Griffiths to the *Uitvoerende Raad*, 12 Jan 1874, R54/74, pp. 94–97, SS 167. TAB.

Forssman supported ideas for general surveys early on, even if he did not fully concur with Griffiths. The government of President Burgers was an ally in efforts to reform inspection and survey, and they obtained standard measures as well as examples of general survey plans from Surveyor-General Abraham de Smidt in Cape Town.[81] Through *De Volksstem*, the newspaper he helped found in 1873, Burgers and his hand-picked editor, Jan Celliers, pointed to the Cape Colony's land survey and registration system as a model despite its own flaws.[82] In November 1873, the President presented his formal proposal for a general survey and a reorganization of the office of the Surveyor-General to the *Uitvoerende Raad*. The proposal included the appointment of a new Surveyor-General, an engineer to carry out the fundamental work of managing the general survey, and a regular stable of sixteen surveyors.[83] The proposal received the council's favor and, with a more specific invocation of a *trigonometrical* survey, figured prominently in Burgers's speech opening the next *Volksraad* session in late September 1874 as a solution to complaints over the moratorium on new inspections and the slowness in dealing with a backlog that promoted unrest among some claimants.[84] Those complaints had gone so far as to prompt *De Volksstem* to mount a defense against "landjobbers" who preferred the "iniquitous system of 'anteekeningen'" to more regular governance.[85] Surveyor and examiner Edwin Griffiths naturally supported the proposal and put forward his own opinion publicly in *De Volksstem*, which was more than happy to print it.[86]

Inertia and an aversion to state expenditure proved impossible to overcome. The general *Volksraad* rejected the general survey bill in October 1874 by a vote of eight to ten, with votes against it from at least two former inspectors; at the start of the next session in May 1875, Burgers declared his reluctance to reintroduce it to them but stated his hope that it might survive in some form.[87] When the *Volksraad* discussed the law again later that month, Burgers was not there to advocate for it, and arguments erupted over the state's liability for bad surveys, the cost, and the public's desire. They finally rejected it again on the

81 A. de Smidt to N.J.R. Swart (Staatsecretaris), 8 Jul 1873, R1445/73, SS 160, TAB; De Smidt to Swart, 28 Oct 1873, R1782/73, SS 162, TAB.

82 "Our Land Registry," *De Volksstem*, 26 Sep 1873.

83 URB Art. 247, 25 Nov 1873, pp. 134–136, UR 5, TAB.

84 "Net zoos jy," letter to the editor, *De Volksstem*, 23 May 1874.

85 Notulen der Verrigtingen van den Hoog-Ed. Achtb. Volksraad der Z.A. Republiek…, 21 Sep 1874, 4, §4, A2075/5, TAB; "The Interregnum Question," *De Volksstem*, 25 Jul 1874.

86 E. Griffiths, Letter to the Editor, *De Volksstem*, 10 Oct 1874.

87 "De Volksraad, Woesdag [*sic*], 14 October," *De Volksstem*, 24 Oct 1874; "The Volksraad, Monday May 3," §12, *De Volksstem*, 8 May 1875.

grounds that its time had not yet arrived, which prompted an accusation from *De Volksstem* that only corrupt, selfish fear of diminishing their own wealth and land could have motivated members to vote against such a public good.[88]

Even without a general survey law, the demand for surveys continued to grow, but that increase did not preclude problems in the work surveyors tendered. Samuel B. Melvill, an English missionary's son who took the post of Surveyor-General after Forssman's death in October 1874, began to demand certificates of beacons' proper erection be tendered with surveys and so made the surveyor responsible as in the Cape Colony, even if inspectors and beacon commissions remained unable to assure landmarks for unsurveyed farms.[89] Surveyors' diagrams were also highly variable in quality and reliability. Melvill engaged in a fair bit of correction of both detail and figure in surveyors' diagrams, and produced a set of regulations for their preparation to assure more reliable data.[90] Nevertheless, in his first full year as Surveyor-General (1875–1876), Melvill reported receiving 167 farm diagrams, of which he found 22 per cent grossly erroneous or wanting enough in detail to be returned to the surveyors.[91] This figure stands out against the 11 per cent that fell afoul of the more stringent standards of the Cape Colony in the same year.[92] Whether this is reflective of insufficient rigor by the surveyors or real uncertainties on the ground is a matter of conjecture, but it was probably a little of both.

Thus when Theophilus Shepstone annexed the ZAR for Britain as the Transvaal Colony in April 1877, the land situation was a pressing concern. The creation and maintenance of boundaries affected security of title, reliability of state revenue, maintenance of peace with chiefs, and economic development generally. Melvill agreed to remain Surveyor-General and did so throughout the British period, but as Administrator, Shepstone faced pressing military issues and put the matter off.[93] The uncertainty of old inspections remained difficult enough that a report on the condition of the Transvaal in August 1878 reported that purchasers of farms were so used to overlapping claims that they

---

88 "De Volksraad, Vrijdag, 28 Mei," *De Volksstem*, 19 Jun 1875 (bijvoegsel); "De Meetwet," *De Volksstem*, 10 Jul 1875.

89 See, e.g., S.B. Melvill to A.L. Devenish, 20 Dec 1875, LMG 78, TAB.

90 Kennisgeving van den Landmeter-Generaal, 4 Nov 1874, in Jeppe and Kotzé, *De Locale Wetten*, 600–602.

91 "Rapport van den Landmeter Generaal over het Jaar eindigent January 31 1876," p. 1, R698/76, SS 206, TAB.

92 CPP G.33-'77, *Report of the Surveyor-General* [for the Year 1876], 56.

93 Melvill to Theophilus Shepstone (Administrator), 12 May 1877, R1539/77, SS 233, TAB.

asked what 'layer' of inspection the title rested upon, and recommended that the problem of land administration be assigned to a competent imperial survey officer.[94] Melvill also appealed directly to Shepstone to resume inspections on a more rigorous model in response to the ongoing receipt of new requests. Melvill argued that because claimants paid no taxes or quitrents, inspection and title were essential to short-term solvency, and the administration had the power to simply require that all commissions include a government land surveyor "or another properly qualified person" to assure some basic degree of precision.[95]

Shepstone's successor as Administrator, W. Owen Lanyon, was far more receptive. Lanyon, however, labored for a year in an 'Acting' capacity under General Garnet Wolseley, his superior in the Colony of Natal, and only truly took control of government in April 1880.[96] Melvill's exertions to bring the Transvaal survey profession in line with its Cape counterpart and promote a general survey of lands found a receptive audience in Lanyon, as did the efforts of David Gill, the Astronomer Royal at the Cape of Good Hope. Gill's plan for a wide-ranging geodetic survey across the entire subcontinent provoked great interest from Lanyon in late 1880, just as it had from Lanyon's ally H. Bartle Frere at the Cape a year before.[97] Lanyon, who felt the Boers to be ignorant and mendacious at best, sought solvency by improving the collection of the taxes and duties that many in the Transvaal had simply disregarded before 1880.[98] A general survey of lands, which required a trigonometrical framework, would go a long way towards that goal and permit the government to sell or lease additional land as well.

---

94 BPP, Further Correspondence Respecting the Affairs of South Africa, 1878, C.2144, at 288. Colonel Charles Warren of the Royal Engineers, who was then in Griqualand West after dealing with land issues there, was the suggested candidate; evidently he was on his way when the war and rising in the Transkei demanded his military services in command of Griqualand West's forces. See Watkin Wynn Williams, *The Life of General Sir Charles Warren G.C.M.G. K.C.B. F.R.S., Colonel Commandant, Royal Engineers* (Oxford: Basil Blackwell, 1941), 101.

95 "Minute: The Surveyor-General to the Honble the Secretary to Govt," 26 Jan 1879, pp. 8–9, LMG 82, TAB.

96 John Laband, *The Transvaal Rebellion: The First Boer War, 1880–1881* (London: Pearson-Longman, 2005), 49.

97 Lanyon to Gill, 30 Sep 1880, pp. 433–434, RGO 15/98, Royal Greenwich Observatory Archives, Cambridge University Library (CUL); Frere to Gill, 20 Sep 1879, pp. 82–83, RGO 15/98, CUL.

98 Bridget Theron-Bushell, "Puppet on an Imperial String? Owen Lanyon in South Africa, 1875–1881" (D.Litt et Phil diss., UNISA, 2002), 177, 194–195, 204, 220–225, 257–258.

By the time Gill's plans reached him, Lanyon and Melvill had in fact already begun to move on the question of survey. Melvill put forward the need for a general survey of Crown lands in March 1880, and within weeks Lanyon put forward the essential points of a proposal to Wolseley.[99] This plan envisioned two parties of surveyors (one to triangulate and one to survey land in the wake of the first), funded with an initial loan of £20,000 that the improved revenue and arrears would repay over time.[100] Wolseley had a fraught relationship with Lanyon, but he had just engaged in wars against African forces on unsurveyed territory, so he endorsed the plan to the Colonial Office in London. At the same time, he urged Lanyon to begin his preparations immediately.[101] Wolseley's handpicked successor in Natal, Major-General George Pomeroy Colley, was even more likely to support Lanyon's aims; after all, he had conducted the first reconnaissance surveys of the western Transkei two decades prior. The inspection system, Lanyon explained to Colley later, grossly dispossessed Africans in particular and so created pointless unrest.[102] The Colonial Office careerists agreed that Lanyon's request fit with the general survey of South Africa that Frere and Gill had already brought before them, but Assistant Under-Secretary R.H. Meade convinced the new Colonial Secretary, Lord Kimberley, to forward the proposal to Colonel Charles Warren of the Royal Engineers for comment.[103]

Warren was a military surveyor and colonial official with extensive experience in South Africa, and he had just returned in 1880 from the post of Administrator in the colony of Griqualand West to head up instruction in surveying at the School of Military Engineering at Chatham.[104] He took less than four days to tender his comments on the matter after receiving the letter from the Colonial Office at the beginning of June 1880. In Warren's opinion, the existing system of inspection was "excellent, cheap, and practical so long as the Government takes care that at least one nominee can be trusted to look to

99 "Memorandum to accompany the Report of the Surveyor-General for the year 1879," 6 Mar 1880, p. 69, LMG 82, TAB.

100 Lanyon to Wolseley (copy), 28 Mar 1880, pp. 499–504, Transvaal No. 7360, CO 291/5, BNA. Lanyon referred to this two-party model as "The Indian system" of survey, although he had no direct experience with India himself.

101 Wolseley to Lanyon (copy), 28 Mar 1880, p. 504, Transvaal No. 7360, CO 291/5, BNA.

102 W.A. Stals, "Die Britse Beleid teenoor en Administrasie van die Swartes in Transvaal, 1877–1881" (D.Phil diss., University of Pretoria, 1985), 444.

103 Memorandum of R.H. Meade (and comment by Lord Kimberley thereupon), 25 May 1880, pp. 491–492, Transvaal No. 7360, CO 291/5, BNA.

104 Williams, *Life of General Sir Charles Warren*, 122–123. Warren had been the choice to handle the abortive settlement of Transvaal land matters in 1878, which may have further affected his selection.

Government interests" and he believed that survey "must follow and not precede the settler."[105] He believed that imposing a survey was impossible because most Transvaal burghers would never accept any survey that they did not initiate, even if the ultimate cost was far higher to them, and so government should abandon the comprehensive survey, but fix up to a hundred points astronomically to support it in the future, and change land law in order to encourage farmers to invite survey. Warren's report had the effect of delaying the implementation of a general survey law Lanyon and his appointed legislative council had already passed, so he wrote to Gill in November to solicit his opinion in order to "combat this absurd proposal."[106] Gill, who had received assurances of support for his survey from Colley in Natal, eagerly pressed his advantage with the telegraphed words "Warren utterly wrong" at the beginning of December 1880.[107]

Gill followed that telegram with a long report full of recommendations that were certainly ambitious and undeniably expensive. He included a familiar litany of the scientific and administrative failings of the old inspection system: many owners could not find their farms; it would be less costly in the long run to perform a precise triangulation and general survey; it could pay for itself over time; it would improve the value of lands by making them findable and limiting overlap; and the finances of the state would require it in time anyhow.[108] Gill and Lanyon shared a dim view of Warren's pragmatic worries.

While Warren's advocacy of the continuation of the old system suggests that he did not fully appreciate the depth of its long-term problems, the aspirations of Gill and Lanyon indicate that they did not appreciate the much more immediate issues of governance and taxation that produced open rebellion and fighting by late December 1880. That conflict led to Colley's death in action at Amajuba in February 1881 and Britain's retrocession of the Transvaal soon after, which rendered the 1880 general survey law a dead letter but did not derail the

---

105 "Colonel Warren's Report on the Proposed Survey of the Transvaal, 1880," 7 Jun 1880, pp. 3, 8, unnumbered document, Pamphlet Collection, NGI; CPP A.104-'80, *Despatches, Correspondence and Papers, &c., relative to Proposed Continuation of the Trigonometrical Survey of the Cape Colony in connection with the Adjacent Territories.*

106 "Survey Law 1880" (draft), RGO 15/98, CUL; Lanyon to Gill, 9 Nov 1880, pp. 460–462, RGO 15/98, CUL.

107 Gill to Lanyon, 19 Oct 1880, pp. 454–457, RGO 15/98, CUL; Gill to Colley, 21 Oct 1880, pp. 460–462, RGO 15/98, CUL; Gill to Lanyon, 7 Dec 1880, p. 465, RGO 15/98, CUL.

108 Gill to Lanyon, 8 Dec 1880, pp. 472–475, RGO 15/98, CUL; "Remarks on Colonel Warren's Report on the Survey of the Transvaal," n.d. [8 Dec 1880], unnumbered document, Pamphlet Collection, NGI.

Cape-Natal part of Gill's scheme. After 1881 survey officials north of the Vaal continued to promote broad reform, but the state settled on an uneven mix of inspections (representing economy and speed) and scientific surveys (representing fidelity and security) to address the egregious unreliability of the old inspection system until financial conditions changed. The old pattern of profiting from position and authority continued almost unabated among the *veldcornetten* and *landdrosten* in rural areas, despite the reform and extension of bureaucracy in Pretoria.[109]

The specialization of central bureaucracy under British colonial government continued through the second republican period of the ZAR, when economic issues demanded ever greater control over and enumeration of the territorial, human, and mineral resources of the state.[110] The ZAR therefore kept its separate Native Affairs department, although its superintendent was usually also the Commandant-General of the military. The negotiations for retrocession included the possibility of maintaining British oversight in the far north, but the Colonial Secretary proposed cleaving off the Zoutpansberg district east of the 30th meridian as a separate 'native territory' outright. The Royal Commission dealing with treaty proposals did not recommend either, but to end conflict over land between white settlers and African households, the settlement included a Native Location Commission that would inspect and set aside lands for certain chiefs under government trust.[111] The terms of the 1881 Pretoria Convention also stipulated that no further inspections or grants of land were to take place in Lydenburg, Waterberg, or Zoutpansberg districts until all the major locations were defined, and that other African purchases of land, also held in government trust, would be permitted.[112]

The Native Location Commission stipulated under the Pretoria Convention of 1881 in fact became a major part of the effort to reconcile flawed inspections and titles with African community landscapes, to the detriment of the latter. Initially, a rotating three-member commission (including one British representative, but no surveyor) was to beacon and inspect chiefdoms' lands to

109 Peter Delius, "Abel Erasmus: Power and Profit in the Eastern Transvaal," in *Putting a Plough to the Ground: Accumulation and Dispossession in Rural South Africa, 1850–1930*, ed. W. Beinart, P. Delius, and S. Trapido (Johannesburg: Ravan, 1986), 184–185.

110 Cohn, *Colonialism and Its Forms of Knowledge*, 8; Scott's discussion of the Stolypin Reforms in Russia are also evocative of this shift; see Scott, *Seeing Like a State*, 39–44.

111 BPP, Report of the Commissioners Appointed to Enquire into and Report Upon All Matters Relating to the Settlement of the Transvaal Territory, Part I, 1882, C.3114, 7, and §139–148 at 29–31.

112 Pretoria Convention, 3 Aug 1881, Arts. 13, 21–22.

forestall expropriation and conflict, effectively by registering them as oversized farms or amalgamations of existing farms, complete with registry numbers that made them addressable and visible to the technicians of the state. The governments initially determined to allot locations to seventeen major chiefdoms.[113] This scheme was related to the indirect, accommodationist system Shepstone had begun to employ in Natal whereby reserves for African societies were defined *in situ* and ruled through chiefs and 'native law,' although its conception by 1881 had weak links to the preservationist ideals of the man himself.[114] The general idea of reserves, with further emendations, was a good fit for recommendations regarding defined African areas as labor reserves that had come out of the 1871 Commission on African Labor and an abortive 1876 law governing African habitation on private farms and in bounded locations, as well as their legal positions, tax obligations, and various other liabilities.[115] Whether it was an effective means of heading off conflict was another matter entirely.

Unlike the model that evolved into the Glen Grey Act in the Cape Colony, the location system that emerged in the Transvaal never envisioned assimilation of Africans into the state or aspired to rule them closely through government headmen. Instead, it augured a sort of indirect rule through a reified chiefly apparatus, headed by the Superintendent of Native Affairs (*Superintendent van*

113 "Notulen der Locatiecommissie," 9 May 1882 art. 8, SN 177, TAB; Bergh, "Grondregte in Suid-Afrika," 45; TKP (unnumbered), *Report by the Commissioner for Native Affairs Relative to the Acquisition and Tenure of Land by Natives in the Transvaal* (Pretoria, 1904), 34; Johan Bergh, "'(To) Reserve to the Native Tribes Such Locations as They May Be Fairly and Equitably Entitled To': The Transvaal Location Commission (1881–1899)," *South African Historical Journal* 54 (2005): 8. The number was later increased, as the ZAR determined that the initial seventeen were meant to be "examples" of qualified groups. No objective measure ever emerged.

114 Jeff Guy, *Theophilus Shepstone and the Forging of Natal* (Pietermaritzburg: University of KwaZulu-Natal Press, 2013), 495–505, 527–529. On location polices, see testimony of T. Shepstone, 12 Sep 1881, in CPP, G.4-'83, *Report and Proceedings with Appendices of the Government Commission on Native Laws and Customs*, §878–929, 1: 55–57; Bridget Theron, "Theophilus Shepstone and the Transvaal Colony, 1877–1879," *Kleio* 34 (2002): 120–121. For a discursively nuanced view of Shepstone's 'system' in Natal and his initial hopes of deeper acculturation and spatial reorganization, see Thomas V. McClendon, *White King, Black Lords: Shepstone and the Colonial State in Natal, South Africa* (Rochester: University of Rochester Press, 2010), 44–46.

115 §42–44 of "Report of the Commission, 7 November 1871," in *'To Make Them Serve…': The 1871 Transvaal Commission on African Labour*, ed. J.S. Bergh and F. Morton (Pretoria: Protea, 2003), 147; "Wet No. 3, 1876," in Jeppe and Kotzé, *De Locale Wetten*, 662–668.

Naturelle Zaken) as manageable fragments on the landscape of the colonial state. The creation of that office also hewed to the principles of an 1873 *Volksraad* resolution to establish a separate department to centralize matters pertaining to Africans and an 1874 proclamation that barred private individuals from purchasing land or making other contracts with African states without approval from Pretoria, so it was easy to incorporate the office into the renewed Republic.[116] The British thus enacted and refined the ZAR's plans for rendering African societies legible, although the results were slow to arrive.

In the renegotiated 1884 London Convention, however, the detailed conditions governing the Native Location Commission and native administration receded to a simple request for the government of the ZAR "faithfully to fulfil the assurances given" in 1880—not in the earlier Convention itself—that they would allow land purchases in trust and that a commission would mark out locations.[117] Inspections in the previously proscribed districts in fact began almost immediately after the London Convention, and the Location Commission carried on without any British input at all and rarely with surveyors on hand. The 'restored' Republic thus became an uneasy amalgam of old and new, with significant consequences for intergroup relations on the notional farms that made up its landscape.

Upon the official resumption of Boer administration in Pretoria in 1881, Melvill had departed for Cape Town and left his capable assistant F.H. (Hendrik) Rissik in the post, but Rissik was not to retain it as he hoped and apparently expected.[118] The appointment fell instead to George Pigot Moodie, a land speculator, railroad company director, and, lastly, land surveyor in special favor with the new governing Triumvirate for his actions on behalf of the Boer cause in London during 1880 and 1881.[119] Moodie proposed revisions to rules for dealing with discrepancies between inspection and survey and restated the need for a surveyor to be part of all future inspection commissions.[120] The

116 Stals, "Britse Beleid," 12; "Proclamatie No. 1705," 14 Dec 1874, in Jeppe and Kotzé, *De Locale Wetten*, 605–606. This did not eliminate the practice, but it did ensure some level of government awareness and approval.

117 London Convention, 27 Feb 1884, Art. XIX.

118 F.H. Rissik to W.E. Bok (Staatsecretaris), 28 Sep 1881, R3921/81, SS 563, TAB. Abraham de Smidt appointed Melvill as Assistant Surveyor-General of the Cape Colony, a post he held until he retired in 1898.

119 Trapido, "Land, Wealth, and Office," 354; A.M. Davey, "Moodie's Road to Fortune," *Pretoriana* 71 (Apr–Dec 1973): 37.

120 G.P. Moodie, "Rapport over de Baken Wet in verband met Volksraad besluit Art 352/81," 25 Apr 1882, pp. 240–244, LMG 83, TAB.

Uitvoerende Raad modified these proposals to include a requirement for a general survey law to be drafted as soon as possible, and the *Volksraad* approved this call in July 1882.[121] Moodie delivered a proposal for a general survey law in January 1883 that required owners to put up corner beacons and relegated surveyors to the task of retracing inspectors' work with more precision and settling the disputes that earlier vagueness hid, but no more.[122]

Moodie was fully aware of the enormous disconnection between titles and actual extents, as well as the great problem of overlap in farm diagrams and inspections, which he described vividly to the Supreme Court in November 1883 while dealing with such a case:

> So long as I have been Surveyor-General I have found that there is a great difference between the survey and the inspection report as to the size of farms. ...The number of [confirmed] farms larger than 3750 [morgen] is 385. There are 119 farms above 5,000 morgen. These farms are in all districts. There are 29 farms over 6,000 morgen; there are 7 confirmed diagrams over 7,000 morgen; one farm of more than 8,000 morgen. ...As a rule, when I surveyed a farm I did not find the beacons erected. ...I have known cases where grondbrieven have been given out for ground that did not exist.[123]

However, Moodie's more muted proposal for a survey law produced nothing that year. Although the Transvaal bureaucracy sought a more reliable geographical archive, the state could not (and those on the land would not) afford it. The land surveyor was meant to limit the excesses of the older system, in order to make it more reliable for producing revenue and title, but only on an irregular basis.

After a six-month vacancy, the post of Surveyor-General passed in August 1884 to the twenty-five-year-old Gideon Retief von Wielligh, a Cape surveyor with specialized training from the relatively new program at the University of the Cape of Good Hope.[124] Von Wielligh was energetic and idealistic, and as a Cape Afrikaner he was especially welcome to the self-consciously Boer

121 URB Art. 251, 5 Jul 1882, p. 233, UR 6, TAB; VRB Art. 744 and 754, 7–8 Jul 1882, in Jeppe and Kotzé, *De Locale Wetten*, 1129.

122 Moodie, "Voorstel van Wet," 26 Jan 1883, R367/83, pp. 126–134, SS 776, TAB.

123 "Bok, N.O., v. Barrett Bros.," *De Volksstem*, 30 Nov 1883.

124 "Plaatselijk en Algemeen," *De Volksstem*, 26 Feb 1884; Von Wielligh to Bok (Staatsecretaris), 15 Aug 1885, R3756/84, SS 908, TAB; C.D. Storrar, *The Four Faces of Fourcade* (Cape Town: Maskew Miller, 1990), 8.

government of the ZAR. Von Wielligh arrived in the Republic only in 1883, but he immediately propounded a rigorous trigonometrical survey of the country for settling questions of land and locality—in short, arranging and correcting the geographical archive of the state, and correcting the poor practices of individuals. His first task was to produce a comprehensive recapitulation of the land situation—grants, inspections, and surveys alike—for the *Volksraad* that may very well have been modeled upon the blue books that laid out a compelling case for survey reform and trigonometrical survey in the Cape Colony in the 1870s, and which were well-known to von Wielligh.[125] In making his case, von Wielligh had an easy target in the bad inspections so rife in the 1870s and before, and he dwelled upon their unsuitability for planning further grants, accurately assaying state resources, or compiling maps. He laid the report before the public in September, and it generated significant public discussion in the following months.[126]

Fortunately, the *Volksraad* already sought a survey law, and von Wielligh overhauled Moodie's earlier proposal to the point of making it unrecognizable. The product he tendered in September was the far-reaching General Survey Law (No. 2) of 1884, which sought to reform the entire survey establishment in the ZAR. As its centerpiece, von Wielligh envisioned a comprehensive trigonometrical survey and a *Staatmeter-Generaal* to coordinate its execution.[127] In the days following the passage of the new law, von Wielligh asked David Gill, the Cape Astronomer Royal, to be the technical advisor to the anticipated project; Gill was all too happy to accept.[128] At the same time, the Surveyor-General moved quickly to issue instructions and to prepare for large-scale surveys of government and private ground. He also heavily revised regulations for land and beacon commissions, in the latter case specifically to prepare for precise survey and, for the first time, to ensure the detection of African settlements on the prospective farms.[129] Von Wielligh anticipated the start of the new survey regime in late May 1885, but it was not to be.[130] In the end financial constraints—including the old resistance of landowners to expensive land surveys, and their inability to pay installment costs that were many times their normal taxes and

---

125 ZPP No. 1-1884, *Rapport van den Landmeter-Generaal.* The Cape of Good Hope Blue Books referred to are CPP G.30-'76 and CPP A.104-'80, respectively.

126 "Correspondence: The Surveyor-General's Report," *De Volksstem*, 14 Nov, 28 Nov, and 19 Dec 1884.

127 "Wet No. 2, 1884," §1, in Jeppe and Kotzé, *De Locale Wetten*, 1281–1282.

128 G.R. von Wielligh to Gill, 1 Dec 1884, p. 2, LMG 84, TAB.

129 "Instructies voor de Baken-Commissie," Gouvernements Kennisgeving No. 369, 22 Dec 1884, in Jeppe and Kotzé, *De Locale Wetten*, 1313, esp. §13.

130 "Rapport van den Landmeter Generaal…1885," pp. 6–11, R4657/85, SS 1103, TAB.

rents—postponed the general survey, and state frugality ruled a trigonometrical survey out completely by 1886.[131]

The collapse of the General Survey Law for lack of funding meant that reforms could only succeed incrementally and synthetically. The need for revision and improvement of poor inspections dating back to the 1860s—or earlier—was still acute, and therefore provided the subject of the Special Commissions Law (No. 3) of 1887 that initially sought to correct the ongoing problems with block surveys in Waterberg district. The critical provisions of that law for geographical questions were the stipulations that a sworn land surveyor was *required* to be a member of such a commission, and that additional commissions could be constituted in other districts, or even in the same district, as needed. This improved inspection regime nevertheless included an encouragement to engage the prior inspectors, who might help the new commission find the old beacons and landmarks.[132] In Nylstroom ward, district Waterberg, surveyor J.E. de Villiers duly sought to appoint a certain Jan Anthonie Smit to replace a departing member of his special commission in February 1888 on these grounds, but the government quietly and wisely denied his request by simply sending someone else.[133]

With the addition of the surveyor and better regulations for beacons, the results of the work were correspondingly more palatable. Even so, the results remained scientifically imprecise and planimetrically inaccurate, as sides still were reckoned in minutes on horseback and corner angles were not determined. These inspections were therefore still less useful than a true survey, even if they were somewhat quicker to execute. The 1888–1889 Special Commission for Middelburg and Lydenburg, for example, conducted 156 inspections over a period of some 11 months—slow compared to the inspections of two decades prior, but faster than detailed surveys.[134] The inspections of the special commissions had only a shadow of the survey's form, but they resolved most disputes and reconciled uncertain boundaries with sufficient precision for title. The general plans were also useful for mapping, but they clearly show how flawed the original inspections were (see map 5.2).

131 Wedepohl, "Historical Review," 11; Von Wielligh to Bok, 3 Dec 1886, p. 63, LMG 84, TAB. See also remarks on von Wielligh's question to government about restarting the survey in 1887; Von Wielligh to Bok, 25 Apr 1887, R2692/87, p. 107, SS 1386, TAB.

132 §3 of "Wet No. 3, 1887," in *De Locale Wetten en Volksraads-Besluiten der Zuid-Afrikaansche Republiek, 1886–1887*, ed. and comp. J.G. Kotzé (Pretoria: J.F. Celliers, 1888), 96.

133 J.E. de Villiers to Bok, 6 Feb 1888, R1343/88, pp. 129–133, SS 1490, TAB; H.S. Lombard and J. de Beer to *Uitvoerende Raad*, 10 Apr 1888, R3276/88, p. 134, SS 1490, TAB.

134 Inspectie Rapporten Middelburg & Lydenburg (voorzitter F.J. Janse van Rensburg), RAK 2744, TAB.

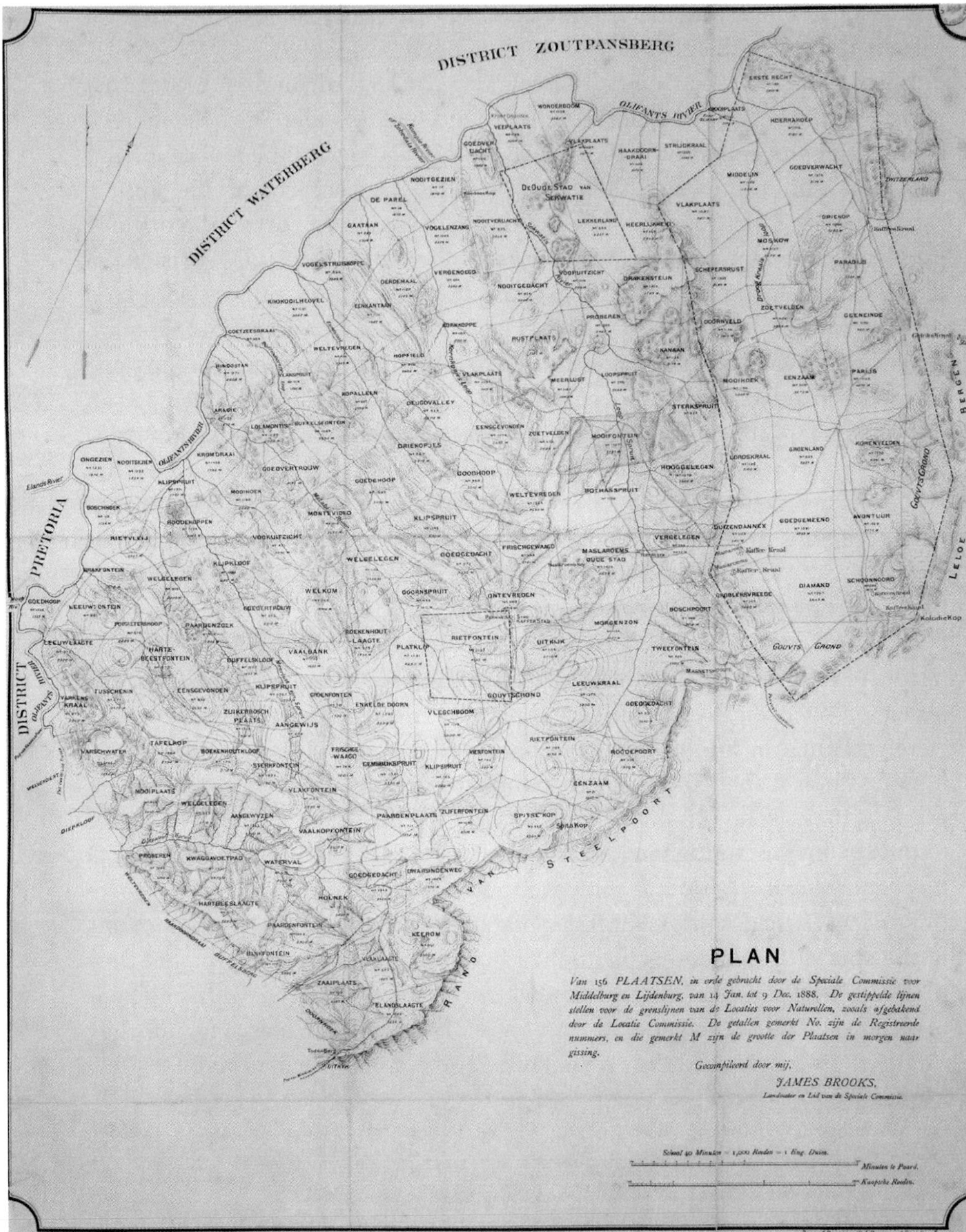

MAP 5.2 *"Plan van 156 Plaatsen, in orde gebracht door de Speciale Commissie voor Middelburg en Lijdenburg, van 14 Jan. tot 9 Dec. 1888," compiled by accompanying surveyor James Brooks. This block was originally inspected and presented as a square grid in 1869 and 1870, and includes on the right the location surveyed for the Pedi regent Kgoloko in 1885 (dotted line).*

SOURCE: MAPS S.2/5L3, TRANSVAAL ARCHIVES DEPOT, NATIONAL ARCHIVES AND RECORDS SERVICE OF SOUTH AFRICA, PRETORIA. RSA STATE COPYRIGHT.

Von Wielligh nevertheless began a strong push for the full execution of the 1884 law in January 1889 in light of changed fiscal circumstances. The government initially let him appoint a highly trained young Cape surveyor, M.C. Vos, to begin working with David Gill to obtain instruments and standards for a geodetic triangulation, master the precise astronomical observations involved, and devise a program of work compatible with the Geodetic Survey.[135] In March, the Surveyor-General asked that President Kruger call for a conference of land surveyors, while urging the preservation of the trigonometrical survey and the requirement that surveyors compute the coordinates of their own diagrams as a bulwark against carelessness.[136] He repeated these feelings with the backing of dozens of land surveyors who attended the general conference in late March, and they produced a petition that he sent forward with his annual report in May as a way to circumvent the few surveyors who disagreed on the trigonometrical survey.[137] In his cultivation of expertise, von Wielligh even invited Sam Melvill, the former Surveyor-General, to take part in the geodetic triangulation.[138] Von Wielligh made further moves in September 1890 to prepare for the general survey of lands that would follow, and assigned surveyors to fifty distinct *meetdistrikten* (survey districts) to begin work.[139] By this time, the Native Location Commission was also employing surveyors regularly, although that was not itself a stipulation of the general survey law. Unfortunately the triangulation would take two years and required an initial cash outlay two and a half times what the existing law provided, which was not acceptable to government.[140]

The second General Survey Law (No. 9) of 1891 that followed this push was in effect a muted revision of the ambitions of the first law. The geodetic survey was no longer a legal requirement, although surveyors were to erect suitable beacons in their *meetdistrikten*; triangulations were generally only required for mineral claims (the Witwatersrand in particular) and the control of block surveys under the 1891 regulations.[141] The most important changes involved

---

135 Von Wielligh to M.C. Vos, 20 Feb 1889, pp. 64–65, LMG 84, TAB.

136 Von Wielligh to S.J.P. Kruger (Staatspresident), 20 Mar 1889, R2632/89, SS 1866, TAB; Von Wielligh to Jurisch, 24 May 1889, pp. 87–88, LMG 84, TAB.

137 "Rapport van den Landmeter Generaal [1888]," 24 May 1889, R4899/89, SS 1933, TAB; Von Wielligh to Gill, 27 Mar 1889, pp. 80–81, LMG 84, TAB.

138 Von Wielligh to C.H.L.M. Jurisch, 24 May 1889, p. 89, LMG 84, TAB.

139 Von Wielligh to W.J. Leyds (Staatsecretaris), 12 Sep 1890, R12527/90 and R12528/90, SS 2515, TAB; "Kennisgeving: Generale Opmeting," 17 Sep 1890, *Staats-courant der Z. A. Republiek* X no. 506 (1890): 889–892.

140 Von Wielligh to Kruger, 27 Jan 1890, pp. 108–109, LMG 84, TAB.

141 "Wet No. 9, 1891, zijnde Wijziging van Wet No. 2, 1884," in *De Locale Wetten en Volksraadsbesluiten der Zuid-Afr. Repupliek...gedurende de Jaren 1890, 1891, 1892, & 1893*, ed. H.J. Coster (Pretoria: Staatsdrukkerij, 1894), §14, 160–161.

modified regulations for beacons, inspections, and surveyors' diagrams, as well as the stipulation that a beacon commission should precede survey to sort out claims and if necessary re-inspect the ground.[142] The relative success of the 1891 survey law, however, may have owed as much to rising land values, greater commerce generally in the country, and the income realized from mineral concessions and monopolies as it did to reconciliation between von Wielligh's ideals and fiscal reality. The setbacks for his scheme of rigorous overall control, however, may have helped to distance his interest in the day-to-day operation of his office; when Johann Rissik took over in 1895, Sam Melvill wrote from Cape Town to congratulate him on an overdue promotion because "you have, as all know, for years been virtually holding the appointment."[143] That lack of general triangulation also meant that the correlation between diagram and ground remained suspect until after the South African War brought the Republic to an end.

The nature of cartography and survey work in the Transvaal changed in the wake of the South African War because the new administration demanded greater legibility and was willing to pay for it. First, it was essential to determine the land that accrued to Africans and Boers alike for purposes of tax assessment and delimitation. Second, putting the Transvaal's cadastral structure on a firmer footing that included a trigonometrical survey would allow the Crown to dispose of land and eliminate nebulous spaces, particularly in the far north, where Africans might support themselves and avoid the labor market. The South African Native Affairs Commission of 1903–1905 (the Lagden Commission) treated spatial questions in its effort to eliminate general inconsistencies in native policy across southern Africa, but the colonial government in Pretoria also reconstituted the Native Location Commission in 1904 in order to settle questions of ownership, resolve overlapping claims between settlers and chiefs, deal with reimbursement, and sometimes create boundaries for the first time.[144] The reorganization of space on the basis of geodetic survey was the long-prized goal of David Gill, who pursued it along with other projects such as the adoption of a single universal South African time zone (realized in

142 Ibid., §16–21, 161.

143 S.B. Melvill to J.F.B. Rissik, 16 Jun 1895, MA1974/761 (Rissik Collection), MuseuMAfricA, Johannesburg.

144 T.R.H. Davenport and C.C. Saunders, *South Africa: A Modern History*, 5th ed. (New York: St. Martin's, 2000), 240–241; Adam Ashforth, *The Politics of Official Discourse in Twentieth-Century South Africa* (Oxford: Clarendon Press, 1990), 35–36; J.H. Cilliers, "Die Administrasie en Benutting van Transvaalse Kroongrond 1900–1906" (D.Litt et Phil diss., UNISA 1978), 153.

1903) and a South African meeting for the British Association for the Advancement of Science (1905).[145]

The imperial government underwrote much of the cost of the geodetic triangulation between 1903 and 1906, but the original plan for secondary and tertiary triangulation as well as a standing topographical survey department fell apart over questions of the colonies' contributions in 1906.[146] The colonies were only willing to underwrite secondary triangulation at that point in time, and only the Free State was surveyed topographically—and then only because of the strong imperial contribution of money and personnel.[147] This selective continuation is not coincidental, because although trigonometrical survey could improve the reckoning of cadastral boundaries, topographical survey had less potential to generate revenue. The notional, numberless topography of the farm diagram was usually adequate for the appropriation and reconfiguration of the broader landscape, but planimetric fidelity struck directly at the colonial treasury.[148] It was necessary not only to refine the cadastral body of the state, but to ensure that it encompassed all people within one set of boundaries, coordinates, and meanings. To do that, the cadastral subdivision of the north needed to be completed, and the accepted spaces for nonwhite ownership and occupancy more clearly defined by its standards.

This is not to imply that the cadastral structure created by surveyors in the Transvaal after 1900 was accurate, only that it promised greater precision. Primary and geodetic triangulations, after all, were of limited use to the survey of land boundaries because the stations were often too far apart and at too high an elevation to be observed by the small instruments and low-lying terrain of the land surveyor. For accuracy the intermediate steps needed to be completed, and in parts of the Transvaal these secondary and tertiary triangulation networks were still under construction as late as the 1950s—by which time some rural black communities had begun to retain their own surveyors.[149]

---

145 Saul Dubow, *A Commonwealth of Knowledge: Science, Sensibility, and White South Africa, 1820–2000* (Oxford: Oxford University Press, 2006), 172–175.

146 Gill to Colonial Secretary, Pretoria, 5 Aug 1902, file 9708/02, CS 121, TAB; W.G. Morris, *Geodetic Survey of South Africa*, vol. 5, *Reports on the Geodetic Survey of the Transvaal and Orange River Colony* (London: HMSO, 1908), xi, xxiii.

147 E.C. Liebenberg, "Mapping British South Africa: The Case of G.S.G.S. 2230," *Imago Mundi* 49 (1997): 134–137.

148 Matthew Edney, "The Irony of Imperial Mapping," in *The Imperial Map: Cartography and the Mastery of Empire*, ed. James R. Akerman (Chicago: University of Chicago Press, 2009), 19.

149 Hofmeyr, *We Spend Our Years as a Tale That Is Told*, 74. Hofmeyr erroneously refers to all of this as primary triangulation, but the point stands.

The lack of a control network meant that surveyors could still relate beacons to other beacons, and triangulate loosely within blocks of farms, but they were building a framework with creeping error the further they moved from a precisely known position. Nevertheless, the colonial presumption was that the performance of a surveyor necessarily conveyed authority to the numerical and graphical depictions of the land so surveyed, just as they did in the Cape Colony.

Aspirational Erasure: Inspection, Survey, and Native Landscapes

Of course, this entire evolutionary process did not happen in a vacuum, but interacted with existing landscapes and the vast majority of people living there. The problems attendant on the inspection system and the complications of precise survey were great enough where settlers could actually take possession, but in places where people already lived in established communities, the situation was more complicated. The development of the landscape in those areas fell into two categories: land where smaller or sparser networks of homesteads existed, and land where larger, more centralized African states held sway. In neither case was there any colonial effort to create small-scale African farming, as there was in the Cape; the ultimate goal was exclusion of African authority over land (sometimes by excluding certain areas themselves) and the subordination of people in a system of either wage or tenant labor. To the government in Pretoria, areas excluded from white settlement were places with retrograde systems of landholding and authority, and the terms 'location' and, later, 'reserve' suggested that they were areas allowed to continue in a kind of primitive splendor or squalor under more indirect rule, perhaps to die out at some future date. In general, the ZAR made official provision for African lands only reluctantly and only for potentially troublesome chiefs or kings.

The inspection system encouraged the effacement of local occupation in two important ways. First, the quick and cursory nature of inspections of lots that were ideally over 25 square kilometers in extent each could easily miss small-scale habitation and would definitely miss transhumance. Second, the things that made land valuable to African farmers and suitable for dense settlement also made it valuable to burghers. The standard instructions issued to the *veldcornetten*, who usually led the commissions, stated that any land containing large African settlements was to be reported to the *landdrost*, who would then decide in consultation with the government whether it might be held for government—a totally subjective measure.[150] Such settlements would have been on or near the best land and sources of water, so there was an incentive to ignore the presence of all but the largest towns and most powerful kings and chiefs. Furthermore, people without such sanction could be characterized as invaders or squatters, and coerced to work or removed by force if necessary once the state had the power to compel them. Of course, some people in that situation voted to move, and the proliferation of farm names that invoke local habitation ('Kafferskraal') or even particular chiefs suggest that a very different landscape existed before the effective white occupation of particular areas, and possibly even afterward.[151]

As one case of erasure, consider the situation of the area that became known as the farm 'Dordrecht,' in the district of Waterberg. The inspection of the farm itself happened in 1869, on an *uittreksel* tendered to Schalk Willem Hendrik Engelbrecht. The director of the inspection was the now-notorious J.A. Smit, who felt confident enough about the land that he deemed it good for wood and water—indeed, he noted precious standing fresh water, which means that he actually saw this plot.[152] The Registrar of Deeds only issued a *grondbrief* on 7 February 1888.[153] The title was based on the initial inspection report, which included a typically vague Smit diagram (see map 5.3) that indicated little more than a cardinal direction. We do not know if the delay in obtaining title owes to the 1877 moratorium on titles in Waterberg pending a general survey law, or to dilatoriness from Engelbrecht, who may not have been in residence or who occupied only a small part and could not afford the expense. The title request may have come solely because of a judgment against Engelbrecht, because it was transferred the next day to the estate of G.J. Verdoorn, which in turn transferred the title on 9 February to the Oceana Transvaal Land Company that held it until December 1889.[154]

Six years after the state awarded the title for the farm to Engelbrecht, a Special Commission set out to re-inspect Smit's blocks of farms in that area.

---

150 VRB, Art. 50, 17 Sep 1858, in Jeppe and Kotzé, *De Locale Wetten*, 97; Delius, *The Land Belongs to Us*, 130.

151 Bergh, "Grondregte in Suid-Afrika," 40–41. It is rarely possible to separate truly abandoned sites from occupied ones based on naming or even inspection, unless a land claim emerges or a later report exists.

152 Inspection report 1171 (244/1888), farm 'Dordrecht,' n.d. Apr 1869, transfer register 201/1888 to 300/1888, Registrar of Deeds, Pretoria (hereafter RA-PTA).

153 *Grondbrief* 244/1888, farm 'Dordrecht,' 7 Feb 1888, transfer register 201/1888 to 300/1888, RA-PTA.

154 Ownership history register LR, entry 578-LR, RA-PTA.

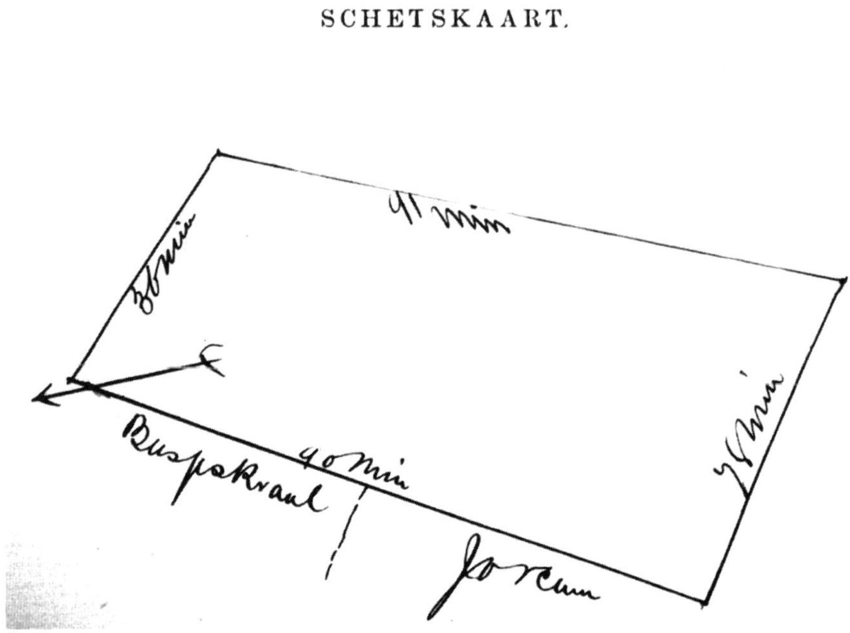

MAP 5.3 *1869 title sketch of farm 'Dordrecht,' copied from the inspection report by the Waterberg land commission under J. A. Smit, April 1869.*
SOURCE: INSPECTION REPORT 1171 (244/1888), "DORDRECHT," N.D. APR 1869, TRANSFER REGISTER 201/1888 TO 300/1888, REGISTRAR OF DEEDS, DEPARTMENT OF RURAL DEVELOPMENT AND LAND REFORM, PRETORIA. RSA STATE COPYRIGHT.

This Commission included American-born government surveyor E.W. Ferguson, and spent October and November 1894 inspecting the hundred or so farms requiring new, non-conflicting diagrams. In the case of Dordrecht, however, the Commission stumbled across a large town—something they apparently did not expect—and they noted its presence on a major road, across from a significant water source that Smit also did not show on his inspection plan (see map 5.4).[155] By then the title had passed to the New Belgium Transvaal Land & Development Company, a speculating organization that owned many farms in the Republic, and who paid to have Ferguson frame a special diagram with numerical angles and sides in the accelerated time-frame of the re-inspections.[156]

155 "Generaal Plan van Plaatsen in het Distrikt Waterberg, Wijken Zwagers Hoek en Nijlstroom Z.A.R.," 1894, Plan GS 10, surveyor E.L. Ferguson, 1894, Office of the Surveyor-General, Pretoria (hereafter SGO-PTA).

156 Diagram 578-LR, Oct-Nov 1894 (framed Apr 1895), SGO-PTA.

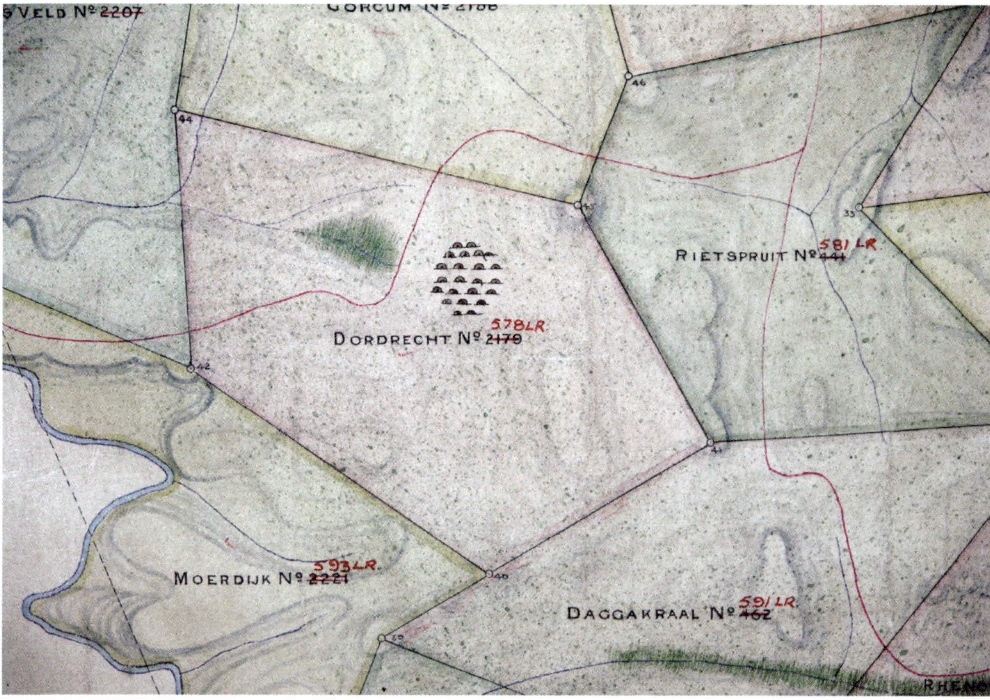

MAP 5.4 *Detail from the Special Commission re-inspection of the block of farms including 'Dordrecht,' 1894. Note the vast difference in geometry from the original sketch of 1869 (5.3), as well as presence of the large town cluster.*

SOURCE: E. W. FERGUSON, "GENERAAL PLAN VAN PLAATSEN IN HET DISTRIKT WATERBERG, WIJKEN ZWAGERS HOEK EN NIJLSTROOM Z.A.R.," 1894, PLAN GS 10, OFFICE OF THE SURVEYOR GENERAL, POLOKWANE. RSA STATE COPYRIGHT.

Who were the inhabitants of Dordrecht, whose town Ferguson so diligently noted? The short answer is that there is no official record of their identity or their fate. The state records of the area are fragmentary, and today the property is part of the Waterberg Biosphere Reserve conservation area. The existence of at least one land restitution claim including the farm suggests that at least some of the earlier inhabitants were still on the farm following the Natives Land Act of 1913, when it was excluded from the areas released for black occupancy. The land company, however, sold the farm, with around sixty others, to English food and shipping magnates William and Edmund Vestey in December of that year for £40,000.[157] The Vesteys, who had acquired large parcels of land around the world, most likely grazed beef cattle for their global operations

157 See transfer 10856/1913 across farms 2164–2223, RAK 3060, TAB.

there and employed conveniently-located tenant labor in the process.[158] In any case, none of the various owners were residents themselves, so the local conditions remain unclear. The government detached a section of the farm for state use in 1939, but it was not the section that included the town and its occupants, which is still in private hands today as part of a lodge and nature preserve.

We know little about the land's conditions or circumstances from the archives, only that the majority of the plot has remained private property ever since it entered the Deeds Registry in 1888.[159] This process repeated many times around the Transvaal and beyond, sometimes with clear written or oral evidence trails, but often without. Silent dispossession had a ready ally in laws that denied Africans the right to contest such actions in court at the time and, arguably, much more recent ones that disallow direct claims predating 1913.[160] Dispossession also had help from the fact that the title deeds' transfer and even their mere existence were rarely known to the people living on the land in question, and who only found out that some distant authority nominally had titled it away when the new legal owner turned up.

Surveyors occasionally, however, reported in detail upon the large towns they encountered on surveys or re-inspections, especially where no prior private claims were involved. August Bechtle, for example, noted one such settlement in his 1888 survey of the 'Kaapsche Blok' for small farms in the Lydenburg district of the eastern Transvaal near the Swaziland border. Bechtle's report, which the Surveyor-General forwarded to the Superintendent of Native Affairs, led to the government's assumption of the farm's title in trust as a reserve.[161] But even in this case of recognition, the exception proves the rule. For the reserved farm, Bechtle clearly identified the chief in question (Matsafeni or 'Mataffin,' chief of the Mdluli Swati), but the general plan he produced with his partner Charles Marais notes many other 'kraals' that received no such reserve status or even occasioned comment from the surveyors.[162] Even such notation was not proof against later dispossession, and Matsafeni was not powerful enough to warrant special consideration in perpetuity. The presence of the Mdluli

---

158 Michael Woods, "The Elite Countryside: Shifting Rural Geographies of the Transnational Super-Rich," in *Geographies of the Super-Rich*, ed. Iain Hay (Cheltenham: Edward Elgar, 2013): 125.

159 Ownership history register LR, entry 578-LR, RA-PTA.

160 Mike Akomaye Yanou, "The 1913 Cut-off Date for Restitution of Dispossessed Land in South Africa: A Critical Appraisal," *Africa Development* (*Afrique et Developpment*) 31, no. 3 (2006): 178–180.

161 Bechtle to von Wielligh 20 Mar 1888, and note of the Superintendent for Native Affairs thereupon, 24 Apr 1888, 58–59, LMG 12, TAB.

162 "Plan van een gedeelte der Kaapschen Goudvelden," Mar 1889, Plan M56, sheet 2, SGO-PTA. As elsewhere, I prefer the identifier 'Swati' to the older 'Swazi.'

settlement amidst a large block of titled farms meant that it was not included among the approved land for black occupation in 1913. The government expropriated the land in 1920 and sold it to a large agricultural concern in 1921, a situation that 6,000 descendants of the Mdluli clan only reversed through the land restitution process in 2003.[163]

This disconnection between people on the land and its depiction in the archive does not mean that people remained ignorant of the Republic's system of titling and did not try to work within or around it, just as Africans did in the Cape. Although *Volksraad* resolutions in 1855 and 1857 had prohibited private African ownership of fixed property, people throughout the Transvaal sought to purchase established and defined *plaatsen* from burghers.[164] Some groups of prosperous Africans began requesting the right to purchase land privately as early as 1868, and these requests increased over time, although only one case resulted in an actual title being issued.[165] During and after the British period, some titles rested in trust with the Superintendent of Native Affairs, and any new private purchases of land by Africans that governments allowed fell into this category.[166] Others purchased land in trust of private individuals and missionaries to circumvent the legal ban on African ownership or simply made private rental arrangements, phenomena that complicated colonial attempts to divine and alter African settlement patterns after 1900.[167] The case of Edward Tsewu in 1905 (see chapter 8) would change the official prohibition, but only temporarily.

In areas abutting (or within) the lands of more powerful chiefdoms distant from Pretoria, such partial or total erasure was impossible. In those cases, local expedient dictated the form, if not the legal technicalities, of relations over land. An 1853 *Volksraad* resolution that chiefs' lands were loan farms occupied at the pleasure of the government, and article 7 of the 1858 *Grondwet* stating that all 'open lands' belonged to the state, had little meaning in these cases.[168]

---

163 Mpumalanga Regional Land Claims Commission, "Advisory: Celebration of Settlement of Mdluli Land Claim, 13 Dec 2003," 9 Dec 2003, accessed 14 Aug 2014, http://www.gov.za/speeches/2003/03120915461001.htm.

164 VRB Art. 235, *Bylaag* 1, 16 Oct 1857, in Breytenbach, *SA Argiefstukke: Transvaal No. 3*, 468.

165 See minutes of *Volksraad* meeting, 5 Oct 1868, in *S. A. Argiefstukke: Transvaal No. 8*, ed. D.C. Joubert (Pretoria: Staatsdrukker, 1989), 28; Stals, "Kwessie van Naturelle-eiendomsreg," 6–7.

166 TKP (unnumbered), *Acquisition and Tenure of Land by Natives in the Transvaal*, 5.

167 See *South African Native Affairs Commission 1903–5*, vol. IV (Cape Town: Cape Times, 1904), §42,095–§42,129, 649–652, for statements by headmen in this regard; see also TKP (unnumbered), *Acquisition and Tenure of Land by Natives in the Transvaal*, 21–33, 66–69, 96–105, for the results of postwar investigations.

168 VRB Art. 124, 28 Nov 1853, in Breytenbach, *SA Argiefstukke: Transvaal No. 2*, 190 (and Bylaag 103/1853, 466–468); Bergh, "Transvaal Location Commission," 3.

These areas were nevertheless not immune to the rush for land in the late 1860s and they, too, encountered the inspection and survey apparatus. Claims for farms, the issue of *uittreksels*, and even a few inspections had happened well within African kingdoms and even Portuguese territory on the lowveld by the 1850s.[169] These claims went ahead despite a few cases (for example, that of the Kopa under Boleu [Maleo] in the early 1860s) where the early Republic had tried to separate African lands to avoid just this problem.[170] Across much of the eastern Transvaal, it was difficult by the 1870s to find a spot where an *uittreksel* or even a *grondbrief* had not been written or could not somehow be applied.[171] The northern districts of Zoutpansberg and Waterberg avoided this situation only by being even worse, but in the eastern lowveld problems of inspection, land speculation, survey, conflict, and native policy also intersected.

One particularly telling example is the inspection and award of farms in the heart of the Pedi polity under Sekhukhune in 1870. *Veldcornet* S.P. Botha in Lydenburg oversaw a block of 113 inspections between 27 July and 26 August 1870 that extended eastward into the fertile valley just west of the Lolu Mountains.[172] Although Botha's inspections were better than his Waterberg counterparts in that many of his sketches show neighboring lands and describe beacons, their quality and detail broke down as he approached the lands under the Lolu Mountains where Sekhukhune's people lived. Many of the *uittreksels* for those easterly lands had in fact been issued only within the previous year, and the detail on the reports diminishes greatly there. The most jarring feature of the reports, however, is the lack of any note of extant settlement, save on a few farms reserved specially for government. It is extremely unlikely that only those few spots were occupied, given that at least 20,000 households were there by 1905 and people cultivated heavily in the area. Other cartographic evidence suggested settlements and regular agriculture and grazing in the area, if only by the presence of forts, streams, and roads.[173]

The likelihood is that homesteads were either not noticed or not noted, as they might have jeopardized the award of such valuable land. Either

---

169 Delius, *The Land Belongs to Us*, 132–133; Erasmus, "Re-thinking the Great Trek," 73.

170 Theodor Wangemann, *Maléo en Sekoekoeni*, trans. J.F.W. Grosskopf (Cape Town: Van Riebeeck Society, 1957 [1868]), 39. This effort was clearly unsuccessful, given that Boer *commandos* destroyed Kopa power in 1864.

171 Erasmus, "Re-thinking the Great Trek," 63.

172 Inspectie Rapporten Lydenburg (voorzitter S. P. Botha), RAK 2795/8, TAB.

173 See sketch map of the Pedi heartland, Maps 3/1164, TAB; "Chief of Staff's Journal of the Military Operations in the Transvaal, 1879," p. 86, CO 291/9, BNA, reproducing the (now lost) drawing by A. Merensky sent to Owen Lanyon; see A. Merensky to Administrator, 24 Jun 1879, R2165/79, SS 348, TAB.

option gives added merit to Delius's suggestion that land speculators were anticipating the destruction of Pedi power.[174] It also explains the anger Sekhukhune displayed over those inspections, which titled land away from him "without his knowledge and against his will."[175] Of the 22 farms inspected for private owners within the area later adjudged to be the Pedi location, the majority were sold by the grantees to land companies or private speculators. Only three farms remained in the hands of their original title recipient, and twelve were transferred to land agents or other purchasers within six months—some several times within a matter of days of the deed's issuance.[176] It is clear that the bulk of this land was never actively used or intended for use by those who laid claim to it, although those owners would welcome rents or generous compensation later. British officials after 1877 themselves recognized the role of such careless or malicious inspections and claims in destabilizing the situation with the Pedi, but to no avail.[177] In upholding the geographical archive, British and Boer governments helped to set themselves on a path that led to protracted war in 1876 that only ended with the destruction of Sekhukhune's independent power in November 1879.

The final orientation, location, and extent of the farms inspected in 1870 were only determined in 1888, after the work of a special commission appointed for that purpose under Law 3 of 1887. That commission faced the difficult task of charting Botha's unmarked farms against the location that had been inspected in the meantime for the late Sekhukhune. Kgoloko, the regent over Sekhukhune's successor, had requested the Location Commission visit in response to the resumption of private farm inspections for speculators in Lydenburg in 1884 and the danger of further loss of land and liability for rents.[178] The Location Commission that came on 29 May 1885, however, had no idea where Botha's inspected farms were, and their initial intent to mark off

174 Delius, *The Land Belongs to Us*, 134.

175 A. Merensky to the *Uitvoerende Raad* (copy), 24 Nov 1873, vol. 8, p. 122, AAS 123 (Shepstone Papers), UNISA Library, Pretoria.

176 Data on these farms was obtained from the publicly accessible Transfer Registers at the office of the Registrar of Deeds, Pretoria, and the office copies of the *grondbrieven* maintained in the basement store there. The transfer volumes unfortunately have no numerical identifiers for citation.

177 Delius, *The Land Belongs to Us*, 130–131, 134; BPP, Further Correspondence Respecting the Affairs of South Africa, 1879, C.2316, at 29–30.

178 J.A. Erasmus to P.J. Joubert (Superintendent of Native Affairs), 23 Aug 1884 and 8 Nov 1884, R4507/84, SS 985, TAB. The response from government recorded on the latter missive was that the Location Commission "zal alles regt maken" (shall make everything right). Surveyors almost never accompanied these early commissions.

nine, then thirteen, farms for Kgoloko produced a much larger area.[179] Some farms seemed to be included in part, and others in their entirety, but there is little evidence that the commission found concordance with whatever established farm beacons existed. Existing land law obliged the government to buy any included private land from its owners, so this was a matter of some confusion, and some of the transfers were not completed until well after 1900.[180] In 1895 the *Uitvoerende Raad* instructed the Superintendent of Natives to modify location boundaries to match cadastral ones, presumably to simplify compensation claims, limit the number of claimants, and effectively define the location as negative space without the survey of additional subdivisions.[181] The ZAR remained silent throughout on the question of Pedi who lived outside of this area, expecting them to hew to the requirements of labor tenants or migrant workers on private farms despite their allegiance to the heirs of Sekhukhune, who had their own internal conflicts.

The geographical archive therefore served to allow the appropriation of land as an idea preparatory to its appropriation in fact—a clear case of the map prefiguring the territory, though on a different scale from the maps that historians usually considered in that light. The creation of locations under various authorities after 1881 was therefore a conceptual retrocession and recognition of limitations, but it was also an important improvement of the legible detail in the archive and a more meaningful schema for reorganizing the landscape. In the far north and northeast, however, larger African populations and even more extensive African state power made the initial phase of clandestine expropriation by inspection more difficult. That greater power, maintained over a longer period, complicated the state's power to rationalize the landscape in unexpected ways.

---

179 "Notulen der Locatiecommissie," 30 May 1885 art. 47, SN 177, TAB.

180 Schoonord 894 (362-KS) was transferred to government in 1904; title to Eerste Regt 1189 (502-KS) was only finally obtained in 1911. See file NA1722/02, SNA 49, TAB; See also File 3487, LDE 307, South African Archives, Pretoria (hereafter SAB).

181 URB Art. 756, 5 Nov 1895, in TKP (unnumbered), *Translations of the Resolutions of the Executive Council of the Late South African Republic, 1895* (Pretoria, 1903), 52.

CHAPTER 6

"Before, the Entire Land Was Ramabulana"

In light of the ramshackle system of land titling and its problems in the South African Republic (ZAR), conflict between this Boer government, its settler populations, and their African counterparts over issues of boundaries and ownership is not surprising. In cases like the Pedi example in Chapter 5, the notional titling of land already thick with grazing herds and African cultivation contributed heavily, if not decisively, to open conflict and the uprooting of title. Measures from 1874 onward sought to place some kind of wall between untrammeled settler acquisitiveness and relations with African polities. But their purpose was more programmatic than pacifistic, because the *Volksraad* still sought to establish settler control over the landscape, and the bureaucracy of the ZAR increasingly pushed to define its boundaries, contents, values, and restrictions. That two-pronged drive to prescribe and enumerate became, in light of growing state wealth after 1886 and pressure for land, the vehicle for a new phase of conflict over land, livelihoods, and authority with kingdoms and chiefdoms that before had considered Pretoria's reach about as notional as it truly was. There were many such states across the districts far from Pretoria, but few had as long or convoluted a history with the Boers as the western Venda kingdom of Ha Ramabulana (see map 6.1), which was arguably the strongest single independent power in the mountains of the northern Transvaal between the first Boers' visit in 1836 and its military defeat in late 1898.[1] The kings of Ha Ramabulana, from Ramabulana himself (r. 1836–1864) to his son Makhado (r. 1864–1895) and grandson Mphephu I (r. 1896–1925), were careful yet assertive in making their own claims to land, and the landscape of Venda communities under them was resilient yet responsive to influences from the south.

As with almost every other activity of the ZAR, the incremental developments in the Republic's system of land inspection and survey rarely had direct meaning for Ha Ramabulana and the other Venda polities in the region. The

1 I employ the name Ha Ramabulana (Ramabulana's country) to focus on change from his era forward, and to define the house's potential reach to clients instead of a particular piece of land. It is not a territorial term that people used regularly or exclusively, but it is consistent with other houses' territorial labels (e.g., Ha Tshivhase). The term Boer here refers primarily to the agrarian white settler population of South African birth who spoke proto-Afrikaans dialects, although their interests often shared little beyond that.

 | DOI 10.1163/9789004282292_007

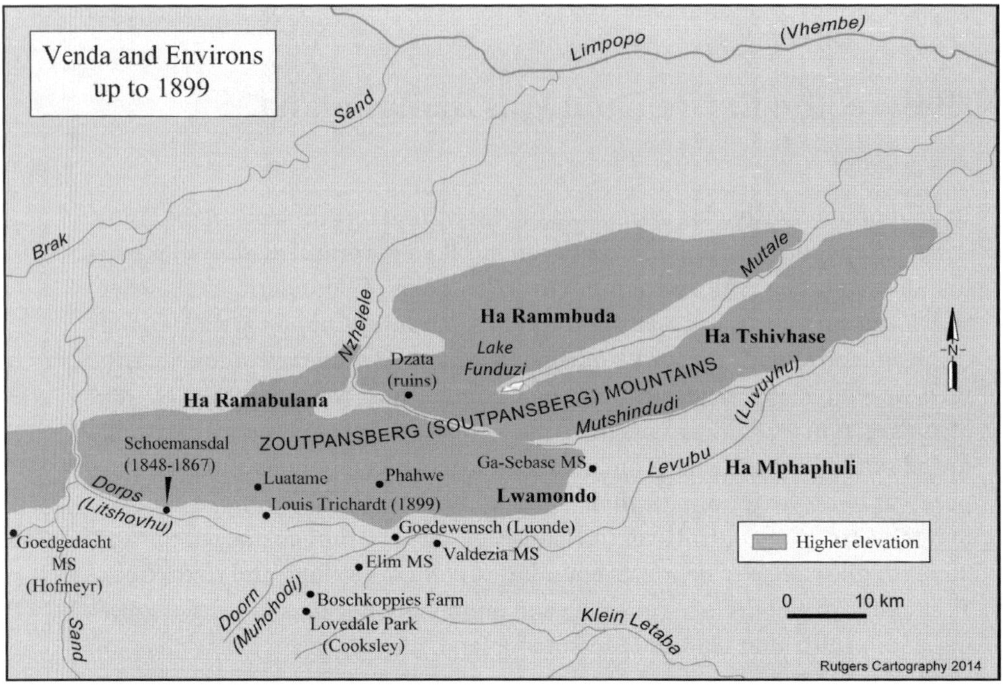

MAP 6.1 *Ha Ramabulana and its neighbors.*

Ramabulanas ejected most Boer presence from the area around the mountains in the 1860s, and kept all agents of external authority, whether ZAR officials or missionaries, at arm's length. That limited state power meant that virtually the entire northern portion of the vast Zoutpansberg district (including the Soutpansberg Mountains themselves) formed a vast and persistent gap in the various archives in Pretoria that extended beyond the lifespan of the ZAR itself. There were few scientific surveys, positional measurements, route sketches, or even inspection drawings of the area before 1900, and those that existed came from missionaries or the handful of explorers who generally avoided the central mountains. Together with a lack of effective authority from Pretoria, general Venda wariness assured that very little reliable data about the landscape was initially available to the ZAR or to the British.

The poor state of European geographical knowledge of the northern Zoutpansberg was clearly visible on the maps that German-born cartographer Friedrich Jeppe produced between 1867 and 1899. Jeppe arguably did more than any other individual to compile maps from the geographical archive and correct them during the era between 1864 and 1899, and his status as a perennial bureaucrat in the various governments of the Transvaal—including the office of the

MAP 6.2 *Detail from F. Jeppe and A. Merensky, "Original Map of the Transvaal or South-African Republic" (Gotha, 1868). Original scale 1:1,850,000. Schoemansdal (Zoutpansberg) is marked as having "100 Inhabitants." The unknown Venda hinterland is extremely compressed and the Ramabulana presence is the only one evident here Although the map went to Gotha after the evacuation of Schoemansdal, Jeppe did not remove the marks of ZAR authority there.*
SOURCE: ORIGINAL COPY IN THE AUTHOR'S COLLECTION.

Surveyor-General—assured him unparalleled access.[2] But his maps naturally reproduced archival lacunae, and nowhere was that process more evident than along the Limpopo River. Jeppe compiled his maps directly from the Surveyor-General and Registrar of Deeds as well as material published in the geographical journals of Europe and sometimes directly from travelers, and his depiction of the area north of the Soutpansberg range changed with each new production. The first map, which Jeppe produced in tandem with German missionary Alexander Merensky in 1868, collapsed the considerable distance between the mountins and the Limpopo river entirely (see map 6.2).[3] Jeppe's major revision of 1875, published in London along with a description in 1877 and with minor alterations until 1881, had the benefit of latitude measurements. But it also stretched the area's features based on sparse verbal descriptions

2 For a brief synopsis of Jeppe's career, see Jane Carruthers, "Cartographical Rivalries: Friedrich Jeppe and the Transvaal," in *Mapping Colonial Conquest: Australia and Southern Africa,* ed. Norman Etherington (Crawley: University of Western Australia, 2007), 108–121.

3 Friedrich Jeppe, "Die Transvaal'sche oder Süd-Afrikaansche Republik," in *Petermanns Geographischen Mittheilungen, Ergänzungsheft* 24 (1868): 1–15, and map with A. Merensky. For the general issue of the map's distortion of geography, see W.C. Watson, "The Jeppe-Merensky Map of the Transvaal 1:1,850,000—1868," *South African Survey Journal* 11, no. 5 (1968): 16–17.

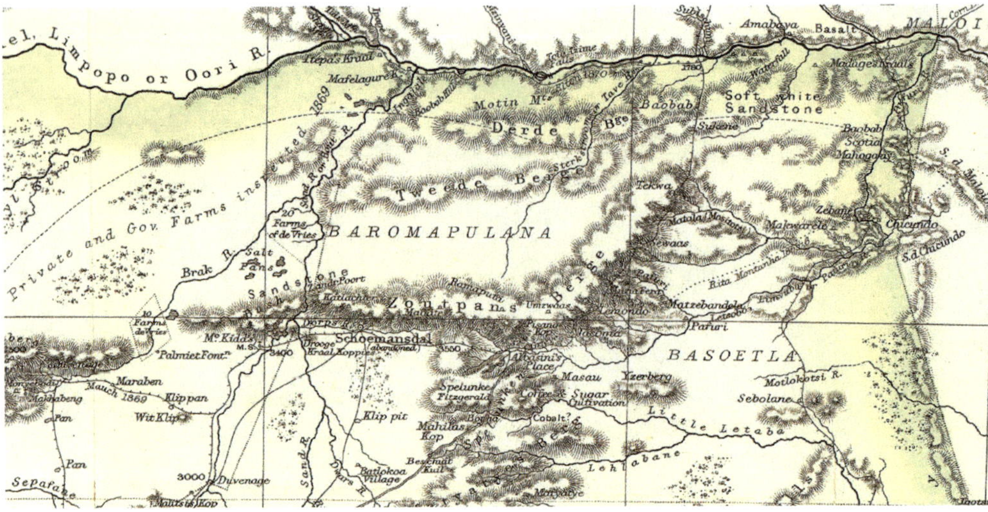

MAP 6.3 *Detail from F. Jeppe "Map of the Transvaal or S. A. Republic and Surrounding Territories" (London, 1877). Original scale 1:1,850,000. Note the "Private and Gov Farms inspected" area label in Waterberg district, as well as the growth of latitudinal distance to reflect the newer measurements of travelers. The elaboration of detail however shows their movement around, not through, Ramabulana areas.*
SOURCE: ORIGINAL COPY IN THE AUTHOR'S COLLECTION.

so as to fill the unknown territory between the river and the southern mountains (see map 6.3).[4]

The lack of information certainly bothered Jeppe, who had an insatiable drive to absorb all available information in compiling maps. For example, he delayed his large map of 1888 for a year in order to redraw the entire Zoutpansberg district and incorporate new data. That data included sketch maps and route measurements from the Swiss missionary Henri Berthoud of Valdezia southeast of the mountains, as well as general plans from re-inspection commissions then in the region that he, working closely with the Surveyor-General in Pretoria, could see before anyone else.[5] The result was a hybrid of topography, cadastral territory, and social topology that was visibly uneven.

4 Friedrich Jeppe, "Notes on Some of the Physical and Geological Features of the Transvaal, to Accompany His New Map of the Transvaal and Surrounding Territories," *Journal of the Royal Geographical Society of London* 47 (1877): 217–250 and map.

5 Friedrich Jeppe to Henri Berthoud, 27 Jan 1890, 1, Berthoud Papers, A1529, TAB; G.R. von Wielligh (Surveyor-General) to W.E. Bok (Staatsecretaris), 24 Jul 1889, R7517/89, pp. 105, 114, SS 2012, TAB. On Henri Berthoud as the "premier explorer" in the area, see Patrick Harries, *Butterflies and Barbarians: Swiss Missionaries and Systems of Knowledge in South-East Africa* (Oxford: James Currey, 2007), 114; see also H. Berthoud, *Carte des Districts du Zoutpansberg et de Lorenzo Marquez* (Geneva: F. Noverraz & Fils, 1886). The commissions in question were

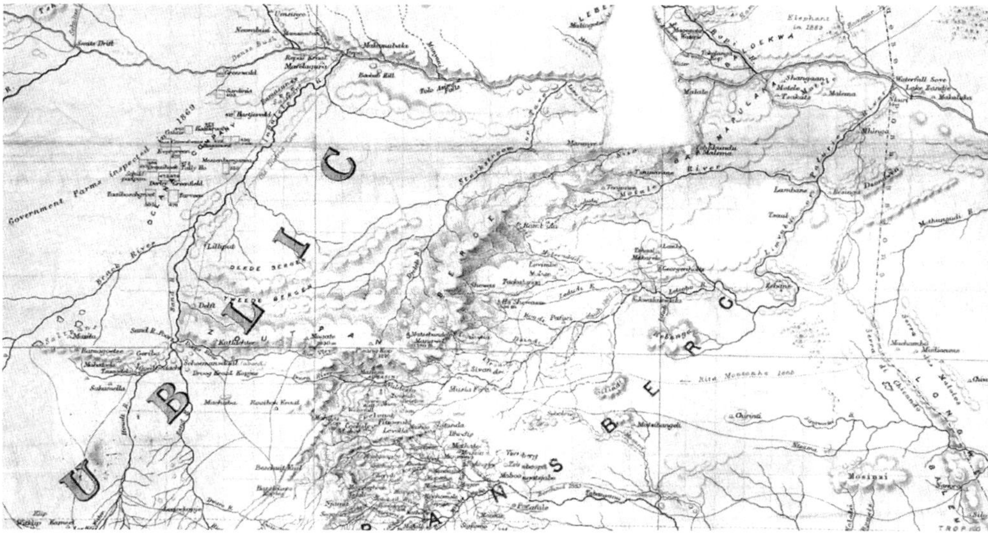

MAP 6.4 *Detail from Jeppe, "Map of the Transvaal or S. A. Republic and Surrounding Territories" (London, 1889), sheet 2. Original scale 1:1,000,000. The isolated cadasters (squares) with farm names in the upper left and a few other spots indicate the few plots in that region which had careful survey diagrams on file in Pretoria at the time. All others were so poorly inspected that Jeppe could include only a note of their presence as he had in 1877. Ethnonyms however diminished visibly, particularly with the addition of material from local informants via the Swiss and German missionaries in the region.*

SOURCE: TAB MAPS 3/1105, TRANSVAAL ARCHIVES DEPOT, NATIONAL ARCHIVES AND RECORDS SERVICE OF SOUTH AFRICA, PRETORIA. RSA STATE COPYRIGHT.

Combined with the novelty of longitude measurements on the Highveld, this information produced a significant lateral correction and new detail—but almost entirely south of the mountains (see map 6.4). Jeppe's map of the Zoutpansberg goldfields in 1893 put the mountains on the northern edge of the map itself and so sidestepped the issue entirely. Even his posthumous map of 1899, the most precise depiction of the Transvaal available anywhere at that time, depicts the northeastern Zoutpansberg district as a vast area with deformed hill-shading and fictitious rivercourses, in contrast to the data that survived the construction process from earlier maps and resurveys (see map 6.5).[6] The lack of imagery such as maps, and scientific edifices such

presumably the three accompanied by surveyors A.L. Devenish and F.H. Rissik in 1888 and 1889; see "Proclamaties aangande de verschillende Speciale Commissies," R1667/96, p. 3, SS 5248, TAB. Jeppe became Chief Draughtsman and Compiler in winter 1889.

6 Fred Jeppe and C.F.W. Jeppe, *Map of the Transvaal or S.A. Republic* (Winterthur: J. Schlumpf, 1899).

MAP 6.5 *Detail from F. Jeppe & C. F. W. Jeppe, "Jeppe's Map of the Transvaal or S. A. Republic and Surrounding Territories" (Winterthur: J. Schlumpf, 1899), Dutch edition, sheets 2 & 3. Original scale 1:476,000. Cadastral plans became more useful sources following on the Occupation Law of 1886, the Special Commissions Law of 1887, and the revised General Survey Law of 1891, which together made this massive six-sheet compilation possible. The Jeppes, father and son, built this map from the ground up and eliminated many African ethnographic or political labels present in earlier maps. Venda hinterland data however remains unreliable, reflecting the active contest there.*
SOURCE: DIGITAL SCAN OF ORIGINAL COPY AT THE CHIEF DIRECTORATE: NATIONAL GEO-SPATIAL INFORMATION, DEPARTMENT OF RURAL DEVELOPMENT AND LAND REFORM, MOWBRAY. RSA STATE COPYRIGHT.

as beacons, meant that Venda territory existed as a nebulous subtraction, and within Jeppe's presentation of the geographical archive, it was "unsurveyed and uninspected government lands" awaiting disposal.[7] Most other depictions of the region before 1900 drew from Jeppe or the same body of sources, and so repeated or even embellished upon his misrepresentations.

In keeping with Berthoud's importance to Jeppe, most of the detailed textual descriptions of the area before 1900 also come from missionaries. Their efforts to understand Venda landscapes and people evolved over time to create an image that historian Alan Kirkaldy describes as an intertwined environmental and human 'darkness'—dense forest with sickness, dangerous wildlife, idolatrous people, and even base savagery—in contrast to the 'light'

7 That text in fact appears across the Venda hinterland on the 1899 map, sheets 2 & 3,in Dutch or English depending on the edition (see map 6.5).

of familiar, visible landscapes, as well as the Christianity and civilization the missionaries propounded.[8] This perception, which extended beyond the Berlin missionaries who were closest to Venda, worked with the cartographic lacunae to established an impression of the far north as a 'Land of Myths and Legends'—an idea that endures today with help from the 'wild Africa' imagery of Kruger National Park located to the east of Venda.[9] Dramatic textual and pictorial imagery of romantic yet threatening vistas hardly apply to the Zoutpansberg region alone—a point Mary Louise Pratt has made convincingly for many other narratives of exploration—but compared to other parts of South Africa, it set deep roots in this era.[10] The Venda landscape was, after all, not merely illegible or notional in Pretoria; rather, it was a landscape of denial with little more than distorted or fragmentary geographical and human features. The evolution of that distortion speaks volumes about the power of territorial definition and the limits of state engineering on distant landscapes, and few landscapes seemed as distant as the far north.

Landscape, Encounter, and Conflict, 1836–1876

During the nineteenth century, Venda political organization consisted of three major entities and a number of smaller ones covering the rugged terrain and abutting plains in present-day northern and northeastern Limpopo province, stretching across the Limpopo (Vhembe) river into southern Zimbabwe. The tripartite division originated in a single large kingdom with common leadership under the dominant Singo group until around 1800, so the rulers' affinities were still close during the ZAR era even though temporal power had effectively fractured.[11] The rulers of Ha Ramabulana enjoyed a nominal stature above the

8 Alan Kirkaldy, "The Darkness within the Light: Berlin Missionaries and the Landscape of Vendaland c. 1870–1900," *Historia* 48, no. 1 (2003): 169–202.

9 The statement about myths and legends (with "beautiful scenery" appended) comes most officially from the Limpopo Tourism and Parks Board, http://www.golimpopo.com(accessed 22 Jul 2013), but it is present in a variety of permutations from other sources; Jane Carruthers, *The Kruger National Park: a Social and Political History* (Pietermaritzburg: University of Natal Press, 1995), 1–3.

10 Mary Louise Pratt, *Imperial Eyes: Travel Writing and Transculturation* (New York: Routledge, 1992), 216–227.

11 Gerhard Liesegang, "New Light on Venda Traditions: Mahumane's Account of 1730," *History in Africa* 4 (1977): 164 *et passim*, M.H. Nemudzivhadi, "The Attempts by Makhado to to Revive the Venda Kingdom 1864–1895" (PhD diss., Potchefstroom U., 1998), 3–4; on Singo ascendancy, see Victor N.M.N. Ralushai, "Conflicting Accounts of Venda History

other major houses of Tshivhase and Mphaphuli, but conflict existed between them over clients and key locales, and arose within houses over questions of succession.[12] As with most polities in the region, individual Venda territorial chiefs (*khosi*, plural *mahosi*) enjoyed a great deal of local autonomy and power within their own communities, though networks of allegiance and a well-developed system of councilors ideally served as a brake on tyranny.[13] The existence of formidable natural defensive positions in the mountains and a deep hinterland also aided the survival of Venda leadership in the face of external threats.[14] Flexibility of governance combined with strong defenses and a relatively large population compared to people further south meant that Venda society was resilient, prosperous, and dynamic, although it was also prone to fracture politically over questions of succession. Conflict arose in part because sitting kings (like other *mahosi*, whether great or small) normally could not designate their heirs, although they certainly expressed preferences and showed favor while alive. Multiple marriages, however, represented fusion between prominent families within the broad general area and links between the great houses, which almost assured that competition would re-emerge and draw upon networks of patronage in succession struggles.

Such a struggle was still underway in 1836, when a party of Boer *trekkers* under Louis Tregardt arrived in the lands south of the Soutpansberg Mountains that the residents called Dzanani, and included the core lands of the western

with Particular Reference to the Role of Mutupo to Social Organisation" (PhD diss., Queen's University Belfast, 1977), 155–172.

12 The primacy of the Ramabulanas in a decentralized but unitary Venda figures strongly into Nemudzivhadi, "Attempts," esp. 5–7; on the historical context and arguments surrounding the issue, see Caroline Jeannerat, 'An Ethnography of Faith: Personal Conceptions of Religiosity in the Soutpansberg, South Africa, in the 19th and 20th Centuries' (PhD diss., University of Michigan, 2007), 175–179, 202–207.

13 In this usage for historical chiefdom, I follow Alan Kirkaldy and Lize Kriel, "Converts and Conservatives: Missionary Representations of African Rulers in the Northern Transvaal, 1870–1900," *Social Sciences & Missions* 18 (2006): 109 n. 1. I use "king" instead of the anachronistic terms *thovele* and *khosikhulu* to distinguish the Ramabulanas among *mahosi*, and prefer "headman" to *gota*. English and Dutch sources tend to refer to all *mahosi* as *kapiteins* or chiefs, and others as *ndunas* (or "indunas") which signified leaders of fighting men or councilors with direct access to the king, but some reports apply the term to *magota* who were local headmen of non-royal origin. On councils and deliberation, see Hugh A. Stayt, *The Bavenda* (Oxford: Oxford University Press, 1931), 215–217.

14 The mountain stronghold was widespread enough that later analysts pointed to it as a standard characteristic of Venda society, even though it arose because of military pressure; see H. du Plessis, "Die Territoriale Organisasie van die Venda," *African Studies* 4, no. 3 (1945): 123, 126–127.

Venda seat.[15] The conflict began about six years earlier with the death of then-king Mpofu and the unseating of his son Ramabulana (also called Ravele or Rasithu) by his younger brother Ramavhoya, resulting in Ramabulana's flight to a town about 50km south of the royal residence of Tshirululuni. The arrival of the small but militarily potent party under Tregardt was fortuitous for Ramabulana's aspirations to regain the throne. With the mediation of Doors (or Doris) Buys, whose family had relocated from the Cape over decade earlier and who had first encountered Tregardt at the salt pan to the west, the two formed a partnership.[16] Tregardt aided Ramabulana in retaking the kingship by luring Ramavhoya out, and after an ambush and a short battle Ramabulana strangled his brother—treachery that would re-emerge in his heirs' mistrust of the Boers.

In return for this assistance and his help against raiding parties from the Kumalo Ndebele under Mzilikazi, Ramabulana evidently gave Tregardt the freedom to occupy land and access to hunting grounds.[17] Tregardt, however, also shared a desire with the *trek* leader A.H. Potgieter to found some kind of trading settlement in the far north, and his party eventually settled near the future site of the Elim mission station to await the latter's arrival. When that did not materialize, Tregardt's shrinking and sickly party departed in August 1837 and headed for the east coast, where he died of fever in 1838. The purported promise of land to Tregardt has remained in narratives of the region's history, and with Potgieter's tacit agreement to found some kind of settlement in the north, it became a prelude to his eventual arrival over a decade later.[18]

15 Nemudzivhadi, "Attempts," 8n27. Nemudzivhadi notes that Dzanani encompassed the central areas of Ha Ramabulana, but its historical limits are unclear so I have not employed it here. Today it is the name of an administrative region that includes the location areas of western Venda (see Chapter 7), while the etymologically related "Tzaneen" applies to a town some 100km south.

16 U. de V. Pienaar, "Karel Trichardt: Pioneer and Explorer," in *A Cameo From the Past: The Prehistory and Early History of the Kruger National Park*, ed. U. de V. Pienaar (Pretoria: Protea, 2013), 133–134. On the origin of the Buys people, see J.W.N. Tempelhoff, *Townspeople of the Soutpansberg: A Centenary History* (Louis Trichardt: Greater Louis Trichardt TLC, 1999), 18–22.

17 Nemudzivhadi, "Attempts," 13–16. A variety of later sources, including Venda accounts, attest to an agreement but disagree about its meaning, with the Boers seeing the land as a cession and Venda seeing it as patronage.

18 See Dorothea Möller-Malan, "Die Donker Soutpansberg," *Historia* 2, no. 1 (1957): 35; Nemudzivhadi, "Attempts," 13; O.J.O. Ferreira, *Montanha in Zoutpansberg: 'n Portuguese Handelsending van Inhambane se Besoek aan Schoemansdal, 1855–1856* (Pretoria: Protea, 2002), 39–40. The origin of the specific agreement between Potgieter and Tregardt seems to be the remembrances of H.J. Grobler many decades later; see P.J. van der Merwe, "Die Matabeles en die Voortrekkers," *AYB* 49, no. 2 (1986): 416 n. 47.

Tregardt, and later Potgieter, did not encounter an empty landscape, but sources for Venda community organization and land use in the era of their *de facto* independence are few compared to those that dwell on other political or religious questions. Still, those few provide useful insight. Tregardt himself made careful notes regarding the health of his animals and people, as well as accounts of the exchange of various animals between his party and important Venda, including both Ramavhoya and Ramabulana.[19] As elsewhere, cattle were particularly important markers of status and wealth, although studies in the 1920s suggested their ownership concentrated in only a few hands before Ramabulana's time.[20] Tregardt also moved at least three times in his efforts to find a sustainable locale, which suggests that the best and healthiest places for permanent residence and intensive cultivation were occupied, and many places between them were in seasonal use, probably for grazing or hunting.[21] Leo Weinthal, who visited Makhado in 1894, noted a thick cover of bush just north of the Doorn River (known as the Muhohodi where it passes south of Ha Ramabulana), followed by the 'Ten Mile Flats' just south of the mountains, the latter being a clear area whose northern reaches accommodated large herds of cattle as well as extensive cultivation.[22]

Such an image fits well with the brief notes of the Berlin missionaries who visited Makhado between 1871 and 1874 in an unsuccessful attempt to establish a station in his lands. The three missionaries who visited in May 1871, under the leadership of Heinrich Grützner, recorded a marked increase in vegetation and running water in the foothills of the mountains. They noted that the foothills and steep slopes supported heavy maize cultivation, but those same slopes were too wet for the sorghum that people on arable land further from the mountain range cultivated, and which provided both food and socially important beer.[23] The model of land use was one of usufruct within the households of a community, where the primacy of occupation determined land tenure, and the ability to bring land under cultivation determined its extent. As was true further south before the introduction of individual tenure, personal boundaries and extents were flexible, but occupation depended in part on

19 T.H. le Roux, ed., *Die Dagboek van Louis Trigardt* (Pretoria: Van Schaik, 1964), 4–80.

20 Stayt, *Bavenda*, 37–39.

21 Ferreira, *Montanha in Zoutpansberg*, 40.

22 Leo Weinthal, "The Magato Visit," *Pretoria Press*, 9 Jun 1894, reprinted as an appendix to R. Wessmann, *The Bawenda of the Spelonken* (London: The American World, 1908), 148–149; Maanda Mulaudzi, "'U shuma bulasi': Agrarian transformation in the Zoutpansberg District of South Africa, up to 1946" (PhD diss., University of Minnesota, 2000), 31–32.

23 Alan Kirkaldy, *Capturing the Soul: The Vhavenda and the Missionaries, 1870–1900* (Pretoria: Protea, 2005), 123. Tregardt discusses Ramabulana sharing beer and festivities in his diary; see entries for 8 Mar and 17 Apr 1837 in Le Roux, ed., *Dagboek*, 18, 32.

patronage, and as king, Ramabulana expected any new clients to acknowledge his primacy and exchange gifts to cement the relationship as Tregardt had.

From their casual questioning, and presumably in tandem with their experience approaching Makhado's defensively situated mountain capital at Luatame at the start of the dry winter season, the German missionaries also concluded that the people of western Venda lived in the mountains "in isolated villages."[24] The idea of isolation presumably came from a misinterpretation of the discrete names of localities and personal or political connections to them; central towns or villages with layouts that reflected social and political hierarchies, each with roughly defined territories for cultivation or grazing, were the common model of settlement. Hugh Stayt, who grew up in the area and conducted research in western Venda during the late 1920s, claimed that large villages in inaccessible places were the norm during the nineteenth century "before the present peaceful conditions were established," presumably referring to the growth of labor tenancy by small numbers of Venda on white-owned farms to the south and southwest.[25]

However, Ramabulana's capital at Tshirululuni was lower on the mountain, and other administrative areas were on even flatter land, so the evolution of strongholds undoubtedly reflected later conflict even if we accept that warfare before 1836 already dictated a defensive-mindedness in the bushy, hilly country of the north.[26] The population had points of concentration in their residence patterns that the homesteads of the western Transkei did not, but even the relatively hardscrabble veld south of the foothills had a purpose for herds. G.G. Munnik, *landdrost* there in the 1890s, described the region as so admirably suited for herding that in the 1840s the Venda "had more livestock than they could use," and white settlers had to exercise caution to avoid claiming the places where people were already in occupation.[27] By all accounts the landscape south of the mountains had significant pasturage as well as thick bush, creating spaces between areas of heavy settlement and agriculture where limited occupation was possible.

Thus when Hendrik Potgieter and his large *trek* party arrived from Ohrigstad in May 1848 to establish a new settlement in the north, land seemed to be there

---

24 Report dated 24 May 1871, *Berliner Missionsberichte* (hereafter BMB) 9–10 (1872): 160.

25 Stayt, *Bavenda*, 29–30.

26 Roger Wagner, "Zoutpansberg: the Dynamics of a Hunting Frontier, 1848–1867," in *Economy and Society in Pre-industrial South Africa*, ed. S. Marks and A. Atmore (London: Longman, 1980), 321–322.

27 G.G. Munnik, *Kronieke van Noordelike Transvaal* (Pretoria: Bienedell, n.d. [1921]), 6–7. Munnik also describes (p. 7) the region as a wilderness of bush, "swarming" with lions and savage natives in an undifferentiated yet inconsistent landscape of danger.

for the taking. Potgieter's people were not especially invested in farming, but rather in hunting, raiding, and the collection of tribute, to feed the trade in ivory and skins to the eastern coast and captured African women and children for the labor market.[28] Venda accounts suggest that Ramabulana initially welcomed their presence and expected them to live within his jurisdiction, but their sheer numbers and their tendency to spread out across the land alarmed him, as they were many times the size of Tregardt's party—well over a hundred people.[29] They set up due south of the hills and mountain of Ramabulana's brother Madzhie, and oddly called their new town Oude Dorp ('Old Town'), which soon became Zoutpansbergdorp or simply Zoutpansberg.[30] Despite its initially disorganized growth and high incidence of malaria, the town became the focus of settler power in the area, and its ivory exports were valuable to the fledgling ZAR.[31] In 1855 the new commandant, Stephanus Schoeman, reorganized the town into a rectangular plan on slightly healthier ground closer to reliable sources of water, and from then on it bore his name as Schoemansdal.[32]

For most of its existence Schoemansdal was a law unto itself, under the rule of successive commandants. These commandants demanded labor (service or *dienstdoen*)—often in the form of hunting parties—from local people who could be coerced, and tribute (*opgaaf*) from polities further afield, although the line between the two was not always clear.[33] The primary purpose of labor was to obtain ivory and other proceeds of the hunt, and most *opgaaf* came in the form of similar commodities. The hunters arranged with kingdoms and chiefdoms further afield for permission to take parties into the area, and crossed the Limpopo into malarial and tsetse-infested regions as wildlife stocks

28 Mulaudzi, "U shuma bulasi," 33–34.

29 Ferreira, *Montanha in Zoutpansberg*, 44; Nemudzivhadi, "Attempts," 18. The party was significantly larger, but the exact size is uncertain. Ferreira claims around 40 households arrived initially, which fits well with accounts placing fewer than 50 homes in Schoemansdal around 1856 and around 70 in the 1860s. On later population figures, see J.C.A. Boeyens, "'Black Ivory': The Indenture System and Slavery in Zoutpansberg," in *Slavery in South Africa: Captive Labor on the Dutch Frontier*, ed. E.A. Eldredge and F. Morton (Boulder: Westview Press, 1994), 194.

30 O.J.O. Ferreira, "Schoemansdal: van Voortrekkervoorpos tot Volksfeesterrein," *Contree* 1 (1977): 5–6.

31 J.C.A. Boeyens, "Die Konflik tussen die Venda en die Blankes in Transvaal, 1864–1869," *AYB* 53 (1990): 1.

32 Ferreira, *Montanha in Zoutpansberg*, 45–47. For the sake of clarity I will refer to the settlement as Schoemansdal, which is the name it carried for most of its existence, and by which it is most widely known.

33 Wagner, "Zoutpansberg," 319–320; Boeyens, "Black Ivory," 195.

thinned in the south. Their dependence on African labor to carry out the hunt increased with time, because horses were unsuitable in the hunting lands of the northeastern lowveld and modern-day Zimbabwe, and soon African gun-carriers became African marksmen (colloquially *swart skuts*, or 'black shots').

The enslavement and trading of women and children as part of the natural bounty of the land was technically illegal in the ZAR by repeated agreements and proclamations, but the practice continued and even grew in the 1850s and 1860s. Although some societies paid *opgaaf* in part with children they had captured—known as *inboekselingen* or apprentices—direct raids and military action against recalcitrant chiefs and headmen generated the majority of the captives, whom traders shipped further afield in an illicit economy of uncertain but significant size.[34] These industries extended beyond Schoemansdal to involve many others in the region, most notably the influential Buys family as well as a newer arrival, the Portuguese-born trader João Albasini, who had a personal following of thousands of Tsonga-speakers later known as 'Shangaans' by 1853.[35] Most of the individual captives have vanished from the record, but some formed a nucleus of acculturated Africans in the republics and could even became fairly powerful through subservience to powerful masters like Albasini.[36] For the communities that experienced these depredations, the decades before 1867 were fearful ones.[37]

However, the uptick in Boer activity at Schoemansdal after 1855 and especially in the 1860s generated greater resistance and conflict, which meant that hunting revenue declined while the taking of captives increased. The government in Pretoria assigned the collection of *opgaaf* to Michael Buys

34 Wagner and Boeyens differ on the centrality of slaving to Schoemansdal's role as a hunting town, but agree on its existence there and in the ZAR more broadly into the 1870s. The only clear claim was "about 1,000" in 1866 alone by the recently-arrived Berlin missionaries. See Wagner, "Zoutpansberg," 315; Boeyens, "Black Ivory," 198, 202.

35 Mulaudzi, "U shuma bulasi," 29; E.A. Eldredge, "Delagoa Bay and the Hinterland in the Early Nineteenth Century: Politics, Trade, Slaves, and Slave Raiding," in *Slavery in South Africa: Captive Labor on the Dutch Frontier*, ed. E.A. Eldredge and F. Morton (Boulder: Westview Press, 1994), 152–153; Boeyens, "Black Ivory," 196, 201, 205; Wagner, "Zoutpansberg," 325. Some Tsonga-speaking people and communities also joined other chiefdoms in the area, including Ramabulana's, although we have no idea of the numbers.

36 Boeyens, "Black Ivory," 205–207. J.B. de Vaal maintained that Albasini was not and could not have been involved, and that the evidence was circumstantial, but relates this specifically to the Delagoa Bay trade and not within the Boer communities or for his own use; see J.B. de Vaal, "Die Rol van João Albasini in die Geskiedenis van Transvaal," *AYB* 16, no. 1 (1953): 125–128.

37 Kirkaldy, *Capturing the Soul*, 38.

(the elder brother of Doors) in 1855 and João Albasini in 1859, because their followings meant they actually stood a chance of collecting, and they could chasten those who did not pay.[38] At the same time, Albasini became the official 'Native Commissioner' for the vast and ill-defined Spelonken ward, and he used this position to coerce tribute. For Venda who provided service to the Boers in hunting parties (including Makhado, the future king), opportunity well offset threat. People who worked for labor-starved Boer farmers in the late 1850s and early 1860s could earn a cow for a season of labor, which appealed to younger sons and others without cattle.[39] But both forms of seasonal labor altered the social order within Venda society by taking people away from homesteads, and Boer demands became more oppressive as their activities grew over time.[40] In this expansion, the ambition of the settlers exceeded their reach and they fell out among themselves. Albasini engaged in intrigue against the Gaza Ngoni kingdom from 1859 to 1862 and tried to arrange an alliance with the Portuguese in Lourenco Marques in a failed effort to secure control of hunting and trade, which led the Ngoni kingdom to close the hunting grounds to the northeast; at the same time his relationship with the Boers in Schoemansdal also deteriorated, and they sowed dissent among Albasini's own clients.[41] The result, by 1864, was peripheral conflict and raiding that alienated virtually all of the regional powers, but most importantly the nearby rulers of Ha Ramabulana.

The effect of the presence of the Boers in Schoemansdal and the nearby traders on the landscape was complex and not entirely clear. They and the African populations who aided them, or increasingly acted as free agents, certainly had a growing and ultimately devastating effect on animal populations. The government in Pretoria responded after 1858 with legal restrictions on the trade in wildlife products and the employment of African marksmen that were more aspirational than enforceable, and Venda hunters took increasing advantage of their control of territory and their ability to hunt during the summer without the Boers' concerns about malaria.[42] The physical landscape changed less, in part because the focus of Schoemansdal was not on its transformation, and there is no indication of problems with woodcutting, overgrazing, or erosion. The town's permanent population was never more than a few hundred whites, although seasonal traders, grazers, or hunters probably added to that

38 Wagner, "Zoutpansberg," 321.

39 Kirkaldy, *Capturing the Soul*, 38–39.

40 Nemudzivhadi, "Attempts," 24–26.

41 Wagner, "Zoutpansberg," 325–328.

42 Jane Carruthers, *The Kruger National Park* (Pietermaritzburg: University of Natal Press, 1995), 10–13; Wagner, "Zoutpansberg," 330–332; Nemudzivhadi, "Attempts," 23–24, 71–74.

number periodically.[43] The enhanced volume of trade and access to firearms, however, augured changes in African settlement patterns and locations, and the unsettled years between 1859 and 1869 also increased the importance of the mountain strongholds and dictated their construction to withstand enemies with firearms—just as African acquisition of the same dictated the transformation of the few outposts of the ZAR in the Zoutpansberg district into veritable and sometimes literal fortresses as well.[44]

The succession to Ramabulana after his death in 1864, like his own resumption of power in 1836, became intertwined with regional politics. The normal system involved siblings in the selection of a new *khosi* or king, with the senior sister (*makhadzi*) identifying the candidate, and the next junior brother by rank (*khosimunene*) confirming it, but this was often honored in the breach.[45] Household connections, ties of obligation, and other practices had as much importance. In the case of Ramabulana's eldest son Davhana, many Venda suspected that he had engineered his father's death and doubted his temperament, concerns which his conduct as heir-presumptive did nothing to allay.[46] Such worries widened the opening for a struggle over succession, and Davhana had many other brothers.

Ramabulana, however, reputedly favored his youngest son Makhado, who was about 25 years old at the time, and he had a tenuous claim through his mother, Limani. The *khosi* of Tshitavhadulu had intended Limani, his daughter, to replace her deceased elder sister as Ramavhoya's great wife, because she had passed before producing an heir; after overthrowing his brother, Ramabulana exercised his option to marry her in his stead, and she soon became Ramabulana's favorite.[47] Limani was politically savvy and, with Ramabulana's support, enjoyed the relative favor of Madzhie (the *khosimunene*) as well as Nyakhuhu (the *makhadzi*); they in turn supported Makhado in 1864. He had further support from other circumcised Venda (Makhado was the first ruler to have undertaken the rite), including those who had served as *swart skuts* for hunters based in Schoemansdal.[48] Foremost among the latter were his friends and confidants,

---

43 J.W.N. Tempelhoff, "Die Okkupasiestelsel in die Distrik Soutpansberg, 1886–1899," *AYB* 60 (1997): 9.

44 Albasini's home at Goedewensch was indeed already fortified in addition to the presence of his client base; see de Vaal, "Rol van João Albasini," 35–37.

45 Ralushai, "Conflicting Accounts of Venda History," 72–73; Kirkaldy, *Capturing the Soul*, 281.

46 It is hard to separate later characterizations from contemporary ones, but different informants agree on these points. See Nemudzivhadi, "Attempts," 34–35.

47 Ibid., 16–18.

48 Nemudzivhadi, "Attempts," 36–37; Boeyens, "Konflik tussen die Venda en die Blankes," 6–7; N.J. van Warmelo, ed., *Contributions towards Venda History, Religion, and Tribal Ritual*

Funyufunyu (known to the Boers as 'Tromp') and Rasivhetshele (known as 'September'), who would remain central figures as advisors in Ha Ramabulana in the following decades, and who enjoyed unfettered access to the king at his capital. They assembled a force sufficient to defeat and expel Davhana and most of his other siblings, and secure Makhado's installation as king—after which he moved his capital from Tshirululuni to the greater visibility and defensive security of a new mountain site at Luatame, just west of the imposing landmark of Songozwi (Hanglip) due north of the present city of Makhado/Louis Trichardt.[49]

According to most accounts and the few photographs of the capital before 1905, Luatame not only benefited from the presence of the sheer rise of the mountain behind it and limited accessibility through collapsible thickets of vegetation, but it was an organized capital. A series of walled passages and village areas helped to maintain hierarchical order within the court itself, but there were clear spaces for government functions.[50] Ernest Creux, the Swiss missionary sent to Makhado as an envoy from the Boers to re-establish peace in 1883, described it in vivid terms that invoked the European picturesque:

> Oh! What a beautiful country! A Swiss missionary really enjoys this pure mountain air and abundant water. What a beautiful chalet one could build here. But we are approaching the chief's kraal. It is 4:30. We reach a labyrinth of enormous rocks of a lilac color. Here and there you see other formations which also fall down from the cliff. The huts are now spread anywhere where there is a wide enough space between the boulders. From here there are walls on either side of the stony path, which leads from one group of huts to another. A forest now separates the village from the cliffs which crown the top of the mountain. ...On our arrival we noticed a group of Natives perched as sentries on top of the rocks that are above the village.[51]

(Pretoria: Government Printer, 1960), 31. Tshamaano's account in van Warmelo, from which Boeyens draws, identifies Rasivhetshele as "Stuurman," although it is unclear whether this is an error or a second name he used.

49 Boeyens, "Konflik tussen die Venda en die Blankes," 8. Rasivhetshele became the primary diplomatic intermediary for envoys from Pretoria, while Funyufunyu's role was primarily connected to military issues, although each possessed territorial power as headmen at some point as well.

50 See the description relative to fighting between Makhado and Davhana in Nemudzivhadi, "Attempts," 115.

51 Letter from E. Creux, Elim, 15 May 1883, in *Bulletin Missionnaire Adressé par la Commission des Missions de l'Église Évangelique Libre du Canton de Vaud* (hereafter BMV) 4, no. 50 (1883): 201, translation courtesy of Charles Leach.

The groups of huts probably corresponded to the extended families of Makhado and his chief councilors based on later descriptions, but Creux did not note this. The height of the mountain promoted the condensation of water vapor that fed the streams (and rich plant life) that could insulate the kingdom against drought and keep the soil rich and productive, as it remains today.

The compound was designed to provide defense and diplomatic seclusion, but its position offered surveillance of the troublesome southern reaches and perhaps a sense of kingship in itself. In 2010 I visited the site as well as the accessible top of the Luatame mountain, and although tree plantations blocked some of the field of view from the capital site itself, I could identify Schoemansdal and Albasini's farm site.[52] Even when low clouds shrouded the summits, the air below them remained fairly clear and I could see thirty or forty kilometers with little difficulty. Visibility was presumably better in the 1860s when pastures and fields in the hills were open, and when less light and air pollution existed. This kind of visibility was not only a matter of security but also offered Makhado an illusion of control over all he surveyed, a sense that may have applied to those under Makhado as well as to the king himself.

The functionaries of the ZAR in 1864 did not agree on what to make of Makhado taking the throne and fortifying it. Some in Schoemansdal supported Makhado morally, if not materially, against Davhana in June and *landdrost* Jan Vercueil remained friendly with him, but 'Native Commissioner' João Albasini had already recognized Davhana as king in May 1864 on behalf of the ZAR, and *veldcornet* Jan Hendrik du Plessis expressed support for Davhana as well.[53] When Davhana took up residence on Goedewensch under the protection of Albasini that winter, it seemed like official opposition to Makhado's leadership of Ha Ramabulana. The inspection of farms and attempted granting of lands on the southern slopes of the mountains just months later could not have improved matters, and increased demand for Venda labor to tend and protect fields and herds—including women who had their own fields to cultivate within households, and whose produce also provided wealth for the state—created further broad discontent.[54] The Boers also constantly demanded the surrender of Venda firearms, which were both militarily and economically essential to Makhado, and so provided ample fuel for suspicion. Makhado soon forbade people under him to labor for the Boers and consistently refused to

52 For an earlier verification (December 1998) see Tempelhoff, *Townspeople of the Soutpansberg*, 379. Overgrowth made the site of Schoemansdal harder to identify from the mountain by 2010. Albasini's position is not directly visible today, but the abutting dam and reservoir bearing his name are, and his family graves are intact.

53 Boeyens, "Konflik tussen die Venda en die Blankes," 7–10, 52–53.

54 Nemudzivhadi, "Attempts," 81–86.

hand over weapons without first obtaining the surrender of Davhana, who had proven impossible for his soldiers to dislodge by force.

The Schoemansdalers themselves laid claim to farms—places—by the terms of the laws of the South African Republic. Although we do not know when the first *uittreksels* were issued, *landdrost* Jan Verceuil had requested the approval of several local burghers to serve on committees in early 1863 and sent some notices to Pretoria for publication that August.[55] The oldest extant inspections close to the mountain seem to date from October and November 1864. Those reports were the work of du Plessis, the *veldcornet* for the Spelonken ward, who initially showed great detail in his work, and he claimed to carry out only one or two per day. Some sketches included not only roads and watercourses, but also notable landforms and the places where people lived. In his first sketch of 'Palmiet fontijn,' a *zaaiplaats* or sowing farm for P.J.C. van Staden,

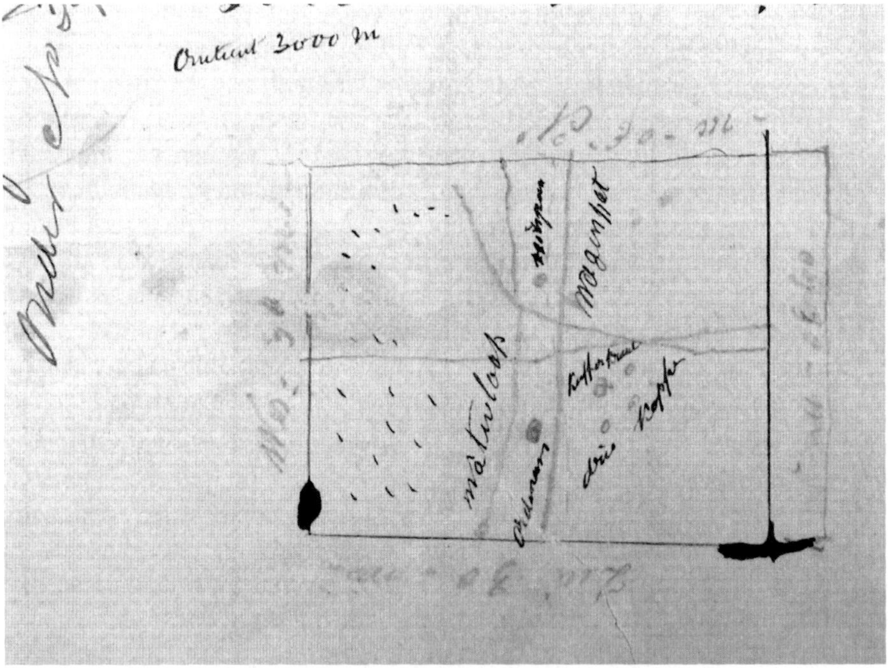

MAP 6.6 *The sketch plan drawn by Jan du Plessis for the farm 'Palmiet fontijn' (later 'Palmietfontein') in November 1864. Note the clear pencil marking of Venda occupation.*
SOURCE: RAK 2777, TRANSVAAL ARCHIVES DEPOT, NATIONAL ARCHIVES AND RECORDS SERVICE OF SOUTH AFRICA, PRETORIA. RSA STATE COPYRIGHT.

55 Verceuil to W.C.J. van Rensburg (acting President) and *Uitvoerende Raad,* 4 May 1863, R340/63, SS 48, TAB; Verceuil to *Uitvoerende Raad,* 4 Aug 1863, R560/63, SS 49, TAB.

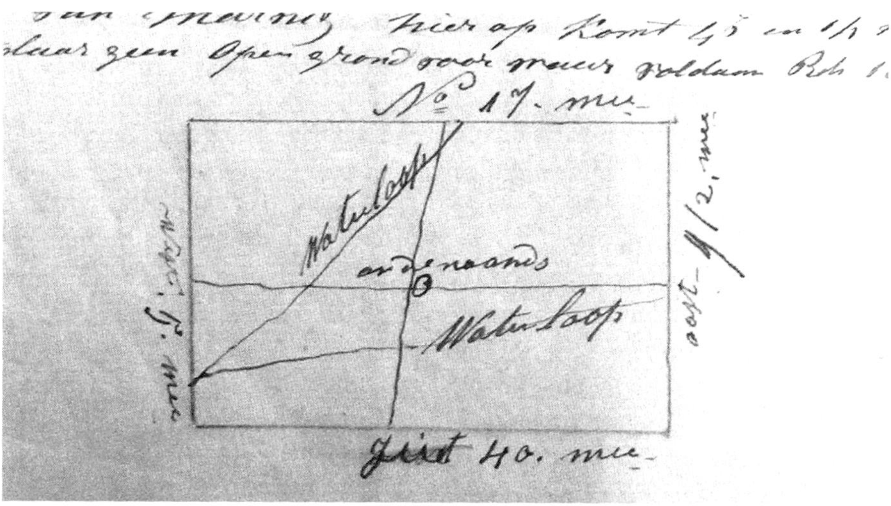

MAP 6.7 *The sketch plan drawn by Jan du Plessis for the farm 'Welgevonden' in November 1864. The detail is more hurried than "Palmiet Fontijn," and the riding times are irregular. Compare this with the later surveyed plan of the same farm from 1897* (*Map 7.1*).
SOURCE: RAK 2777, TRANSVAAL ARCHIVES DEPOT, NATIONAL ARCHIVES AND RECORDS SERVICE OF SOUTH AFRICA, PRETORIA. RSA STATE COPYRIGHT.

du Plessis indicates a 'Kaffer kraal' located on hills along the road through the parcel leading towards Schoemansdal (see map 6.6).[56] He says nothing about the people living there, but he shows clear land on their side of the watercourse, which suggests activity. On each of the first four sketches, African occupation is clearly indicated, but it is unclear if any burgher homes or other structures existed.

But after the fourth inspection, human geography vanishes completely. The fifth inspection, of 'Bergvliet' (which would form part of the Louis Trichardt/Makhado town lands after 1898) was delayed by six days, to 25 October 1864, and shows dwelling-like features that are not labeled or explained. The remaining inspections followed one per day (excluding Sunday) up to 8 November, and only watercourses and the starting point of the inspection appear within each sketch (see map 6.7). At the end of the seventeen inspection reports, du Plessis added a note about five farms intended for inspection in June 1865, in order to claim pay for entering them into the *landsboek*.[57] These inspections

56 Inspection report for 'Palmiet fontijn,' 17 Oct 1864, No. 1 in "Inspectie Rapport van J.H. du Plessies Zoutpansberg wyk Spelonken October 1864," RAK 2777, TAB.
57 Note on "Aangetekende plaatzen voor genoemde inspektie den 12 Junij 1865," in "Inspectie Rapport van J.H. du Plessies Zoutpansberg wyk Spelonken October 1864," RAK 2777, TAB.

formed fragments of supposedly known and controlled land that had become places on a Boer landscape. But there is no evidence that those five inspections ever happened or that the burghers who claimed any of these 22 farms actually occupied them, and the reports themselves did not go to Pretoria until the end of 1867, by which time Schoemansdal was in ruins.[58] Nevertheless, officials of the ZAR referred to many of these areas by those assigned names thereafter.

The general reason for the hastening of those inspections, and the abortive nature of many others, almost certainly involved the growing hostility of Makhado and Madzhie in the mountains. The first four inspections took place eight kilometers or more south of the mountains, but the remaining thirteen were so close that most included significant portions of the Soutpansberg foothills. This act of appropriation was certainly anticipatory, but the lack of extant settlement on the sketches suggests both unrest in the area and haste on the part of du Plessis. Some people were claiming ground even closer without inspections; one complaint mentioned that the acting *veldcornet* Stephanus Janse van Rensburg had claimed a grant from government in the immediate vicinity of Madzhie.[59] This surprising reach into the mountains reflected the expectation of peaceful Venda acquiescence as well as a presumption that the ZAR could and would enforce the claims. It also suggests that Venda tribute was no longer reliable and a greater need for fertile land had arisen—and perhaps, coming as it did in the spring, part of the plan included appropriating existing fields, or areas temporarily vacated by communities that retreated further into the mountains to avoid the many-sided succession conflict.

But as Boers laid out farms on the mountain slopes, Makhado had been confirming his own network of clients and circulating to assure that the *mahosi* of the other great houses—particularly Tshivhase, Mphaphuli, and Rammbuda, but also the nearby Lobedu 'rain queen' Modjadji—supported him or at least recognized him. In this he was generally successful, and in tandem with a reorganization of the military, he forged the basis for a unified front against both internal and external enemies.[60] This became necessary by April 1865, when local commandant S.M. Venter, Albasini, and Davhana, together with soldiers under them, attacked the town of Phahwe ostensibly in pursuit of a fugitive Tsonga chief. In Phahwe and the surrounding areas, they killed some ninety

58 R.A. van Nispen to *Uitvoerende Raad*, 11 Dec 1867, R10/68, SS 95, TAB. The dating of the reports themselves is suspect, because van Nispen became *landdrost* in January 1866, and du Plessis refers to him for approval while calling himself the "former *veldcornet* at Zoutpansberg" which suggests a date after 15 Jul 1867.

59 J.C.J. Herbst to M.W. Pretorius (Staatspresident), 10 Nov 1864, R1022/64, SS 61, TAB.

60 Nemudzivhadi, "Attempts," 44–54, 92–93.

people, including the *makhadzi* Nyakhuhu, and took other women and children into servitude. Although *landdrost* Vercueil condemned this act to Makhado's enraged envoy later in the month and complained to Pretoria, it began a series of raids that brought Venda retaliation and progressively pushed the population in and around Schoemansdal into defensive laagers for the next two years.[61]

Neither Madzhie nor Makhado would in any case contemplate concessions as long as Davhana remained under Albasini's shield, especially in light of the attack on Phahwe. Makhado stated this repeatedly through his envoys and to Venter at a personal meeting on 5 June 1865 that produced a tentative agreement and a promise of a two-month truce that rapidly collapsed with Venda raids on Shangaans in the area and the Boer arrest of Makhado's envoys to a commission later that month.[62] With Albasini and the civil authorities at loggerheads, and the government in Pretoria unable to pay for adequate equipment or raise sufficient volunteers to form a burgher force, matters deteriorated further, with a particularly brutal assault by Albasini on the *khosi* Magoro in August 1865 on the grounds of his refusal to pay *opgaaf* and his support for Makhado.[63] Boer attacks on the strongholds of Madzhie and another *khosi*, Lwamondo, in September 1865 failed, and Albasini characterized virtually every Venda leader of stature as a rebel in an effort to rally help from Pretoria. Makhado's basic demand for the surrender of Davhana and steadfast refusal to hand over guns and ammunition did not change, but by mid-1866 Makhado and Madzhie recognized that Schoemansdal and its claims to territory and sovereignty were an intractable problem. By then Venda families who had retreated into the mountains sought to return to former homesteads and towns south of it (and even took up hunting parties again by the end of that year), while white farmers resolved to return to the same lands based on their own claims. Makhado expected white settlers to compensate him before they could return, and was adamant that any *opgaaf* from his clients must go through the Ramabulanas and not to ZAR functionaries directly.[64]

Little else happened to break the impasse in 1866 and early 1867. Despite pleas from Schoemansdal for assistance, Boers to the south were not apt to risk their lives to secure a distant, malarial place where they believed the law had

61 Wagner, "Zoutpansberg," 328.

62 Boeyens, "Konflik tussen die Venda en die Blankes," 14–19, 23–25.

63 Ibid., 23, 36–39. Besides 300 deaths and the taking of hundreds of cattle, Albasini's force of sixty whites and nearly a thousand Shangaan soldiers took well over a hundred children and an unknown number of women captive.

64 Ibid., 53–54, 60.

little meaning.[65] Commandant-General Paul Kruger was ordered to assemble a commando of around 1,250 men from various districts in June 1866, but when the appointed day came, only 161 showed up. The second attempt in June 1867 was more successful, but still only about 400 appeared, and they were arguably short on supplies.[66] With Albasini's help, they attacked Madzhie on 20 June 1867 anyhow, but failed to breach the defenses and retreated, even though the only significant casualties seem to have been several Shangaans shot in error by members of the commando.[67] Afterward, with no prospect of reinforcement and little chance of prevailing against an expected attack from the mountains, the commando served only to cover the evacuation of the entire town population on 15 July 1867. Venda soldiers affiliated with Madzhie came down and destroyed the empty town within a day or two, and Funyufunyu reputedly took material from the church to build his own house elsewhere.[68] Proposals in the field to build a new town in the vicinity—including one proposal to place it even *closer* to Luatame, on the present site of Makhado/Louis Trichardt—proved impossible, so the evacuees ultimately formed the new town of Marabastad farther south.[69]

The departure of the Schoemansdalers left only Albasini's fortress as an outpost of the ZAR, although the government rescinded his appointment in July 1868, and further attempts to raise commandos failed to field an effective force even when the President, M.W. Pretorius, himself led it.[70] Stephanus Schoeman took over military matters from Albasini, and was able to convince the Gaza Ngoni and a group of Swati chiefs to send separate military expeditions in 1869 that were fiascos and failed to achieve anything decisive, despite a falling-out between Makhado and Madzhie that led to the latter's flight westward in 1870.[71] The government in Pretoria sent a commission to conclude treaties and restore peace in November 1869, but the great *mahosi* and Makhado himself

65 A.J. Potgieter, "Die Vestiging van die Blanke in Transvaal (1837–1886)," *AYB* 21, no. 2 (1958): 169.

66 Report of H. Grützner, n.d., *BMB* 7 (1868): 101.

67 Boeyens, "Konflik tussen die Venda en die Blankes," 68–69.

68 Ibid., 77.

69 Ibid., 78–79. See also "Journal van Diplomatiek Agent S. Schoemen voor de (Naturellen) Zaken in het District Zoutpansberg, 1868," 5 Jan 1869, Supl 1/69, p. 32, SS 118, TAB.

70 Nemudzivhadi, "Attempts," 108–9.

71 G.G. Munnik, *Kronieke van Noordelike Transvaal*, 33; Boeyens, "Konflik tussen die Venda en die Blankes," 108; Johannes Flygare, *De Zoutpansbergen en de Bawenda Natie* (Pretoria: De Volksstem, 1899), 12. By some accounts Madzhie died soon after his flight to the west, but the British encountered a "Katlachter" in 1880 and Stefanus Hofmeyr reported that Makhado's "uncle, at the same time also under-captain, Katlagh" went to Modjadje to ask for rain in summer 1884. See S. Hofmeyr, *Twintig Jaren in Zoutpansberg: Een Verhaal van*

did not dignify the proceedings beyond sending envoys to broadcast their positions as fact. Nevertheless, the commission obtained the marks of a few lower-ranking *mahosi* and headmen on documents agreeing to abide by the laws of the ZAR and pay tribute as subjects, and assessing an indemnity against Madzhie for the loss of Schoemansdal.[72] Makhado, the other great *mahosi*, and virtually all of the minor ones as well, never assented, but the ZAR considered it binding anyway. They simply lacked the power to enforce it. The Republic reinstalled Albasini as their local representative, but he remained ineffective as a collector of *opgaaf* and taxes from Venda *mahosi*, and his shielding of Makhado's brothers reinforced Venda suspicion throughout Albasini's on-again, off-again appointments as Native Commissioner and Justice of the Peace (*vrederechter*) in the Spelonken into the 1880s.[73]

For nearly thirty years, only Albasini and a handful of traders and missionaries kept a presence among the Venda polities. Although suggestions abound that Makhado made declarations of his boundaries at that time—sometimes quite expansive ones—we have no contemporary evidence of any proclamations or statements before 1887.[74] All sources, however, agree that Makhado considered the Doorn River an important marker, although whether he promised death to those who crossed it, or simply declared that he would not pursue his enemies south of it, is a matter of dispute. The evacuation and destruction of Schoemansdal in 1867 proved to be the key event in the rollback of direct Boer influence and cemented their image of the undefeated Makhado, who became the 'Lion of the North' to the white public of the ZAR over time.[75] Albasini was secure and continued his role as a theoretical government

---

Twintig Jarigen Arbeid onder de Heidenen in de Transvaal (J.H. Rose & Co., Cape Town, 1890), 264.

72 Nemudzivhadi, "Attempts," 121–123; Boeyens, "Konflik tussen die Venda en die Blankes," 106–107.

73 The nature and timing of Albasini's various appointments were, and remain, unclear. De Vaal, "Rol van João Albasini," 123–124; W.A. Stals, "Die Britse Beleid teenoor en Administrasie van die Swartes in Transvaal, 1877–1881" (D.Phil diss., University of Pretoria, 1985), 56–61.

74 See Nemudzivhadi, "Attempts," 105–107; Mulaudzi, "U shuma bulasi," 36–37; Munnik, *Kronieke van Noordelike Transvaal*, 35–36. Two writers state that Makhado proclaimed all of his boundaries around 1867–1870, but neither cites contemporary evidence, and each differs in the rivers they name. See Dorothea Möller-Malan, "Die Donker Soutpansberg," *Historia* 2, no. 2 (1957): 169; Dorothea Möller-Malan, *The Chair of the Ramabulanas* (Cape Town: Central News Agency, 1953), 159; L. Changuion and B. Steenkamp, *Disputed Land: The Historical Development of the South African Land Issue, 1652–2011* (Pretoria: Protea, 2012), 71.

75 This respect continued after his death, even among many of his opponents. See G.G. Munnik, *Memoirs of Senator the Hon. G.G. Munnik* (Cape Town: Maskew Miller, 1933), 145.

official, but his actual reach only extended to the people under his power south of the mountains, and few independent Venda *mahosi* ever paid anything to him.

Despite Albasini's presence, Boer landhunters and other speculators therefore generally remained far to the south around the town of Marabastad.[76] This southward retreat was strongest around Ha Ramabulana, but in fact the 1870s saw a general retreat from northward expansion in the Transvaal, and those who did take up residence in northern Zoutpansberg or Waterberg often did so in a tributary arrangement with local Africans.[77] A few commercial entrepreneurs crept north to establish coffee plantations, but obtaining labor legally was difficult in light of limited coercive power and the availability of better wages for migrants at the diamond mines of New Rush (Kimberley).[78] Immediately following their imposed settlement, the ZAR, however, went back to work constructing its notional proprietorship over land in Zoutpansberg as well as Waterberg through massive block inspections (see Chapter 5), although virtually all new private registrations in Zoutpansberg before 1877 were leaseholds.[79]

Veldcornetten Jules Franck of Rustenberg (as *voorzitter*) and J.A. Esterhuizen of Lydenburg in fact began a block inspection of ground in the Spelonken ward for government in October 1869, while the peace commission was still underway.[80] In their work, the commission poked north of the rivers to maintain a fiction of state control and knowledge, but the 200 inspections they produced were cursory, confused, unreliable, and even provocative. Indeed, Franck and Esterhuizen carried out inspections at the rate of 14 or 15 a day, and the pace slowed only slightly in November. According to local *veldcornet* and Schoemansdal evacuee H.R. Schnell, their primary source of reckoning involved periodic hikes to low peaks south of the Soutpansberg Mountains and travel along rivers between them, and in the process they claimed to have inspected the lands of *mahosi* Tshivhase, Mphaphuli, and Lwamondo.[81] They also traveled along the

76 Kirkaldy and Kriel, "Converts and Conservatives," 111, 114.

77 Peter Delius, *The Land Belongs to Us: The Pedi Polity, the Boers, and the British in the Nineteenth Century Transvaal* (Johannesburg: Ravan, 1983), 104; Mulaudzi, "U shuma bulasi," 38–39.

78 De Vaal, "Rol van João Albasini," 137.

79 Mulaudzi, "U shuma bulasi," 38; Tempelhoff, "Okkupasiestelsel," 33.

80 See inspection reports of 1869 Land Commission under J. Franck (untitled book "70"), RAK 2777, TAB. The third member of the commission was Willem van Heerden.

81 Statement of H.R. Schnell. 30 Dec 1872, in D. S. Maré (*landdrost*) to *Uitvoerende Raad*, 2 Jan 1873, R81/73, pp. 155–157, SS 153, TAB.

foothills south of the Zoutpansberg in late November after the peace commission had completed its work, and inspected several farms that João Albasini had requested in late 1868, abutting the earlier work of J.H. du Plessis.[82] In the process the local *veldcornet*, H.R. Schnell, and another ex-Schoemansdaler, J.P. Jacobs, accompanied them, and they also retained five Africans—at least two of them Albasini's Shangaans—to assist them and presumably smooth matters over with local people. Only the wagon driver Platje was asked to make a statement about the work, but he would attest only to the identities of those present.[83]

The second commission, in September or October 1871, convened under Esterhuizen and included surveyor A.H. Walker, and worked much further south. Its formation and composition likely reflects the *Volksraad* resolution on 12 September that closed much of the eastern Zoutpansberg district to settlers, in order to reserve possible goldfields to the state.[84] According to Jacobs, this party not only crossed over the old inspection line, but deliberately cut into Modjadji's lands with the future in mind.[85] With Walker in tow, at least their work was less brazenly incorrect, but overlap was evident as soon as they tendered their work, and Esterhuizen later stated his belief that in 1869 they had not gone as far south as Franck claimed.[86] The result was an inquest between 1872 and 1875 that encapsulated the worst problems attendant on block inspections and certainly figured into the legal battles of the 1870s over the creation and division of territory.[87] In the end, the *Uitvoerende Raad* in May 1875 established a commission that drew in the Surveyor-General, a senior land surveyor, and the Registrar of Deeds, but also put two surveyors in the field.[88]

82 De Vaal, "Rol van João Albasini," 137; Entries 359–362, Zoutpansberg Plaasregister, RAK 3092, TAB.

83 Statement of Platje, 30 Dec 1872, in D.S. Maré to *Uitvoerende Raad*, 2 Jan 1873, R81/73, p. 159, SS 153, TAB.

84 VRB Art. 42, 12 Sep 1871, in *De Locale Wetten der Zuid-Afrikaansche Republiek 1849–1885*, ed. and comp. F. Jeppe and J.G. Kotzé (Pretoria: J.F. Celliers, 1887), 421.

85 "Rapport van de Commissie benoemd door Uitv. Raads Besluit d.d. Mei 10 1875, in Zake de Inspectie van Esterhuyse en Frank in Distrikt Zoutpansberg," 3 Jun 1875, R1239/75, RAK 2794, TAB; Statement J.P. Jacobs, 30 Dec 1872, in D.S. Maré to *Uitvoerende Raad*, 2 Jan 1873, R81/73, pp. 160–161, SS 153, TAB.

86 "Notulen der Verrigtingen van de Commissie," n.d. [May-Jun 1875], R1239/75, RAK 2794, TAB.

87 Despite the ongoing inquest, both Franck and Esterhuizen had been elected to the *Volksraad* in 1872; see annexure dated 28 Jun 1872, A2075/4, TAB.

88 URB Art. 121, 20 May 1875, pp. 315–316, UR 5, TAB. An earlier resolution (URB Art. 186, 9 Dec 1874) had only called for another three-person commission, so the specificity was a major change.

The surveyors concluded that the earlier inspection was for all intents and purposes not done, because the area in question was between one-fourth and one-third the size necessary to include the two hundred farms Franck situated there. On that basis the government canceled all of the 1869 work that could not be proven to lie north and west of the later inspection line *and to actually exist*, which at least saved Albasini, although he would not see his *grondbrieven* until 1887.[89] The inspectors in turn had to refund their fees to the state.

As for the 17 inspection diagrams from 1864 that Jan du Plessis forwarded to the government, they went to the Registrar of Deeds and did result in *grondbrieven*. These *plaatsen* became notional territory in the heart of Ha Ramabulana, and much like Albasini's farm inspections, they were allowed to stand. Only one inspection did not pass muster, but a second went to government, and the claimant on a third did not take a title deed. Of the remaining 14, all received titles between February 1870 and September 1876, with gaps corresponding to the general moratoria on new titles (see Chapter 5).[90] The spacing presumably also indicates poverty or laxness on the part of the recipients, but some of these titles eventually entered the portfolios of land companies or others who were willing to pay the taxes in anticipation of one day taking ownership. It would be a long wait.

Briton, Boer, and Venda, 1871–1887

With the major Boer enclave gone, Makhado could consolidate his position and control influx to a degree. Albasini and Davhana remained a problem, but one that the king and his *mahosi* could manage. Both white and black traders continued to do business in western Venda, where local hunters offered a good return, and sometimes white hunters or other travelers gained entry as well. The arrival of German and Swiss missionaries in the area, however, represented a new factor that offered both opportunity and threat, even though they were not the first. Madzhie had made overtures in the 1860s to the Dutch Reformed Church missionary Stefanus Hofmeyr, whose primary mission was among the Buys people, but Makhado remained skeptical and only treated with him after 1870.[91] In 1871, the Berlin Missionary Society

89 URB Art. 152, 12 Aug 1875, pp. 342–344, UR 5, TAB.

90 The exceptions were Pisanghoek (Inspection no. 14), Ledig (No. 7), and Brakspruit (No. 2) respectively; see "Inspectie Rapport van J.H. du Plessies Zoutpansberg wyk Spelonken October 1864," RAK 2777, TAB.

91 Nemudzivhadi, "Attempts," 128–129; Hofmeyr, *Twintig Jaren in Zoutpansberg*, 38–39.

sought unsuccessfully to establish a station in his lands, although they successfully placed one with Ligegise Tshivhase to the east in 1872 (called Ga-Sebase) and two other stations with minor Venda *mahosi* as well in 1874 and 1877.[92] Swiss missionaries arrived in 1875, and focused their work on Tsonga-speakers, which led them across the border of Mozambique at times. They established their first station on a titled farm near Albasini in 1875, and called it 'Valdezia' after their *Mission Vaudois* in an undisguised act of appropriation.[93] Another followed later at Elim, near Louis Tregardt's former camp, and a third at Shiluvane in 1886. The three missionary elements would become occasional visitors and sometimes intermediaries to Makhado, even though he kept them studiously at arm's length. Hofmeyr in particular found this frustrating, and by 1887 considered simply erecting a station without his approval.[94] This accessibility, though guarded, nullifies the popular idea that Makhado would kill people who entered his lands. His goal was to avoid surrendering the pastures, fields, and watercourses central to Ha Ramabulana itself, and to avoid openings that could expose the workings of the state and its clients to outside influences. The vague extent of his power was an ally that worked more effectively than any firm claim of boundaries could.

For nearly a decade after 1869, the settler government to the south had little presence on the landscape of Ha Ramabulana. The notional landscape of white-owned farms and titles remained as the ultimate aim of the ZAR, presumably with a return to a system whereby Africans tendered labor and tax according to law. With Albasini unable to collect anything like a regular tax, Makhado and the various Venda *mahosi* largely ignored his authority, and he did not press for advantage. Makhado continued to feel pressure, however, and intimated that a state of war still existed when he met the Berlin missionaries a second time in 1872.[95] His search for effective means of defense ranged from the simple acquisition of weapons and the investiture of his own position to more radical experiments, notably an ill-advised foray into medicines intended to stop bullets that he wisely abandoned after a failed demonstration in 1875.[96] The ZAR government continued to warn Makhado against interfering with Davhana, but refused to remove him from the area despite efforts by local officials to address the matter.[97] Albasini, demoted

92 Kirkaldy, *Capturing the Soul*, 25–27.

93 Harries, *Butterflies and Barbarians*, 22, 115; Nemudzivhadi, "Attempts," 135–136.

94 Hofmeyr, *Twintig Jaren in Zoutpansberg*, 317.

95 B. Beyer, Report on the founding of Ga-Sebase, Mar 1872, *BMB* 7 & 8 (1874): 127.

96 Nemudzivhadi, "Attempts," 172–175; "Een Wonderlijke Profeneming," *De Volksstem*, 30 Oct 1875. The Berlin Missionaries also commented on this in November 1875.

97 URB Art. 135, 3 Aug 1875, UR 5, TAB.

again in 1875, was reduced to contracting with mines in Kimberley to provide labor, but they refused to pay him any fees for recruitment when he and the laborers arrived in July 1875. He was only saved from poverty by a number of prominent Boers, presumably including *landdrost* Maré, who collected Albasini's farm titles on a debt of £2,000 as soon as their grants passed in October 1887, and conferred 9/20 ownership shares on members of his own family.[98]

The remaining Boers in the Zoutpansberg were aware of this weakness and showed alarm at almost anything Makhado did, in part because of the impending confrontation with the powerful Pedi state under Sekhukhune. Makhado wrote at the end of June 1876 to the *landdrost*, D.S. Maré, that he intended to attack Shangaans under Albasini who had invaded his land and that people should not keep their cattle there, but he also reiterated that he was the sole conduit for any tribute to government, and his clients on the plains and hills to the south would not abide by the recent law (No. 3 of 1876) demanding taxes from them directly.[99] Maré suspected something else was afoot, because Makhado had not made good on such threats since his attacks against Davhana over ten years before.[100] Indeed, Maré tasked the *veldcornet* of Spelonken, W.J. Grieve, to write to the king as a warning against interfering with the Sekhukhune matter, based on information from unnamed spies that most of Makhado's people sympathized with Sekhukhune and that he had received new cattle.[101] Whatever the Venda opinion of the Republic's war against Sekhukhune, Makhado seemed uninterested in intervention, but took care to remind them of his active presence, and so kept the fields and mountains clear for Venda herds and farms.

Venda generally welcomed the retraction of the Republic's effective authority in the 1870s and its dismal campaign against Sekhukhune in that light, but Theophilus Shepstone's annexation of the Transvaal for Britain in April 1877 was certainly a surprise. The partial, then full, restoration of Albasini as the local Native Commissioner was probably less of a surprise, even though he theoretically was subordinate to Danish-born Captain Oscar Dahl, the district Commissioner since the post's establishment in 1876, as well as the new Secretary for Native Affairs, Theophilus Shepstone's son Henrique.[102] Before

98 De Vaal, "Rol van João Albasini," 141; Entries 359–362, Zoutpansberg Plaasregister, RAK 3092, TAB.

99 Makhado to D.S. Maré, 30 Jun 1876, p. 291–292, SS 212, TAB. For the conditions in question, see "Wet No. 3, 1876," §4–6, in Jeppe and Kotzé, *De Locale Wetten*, 663–664.

100 Maré to N.J.R. Swart (Staatsecretaris), 21 Aug 1876, R2225/76, pp. 265–266, SS 214, TAB.

101 W.J. Grieve to D.S. Maré, 24 Aug 1876, R2259/76, p. 357, SS 214, TAB.

102 Stals, "Britse Beleid," 50, 89. Dahl, like Maré, was kept on by the British.

annexation, Dahl, camped in his fortified residence of Klipdam, was even less effective than Albasini had been. On his first visit to Makhado in 1876, the king purportedly showed him the vista from Luatame, and told him with disdain to report back to Pretoria that all the land he could see had been Ramabulana's, and he would defend it.[103] Dahl had no support from above or below; when he reported a raid by Makhado against Davhana in the vicinity of the (again) temporarily disempowered Albasini, it only brought a shrug from the government and a visit to ask Makhado to return stolen cattle, not any effort at confrontation and no attempt to delimit the king's reach.[104] The government of the ZAR was unwilling and unable to challenge Makhado, who could openly dismiss them.

The records of relations directly between British administrators and Venda *mahosi* in Ha Ramabulana are scattered and fragmentary, but they clearly met on several occasions, and Makhado could not be ignored in the work of Dahl or the new Special Commissioner for Waterberg and Zoutpansberg, an office designed to mediate between H.C. Shepstone in Pretoria and local officials.[105] The first of those special commissioners, Morrison Barlow, responded credulously to Albasini's fear of an attack, with a plan to rally dependable chiefs and raise a force to attack Makhado "in his own stronghold," but he wisely waited for instructions.[106] Dahl, for his part, had gone to Makhado to ask him what his position to the new government would be, and recorded that most of the older people at the meeting were in favor of paying tax, while the younger people were not for paying, but for fighting, and if defeated they would retreat to the Limpopo and build fortresses there—leading Dahl to characterize him broadly as an independent chief who would never pay taxes to any government.[107] H.C. Shepstone instructed the pair to tour the district at the end of July 1877, and they reached the foot of the mountains on the 29th.[108] There they met Rasivhetshele, who had come to assure that "it was not Mr. Finny," a prior emissary from Theophilus Shepstone, and promised that the king would come down the next day.[109]

103 Oscar Dahl, "The Native Question" (Letter to the Editor), *Zoutpansberg Review*, 17 Feb 1892.

104 See, e.g., O. Dahl to Swart, 10 Jan 1877 (with reply in marginalia), R267/77, pp. 375–376, SS 227, TAB.

105 Stals, "Britse Beleid," 32–35.

106 M. Barlow to Swart (as Acting Government Secretary), 9 Jul 1877, R2616/77, pp. 200–203, SS 240, TAB.

107 O. Dahl, journal entry for 21 May 1877, with R7451/95, p. 56, SS 4908, TAB.

108 O. Dahl, journal entries for 20 and 23 Jul 1877, with R 7451/95, p. 64, SS 4908, TAB.

109 O. Dahl, journal entry for 29 Jul 1877, with R7451/95, pp. 66–67, SS 4908, TAB. "Mr. Finny" was probably Frederick Bernard Fynney, Theophilus Shepstone's special commissioner to Zululand, who reputedly had postured as a 'chief' to Makhado.

When Makhado indeed came at around 11 the next morning, he brought most of his local headmen and councilors with him so all could listen. In response to Barlow's statement that the British had taken over the territory and would be administering matters, Makhado reportedly expressed his satisfaction with the fact and recognized their claim to govern up to the Limpopo. His objections, as recorded by Dahl, were connected to questions of patronage and territory. Makhado had one important objection to being called Ramabulana, because

> That was his father's name and until the Copis [Kopjes] namely Machow [Mashau] Lebula Machambu & Magoro was given back to him he should not be called by that name, Said Copis was his father's and which Albasini had taken from him, the respective Chiefs of said Copis are Refugis here at my Kraal & I wish you as Sp Com of this District to give them right to goe back to their old places.[110]

Barlow listened carefully and promised to investigate. Makhado added his account of his history with Albasini, Davhana, and the Shangaans, who he said were behind "all the rows in this Country." As a show of goodwill to the new order, Makhado invited their party up to Luatame the following day, where they had a long visit and the king presented them with small gifts in hopes of a better relationship than Albasini or the ZAR, had offered, including possibly the return of his network of *mahosi* to lands in the southeast.[111] Barlow held a dim view of Albasini's extralegal role as a chief, which alone was an encouraging sign, and they reciprocated Makhado's gesture of gifts the following September.[112] Barlow and Dahl, however, made no decisions about Makhado's boundaries, though they visited a chief they identified as 'Katlachter' (Madzhie) and told him that he must not take possession of any disputed areas from Makhado "until Government could lay down a line between him and said Chief"—a clear statement of British intent, eventually, to build boundaries and rational, legible landscapes.[113]

Indeed Makhado kept *veldcornet* Grieve and commissioner Dahl informed of the purpose of his movements: the emplacement of new chiefs, the mobilization of force against others (as in the case of Lwamondo in November 1878),

110 O. Dahl, journal entry for 30 Jul 1877, with R7451/95, p. 67, SS 4908, TAB.
111 O. Dahl, journal entry for 31 Jul 1877, with R7451/95, p. 68, SS 4908, TAB.
112 O. Dahl, journal entry for 1 Sep 1878, with R7451/95, p. 275, SS 4908, TAB.
113 O. Dahl, journal entry for 3 Oct 1877, with R7451/95, p. 96, SS 4908, TAB.

and anything else that might be misconstrued as directed against the government. He continued to make gestures towards Barlow, in one case sending a gift of two dozen head of cattle under three of his headmen.[114] Barlow, for his part, agreed that Makhado had a right to aid the defense of his client *mahosi* and headmen against Lwamondo, but did not approve of reprisal attacks. Nevertheless, Makhado followed this with a message asking "as a child to his father" for "a little ammunition" to fight against Lwamando, a request Barlow refused sympathetically, but he conveyed his appreciation of the king's acquiescence to Barlow's wish only to defend his allies, and he offered the gift of a saddle and bridle from the Administrator in Pretoria—things Makhado had sought from the Berlin missionaries in 1872.[115] Barlow made no territorial claims, demanded no onerous taxes, exchanged gifts and patronage, and largely respected his autonomy, all things that gave Makhado a better opinion of British rule compared to the very low bar of his relations with the ZAR and Albasini. This state of affairs continued when military officer Charles Creagh replaced Barlow at the beginning of 1880, in a merger of Barlow's office with that of the former special commissioner to Lydenburg, although Dahl remained in place and Albasini had regained his status as a local commissioner.[116]

Albasini began raising alarms about Makhado planning attacks to "destroy the Spelonken by force of arms" and aiding enemies of the British almost immediately, which required Creagh's investigation in February 1880; after a friendly visit with the king, he found these accusations to be without merit and proclaimed that Makhado was perfectly loyal.[117] In December 1880, as armed rebellion broke out among the Boers, Albasini reported that Ligegise Tshivhase told him that Makhado was "planning some great undertaking," and that two of Albasini's police had been chased off the mountain after inquiring about one of his client *mahosi*, Mahulume, who reputedly claimed that Albasini was trying to "steal him" from Makhado by ordering his headmen to go to Goedewensch and pay taxes.[118] Although Mahulume later denied saying that he had to go to

114 O. Dahl, journal entry for 20 Dec 1878, with R7451/95, pp. 342–343, SS 4908, TAB.

115 O. Dahl, journal entry for 4 Mar 1879, with R7451/95, pp. 394–395, SS 4908, TAB; B. Beyer, Report on the founding of Ga-Sebase, Mar 1872, *BMB* 7 & 8 (1874): 135.

116 Stals, "Britse Beleid," 38. Barlow was reassigned to adjudicate the Swaziland boundary.

117 Albasini to C.F. Ziervogel (*landdrost*, Zoutpansberg), 29 Dec 1879, under minute paper N6/80, SN 3, TAB; Albasini to H.C. Shepstone (Secretary for Native Affairs), 22 Dec 1879; Barlow to H.C. Shepstone, 2 Jan 1880; and comment of C.A. Creagh, 13 Feb 1880; all under minute paper N7/80, SN 3, TAB. Albasini transmitted some of these accusations directly from Davhana.

118 Albasini to H.C. Shepstone, 13 Dec 1880, SN 4, TAB.

Makhado for permission to send his headmen out, or to pay taxes to Albasini, the king certainly viewed Albasini's motives with far more suspicion than the intentions of Creagh or even Dahl.[119] Makhado in fact contributed 'native police' to Dahl in late 1880 and paid some taxes, despite his continued assertion of *de facto* sovereignty on the landscape of Ha Ramabulana.[120]

The Boer rising at the end of 1880, however, proved impossible for the British to contain, although African states refused Boer enticements to aid them, and the British refused to permit them to help.[121] According to the Native Commissioner in Waterberg district, Makhado threatened to burn down Stefanus Hofmeyr's mission station at Goedgedacht if the Buys people or others from the mission went to aid the Boers (although Hofmeyr himself years later maintained that Makhado *supported* the Boers), and other chiefs stated their intent to chase the Boers out yet again if Britain quit the territory.[122] Nevertheless an armistice followed the British defeat at Amajuba on 28 February 1881, and the Royal Commission that followed set out the conditions for retrocession under a vague imperial suzerainty. That commission asked a number of administrators for their input, and in response to the urging of H.C. Shepstone, they agreed to hear from a number of chiefs or their representatives.[123] But they rejected the idea of separating the bulk of the Zoutpansberg from the restored Republic and maintaining British rule there, despite Dahl supporting the idea out of a prescient belief that uncertainty over land and local disdain for Boer governance would lead to further conflict.[124]

A "sort of conference" of chiefs and representatives in Pretoria on 2 August 1881 broadcast the terms reached for the Pretoria Convention, including the provision for a Native Location Commission and a British promise to mind the

---

119 See statement of Mahulume (unnumbered), 16 Dec 1880, SN 5, TAB.

120 Brievenboek, N.C. Zoutpansberg, under R7451/95, p. 47, SS 4909, TAB; O. Dahl to P. Joubert (Commandant General and Superintendent for Native Affairs), 3 Oct 1884, R 4742/84, pp. 142–143, SS 989, TAB. Makhado and Dahl alike preferred to exclude Albasini from their relations.

121 John Laband, *The Transvaal Rebellion: The First Boer War 1880–1881* (London: Longman, 2005), 187. Laband calls the people who took control of government property in Waterberg and offered assistance "Venda," but his sources do not make that attribution.

122 BPP, Further Correspondence Respecting the Affairs of South Africa, 1881, C.2950, at 173–174; BPP, Report of the Commissioners Appointed to Inquire into and Report upon All Matters Related to the Settlement of the Transvaal Territory…Part I, 1882, C.3114, at 164–165, 172; Hofmeyr, *Twintig Jaren in Zoutpansberg*, 255.

123 BPP, Report of the Commissioners Appointed to Inquire into and Report upon All Matters Related to the Settlement of the Transvaal Territory…Part II, 1882, C.3219, §1765–81 at 83–84.

124 Ibid., §1350–54 at 66–67.

welfare of Africans.[125] The signatories of the Convention named seventeen chiefdoms in need of delineation, specifically including the lands of Makhado and the major Venda *mahosi* separately, although the government later called these 'examples' and not a full or legally binding list.[126] Such lands in Waterberg, Zoutpansberg, and Lydenburg were to be inspected and beaconed before any new grants of land would take place, a condition eliminated in the succeeding 1884 London Convention, and the commission initially also included the British Resident as one of its members. The process of the Location Commission was to determine the amount of land African polities were 'entitled' to occupy based on a minimum acreage per household as determined by census, a model employed at the Cape as well as in other settler societies.[127] This number was difficult for the commission to settle upon in the face of efforts by the *Uitvoerende Raad* of the Republic to keep it as small as possible, not just to open land for settlers but to extract sought-after tenant and migrant labor for rural settlers.[128] The push for some reserve areas to be smaller also involved compensation rights to burghers whose farms were adjudged to fall into a reserve, which could be expensive—if owners were willing to sell at all.[129]

Such theoretical provisions, worries, and assignations that the Location Commission intended to apply to Ha Ramabulana were of limited relevance in light of the actual situation on the ground. Makhado was particularly unlikely to hew to fantastic ideas of state power imagined in far-away Pretoria by a new generation of Boers, headed by Paul Kruger, the commander he had run off in

125 "De Koninklijke Commissie en de Inlandsche Opperhoofden," *De Volksstem*, 10 Aug 1881.

126 "Notulen der Locatiecommissie," 9 May 1882 art. 8, SN 177, TAB; Johan Bergh, "Grondregte in Suid-Afrika: 'n 19de Eeuse Transvaalse Perspektief," *Historia* 40 (1995): 45; TKP (unnumbered), *Report by the Commissioner for Native Affairs Relative to the Acquisition and Tenure of Land by Natives in the Transvaal* (Pretoria, 1904), 34; Johan Bergh, "'(To) Reserve to the Native Tribes Such Locations as They May Be Fairly and Equitably Entitled To': The Transvaal Location Commission (1881–1899)," *South African Historical Journal* 54 (2005): 8.

127 See, for example, Cole Harris, *Making Native Space: Colonialism, Resistance, and Reserves in British Columbia* (Vancouver: UBC Press, 2002), 92–94; Bruce Berman and John Lonsdale, *Unhappy Valley: Conflict in Kenya and Africa, Book One: State and Class* (London: James Currey, 1992), 115–116.

128 Bergh, "Transvaal Location Commission," 8–9. The Commission recommended from five up to ten "English acres" of arable land per household, while the Executive Council sought to push it down to two or three morgen (about 4.2 to 6.3 acres), with later adjustments permitted for the quality of terrain and grazing needs. See "Notulen der Locatiecommissie," 3 Oct 1882 Art. 15, SN 177, TAB; Bergh, "Transvaal Location Commission," 8.

129 Bergh, "Transvaal Location Commission," 11–12.

1867. The new government sought to use the momentum of the British era to maintain hut-tax and pass-tax receipts, and give force to legal measures restricting African residence on private farms and their movements that had defied even the British. But the retrocession of the Transvaal to the Boers had ended any threat of military danger from British arms, which had been the only factor able to overcome the Zulu and Pedi kingdoms. In the eyes of Makhado and other rulers in the Limpopo region, the resumption of local rule in Pretoria in 1881 was in the short term a positive development for their security.

Makhado and the other kings and chiefs of the north were thus understandably dismissive of any fresh pretensions of imposition from Pretoria when they made their first attempt to exert power over him. As Dahl had predicted, Makhado and his clients in 1882 were resistant to taxation, with one Tsonga headman under him unwilling to pay the new Native Commissioner, João Albasini's son Antonio, on the grounds that Makhado forbade it.[130] Dahl did not press the matter during his tax collection tour in September 1882, but two of Makhado's headmen came to Dahl's fort at Klipdam in October to deny accusations that he was orchestrating defiance and sought to make war—but they also would not say that the king would pay tax.[131] Whether he was demanding no taxes be paid, or his subordinates were using the king as an excuse not to pay taxes, a number of them evidently told Dahl that they feared reprisal from Makhado should they pay him.[132] Antonio Albasini recommended in January 1883 that no attempt to collect tax be made for fear of a general rising, because none of them would pay until Makhado did.[133]

The Zoutpansberg district was, however, also in the grips of a devastating drought and famine between 1881 and 1883, which took matters even further out of the ken of the ZAR. It hit the houses of Tshivhase and Mphaphuli hardest, which encouraged Makhado to send his sons Mphephu and Sinthumule with their regiments on campaign against certain disputed client communities that he might wrest from Tshivhase in particular. Both Makhado and *khosi* Ligegise Tshivhase fought in favor of different candidates to the disputed throne of Rammbuda beginning in 1882.[134] Makhado categorically did not ask or even notify Antonio Albasini about that military action against Bele Rammbuda in 1882, his intervention in the succession to Maboho Lwamondo

130 A.A. Albasini to C.J. Joubert (Superintendent of Native Affairs), 30 Apr 1882 (two letters), R 2784/82, pp. 199–202, SS 665, TAB.

131 O. Dahl, "Boodschap van Magato," 1 Oct 1882, R6481/82, p. 206, SS 750, TAB.

132 Namudzivhadi, "Attempts," 151.

133 A.A. Albasini to P. Joubert, 17 Jan 1883, SN 80, TAB.

134 Nemudzivhadi, "Attempts," 183–193, 201–17.

later that year, or his clashes with Ligegise Tshivhase in 1883; when he moved against his brother Nthabalala to the south in early 1883, Albasini wrote to Pretoria that the king's true goal was to bring all "government people" and Boer lands under his control.[135] Stefanus Hofmeyr noted that some Venda communities near his mission station with the Buys people supported Davhana but paid taxes to Makhado, and the missionary's presence there annoyed and constrained the king.[136] Matters south of the mountains spiraled into fighting that drew in a local force led by several dozen burghers under the district Commandant, 'Swart' Barend Vorster Sr., which forced Makhado to withdraw and led to efforts at parley in February and March 1883.[137]

The discussion, as described by the Swiss missionary Ernest Creux, turned on boundaries and taxes. The Special Commissioner, Christiaan Joubert, aproached wh a small group of armed Boers, but Creux and Berlin missionary Carl Beuster handled the mediation. The key demand was for Makhado to cease his military operations and hew to the boundaries "set by the British Government" pending the Location Commission's arrival, and make a good-faith payment of £1,000, which he agreed to in a declaration on 9 April.[138] But those boundaries, according to Makhado, did not even exist—and some parties vocally refused to submit to Boer rule.[139] Still, the potential for trouble was apparent. After initial hesitation, Makhado eventually paid about £300 of the £1,000 demanded of him in arrears, and the group that Joubert had assembled returned home.[140] At the same time, Albasini accused Makhado of claiming that he had "bought the land in Zoutpansberg earlier belonging to Ramabulana from the Special Commissioner" for the agreed £1,000 and that his cooperation was all a ploy, presaging greater difficulties as soon as the commission and its military support departed.[141] Indeed the king continued to posture, and some

---

135 Declaration of Shimaangie, 15 Jun 1882, SN 176/3, TAB; A.A. Albasini to C.J. Joubert, 8 Feb 1883, R957/83, pp. 163–164, SS 787, TAB. The first declaration maintains that Makhado was assisting Ligegise Tshivhase against Bele, whom neither ruler supported as the successor, but that seems odd in light of the competiton between the two; see Nemudzivhadi, "Attempts," 204.

136 Hofmeyr, *Twintig Jaren in Zoutpansberg*, 255.

137 Nemudzivhadi, "Attempts," 152–155.

138 Statement of Makhado, 9 Apr 1883, R1764/83 (under R13217/91), pp. 84–85, SS 3062, TAB.

139 Letter from E. Creux, 15 May 1883, *BMV* 4, no. 50 (1883): 206–207.

140 Kassaboek, Comissaris van Naturellen, Zoutpansberg, R7451/95, pp. 90, 100, SS 4912, TAB; Stals, "Britse Beleid," 195; Nemudzivhadi, "Attempts," 156–161.

141 A.A. Albasini to C.J. Joubert, 7 Apr 1883, R1764/83 (under R13217/91), pp. 74–75, SS 3062, TAB.

of the few white settlers in the area stayed in defensive laager with the Buys people and missionary Hofmeyr into May and June.[142]

It was true that beyond the money itself, Makhado had surrendered nothing of substance. No meaningful boundaries existed, while his military actions in 1882 and early 1883 had actually led to the strengthening of his hold over key *mahosi* and the expansion of his power. The drought even provided an opportunity to strengthen ties with the spiritually powerful Lobedu rain queen, Modjadji, to the south.[143] Dahl made careful note of Makhado's expanded power when urging caution to the government in dealing with him later in 1884.[144] A December 1884 visit to Makhado from the Commandant-General and Superintendent of Native Affairs, Petrus Jacobus (Piet) Joubert, produced an agreement for him to assemble people to pay Albasini as Native Commissioner, but no money changed hands.[145] The British High Commissioner, Hercules Robinson, apparently even mocked Dahl in late 1885 for the Republic's inability to collect taxes, as a sign of its lack of respect among Africans who would prefer British rule.[146] Makhado indeed continued to refuse to pay taxes in the manner, form, and amount prescribed by Pretoria, and told Albasini in June 1886 that he was the sole recipient of his people's tribute and would pay tax for all of them in one sum, not individually.[147] He also sent cattle of uncertain health, which had to be valued against a supposed tax liability that depended on a nonexistent census.[148]

The enumerative drive of the ZAR would not accept this condition indefinitely. The State President himself, Paul Kruger, held a meeting at Klipdam in October 1886 to announce to the roughly two thousand chiefs and people in

---

142 Hofmeyr, *Twintig Jaren in Zoutpansberg*, 256.

143 Ibid., 264; Hofmeyr states that the king sent Madzhie on the errand, which would both demonstrate Madzhie's acceptance of Makhado's authority while honoring the queen with a visit from the *khosimunene*—assuming Hofmeyr's identification is reliable.

144 O. Dahl to P. Joubert, 3 Oct 1884, R 4742/84, pp. 140–142, SS 989, TAB. Makhado was likely playing Dahl and the younger Albasini against one another as the two fought over jurisdiction. See A.A. Albasini to D.S. Maré, 4 Oct 1884, R4767/84, pp. 146–148, SS 989, TAB; A.A. Albasini to P. Joubert, 4 Oct 1884, R4751/84, pp. 151–155, SS 989, TAB; Nemudzivhadi, "Attempts," 233–234.

145 Nemudzivhadi, "Attempts," 234.

146 Minute van eene Conferentie Gehouden ten Landrrostkantoore te Marabastad op den 13den January 1886," enclosure C in P. Joubert to S.J.P. Kruger, 20 Jan 1886, R359/86, p. 67, SS 1160, TAB.

147 A.A. Albasini to P. Joubert, 11 Jun 1886, R2899/86, p. 123, SS 1232, TAB.

148 A.A. Albasini to P. Joubert, 23 Jul 1886, R2899/86, p. 126, SS 1232, TAB; Memorandum by H. Stiemens, 24 Aug 1886, R2899/86, p. 120, SS 1232, TAB.

attendance that, in the interests of ending conflict among black and white alike, a surveyor would come to divide the land, the Location Commission would assure that everyone received their rightful territories, and then all could live in peace. At the same time, he stated that all back taxes were to be paid by the end of the year and all huts counted, and Africans living on private farms were to obey the owners and not consider themselves to be in charge.[149] Makhado and the *mahosi* of Venda did not attend and certainly did not sanction these claims to authority, but they would become the Location Commission's very next targets.

Location and Provocation, 1887–1890

The process of extending state authority over Ha Ramabulana had several components, each intended to produce the legibility necessary to confine, restrict, and exploit land and labor around it. Some of these elements were active in 1883 and 1884, but after 1887 it would become a constant refrain from the representatives of the ZAR that Makhado navigated by limiting Boer access to the landscape and manipulating the state's functionaries. The state in Pretoria sought Venda submission to government, as they had unilaterally declared in 1869, but Makhado treated it as a tributary relationship with the government or its leadership (Piet Joubert or Paul Kruger) as his real peers. But beyond that, they expected to confine and tax Africans within the Republic's stated boundaries, which required censuses and the creation of locations that branded certain lands as inside or outside of African control based on law defined in Pretoria. Communities outside of adjudged locations fell under various regulations formalized in the *plakkerswet* (squatters' law) of 1887 and revised in 1895, which enshrined a maximum of five non-white family households on any private farms—even if Africans owned the land in trust—which would ideally spread labor across a white settler landscape.[150] Beyond that, a location would imply that the land (and potentially other *mahosi*) outside of it were beyond Makhado's power. Venda politics between 1882 and 1895 turned heavily on the expansion of Ramabulana networks of authority, arguably in pursuit of a true Venda kingdom, and locations with inviolable boundaries would accept the Boer paradigm

149 O. Dahl to P. Joubert, 29 Oct 1886, SR 615/86, SN 12, TAB.

150 J.S. Bergh, "Grondverdeeling tussen Blank en Swart in Suid-Afrika: 'n 19de-Eeuse Transvaalse Perspektief," *Genl. J.B.M. Hertzoggedenklesing* XXXIV (2005): 18–19. The laws were No. 11 of 1887 and No. 12 of 1895.

of fragmentation and submission.[151] On the side of the ZAR, the dismantling and freezing of Venda as a series of separate chiefs in locations was preferable to the loosely bounded, opaque networks of kinship and patronage that supported Makhado, who could apply force to sustain them.

The government therefore moved to define locations for Makhado and others in the Zoutpansberg district at the beginning of 1887, at which point Piet Joubert, in his role as Superintendent of Native Affairs, recognized that the Location Commission needed to consider the matter afresh. The timing had a great deal to do with matters of state and the need to reach an accommodation with Makhado, if one was possible. The passage of the *Occupatiewet* (Occupation Law, No. 6 of 1886) promised to further white settlement and state reach through the grant of small farms in Zoutpansberg on condition of personal occupation and the establishment of a new town, Pietersburg (today Polokwane).[152] The occupation farms would ideally generate taxes as well as bodies for a militia, but the matter of knowing which lands could actually be given away concerned the Location Commission as well as the first Special Commissions that formed the following year.[153] The discovery of vast gold reserves at the Witwatersrand was another contributor, because beaconed locations and taxes could push labor into the market—but if matters reached an impasse, it might also pay for the force necessary to compel a resolution. The fact that the Superintendent of Native Affairs and chairman of the commission was also the Commandant-General of the Republic's armed forces further suggests that an element of confrontation was endemic to the process. Makhado was also determined to oppose any social and spatial partition, and did so a number of times between February 1887 and his death in September 1895.

The Location Commission in Zoutpansberg under Piet Joubert and Antionio Albasini set its first task as settling with Makhado. They arrived around midday on 22 February 1887 near the former capital of Ramabulana that lay below Luatame, known to Venda as Tshirululuni but to the Boers as 'Rietvlei,' the name J.H. du Plessis registered for it in the 1860s.[154] Together with former

---

151 Nemudzivhadi, "Attempts," 239–240, 251. The idea of a 'restoration' of Venda kingship is at the heart of Nemudzivhadi's study, but one need not embrace that interpretation to recognize this expansion and security.

152 On the passage of the *Occupatiewet* and its preconditions, see Tempelhoff, "Okkupasiestelsel," 12, 20–22. The occupation farms under the *Occupatiewet* were smaller than full-size Boer farms (500–1,500 morgen as opposed to 3,000) in order to build up a standing military reserve.

153 The Special Commissions operated under Law 3 of 1887, and re-inspected lands with a surveyor present. See Chapter 5.

154 P. Joubert *et al.* to S.J.P. Kruger (Staatspresident), 24 Feb 1887, R1526/87, p. 70, SS 1364, TAB. Rietvlei was one of the farms J.H. du Plessis inspected in the foothills in 1864, and it had

acting Surveyor-General F.H. Rissik, Captain Adolph Zboril of the Mounted Artillery, local intermediary Christoffel Snijman, and their secretary Fritz Stiemens, the commissioners met with Makhado and his advisor (and purportedly translator) Rasivhetshele by invitation the following day. The prompt invitation notwithstanding, Makhado immediately made clear that he felt the status quo was in no need of modification and that all he needed to say he had already told Albasini before—presumably referring to his position as ultimate arbiter of his lands and people.[155] Joubert's response, however, addressed the influx of people to the mines, with some taking up occupation lands in the north, and stated that

> ...the government sent me to see and beacon the Locations, so that the natives also know what their land is and cannot be oppressed. ...then the government shall see to [it] and also help the natives not to be oppressed and punish trespassers, but because the government wants to be able to do this before people move in [they want] to make up the beacons and have the [boundary] lines beaconed off.[156]

This implied threat of pressure and loss from new arrivals would have been familiar to people around the Kei far to the south, as would the paternalistic guarantee of government to uphold 'native rights.' The government had indeed already announced the opening of Spelonken, the vast ward including the Soutpansberg Mountains, under the *Occupatiewet* on 6 October 1886, and inspections for occupation farms began about the same time that the Location Commission was visiting Luatame.[157]

Makhado responded curtly to the commission's divisive tactics and questionable assessments but, according to later reports, remained congenial throughout.[158] His initial response to Joubert was that yes, he knew all of these things, and that there were foreign farm claims on the flatlands where his people already grazed sheep and cultivated gardens. Makhado further advised that before anything was decided, Joubert should speak with the other chiefs. Joubert's response, that each chief would get their own location and that Makhado needed to deal with the commission separately, did not sit well with the king. Makhado refused to accept such piecemeal arrangements among his

---

received a title. Today it forms the eastern half of Makhado/Louis Trichardt. On this entire episode, see Nemudzivhadi, "Attempts," 239–246.

155 Transcript of Conference, 23 Feb 1887, R1526/87, p. 73, SS 1364, TAB.

156 Transcript of Conference, 23 Feb 1887, R1526/87, pp. 73–74, SS 1364, TAB.

157 Tempelhoff, "Okkupasiestelsel," 43.

158 "De Superintendent van Naturellenzaken...," *De Volksstem*, 10 Mar 1887.

clients, which threatened the plains south of the mountain that fed people and animals, as well as the less arable region north of the mountains where some people moved seasonally. Their request for a census from Makhado, so they could assign a location size, met with the wry retort that he had already told C.J. Joubert years before that if he wanted to know the population, he could go count the people himself.[159] Makhado had responded to Dahl's call for a census and tax payments in 1884 with the statement that his huts were too widely spread and people not under him might shoot a white man, so Dahl could just count the people as they came down to pay him—an offer he did not repeat to Piet Joubert.[160] Attempts to convince the king to delegate the task to his subordinates, together with a lack of any guarantee of his patronage over lands, further roused his ire. Makhado declared that he could not tell Joubert the limits of his lands because he really did not know them. He explained that the uncertainty arose because "before, the entire land was Ramabulana," a blunt statement that his land reached as far as his power, and that *any* settler land occupation in the area represented hospitality and sufferance from Makhado.[161]

But there were other elements to Makhado's position, given that he could not enforce the links of patronage between himself and his *mahosi* as easily across policed boundaries, and the Venda use of labor levies to cultivate state crops required people and fertile lands that the king could not reasonably partition.[162] Makhado's statements were articulations of sovereignty and control over the landscape. For the ZAR, boundaries were financial and administrative matters, allowing them to draw revenue by incorporating or alienating land, breaking ties of patronage between African leaders, and uprooting labor in quantifiable ways. If this basic misalignment in the assumptions behind the two positions was not clear to Joubert and Makhado, it would be to their successors. The timing of engagement (and attempted engagement) between the Location Commission and the leadership of Ha Ramabulana in fact turned upon the kings' changing power relative to Pretoria.

The only definite information the commission got out of Makhado in 1887 was a statement of what the *onderste veld* or closest fields were. According to Makhado, those boundaries ran west along the Doorn River from the Luvuvhu

159 Transcript of Conference, 23 Feb 1887, R1526/87, p. 75, SS 1364, TAB.

160 Dahl to P. Joubert, 3 Oct 1884, R 4742/84, p. 142, SS 989, TAB.

161 "Vroeger was het geheele land Ramapoelanie zijn." Transcript of Conference, 23 Feb 1887, R1526/87, pp. 75–76, SS 1364, TAB.

162 Marcel Dreier, "Years of Terrible Drought: Surviving the 1895–1897 Supply-Crisis in the Limpopo Area" (Limpopo Research Project, University of Basel, 2005), 3, accessed 28 Jan 2012, http://pages.unibas.ch/afrika/limpopo/papers/limpopo_pdf/limpopo_dreier.pdf.

River confluence, then parallel to the mountains from the source of the Doorn to Machaba, back towards the Soutpansberg Mountains along the Brak River, including the salt pans to the west of the mountains, and from there to the Limpopo river and around to the Luvuvhu.[163] This representation of boundaries was unnatural to Makhado. As with other major rulers of the north, he defined the extent of the kingdom not by arbitrary lines but through the networks of individuals under his patronage, and there were many.[164] Joubert would not guarantee such an extent, stating that it was the surveyor (Rissik) who would ultimately decide on the extent of land Makhado could retain based on his census. This was unacceptable to Makhado, who expected that tendering taxes to Pretoria—mostly in cattle, the form of an exchange between equals—should exempt his lands from "being cut up." The king made no concessions, preferring instead to offer vague agreements with sentiments for peace and fairness while listening intently to the statements Joubert made about locations to gauge their intent. Joubert offered safe passage to Pretoria if Makhado had complaints or wished to say anything further, because the commission needed to move on—and they had no power to compel his agreement.[165] Makhado, on the other hand, recalled the fate of his uncle Ramavhoya when he met Louis Tregardt's trek party on their terms in 1836, and that Davhana was pointedly still alive.[166]

After the commissioners had retired to a nearby camp the next day, Joubert sent a letter to Makhado stating that they had assayed the land and the mountain, and noted that even the area Makhado claimed as his core was about "600 Boer farms stretched out" (15,420 square kilometers), which included a missionary station, the former grounds of Schoemansdal, and about sixty titled farms.[167] Joubert could not accept this for the government in Pretoria because the Commission's land-area reckoning would require that Makhado's population be about 300,000 households paying a total of £150,000 each year, but his total payment since 1881 was only £384—totally inadequate for even a fraction of that estimate. Joubert offered instead to beacon about twenty farms' equivalent (60,000 morgen or 514 square kilometers) for Ha

163 Transcript of Conference with Makhado, 23 Feb 1887, p. 92, SN 179, TAB. This appears to be the earliest clear statement of territorial boundaries from Makhado. Refer to map 6.1.

164 Mulaudzi, "U shuma bulasi," 44.

165 Transcript of Conference, 23 Feb 1887, R1526/87, pp. 77–79, SS 1364, TAB.

166 He would occasionally voice this recollection, as he did through missionary Creux in 1883; see "Antwoord van het Opperhooft Makatu [*sic*]," 4 Apr 1883, R1764/83 (under R13217/91), p. 60, SS 3062, TAB.

167 P. Joubert to Makhado, 24 Feb 1887 (unpaginated), SN 179, TAB.

Ramabulana, based on his estimate of 10,000 households, requiring a hut tax of £5,000 per year to be paid, and suggested that the government might ask for arrears of at least £15,000. Joubert followed this statement with a wry apology that he could not recommend the area Makhado claimed, at least not without a census.[168]

Makhado's opinion of this remarkable letter is unknown, but the lack of a response is telling on several levels. It would have been insulting to say the least that Makhado's claim to land was too large and incompatible with the presence of white farmers and missionaries under his authority. But it also says a great deal about the way Joubert and the commission considered 'native title' in terms of an allowance per household, exclusive of any other claims to the land (save possibly mission stations). The idea of overlapping authority and land use was not alien to Venda social networks, but the ZAR and its Location Commissions were unwilling to recognize such broad and shifting claims. Like other independent rulers in the north, Makhado recognized the threat that locations represented, and like many of them, he refused to conduct a census that would serve to legitimize its formulas for taxes and land restrictions and place limits on his patronage besides.[169] The claims of Makhado made it impossible to undertake any beaconing in the Spelonken without revised instructions, and the commissioners sent a resolution to that effect to the government along with reports of the proceedings, but no map.[170] A map, no matter how flawed, would have granted undesirable legitimacy to Makhado's vision.

The Location Commission only reconvened in Zoutpansberg in February 1888 at Oscar Dahl's fortress at Klipdam, and made a raft of resolutions regarding reserves in the Zoutpansberg district, including, as their last order of business, the case of Makhado. The commissioners again included Joubert and Albasini, as well as Dahl, but no surveyor. Albasini related directly that he believed Makhado had only 3,000 households, many on private farms, and further that the king was not obeying government regulations or paying taxes at all. The only resolution the commission reached was to grant him a location as an independent chief, and although they never articulated what that meant, they skipped past the question of Lwamondo because Albasini identified them as being under Makhado.[171] Settlers in the district at the same time pressed for

168 Ibid.

169 Mulaudzi, "U shuma bulasi," 43–44.

170 Tempelhoff, "Okkupasiestelsel," 268; Notulen der Locatiecomissie, Art. 65, 24 Feb 1887, p. 37, SN 177, TAB; Joubert *et al.* to Kruger, 24 Feb 1887, R1526/87, pp. 71–72, SS 1364, TAB.

171 "Notulen der Locatiecommissie," Art. 114 & 113, 9 Feb 1888, p. 66, SN 177, TAB.

the definition of locations by survey as a security issue, because people were sowing and living freely on titled lands, not to mention government lands, whereas legal owners and their labor tenants were paying taxes—if they had not simply been driven out.[172] Beaconing locations would not change any of this, but it would change the meaning of these conditions and acts, and perhaps bring a military response from Pretoria. The legal ambiguity over the landscape evoked chaos but kept the peace.

Certainly Makhado only stood to lose by making any firm arrangement on the terms of the ZAR. It was also abundantly clear that government officials were not neutral in the location process. João Albasini's Shangaans, for example, received recommendation for their own location of about 260 square kilometers (30,000 morgen) from the commission in early February 1888. In this arrangement, the fact that Antonio Albasini was the local Native Commissioner and *de facto* chief certainly helped his case.[173] The younger Albasini seems to have taken an expansive view of his dual role. In June 1888, after the harvest, Joubert met with two representatives from Makhado, who complained that Albasini had demanded that some of their people leave their lands on Rietvlei. Joubert responded that Makhado himself was guilty because the farms had boundaries and beacons, as did missionary stations, but his location did not and so he could not contest those lands until he submitted to a census.[174] Makhado made his disapproval of any imposed land settlement clear in August, and refused to aid in any census while disavowing responsibility for what might happen if Dahl or Joubert tried to do it themselves.[175] Joubert recognized that only a surveyor's precision would suit the needs of the state relative to independent people on ostensibly government property in the far north, and it would prevent complaints or adjustments that might undercut their authority—but a census was still a necessary precondition.[176] At the behest of surveyor F.H. Rissik, Antonio Albasini broached the subject of a census and location survey to Makhado yet again in February 1889, but found his response unchanged.[177]

---

172 Memorial of W.J. Jacobs and 70 others, Zoutpansberg, 12 Apr 1888, R4806/88, p. 100, SS 1633, TAB; Memorial of A.P. Botha and 19 others, Zoutpansberg, 26 Jun 1888, R6119/88, p. 124, SS 1671, TAB.

173 "Notulen der Locatiecommissie," Art. 111, 9 Feb 1888, pp. 64–65, SN 177, TAB.

174 Minutes of meeting of P. Joubert with Mambogor and Pompey, R11807/88, 11–14 Jun 1888, pp. 103–106, SS 1795, TAB.

175 Tempelhoff, "Okkupasiestelsel," 268; "Extract uit brief dd. 12 Sept 1888," R11807/88, p. 108, SS 1795, TAB.

176 Memorandum of P. Joubert to W.E. Bok (Staatsecretaris), 2 Oct 1888, R8760/88, pp. 44–45, SS 1725, TAB.

177 Nemudzivhadi, "Attempts," 247–248.

Unable to hem in Makhado with his active consent, the administrators of the ZAR sought to achieve it through implicit threat. The establishment of forts ever nearer his capital, some encroaching on land he had claimed, was openly provocative—as was the parceling out of occupation farms in the forts' shadows, which brought European grantees into conflict with people already living on the land. To the local administrators, this was a vital response to unrest in the area that was driving white farmers off of land and generating complaints of theft and trespass.[178] Piet Joubert therefore visited the Zoutpansberg between June and October 1889 with a few soldiers from the Transvaal artillery corps, in order to devise a strategy for bounding and policing the area.[179] Ultimately he reversed the initial location plan and instead sought to beacon the locations of less powerful groups first to neutralize them, while placing a fort close to Makhado's capital to coerce him towards a settlement—a provocation against which Makhado categorically warned him.[180] At the same time, Makhado was in intermittent conflict with Ligegise Tshivhase while consolidating his own authority, and the latter had appealed through the missionary Carl Beuster for help as "a trusted servant of the Government…and as a friend of the white nation."[181] Makhado consequently refused to meet with Joubert or send any representatives to negotiate with him, in a slight that incensed the Superintendent.[182] Joubert considered simply cordoning Makhado's location with the backing of a military detachment, and made inquiries about the resources available locally.[183] At the same time, he called on Makhado's *mahosi* and headmen to pressure the king, and sent his own offer to mediate between Makhado and Tshivhase and, unsurprisingly, to beacon his location.[184] Makhado declined to respond, but Davhana kept abreast of the news and

178 Tempelhoff, "Okkupasiestelsel," 269.

179 P. Joubert to S.J.P. Kruger, 2 Jun 1889, R6732/89, pp. 64–71, SS 1991, TAB.

180 Minutes of meeting 5 Aug 1889, SN 178, TAB; Minutes of meeting between P. Joubert and representatives of Chief Umswaas and Chief Lerami, 16 Aug 1889, 2, SN 178, TAB; P. Joubert to S.J.P. Kruger, 6 Aug 1889, R8210a/89, pp. 62–63, SS 2037, TAB. The Umswaas mentioned was not the Swati king, but a minor ruler east of Luatame.

181 C. Beuster to P. Joubert, 5 Feb 1889, S.R.85a/89 (under R5310/93), p. 177, SS 3731, TAB.

182 Transcript of remarks from P. Joubert to Machinga and Jan (Makhado's messengers), 16 Aug 1889, enclosure D in P. Joubert to S.J.P. Kruger, 12 Oct 1889, SN 178, TAB; minutes of meeting between P. Joubert and messengers Salomon & Jan, 20 Aug 1889, SN 178, TAB.

183 P. Joubert, Draft minute, n.d. [just before 12 Aug 1889], enclosure D in P. Joubert to S.J.P. Kruger, 12 Oct 1889, SN 178, TAB; D.S. Maré to P. Joubert, 5 Sep 1889, SN 178, TAB.

184 Transcript of meeting between P. Joubert and Piet & Rakatha, 10 Aug 1889, SN 178, TAB; P. Joubert to Makhado, 8 Aug 1889, p. 114, SN 179, TAB.

repeatedly asked the Swiss missionaries if the Boers were finally coming to kill the king.[185]

The government, however, would not allow Joubert to provoke Makhado too openly for fear of starting a real war. The State Secretary of the ZAR was alarmed enough to send a telegram categorically refusing to allow Joubert to erect the fort or to demonstrate military force near Makhado, even though they felt that his claims and Joubert's counterproposal in 1887 were both unacceptably vast.[186] The fort, a collapsible steel structure of Austro-Hungarian manufacture, instead went up further south on the farm 'Boschkoppies,' where it became known as Fort Hendrina after Joubert's wife.[187] The fort was close to Lovedale Park, the estate and store of John Skinner Cooksley, and its erection there served to make it visible to Venda and others who often came to buy from Cooksley; indeed in 1894 Leo Weinthal of the *Pretoria Press* suggested that Lovedale Park protected the fort, not the other way around.[188] The government went so far in its efforts to avoid confrontation in 1889 as to order Joubert to "put Magato on notice that the government by itself ceased the Occupation across the Doorn River [because] it may appear that the present location may be too small" but also to remind him that "the goal is to keep the peace."[189]

Joubert duly transmitted this statement to Makhado in a roundabout way. He sent a message on 25 September 1889 that described a preliminary location with a large extent behind the mountains—roughly 6,200 square kilometers—but had a convoluted southern line that cut off much of his area south of the mountains but north of the Doorn River occupation line.[190] Its landmarks spoke to the curious geography of interaction between Ha Ramabulana and the Republic, in that most of the points on his line were either the beacons of farms J.H. du Plessis inspected in 1864, or the sites of stores belonging to traders who dealt with Makhado. Joubert wrote that the line could be adjusted later after a reliable census, but he demanded that the king keep his people and herds within its confines—an unacceptable order, if not an impossible one. Venda communities thus remained in effective control of the territory between

185 Letter from M.H. Schaefli, 14 Oct 1888, *Bulletin Missionaire des Eglises Libres de la Suisse Romande* (hereafter *BMSR*) 7, no. 51 (Dec 1888): 176.

186 Staatsecretaris (W.J. Leyds) to P. Joubert (telegram), 5 Sep 1889, SN 178, TAB; Tempelhoff, "Okkupasiestelsel," 269; Leyds to P. Joubert, 5 Sep 1889, BB 2911/89, SS 8683, TAB.

187 Nemudzivhadi, "Attempts," 248.

188 Weinthal, "The Magato Visit," 148.

189 Staatsecretaris (W.J. Leyds) to P. Joubert, 7 Sep 1889, SN 178, TAB.

190 P. Joubert to Makhado, n.d. [25 Sep 1889], pp. 186–189, SN 179, TAB.

the occupation line and the 'location.' The young *Zoutpansberg Review*, published in Pietersburg, was under no illusion that Makhado would accept a location peacefully, and maintained that other *mahosi* in the mountains would not accept government authority as long as he refused.[191] The death of João Albasini in 1888, the severing of the link between the office of Spelonken Native Commissioner and the Albasinis with the appointment of a German-born military officer named Adolf Schiel in June 1889, and finally the death of Antonio Albasini in early 1890 may have provided some sense of relief to Makhado.[192] But the new thrust of settler power northward and the coziness between the new ZAR officials and the 'government people,' not to mention Davhana, kept him wary. Peace meant leaving the boundaries of Ha Ramabulana in Makhado's hands, but the physical and notional space for ambiguity continued to shrink.

The Settler State and the Territorial Question, 1890–1895

The moratorium on new occupation farms north of what became known, misleadingly, as the 'Joubert Line' further underscored the incompatibility between European models of landholding and African authority in Pretoria, a stance that ran counter to earlier varieties of coexistence, however unequal.[193] The jagged edge of the inspected farms in fact only appeared in published form on Fred Jeppe's 1893 map of the Zoutpansberg Goldfields in the Royal Geographical Society's *Geographical Journal*, attached to an article where he stated that

> [n]egotiations are still pending with regard to the territory claimed by Magato, who occupies a stronghold in the Zoutpansberge, considered almost impregnable. The Republic has been several times on the point of deciding the dispute with this pugnacious and impertinent chief by force of arms, but the wish to avoid bloodshed and arrange matters in a peaceful manner has been predominant with the authorities.[194]

---

191 "Natives and their Locations," *Zoutpansberg Review*, 8 Oct 1890.

192 After 1890 the group fractured but remained "government people." See the last (unnumbered) page of F. Martins, "Joao Albasini and the Colony of St. Louis," and J. Albasini III, "Matshangaan 1825," p. 6, typescripts in the Albasini Papers, AAS 53, UNISA; Nemudzivhadi, "Attempts," 249.

193 Leonard M. Thompson, "Co-operation and Conflict: The Highveld," in *The Oxford History of South Africa*, ed. Monica Wilson and Leonard M. Thompson (Oxford: Oxford University Press, 1969), 1:442.

194 Friedrich Jeppe, "The Zoutpansberg Goldfields in the South African Republic," *Geographical Journal* 2, no. 3 (Sep 1893): 288 (map), 216.

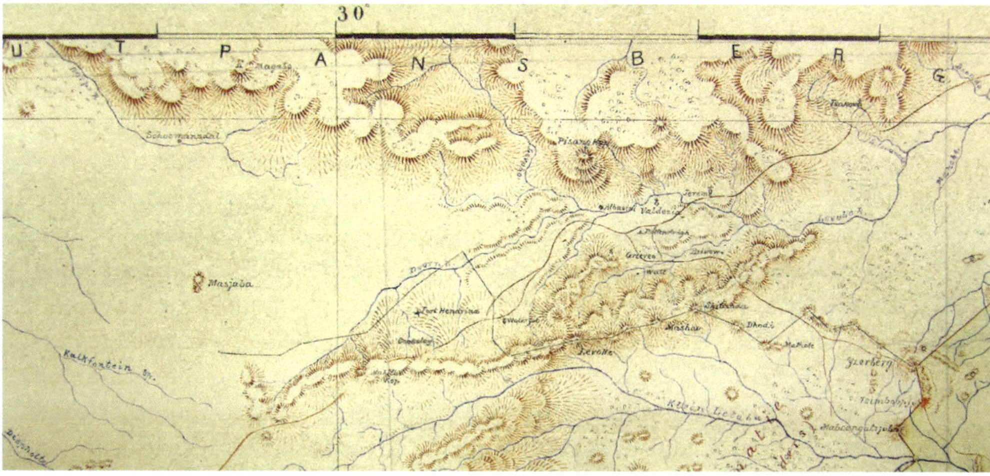

MAP 6.8 *Detail of Jeppe's 1892 manuscript map of the Zoutpansberg Goldfields, showing the incompletely-redefined cadastral edge at the 'Joubert Line' around 30 degrees east at the Doorn River. Note the presence of a variety of places on the settler landscape, and the absence of Venda ones aside from Makhado's own just below the P in 'Zoutpansberg.'*

SOURCE: TAB MAPS 3/1114, TRANSVAAL ARCHIVES DEPOT, NATIONAL ARCHIVES AND RECORDS SERVICE OF SOUTH AFRICA, PRETORIA. RSA STATE COPYRIGHT.

The version Jeppe produced at the same time for the official purposes of the State Mining Engineer, Josef Klimke, does not include the line even though part of it appears on the draft version of the map from May 1892 (see map 6.8). The reluctance to show this tentative boundary on any official map issued through a government department is clear, given that other bounded native locations were clearly shown on all states of the map.[195] Jeppe, however, did not depict the more northerly line Joubert described to Makhado in 1889, either because he did not know of it or because the landmarks Joubert described were not familiar.

Venda households in Ha Ramabulana had as little incentive to accept impositions on their territory as Makhado did. Editor and emissary Leo Weinthal

---

195 The manuscript draft that includes the eastern part of the cadastral edge is "Schets Kaart aantonende de Zoutpansberg Goudvelden verzameld op Grond van Metingen, Inspectien, en Persoonlijke Waarnemingen van den Staats Mijn Ingenieur J. Klimke, door Fred. Jeppe Landmeter Generaals Departement Mei 1892," Maps 3/1114, TAB. The published version without the boundary is F. Jeppe, "Schets Kaart aantonende de Zoutpansberg Goudvelden gecompileerd van Metingen en Inspectien door Fred. Jeppe, Landmeter Generaals Departement Februari 1893," copy at Maps 3/1115, TAB; the map is described officially in ZPP, *Rapport van den Staats-mijningenieur aan de Hoog Edele Regeering over het Jaar 1892* (Pretoria, 1893), 1.

remarked as late as 1894 on their healthy crops and vast herds—key measures of African wealth and effective land use.[196] In particular, he commented on abundant "mealie plantations," smaller cornfields, and even tobacco farming, which attests to a rapid growth of commercial activity in Ha Ramabulana.[197] Laborers to the mines could afford guns and other implements, but people could also sell or trade valuable hardwoods and salt from the pan west of the mountains, while the grain surplus for sale to the coast and inland towns increased as infrastructure improved and greater numbers of people came to the area.[198] The long-standing rumors of gold-bearing ore south and east of the mountains presaged the proclamation of goldfields in the years after 1887 (six by 1893, which prompted Jeppe's map and article) and drove the movement of non-farming consumers into the area, which likewise improved the market for Venda produce and other commodities.[199] New road construction south of the mountains further encouraged regional commerce, which included the arrival of traders to service new landholders as well as African communities in the far north.[200] Makhado exercised some control in admitting outside traders, and traveled to see friendly merchants south of the mountains to meet prospective new vendors, while Cooksley used his friendship with the king to establish at least two additional stores situated at intervals around the mountains.[201] The local Traders' Association in fact took a dim view of calls for war against Makhado, which they felt the publisher of the *Zoutpansberg Review* was particularly guilty of stoking.[202]

The cessation of new grants north of the Doorn River did not stop the further extension of the general immigration to the area, which put pressure on the survey apparatus of the state to divide and register new parcels of land. In the Spelonken wards, this process began before the *Occupatiewet* became law in

---

196 Weinthal, "The Magato Visit," 149; Dreier, "Years of Terrible Drought," 5.

197 Weinthal, "The Magato Visit," 148–149; Mulaudzi, "U shuma bulasi," 31–32.

198 See Mulaudzi, "U shuma bulasi," 31–32. This also suggests strongly that many of the new white farmers struggled compared to established Venda producers, and the latter apparently even built their own roads for trade purposes; see Weinthal, "The Magato Visit," 145, 149.

199 For the proclamations, see Jeppe, "The Zoutpansberg Goldfields," 218–222.

200 Tempelhoff, "Okkupasiestelsel," 268.

201 B.H. Dicke, *The Bush Speaks: Border Life in the Old Transvaal* (Pietermaritzburg: Shuter and Shooter, 1936), 375; Retlaw Yelihw [Walter Whiley], "Interviewing Magato and His Lady," *Zoutpansberg Review*, 11 Dec 1889; Nemo [pseud.], "Ten Days in a Spider (Part 2)," *Zoutpansberg Review*, 10 Jun 1891.

202 See copy of W. Brown to W.R. McNal, 17 Jul 1893, under R13496/93, p. 181, SS 4000, TAB, wherein Brown uses the call for "smashing Magato" to threaten the Association against a boycott of the paper.

1886. The wards only had their own geographical definitions settled after 1885, because the highly imprecise reckoning of the four wards in Zoutpansberg from 1883 had proven to be geographically impossible, and one German cartographer found even the corrected proclamation to be rife with errors.[203] With such poor schematic knowledge of the area around Ha Ramabulana in the geographical archive, surveyors were both starting over and trying to reconcile a fictitious partial landscape of *plaatsen* with physical and human geographies that were especially unclear to them. Surveyors moved successively from correcting old inspections under the Special Commissions law (No. 3) in 1887 to conducting new surveys under the revised General Survey Law (No. 9) of 1891 for occupation farms and mining stands, while survey authorities helped to monitor the working of the *Occupatiewet* in Zoutpansberg.[204] However, survey activity in the area locals increasingly called 'Magatoland' arrived quite late.

Five special inspection commissions worked partially or wholly in the vast Klein Spelonken ward between 1888 and 1896. Initially F.H. Rissik drew the work, but later commissions used P.A. van Breda, and finally A.L. Devenish, who after 1890 was the assigned surveyor for the *meetdistrikt* that included Ha Ramabulana, took the bulk of new work.[205] The presence of surveyors could expose overlap in the process of repeating it; Devenish, for example, had to write to government in July 1889 to complain that his special commission far to the south of Venda had cut out some fifteen occupation farms that people under chief Mphatele used for agriculture and residences, and that they occupied even more ground than that beyond his commission's work.[206] By census, the Location Commission decided they were only 'entitled' to nine farms and portions of three others, and although they obtained its slight enlargement, they did not receive the area Devenish initially noted, and Mphatele had to move his own residence to be inside of it.[207] The special

203 B.J. Vorster, Jr. (Acting *landdrost*, Zoutpansberg) to Bok, 29 Dec 1883, R6/84 (with map), pp. 70–71 (map at p. 72), SS 1184, TAB; H. Raddatz to Bok, 15 Jun 1885 (with map), R3130/85, pp. 75–76 (map between pp. 71 and 72), SS 1184, TAB; H. Raddatz to Bok, 12 Oct 1885, R5236/85, p. 77, SS 1184, TAB.

204 There were in total nine commissions over the Occupation Law. See Tempelhoff, "Okkupasiestelsel," 56–70.

205 "Proclamaties Aangaande de Verschillende Speciale Commissies," n.d. [1896], R1667/96, p. 3, SS 5248, TAB; *Staats Courant der Z.A. Republiek*, 17 Sep 1890, 892. The *meetdistrikten* later increased in number, but Devenish and his partner, C.A. Rühs, seem to have kept the kingdom within their area.

206 A.L. Devenish to D.S. Maré, 15 Jul 1889, R7418/89, pp. 46–47, SS 2009, TAB.

207 "Notulen der Locatiecommissie," 6 Nov 1889, pp. 67–68, 97, SN 177, TAB; Tempelhoff, "Okkupasiestelsel," 61; "M'Phatlele's Location," Map 3/1486, TAB.

commissions and surveys, far from safeguarding African lands, absolutely diminished them.

Although surveyors often complained about the tariffs paid for surveys, some had a personal stake in the resolution of ambiguity surrounding Makhado and other rulers of the north. Beyond occupation farms, the Location Commission was another source of revenue, and Devenish himself took up the survey of the locations they assigned to the Shangaans ('Knobneuzen') and Davhana ('Tabaan') in 1892, as part of four location surveys that brought him £166 10s for a month and a half of work.[208] Devenish took up speculation as well, and bought one of the farms Jan du Plessis inspected in 1864, 'Welgevonden,' from an absentee owner at the Cape; he was also a partial owner of the prospecting farm 'Frischgewaagd' to the south (which he had surveyed himself) and had stakes in other properties besides.[209] He acquired most of those fairly cheaply as they were virtually worthless without a resolution of the situation with Makhado, but without that impediment Devenish, like the Assistant Surveyor-General, Johann Rissik, was sure that buying up land and mineral claims in the Spelonken would have a superb return.[210] Indeed, after the king's death Devenish would become a very familiar figure in the area. He was already well known in Pietersburg during the early 1890s for his stranglehold on surveys and the proceeds he derived from them in land and money, and in some circles he was openly reviled because of it—to the point that Devenish even had to drag *landdrost* Munnik to the Supreme Court for defamation in 1896.[211]

Further conflict over the land was therefore an absolute certainty. White landholders close to the mountains complained about the presence of people, presumably under Makhado, who forced them to vacate in 1890 and 1891.[212] In May 1890, the ZAR therefore sanctioned the construction of a town on Albasini's former farms less than 20 kilometers to the east of Luatame, and resolved in August the following year to establish a town directly on Rietvlei and declared

208 "Notulen der Locatiecommissie," 6 Nov 1889, pp. 100–103, SN 177, TAB; Devenish to P. Joubert, 5 Sep 1892, SR938/92, SN 21, TAB.

209 "Local and General," *Zoutpansberg Review*, 7 May 1890; E.F. Short (Devenish), "Twenty Years in the Transvaal Republic," ed. A.D. Irvine. *Pretoriana* 107 (Nov 1995): 6, 41–42.

210 See J.F.B. Rissik to F.H. Rissik, 31 Jan 1888, p. 33, MA1974/759 (Rissik Collection), MuseuMAfricA, Johannesburg.

211 "We Want to Know," *Zoutpansberg Review*, 5 Jan 1893; "The General Survey," *Zoutpansberg Review*, 10 Feb 1893; A.L. Devenish vs. G.G. Munnik, Case 3451/1897, pp. 488–545, ZTPD 5/1431, TAB. Eventually this case, and a matching countersuit from Munnik, were dropped, and each continued in his respective office.

212 Tempelhoff, "Okkupasiestelsel," 269.

their intent to Makhado.[213] The former settlement, however, developed poorly and, despite preparations to survey the land and move Fort Hendrina to Rietvlei, Joubert ultimately could not recommend it while Ha Ramabulana remained autonomous under Makhado.[214] That Rietvlei and other low-lying areas were malarial in summer and Makhado had not yet assented did not appear to matter to commentators who believed it might go forward in winter 1892 as a matter of security.[215] Ultimately the military element moved to the residence of Native Commissioner Schiel instead, and Makhado remained in possession of the ground.[216]

Though the state preferred assent to confrontation, its functionaries were not as accommodating. Adolf Schiel's initial dealings with Makhado after his appointment as Native Commissioner in 1889 had been "unusually friendly," and Makhado had casually told Schiel in December 1889 that he was the child [client] of government and would pay his taxes.[217] Schiel's effort in January 1890 to obtain a census bore less fruit. Makhado called together people from towns in the mountains and produced 2,150 adults and 1,172 children, but he said it was impossible to call all of them in the summer, and Schiel agreed to go back to count people and huts in the winter.[218] By March, Makhado had collected £592 7s in total for Schiel, which the king felt should be satisfactory. Schiel, expecting many times that amount, demanded more. It was impossible to collect more, the king told him, because the people kept no more money and they were afraid to leave the kingdom to work.[219] This last comment is interesting in its own right because it speaks to the relative prosperity of the country on its own terms. The imposition of taxes had as one of its goals the uprooting of labor, but that had been a sore point in the 1860s. Venda traders were more prosperous, but they did not seek to build up cash reserves when they could obtain cattle or other useful goods like plows or guns. Besides, the wage labor market in the vicinity was already heavy with people under his enemies and rivals. The Boers also paid farm laborers very little, just as

213 Tempelhoff, "Okkupasiestelsel," 136–137; A. Schiel (Native Commissioner, Spelonken) to P. Joubert, 6 Aug 1891, R9494/91 (under R5310/93), p. 113, SS 3731.

214 G. Munnik (*landdrost*, Zoutpansberg) to P. Joubert, R9493/81 (under R5310/93), p. 111, SS 3731, TAB; P. Joubert to W.J. Leyds (Staatsecretaris), R15686/91 (under R5310/93), p. 124, SS 3731, TAB.

215 "Local and General: Spelonken Specimens," *Zoutpansberg Review*, 13 Feb 1892.

216 Leyds to P. Joubert, 28 Dec 1891, R15686/91 (under R5310/93), p. 125, SS 3731, TAB.

217 Schiel to P. Joubert, 31 Dec 1889, R442/90, pp. 10–12, SS 2206, TAB.

218 Schiel to P. Joubert, 14 Mar 1890, R442/90, pp. 16–27, SS 2206, TAB.

219 Schiel to P. Joubert, 14 Mar 1890, R442/90, pp. 18–20, SS 2206, TAB.

Makhado had told Antonio Albasini in 1886, and only those who worked in the mines might have money to pay on demand.[220]

Later, when Schiel returned and persisted, the interactions were less friendly. The headmen and *mahosi* obstructively answered "a hundred" to any request Schiel made for counts of huts, men, women, children, and lands, and when he tried to begin a census himself, people went missing or declared they did not belong to those areas.[221] There are a number of reasons for this obstruction, including the demonstration of Schiel's utter lack of knowledge about the landscape and his reliance on Venda consent, as well as a desire to keep Europeans from crossing the land to assay and divide people in a threat to the temporal and spiritual power of a *khosi* or a king. Indeed, the census and its consequences created those precise problems in colonized Zululand in 1904 and contributed to uprisings there in 1906.[222] The stance Makhado assumed against taxes and census by 1892 led Piet Joubert, at a meeting in the district, to threaten him in absentia with the total destruction, dispossession, and scattering visited on the Ndzundza chiefdom in 1883 if he persisted.[223] Joubert's goal was largely to dissuade other groups from following his lead in the face of rising hut and road tax levies, but the threat against land and society was a rhetorical escalation. The obstruction even exasperated the Commandant of the Mounted Artillery and Police, Henning Pretorius, who as head of the Location Commission in July 1892 told an unwilling chief that he could either accept a census and location, leave the country, or go to Makhado—but that if he went to Makhado, there would still be a day of reckoning.[224]

Makhado also came to see Schiel as a threat because the commissioner exerted authority over the king's enemies, including the Shangaans and Davhana (until his death in June 1894), and he sought to inflate the recurring clashes between Makhado and Ligegise Tshivhase over the succession in Ha Rammbuda into reasons for diplomatic disengagement or worse.[225]

---

220 Nemudzivhadi, "Attempts," 235.

221 Adolf Schiel, *23 Jahre Sturm und Sonnenschein in Südafrika* (Leipzig: Brockhaus, 1902), 249–251.

222 Benedict Carton, *Blood From Your Children: The Colonial Origins of Generational Conflict in South Africa* (Charlottesville: University Press of Virginia, 2000), 86.

223 "The General in Rhenosterport," *Zoutpansberg Review*, 30 Mar 1892. On the Ndzundza case and its consequences, see Peter Delius, "The Ndzundza Ndebele: Indenture and the Making of an Ethnic Identity, 1883–1914," in *Holding Their Ground: Class, Locality, and Culture*, ed. P. Bonner, I. Hofmeyer, D. James, and T. Lodge (Johannesburg: Ravan, 1987), 227–258.

224 "Notulen der Locatiecommissie," 26 Jul 1892, p. 119, SN 177, TAB.

225 Nemudzivhadi, "Attempts," 260.

'Swart' Barend Vorster (Sr.) very nearly launched an attack upon Luatame based on this faulty information and was only dissuaded by a telegram from Kruger and the intervention of Munnik, who visited Makhado personally in August 1891.[226] In October 1893, another complaint from Ligegise Tshivhase about an attack from Makhado drew a cynical response from Schiel that it was useless to investigate because Makhado ignored all warnings, and the two always blamed each other for any fighting anyway.[227] Schiel and the king were at an impasse.

In this non-cooperative atmosphere, Makhado sent contradictory signals to maintain his initiative. Although *landdrost* Munnik in Pietersburg reported that Makhado was prepared to accept a location and pay taxes in June 1894, Leo Weinthal of the Pretoria *Press*, as an unofficial envoy, reported just weeks later that Makhado was willing to pay taxes to President Kruger (and not to Schiel), but that he would not move to a location.[228] When one of Makhado's subject *mahosi* permitted a census in October for Barend Vorster Sr., as Native Commissioner for Kalkbank ward, he came under attack from the forces of the king.[229] Vorster was ordered not to precipitate conflict while the ZAR was busy with other campaigns, but apparently he was able to obtain information from a few *mahosi*. Makhado purportedly sent word to the elder Vorster through Rasivhetshele that he had given a general order to allow a census and pay taxes, but when Schiel was to be sent to the mountain, Vorster's son—Barend Vorster, Jr., a member of the *Volksraad*'s second chamber—wrote to object and soon became a candidate for Schiel's position.[230] When Schiel sought to take the census and collect taxes, Makhado refused, and word of the king's opposition to Schiel quickly reached Joubert.[231]

Schiel complained bitterly about the self-interested Vorster, who had arranged a mineral concession covering all of Makhado's lands for the speculator Edward P. Scrutton in January 1894 by claiming to represent Makhado in

226 Ibid., 253–257; Munnik, *Memoirs*, 145–148.

227 Memorandum by A. Schiel, 12 Feb 1894, R13496/93, pp. 176–177, SS 4000, TAB.

228 M.H. Nemudzivhadi, "The Conflict between Mphephu and the South African Republic, 1895–1899" (master's thesis, UNISA, 1977), 27–28; B. Vorster, Jr. to P. Joubert, 26 Jun 1894, CR2084/94, KG 81, TAB; Weinthal, "The Magato Visit," 142–143.

229 B. Vorster, Sr. to P. Joubert, 12 Oct 1894, SR1496/94 (under R10366/94), pp. 25–26, SS 4485, TAB; B. Vorster, Sr. to P. Joubert, 9 Oct 1894, SR1522/94 (under R10366/94), p. 46, SS 4485, TAB.

230 B. Vorster, Jr. to Kruger, 29 Nov 1894, R11901/94 (under R10366/94), pp. 50–51, SS 4485, TAB; Nemudzivhadi, "Attempts," 261–262. The latter does not differentiate between the two Vorsters; the younger however was known as 'Klein' or 'Kreupel' Barend.

231 P. Joubert to Makhado, 13 Dec 1894 (unnumbered), SN 115, TAB. It is possible that Rasivhetshele was acting on his own unsanctioned initiative.

order to register Scrutton's rights with the ZAR's Registrar of Deeds.[232] Scrutton, who claimed to have lived near Makhado since 1890, had been inquiring since April as to the state of matters because of this concession. In his inquiry, Scrutton invoked the interest of other parties in hiring land for plantations in the locations and the possibility of capital investment; to aid matters, he offered to mediate, erect beacons, and do anything necessary to settle the matter.[233] Vorster claimed in October that Rasivhetshele had again declared Makhado's willingness to allow a census and pay taxes, while Pretorius had performed military reconnaissance in the area to "look behind the fortifications" and collect tactical information about the kingdom, although he took the elder Vorster so as not to arouse fresh suspicion from Makhado.[234]

By the end of 1894, ZAR military actions against other powerful kings and chiefs in the north using powerful new weapons enjoyed devastating if hard-fought military successes, which did not fail to impress Makhado, if not alarm him outright.[235] His cultivation of British contacts from the north may have been related to this concern. Several Rhodesian officers reportedly visited with Makhado in the 1890s and developed friendly relations in a direct affront to the Republic's claims of sovereignty over the kings and chiefs within its boundaries, which the Boers also noted with some worry.[236] When the Berlin missionary Reinhold Wessmann visited Luatame in early 1895, Makhado stated again that he would put himself *directly* under government and pay taxes to Pretoria, but he would not hear of locations or censuses.[237] The conflicting reports from Vorster, Scrutton, Munnik, and Schiel clearly required some sort of official commission to sort out, as did the truth of Makhado's complaints against Schiel as Native Commissioner.[238] In hopes that Makhado would be receptive to meeting the Location Commission, the *Uitvoerende Raad* published a resolution in early April 1895, and the new commission chair, again Henning

---

232 "Precis of that Portion of Minute R12007/96 relating to Scrutton's Concession," n.d. [1906], 1, file 477a, SGO-PTA; Contract 360/1894, 8 Jan 1894, in J.H. Scrutton & E.P. Scrutton v. L. Ehrlich & Co., New District Development Co., Ltd., & H.E. Proprietary Ltd., Case 80/1908, pp. 682–693, ZTPD 5/649, TAB.

233 J.H. Scrutton (qq. E.P. Scrutton) to P. Joubert, 10 Apr 1894, SR793/94, SN 26, TAB;.

234 B. Vorster, Jr., to P. Joubert, 15 Oct 1894, SR 1536/94 (under R10291/94), pp. 47–48, SS 4485, TAB; H.P.N. Pretorius to P. Joubert, 22 Oct 1894, R10613/94, SS 4496, TAB.

235 Tempelhoff, "Okkupasiestelsel," 270–271.

236 Ibid., 274; Nemudzivhadi, "Attempts," 262–264.

237 R. Wessmann to P. Joubert, 16 Jan 1895, R1198/95 (under R10366/94), pp. 60–61, SS 4485, TAB.

238 "Kopie Memorie…J.J. Roos, L. Jordaan, en 53 anderen," Apr 1895, R6268/95 (under R10291/94), pp. 142–143, SS 4485, TAB.

Pretorius, requested that a surveyor be held in readiness.[239] Pretorius embarked after hearing from the self-interested and openly solicitous E.P. Scrutton that Makhado would at last permit a census and beaconing, although the commission did not take the surveyor yet.[240] They arrived on Rietvlei on 8 May and demanded to see Makhado.

This meeting, unlike earlier occasions, was much more formal in protocol. A body of 60 or 70 armed soldiers met and escorted the commission into the mountains to the village of one of Makhado's junior wives, and Pretorius noted the presence of "many armed Kaffers on both sides of the path," a show of military power that was certainly intentional.[241] At the capital, the commissioners did not meet Makhado, but a number of '*indunas*' along with Funyufunyu, whom Pretorius labeled the 'head *induna*.' Funyufunyu was indeed Makhado's most reliable commander—and in confrontational matters spoke with that power as his eyes, ears, and shield.[242] Funyufunyu stated plainly that his purpose was to convey the words of Makhado that he refused to allow a count of huts or a census of people, and he also would not allow the land to be divided. He disavowed any acquaintance with Scrutton (he was not in fact a signatory to the concession), suggesting that Scrutton misled the commission for reasons of his own, given that mineral concessions over an undefined territory were of dubious value. Funyufunyu further castigated them for breaking the government's word regarding the location question:

> Tromp also said: "See what Barend Vorster [Jr] has done; he promised the land from the Doorn River to Witklip and from there past the Zoutpan to the Krokodil [Limpopo] River to us, and he [Vorster] and his father had [*sic*] already taken away a further portion of this ground."[243]

---

239 F.C. Stiemens to P. Joubert, 9 Apr 1895, p. 232, SN 179, TAB.

240 Scrutton went so far as to send a draft authorization and instructions to Pretoria for signature; see "Opdracht en Instructies voor den Heer Scruten [*sic*]," SR639/95 (under R10291/94), p. 134, SS 4485, TAB.

241 H.P.N. Pretorius to P. Joubert, 13 May 1895, R4808/95, pp. 165–166, SS 4805, TAB; "Notulen der Locatiecommissie," 8 May 1895, p. 165, SN 177, TAB; Nemudzivhadi, "Attempts," 270.

242 The position involved distilling visitors' business for a chief or headman, and required direct access, so Funyufunyu was *nduna*, but we do not know if he held additional titles at this time. Rasivhetshele was sometimes also 'head *induna*' to visitors, but Funyufunyu seems to have held slightly higher esteem.

243 "Notulen der Locatiecommissie," 8 May 1895, p. 166, SN 177, TAB; "Zitting van de Locatie Commissie te Rietvley onder Magato's Hoofstad 8 Mei 1895," SR 869/95 (under R10291/94), pp. 112–113, SS 4485, TAB.

That the Vorsters might have made such a promise beyond their authority, and inevitably broken it, was in keeping with the "ambitious and haughty" behavior that helped 'Swart' Barend provoke a war with the chief Mmalebogo to the west in 1894.[244] Certainly such an accusation furthered the king's efforts to pit the Vorsters against Schiel. But a more important issue lies in the connection between Scrutton and the younger Vorster. For them, promoting Makhado's expansive claims and seeing them enter the state's geographical archive was the next step in realizing the maximum value of those mineral rights, and the concession could have been a vehicle to achieve Makhado's territorial aims as well. The matter clearly required direct communication between the king and the commission. Funyufunyu reiterated that he spoke for Makhado, who would not allow the land to be divided or a census taken, and that the money the king already paid was "for the corn that we eat and the land upon which we live." Makhado, who wished to be perfectly clear about the matter, soon sent word that he would meet with the Commision in person the following morning.[245]

The audience at Luatame served simply to put an official stamp on Funyufunyu's words. When asked directly if that answer was final, Makhado responded that his *mahosi*—all still present at this meeting—could speak freely on the matter, at which point all echoed Funyufunyu's sentiments. The response of Pretorius showed how little had changed in the eight years since Joubert first made his arguments—that the demarcation line conveyed in 1889 was not binding on the government (for it was neither beaconed nor surveyed), that new immigrants would continue to come in, and without a census the boundaries could not be fixed and Venda lands assured. Makhado still recognized that acceptance of boundaries meant the loss of land and the true abdication of sovereignty. His final response to Pretorius was that it was unnecessary to talk further, because the southern boundaries were good as they were, loosely at the Doorn and Sand Rivers as he stated Vorster had indicated—and which was in keeping with the state of affairs since 1887—and for the moment Pretorius let it stand.[246] But such boundaries were imprecise, the area was vast, and it did not confer the kind of legibility and control over the people and landscape of Ha Ramabulana that the government in Pretoria sought. Besides,

244 *Dictionary of South African Biography*, ed. W.J. de Kock (Pretoria: Nasionale Boekhandel, 1968–81), s.v. "Vorster, Barend Jacobus, the younger"; Lize Kriel, "African Reaction to White Penetration: The Hananwa of Blouberg, ca. 1886–1894," *Historia* 45, no. 1 (2000): 60.

245 "Notulen der Locatiecommissie," 8 May 1895, p. 166, SN 177, TAB.

246 "Notulen der Locatiecommissie," 9 May 1895, pp. 166–167, SN 177, TAB; Report of the Commandant-General, 13 May 1895, R4809/95, pp. 159–160, SS 4805, TAB; Tempelhoff, "Okkupasiestelsel," 270.

Joubert recognized that the other major Venda *mahosi* would refuse censuses and locations so long as Makhado could, even though they pretended to cooperate with the ZAR for their own reasons.[247]

After hearing of the commission's total failure to exact concessions, Piet Joubert proposed a shift to more forceful measures to pressure Makhado, including new military encroachment.[248] Although concern about a general rising of Venda stopped any immediate action, Joubert was preparing for the possibility of a campaign in winter 1896 once military matters with people to the south had been settled.[249] But Makhado's death in September 1895, possibly from poisoning by a conspiracy that included his uncle Mutheiwana, his advisor Rasivhetshele, and his senior wife Nwaphunga, changed matters entirely. Indeed, he may have been removed to allow the pursuit of a more conciliatory attitude towards the ZAR, as Rasivhetshele and Nwaphunga had expressed their concerns with the king's machinations to Wessmann in January, and Makhado had named Nwaphunga's son Maemu Malise as his preferred successor a few years before.[250] If poison was the culprit, however, then the conspirators severely miscalculated the ultimate effects of Makhado's removal. But they also could not have anticipated the role of external factors in reshaping the landscape of Ha Ramabulana.

---

247 P. Joubert to Leyds, 4 Nov 1891, R13574/91, SS 3071, TAB. Although the ZAR hoped to beacon other Venda locations in 1888, no serious effort followed until after Makhado's death, and then was refused. See "Notulen der Locatiecommissie," Arts. 110 & 113, 9 Feb 1888, pp. 63 & 65–66, SN 177, TAB; H.P.N. Pretorius to P. Joubert, 1 Jun 1896, R6286/96, SS 5456, TAB.

248 "Binnenland," *De Volksstem*, 19 Jun 1895.

249 Tempelhoff, "Okkupasiestelsel," 272. It may have helped the calculus against war that new reports of English officers visiting Makhado's capital began to arrive; see Schiel to P. Joubert, 20 May 1895, CR 2381/95, KG 122, TAB.

250 R. Wessmann to P. Joubert, 16 Jan 1895, R1198/95 (under R10366/94), p. 60, SS 4485, TAB; Nemudzivhadi, "Conflict," 29–32.

CHAPTER 7

The Fall and Rise of Mphephu

The passing of Makhado marked a powerful political shift for a landscape that had already changed. During his lifetime, Ha Ramabulana had become a semi-commercial enclave that benefited from connections to the south and east, but one that retained an insular character. The machinery of colonial knowledge and subjection that bounded African lands and dictated changes in social and spatial order elsewhere had not made the same inroads in the kingdom or in the major Venda polities to the east. Makhado, at least, had exposed its demands and threats as primarily bluster that could be negotiated or manipulated away, with the result that Venda occupation of the lands between the Doorn, Sand, and Limpopo rivers west of his neighboring great *mahosi* remained uninterrupted. But without the central presence of the king, an opening existed for the ZAR to weaken the political order in a way they could not in 1864, and it came at a time when Venda households and communities faced some of the greatest environmental and ecological dislocations in memory. The result was ultimately the achievement of the stated goals of the South African Republic and its successors in dividing and categorizing land, but the landscape that emerged was not the same on the ground as it was in the archive—in part because the rulers of Ha Ramabulana and the Venda households there continued to exert their influence on that landscape.

This disconnected set of landscapes—one notional but ever more precise, and the others built on local knowledge—reflected adaptation to changing conditions. Before the South African War (1899–1902), Venda leadership tried to operate in the same way as before, using carefully measured policy shifts towards the ZAR to keep them at arm's length; that strategy ultimately failed at the end of 1898, when the demands of consolidation collided with the ambitions of the Republic. During and after the South African War, however, Venda leadership shifted strategies to work around, but not directly against, the new British colonial authorities who vexingly took up the notional landscape of the ZAR they superseded and peppered the mountains with privately-owned farms. In the years after 1900, Makhado's son Mphephu and his supporters used legal and social interventions to obtain the return of the king himself and restore much of their authority over the people, who still dominated the landscape even where they had no place in the colonial state's geographical archive. In essence, the endurance of Ha Ramabulana turned on a few patches of land and vast networks that formed a 'shadow state,' stretching far across the

 | DOI 10.1163/9789004282292_008

Soutpansberg range from the Nzhelele Valley where the British colonial government assigned Mphephu a location. The landscape became much more complicated and challenging for Venda livelihoods, but the Ramabulana kingship maintained a surprisingly strong geographical reach and the ability to employ every measure short of force to enhance its position. The South African government's 2010 recognition of Mphephu's lineage as holders of the controversial 'traditional' office of king (*thovele*) over all Venda houses in perpetuity, one of only seven such houses across South Africa, suggests the eventual extent of their success in redefining the relationship between authority, society, and territory.[1]

On the land, that success after 1900 meant that Venda homesteads remained in more extensive occupation of land, with greater wealth, than many others in South Africa. But their landscapes also changed in response to the acceptance of colonial rule and its enumerative drives. The emergence of white-owned farms on the mountains and the progressive surveying and dividing of lands within Ha Ramabulana created new obstacles to Venda security and livelihoods outside of the relatively small locations the British colonial government recognized after 1902. That extension of white farming and tax liability, together with the end of direct conflict between the ruling houses of the region, augured a broader dispersal of people across the landscape than existed before, but matters rarely unfolded the way governments in Pretoria intended. Although the experience of the king, Mphephu, is central to considering the endurance of Ha Ramabulana, everyone experienced the fracturing landscape in different ways.

Interstate Confrontation and Collapse, 1895–1899

Regardless of the cause of Makhado's death in 1895, it caused the leadership of Ha Ramabulana to fragment in dramatic fashion. As it had been for Ramabulana and Makhado, the struggle for succession was the issue that widened the cracks that already existed. Initially, Makhado's youngest son Maemu Malise claimed the throne on the strength of the king's preference and the simple fact

1 Department of Cooperative Government and Traditional Affairs (South Africa), "Report on the Position of the Paramount Chiefs," 29 Jul 2010, 599–664. On the Ramabulana claim to kingship and the idea of cultural homogeneity in Venda, as well as the historical development of the idea of a single Venda throne, see Caroline Jeannerat, "An Ethnography of Faith: Personal Conceptions of Religiosity in the Soutpansberg, South Africa, in the 19th and 20th Centuries" (PhD diss., University of Michigan, 2007), 175–179, 202–207.

that he was actually at Luatame when his father died. His supporters, including his mother Nwaphunga, his maternal uncle Mutheiwana, and Rasivhetshele moved quickly to install Maemu precisely because he had very little support, and although they did not have the approval of the *makhadzi*, they clearly did not consider it insurmountable.[2] The initial weakness of his claim meant that Maemu and his confederates immediately embraced the ZAR, offered their fealty, and sought its support.

The key challenger was Mphephu, Makhado's eldest son, who had important allies and a strong claim from two major sources: his mother and his paternal aunt—the *makhadzi*. His mother, Midana of Phahwe, was not the senior wife but, because her bridewealth was paid with cattle of royal lineage (*dzekiso*), she was Makhado's great wife. The *makhadzi*, Ndalammbi, was also married at Phahwe, suggesting strong bonds between these two powerful women who supported Mphephu.[3] Mphephu further enjoyed the support of his paternal uncle Raliphaswa as well as some of Makhado's closest and most senior *mahosi*, particularly Funyufunyu, who remained his military commander and secretary of state.[4] But at the time of his father's death, Mphephu was in exile at the mines in Kimberley, together with comrades from his age-set and a number of elders.[5] Makhado's second son Sinthumule, another possible claimant, had been at the Rhodesian post of Tuli since late 1894, likely as his father's liaison to the British South Africa Company (BSAC) and possibly as a conduit for purchasing weapons.[6]

2 Alan Kirkaldy, *Capturing the Soul: The Vhavenda and the Missionaries, 1870–1900* (Pretoria: Protea, 2005), 281; M.H. Nemudzivhadi, "The Attempts by Makhado to Revive the Venda Kingdom 1864–1895" (PhD diss., Potchefstroom U., 1998), 194.

3 On the importance of Phahwe and Ndalammbi, see Nemudzivhadi, "Attempts," 166, 178; on relative position of the wives, see M.H. Nemudzivhadi, "The Conflict between Mphephu and the South African Republic, 1895–1899" (master's thesis, UNISA, 1977), 36.

4 Nemudzivhadi, "Conflict," 34–35. Funyufunyu's prominence in fact led to speculation that he had taken over; see "Dood van Magato: Tromp in Zyn Plaats," *Land en Volk*, 26 Sep 1895.

5 Nemudzivhadi, "Attempts," 193; Nemudzivhadi, "Conflict," 37; M.M. Motenda, "History of the Venda and of the Lemba," in *The Copper Miners of Musina and the Early History of the Zoutpansberg*, ed. and trans. N.J. van Warmelo (Pretoria: Government Printer, 1940), 59. Mphephu may have spent some of his time in and around Johannesburg and evidently was even in the mountains at times; see "Magato's Tribe," *Zoutpansberg Review*, 20 Mar 1896; "Onderhoud met Umpifo zoon van Magato Zoutpansberg," 28 Feb 1893, SR243/93, SN 22, TAB; Adolf Schiel, *23 Jahre Sturm und Sonnenschein in Südafrika* (Leipzig: Brockhaus, 1902), 244–246.

6 Nemudzivhadi, "Attempts," 263–264; Nemudzivhadi, "Conflict," 84; Report of J.T. Bain (Commandant Fort Hendrina), 29 May 1896, R13089/96 (under R6826/96), pp. 148, SS 5456, TAB; Report of D. du Preez (Commandant, Zoutpansberg), 22 Jul 1896, SR1717/96, SN 38, TAB.

PHOTO 7.1 *Mphephu and one of his father's wives, probably in 1897.*
SOURCE: TAB FOTO 14549, TRANSVAAL ARCHIVES DEPOT, NATIONAL ARCHIVES AND RECORDS SERVICE OF SOUTH AFRICA, PRETORIA. RSA STATE COPYRIGHT.

The *mahosi* opposed to Maemu sent runners who retrieved the brothers from their distant posts, and when the two returned, they moved in concert against him. The result was a quick rout of Maemu's supporters, who fled south to the protection of the ZAR in Pretoria, and the installation of Mphephu as king in the mountain capital at Luatame at the end of December 1895.[7]

7 Nemudzivhadi, "Conflict," 35–41.

Mphephu put Sinthumule in charge as *khosi* of low-lying land at Tshifhefhe to the southeast, both because of its importance and because it was not especially defensible. The Boers initially regarded Mphephu as a usurper, but it quickly became apparent that Maemu had little if any following in comparison, so they had no choice but to treat him as a legitimate king.[8]

In the tumult following Makhado's death, Piet Joubert had already divined an opportunity to overcome the stubborn failure of previous Boer efforts to confine the Ramabulanas and establish themselves fully in the far north. In November 1895, while the succession was still extremely volatile, Joubert requested the dispatch of another Location Commission to arrange a census and beacon a location, despite receiving no indication from Mphephu that he would receive such a commission.[9] He again called upon Commandant Henning Pretorius to lead the party, and he held Anthony Lennox Devenish in readiness to join the commissioners as soon as Mphephu acquiesced to survey.[10] But Joubert also admonished Pretorius to collect a great deal of clandestine information on matters that were more important to military and diplomatic posturing than to the work of census or survey.[11] Despite his suspicions, Mphephu also made some noises about changing course and meeting with representatives of the Republic, if only to blunt their support for his brothers and buy time to consolidate his office.

This commission, however, had a false start. On their first visit in December 1895, Pretorius and his fellow commissioners had a good reception and even began to make a census, but Mphephu requested a delay on the grounds that he had not yet been fully installed, Makhado was "not yet buried according to native law," that his people would not go to the north in summer owing to fever, and that many people had plowed in places they would not leave before harvest. The commissioners duly departed, but Pretorius's attempt shortly thereafter to mediate between Ligegise Tshivhase and Mphephu over candidates to the Lwamondo leadership led Mphephu to order the four Boer sentries Pretorius had left behind to leave the mountain on the grounds that the government could not back three camps.[12] At that moment the government in Pretoria had a very different concern in the Jameson Raid, the failed overthrow

8 Ibid., 61–62.

9 P. Joubert to S.J.P. Kruger, 20 Nov 1895, R11316/95, SS 5076, TAB.

10 P. Joubert to H.P.N. Pretorius, F.C. Stiemens, and J.J.H. Wolmarans (Confidential), 20 Nov 1895, R11316/95, p. 123, SS 5076, TAB.

11 Copy of P. Joubert to H.P.N. Pretorius, 25 Nov 1895, R11316/95, SS 5076, TAB.

12 H.P.N. Pretorius to P. Joubert, 6 Jan 1896 (with enclosures), R6268/95 (under R10291/94), pp. 144–161, SS 4485, TAB.

attempt from the British South Africa Company (BSAC) in the few days surrounding the New Year. That event diverted attention and resources, but it also reinforced the importance of settling matters in Venda, given prior contact between the Ramabulanas and the BSAC. During 1896 a number of reports of new contacts and foreign interference in Venda reached Pretoria, as did a variety of rumors, and the *Volksraad* put pressure on Joubert to send out another Location Commission.[13]

No proper commission ever actually took the field. President Kruger was of the opinion in February that the time was not ripe for trying to compel a census of Mphephu's people, but that it should be brought up in March, at which point Joubert was of the opinion that unrest was too great to move forward.[14] Indeed Mphephu continued to make military interventions to shore up his father's client network and establish his own authority, especially against the house of Tshivhase. These acts furthered the accusations of Maemu and later Sinthumule that Mphephu was a warmonger, but officers of the ZAR considered the matter akin to "two dogs fight[ing] over a bone" and did not see it as necessarily prohibitive to their work.[15] At the end of March 1896, Joubert promised that the commission would decamp around the first of May barring any trouble, and Pretorius even felt confident enough on 1 April to give Barend Vorster, Jr. a very rough idea of the likely area that would be included, based a sketch map Vorster sent and his own impressions from the prior summer.[16] But the government canceled their departure in late April, and did not call them up again.[17]

Although matters internal to Venda continued to concern Mphephu most heavily, the representatives of the ZAR pressed forward with their intent to

13 Report of J.T. Bain (Commandant Fort Hendrina), 29 May 1896, R13089/96 (under R6826/96), pp. 147–148, SS 5456, TAB; Report of D. du Preez (Commandant, Zoutpansberg), 22 Jul 1896, SR 1717/96, SN 38, TAB; "Spelonken Notes," *Zoutpansberg Review*, 24 Feb 1896 and 24 Apr 1896; Acting Staatsecretaris to P. Joubert, 12 Feb 1896, BB176/96, pp. 238–239, SS 8719, TAB.

14 Memoranda of Staatspresident (Kruger), 13 Feb 1896, and P. Joubert, 23 Mar 1896, R11316/95, pp. 112 & 114, SS 5076, TAB.

15 G.A. du Toit, Report on Conditions at Ramputa [Rammbuda], Feb 1896, R4357/96, p. 81, SS 5509, TAB; Nemudzivhadi, "Conflict," 112–113; TA, Report of meeting with Mahimo [Maemu] and September [Rasivhetshele], 10 Sep 1896, SR1883/96, SN 32, TAB.

16 Memorandum of W.J. Leyds, 30 Mar 1896, R11316/95, pp. 114–115, SS 5076, TAB; B. Vorster, Jr. to H.P.N. Pretorius, 1 Apr 1896 (and reply of the same date thereon), R12007/96, under J.H. Scrutton & E.P. Scrutton v.L. Ehrlich & Co., New District Development Co., Ltd., & H.E. Proprietary Ltd., Case 80/1908, p. 773 and p. 776 (map), ZTPD 5/649, TAB.

17 Memorandum from F.C. Stiemens, 27 Apr 1896, R11316/95, p. 116, SS 5076, TAB.

enumerate and encapsulate Ha Ramabulana by degrees. Joubert sent a letter to Mphephu at the beginning of May announcing the departure of Adolf Schiel as Native Commissioner and his replacement by J.J.H. Wolmarans, but also informing him that *veldcornet* Tom Kelly and resident surveyor (and local landlord) Anthony Lennox Devenish were coming with a Special Commission—not a Location Commission.[18] The purpose of the Special Commission was to re-inspect and beacon farms in the Spelonken ward that bore titles based on the flawed inspections of the 1860s, including those quite close to the mountains. A full survey to divine precise coordinates for these long-notional yet registered plots would follow later, to enact colonial names and numbers upon a landscape that was not yet theirs. Joubert was, however, clear that the task was also a step towards a census and a location, and he trusted that Mphephu and his people "shall help the Surveyor and the Commission to make up the beacons."[19] Mphephu and Legigise Tshivhase, each suspicious of the other, failed to send promised envoys to a meeting meant to introduce Wolmarans, but Mphephu was more receptive to Joubert's approach and indirectly declared himself to be in accord with it.[20] Kelly, when he approached Mphephu about the matter directly at the end of May, in fact got a better response than from the other major Venda leaders, who refused to sanction any such activity; Mphephu reportedly responded only that "it is good."[21]

Devenish had visited the king at least four times by the second week of June, and after finally hearing the details, Mphephu consulted a large council of advisors and agreed to aid the work of the commission.[22] Although the king allowed Devenish to erect beacons in the foothills for the farms Jan du Plessis inspected in 1864, the surveyor was neither prepared to survey a location, nor

18 P. Joubert to Mphephu, 9 May 1896, R6826/96, pp. 128–130, SS 5456, TAB.

19 J.F.B. Rissik (Surveyor-General) to Leyds, 11 May 1896, R5364/96, SS 5393, TAB; "Spelonken Notes," *Zoutpansberg Review*, 8 Jun 1896; P. Joubert to Mphephu, 9 May 1896, R6826/96, pp. 128–130, SS 5456, TAB.

20 Schiel to P. Joubert, 27 May 1896, SR1179/96, SN 36, TAB; Report of J.T. Bain (Commandant Fort Hendrina), 29 May 1896, R13089/96 (under R6826/96), pp. 150–151, SS 5456, TAB.

21 J.T. Kelly (*veldcornet*, Spelonken) to P. Joubert, 21 Oct 1896, CR6965/96 (under R6826/96), pp. 157–158, SS 5456, TAB.

22 A.L. Devenish to P. Joubert, 11 Jun 1896, SR1320/96 (under R6826/96), p. 135, SS 5456, TAB; G.G. Godson to P. Joubert, 11 Jun 1896, SR1355/96 (under R6826/96), pp. 137–138, SS 5456, TAB; "M'pefu," *Zoutpansberg Review*, 15 Jun 1896. The *Review*, however, appears to have conflated his agreement on the matter with the actual work of the commission, which did not include actual location surveying.

was it part of his assignment.[23] In any case, Mphephu maintained a certain reticence about the matter, and internal dissent meant he could not seem too eager—especially if Devenish really intended to put a beacon next to the capital at Luatame, as one report maintained.[24] Although such a beacon would have been useful in a technical sense to triangulate farm beacons, it would also have been a powerful symbol of the incorporation of Ha Ramabulana into the colonial landscape, and although Devenish reportedly built a series of hill beacons, there is no indication that he built one in such a sensitive place.[25] Mphephu even put his mark on a note to Piet Joubert that stated his willingness to accept a census and a location, and requested that Pretoria send a commission.[26]

Mphephu's initial cooperation, however, fell apart when hostilities broke out between him and Sinthumule in July, and the broader scheme collapsed not long after. After several sharp engagements, Sinthumule too sought the protection, if not support, of the Boers, and eventually made common cause later in 1896 with Maemu. Maemu's supporters at the same time portrayed Mphephu as a violent usurper who really sought to attack whites in the Zoutpansberg and would oppose government as soon as his position was secure, while Mphephu in return saw the ZAR's harbouring of his enemies as interference with internal political matters—just as his father had in 1864.[27] The other two great houses of Venda roundly refused Joubert's request to submit to a location survey despite their ostensibly friendlier relationships with

23 J.T. Kelly to P. Joubert, 21 Oct 1896, CR6965/96 (under R6826/96), p. 158, SS 5456, TAB; Nemudzivhadi, "Conflict," 56–58. Nemudzivhadi errs in calling Devenish the head of a Location Commission, when he was in fact the head of a Special Commission under Law 3 of 1887.

24 Devenish to P. Joubert, 11 Jun 1896, SR1320/96 (under R6826/96), p. 135, SS 5456, TAB; "The Surveying," *Zoutpansberg Review*, 22 Jun 1896. The *Review*, like most of the *veldcornetten* and other officials, erroneously refer to the work as surveying (*opmeting*), but Devenish correctly calls it inspection (*inspectie*). The *Review* also is in error in describing the laying out of a township as part of his labor, although he did beacon those farms.

25 "Spelonken Notes," *Zoutpansberg Review*, 6 Jul 1896; see also C.A. Rühs, "Generale Plan van 52 Plaatsen Gelegen in de Wijk Spelonken…Gemeten in September en October 1897," GS 94, Office of the Surveyor-General, Polokwane (hereafter SGO-PKW). Rühs does not indicate any such reference beacons on his plan.

26 Minutes of Correspondence, pp. 8–12, R11316/95, SS 5076, TAB; Declaration of Mphephu, 18 Jun 1896, Appendix VI in Nemudzivhadi, "Conflict," 176. As Mphephu was not literate, there is doubt whether he fully concurred with the contents.

27 Statement of Moetsiwan [Mutheiwana], 20 Feb 1896, in G.A. du Toit (Lieutenant, Mounted Police) to P. Joubert, 3 Mar 1896, R2527/96, pp. 167–168, SS 5277, TAB; Nemudzivhadi, "Conflict," 59–61.

the Republic.[28] In October, Joubert's successor as Superintendent of Native Affairs, General Pieter Arnoldus (Piet) Cronjé, reported that the demarcation of a location for Mphephu simply could not be done that year, never mind locations for any of the other great *mahosi*.[29]

A.L. Devenish, the surveyor, saw his own problems over land in Ha Ramabulana grow at the same time. Because Devenish was the primary surveyor in the Zoutpansberg, he had obtained a number of pieces of land and mineral claims, some within Venda regions. Initially Devenish felt that his 1896 experience with Mphephu and his *mahosi*, together with his regular contact with people under the king, gave him enough cachet to offer his help actively. The surveyor proposed in August 1896 to conduct the census and assess tax himself, with the help of a few select clerks and some native police, after which the Location Commission could come and he would immediately beacon the location.[30] The response was negative, and he offered his help again as a special intermediary directly to government the following year, which they also refused.[31] Devenish did not demonstrate his abilities well. In October 1897 he not only complained to government of unnamed Africans working his mineral claims, but also of large numbers of Venda under one of Mphephu's headmen, Makatu, occupying his farm Welgevonden in the foothills of the mountains.[32] In the latter case, they refused to leave, to pay rent, or to permit Devenish to take up residence. According to his widow, the surveyor

> ...later on went with the Field cornet of the district to lay formal claim to it, with the result that the natives ordered them off in a most threatening manner, a hint they thought best to take. ...[T]he sheriff was sent to the natives with a writ of ejectment, unless they quietly submitted to his occupation. On the sheriff's arrival he was met by the Head Induna of the kraal to whom he handed the writ. This document was contemptuously torn up in his presence and the Chief told him that if he did not instantly

28 H.P.N. Pretorius to P. Joubert, 1 Jun 1896, R6286/96, SS 5456, TAB; H.P.N. Pretorius to P. Joubert, 31 Jul 1896, SR1669/96 (also labeled R10582/96), p. 3, SN 37, TAB.

29 Memorandum by P.A. Cronjé, 12 Oct 1896, R12007/96, in J.H. Scrutton & E.P. Scrutton v.L. Ehrlich & Co., New District Development Co., Ltd., & H.E. Proprietary Ltd., Case 80/1908, p. 779, ZTPD 5/649, TAB.

30 Devenish to P. Joubert, 28 Aug 1896 (unnumbered), SN 80, TAB.

31 Devenish to *Uitvoerende Raad*, 10 Sep 1897 (with reply), R12996/97, pp. 28–31, SS 6725, TAB.

32 See P.A. Cronjé to Staatsecretaris, 21 Feb 1898, R2206/98, SS 7031, TAB; Staatsecretaris to Staatsprokurer (Attorney General), 6 Jan 1898, SPR 176/98, SP 158, TAB; Zoutpansberg Board of Executors & Trust Co. to Leyds, 21 Oct 1897 (and memorandum appertaining), R14816/97 (under R9125/94), pp. 179, 188–190, SS 4428, TAB.

> take himself off, his person would be treated in the same manner. He further emphasised his threat by ordering a score of armed warriors to escort them with all speed off the farm.[33]

The officer of the court (and former assistant *landdrost*) who went to Welgevonden to order the people under Makatu to leave the farm and pay compensation, John William Johnson, indeed reported that the headman answered that his people would not leave and would not pay, but if Johnson did not leave they would take knobkerries to him.[34] Any confidence Devenish had in his diplomatic ability with Mphephu was clearly misplaced, and he sold his interest in the property at some point in the following six months.

This low-level conflict with Devenish did not prevent his junior partner, German immigrant Carel Abraham Rühs, from surveying the farms in the area in September and October 1897. Devenish wanted the work to follow the final publication of his inspections in June 1897 as closely as possible, so as to incorporate location boundaries and prevent any drift.[35] Nevertheless, the inbreeding of special commissions and surveys drew attention from F.H. Rissik, who wrote his brother (the Surveyor-General, Johan Rissik) to express his concern that Devenish was effectively creating a personal monopoly over hundreds of farm surveys in the area by controlling so much land inspection.[36] Rühs carried out the work with no dire problems, but although his general plan of the 52 farms he surveyed shows sparse, artistic renderings of landforms, rivers, roads, and even vegetation, not a single sign of human habitation appears that might potentially legitimize it.[37] In Rühs's rendering of Devenish's own 'Welgevonden,' for example (see Map 7.1), the only hint of Makatu's people and their town is a road that leads to nothing.

Even with the extension of the spatial apparatus of the state, matters in 1896 and 1897 might not have become perilous to Mphephu were it not for ecological factors beyond anyone's direct control. The first involved food. Between 1895 and 1897, the northern Highveld experienced consecutive years of drought and the arrival of locusts, dropping crop yields dramatically at the same time that political unrest depressed the scale of cultivation. This alone was not

---

33 E.F. Short (Devenish), "Twenty Years in the Transvaal Republic," ed. A.D. Irvine. *Pretoriana* 107 (Nov. 1995): 42. The identity of the "sheriff" is not stated.

34 Declaration of J.W. Johnson, 18 Oct 1897, R14816/97 (under R9125/94), p. 191, SS 4428, TAB.

35 Devenish to J.F.B. Rissik, 28 Jun 1897, No. 1844, LMG 56, TAB.

36 F.H. Rissik to J.F.B. Rissik, 1 Feb 1898, No. 274, LMG 58, TAB.

37 C.A. Rühs, "Generale Plan van 52 Plaatsen Gelegen in de Wijk Spelonken…Gemeten in September en October 1897," GS 94, SGO-PKW.

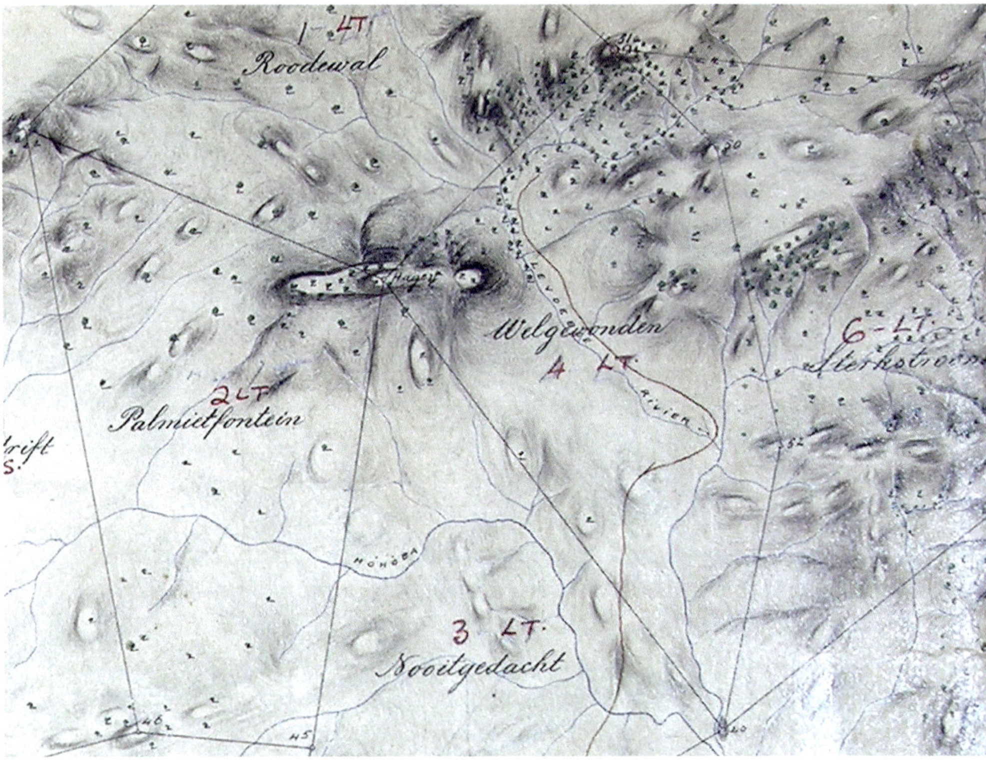

MAP 7.1 *Detail of 'Welgevonden,' the farm of A.L. Devenish in Ha Ramabulana, surveyed by C.A. Rühs in 1897, with the nearby farm 'Palmietfontein.' Note the stylized shading, vegetation, and the road leading to the undepicted village and homesteads of Venda headman Makatu. Compare these representations with their square 1864 inspection plans (Maps 6.6 and 6.7).*

SOURCE: PLAN GS 94, OFFICE OF THE SURVEYOR-GENERAL, POLOKWANE. RSA STATE COPYRIGHT.

necessarily devastating, in that the people knew how to deal with times of want through alternate sources of nutrition, opening stockpiles from years of plenty, and if necessary consuming livestock. In March 1896, still the early days of the drought, *landdrost* G.G. Munnik had in fact gone to Mphephu in part to recruit men for the mines, but the king responded that he could not send away married men who were needed at productive homesteads, and young men were already going out to work in numbers that reduced the total mouths to feed and provided money to buy food for displaced homesteads.[38] Although it

38 "Magato's Tribe," *Zoutpansberg Review*, 20 Mar 1896; "The Drought," *Zoutpansberg Review*, 27 Mar 1896.

is possible that Mphephu exaggerated the latter fact in order to retain his fighting regiments, the drought was an adequate explanation for Munnik and others in the Zoutpansberg district.

But other processes of colonization had changed the calculus and assured that the crisis would grow rapidly. The growth of commercial trade had encouraged the sale rather than stockpiling of maize in the 1880s and 1890s, and the price of buying food exploded during the drought. The gradual encroachment of *Occupatieplaatsen* further limited the area over which people could forage for 'famine breakers,' wild roots or fruits that were unpalatable but adequate for survival. The result was that many people turned to raiding, sought relief at mission stations or retreated to the security of chiefs in the mountains, had to seek labor (often with the aid of the chiefs), or even sold children into slavery or otherwise committed their labor.[39] As if this situation were not already difficult enough, the devastating cattle epizootic of *rinderpest* was already burning its way south. The first effects of the disease were connected to forestalling its spread in May 1896, when Munnik promulgated severe regulations regarding the movement of cattle, although it had limited effect around the mountains.[40] The disease actually entered the region in early 1897, killing well over 90% of the cattle and creating a situation of general dislocation, besides wiping out transport and so raising the price of grain even further.[41]

Venda communities therefore faced social breakdown and the loss or displacement of perhaps a third of their populations at the same moment that it faced deepening internal and external political crises.[42] The land was not producing or supporting herds, and therefore seemed in disuse, so many homesteads sought productive places in the short term. The *Volksraad* of the ZAR had already revised its 1887 *plakkerswet* (squatters' law) in consultation with the Orange Free State in 1895, with the goal of eliminating African sharecropping and regulating the numbers of nonwhites on white farms so as to distribute labor evenly, though its enforcement was slow and fraught because many people could simply move to unoccupied land.[43] The *Volksraad* in 1897 thus

39 Marcel Dreier, "Years of Terrible Drought: Surviving the 1895–1897 Supply-Crisis in the Limpopo Area," Limpopo Research Project, University of Basel (2005), 4–7, accessed 28 Jan 2012, http://pages.unibas.ch/afrika/limpopo/papers/limpopo_pdf/limpopo_dreier.pdf.

40 "Rinderpest Proclamatie," *Zoutpansberg Review*, 11 May 1896 (extra)' "Spelonken Notes," *Zoutpansberg Review*, 1 Jun 1896.

41 Dreier, "Years of Terrible Drought," 6; ZPP, *Rapport van den Superintendent van Naturellen over het Jaar 1897* (Pretoria, 1898), 2.

42 Kirkaldy, *Capturing the Soul*, 23–24.

43 TKP (unnumbered), *Memorandum by the Commissioner for Native Affairs on the Subject of the Transvaal Squatter's Law* (Pretoria, 1904), 1–5.

advanced stringent new regulations prohibiting African occupation of "government farms"—in effect, any land inspected but not yet apportioned or sold, regardless of its *de facto* ownership. At the beginning of 1898 Cronjé further demanded the collection of all tax arrears as well as a massive new levy of £2 per household.[44] In these changed conditions, which further diminished the strength of Mphephu's state by continuing the dispersal of its fighting men as migrant labor and its productive women and male heads of household as tenants on white-owned farms, Pretoria could for the first time consider enforcing these measures.

The exactions of natural catastrophe encouraged the ZAR to play kingmaker, just as those same conditions demanded that the king to take stronger measures to consolidate and extend his rule. Mphephu saw the Republic's relationships with Sinthumule and Maemu as an attack on his kingdom and interference with internal matters, although the involvement of the Boers had a precedent. Makhado, after all, had to deal with Albasini and the Shangaans protecting Davhana after 1864. But the ZAR was never before capable of creating such permanent weakness in the succession by putting the full power of a colonial state behind these alternates. Despite drought and *rinderpest*, Mphephu sought to neutralize his brothers and their supporters through armed incursions throughout late 1896 and 1897. Any Boer efforts to impose taxes and beacon a location were unlikely to succeed long as drought and disease existed, and it did not help that Pretoria shielded Mphephu's enemies. The ZAR, on the other hand, tried to emplace Sotho-speaking trader Henry Thomas Austin, who had a store on the mountain nearby, as government representative over Mphephu in November 1896.[45] Austin had been a trader in Schoemansdal decades before, and he encouraged Piet Cronjé to believe that his personal relationship with the Ramabulanas would allow him to rein in the new king peacefully.[46] Mphephu accepted Austin's mediation but included a

44 ZPP, *Rapport van den Superintendent van Naturellen over het Jaar 1897*, 3, and appendices G and H.

45 "Onderhoud met Mpefu waarbij Tegenwoordig Tromp [Funyufunyu]," 29 Oct 1896, appendix D in P.A. Cronjé to *Uitvoerende Raad*, 7 Nov 1896, SR 2402/96 (also marked R15515/96), pp. 3–4, SN 176, TAB.

46 J.B. de Vaal, "The Bygone Days of the Soutpansberg: Schoemansdal, the former Zoutpansbergdorp (Soutpansberg Town) (1848–1867)," in *A Cameo From the Past: The Prehistory and Early History of the Kruger National Park*, ed. U. de V. Pienaar (Pretoria: Protea, 2013), 179; P.A. Cronjé to J.J.H. Wolmarans, 7 Nov 1896, p. 1, SN 114, TAB; Cronjé to Austin, 14 Nov 1896, SR2042/96 (also marked R15515/96), SN 176, TAB; P.A. Cronjé to Leyds, 11 Dec 1896, R17412/96, p. 17, SS 5960, TAB.

stern warning that he would expel the trader if he proved a nuisance, and he soon shut Austin out so completely that he was barely an observer.[47]

Despite this deteriorating physical and political environment, the ZAR still hoped to constitute a Location Commission. The first push came from resolution of the first chamber of the *Volksraad* in May 1897, which supported a popular request from two families who sought to occupy the site of Schoemansdal, and who wanted any Ramabulana location to be pushed northwards to allow them to take care of the graves of "our voortrekkers" as "white and trusty burghers" ought.[48] Officials in the Spelonken ward also sent a steady stream of spies to look for new fortifications and weapons, and report on Mphephu's disposition.[49] At some point in the early months of 1898, *landdrost* G.G. Munnik and the district Commandant, Daniel du Preez, visited Mphephu at Luatame. They conveyed the demand of the government for a census within a month, in preparation for a location survey. According to Munnik, Mphephu responded in a manner worthy of his father:

> Without a moment's delay, he [Mphephu] said, "Tell the Government I know the boundaries of my location, and if anyone comes here to mark off those boundaries I will put him outside of them."[50]

The exact words are questionable, but the insistence on self-defined borders is consistent both with Ramabulana precedent and actual practice. Munnik later recalled that the government sent Commandant du Preez and A.L. Devenish back a month later to obtain this information and beacon the location, whereupon Mphephu's soldiers promptly escorted them back across the Doorn River and "told them that if they came back, there would be trouble."[51] Venda testimonies collected in the 1930s and 1940s also include an account of "chosen warriors" chasing away a survey party in the fall or winter of 1898.[52] Although

47 J.J.H. Wolmarans to P.A. Cronjé, 21 Jan 1897, R17412/96, pp. 24–25, SS 5960, TAB.

48 W.J. Fockens (First *Volksraad*) to P.H. Cloete Sr., J.M. Cloete, and 191 others, 12 May 1897, EVRBB220/97, p. 731, EVR 554, TAB; J.L.H. du Preez (*veldcornet*, Rhenosterpoort ward) to *Uitvoerende Raad*, 10 Apr 1896, SR1194/97 (also marked R7033/97), SN 42, TAB.

49 See, e.g., J.J.H. Wolmarans to P.A. Cronjé (with enclosures), 28 Oct 1897, SR2465/97 (also marked R15636/97), SN 45, TAB.

50 Munnik, *Memoirs*, 154; Anon., "Devenish and the M'Pefu War," *Pretoriana* 2, no. 1 (1952): 7–8.

51 Munnik, *Memoirs*, 156. This probably happened in April 1898, given that Cronjé called up the 1895 file in April 1898. See Minutes of Correspondence, p. 13, R11316/95, SS 5076, TAB. No direct report has yet been found.

52 Dorothea Möller-Malan, *The Chair of the Ramabulanas* (Cape Town: Central News Agency, 1953), 197.

they do not identify the surveyor, if it was Devenish, then it happened before his sudden death in early May.

Mphephu and those living within Ha Ramabulana actively continued to assert their right to land and autonomy, a fact so clear that Munnik considered it to be the major cause of the ZAR government's eventual decision to send a military force in 1898.[53] Mphephu's attempts to cement his own position and collect taxes from other groups of people including the Buys families, his unwillingness to pay taxes to the ZAR, his shielding of a subordinate accused of murdering a number of Shangaans in a raid south of the Doorn River two years prior, and Boer fears that Mphephu's defiance was attracting other groups of people to his banner, all provided additional fodder for war.[54] Piet Joubert, still in his capacity as Commandant-General, clearly intended this confrontation to finish the matter one way or another and made arrangements to bring his iron forts along with other provisions for a permanent presence. In response, the Surveyor-General telegraphed C.A. Rühs on 3 October 1898 to be ready to go to Rietvlei to lay out the long-awaited township, and undertake any other work Joubert might require. Rühs bluntly refused, but the much senior H.M. Anderson readily agreed to go instead.[55]

When faced with the crossing of the first thousand or so burghers on 17 October 1898 just under the mountain, Mphephu sent a translator to invite Joubert for a conference; Joubert felt he might be a spy, but sent back an invitation to come settle all matters and answer all charges peaceably—in short, to hand himself over—to which the king repeated his initial invitation to Joubert, creating an impasse. At the same time, Joubert sent letters to other *mahosi* to urge them to support him or at least remain neutral, and resolved to request an additional two or three thousand burghers. A Venda force attacked the commando on 21 October, before its reinforcement, in an attempt to seize their cattle and horses and perhaps to force a parley. The response was cannon fire and pursuit on horseback that drove the attackers back into the mountains with no loss of life among the burghers and limited Venda casualties. Mphephu sent word that he had not ordered the attack, but another attack on 22 October against another camp, also without Boer casualties, confirmed the eventual

53 Munnik, *Memoirs*, 156.

54 P.A. Cronjé to Staatsecretaris, 14 Mar 1898, Appendix III of Nemudzivhadi, "Conflict," 172–173; Wessmann, *The Bawenda*, 120.

55 J.F.B. Rissik to C.A. Rühs, 3 Oct 1898, p. 194, LMG 137, TAB; C.A. Rühs to J.F.B. Rissik, 15 Oct 1898, No. 2766, LMG 61, TAB; J. Luttig (Assistant Surveyor-General) to H.M. Anderson, 21 Oct 1898, p. 652. LMG 120, TAB. The date of Anderson's arrival is not clear.

course: that Joubert would await the remainder of his commando and his African allies before attacking in force.[56]

Mphephu's efforts to dissuade the commandos through negotiation and skirmish had failed. But he had prepared for the eventuality by contacting the British administrator in Bulawayo seeking refuge.[57] On the ZAR side, after assuring the neutrality of other Venda and Tswana groups and acquiring the support of Swati and Shangaan regiments, the combined expedition stormed the capital in a carefully executed operation on 16 November that put Mphephu and his supporters to flight. In all likelihood, they were well aware of the capabilities of Joubert's artillery, and had already prepared to withdraw. Mphephu's remaining client *mahosi*, including his third brother Kutama, resisted briefly but sued for peace over the following week, whilst the king remained at large.[58] Three days after occupying the capital, the members of the commando dynamited it as well as the nearby sheltered positions.[59] People throughout the mountain fled the roving squads of Africans and Boers who scoured the area, but their departure was temporary. As a sign of Boer permanence, Anderson soon situated the township they had long sought to place at the foot of Luatame, and the commando gave it an ironic piece of historical backdating by naming it Louis Trichardt after the early traveler whose aid had helped put Mphephu's grandfather back on his throne in 1836.[60]

From Luatame, Mphephu retreated northeast to a spiritually important location across the Nzhelele River, hoping for active help from the BSAC and collecting his people, but the Company refused to intervene and left his party exposed. By the time the Boer commando, with some help from the house of Tshivhase, reached Mphephu's new stronghold on 30 November, the *khosi* had

56 "Verslag of Algemeen Overzicht van den Commandant Generaal der ZAR over den oproerigen kafferstam van M'pefu te Zoutpansberg," 6 Apr 1899, R5123/99 (under R11440/98), SS 7412, TAB.

57 Resident Commissioner, Salisbury, to G.Y. Lagden (High Commissioner, Johannesburg), 21 Aug 1901, NA Misc 33/01, SNA 1, TAB.

58 "Verslag of Algemeen Overzicht van den Commandant Generaal der ZAR over den oproerigen kafferstam van M'pefu te Zoutpansberg," 6 Apr 1899, R5123/99 (under R11440/98), SS 7412, TAB.

59 Journal entry, 19 Nov 1898, "Dag Boek M'pefu's Commando," KG 655, TAB.

60 H.M. Anderson to J.F.B. Rissik, 15 Dec 1898, No. 3146, LMG 61, TAB; H.M. Anderson to J.F.B. Rissik, 11 Aug 1899, LMG 64, TAB. It helped that the grandson of Louis Tregardt was commander of the artillery against Mphephu. See S.P.E. Trichard, *Geschiedenis, Werken, en Streven van S.P.E. Trichard*, ed. and comp. O.J.O. Ferreira (Pretoria: Raad vir Geesteswetenskaplike Navorsing, 1975), 106n65.

already escaped with a sizeable party including Funyufunyu.[61] Summer conditions and the incidence of malaria and other sicknesses hampered further pursuit.[62] On 21 December 1898, Mphephu's party—over a thousand people with some 250 cattle—crossed the Limpopo and entered Southern Rhodesia, joining many hundreds of others who had crossed since 25 November.[63] Only at that moment did the BSAC choose to protect Mphephu. When the ZAR on 30 December 1898 demanded his extradition, Lieutenant-General W.F. Butler (acting British High Commissioner for South Africa) refused, both on the grounds that no extradition treaty existed and because Mphephu was "a man who can only be regarded as a political refugee having sought shelter in the Queen's Jurisdiction."[64] Mphephu's account of the conflict, which his party conveyed to Rhodesian officials at a formal meeting in Bulawayo on 3 January 1899, certainly played a role in the decision. To accommodate the uprooted king, the Company allotted lands to his party at Vhuxwa, district Belingwe, in early 1899.

Those *mahosi* opposed to Mphephu, or who had stood aside, entered the Republic's system of subordination. Sinthumule's acquiescence to the Republic's authority led Pretoria to recognize him as the successor to Makhado.[65] It also led to the creation of a location of about 16,000 morgen for Sinthumule around his old town at Tshifhefhe just south of the Dorps River, which the surveyor H.M. Anderson inspected and sketched in August 1899.[66] The state emplaced Maemu and his smaller group on the farm Rondebosch, abutting the southern edge of the new town lands, and moved him about 40km further southeast later, although the *mahosi* already there apparently wanted little to do with him.[67] The Boers soon released Kutama and most of the

61 Trichard, *Geschiedenis, Werken, en Streven*, 102.

62 J.I. Rademeyer, "Die Oorlog teen Magato (M'pefu), 1898" (master's thesis, University of Pretoria, 1943), 68–69.

63 Declaration of Madzihandela, 15 Dec 1898, pp. 132–133, CR72/99 (under R17221/98), SSA 737, TAB; Nemudzivhadi, "Conflict," 154–155.

64 F.W. Reitz (Staatsecretaris) to Edmund Fraser (British Agent), 30 Dec 1898, RA5049/98, p. 145, SSA 735, TAB; Fraser to Reitz, 9 Jan 1899, RA136/99, pp. 128–129, SSA 736, TAB; the interview, held at Bulawayo, is transcribed as Appendix IX to Nemudzivhadi, "Conflict," 179–182.

65 Nemudzivhadi, "Conflict," 164–166; Trichard, *Geschiedenis, Werken, en Streven*, 102, 106; Native Location Commission, "Report on Senthimula and Mahimo's Location," 8 Apr 1907, 1–2 and appendices, C27/21, TAB.

66 Möller-Malan, *Chair of the Ramabulanas*, 193; H.M. Anderson to J.F.B. Rissik, 11 Aug 1899, LMG 64, TAB.

67 J.W.N. Tempelhoff, "Die Okkupasiestelsel in die Distrik Soutpansberg, 1886–1899," *AYB* 60 (1997): 277; F.J. Newnham (Secretary, Location Commission) to Secretary for Lands,

surrendered *mahosi* who had supported Mphephu and they, like other former enemies and clients alike, became vehicles for the cadastral fission of Ha Ramabulana in small locations or on private farms. In all cases, the imperative of government was that their potential enemies should be on flat, indefensible territory.[68] In the wake of Mphephu's dramatic flight, the other major Venda rulers agreed to censuses, hut taxes, and locations, although the South African War would forestall any attempt to make good on those agreements.[69]

The government in Pretoria rather naively intended to clear the mountains and open Magatoland to settlers and speculators, on the basis that Mphephu was a rebel and had forfeited it. But squatters precipitously moved into the more fertile areas despite official prohibitions and, together with the return of dislocated Venda farmers in "great numbers" during 1899, their incursions generated decades of administrative chaos.[70] The survey of lands, which was a precondition to any grants, was not even underway when war broke out between the British and the Boers of the ZAR and Orange Free State in October 1899.[71] By that time, the first inhabitants of Louis Trichardt were in residence, while prospectors and planters already had feelers out for large grants, and individual requests for smaller farms abounded.[72] One farmer, P.S. Jacobs, even wrote to ask if he could reoccupy the farm on the mountain that he had left in 1867, and which had been occupied by towns under Makhado and Mphephu ever since—only to find that it had already been sold for non-payment of taxes, and the new owners did not seem so concerned with taking occupation.[73] The people under Mphephu, furthermore, were rapidly returning to their lands.

Pretoria, 15 Feb 1906, File 1082/18, LDE 202, SAB.

68 It is noteworthy that Mphephu and then the ZAR allotted Sinthumule low ground for precisely the same reasons; see Nemudzhivadi, "Conflict," 44–46.

69 J.J.H. Wolmarans to P.A. Cronjé, 24 Dec 1898, SR5938/98, SN 58, TAB; Acting Commandant (Trichard) to P. Joubert, 13 Dec 1898, R16410/98, p. 18, SS 7607, TAB.

70 P. Joubert to Reitz, 3 Mar 1899, R3215/99, SS 7737, TAB; Post Commander, Nijlstroom (District Waterberg) to J.C. Smuts (State Attorney), 28 Jan 1899, GCPM 23/99, SP 885, TAB.

71 Minute of H. de Cock (clerk to Staatsecretaris), 7 Sep 1899, RBB1476/99, SS 8794, TAB.

72 See G.J. du Toit to M.T. Steyn (Staatsecretaris) and précis of correspondence thereupon, 8 Jun 1899, R8894/99, pp. 87–98, SS 7931, TAB; M.W. Pretorius to S.J.P. Kruger, 11 Sep 1899, R12699/99, SS 8034, TAB; J. Flygare to S.J.P. Kruger and Uitvoerende Raad, 1 Jun 1899, R8235/99, pp. 40–44, SS 7894, TAB; Précis of correspondence, R16746/98, pp. 26–59, SS 7620, TAB.

73 P.S. Jacobs to S.J.P. Kruger (and comments thereupon), 26 Jan 1899, R1613/99, pp. 66–72, SS 7691, TAB.

In Rhodesia it was not loyalty to Mphephu or his father that led the BSAC to shield the king and his party. There were both long-term and short-term reasons for refusing extradition. In the long term Mphephu was a useful ally, because Venda lived on both sides of the Limpopo and many still recognized the legitimacy and authority Mphephu possessed. In fact, the ZAR government specifically stated their desire that the British not recognize Mphephu as a paramount chief out of their concern over his stature in exile.[74] In the short term, the Native Commissioner of Matabeleland hoped that the expected influx of some ten thousand impoverished Venda would mean an increased supply of cheap labour for mining in particular.[75] But as of late 1899, fewer than three thousand Venda were living in the location, and besides being "too fully occupied in building their kraals and laying out their gardens to go out to the mines for work," they were also unwilling to perform mine labour for the low wages offered.[76] Mphephu duly paid the Company's hut tax of ten shillings per household all the same, possibly through his own funds or via the receipt of periodic tribute from Venda south of the Limpopo.[77] That a great many Venda *mahosi* and people in the mountains continued to pay homage to Mphephu is clear, as is the fact that the Limpopo River was no impediment to their ability to consult with him.[78] Indeed, to pay hut taxes for his Location in June 1900, Mphephu unsuccessfully sought Company permission to cross the Limpopo to collect tribute directly, and various *mahosi* made visits from one

74 Reitz to Fraser, 11 Jan 1899, RA5049/98, pp. 148–149, SSA 736, TAB.

75 "Report by the Deputy Administrator of Matabeleland (A. Lawley)," in *Reports on the Administration of Rhodesia, 1897–1898* (London: BSA Company, 1899), 109; Per Zachrisson, *An African Area in Change: Belingwe, 1894–1946* (Gothenburg: Dept of History in Gothenburg, 1978), 147.

76 "Report by the Administrator of Matabeleland (Sir Arthur Lawley)," in *Reports on the Administration of Rhodesia, 1899–1900* (London: BSA Company, 1900), 28; Zachrisson, *African Area in Change*, 147; Resident Commissioner, Salisbury, to G.Y. Lagden (Native Commissioner, Johannesburg), 21 Aug 1901, NA Misc 33/01, p. 49, SNA 1, TAB; Nemudzivhadi, "Conflict," 132.

77 Nemudzivhadi, "Conflict," p. 163.

78 Dorothea Möller-Malan, "Die Donker Soutpansberg," *Historia* 3, no. 4 (1958): 258; T.G. Trevor, *Forty Years in Africa* (London: Hurst & Blackett, 1932), 188. On the general porosity of the Limpopo barrier in this era, see Teresa Barnes, "Virgin Territory? Travel and Migration by African Women in Twentieth Century South Africa," in *Women in African Colonial Histories*, ed. Jean Allman, Susan Geiger, and Nakanyike Musisi (Bloomington: Indiana University Press, 2002), 172. On the returns of Mphephu in detail, see L.F. Braun, "The Returns of the King: The Case of Mphephu and Western Venda 1899–1904," *Journal of Southern African Studies* 39, no. 2 (2013): 271–291.

side to the other.[79] That particular request, made as the South African War seemed to be near an end, however, had a more important and consequential motive than the tender of tax money to an official in Bulawayo.

The Return of Mphephu, 1900–1902

Despite the capture of Bloemfontein and Pretoria by the winter of 1900, many areas of the former Boer Republics that were away from the early fighting remained nominally in Boer hands well into 1901. Perhaps the farthest-flung of these areas was the Zoutpansberg district, which was not a priority for the British military despite the existence of telegraph lines going through Pietersburg (Polokwane) all the way to the nascent town of Louis Trichardt. The squatter stands in Magatoland were mostly empty by that time, and extant official records are silent about any friction in the area but they also suggest an absence of meaningful ZAR authority in the mountains. Such a lack of reach allowed Venda homesteaders in the mountains and foothills to rebuild their old dwellings and resume their grazing and farming activities.[80] Many of those who reoccupied their vacated lands expected, like other African farmers around the Transvaal, that a British administration would restore their rights to ancestral land and perhaps livestock confiscated by the ZAR, or allow them to keep cattle taken from Boer farms.[81]

In legal reality, the British would restore the rights of the Boers to their titled land by the terms of the Treaty of Vereeniging (1902) and offer them reparations besides. In addition, the British enforced the collection of hut taxes more systematically, and as a result they encountered broad resistance in the countryside from people insistent on their right to the land they occupied and angry at taxes that they had previously avoided, ignored, or that simply had not been collected.[82] In the far north, the British trod comparatively softly across a

---

79 Zachrisson, *African Area in Change*, 71.

80 Maanda Mulaudzi, "'U shuma bulasi': Agrarian transformation in the Zoutpansberg District of South Africa, up to 1946" (PhD diss., University of Minnesota, 2000), 72–73.

81 Krikler, *Revolution from Above, Rebellion from Below: The Agrarian Transvaal at the Turn of the Century* (Oxford: Clarendon Press, 1993), 19–23; Peter Warwick, *Black People and the South African War 1899–1902* (Cambridge: Cambridge University Press, 1983), 164–165; F. Morton, *When Rustling Became an Art: Pilane's Kgatla and the Transvaal Frontier, 1820–1902* (Cape Town: David Philip, 2009), 265.

82 Krikler, *Revolution from Above*, 143–144, 196.

landscape the Boers had largely abandoned, which may have reinforced the idea that the end of Boer rule meant the restoration of land rights. Mphephu and his *mahosi* were doubtless also expectant of restoration to their old lands and homes, but he did not wait passively to find out.

Mphephu obtained his leave to cross the Limpopo in April 1901 from Herbert Taylor, the Chief Native Commissioner in Bulawayo. The king managed this by offering the services of his men as scouts in the pursuit of Boer commandos, on the condition that he was in direct charge of his own people.[83] After he crossed the Limpopo with a small British detachment sometime in May, Mphephu and a number of influential *mahosi*—including Funyufunyu—soon made their way back to the old capital, where many of the king's councilors and family members had already relocated. His hope was apparently that he could reinvest his position relative to his siblings in these chaotic conditions (as other former foes of the ZAR in the north had managed), and that his service in the war would obligate the British to him.[84] In the short run, the British hoped Mphephu would dissuade Boer guerrillas from occupying the difficult terrain of the mountains. The northern part of the Zoutpansberg district had not been subject to the same scorched-earth, anti-guerrilla tactics employed further south, in part because of the large Venda and Tsonga/Shangaan populations, and therefore cultivation and supply were profitable activities—a marked shift from the lean years of 1896–1898. Boer generals in the field also recognized the area as the only one in the Transvaal that still produced food, but lamented by early 1902 that local African power had made any attempt at raiding for supplies ultimately counterproductive.[85]

This meant that the parts of the Zoutpansberg District that were still in Boer hands when Mphephu returned to his mountain were in dire straits. When a detachment of the British northern force finally occupied Louis Trichardt on 9 May 1901, its condition was reportedly atrocious, with widespread incidence of various fevers and hunger, not to mention poor water supplies and even worse sanitation.[86] Strategic and humanitarian goals coincided in this instance.

83 H.J. Taylor (Chief Native Commissioner, Bulawayo) to P. Dalton (Staff Officer, Rhodesia), 14 Oct 1901, NA 14/01, SNA 3, TAB.

84 H.J. Taylor to F. Enraght-Moony (Native Commissioner, Spelonken), 28 Sep 1901, 11–12, NA 209/1901, SNA 8, TAB; L. Kriel, "African Reaction to White Penetration: the Hananwa of Blouberg, ca. 1886–1894," *Historia* 45, no. 1 (2000): 61–62.

85 Bill Nasson, *The War for South Africa: The Anglo-Boer War, 1899–1902* (Cape Town: Tafelberg, 2009), 248.

86 A.S. Hickman, *Rhodesia Served the Queen: Rhodesian Forces in the Boer War, 1899–1902* vol. 2 (Salisbury[Harare]: Government Printers, 1975), 338.

The British military leadership duly ordered the removal of the local population to Pietersburg and tasked Captain Alfred 'Bulala' Taylor, a Rhodesian officer of uncertain status and dubious morality, with burning the town.[87] Taylor reportedly enlisted locals to carry out the order during the following weeks, and those people—including Venda from the environs of Luatame with allegiance to Mphephu—performed the task with understandable enthusiasm.[88]

Once Mphephu was encsconced at Luatame a few weeks later, Taylor sought to co-opt his significant power base. Oral accounts maintain that 'Bulala,' the killer, summarily tried and executed some of Mphephu's enemies in June, but they disagree on details, and no other sources exist.[89] It is clear in any case that Mphephu rapidly regained political strength after returning to Luatame. At the end of July, the Chief Native Commissioner in Matabeleland reported that Mphephu's people were drifting back to Ha Ramabulana and that the movement would be difficult to stop.[90] At that point it became clear that the civil administration in the Transvaal had no idea that any of this was happening, but they held the matter over until the arrival of the new colonial Native Commissioner, Godfrey Lagden.

In August and September, matters grew more complicated for Taylor and the king. Besides his implication in the emerging scandal of the Bushveldt Carbineers, Taylor's relationship with Mphephu also deteriorated greatly. Much like the ZAR officials before him, Taylor greatly underestimated the robustness of allegiance to Mphephu among people in the Zoutpansberg. According to a letter in mid-September enclosing complaints against Mphephu,

---

87 Report of E. Gottschling, 15 May 1901, *Berliner Missionsberichte* (Sep 1901): 342–343; J.W.N. Tempelhoff, *Townspeople of the Soutpansberg: A Centenary History* (Louis Trichardt: Greater Louis Trichardt TLC, 1999), 47; Memoir of H.R. Mingard, 8 Sep 1901, in *Breaker Morant and the Bushveldt Carbineers*, ed. A.M. Davey (Cape Town: Van Riebeeck Society, 1987), 45–46. On the reputation of 'Bulala' (Killer), see William Woolmore, *The Bushveldt Carbineers and the Pietersburg Light Horse* (McCrae: Slouch Hat, 2002), 306–307; Davey, *Breaker Morant*, xlvii–xlix.

88 Memoir of H.R. Mingard, 8 Sep 1901, in Davey, *Breaker Morant*, 45–46; Woolmore, *Bushveldt Carbineers*, 58.

89 Nemudzivhadi, "Conflict," 167 and n. 42. The accuracy of the oral history on this point is uncertain. The informants were not unanimous about the reason that Maemu and Sinthumule escaped capital punishment, and many of Maemu's confederates vanish from the historical record at this time, but not all (see the list enclosed in C.G. Murray to C.A. Wheelwright, 12 Sep 1902, NCS 106/02, KLT 2/1/1, TAB). Taylor's agency also figures in Motenda, "History of the Western Venda and of the Lemba," 61, 168.

90 Copy of W.H. Milton (Administrator, Southern Rhodesia) to Resident Commissioner, Salisbury, 31 Jul 1901 , HC 1/01, p. 4, SNA 1, TAB.

Taylor had already written to his superior at Military Intelligence in Pretoria in August to state that Mphephu was "a public nuisance," and his efforts to reclaim his influence and "pose as a Paramount Chief" augured so much trouble that he should be send back to Rhodesia permanently.[91] Taylor further indicated that his warnings to Mphephu had gone unheeded since then, and that he could not really enforce directives upon those under the king so long as he remained in the mountains.[92]

The complaints against Mphephu came from Sinthumule and his allies, who attested that towards the end of August 1901 Mphephu started sending people he considered loyal to challenge Sinthumule's power to apportion land, by picking "those same gardens [as Sinthumule's people were] claiming them as theirs, on account that the country belonged to M'Pefu before the Boers drove M'Pefu from the Mountains."[93] In the following weeks, Sinthumule complained further that Mphephu sent people to drive Maemu and others from their homesteads because "the country belongs to him," and that they were powerless to stop him on their own.[94] Some of these people were tenants on land that Mphephu knew had been granted to white settlers before the war, but it is impossible to know whether he was making a claim to the ground itself or merely challenging the presence of his enemies there. Sinthumule and Maemu certainly had incentive to portray it as a challenge to British authority, and Lagden was receptive to the idea that chiefs sought "to take advantage of the present confusion to gain ascendancy."[95]

By mid-August Lagden was in Johannesburg, and on 29 August Francis Enraght-Moony took up his post of Native Commissioner in Pietersburg, where he found that Taylor was virtually a law unto himself in the far north. Clearly he needed to be removed as soon as possible, but it took over a month to engineer the feat—a month in which Taylor carried on with "working trouble in the north."[96] Eventually they got their wish, and the commander-in-chief, Lord

---

91 Quoted in A. Taylor to Enraght-Moony, 16 Sep 1901, NA 14/01, pp. 18–19, SNA 3, TAB. Taylor's original letter is missing.

92 Ibid.

93 Copy of "Case against M'PEFU" [Statement of Sinthumule], 9 Sep 1901, enclosure to A. Taylor to Enraght-Moony, 16 Sep 1901, NA 14/01, p. 22, SNA 3, TAB.

94 "Case of Sinthoomoola against M'Pefu" and "Statement of Molimo [Maemu], brother to M'Pefu," enclosures to A. Taylor to Enraght-Moony, 16 Sep 1901, NA 14/01, p. 23–25, SNA 3, TAB.

95 Lagden to D. Henderson (Director of Military Intelligence, Pretoria), 21 Nov 1901, NA 187/01, p. 161, SNA 7, TAB.

96 Henderson to Lagden, 24 Sep 1901, NA 13/01, pp. 124–126, SNA 2, TAB.

Kitchener, met with Enraght-Moony and Lagden in late September with the expectation that Enraght-Moony himself would take over from Taylor and his agents.[97] Another of the main subjects of this discussion, however, was the removal of Mphephu. Although no minutes of the meeting survive, it is clear that all agreed on the point, although Lagden did not agree with the military authorities who suggested that he should simply be ordered or driven out of the country.[98]

We have no account of how Enraght-Moony was able to convince Mphephu to leave the mountains. He dared not charge in and arrest the king, yet he somehow managed the feat without provoking active opposition. Mphephu eventually travelled to Pietersburg under escort on 28 October, and then to Pretoria, where he and six *mahosi* (including Raliphaswa, but apparently not Funyufunyu), were to stay "until cessation of hostilities & report by post."[99] After two or three months, however, they returned to Vhuxwa with the apparent impression that they could return after the war. Mphephu nevertheless maintained pressure for his permanent return while his *mahosi* in the Zoutpansberg did the same.[100] Lagden was inclined to support Sinthumule, but would not recommend an official recognition given the open question of Mphephu's return and the king's indisputably large constituency.[101] This deferral ran headlong into the desires of Mphephu's allies in the Transvaal, and caught the nascent British colonial presence in the north at a huge disadvantage in power, knowledge, and experience.

These disadvantages accrued in the person of the new Native Commissioner of the Spelonken ward in March 1902, a 25-year-old English patrician named Charles Gideon Murray. Murray's prior posts as resident magistrate in New Guinea and six months as Lagden's private secretary in Johannesburg gave him the dubious honor of being the best candidate for the post, not to mention the only applicant, when Enraght-Moony departed for Swaziland in January.[102] Although Murray soon blamed Mphephu's temporary return in 1901 for

97 Lagden to Enraght-Moony, 25 Sep 1901, NA 13/01, p. 127, SNA 2, TAB.

98 Enraght-Moony, "Points for discussion with Lord Kitchener," n.d. [27–29 Sep 1901], NA 13/01, p. 132, SNA 2, TAB; Memo of G.Y. Lagden, 4 Oct 1901, NA 14/01, p. 2, SNA 3, TAB.

99 Enraght-Moony to Lagden, 27 Oct 1901 and 2 Nov 1901, NA 211/01, pp. 18–22, SNA 8, TAB.

100 W.H. Milton (Adminstrator, Southern Rhodesia) to Lord Milner (Governor and High Commissioner), 4 Feb 1902, NA 424/02, p. 79, SNA 17, TAB.

101 Lagden to C.A. Wheelwright (Native Commissioner, Northern Areas), 18 Dec 1902, NA 2645/02, file 191/335, BAO 6746, SAB.

102 *The Transvaal Civil Service List 1905* (Pretoria: Government Printer, 1905), 58; Viscount Elibank [C.G. Murray], *A Man's Life: Reflections and Reminiscences of Experiences in Many Lands* (London: Hutchinson & Co., 1934), 79.

disrupting the expected drift of *mahosi* and people to Sinthumule, he noted after his first visit in late July to Sinthumule's location and the towns around Luatame that Mphephu retained a great following from the Doorn River all the way to the Limpopo—in effect, across all of Ha Ramabulana.[103] The *mahosi* petitioned him for Mphephu's return on many occasions starting in mid-1902, including one episode where Murray claimed to have been offered £200 in "golden sovereigns [to] secure his repatriation," which Murray looked upon as a personal bribe and not as an installment or gift that would have been more in keeping with the desultory tributes paid to government by Mphephu and Makhado in the past.[104] In any case, he urged an early settlement of the issue of Mphephu's return because it was impossible for him to navigate Venda politics himself and he felt that it would be simpler to deal with one individual, be it Mphephu or some other designee.[105]

These complications included struggles between Mphephu's *mahosi* and his brothers, as well as friction between the returning Venda and the Boers who, once again, had begun squatting on the lands of the north.[106] Although Murray ordered Mphephu's *mahosi* and people not to interfere with other groups in the area, his commands rang hollow in Venda ears. Some families began to move into Sinthumule's area and refused to recognize his authority or comply with Murray's demand that they vacate. The situation became dire enough for Sinthumule to complain to the South African Constabulary directly that people were being turned out of their compounds, and Murray characterized the situation as being "a 'try on' on the part of [Mphephu's people] to reclaim what was once Mpefu's ground" that he promised to defuse by arresting the offenders if needed.[107] Sinthumule, Maemu, and people under them also enlisted Murray's judicial authority to try to reverse old disputes from July 1902 forward, whether the issues involved cattle, wives, or the occupancy of land, which did not enhance Murray's cachet with Mphephu's retainers.[108] The colonial record of such disputes does not recognize that many people under Maemu or

103 Murray to Wheelwright, 12 Sep 1902, NCS 106/02, pp. 4–5, KLT 2/1/1, TAB.

104 Elibank, *A Man's Life*, 82.

105 Murray to Wheelwright (Confidential), 20 Jan 1904, NCS 1/04, p. 2, file 191/335, BAO 6746, SAB; Murray to Wheelwright, 12 Sep 1902, NCS 106/02, pp. 4–5, KLT 2/1/1, TAB.

106 Murray to Wheelwright, 14 Sep 1902, sub-file N2/1/21, KLT 2/1/1, TAB; Wheelwright to Lagden, 26 Nov 1902, SNAZ 691/02, file 191/335, BAO 6746, SAB.

107 J.S. Nicholson (Colonel, South African Constabulary) to Lagden, 14 Aug 1902, NA 1724/02, pp. 154–155, SNA 49, TAB; Murray to Wheelwright, 7 Sep 1902, NA 1724/02, pp. 161–163, SNA 49, TAB. No arrests took place.

108 Register of Civil Cases (Spelonken, Zoutpansberg), Cases 7, 29, 31, 39 (1902), and 97 (1903), LLT 13/2/2/1, TAB.

Sinthumule might have considered themselves as being under Mphephu as well, but the stated affiliations in the records depict an active struggle between the brothers' independence and Mphephu's ongoing claim to central authority even in exile. But political battles formed only one aspect of the changing landscape of Ha Ramabulana.

The Struggle for Magatoland

With the end of hostilities in May 1902, the unsettled question of Magatoland soon re-emerged. Boer squatters, mostly poor opportunists or former members of the commando against Mphephu, began to return to the lots they had abandoned during the South African War. One of the first agencies they dealt with was the Transvaal Land Board, a quasi-governmental entity that sought to promote settlement schemes and facilitate repatriation through the purchase and distribution of land and stock.[109] However, its powers were so ill-defined, and its knowledge so lacking, that initially they took steps to grant farms on the mountains, with one report in October 1902 stating that "a party of Government Land Surveyors" had gone into the area to begin settlement.[110] These surveyors, probably Ralph Antrobus and Alexander Simms, were in areas that Mphephu's people actively occupied. Those people in turn complained through C.G. Murray to Lagden, who recognized the peril inherent in antagonizing them. The colonial government concurred and ordered any such peri-legal activity to end, but the episode surely did not sit well with Venda residents.[111]

At the same time, the Land Board claimed it was exercising the greatest care and that its local inspector, Edward Mostyn Jones, had done nothing to suggest a final settlement.[112] Mostyn Jones was in fact in the mountains in September and October 1902 with an unspecified group, to report on conditions and prospects there with an eye to the division of land. His report glowed about the

---

109 On the ambit of the Land Board, see L.C.A. Knowles and C.M. Knowles, *The Economic Development of the British Overseas Empire* vol. 3 (London: George Routledge & Sons, 1936), 54–55.

110 E. Mostyn Jones (Inspector, Land Board) to P. Eastwood (Secretary, Land Board), 16 Oct 1902, file 850/02, LDE 187, SAB; A. Lawley (Lieutenant-Governor, Transvaal) to W.E. Davidson (Colonial Secretary), 11 Oct 1902, LG347, file 44/2, LTG 41, TAB.

111 J.H. Cilliers, "Die Administrasie en Benutting van Transvaalsse Kroongrond 1900–1906" (D. Litt et Phil diss., UNISA, 1978), 151; H. Tennant (Law Department) to W.E. Davidson. 2 Sep 1902, file 10390/02, CS 132, TAB.

112 P. Eastwood to A. Lawley, 18 Oct 1902, file 44/2, LTG 41, TAB.

commercial potential for fruit, potatoes, tobacco, and food generally in the foothills and valleys, with little irrigation necessary, even in connection with the "probably malarial" land along the rivers. He also noted that a "considerable number of people"—meaning Boers—were already squatting in the valleys near the base of the mountains, and recommended that no more be allowed to go up until the mountains had been surveyed.[113]

Mostyn Jones, however, also visited a great many Venda on the mountains, and saw them much more prominently than the newer arrivals. He noticed a "beautiful" patch of wheat, peach trees, tobacco, and corn under their cultivation, and although the farmers had relatively few cattle and sheep, they were on and around Luatame in "considerable numbers." Being under Mphephu, they were friendly but "not too respectful" to Mostyn Jones as an Englishman, but they were clear that they would have no dealings with the Boers. Nevertheless, the inspector suggested leaving the people where they were and titling the land away under them, leaving each settler to make arrangements with "his natives" who, if they refused, could go to Rhodesia. This expectation is especially surprising when, in the very next sentence, the inspector complained that *mahosi* had promised him labor but he had received none, and that some Venda had rifles and were hunting game.[114]

Clearly the Venda on the mountain suffered neither for sustenance nor for prosperity, even later when taxation and rents became operative and the dislocation of the war receded into the past. According to testimony before the Transvaal Indigency Commission in 1907, the people in the mountains could not be induced to work for wages locally since the war—not even for the surveyors working in and around the mountains between 1902 and 1906—and they preferred to go to company-owned properties or government farms where "there is no white man to look after them and they can make their wives work."[115] Its opinion of the sexual division of labor aside, this comment suggests that people had some success pursuing their own livelihoods in the short term. The white squatters, on the other hand, had a harder time. They were not cultivating extensively, and the police detachment at nearby Fort Edward reported a total of only 81 acres under cultivation in January 1903, with no more than 16 acres accruing to any one party.[116] These people were ordered off the

113 Mostyn Jones to Eastwood, 4 Oct 1902, file 850/02, LDE 187, SAB.

114 Ibid.

115 Testimony of Rev. L.E. Brandt, 2 Apr 1907, in TKP T.G. 11-'08, *Minutes of Evidence: Transvaal Indigency Commission, 1906–8* (Pretoria, 1908), 204.

116 Report of J.M. Moore (Sergeant, South African Constabulary), 26 Jan 1903, file 1000, LDE 191, SAB.

mountain until claims were figured out, but any who left were not gone long. In April 1903 Mostyn Jones, writing for the newly-formed Zoutpansberg Land Commission, reported to the Lieutenant Governor that "a state of chaos may be said to exist in regard to land tenure" among the white claimants in the mountains, but despite a patchwork of overlapping claims and a variety of rationales for them, the commission recommended some 55 of the first 69 claimants for grants.[117]

Even before deciding on the merits and approving grants for that first group of claimants, the government was already well along on the project of dividing the land in the mountains. Two of the surveyors working for the Land Board, Antrobus and Simms, were fresh from work on the Geodetic Survey of Southern Rhodesia (1897–1901) for David Gill.[118] The pair was already in the mountains surveying in September 1902, but lacked data to connect with the work Rühs had carried out in 1897 and could not find the northern farm beacons Devenish had erected in 1896, suggesting that they were poorly marked or, more likely, had been destroyed.[119] The pair carried out surveys of some 52 farms on the mountain between 1902 and 1904 for Mostyn Jones and the board's chair, W.H. Gilfillan, who happened also to be the acting Surveyor-General until 1903.[120] Their work preceded the passage of the Geodetic Survey, so it was dependent on neighboring farm surveys and very few reference beacons, but speed was essential to the British effort to control the colonization of 'Magatoland.' The Surveyor-General further reminded Simms in 1903 to erect and describe trigonometrical stations during his work, covered with cairns of monumental size—"six feet is ample"—in order to have them available for the approaching Geodetic Survey party.[121] The beacons seem to have survived at least that long.

117 Mostyn Jones to A. Lawley, 23 Apr 1903 ("Second Report"), file 1000, LDE 191, SAB. The list of "Magatoland Squatters" in manuscript has separated from this report but is still in the file.

118 See D. Gill, *Geodetic Survey of South Africa* vol. 3, *Report on the Geodetic Survey of Southern Rhodesia* (Cape Town: Cape Times, 1905), iv–viii.

119 R. Antrobus to W.H. Gilfillan (Acting Surveyor-General), 24 Sep 1902, p. 1416, LMG 65, TAB; R. Antrobus to W.H. Gilfillan, 12 Oct 1902, 12 Oct 1902, p. 1635, LMG 65, TAB.

120 W.H. Gilfillan to Lagden, n.d. [20 Jun 1903], file 202-MT (vol. 1), SGO-PKW.

121 W.H. Gilfillan to A. Simms, 25 Feb 1903, p. 839, LMG 129, TAB; H.M. Jackson (Surveyor-General) to A. Simms, 17 Jun 1903, p. 114, LMG 130, TAB. This was also a requirement of Law 9 of 1891, which was still in force. Simms himself would take part in the Geodetic Survey by measuring baselines in late 1903; see W.G. Morris, *Geodetic Survey of South Africa* vol. 5, *Report on the Geodetic Survey of the Transvaal and Orange River Colony* (London: Harrison & Sons, 1908), 8, 203–206.

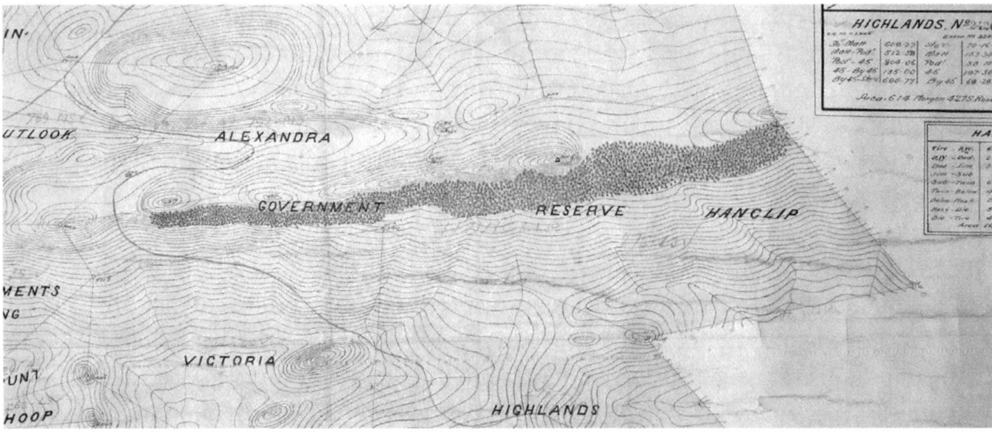

MAP 7.2 *Detail of the 'farm' on which the capital and the two mountains of Songozwi and Luatame are located ('Hanglip'), by Ralph Antrobus in 1904. Note the contour lines, the carefully drawn forest, and most importantly, the total omission of the capital site or any sign of human presence at all on the mountains beyond roads. The mountain gravesites are on 'Alexandria,' just above 'Hanglip.'*
SOURCE: PLAN M591, OFFICE OF THE SURVEYOR-GENERAL, POLOKWANE. RSA STATE COPYRIGHT.

The surveyors rendered the mountains into distinct plots for the Land Department, and the assignment of names and registry numbers that followed made the landscape at the heart of Ha Ramabulana legible and addressable to government. But property lines alone were inadequate for the colony, so Antrobus took a plane-table into the mountains in October 1903 and conducted a basic topographical survey.[122] His general plans consequently contained contour lines to depict relative heights and landforms more precisely than hill shading allowed, even though they included no numerical values for those lines.[123] This precision therefore lacked any connection to accuracy, but it still provided the necessary illusion of knowledge and control to British administrators. Among these lands were the mountains of Luatame and Songozwi, which Antrobus carefully populated with thick forests of trees in contrast to his more spartan treatment of other lands on the mountain (see Map 7.2).

---

122 R. Antrobus to H.M. Jackson, 12 Oct 1903, LMG 87, TAB.

123 R. Antrobus, "General Plan of 52 Farms Situate in the District of Zoutpansberg," n.d. [Jul–Sep 1904], Plan M59, SGO-PKW.

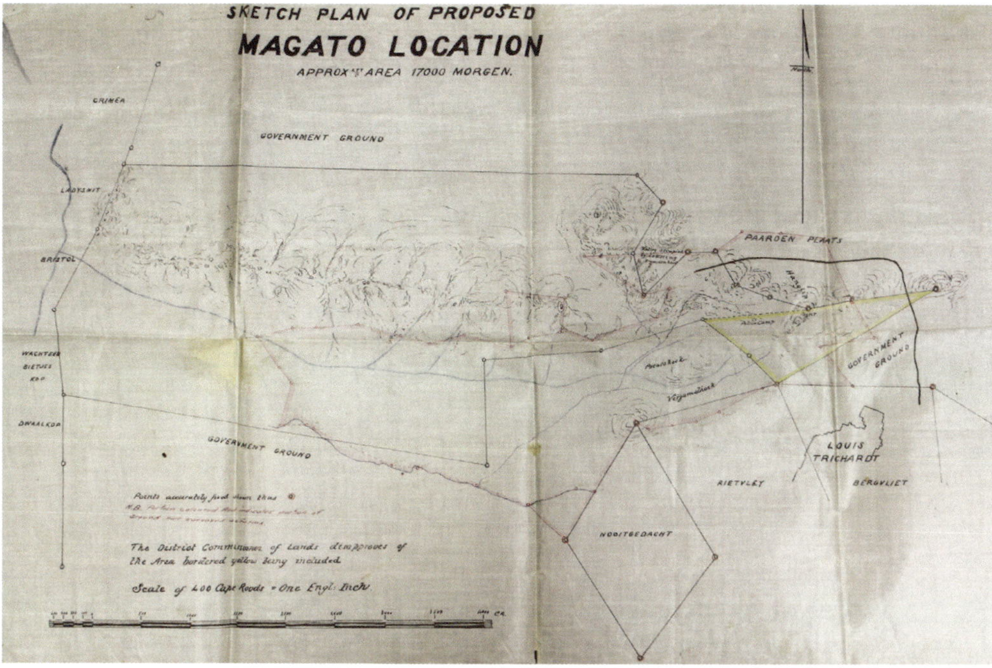

MAP 7.3 *The 'Magato Location' beaconed by Ralph Antrobus and the Delimitation Commission in mid-1903, including the mountains. This sketch copy also shows the boundaries of the farms awarded to white settlers at the same time. Luatame is in near the right point north of Louis Trichardt. The actual location would be entirely northeast of this area; see Map 7.5.*

SOURCE: FILE N2/8/3, KLT 2/1/6, TRANSVAAL ARCHIVES DEPOT, NATIONAL ARCHIVES AND RECORDS SERVICE OF SOUTH AFRICA, PRETORIA. RSA STATE COPYRIGHT.

The surveyors' work also ideally provided boundary coordinates for whatever location the British would devise for the Ramabulanas. The rough area the British considered in 1902 relied on the 1887 and 1889 assays by the Location Commission and covered much of the western mountains and the lowlands to their southwest, including the land of Sinthumule, with the Chief Native Commissioner in Pietersburg, Charles Apthorp Wheelwright, warning that if Mphephu were to return, then the plan must be "altered entirely."[124] Antrobus himself assisted the 'Magato Delimitation Commission' at the end of July 1903 to beacon a similar reserve in the western mountains north of Sinthumule's lands (see Map 7.3). Those reserves ultimately had to be scrapped as

124 SA, BAO 6746, file 191/335, former NA 2645/02, Wheelwright to Lagden, 26 Nov 1902, p. 2, and sketch plan (modified from SNA Z691/1902).

"impossibly hopeless" in mid-1904 because Land Commission decisions and further surveys had somehow failed to account for them, and so carved up the same ground.[125] The various technicians of the state were at cross purposes in their pursuit of rational order.

This collision also played out on the ground, as Venda noticed the surveyors working and more white farmers taking up lands, even past the north side of Luatame and by tributaries of the Nzhelele River. Murray wrote to Wheelwright with increasing concern at the beginning of June 1903, by which time the land matter had assumed "a different complexion" because the Zoutpansberg Land Commission had adjudged the squatters' claims in April with undue haste and had, in his view:

> practically granted the Boer farmers the land they were then and are still occupying and in addition given them to understand that such rights to the farms have been granted to them that they will have full control over them even as regards the native side of the question and that the natives will leave as soon as their crops are reaped. ...[I]t was wrong of the Commission to inform the Boers, without having more settled ideas as to the site of the Location, that the natives would leave when their crops were reaped.[126]

The lands in question after all included the heart of the old kingdom, and the Boers squatting there had no titles or diagrams to indicate ownership, so multiply overlapping claims were widespread. The entire matter was careening towards administrative disaster, and government sought to define locations and farms, while separating 'whites' and 'natives' to defuse the tension. When Antrobus went to identify particular encroachments from Boers in July 1903, he was unable to find the particular squatters, but he recognized the vastness of the area as a problem.[127] In November 1903, G.G. Hay, the resident Justice of the Peace and District Surgeon, reported that the people in the area around Louis Trichardt were mostly impoverished Boer *bywoners* (tenants) and squatters who had no deeds and were unruly at best, but he was silent on the question of Venda households, and his sample size was small—even four years later, Hay identified only 193 white families in the town and surrounding area, none of

125 R. Antrobus to H.M. Jackson, 13 May 1903, S.G. 2966, LMG 67, TAB; Mostyn Jones to W.N. Bolton (Resident Magistrate, Pietersburg), 25 Apr 1904, file 202-MT (vol. 1), SGO-PKW; Wheelwright to Lagden, 24 Jun 1904, sub-file N/2/8/3, KLT 2/1/6, TAB.

126 Murray to Wheelwright, 4 Jun 1903, pp. 2–3, former NCS 276/03, file 191/335, BAO 6746, SAB.

127 R. Antrobus to Bolton, 31 Jul 1903, file 191/335, BAO 6746, SAB.

whom were affluent.[128] Although the Zoutpansberg Land Commission in 1903 and the Crown Land Commission through 1908 struggled mightily to untangle the competing claims of whites to land prefatory to issuing titles, they implicitly invalidated any Venda claims through the British right of succession to the ZAR, and so any location would have to be outside of the commissions' decisions, and the prior inhabitants of Ha Ramabulana were left with uncertainty.[129]

Re-establishing Mphephu, 1903–1906

As the local officer, C.G. Murray recognized how precarious this situation was, but he had little power to alter it. In an effort to buttress his standing and show the paternal empathy required of a British colonial official, Murray met with 35 of Mphephu's *mahosi*, including Funyufunyu, on 9 June 1903. When Murray told them that the government had no answer to the question of the king's return, Funyufunyu replied that the people would like to know "what he [Mphephu] has done that he can't come back" and if a decision would ever be made.[130] Murray promised to forward their pleas, but he committed to nothing, and neither side broached the land question. Murray carefully reported this visit to Wheelwright, and added that he now supported the return of Mphephu under certain conditions, one of which was his confinement to a location that clearly did not include the former capital.[131] But if Murray hoped his meeting would serve to mollify the Venda *mahosi* and prove Britain's dedication to fair governance, he was mistaken. Taken together with recent events, it had instead shown them that the young Murray was impressionable but politically weak—an assessment which reached Mphephu as well. Venda households paid British taxes faithfully, and they expected something in return.[132]

128 G.G. Hay to Bolton, 25 Nov 1903, p. 62, LLT 5/1/1, TAB; Statement of G.C. Hay [*sic*], District Surgeon, Louis Trichardt [1907], in TKP T.G. 11-'08, *Minutes of Evidence: Transvaal Indigency Commission*, 384.

129 Cilliers, "Administrasie en Benutting," 151–152; TKP T.G. 28-'08, *Report of the Crown Land (Zoutpansberg) Land Commission 1907–1908* (Pretoria, 1908), 8–11.

130 "Minutes of meeting between SNC Spelonken and deputation of *indunas*," 9 Jun 1903, NA 1410/03, file 191/335, BAO 6746, TAB.

131 Murray to Wheelwright (Confidential), 11 Jun 1903, NCS 1/03, pp. 3–4, file 191/335, BAO 6746, SAB.

132 TKP (unnumbered), *Transvaal Native Affairs' Department: Annual Reports for the Year Ended 30th June 1905* (Pretoria, 1905), B.27.

The campaign for repatriation duly intensified, but now it used Murray as a lever. At the beginning of 1904, Wheelwright reported that his subordinate was encountering a much stronger, broader push:

> Petitions from the Indunas have now become incessant and barely a week passes without a body of them waiting upon Mr Murray the S.N.C. Spelonken on the matter. I enclose in these papers a letter from Mpefu to his mother Midana asking her to petition the Government on his behalf to be allowed to return to the Transvaal. The people unfortunately are even going outside of us and are asking some white people in the District to intercede on their behalf.[133]

Midana of Phahwe still resided near Luatame and, through her allies (including the *makhadzi*, Ndalammbi) and her position as Queen Mother, she possessed a great deal of authority to mobilize the king's *mahosi* on his behalf. The letter was drafted in English as dictated to the Assistant Native Commissioner, Bulawayo, in October 1903, and was very clearly intended to be seen by Murray and his superiors. Its effect on Venda listeners must, however, also have been considered. Mphephu could already communicate with his *mahosi* across the Limpopo directly, but this written letter came to Makhado's great wife, and her use of it tacitly underscored Mphephu's legitimacy as sole heir. In the letter, Mphephu characterized himself as a prisoner charged with no crime, without even the opportunity to defend himself and prove his innocence.[134] The letter actively played upon the right to speedy trial, calculated with British jurisprudence in mind, and requested Midana to take his case to the legally-constituted colonial authorities, after enquiring about "the health of all his indunas and people" and so invoking his own patriarchal legitimacy.[135] The rhetoric of the letter suggests that Mphephu understood the technical rights of a subject under British rule and how best to articulate them—as well as the ways he might reclaim his own position within its constraints.

At about that same time, Murray reported that many people spoke openly of a mass-migration to Rhodesia to join Mphephu rather than wait longer to hear from government. Regardless of whether the feeling was spontaneous or represented an act of brinksmanship by Funyufunyu, Midana, and other allies of Mphephu, Murray did not consider this an idle threat. He characterized it in terms of the loss of "at least 1,000 to 1,500 able-bodied men apart from women

---

133 Minute from Wheelwright to Lagden, 26 Jan 1904, Z164/04, file 191/335, BAO 6746, SAB.

134 Mpepu [Mphephu] to Midana, 17 Oct 1903, file 191/335, NTS 7787, SAB.

135 Ibid.

and children which the country can ill afford at the present moment," besides the liability it would create for Murray himself as a vote of no confidence.[136] It was also vital, Murray stated, that Sinthumule's separate location be fully surveyed and beaconed to British satisfaction before Mphephu returned, in addition to one for the king, to forestall any attempts to reform a single western Venda authority.[137] Such a dilatory course of action, however, only strengthened Mphephu's support: Sinthumule's prior acquiescence to the ZAR and his continued reliance on colonial power still tainted his viability as an alternative, while Mphephu's ongoing exile offered a powerful symbol of British hypocrisy and injustice given that they permitted his other enemies and even their own Boer foes to live freely in the Colony.

Such injustices were not only confined to the past, especially where they concerned land. Despite British efforts to stop land-hunting and address the matter legally, the prospect of further conflict over land was increasingly likely. The latitude the British gave mineral concessionaries from before the war, including the confederates of E.P. Scrutton, suggested further impending exactions upon Venda households and lands at the hands of outside parties.[138] By early 1904, both Murray and Wheelwright were exasperated enough to accept the possibility that the return of the exiled Mphephu, and his co-optation, was the most efficacious way to solve the problem of trust in the north. Ironically, at the very same time, the Executive Council of the Transvaal resolved to go ahead with a demarcation and governance strategy that presupposed the recognition of Sinthumule.[139]

The summary of Venda history that the Native Affairs Department in Pretoria produced in January 1904 for the use of a new Native Location Commission was just one such sign of their disconnection from the situation on the ground. That memorandum placed the blame for the position of Mphephu and the people of Ha Ramabulana firmly on their leadership—namely Makhado and Mphephu—for failing to pay their taxes and take the census asked of them.[140] This uncritical presumption of the Boers' territorial and legal rights was not surprising given that the British intended to inherit

136 Murray to Wheelwright (Confidential), 20 Jan 1904, NCS 1/04, pp. 3–4, file 191/335, BAO 6746, SAB.

137 Ibid., p. 6.

138 Notes on H.C. Hull to Commissioner for Native Affairs (G.Y. Lagden), 27 Jun 1903, file 191/335, BAO 6746, SA.

139 Copy of Resolution E.C.N.A. 26/04, 24 Feb 1904, SNA 551, TAB; Lagden to Pollock (Commissioner for Lands), 19 May 1904, NA 2307/04, SNA 236, TAB.

140 "Baramapulana or Bavenda Tribe under Magato" n.d. [Jan 1904], C27/16, TAB. A working draft of this summary exists in file 191/335, BAO 6746, SAB, attesting to its origin.

them, but such an attitude seemed profoundly unjust to Venda who encountered it.

The initiative was ultimately, however, not in British hands. Mphephu himself made that manifest when he vanished from Matabeleland at the end of July 1904, leading the government secretary of Rhodesia to telegraph Lagden directly in order to warn his department that "Mpefu has left without permission presumably for Transvaal Police and Native Commissioners informed."[141] Such alarm carried additional weight coming on the heels of over a month of unfounded but widespread rumours of impending uprisings in the far north and a general unease in the rural areas of the subcontinent.[142] Unlike those rumors, however, real justification existed for suspicion over Mphephu's whereabouts, given that he suddenly appeared at Wheelwright's office in Pietersburg on the morning of 8 August in the company of six *mahosi*. He carried only the pass issued on 18 July by the Native Commissioner in Bulawayo, meant for "travelling in District, etc." for twenty days.[143] Mphephu had used that twenty days to cross to Luatame and surround himself with his most trusted advisors before going to Pietersburg to place himself "in the hands of the Government and to learn what is to become" of him.[144] It is telling that Mphephu bypassed Murray entirely, suggesting his awareness of Murray's lack of effective influence and his relative youth, and that he also did not attempt to journey to see Lagden in distant Johannesburg, for he had sent the king back to Rhodesia before. Thus, Mphephu and his *mahosi* deliberately forced the issue of the king's return before an increasingly sympathetic official of significant rank at a crucial juncture in colonial deliberations over western Venda land and leadership, and at a time of greatly heightened anxiety over the 'native question.' Wheelwright, to his credit, understood the deliberate nature of the timing and its strategic importance.[145]

Mphephu's party stayed in Pietersburg for a few weeks while the government devised the conditions under which he could remain in the Transvaal Colony. There was a conspicuous lack of any objection to the king's return itself, in part because he appeared before Wheelwright voluntarily and professed loyalty, but also because he came with the *mahosi* who might relay the

---

141 Chief Secretary, Rhodesia to Lagden, 2 Aug 1904, NA 1817/04, file 191/335, BAO 6746, SAB.

142 Jeremy Krikler, "Social Neurosis and Hysterical Pre-Cognition in South Africa: A Case-Study and Reflections," *Journal of Social History* 28, no. 3 (1995): 493–499.

143 British South Africa Company Pass 8258, 18 Jul 1904, NA 1817/04, file 191/335, BAO 6746, SAB. Nobody seems to have questioned what 'etc.' was originally meant to entail.

144 Wheelwright to Lagden, 8 Aug 1904, NA 1817/04, file 191/335, BAO 6746, SAB.

145 Wheelwright to Lagden, 13 Aug 1904, sub-file N2/8/3, KLT 2/1/6, TAB.

response. Even more surprisingly, Wheelwright stated that he now had no objections to Mphephu reoccupying his old mountain towns around Luatame and Songozwi, a sentiment that the government adamantly opposed. But Wheelwright agreed that Mphephu's lands should be marked off and separated from those of Sinthumule as clearly as possible—indeed, he felt it was 'the most essential point' surrounding Mphephu's return.[146] Lagden's opinion was that Mphephu's obligations and lands must be defined, but also that he should not be allowed "under any circumstances to recall people living on farms or living with other chiefs who may formerly have been his or his fathers adherents" onto his lands, a clear statement of intent to frustrate any reformation of the larger social and political body despite the inability of the British to stem Venda allegiance to him.[147] The Executive Council agreed to these conditions for Mphephu's return at the beginning of September and voided their earlier resolution to emplace Sinthumule.[148] People on the mountains north and west of Louis Trichardt were warier, and when G.G. Hay visited those lands, the topic of broadest interest was the relationship that would exist between the new white population and the existing Venda one, as friction between them was increasing with that uncertainty.[149] Although Hay suggested comprehensive squatting regulations as the solution and did not mention Mphephu, the king could have been an important ally in defusing tension and keeping the peace. The remarkable lack of press commentary on his return suggests that this feeling was fairly widespread.[150]

Despite the officious rhetoric of government, Mphephu therefore came out ahead in the episode. He had forced the issue upon the Transvaal government at a time of his choosing, knowing full well at that point that the British dared not expel him if they expected peace in the north. Therefore, their approval of his return did not bear the same semantic imprimatur of colonial supremacy that his rivals' agreements with the ZAR and the British did. Wheelwright knew that under the circumstances any arrangements made without Mphephu's approval were untenable, but he still had his order to mark off a location. He therefore included Mphephu and his chosen *mahosi* in the inspection and provisional beaconing of a location "about 30,000 to 40,000 morgen" in extent on

146 Minute of Wheelwright to Lagden, 13 Aug 1904, file 191/335, BAO 6746, SAB.

147 Memorandum of the Native Affairs Department, 15 Aug 1905, 2–3, file 191/335, BAO 6746, SAB.

148 Copy of Resolution E.C.N.A. 93/04, 7 Sep 1904, SNA 765, TAB.

149 G.G. Hay to Bolton, 5 Sep 1904, pp. 99–105, LLT 5/1/1, TAB.

150 Unfortunately no complete copies of the relevant editions of the *Zoutpansberg Review* and its sister papers in Pietersburg survive, but no clippings or discussions of press opinion anywhere appear in the records of Mphephu's return.

19 September 1904.[151] The area Wheelwright pointed out was directly north of the old mountain capital, in the central valley of the Nzhelele River, which conveniently was also an area not yet under pressure from land-hunting white settlers. Because they conducted no survey at the time, the British poorly understood the extent of the land, and they were clueless of the conditions there. Wheelwright, however, sought to move people there as soon as possible because "delay may cause serious trouble."[152] Over the next few months, many *mahosi* and their immediate communities moved, in time to plant and plow that spring in the more difficult Nzhelele valley. Sinthumule retained the separate reserve on the southern flats as before, joined in time by Maemu and Kutama.

Mphephu had his own reasons to agree to the Nzhelele territory, even though it was not as fertile as the lands to the south. The valley represented a secure holding that might further extend north and east onto land that was not yet surveyed, and from which the king could exert authority over a sort of shadow state among Venda tenants to the south and west. Indeed, Mphephu had tried to site his new compound well outside the lands designated for him, although this had more to do with arability than boundaries.[153] Murray eventually promoted an eastward extension of some 8,000 acres in early 1905 to cover more of the fertile land at the confluence of the two major waterways, where some people had erected dwellings and sowed crops on unsurveyed land outside of the boundary markers (see Map 7.4).[154] Furthermore, the historic ruins of the long-abandoned Venda capital at Dzata were in the proposed extension, a point Murray and Wheelwright made in justifying its award, but a rationale that was also at odds with their stated intent to frustrate Mphephu's claims to broader authority.[155] The situation of the location was also important for the many Venda households claiming allegiance to him but living on various white-owned farms as labor tenants—as much as seventy percent of the people under his leadership—whom, Wheelwright's lieutenant later reported, Mphephu had ordered to remain on the farms to retain his presence in the

151 Wheelwright to Lagden, 10 Sep 1904, file 191/335, BAO 6746, SAB; J.S. Marwick (Assistant Secretary for Native Affairs) to Wheelwright, 12 Sep 1904, file 191/335, BAO 6746, SAB; Wheelwright to Lagden, 13 Sep 1904, file 191/335, BAO 6746, SAB; Location Overview, n.d. [Jan 1906], File 1082/17, LDE 202, SAB.

152 "Sketch Plan of Proposed M'Pefu Location, District Zoutpansberg," n.d. [Oct 1904], Maps 2/1200, TAB; Wheelwright to Lagden, 10 Oct 1904, file 191/335, BAO 6746, SAB.

153 H. Oftebro (Acting Native Sub-Commissioner, Spelonken) to Wheelwright, 4 Oct 1904, sub-file N2/8/3, KLT 2/1/6, TAB.

154 C.G. Murray, "Sketch Map of Proposed Mpefu Location," 20 Mar 1905, Maps 3/1473, TAB.

155 Wheelwright to Lagden, 5 Apr 1905, N2/8/3, KLT 2/1/6, TAB.

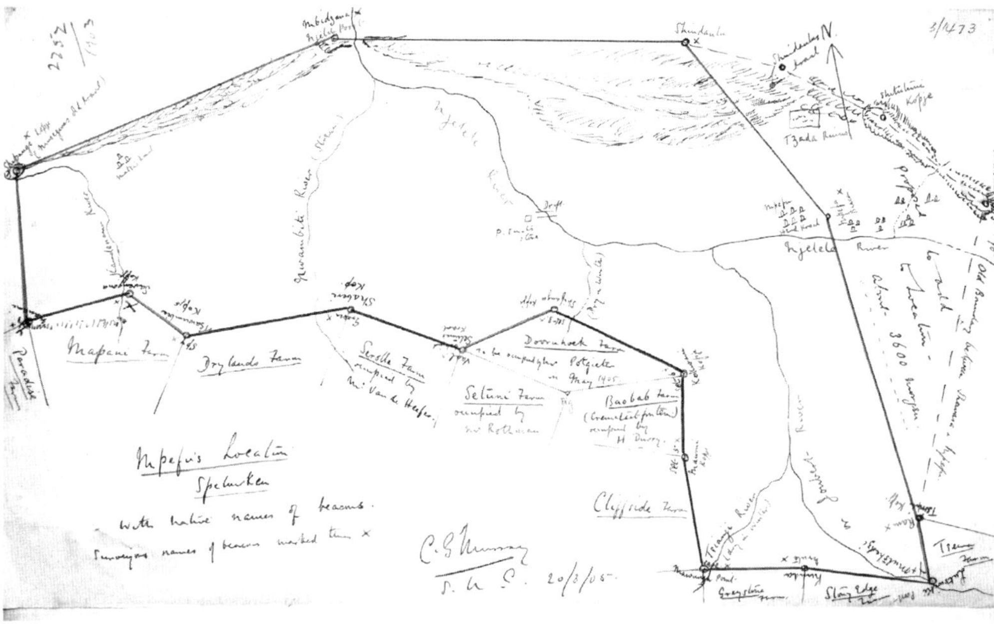

MAP 7.4 *C.G. Murray's March 1905 sketch plan of the proposed 'Mpefu's Location' in the Nzhelele Valley after the king's return, showing the proposed eastward extension and extant towns.*

SOURCE: MAPS 3/1473, TRANSVAAL ARCHIVES DEPOT, NATIONAL ARCHIVES AND RECORDS SERVICE OF SOUTH AFRICA, PRETORIA. RSA STATE COPYRIGHT.

broader area and "court popularity" among the farmers.[156] In addition to having the symbolic Dzata ruins, Mphephu's location enjoyed well-worn paths to Luatame and more recent royal grave sites, including that of his father, Makhado.

This last point was ultimately the most important, because it struck at the heart of Mphephu's leadership. Mphephu was reportedly alarmed that rivals were moving people onto unnamed sites his people were vacating—possibly including some of the mountain lands—and that some of Makhado's widows and others were moving elsewhere rather than go to the valley.[157] Whether or not this threat to Mphephu's control was as dire as Murray made it sound, he clearly felt a necessity to keep a presence at the old capital, despite its position on ground designated for white settler ownership and the colonial government's demand that he relocate totally to the valley. According to Murray's

156 W.E. Peachey (Acting Native Commissioner, Pietersburg) to W. Windham (Secretary for Native Affairs), 29 May 1907, NA 1489/07, SNA 361, TAB. The figure is based upon the Location Commission summary in C27/22, TAB, and the location census in the "Memorandum of the Sub-Native Commissioner," 29 Feb 1907, file 191/335, BAO 6746, SAB.

157 Murray to Wheelwright, 2 Jan 1905, former NZ 100/05, file 191/335, BAO 6746, SAB.

official protest in July 1905, Mphephu had been moving to invest himself at the old capital ever since he returned the year before, and spent much of his time there living in a house that was "more or less an emblem of his residence there," which Murray feared would "give the natives the idea that he has still a perfect right to reside there."[158] Mphephu claimed a need to guard corn buried in pits there, and then in March stated that he needed the time to arrange its transport. Murray inadvertently legitimized his occupation by charging him the rent due on Crown lands, but demanded that he pull his house down by August lest he send people to do it.[159] At the beginning of September, Mphephu had still made no moves to leave the capital, and Murray wrote the South African Constabulary post to send a force to pull down the house.[160] After that was completed on 8 September, Murray gave Mphephu until 12 November to vacate the capital entirely.[161]

At the same time that Murray and his superiors sought to expel the king from Luatame, Mphephu was pursuing his own strategies aimed at staying there. In early October 1905, Mphephu retained an attorney from Pretoria, C.P. Bawden, and sought through him to make representations against his removal directly to the Lieutenant-Governor, Arthur Lawley, who was visiting the district for a group meeting.[162] The act of communicating through an attorney presumed a legal negotiation between equals, an idea that was immediately offensive to the paternal, if not autocratic, hierarchy of native administration. Lawley responded through Murray that Mphephu must make his case "through the proper channel which is that of the Native Affairs Department," but that Lawley would still deign to hear him out.[163]

The meeting itself, on 18 October, was typically imperial in its paternalism. It was a group meeting, with many chiefs and headmen from around the region, and Lawley spoke through an interpreter. Lawley opened with an admonishment for chiefs not to bring in "outside parties, black or white" in communicating, for he clearly considered himself a greater paramount chief who presided over children. The welcome the delegation gave him was extremely self-effacing, meant to stroke Lawley's ego while making muted complaints about the burden of taxes and rents. Lawley's response was that

158 Murray to Wheelwright, 30 Jun 1905, former 1123/05, file 191/335, BAO 6746, SAB.

159 Receipt of M'pefu for Native Squatters' Rent Paid, No. 6106, 16 May 1905, file 191/335, BAO 6746, SAB.

160 Windham to SAC post, Fort Edward, 4 Sep 1905, NA 346/1905, SNA 252, TAB.

161 Memorandum by Murray, 12 Sep 1905, file 191/335, BAO 6746, SAB.

162 C.P. Bawden to Murray, 12 Oct 1905, file 191/335, BAO 6746, SAB.

163 Undated draft reply on verso of C.P. Bawden to Murray, 12 Oct 1905, file 191/335, BAO 6746, SAB.

whites paid taxes too, that it was expensive to run a country, and that there was plenty of work for them in the mines. Furthermore, the rents they paid covered land beyond their colonial entitlement, and a new Location Commission then empaneled in Pretoria would address any complaints.[164]

Mphephu's petition was another matter. The petition introduced him as 'paramount' of Venda (a point that tellingly brought no objection from Sinthumule or the other *mahosi* present), and claimed that he, as direct successor of Makhado, should hold trusteeship over "the Magato lands." The king further complained that the British colonial government had deprived him of vital parts of his rightful territory. Not only did these areas include the old capital, but also included the graves of previous kings, which he claimed on the basis that "the successors and people shall look over and guard" them. Finally, Mphephu carefully reserved "with all due deference to Your Excellency any right I may have in the event of Your Council [*sic*] not conceding to me, what I deem to be my own, of appealing to your Supreme Court and if necessary to the Privy Council [in London]."[165] It is not clear what boundaries he envisioned, as he did not articulate them, but his specification of the capital and the graves spoke directly to the heart of his legitimacy. The righteous tone and the reservation of legal recourse in the petition were also highly irregular; the legal caveat may owe to the attorney's advice, but the goal was certainly his own, as he made clear to Lawley and the others present.

This unexpected attitude from Mphephu took Lawley aback, and his response was curt. In response to the legal reservations, Lawley accused Mphephu of trying to scare him and of speaking to him as a child, and scolded him like one in turn. The Lieutenant-Governor furthermore stated that the decision over the land was his, and that he had made it. Mphephu, Lawley maintained, lost his rights to any land after the war of 1898, and the British were not inclined as heirs to the ZAR to reverse it, and they had proven their kindness simply by allowing him to return. Furthermore, Lawley repeated the conditions of Mphephu's return, and demanded that he leave the capital and move to the location. Mphephu held that his people were dying because the valley had no shade, it was too hot, and it was good only for cattle—conditions Lawley promised to investigate for himself.[166] It is doubtful Mphephu found this response convincing, because he remained at the capital at the end of

164 "Memorandum of Proceedings," 18 Oct 1905, 1, 2, 9–11, file 191/335, BAO 6746, SAB.

165 Petition of Mphephu to the Transvaal Government, n.d. [Oct 1905], file 191/335, BAO 6746, SAB.

166 "Memorandum of Proceedings," 18 Oct 1905, 3–7, file 191/335, BAO 6746, SAB.

November and reportedly told Murray he intended to mount a further legal challenge against his removal.[167]

Godfrey Lagden, however, was adamant that a variety of factors besides the agreed conditions militated against designating the capital as part of Mphephu's lands, not least the defensibility and "its position with European settlers all round," which might embolden Venda working on those farms.[168] The Native Commissioners therefore began to make plans to demolish the huts and structures in December, with the blessing of the Executive Council and in the presence of Mphephu.[169] In the meantime, more people had apparently moved into the old capital and built new structures and gardens. Their numbers were great enough that Wheelwright did not feel he could eject them during the summer, before their crops were ready for harvest.[170] The discovery was especially frustrating given that the Surveyor-General, W.H. Gilfillan, postponed the surveys of surrounding farms in November 1905 pending the firm settlement and survey of location boundaries.[171] Mphephu's remaining people finally left Luatame early in 1906, although many others remained on the mountains as labor tenants or renters.

Spatial and Social Interventions, 1906–1916

Mphephu's move to the Nzhelele valley did not end his contests, nor did the colonial government's tacit recognition of his position. Colonial officials refused to alienate Luatame (now on a plot named 'Hanglip') in 1906, unanimously stating it "impolitic" to do so, nor would they grant the land on which a number of ancestral graves lay ('Alexandria').[172] Mphephu petitioned the Native Affairs Department in April 1907 through his attorney, asking for permission for people to return to the mountains and tend the graves, on the grounds that the land was not special to the British, that his people would pay rent, and that Venda were "naturally a mountain tribe" and so were dying in the valley.[173] The Minister for Native Affairs, former Surveyor-General Johann Rissik,

167 Wheelwright to Windham, 24 Nov 1905, file 191/335, BAO 6746, SAB.

168 Lagden to Windham, 29 Nov 1905, No. 96/05, file 191/335, NTS 7787, SAB.

169 Lagden to Windham, 30 Nov 1905, file 191/335, BAO 6746, SAB.

170 Wheelwright to Windham, 2 Jan 1906, file 191/335, BAO 6746, SAB.

171 Department of Lands Minute 3402, 3 Nov 1905, file 1082, LDE 202, SAB.

172 Murray to Wheelwright, 24 May 1906, NA 1923/1906, SNA 368, TAB; Lagden to Commissioner of Lands, 16 Jun 1906, NA 1923/1906, SNA 368, TAB.

173 "Petition of M'Pefu," n.d. [Apr 1907], NA 1489/1907, SNA 361, TAB.

interviewed Mphephu on 16 April. Rissik was adamant that Mphephu could not occupy the old capital or the mountains, but promised to do what he could on the question of the graves and find other land if the location was unhealthy.[174] Though the local commissioners concurred that the lowlands were fever-prone in summer and unproductive in dry seasons, they laid the blame on the idleness and superstition of Venda for being disposed against the waters of the Nzhelele river and not practicing irrigation in land that might otherwise be fertile.[175] When faced with Mphephu's ultimate appeal, the imperial government in London deferred to the Transvaal government's recommendations.[176]

The Transvaal Colony's goal was to harden location boundaries through the completion of the work of the ZAR's Location Commission. This new commission included a surveyor, W.E. Kolbe, among its three members. Kolbe would survey the locations himself once they were set down, so his opinion on land carried extra weight with the authorities. The reconstituted Location Commission met on Mphephu's lands to consider the question of his boundaries and claims on 16 August 1906, and made its recommendations the following May. In the meantime, they collected further information, to decide on the question of lands and official recognition for Mphephu as a chief. Kolbe believed that Mphephu should not be recognized as paramount, an opinion that S.P.E. Trichard, who had elevated Sinthumule in 1899 following the campaign against Mphephu, seconded in March 1907.[177] No official recognition was forthcoming until 1910, and even when it did, it did not give Mphephu any official power over his half-brothers.[178]

The Location Commission as a whole in fact sought to *attenuate* Mphephu's power. Kolbe in particular felt that the Nzhelele valley was of too much strategic importance as well as too unhealthy for Mphpehu to possess, while other members of the commission felt that the reserve pointed out was excessive and should be reduced by five-sixths (from about 18,000 to 3,000 morgen), both points with which the two Native Commissioners differed. Rather, they believed the reserve should be granted "as pointed out by Mr Wheelwright," fearful that a sudden diminution of Mphephu's lands or an order to move

174 J.F.B. Rissik to Mphephu, 17 Apr 1907, NA 500/07, SNA 354, TAB.

175 W.E. Peachey to Windham, 29 May 1907, 4–5, NA 1489/1907, SNA 361, TAB.

176 Lord Elgin (Secretary of State for the Colonies) to Lord Selbourne (Governor and High Commissioner), 12 Jul 1907, NA 1489/1907, SNA 361, TAB.

177 Trichard to Kolbe, 8 Mar 1907, C27/20, TAB.

178 See Motenda, "History of the Venda and of the Lemba," 61. In a rhetorically suggestive move, Motenda juxtaposes the timing of Mphephu's recognition with the accession of George V to the British throne that same year.

elsewhere would provoke trouble—a concern underscored by the suspicion Mphephu expressed about boundary markers erected by mineral prospectors in the valley in 1907.[179] The idea of moving a distance away to purportedly better land was also anathema to Mphephu, who responded that they could not consent to "leave the ground of their forefathers."[180] Johann Rissik, upon whom the decision devolved, chose to follow the advice of the local native commissioners and the Executive Council set aside the area by resolution on 10 January 1908.[181]

The final shape and extent of Mphephu's reserve turned on the colonial government's relative lack of knowledge. The Native Affairs Department recommended that the location should be extended to the west and contracted in the north; later, they opted to expand it to the east instead.[182] The Surveyor-General fixed the date of the location survey as 2 November 1908, as the last of his charges in the Zoutpansberg district.[183] But Kolbe moved very slowly and only completed a rough preliminary survey, mostly based upon the farm beacons to the south, by May 1909.[184] That survey included Murray's eastward extension as well as a westward one, but did not extend as far north—a meaningless contraction to the Venda because no farms were yet defined on any of those three boundaries (see Map 7.5). Based upon the preliminary survey, the reserve came out smaller than believed—just under 15,585 morgen (33,000 acres)—but for those living on the ground, it looked like an effective increase in territory. The full definition of the location's boundaries waited until 1916, when the Surveyor-General again retained Antrobus to carve new farms of 1,000 to 1,500 morgen to the north and west of the location—work that required the settlement of that boundary.[185] Antrobus's survey changed the reserve's shape yet again. It returned the land's northern and western boundaries to the 1904 extent, but they were careful to still include the eastern extension Murray had suggested in 1905 and Kolbe had included in 1909, where many people kept

179 "Report of the Sub Native Commissioner, Spelonken on the recommendations of the Locations Commision re Mpefu's Location," 2, former NA 1461/1907, file 191/335, BAO 6746, SAB; "Report by Location Commission on Mpefu," minute by E. Stubbs, 29 Feb 1907, file 191/335, BAO 6746, SAB.

180 Dales to Wheelwright, 26 Jun 1907, former NCS 394/07, file 191/335, BAO 6746, SAB.

181 "Mpefu's Location," n.d. [1908], file 191/335, BAO 6746, SAB.

182 Acting Secretary for Native Affairs to W.H. Gilfillan, 10 Jul 1908, File 702, SGO-PTA.

183 H.E. Schoch (Assistant Surveyor-General) to Kolbe, 29 Sep 1908, p. 17, File 1747B vol. 2, SGO-PTA.

184 Report on the Survey of the Native Locations in the Zoutpansberg District, Transvaal, n.d. [Jan–Feb 1911], p. 103, File 1747B vol. 2, SGO-PTA.

185 Schoch (as Surveyor-General) to R. Antrobus, pp. 26–28, File 1747B vol. 2, SGO-PTA.

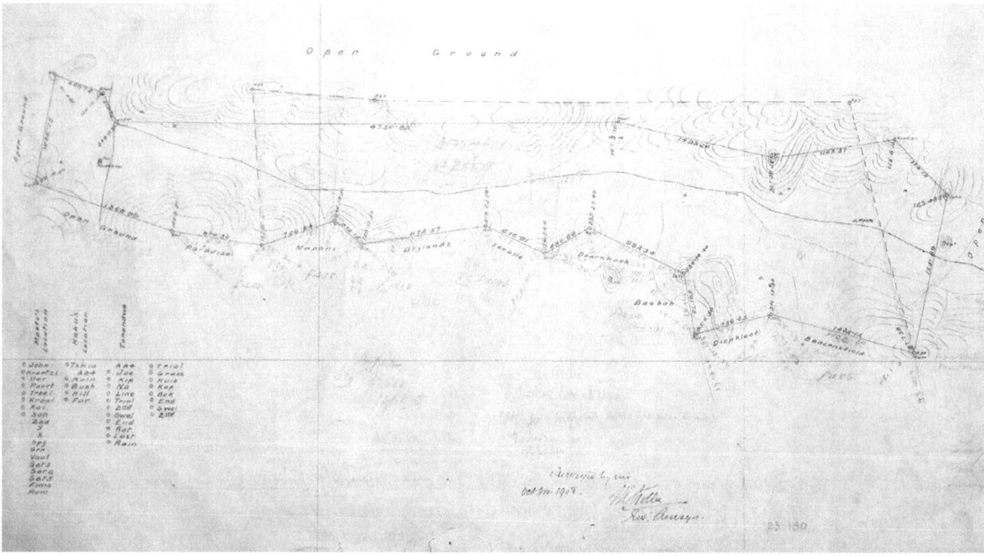

MAP 7.5 *Detail of Mphephu's final location from the plan of reserves on the Nzhelele Valley by W.E. Kolbe in 1908. The dotted line indicates the original extent as pointed out. Note the absence of any farms to the north, east, or west. The final 1916 survey recognized those dashed lines, but added Murray's eastern extension and the western annex .*
SOURCE: PLAN M666, OFFICE OF THE SURVEYOR-GENERAL, POLOKWANE. RSA STATE COPYRIGHT.

stock and crops. The territory grew over a tenth in size officially, but it remained open to government land in any case, in stark contrast to the locations of Mphephu's brothers (see Map 7.6).

Even so, these boundaries had only limited significance for Venda livelihoods at the time. When government finally surveyed the lands to the north of the mountains during the 1900s and 1910s into farms, only a few speculators took up leases, leaving the majority of the land legally unoccupied past the date of the 1913 Land Act.[186] The land companies, absentees, and large stock farmers were particular villains to Pietersburg magistrate W.N. Bolton, who complained in 1907 that the only thing they cultivated was African rent, which

186 This vacancy held as late as 1940, and most of the speculative leaseholds began only in the 1930s. One effect is that up to 90% of commercial farmland faces land restitution claims today. See Zoutpansberg farm registers, RAK 3090–3096 *passim*, TAB; Michael Aliber, Themba Maluleke, Tshililo Manenzhe, Gaynor Paradza, and Ben Cousins, *Land Reform and Livelihoods: Trajectories of Change in Northern Limpopo Province, South Africa* (Cape Town: HSRC Press, 2013), 35, 38.

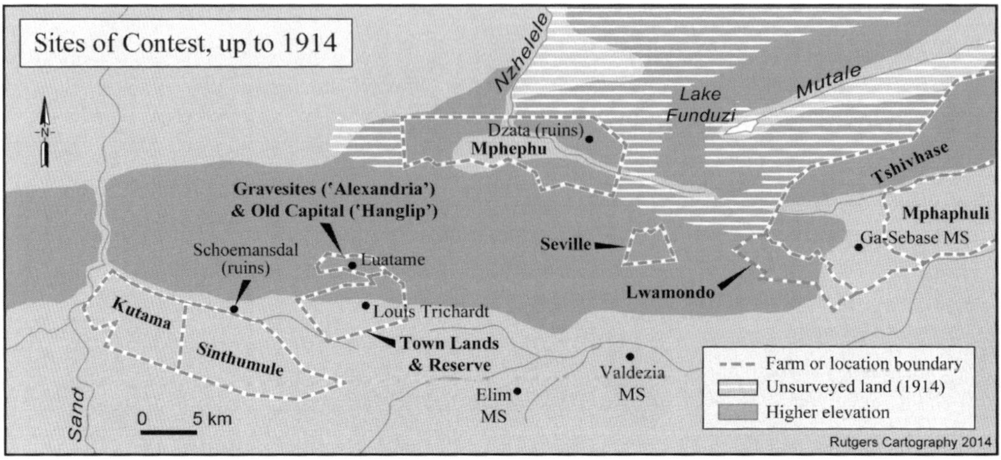

MAP 7.6 *Location areas and sites in colonized Ha Ramabulana. Much of the unsurveyed land became part of the later Venda bantustan under apartheid.*

Venda families and the few poor whites on those lands evidently could shoulder.[187] Rents on the vast extents of Crown lands before survey, and on farms still in the hands of the Crown after, were also bearable if even paid. These were difficult lands to promote to individual buyers owing to ecological factors, and Venda populations could occupy arable government-held farms as tenants or squatters.[188] This capacity for exit and circumvention nullified any plan to disperse the people of Ha Ramabulana actively among white farmers, and so weaken Mphephu's distributed client base. Conciliation remained essential to maintaining the cooperation of the people and the king in the present, while lines on the map might be enforceable at some more convenient time for the state.

The first Prime Minister of the Transvaal Colony after the resumption of self-government in March 1907, former Boer general Louis Botha, believed that the real stumbling block in mollifying Mphephu was not location boundaries but the issue of the gravesites just behind Luatame. Botha acceded early on to the king's request to allow "a limited number of families…to take up their residence on this [gravesite] reserve," after which he believed Mphephu and his people would be satisfied.[189] The government set aside about 160 acres for five

187 Testimony of W.N. Bolton, 2 Apr 1907, in TKP T.G. 11-'08, *Minutes of Evidence: Transvaal Indigency Commission*, 235.

188 Edward Lahiff, *An Apartheid Oasis? Agriculture and Rural Livelihoods in Venda* (London: Frank Cass, 2000), 64–65.

189 Prime Minister's Minute 230, 13 Jun 1907, NA 1489/1907, SNA 361, TAB.

families of Mphephu's choosing near the ancestral gravesites on the farm 'Alexandria,' giving the king a key marker of legitimacy.[190] The gravesites themselves, a few of which were in the foothills near town, were surveyed and excluded from disposal. The government moved a few years later to mark and merge both the former capital and the gravesites as its own version of sacred space, forest reserves, and thereby make them inalienable. The colonial government justified the designation on the grounds that "native tradition will be less likely to be interfered with than if the ground were to become private property," but those words hid the obvious concern for direct conflict.[191] That solution still remains in operation and, despite the later advent of timber plantations on those lands, the immediate areas of the old capital and the gravesites remain a mix of open land and dense, old-growth forest.

The government cessions of 1908 naturally did not mark the end of Mphephu's efforts to reclaim the capital. Mphephu represented the land given to the caretakers of the graves as unsuitable for agriculture, and requested that more land be granted for agriculture on another part of the mountain. The response from Murray's successor as Native Commissioner, Ernest Stubbs, was that this complaint was a wedge strategy typical of "Mpefu's insidious attempts to resettle his people on the Magato Mountain in the vicinity of the old Hoofdstad" and must be opposed.[192] Indeed, Stubbs believed that all territorial requests were aimed at reclamation of the capital, and any concession would have "the effect of encouraging them to believe that the government is gradually giving way to their agitation—which is by no means dead—to get back to the tribal lands."[193] The intransigence of Stubbs on this point seems odd given his growing embrace of territorial segregationism, which only grew stronger over time. But Stubbs's response makes more sense in light of his perception of Mphephu as an unusually powerful figure who already had an uncomfortable pull over people in the area of Ha Ramabulana, especially Venda tenants on the old lands of the mountains or laborers further afield.[194] Stubbs was in fact correct in his presumption of Mphephu's ultimate goal, even if he did not understand its full reasoning and resonance.

---

190 Rough Sketch of Lands Proposed for Reserve, 5 Nov 1908, file 191/335, BAO 6745, SAB; G.R. Hughes (Secretary for Lands) to Windham, 22 Jul 1908, C.3505, LDE 307, SAB.

191 Chief Conservator of Forests to Secretary for Native Affairs, 3 Oct 1911, F/6048, file 191/335, BAO 6745, SAB.

192 Minute of E. Stubbs (Sub Native Commissioner, Northern Division), 18 Dec 1909, SNCKS 336/09, NA 1489/1907, SNA 361, TAB.

193 Minute of E. Stubbs, 16 May 1908, 4, NA 1489/1907, SNA 361, TAB.

194 On Stubbs and territorial segregation, see Paul Rich, "The Origins of Apartheid Ideology: The Case of Ernest Stubbs and Transvaal Native Administration, c.1902–1932," *African Affairs* 79, no. 315 (1980):171–194.

After the creation of the Union of South Africa in 1910, Mphephu continued his agitation and retained new legal counsel in 1912 to make the case that he should be allowed to move from the valley to what unoccupied land remained on the mountain, in turn giving up the valley for white settlement; he reportedly circulated petitions in the area to defuse the claim that local farmers would be endangered.[195] Stubbs remained unmoved, in large part because he did not feel the gain in available labor Mphephu promised offset the political value of regaining the capital or that his people would ever actually vacate the valley, and felt the support of farmers near Louis Trichardt for the plan was misguided.[196] The government concurred in this, but they also approved his strategic purchase of a private farm ('Seville') that lay midway between himself and the location of Lwamondo in 1914.[197] Although there is no evidence that directly links these two moves, and no public objections attended the purchase of the farm, the strategic importance of both acquisitions to Venda politics is readily evident.

At the same time that he pursued the lands of the old capital and acquired other lands in trust, Mphephu actively exercised his reach to lands and people outside the location but within Ha Ramabulana in other ways. Between 1909 and 1911, Mphephu made inroads with people living in and around his half-brother Kutama's lands, notably through the agency of family members such as his *makhadzi* Ndalammbi and her people, who refused to accept the authority of Sinthumule or Kutama and reportedly subjected the latter to "all sorts of indignities."[198] Mphephu's direct involvement was confirmed by the enquiry of his legal counsel, C.P. Bawden, into the eviction notice Stubbs served his aunt.[199] That step did not end the matter, for it arose again in 1910 and the solution was to move troublesome headmen to Mphephu's area or, at the very least, away from Kutama. When confronted by Stubbs and Kutama, Mphephu reportedly

> ...was most unreasonable and arrogant in his attitude towards Kotama. He did not deny that he had been guilty of want of etiquette towards

195 S.P.J. Daneel (attorney) to J.B.M. Hertzog (Minister for Native Affairs), 10 Aug 1912, file 191/335, BAO 6745, SAB; "Louis Trichardt Notes," *Zoutpansberg Review and Mining Journal*, 25 Oct 1912.

196 Stubbs to Wheelwright, 2 Sep 1912, file 191/335, BAO 6745, SAB; Stubbs to Wheelwright, 29 Oct 1912, sub-file N/2/8/3, KLT 2/1/6, TAB.

197 Prime Minister's Minute No. 2015, n.d. 1914, URU 197, SAB.

198 Stubbs to Windham, 30 Apr 1909, sub-file 2/1/21, KLT 2/1/1, TAB.

199 C.P. Bawden to Stubbs, 4 Jun 1909, sub-file 2/1/21, KLT 2/1/1, TAB.

> Kotama and practically stated that he could treat his induna's [*sic*] as he pleased and they had no right to complain; that if his conduct did not meet with Kotama's approval he, Kotama, could do as he pleased; that he would withdraw from Kotama's control that section of his people living on farms adjoining Kotama's Location and either himself control them or place them under another of his Indunas. ...I was satisfied the fault in this instance lay with him [Mphephu]; that he had in effect made Kotama an outcast.[200]

This was not a directly territorial claim, although the suggestion that he could withdraw people from Kutama's control did not necessarily mean he planned to relocate them. When the question was put directly to people on the farms, few indicated a desire to remain under Kutama as an independent chief.[201] Stubbs saw this as a campaign to "secure labour among the farms situate south of the mountains from Verzamelhoek to Zandrivier," although he did not understand the ultimate objective relative to Mphephu's brothers.[202] After several more years of such friction involving the king's efforts to place family members or loyal headmen on private farms among laborers or rentiers, Stubbs resigned himself to the solution he had resisted since taking office. The only avenue he had left by 1916 was to require any people not actively in labor contracts on farms either to go to Kutama's location, or else to accept Mphephu as chief, effectively ceding authority over Venda homesteads on private or government farms to a king the state technically did not recognize.[203] Mphephu does not appear to have harassed Sinthumule so directly, but the lack of any protest is telling.

Mphephu in the end won back substantial power within Venda through the pursuit of territorial rights and the manipulation of legal machinery, despite the loss of soverignty. More than this, his campaign represented a shift from the strategy of direct confrontation he and his father had pursued earlier, and it created a shadow state of sorts on the landscape—one of places and networks meaningful to Venda, but one that conceptually sidestepped the

200 Stubbs to Secretary for Native Affairs, 31 Mar 1911, No. 479/10, sub-file 2/1/21, KLT 2/1/1, TAB.

201 H. Aston Key (Sub-Native Commissioner, Blaauwberg) to Stubbs, n.d. [3 Aug 1912], sub-file 2/1/21, KLT 2/1/1, TAB. Kutama was recognized as a separate chief by government in June 1911 as a way to undercut Mphephu; see Native Affairs memorandum, 28 Jun 1911, sub-file 2/1/21, KLT 2/1/1, TAB; Stubbs to Wheelwright, 31 Mar 1911, sub-file N1/1/3, KLT 2/1/2, TAB.

202 Stubbs to Wheelwright, 26 Oct 1912, sub-file N/2/8/3, KLT 2/1/6, TAB.

203 Minutes of meeting held at Louis Trichardt, 16 Mar 1916, p. 8, sub-file N1/1/3/1, KLT 2/1/1, TAB. Sinthumule was also present at this meeting with Kutama and Mphephu, but again did not object to the proposed solution.

restrictions of new boundaries and white settler ownership. Although colonial land policies eventually divided and even alienated much of the land previously within Ha Ramabulana, direct and indirect action circumscribed their freedom in doing so without resorting to open conflict. Through law and custom, Mphephu managed to gain access to, if not control of, key spaces and loyalties important to his standing, and successive governments respected those implied agreements. The South African authorities in fact reconfirmed the five caretaking families' rights to live at the gravesites in 1936, noting that "the whole of the Bavenda Tribe in this district is interested in the matter and not only the Mpefu section."[204] The recognition that the graves were important to people under all of the various Ramabulana *mahosi* underscores Mphephu's victory in holding a symbolically central position long after his own burial there in January 1925.[205] His successor, Mbulaheni George, not only had the support of his father before his death, but the new *makhadzi* also wrote the sub-Native Commissioner later in the month after assuring community support for the succession.[206] In so doing, she maintained the tradition of presenting the settler state with a *fait accompli* that needed only their official stamp a week later.

The kingdom thus endured in an important fashion, although it had become a shadow enacted primarily through Venda society and politics, woven around and underneath the cadastral structure that divided the landscape, yet able to use that same structure to the benefit of the royal house. This shadow state proved unable to prevent the disruptive visitations of nationwide Betterment policy and related state interventions from 1939 onward, but it may have played an implicit role in the development of opposition. The policies that brought forced relocation, villagization, bounded land allotments, and stock management to Venda provoked popular opposition from the very start that involved remarkable cohesion between chiefs and people, who lamented the loss of chiefs' power over the land.[207] Despite the diminished territorial presence of

---

204 Secretary for Agriculture and Forestry to Secretary for Native Affairs, 9 Dec 1936, file 191/335, BAO 6745, SAB; Native Commissioner, Louis Trichardt, to Native Commissioner, Northern Areas, 24 Dec 1936, file 191/335, BAO 6745, SAB.

205 See Masindi M. Ramabulana to J.C.V. Lyle (Sub-Native Commissioner, Louis Trichardt), 2 Jan 1925, and Lyle to Forestry Officer, Louis Trichardt, 3 Jan 1925, both sub-file N1/1/3/1, KLT 2/1/1, TAB. The year of Mphephu's death is often given as 1924, but letters reported 2 January 1925 as the actual date.

206 Fundzane Ramabulana to Lyle, 28 Jan 1925, sub-file N1/1/3/1, KLT 2/1/1, TAB.

207 Although the particulars of betterment and rehabilitation policies are outside the scope of this study and historians have an unclear picture of the full effects relative to Venda, it was clearly a major new disruption that provoked powerful action there. See Baruch

the kingdom that existed before, the idea of unity connected to its hierarchy persisted in matters connected to the land. The heirs of Mpephu proved adept at using that cachet to build claims to broader leadership later, whether at the head of the Venda homeland under apartheid, or in assuring their state recognition as hereditary kings in the new South Africa.

Hirson, "Rural Revolt in South Africa 1937–1951," *Collected Seminar Papers, Institute of Commonwealth Studies* 21 (1977): 115–132; Peter Delius, "Sebatakgomo and the Zoutpansberg Balemi Association: The ANC, the Communist Party and Rural Organization, 1939–1955," *Journal of African History* 34, no. 2 (1993): 296, 303–306; Thiathu Nemutanzhela, *Ploughing Amongst the Stones: The Story of 'Betterment' in the Zoutpansberg 1939–1944* (Johannesburg: Ravan, 1999); Lahiff, *An Apartheid Oasis*, 66–68; Aliber et al., *Land Reform and Livelihoods*, 44–47.

CHAPTER 8

Objections and Objectives: SANAC, the Tsewu Case, and the Land Act

Fixing a National Landscape

The drives to discern, enumerate, and modify African landscapes that enervated the policies of South Africa's precursor states did not abate in the wake of the South African War, when Britain finally exercised authority in all parts of the country. As we have already seen, British colonial policies pushed ahead with the same imperatives, although government and geographical archive tended to act in closer accord than they had in the Boer Republics. However, suzerainty over the entire region permitted the British to envision a union of the four colonies—as would happen on 31 May 1910—and their handover of a unified body of knowledge with, theoretically, a consistent policy for managing African lands and societies. The period between the end of the South African War in 1902 and the enshrinement of the Natives Land Act (No. 27) in 1913 was consequently one of struggle between groups of people with a wide array of identities and philosophies, ironically at the same time that governments charged towards eventual merger in 1910. The struggle between segregationists and assimilationists in questions of African landholding and labor was a major fracture, and one that created wide variances for local policy within the states that would form the Union of South Africa. Even though the Cape remained resistant to the full enshrinement of segregation, the broad contours of a dominant policy emerged in the Natives Land Act of 1913. That Act prescribed a legible state landscape, wherein objectively bounded and deeded territories formed units that could be mobilized for social, political, and economic management on an unprecedented scale. As was the case before 1913, however, the reality on the ground was very different, and it would remain a fugitive landscape of local meanings and negotiated settlements.

The first major inquest specifically regarding the future of native policy across South Africa paid a great deal of attention to Africans' position within the territorial and legal bodies of the state. The commission charged with the inquest, the South African Native Affairs Commission (the Lagden Commission or simply SANAC), held hearings in various towns around the subcontinent between 1903 and 1905 under the chairmanship of the Transvaal Commissioner for Native Affairs, Godfrey Lagden. The commission's inception in September

 | DOI 10.1163/9789004282292_009

1903 followed on an inter-colonial conference held in Bloemfontein earlier in 1903, and specifically envisaged "the coming Federation of South African Colonies" including Basutoland and Rhodesia. SANAC expected to consider six key areas, the first of which was "the lines on which natural advancement should proceed," and the second of which was African land tenure and the state's obligations regarding it.[1] The primacy of detailed questions relevant to African land and ownership indicates their centrality to the colonizers' search for knowledge and control, true to Cohn's description of survey and enumerative modalities in India.[2]

A comprehensive analysis of SANAC and its procedure is beyond the scope of the present study, but the varying level of involvement of administrators, surveyors, and key African witnesses in providing evidence to the commission in 1903 and 1904 is well worth noting.[3] No surveyors or survey officials from the Transvaal tendered any evidence to the commission or were asked to do so, though one member of the postwar Location Commission did give evidence in his capacity as Resident Magistrate. In the Cape Colony, on the other hand, both the Assistant Surveyor-General (A.H. Cornish-Bowden, who later became Surveyor-General himself) and the lead location surveyor, E. Gilbert Hall, testified regarding surveys under the Glen Grey Act. Agitators for African land rights testified in Transvaal and at the Cape, including editors John Tengo Jabavu and Solomon Plaatje, and most came from the mission-educated elite. Others were invited to give evidence but could not, including Max Jurisch, the Cape Surveyor-General, and a few members of the Eastern Cape's prominent Soga family.[4] The majority of the evidence came from European officials and mission-educated Africans, while the average African farmer was entirely absent—underscoring the colonial belief that 'native opinion' was something intangible and knowable only through the mediation of trained specialists or outsiders with long acquaintance.[5] A variety of opinions nevertheless entered the record.

At the Cape, the questions turned heavily on the Glen Grey Act and the social and material progress of the people. Veldtman Bikitsha, that great

1 A. Lawley to G.Y Lagden, 21 Sep 1903, in *South African Native Affairs Commission 1903–5* (hereafter *SANAC*), *vol. I* (Cape Town: Cape Times, 1905), Annexures No. 2, 7–8. British Bechuanaland also eventually contributed.

2 Bernard S. Cohn, *Colonialism and its Forms of Knowledge: The British in India* (Princeton: Princeton University Press, 1996), 3–5, 7–8.

3 The best general discussion of SANAC and its meaning is in Adam Ashforth, *The Politics of Official Discourse in Twentieth-Century South Africa* (Oxford: Clarendon Press, 1990), 22–68.

4 No reasons for their inability to appear are given. See List of Witnesses Alphabetically Arranged, in *SANAC*, Annexure No. 6, 1:13–26.

5 Ashforth, *Politics of Official Discourse*, 34.

proponent of individual tenure and virtual chief of Fingoland, conflated land survey with the administrative changes under the Glen Grey Act as a necessary advance in accountability and security. But Solomon Zazela, a headman in Nqamakwe, described individual tenure in far less flattering terms that suggested ongoing annoyance with state imposition upon client relationships through the granting of land.[6]

Other witnesses were even less enthusiastic. The Ngqika chief Edmund Gonya Sandile spoke as the ranking authority for Ngqika and Gcaleka households in Gcalekaland, where the administrative provisions of the Glen Grey Act had only recently been extended. Sandile demanded the preservation of beer drinks and ritual dance while also speaking against the concept of survey and the presence of independent schools as things that attacked the fabric of society. On the question of land survey he was unequivocal:

> We do not want the survey at any price—all we Gaikas and also the Gcalekas. First we object to the survey because it brings about a lot of little disputes and troubles. As soon as you have survey it means that you are going to have quarrels and rows, such as over a foal trespassing on that plot, or a goat gets on to that ground and the owner says, "This is my ground and I impound it." Or it may be a sheep, and so on. It means that a man has not got a large bit of ground where he can run his own stock. … Immediately these disputes take place, they are followed by fights with sticks. …We agreed to a Magistrate, and we thanked the Government for a Magistrate. …and they [Sandile and the Magistrate] worked well together, and they agreed.[7]

Sandile raised the additional concern that small fixed patches of land were incompatible with the broader social responsibilities of the head of a household to multiple sisters or wives. He further noted that the Ngqika were not from Kentani, but from "across the Kei…where I wish to die, as a Gaika," and therefore they did not want to receive ground in lands belonging rightfully to Gcaleka.[8] The connection of authority, autonomy, culture, and land were thus complete for Edmund Sandile. At the prompting of W.E. Stanford, the former Chief Magistrate of the Transkei, Veldtman faithfully responded to Sandile's charges as uninformed and baseless. Veldtman stated that individual titles

6 Statements of Capt. Veldtman and S. Zazela, 15 Mar 1904, in *SANAC*, 2:943–45. Veldtman, it may be recalled, was granted a large surveyed farm carved in Gcalekaland in 1883 by order of the Cape Government.

7 Statement of Edmond Sandili [*sic*], 15 Mar 1904, in *SANAC*, 2:946–947.

8 Testimony of Edmond Sandili [*sic*], 15 Mar 1904, in *SANAC*, §13,113, 2:948.

might have prevented the loss of Ngqika territory in the first place, by giving non-rebels the right to prove loyalty and retain their land instead of being dispossessed *en masse*—a point that prefigured the petition of Tiyo Burnside Soga three decades later.[9] The authority of the colony to dispose of the land according to rules it devised went unquestioned, as did the actual needs and desires of others with or without land. Veldtman, however, enjoyed the best of both worlds as a headman and a modern, titled landowner.

Veldtman deliberately did not address the other questions of social cohesion and authority that Edmund Sandile felt were linked to the question of land, possibly because he agreed with their preservation. The Resident Magistrate of Kentani, N.O. Thompson, was in favor of individual tenure for a corollary reason, that without it "you can do nothing at all with [natives] under the present system, where a man, without regard to character or ability, capability, or anything else, simply marches up to the Headman and demands the land. ...There is no inducement for the man to progress or move forward in any way."[10] The presence of an illegible social hierarchy in Kentani and Willowvale, however, meant that such an imposition remained totally unadvisable, and indeed neither district ever came under individual tenure, pointing directly to the limits of colonial intervention in African territory.

In the Transvaal, SANAC found that officials harbored similar kinds of opinions. William Windham, Secretary for Native Affairs, believed that individual landholding should be an eventual goal because under communal tenure the individual was treated "as a child" by chiefs and headmen. At the same time, he believed that Africans should not be allowed to purchase land because he did not think they were "sufficiently responsible to deal with such important property as land property" even though many had the means and desire to buy farms.[11] Windham considered the system used in the Transvaal where Africans could not own land in their own names to be a good one, and the people in the Zoutpansberg especially to be "in a very raw state indeed, and totally unripe for individual holdings," much less large gatherings and participatory government on the Glen Grey model.[12] Charles Wheelwright, the Native Affairs Commissioner in the northern Transvaal, saw no problem with the concept of survey for individual tenure but only when a "Native there living [in a location] shows himself to have improved to such an extent as to make him eligible."[13]

9 Testimony of Capt. Veldtman, 15 Mar 1904, in *SANAC*, §13,114, 2:950.

10 Testimony of N.O. Thompson, 15 Mar 1904, in *SANAC*, §13,182, 2:959.

11 Testimony of W. Windham, 3 Oct 1904, in *SANAC*, §39,768, §39,775, §39,776–836,779, 4:429–430.

12 Ibid., §39,773, §39,780–§39,782, 4:430–431; §39,910, 4:443.

13 Written statement of C.A. Wheelwright, 13 Nov 1903, in *SANAC*, 5:296.

The former *landdrost* of Zoutpansberg, G.G. Munnik, underscored the point before the Native Location Commission in 1906 by stating that Africans were "not sufficiently advanced" for individual tenure and should remain under communal holdings and identifiable chiefs lest they simply dispose of their land and become vagrants.[14] Provided the leadership and boundaries were known, optimal legibility for government already existed.

Officials in the Transvaal colony thus applied typically evolutionary assumptions to systems of land and authority, whereby improvement led to ownership through survey and registration. This application was largely self-serving because it explained the relatively greater power of African authorities in the Transvaal as unenlightened and inertial compared to their Kei Valley counterparts. The processes of fragmentation and atomization were therefore a series of stages to colonial officials. E.H. Hogge, a member of the Transvaal Native Location Commission and formerly a magistrate in the Transkei, indeed said outright that he would "consider these Natives are at least twenty to twenty-five years behind those of the Cape Colony," and as such any application of a Glen Grey style of survey and representation might be useful "in years to come, but not at the present time."[15] The laws of the chiefs and communal tenure, Hogge suggested, were best left in place, along with other policies in line with the ZAR's precedent.[16] Hogge's statements, and his subsequent participation in defining native reserves according to colonial practice, were convenient concessions to the path of least administrative resistance.

A few Transvaal chiefs gave evidence before SANAC, but seemed unsure of their long-term position relative to the land. Many were plowing on private ground bought in trust, held under another name or by the government, because they did not possess the right to register land in their own names. A few had no idea what the commission wanted to know from them or what the possible effect of their words might be.[17] Solomon Makapan, a Kgatla chief who lived on two farms purchased in trust near Pretoria, stated that they "were not given sufficient time to understand the matters that were going to be asked of us, and the language written on the papers is English, and we have to take time to understand the meanings of the headings."[18] Such caution reflects long

14 Testimony of G.G. Munnik, 19 Oct 1905, 1–2, C27/2, TAB.

15 Testimony of E.H. Hogge, 3 Oct 1904, in *SANAC*, §40,048, 4:454; §40,078, 4:458.

16 Ibid., §40,075–§40,079, 4:458.

17 Testimony of S. Mulota *et al.*, 10 Oct 1904, in *SANAC*, §42,118–§42,125, 4:650–651.

18 TKP (unnumbered), *Report by the Commissioner for Native Affairs Relative to the Acquisition and Tenure of Land by Natives in the Transvaal* (Pretoria, 1904), 97; Testimony of S. Mulota *et al.*, 10 Oct 1904, in *SANAC*, §42,124, 4:651.

experience with the capricious nature of colonial rule, which demanded participation on its own terms, but also speaks to the instrumental inaccessibility of its legal and representational forms. As a group, the nine chiefs present requested more time to compose their statements, but mentioned immediately the policy of the ZAR that prevented nonwhites owning land in their own names—a policy the British had opted to continue.[19] They presented their statement the next day, complaining of unfair treatment that denied them access to markets and education, and hoping for land and voting rights as well as continued autonomy in laws and customs regarding the use of that land.[20]

The consultation of chiefs throughout South Africa had an undeniably cursory quality. At the Cape, questioning occurred in the context of large meetings before magistrates, and sometimes, as in the case of Veldtman Bikitsha, officials and witnesses may have arranged their testimonies beforehand. In the case of the Transvaal, most of the chiefs summoned came from near Pretoria, did not know the purpose of their visit before they arrived, were never even asked about questions of land tenure, and spent less time before SANAC than virtually any other witnesses. SANAC weighted the words of officials, capitalists, and settlers far more heavily in making such decisions, and simply presumed the existence of separate "tribes" that might be defined and divided however the state wished.[21] There is no evidence whatsoever that the words of African informants changed any minds at all, but rather represented viewpoints to be explained away. The fact that the various colonial experts had different opinions was far more meaningful.

The final report of the Lagden Commission resolved regarding the system of landholding by Africans that

> [r]ecognising the attachment of the Natives to and the present advantages of their own communal or tribal system of land tenure, the Commission does not advise any general compulsory measure of sub-division and individual holding of the lands now set apart for their occupation; but recommends that movement in that direction be encouraged…[22]

19 Testimony of S. Mulota *et al.*, 10 Oct 1904, in *SANAC*, §42,126–§42,129, 4:651–652; J.H. Cilliers, "Die Administrasie en Benutting van Transvaalsse Kroongrond" (D. Litt. et Phil. diss., UNISA, 1979), 146.

20 Testimony of S. Mulota *et al.*, 11 Oct 1904, in *SANAC*, §42,814–§42,847, 4:715–718.

21 Ashforth, *Politics of Official Discourse*, 30, 40–42.

22 Report of the Commission, in *SANAC*, §147, 1:26.

Although the commission report looked favorably upon the progressive and conservationist ends of the land tenure provisions of the Glen Grey Act, they omitted any suggestion that it should be a direct instrument for labor provision and in fact noted the utter failure of the labor tax. The commission also recommended that the location system at work in the Transvaal and other colonies should offer greater security of tenure than the simple retention of location ground as unalienated Crown land. The final report indeed employed language markedly different from the earlier coercive utterances of reports and correspondence in the South African Republic and the Cape Colony alike.[23] Despite its clear purpose in developing a unified system for native administration across South Africa, SANAC's language about creating sustainable or uniform land policy for those areas was remarkably restrained.[24]

At the same time, SANAC made strong pronouncements regarding patterns of African occupation that had developed to preserve the viability of societies under pressure. The report indeed refers to African systems of agriculture and landholding as retrograde vestiges of primitive and inferior societies, as with beer-drinks and other communal activities. Regarding Africans who lived outside of the defined reserves, SANAC declared that "unrestrained squatting of Natives on private farms, whether as tenants or otherwise, is an evil" and that only servants under contract should be allowed to do so—pushing the proletarianization as well as the enumeration of the African population, and illusorily separating those aspects of policy from the question of African land tenure.[25]

Furthermore, the report of the commission expressed their belief that "there is a manifest effort on the part of Natives to-day being made to possess land which is not counteracted by any reluctance on the part of European holders to dispose of it," and resolved that "it is necessary to safeguard what is conceived to be the interests of the Europeans of this country" by restricting African land purchases to certain areas of the country and prohibiting any purchases that would "lead to tribal, communal, or collective possession or occupation by Natives."[26] W.E. Stanford registered a strong dissent to the effect that such restrictive separations were unworkable, had been circumvented in the past in the Boer republics, and that the European seizure of African lands was much more the norm in any case—perhaps inadvertently suggesting that

23 Ibid., §149–167, 1:27–30.

24 The restraint may reflect the British belief that they had established their legitimate sovereign rights over the land. See Ashforth, *Politics of Official Discourse*, 35.

25 Report of the Commission, in *SANAC*, §181, 1:32–33.

26 Ibid., §191–193, 1:35.

restrictions against African land acquisition be matched with restrictions against Europeans in the future.[27] Stanford did not contest the foundational assumption of separation the recommendation entailed. Ultimately, the official mind of the colony was in agreement on the desirability of separate spheres of citizenship and territoriality within the body of the state, and that single point of agreement solved the incongruity of different systems of tenure for Africans.[28]

One witness before SANAC would eventually create the legal crisis that pushed forward the Lagden Commission's recommendations for separate spheres of citizenship and territory. That witness was Edward Tsewu, a Presbyterian Fingo preacher from the Eastern Cape who became a central figure in challenging the denial of land rights to nonwhites in the Transvaal Colony. Tsewu represented the new generation of Western-educated, Christian Bantu-speaking Africans, a "modern elite" that was in some ways even more alarming to the colonial order in South Africa than the older chiefs and headmen like Mphephu or Edmund Sandile. People like Tsewu could mobilize the colonialists' own signs and language to contest their exclusion from equal rights in the unified South Africa then under design. The new generation included people from many places who spoke from a point of view that reached beyond tribalized ethnicity and borders, and applied experiences from far afield to new localities. Tsewu, for example, aligned with the strident, American-based African Methodist Episcopalian Church for a number of years.[29] Tsewu eventually brought the expectations of modern, educated Africans up against the legal regime of the Transvaal—and in doing so successfully, forced the colonial state to articulate and enshrine its segregationist trajectory in law.[30]

Tsewu was already known to colonial officials in the Transvaal before 1904 for his lack of deference, addressing them directly by name in English instead

27 Ibid., §198, 1:36–37.

28 Ashforth, *Politics of Official Discourse*, 36–37.

29 James T. Campbell, *Songs of Zion: The African Methodist Episcopal Church in the United States and South Africa* (Oxford: Oxford University Press, 1995), 137, 145.

30 Martin Chanock, *The Making of South African Legal Culture 1902–1936: Fear, Favour and Prejudice* (Cambridge: Cambridge University Press, 2001), 361–362. Chanock specifically describes the march to the 1913 Natives Land Act as an effort to rebuild the old prohibitions. See Chanock, *South African Legal Culture*, 362–405 *passim*. My emphasis on Tsewu as a distinctly *modern* actor comes from Jacob Dlamini, "Edward Tsewu and the Struggle for African Property Ownership: Rethinking the Prehistory of the 1913 Natives Land Act," plenary presentation at the Land Divided Conference, University of Cape Town, 25 Mar 2013.

of speaking in metaphor to their interpreters.[31] For SANAC, he led a delegation of five others to testify on all matters before the commission. On the question of land tenure, he stated very plainly that "the Natives ought to be allowed to buy land in their own names, and have title deeds in their own names…because some of them are brought up in cultivating land, and they are quite capable of having land of their own, and using it properly, and supplying the market."[32] Tsewu stated that he expressed the views of Africans in the Cape Colony *and* the Transvaal, and indicated that he himself was buying a piece of land and intended to register it in his own name.[33] As Secretary of the Native Vigilance Committee and leader of the Transvaal Native Landowners' Association, Tsewu had already inquired of Lagden whether a prohibition existed, asked for its repeal if so, and stated his intent to "apply to the Supreme Court of this Colony for Protection as British Subjects *re* this subject."[34] Lagden in turn had dismissed Tsewu's delegation as representing "a very small section of educated natives" and declared their demands to be premature based on his vast knowledge "in the position of your father in this matter."[35] The entire delegation expressed its dissatisfaction with the lack of redress, for they expected better from a British government. But like other delegations before them, Lagden had responded with overt paternalism.[36]

The response of Tsewu was different, for he chose to press the matter once he had "the satisfaction of knowing the mind of the office" at the same time the Transvaal legislature sought to pass a law affirming the prohibitions.[37] As Tsewu mentioned before SANAC, he intended to purchase land, and implicitly to register its title under his own name. The land was an expensive freehold lot in a township, which the Registrar of Deeds refused to enter under Tsewu's name in December 1904.[38] Tsewu challenged that prohibition and took his case to the Supreme Court of the Transvaal, where the full court ruled in his favor, ordered the registration of the lot in his own name, and effectively overruled any attempt to re-legislate the prohibition under British legal authority.[39]

31 Campbell, *Songs of Zion*, 151–152.
32 Testimony of E. Tsewu, 14 Oct 1904, in *SANAC*, §43,552–§43,553, 4:787.
33 Testimony of E. Tsewu, 14 Oct 1904, in *SANAC*, §43,567–§43,572, 4:878–888.
34 Tsewu to Lagden, 7 Jul 1904, 3, NA 1555/1904, SNA 226, KAB.
35 Minutes of Meeting, 8 Jul 1904, 12 (9), NA 1555/1904, SNA 226, KAB.
36 See J.B. Mgweba to J.S. Marwick (Assistant Secretary for Native Affairs), 7 Aug 1902, 151–152, NAM 9/1901, SNA 1, TAB; Minutes of meeting between Lagden and delegates, 3 Sep 1902, 156, NAM 9/1901, SNA 1, TAB.
37 Minutes of Meeting, 8 Jul 1904, 19 (16), NA 1555/1904, SNA 226, KAB; TKP (unnumbered), *Transvaal Native Affairs Department Report for the Year Ended 30 June 1905*, A.5.
38 Case 286/1905, Tsewu vs. Registrar of Deeds, Affadavit of E. Tsewu, 329, ZTPD 8/732, TAB.
39 Case 286/1905, Tsewu vs. Registrar of Deeds, Judgment (*ex parte Tsewu*), 4 Apr 1905, p. 346, ZTPD 8/732, TAB; Chanock, *Making of South African Legal Culture*, 361; André Odendaal,

The decision *ex parte Tsewu* alarmed many within the Transvaal, especially among the northern Boers. G.G. Munnik stated unequivocally to the Location commission that "the natives are taking advantage of a recent judgment of the Supreme Court...[t]his question requires immediate legislation to prevent trouble."[40] P.J. Potgieter, Munnik's former colleague from the district of Waterberg, declared that the unprecedented wealth of some Africans and their acquisition of land would, if "allowed to go on, in 25 years it will be impossible for white men to live in this country" because African landholders would be scattered everywhere.[41] Their alarmist predictions and demands for a return to the restrictions of the old Republic in matters of title and its location reflected a presumption that the legal *status quo ante*, and not the facts on the ground, should provide the basis for any changes. The reality, of course, was that Africans already lived all over the Transvaal as labor tenants and wage laborers, but unrestricted private ownership was a different matter to the state and white landowners.

Edward Tsewu's court victory indeed created a legal precedent for legal parity and true assimilation within the body of the state. True to the predictions of its critics, the decision allowed for the expansion of African land purchases and repurchases; historian Harvey Feinberg calculates that between 1905 and June 1913, African buyers in the Transvaal acquired 399 surveyed farms in their own names, without restrictions on subdivision.[42] The Surveyor-General of the Transvaal, W.H. Gilfillan, was well aware of *ex parte Tsewu*, and the Native Location Commission asked him about its implications in 1906. Gilfillan stated his belief that denying such access would contribute to unrest in South Africa at large, but also that African rights to purchase and lease land on the Cape model did not mean that "he should go [just] anywhere."[43] When the question of Crown lands came up, Gilfillan responded that "[y]ou must decide where the suitable land is and say to the native 'You must purchase or lease it'," implying that any such piece of land would need to be created within the geographical archive and made legible first.[44] Lagden himself reported in 1906 that a "principle [*sic*] obstacle" to leasing Crown land and collecting rents was the

The Founders: The Origins of the anc and the Struggle for Democracy in South Africa (Johannesburg: Jacana, 2012), 273–274.

40 Testimony of G.G. Munnik, 19 Oct 1905, 2, C27/2, TAB.

41 Testimony of P.J. Potgieter, 11 Oct 1905, 3, C27/2, TAB.

42 Harvey M. Feinberg, "Pre-Apartheid African Land Ownership and the Implication for the Current Restitution Debate in South Africa," *Historia* 40, no. 2 (1995): 50.

43 Testimony of W.H. Gilfillan, 5 Apr 1906, pp. 3–4, 7–8, C27/2, TAB.

44 Ibid., p. 7, C27/2, TAB.

lack of reliable records.[45] Matters thus revolved entirely around the need for cadastrally-defined plots of ground enumerated within the state's archive, be they locations, lots, or farms.

Tsewu's victory did not go unchallenged for long. Once the creation of the Union of South Africa in 1910 removed direct British legal authority over internal affairs, the creation of openly discriminatory legislation was easier, and the settler-dominated Union government began working almost immediately. The Natives Land Act (No. 27) of 1913 that emerged was the outcome of a potent mixture of paternal racism, capitalism, and fear that all promoted territorial segregation to an overwhelmingly white electorate.[46] The Land Act designated areas for white and black occupation for the first time, and set aside less than 8% of the state's territory for black ownership with the promise of further assignments of land later, as well as a provision for exceptions with government approval.[47] The Cape Province, with its color-blind, qualified franchise for black South Africans, was exempt until those voting rights were shunted into a Glen Grey-like system of council governance with the Natives Trust and Land Act in 1936.[48] The government trustees were, however, surprisingly permissive in their approval of black purchasers' requests for exceptions, although it is impossible to measure the skewing effect the law had on prices and petitions.[49] Even so, the principles were enshrined, and subsequent legislation until 1990 increasingly sought to realize the impossible goal of territorial segregation.

The barriers that the Natives Land Act created in the transfer of land between Africans and Europeans were of course based on the geographical archive and the desire to control its notional landscape, which in turn inaugurated a new effort to make reality reflect the map's characterization of spaces

45 TKP (unnumbered), *Transvaal Native Affairs Department Report for the Year Ended 30 June 1906* (Pretoria, 1906), A.12.

46 See Harvey M. Feinberg, "The 1913 Natives Land Act in South Africa: Politics, Race, and Segregation in the Early 20th Century," *International Journal of African Historical Studies* 26, no. 1 (1993): 65–109.

47 Although the Act initially envisaged further releases within a few years, they officially did not occur until 1936; see Harvey M. Feinberg and Andre Horn, "South African Territorial Segregation: New Data on African Farm Purchases, 1913–1936," *Journal of African History* 50 (2009): 42.

48 The constitutionality of this exemption was confirmed in the 1917 court case *Thompson v. Kama*; see Ian Loveland, *By Due Process of Law? Racial Discrimination and the Right to Vote in South Africa 1855–1960* (Oxford: Hart Publishing, 1999), 148.

49 Feinberg and Horn, "South African Territorial Segregation," 41–60.

as 'white' or 'black.'[50] That the map's notional spaces and boundaries settled in form at about the same time was thus not coincidence, but a necessary condition for the often-farcical social engineering of the later Union and apartheid eras. In an almost Newtonian association, this notional landscape was also necessary for the creation of a national African political opposition movement. The South African Native National Congress (today the African National Congress) first organized in January 1912 specifically to oppose bills aimed at territorial and legal segregation, and Edward Tsewu was one of the three nominees to be its first president.[51]

The judgment in *ex parte Tsewu* and the Natives Land Act's subsequent legal assault on ownership and occupancy were both important, but they were not challenges or changes to the cadastral structure of the state. Both in fact reinforced the sanctity of the geographical archive, just as the similar shift from oral culture to print literacy had aided state control and legibility in England three centuries prior and empowered the creators of texts.[52] Tsewu and others in the Transvaal advocated the right of Africans to buy titled land to use as free and equal proprietors under colonial law, by definition within the geographical archive and already defined by its terms of reference. The Natives Land Act determined that such a right should be territorially limited to certain areas within state-defined boundaries but said nothing about the nature of landholding within those boundaries themselves, thus allowing varying tenures to exist only in those spaces. Exemption from, disqualification of, and later modifications to certain clauses in the Act turned on the right to acquire defined plots of land or the power of government to allow purchases of defined plots across the Act's racialized boundary.[53] The surveyed body of the state had thus become a normal frame of reference and discourse for all South Africans, whether citizen or subject.

Edward Tsewu thus shared with Tiyo Burnside Soga a fundamental acceptance of the surveyed territorial boundaries of the colonial state as the stage

---

50 Sol T. Plaatje, *Native Life in South Africa* (Johannesburg: Ravan, 1982 [1916]), 24; Feinberg, "Pre-Apartheid African Land Ownership," 50; for the relationship of power, the map, and transformation, see James C. Scott, *Seeing Like a State: How Certain Schemes to Improve the Human Condition Have Failed* (New Haven: Yale University Press, 1998), 87.

51 André Odendaal, *Vukani Bantu!: The Beginnings of Black Protest Politics in South Africa to 1912* (Cape Town: David Philip, 1984), 256–257, 275.

52 Adam Fox, *Oral and Literate Culture in England, 1500–1700* (Oxford: Clarendon, 2000), 259–298; Walter Mignolo, *The Darker Side of the Renaissance: Literacy, Territoriality, and Colonization* 2nd ed. (Ann Arbor: University of Michigan Press, 2003), 121–122.

53 See H.M. Feinberg, "Protest in South Africa: Prominent Black Leaders' Commentary on the Natives Land Act, 1913–1936," *Historia* 52, no. 2 (2006): 122–123.

for struggle against it. Thus our study comes full-circle, returning to the conceptual inviolability of the colonizer's legal landscape and the geographical archive. The diagram and the title may represent the crystallized output of negotiation over land and boundaries, but their very existence testifies to an ongoing governmental drive for legibility and control over landscapes that remained unruly at best. Ironically those documents attained a veneer of objectivity and formed the skeletal framework for territorial separation and racial policy in the segregation and apartheid eras—and beyond.

Conclusion: Shadows on the Land

With regards to the broader relationship between native landscapes and colonialism, what do these South African experiences tell us? In short, they tell us that the nature and form of spatial interventions by the state had a close relationship with local priorities and differing ideas about landscape. Those ideas and needs could and did alter the work of surveyors, just as understandings of the surveyors' work then formed a new framework for contests. This is not to suggest that the colonial property mosaic, and cadastral politics, became hegemonic everywhere; David Hughes, for example, shows how two different colonial regimes (in present-day Zimbabwe and Mozambique) produced different situations in immediately adjoining areas: one where settler-driven cadastral politics took over in African communities, and one where land division was not so invasive and the control of named and metricated spaces was less important.[54] The local contingencies and interactions, mediated by agents like surveyors, were crucial to the ways that social and cultural landscapes changed, and the echoes continue to affect those societies now. We can extend this to the broader colonial world and see each experience of land and colonization as neither a simple matter of policy fulfillment nor a struggle between colonizer and colonized. Actions and negotiations did not boil down to collaboration or resistance relative to state power, but reflected more immediate concerns. Native landscapes were thus co-produced frameworks that created certain spatial constraints for future interactions, but they did not have the same meaning to everyone, and those meanings have changed everywhere since.

For the discussion of geographical science and territorial delineation in the colonial era, I used Fingoland in the Cape Colony and Ha Ramabulana in the

54 David McDermott Hughes, *From Enslavement to Environmentalism: Politics on a South African Frontier* (Seattle: Univeristy of Washington Press, 2006).

Transvaal because they represent greatly disparate examples. State geography and local landscapes had vastly different characteristics in each case, and they interacted in correspondingly different ways that involved strange combinations of negotiation, contingency, and circumvention. In both cases the state's aspiration to assay and control landscapes grew helically with its technicians' faith in their ability to render lands and people legible, despite the enduring disjoint between their understandings and the knowledge of the people on those landscapes.[55] In both regions, surveyors and settlers sought to bound lands, define them, and incorporate them into an overall system of geographical knowledge in order to gain access to the 'surplus' land and the labor of Africans, while also extending their control over a previously unruly settler landscape.[56]

Ultimately, the differences in how the two broader systems of spatial rationalization in the Cape and Transvaal unfolded before 1913 reflect the interactions of successive governments, white settlers, African authorities, and African landholders. A variety of relationships existed among these parties, and settler state's drive to create and define space and place on a knowable landscape encountered potent contests all along the way. Those contests required new strategies and negotiations, and eventually the abandonment of direct attempts at invasive spatial control. The single most crucial element was the capacity of African societies to defend their spatial integrity or, failing that, exact concessions from the colonial state that would preserve key elements of self-determination, social power, and authority as dictated under their own understandings of space and place.

In the Cape Colony, those concessions at first involved an exchange of colonial recognition and guaranty to chiefs in return for the acceptance of boundaries. The land system required some knowledge and survey of the land before that exchange could happen, and that agreement was absolutely necessary before the Cape Colony or its precursor states in the valley could alienate the land. Schemes to settle standing military forces in the region in the mid-1800s also required basic surveys to give authority to the titles and diagrams entered into the geographical archive. When the Colony incorporated the land

55 Scott, *Seeing Like a State*, 88–90; Cohn, *Colonialism and its Forms of Knowledge*, 10–11; C.A. Bayly, *Empire and Information: Intelligence Gathering and Social Communication in India, 1780–1870* (Cambridge: Cambridge University Press, 1996), 365–367.

56 John C. Weaver, *The Great Land Rush and the Making of the Modern World, 1650–1900* (Kingston, ON: McGill-Queens University Press, 2003), 151–152, 176–177; Cole Harris, *Making Native Space: Colonialism, Resistance, and Reserves in British Columbia* (Vancouver: UBC Press, 2002), 14–15.

of allied kings and chiefs, colonial officials only reluctantly conceded any power over land even though they lacked the ability truly to uproot it. The Colony more readily incorporated 'chiefless' Bantu-speakers, particularly the Fingoes, and sought to atomize them further using the system of land survey and individual tenure. Nevertheless, local social networks and hierarchies prevented the unmediated imposition of survey and title to the people of Fingoland. In other areas, like Gcalekaland, survey and title never gained traction at all.

The Cape government nevertheless persisted in pressing survey and title in the Kei valley as a solution to agricultural labor problems and as a manifestation of its own paternal colonial beliefs. This pressure culminated in the Glen Grey Act, which sought to engineer a broader solution rather than hope that extra-colonial authority would simply wither away in the face of European systems of spatial organization. Surveyors and magistrates instead encountered objections from African headmen and farmers who forced compromise in the creation of individual tenure systems, and later simply circumvented restrictions or boundaries that they found onerous. Government nevertheless honored the forms of survey and used its data to frame policy and cartography alike, presenting a perfect landscape of location management that simply did not exist. Closer administration and survey only gained meaningful purchase in African areas through the costly medium of direct mediation between African landholders and surveyors, and then only when the former group received significant concessions. Only the era of Betterment in the 1940s would change this dynamic.

In the Transvaal, the South African Republic represented a settler-driven, land-hunting state that initially paid miniscule attention to the reality of the situation on the ground in making its claims. The *ad hoc* system of land claims and titles under the Republic was very deliberately not dependent on surveyors, who were conspicuous through the enormous problems they encountered in establishing themselves at all. The fundamentally flawed geographical archive the system of inspection created was useful not, as Transvaal Surveyor-General M.W. Wedepohl observed in 1958, because it "met changing circumstances with good effect," but because it allowed the state to create a fiction of authority and knowledge in complete defiance of whatever situations may have existed in reality.[57] The most generous figures *circa* 1896 indicate that the total European population in the ZAR was never more than 15% of the whole,

57 M.W. Wedepohl, "Historical Review of Legislation Affecting Survey and Registration of Land in the Transvaal," *South African Survey Journal* 9, no. 2 (1958): 25.

even before taking account of the likely underestimation of the African population.[58] The citizen population was far smaller. In contrast, the European population in the Cape was larger in both size and proportion, and it enjoyed a direct connection to British imperial power. The policy of the ZAR until the 1880s was therefore completely dependent on a combination of selective application of force and negotiation of boundaries with African states within its own theoretical boundaries initially not by survey, but by reckoning, with a helpful dose of ambiguity.

After 1881, the policies of the ZAR towards African societies turned on a location system for inspecting and beaconing the lands of powerful African states. Reconciling existing landscapes with location boundaries was difficult and sometimes worked further to compromise any veneer of objectivity in the geographical archive, even as the data purportedly became more accurate. That enumerative drive, however, defined all other land as available to white settlers or land companies by default, accomplishing through survey and assignment what the inspection system had done before using omission. Beyond that problem, the push to rationalize and enumerate African space within the theoretical body of the Republic ran afoul of the powerful states of the far north. In the case of Makhado and Mphephu, statecraft and spatial delimitation existed in tension and confronted the pretensions of the colonial state with the reality of Venda power. When the British took over, they chose to take the geographical archive of the ZAR as their own, and render effective its claims. The British sought to complete the Transvaal's location system, but they too encountered the power and determination of African states like Ha Ramabulana, and ultimately made key concessions to secure acquiescence. The ZAR and Transvaal governments created no spaces for private African ownership, nor did they attempt to introduce individual tenure—with the result that after the South African War, Africans sought to obtain land on their own terms and force the issue within the confines of the new dispensation.

The rise of a settler-dominated government with Union in 1910 and the fusion of conservative rural interests with those of industrial capital assured that the response to the challenge of *ex parte Tsewu* and the question of proprietorship models for black South Africans would be the intensification of segregation, seen in the Natives Land Act of 1913, but much more strongly in its

58 See *Whitaker's Almanack, 1899* (London: J. Whitaker & Sons, 1899), s.v. "South African Republic," which cites estimates of 150,000 'white,' 63,000 of whom were *burghers*, and 1,000,000 'black.' Available census figures were uneven at best until after the South African War, when a unified enumerative mission took priority across the colonies and then the Union. See Cohn, *Colonialism and its Forms of Knowledge*, 8.

successors.[59] The variety of negotiated landscapes in places like Fingoland and Ha Ramabulana thus came under the authority of the Union of South Africa to create a single entity within its conceptual world called "native lands." This compartmentalization allowed for variability in African legal and social landscapes while increasingly separating them from parallel white-proprietor landscapes, thus normalizing Africans' subject status in those white areas outside of the Cape Province until it, too, came under the operation of segregationist land law in 1936.[60] Although deteriorating systems of individual tenure in Fingoland and neighboring areas remained, the Lagden Commission made clear that the least common denominator for all was territorial segregation under a model of internal colonialism by indirect rule, one that created a single regime for the various localities and left their internal settlements to ever more artificial models of local self-government.[61] Step by step, the Union government moved in that direction.

But this model of indirect rule remained interventionist when it came to the landscape. Subsequent national governments became progressively *more* severe in their territorial and legal interventions as the twentieth century wore on, in their endeavors to engineer a stable settler-dominated social, political, legal, and economic order in South Africa. The alluring illusion of cartographic legibility implied that it was possible, and a declensionist narrative of environmental catastrophe and African ineptitude suggested that it was urgent. The results were the post-1936 policies of Betterment and Rehabilitation, which brought an additional wave of regimented landscape transformation down atop earlier survey frameworks.[62] Architect Jennifer Beningfield describes their effect as an interruption of local lives "by distant scratchings of drawing implements held by faceless individuals, struggling to overlay political will onto the surface of the ground," which exaggerates the physical remove of technocrats from native landscapes, but perhaps captures the conceptual distance involved.[63] Local chiefs and headmen became compulsory accomplices in 1951, and government applied increasing levels of ultimately unsustainable

---

59 Saul Dubow, *Racial Segregation and the Origins of Apartheid in South Africa, 1919–36* (London: Macmillan, 1989), 3–4.

60 See Ashforth, *Politics of Official Discourse*, 28 (esp. n. 20).

61 Mahmood Mamdani, *Citizen and Subject: Contemporary Africa and the Legacy of Late Colonialism* (Princeton: Princeton University Press, 1996), 70.

62 William Beinart and Lotte Hughes, *Environment and Empire* (Oxford: Oxford University Press, 2007), 284–286.

63 Jennifer Beningfield, *The Frightened Land: Land, Landscape, and Politics in South Africa in the Twentieth Century* (New York: Routledge, 2006), 111.

force in their attempts to enact visions of native landscapes that earlier generations of surveyors and administrators had wisely ignored or abandoned.

The naturalization and use of distinctly artificial boundaries was one of the many contradictions of segregation and apartheid, but it has endured past the end of those regimes. Since 1994, the redress of past injustices involving forced removals, expropriations, and other spatial restrictions has occupied a central position in the national discourse. At the heart of the matter is land, represented by the titles and accompanying precise measurements of area and land quality first set down over a century ago. The possession of land through those documents remains a central government metric for transformation and the redress of inequality, although those have all become separate things in practice.

As if to underscore the importance of the South African geographical archive, the land reform process has not recognized claims for direct restitution dating from before 19 June 1913, when the Natives Land Act came into operation and state-sanctioned African land ownership covered less than ten per cent of the country.[64] That cut-off date for direct restitution, enshrined in Section 25 of the South African Constitution, implicitly closed the door on precolonial or noncolonial patterns of occupation and use in favor of the property system laid down by that date through survey and title. Older or weaker claims remained eligible for redistribution through purchase from willing sellers, and tenure reform aspired to secure ownership for long-term labor tenants and other leaseholders.[65] Specialists have pointed out that pre-1913 political and social issues retain importance and must be understood for land restitution to be satisfactory, even if the terms of reference in oral accounts remain tied to the bounded spaces set down in the archives.[66] The need to consider this larger halo of connections—nodes and networks—in time and space remains an issue that severely complicates government attempts at land reform; political maneuvering never stopped on the landscape the archive purports to describe, and cadastral boundaries do not confine society or memory.

---

64 Cherryl Walker, "The Limits to Land Reform: Rethinking 'the Land Question'," *Journal of Southern African Studies* 31, no. 4 (2005): 815.

65 For an excellent summary of the distinctions between categories of restitution, redistribution, and reform, see Deborah James, Alex X. Ngonini, and Geoffrey Mphahle Nkadimeng, "(Re)Constituting Class?: Owners, Tenants, and the Politics of Land Reform in Mpumalanga," *Journal of Southern African Studies* 31, no. 4 (2005): 828.

66 See F.C. de Beer, "Determining the Merits of Land Claims: A Challenge for the Anthropologist," *Anthropology Southern Africa* 26, no. 3–4 (2003): 131–142. De Beer's essay is particularly salient, as it deals with patronage and a local legacy tied to the 1898 war between the ZAR and Mphephu.

The pace of land reform has been very slow as a result. The South African government set a goal to transfer thirty percent of the country's agricultural land area (amounting to 24.5 million hectares, or 60.5 million acres) to black ownership by 1999, but pushed back that target several times when it became obvious that meeting the deadline would require disbursements the government could not support at a rate they could not predict.[67] Less than 2.9% of the country's agricultural land had passed to new ownership by March 2004, which prompted an effort to accelerate the process.[68] The Department of Rural Development and Land Reform reported the discharge of nearly 95% of the total number of claims lodged—75,844 out of 79,696 by their count—by April 2010, but that included many thousands of cases that were adjudicated but remained unresolved on the ground as of October 2013.[69] Making the 2014 date would have required an unrealistic schedule of hearings and investigations, as well as the power ultimately to compel land sales and transfers in court. One estimate stated that over two million hectares (around five million acres) per year would have needed to be transferred annually from 2004 to 2014—eight times the actual yearly transfer of land between 1996 and 2004, and in total almost four times the amount of land (6.7 million hectares, or 16.6 million acres) actually transferred up to March 2012.[70] The unfinalized claims include a number of rural cases regarding vast or sensitive areas including the Soutpansberg Mountains and parts of the Kruger National Park, and some of the remaining claims overlap with one another, pointing to the confusion that

---

67 Ruth Hall, "Reconciling the Past, Present, and Future: The Parameters and Practices of Land Restitution in South Africa," in *Land, Memory, Reconstruction, and Justice: Perspectives on Land Claims in South Africa*, ed. C. Walker, A. Bohlin, R. Hall, and T. Kepe (Athens: University of Ohio Press, 2010), 36–37.

68 Ben Cousins, "Agrarian Reform and the 'Two Economies': Transforming South Africa's Countryside," in *The Land Question in South Africa: The Challenge of Transformation and Redustribution*, ed. Lungisile Ntsebeza and Ruth Hall (Cape Town: HSRC Press, 2007), 223–225, 211.

69 Department of Rural Development and Land Reform, Republic of South Africa (hereafter RDLR), *Annual Report, 1 April 2009–31 March 2010* (Pretoria: RDLR, 2010), 6; Ben Cousins and Rebecca Pointer, "New Land Policies Further Entrenching Poverty and Inequality," *Another Countryside* (blog), 14 Oct 2013, http://www.plaas.org.za/blog/new-land-policies-further-entrenching-poverty-and-inequality. Cousins and Pointer put the number of unresolved claims at around 20,000.

70 Ruth Hall and Edward Lahiff, "Budgeting for land reform," PLAAS Policy Brief 13 (2004), University of the Western Cape; G.E. Nkwinti, 2012 Policy Speech: Rural Development and Land Reform (Vote 32), 15 May 2012, accessed 19 Nov 2012, http://www.info.gov.za/speech/DynamicAction?pageid=461&sid=27380&tid=67999.

was inherent in defining boundaries and domains and the shifting politics of identity and memory between then and now.[71] To complicate matters further, Parliament recently passed a new Restitution of Land Rights Amendment Act (No. 15 of 2014) that reopened the window for lodging of land claims until the end of June 2019.

At the same time, continuous pressure exists to re-open the 1913 historical limit for direct restitution. Many in government, and outside commentators as well, recognize the importance of the pre-Land Act colonial past in creating the situation written into law after 1913; South African sociologist Cherryl Walker refers to the extent of white-owned lands before the Act as "the unexamined measure of both loss and redress."[72] The Department of Land Affairs (now Rural Development and Land Reform) opposed any cut-off extension in May 2007, but the Policy Conference of the African National Congress in June 2012 recommended the government consider the public call to permit new and formerly ineligible claims.[73] In promoting the Land Rights Amendment Bill in 2013 and early 2014, the government implied that the 1913 cut-off might be waived, but critics pointed out the lack of any such provision in the text of the bill despite the early spin of exploring exceptions, and indeed the Act made no provision for such claims.[74] Thus the post-1913 territorial framework remains the conceptual starting point for the South African state, and the governing ANC seems disinclined to tinker too much with the comfortable cadastral certainty of the native landscapes it inherited after 1994. Indeed, basic constitutional struggles over community leadership and security of tenure in former location

71 Mark Everingham and Crystal Jannecke, "Land Restitution and Democratic Citizenship in South Africa," *Journal of Southern African Studies* 32, no. 3 (2006): 548. Memory can also expose real problems of overlap; see Hughes, *From Enslavement to Environmentalism*, 9.

72 Everingham and Jannecke, "Land Restitution and Democratic Citizenship," 547; Mike Akomaye Yanou, "The 1913 Cut-off Date for Restitution of Dispossessed Land in South Africa: A Critical Appraisal," *Africa Development (Afrique et Developpment)* 31, no. 3 (2006): 177–188; Walker, "Limits to Land Reform," 808.

73 Department of Land Affairs [RDLR], Republic of South Africa, "Restitution Amendment Bill Proposal: Cut-off dates of 19 June 1913 and 31 December 1998, Public Hearings by the Portfolio Committee on Agriculture & Land Affairs 29 May 2007," accessed 14 Apr 2014, http://www.pmg.org.za/docs/2007/070529gwanya.pdf; RDLR, "National Restitution Workshop Executive Summary [6 Oct 2011]," accessed 3 Apr 2014, http://www.ruraldevelopment.gov.za/phocadownload/Restitution/2012/restitutionworkshop-08052011.pdf; African National Congress, "Land Reform Policy Discussion Document, June 2012," 3, 8, accessed 17 Jan 2014, http://www.anc.org.za/docs/discus/2012/landpolicyproposals_june2012g.pdf.

74 See, for example, Nomboniso Gasa and Nolundi Luwaya, "Empty Promises to Rural People," *Custom Contested: Views & Voices* (blog), 4 Apr 2014, http://www.customcontested.co.za/empty-promises-rural-people/.

areas centered upon the roles of chiefs and headmen, whose powers waned and waxed during the twentieth century; these figures now clamor to retain special authority in the new South Africa, including the sole power to claim communal land restitution and administer it, based on traditions of a distinctly recent vintage.[75]

The landowners' defense against these pushes for restitution and redistribution however also turns heavily on the construction of the legal and cadastral framework. The most notable recent intervention has been the 2011 publication of *Omstrede Land* (in English as *Disputed Land*), sponsored by the H.F. Verwoerd Trust, a lightly-researched popular work (and political prop) that candidly advocates the sanctity of the laws and customary rights that created the property mosaic, as well as the retroactive inviolability of survey and titling processes.[76] That book seeks to make a case for the settler right to most of the land based on its occupation, division, and titling, together with a few supplemental arguments about land and race that I can best describe as coming from another era. Its purpose is to call into doubt the sheer breadth of land claims postdating 1913 and argue against the validity of any pre-1913 land claims, but it is silent about the fraught circumstances of production that afflict the archive it extols. The production of colonial landscapes and the roles of the technicians charged with creating them clearly require further critical exploration and expatiation, if we are to understand the competing worldviews that underlie these claims and counter-claims.

---

75 Although current legal battles and accommodations between the ANC, traditional authorities, and communities regarding land fall outside the scope of this study, see Lungisile Ntsebeza, *Democracy Compromised: Chiefs and the Politics of the Land in South Africa* (Leiden: Brill, 2004), 256–294; Ben Cousins, "More than Socially Embedded: The Distinctive Character of 'Communal Tenure' Regimes and its Implications for Land Policy," *Journal of Agrarian Change* 7, no. 3 (2007): 281–315; Peter Delius, "Contested Terrain: Land Rights and Chiefly Power in Historical Perspective," in *Land, Power, & Custom: Controversies Generated by South Africa's Communal Land Rights Act*, ed. Aninka Claassens and Ben Cousins (Athens: Ohio University Press, 2008), 211–37; J. Michael Williams, *Chieftaincy, the State, and Democracy: Political Legitimacy in Post-Apartheid South Africa* (Bloomington: Indiana University Press, 2010), 94, 103–104; Derick Fay, "Dilemmas of 'Indigenous Tenure' in South Africa: Traditional Authorities and the Constitutional Challenge to the 2004 Communal Land Rights Act," in *Indigenous Knowledge and the Environment in Africa and North America*, ed. David M. Gordon and Shepard Krech III (Athens, OH: Ohio University Press, 2012), 287–306.

76 Louis Changuion and Bertus Steenkamp, *Disputed Land* (Pretoria: Protea, 2012). The roots of the book in the geographical and legal archives are further evident by their silence on questions of tenure reform and tenancy, which make up a significant number of claims.

Regardless of the positions within the current debate over land reform, what remains clear is the centrality of the framework laid down during the colonial era. Whether a person is discussing allotments in a location area, long-term labor tenancy, direct claims on a block of land, or simply describing a place, the cadastral body of the state determines the labels and the markers. The meanings that people pour into those landscapes may be quite different depending on background, and may even—as in the case of T.B. Soga in Chapter 2—be a syncretic understanding that merges the historical and the memetic with the archival to produce new boundaries, spaces, and networks of place. In both reflecting and confining discourses on the land, the processes that produced native landscapes in nineteenth-century South Africa—and across much of the formerly colonized world—continue to cast their shadows over the land in the twenty-first.

Bibliography

Author's Note

The Department of Rural Development and Land Reform has devolved the old provincial offices of the Surveyors General to the new provincial structure, and between 2010 and 2012 many records I had consulted at offices in Pretoria and Cape Town went to Polokwane and East London respectively. Where I could physically confirm a later move I have changed the citation, but researchers should be aware that some of my repository attributions may be obsolete.

Manuscripts

South Africa

Cape Archives Depot, Cape Town

Chief Magistrate, Tembuland and Transkei (CMT 3)
Chief Magistrate, Transkei (CMT 2)
Colonial Secretary, Cape Colony (CO)
Department of Native Affairs (NA)
Deputy Surveyor-General, British Kaffraria (DSGBK)
Fingo Agent (FA)
Government House/Governors' Papers (GH)
Government of British Kaffraria (BK)
Inspector of Native Locations, Queenstown (INQ)
Map Collections (M series)
Ministry of Lands, Department of Agriculture (LND)
Orphan Chamber, Estates (MOOC)
Papers of the Prime Minister's Office (PMO)
Resident Magistrate, Butterworth (1/BUT)
Resident Magistrate, Glen Grey/Lady Frere (1/LDF)
Resident Magistrate, Idutywa (1/IDW)
Resident Magistrate, Kentani (1/KNT)
Resident Magistrate, Nqamakwe (1/NKE)
Resident Magistrate, Tsomo (1/TSM)
Resident Magistrate, Willowvale (1/WVE)
Surveyor-General, Cape Town (SG)

Transvaal Archives Depot, Pretoria

Berthoud Papers (A1529)

Typescript *Volksraadsnotulen* and *besluiten* (A2075)
Native Location Commission, Transvaal Colony (C27)
Colonial Secretary, Pretoria (CS)
Eerste Volksraad/Legislature (EVR)
Kommandant Generaal, ZAR (KG)
Native Commissioner, Louis Trichardt (KLT)
Magistrate, Louis Trichardt (LLT)
Landmeter Generaal/Surveyor-General, Pretoria (LMG)
Registrar of Deeds (RAK)
Superintendent van Naturelle, ZAR (SN)
Secretary for Native Affairs, Transvaal Colony (SNA)
Staatsprokurer/Attorney General (SP)
Staatsecretaris/Government Secretary (SS)
Map Collections (TAB Maps)
Uitvoerende Raad/Executive Council (UR)
Supreme Court, Pretoria (ZTPD)
Landdrost, Zoutpansberg (ZZG)

South African National Archives Depot, Pretoria

Department of Lands (LDE)
Office of Bantu Administration (BAO)
South African Native Trust (NTS)

Office of the Surveyor-General, Cape Town

Miscellaneous Plans Collection (Plans)
Transkei General Plans (Tskei Plans); these are most likely in East London
Bound Files (all include subfiles; unbound subfiles may now be in East London):
- S.64 (Tsomo)
- S.140 (Queenstown)
- S.183 (Nqamakwe/Ngqamakhwe)
- S.489 (Willowvale/Gatyana)
- S.622 (Butterworth Commonage)
- S.975 (Correspondence re: Surveyors)
- S.1429 (Kentani/Centane)
- S.2150 (Oxkraal and Kamastone)
- S.5237 (Native Areas, Various)
- S.3505 (Idutywa/Dutywa)
- S.6864 (Farm Nkondwane)
- S.8102 (Tambookie Location)

S.8140 (Butterworth/Gcuwa)
S.8168 (Glen Grey/Lady Frere)
S.8710 (Surveyors' Documents)
S.8676 (Engcobo)
S.10819 (Gaika Surveys)
Loose Files (may now be in East London)
File Stut.5 (Stutterheim)

Office of the Surveyor-General, Pretoria

Correspondence Volumes (miscellaneous), 1902–1910
File 477 (Northern Areas, Claims) and subsections.
File 702 (Locations, Surveyor Kolbe)
File 1747 (Native Locations) and subsections.
"G.P. Index of Surveyors" (bound manuscript volume)
General Survey Plans (GS Series)
Miscellaneous Files, Kelder (Reports, Correspondence)
Miscellaneous Plans Collection (M Series)
Superseded Diagrams, Kelder ("Ou plaasdiagramme")

Office of the Surveyor-General, Polokwane

General Survey Plans (GS Series)
Miscellaneous Plans Collection (M Series)
Property files (various)

National Geospatial Information, Mowbray (Cape Town)

Historical Documents, H2 Series (Geodetic Survey & Observatory)
Historical Documents, H3 Series (Secondary Triangulation)
Historical Documents, H4 Series (Miscellaneous)
Pamphlet Collection, Library

UNISA Library, Muckleneuk (Pretoria)

Albasini Collection (AAS 53)
Shepstone Papers, typescript (AAS 123)

Other South African Repositories

Photographic Collections, George E. Cory Library, Grahamstown
Rissik Collection, MuseuMAfricA, Johannesburg
Administrative files: Chiefs and Headmen, Umtata Archives Depot, Mthatha
Transfer Registers, Ownership Histories, and *Grondbrieven*, Registrar of Deeds, Pretoria

United Kingdom

British National Archives, Kew

Colonial Office, Correspondence Files (CO)
Colonial Office Maps (CO 700)
Maps Oversize (MR, MPH, MPG)

Cambridge University Library, Cambridge

Royal Greenwich Observatory Archives, Cape Observatory Records (RGO 15)

Published Primary Sources

Contemporary Periodicals

Cape of Good Hope Government Gazette
Berliner Missionsberichte
Bulletin Missionnaire Adressé par la Commission des Missions de l'Église Évangelique Libre du Canton de Vaud
Bulletin Missionaire des Églises Libres de la Suisse Romande
Cape Times
Imvo Zabantsundu
Land en Volk
Kaffir Express/Christian Express
South Africa
De Volksstem
Z.A.R. Staatscourant
Zoutpansberg Review

Government Reports

Numbered Cape Parliamentary Papers (Blue Books)

G.37-'56	G.34-'73	G.33-'79
G.1-'59	G.21-'75	A.104-'80
A.102-'61	G.30-'76	G.13-'80
G.26-'63	G.12-'77	G.33-'80
A.14-'67	G.33-'77	G.53-'81
G.41-'72	G.38-'78	A.51-'83
A.102-'73	G.29-'79	G.4-'83
G.8-'83	G.4-'93	G.58-'97
A.14-'83	G.9-'94	A.33-'98
G.3-'84	A.16-'95	G.15-'98

G.17-'85	A.19-'95	G.42-'98
G.12-'87	G.6-'95	G.11-1900
G.8-'88	G.47-'96	G.10 & G.10*-1904
G.23-'92	G.19-'97	G.29-1907

Numbered Transvaal Colonial Publications and Union Blue Books

T.G. 11-'08
T.G. 28-'08
U.G. 8-'18
U.G. 42-'22

British Parliamentary Papers (House of Commons)

C.2144 (1878)	C.2950 (1881)	Cd. 2684-46 (1906)
C.2252 (1879)	C.3114 (1882)	
C.2316 (1879)	C.3219 (1882)	

Other Official Documents and Reports

African National Congress, "Land Reform Policy Discussion Document, June 2012," 8. Accessed 28 November 2012. http://www.anc.org.za/docs/discus/2012/landpolicyproposals_june2012g.pdf.

British South Africa Company. *Reports on the Administration of Rhodesia, 1897–1898*. London: BSA Company, 1899.

——. *Reports on the Administration of Rhodesia, 1899–1900*. London: BSA Company, 1900.

Cape of Good Hope. *Proceedings of the Committee of the Legislative Council appointed to Examine and Report on the Papers Laid by His Excellency the Governor upon the Council Table Relative to the 120 Diagrams*. Cape Town, 1856.

——. *Proceedings of the Committee of the Legislative Council Appointed to Take into Consideration the Present State of the Law with Regard to Disputed Land Beacons*. Cape Town, 1857.

——. *Proceedings of, and Evidence Taken by, the Commission on Native Affairs*. Cape Town, 1865.

——. *Statistical Register of the Cape of Good Hope for 1906*. Cape Town: Cape Times, 1907.

Department of Land Affairs, Republic of South Africa. *Commission on the Restitution of Land Rights Annual Report for the Year Ended 31 March 2006*. Pretoria: DLA, 2006.

——. "Restitution Amendment Bill Proposal: Cut-off dates of 19 June 1913 and 31 December 1998, Public Hearings by the Portfolio Committee on Agriculture & Land Affairs 29 May 2007." Accessed 14 April 2014. http://www.pmg.org.za/docs/2007/070529gwanya.pdf.

Department of Rural Development and Land Reform, Republic of South Africa. "National Restitution Workshop Executive Summary [6 Oct 2011]." Accessed 3 April 2014. http://www.ruraldevelopment.gov.za/phocadownload/Restitution/2012/restitutionworkshop-08052011.pdf.

——. "G.E. Nkwinti, 2012 Policy Speech: Rural Development and Land Reform (Vote 32), 15 May 2012." Accessed 19 November 2012. http://www.info.gov.za/speech/DynamicAction?pageid=461&sid=27380&tid=67999.

——. *Annual Report, 1 April 2009–31 March 2010*. Pretoria: RDLR, 2010.

——. *Annual Report, 1 April 2010–31 May 2011*. Pretoria: RDLR, 2011.

——. *Annual Report, 1 April 2011–31 May 2012*. Pretoria: RDLR, 2012.

Gill, David. *Geodetic Survey of South Africa*. Vol. 3, *Report on the Geodetic Survey of Southern Rhodesia*. Cape Town: Cape Times, 1905.

Hendrikz, D.R. *South African Units of Length and Area*. Special Publication No. 2. Pretoria: Department of Lands, 1944.

High Commission for South Africa. *South African Native Affairs Commission 1903–5*. 5 vols. Cape Town: Cape Times, 1904–1905.

Maclear, Thomas. *Verification and Extension of La Caille's Arc of Meridian at the Cape of Good Hope*. 2 vols. London: HMSO, 1866.

Morris, W.G. *Geodetic Survey of South Africa*. Vol. 5, *Reports on the Geodetic Survey of the Transvaal and the Orange River Colony*. London: HMSO, 1908.

Transvaal Colony. *Report of the Transvaal Labour Commission: Together with Minority Report, Minutes of Proceedings and Evidence*. Johannesburg, 1903.

——. *Translations of the Resolutions of the Executive Council of the Late South African Republic, 1895*. Pretoria, 1903.

——. *Memorandum by the Commissioner for Native Affairs on the Subject of the Transvaal Squatter's Law*. Pretoria, 1904.

——. *Report by the Commissioner for Native Affairs relative to the Acquisition and Tenure of Land by Natives in the Transvaal*. Pretoria, 1904.

——. *Transvaal Native Affairs Department Report for the Year Ended 30 June 1905*. Pretoria, 1905.

——. *Transvaal Native Affairs Department Report for the Year Ended 30 June 1906*. Pretoria, 1906.

Zuid-Afrikaansche Republiek. No. 1-1884. *Rapport van den Landmeter-Generaal, gevende een historisch overzicht van de wijze van de vervreemding en het inspecteeren van gronden, gelegen in de Zuid-Afrikaansche Republiek en van Landmeten in het Algemeen*. Pretoria, 1884.

——. *Rapport van den Staats-mijningenieur aan de Hoog Edele Regeering over het Jaar 1892*. Pretoria, 1893.
——. *Rapport van den Superintendent van Naturellen over het Jaar 1897*. Pretoria, 1898.

Collections of Documents

Bergh, Johan, and Fred Morton, ed. and trans. *"To Make Them Serve...": The 1871 Transvaal Commission on African Labour*. Pretoria: Protea, 2003.
Breytenbach, J.H., et al., ed. *SA Argiefstukke: Transvaal*. 8 vols. Cape Town: Staatsdrukker, 1949–89.
Brownlee, Frank, comp. *The Transkeian Native Territories: Historical Records*. Lovedale: Lovedale Institution Press, 1923.
Coster, H.J., ed. *De Locale Wetten en Volksraadsbesluiten der Zuid-Afr. Republiek... gedurende de Jaren 1890, 1891, 1892, & 1893*. Pretoria: Staatsdrukkerij, 1894.
Davenport, T.R.H., and K.S. Hunt, eds. *The Right to the Land*. Johannesburg: David Philip, 1974.
Jeppe, Friedrich, and John Gilbert Kotzé, ed. and comp. *De Locale Wetten der Zuid-Afrikaansche Republiek 1849–1885*. Pretoria: J.F. Celliers, 1887.
Kotzé, John Gilbert, ed. and comp. *De Locale Wetten en Volksraads-Besluiten der Zuid-Afrikaansche Republiek, 1886–1887*. Pretoria: J.F. Celliers, 1888.
Macfayden, A.N., ed. *Statutes, Proclamations, and Government Notices in Force in the Native Territories of the Cape of Good Hope on the 30th June 1907*. Cape Town: Cape Times, Ltd., 1907.
Proclamations and Government Notices Relating to The Establishment of Councils for the Administration of Local Affairs and the Granting of Allotments in the Transkeian Territories. Cape Town: Cape Times, 1903.
Theal, G.M., ed. *Records of the Cape Colony*. 36 vols. Cape Town: Saul Solomon, 1897–1905.

Memoirs, Correspondence, and Compilations

Butler, W.F. *The Life of Sir George Pomeroy-Colley*. London: John Murray, 1899.
Cripps, George St. Vincent. "Highlands and Lowlands of Kafirland." *Cape Monthly Magazine*, n.s., 14 (1877): 310–322, 325–341.
Davey, A.M., ed. *Breaker Morant and the Bushveldt Carbineers*. Cape Town: Van Riebeeck Society, 1987.
Dicke, B.H. *The Bush Speaks: Border Life in the Old Transvaal*. Pietermaritzburg: Shuter and Shooter, 1936.

"Een Hollander" [K.J. de Kok]. *Toen en Thans: Mededeelingen en Beschouwingen omtrent de Twee Republieken in Zuid-Afrika.* Cape Town: Jacques Dusseau, 1898.

Flygare, Johannes. *De Zoutpansbergen en de Bawenda Natie.* Pretoria: De Volksstem, 1899.

Hofmeyr, Stefanus. *Twintig Jaren in Zoutpansberg: Een Verhaal van Twintig Jarigen Arbeid onder de Heidenen in de Transvaal.* J.H. Rose & Co., Cape Town, 1890.

Hook, David Blair. *With Sword and Statute on the Cape of Good Hope Frontier.* Cape Town: Juta, 1907.

Maclean, J., ed. *Compendium of Kafir Laws and Customs.* London: Frank Cass, 1858.

Munnik, G.G. *Kronieke van Noordelike Transvaal.* Pretoria: Bienedell, n.d. [1921].

——. *Memoirs of Senator the Hon. G.G. Munnik.* Cape Town: Maskew Miller, 1933.

Orpen, J.M. *Reminiscences of Life in South Africa from 1846 to the Present Day.* Cape Town: Struik, 1964 [1908].

Schiel, Adolf. *23 Jahre Sturm und Sonnenschein in Südafrika.* Leipzig: Brockhaus, 1902.

Scully, William Charles. *Further Reminiscences of a South African Pioneer.* London: T.F. Unwin, 1913.

Short [Devenish], E.F. "Twenty Years in the Transvaal Republic." Edited by A.D. Irvine. *Pretoriana* 107 (Nov. 1995): 6–48.

Stanford, W.E. *Reminiscences of Sir Walter Stanford.* 2 vols. Edited by J.W. Macquarrie. Cape Town: Van Riebeeck Society, 1962.

Streatfeild, F.N. *Reminiscences of an Old 'Un.* London: Eveleigh Nash, 1911.

Trichard, S.P.E. *Geschiedenis, Werken, en Streven van S.P.E. Trichard.* Edited and compiled by O.J.O. Ferreira. Pretoria: Raad vir Geesteswetenskaplike Navorsing, 1975.

Wangemann, Theodor. *Maléo en Sekoekoeni.* Translated by J.F.W. Grosskopf. Cape Town: Van Riebeeck Society, 1957 [1868].

Wessmann, Reinhold. *The Bawenda of the Spelonken.* Translated by Leo Weinthal. London: Africa World, 1908.

Wright, H.M., ed. *Sir James Rose Innes: Selected Correspondence 1884–1902.* Cape Town: Van Riebeeck Society, 1972.

Secondary Sources

Reference Works and Indexes

De Kock, W.J., ed. *Dictionary of South African Biography.* 5 vols. Pretoria: Nasionale Boekhandel, 1968–87.

Venter, P.J. *Government Departments of the Cape of Good Hope 1806–1910.* Cape Town: Cape Archives, 1933.

[Zuid-Afrikaansche Republiek.] *Index der Staatscouranten over de Jaren 1857 t/m 1870.* Pretoria: Staatsdrukkerij, 1897.

Books

Adas, Michael P. *Machines as the Measure of Men: Science, Technology, and Ideologies of Western Dominance*. Ithaca: Cornell University Press, 1989.

Aliber, Michael, Themba Maluleke, Tshililo Manenzhe, Gaynor Paradza, and Ben Cousins. *Land Reform and Livelihoods: Trajectories of Change in Northern Limpopo Province, South Africa*. Cape Town: HSRC Press, 2013.

Anderson, Benedict. *Imagined Communities*. Revised ed. London: Verso, 2006.

Ashforth, Adam. *The Politics of Official Discourse in Twentieth-Century South Africa*. Oxford: Clarendon, 1990.

Barrow, Ian J. *Making History, Drawing Territory: British Mapping in India, c.1763–1905*. Oxford: Oxford University Press, 2003.

Bayly, C.A. *Empire and Information: Intelligence Gathering and Social Communication in India, 1780–1870*. Cambridge: Cambridge University Press, 1996.

Beinart, William. *The Political Economy of Pondoland, 1860–1930*. Johannesburg: Ravan, 1982.

——. *The Rise of Conservation in South Africa: Settlers, Livestock, and the Environment 1770–1950*. Oxford: Oxford University Press, 2003.

Beinart, William, and Colin Bundy. *Hidden Struggles in Rural South Africa*. Johannesburg: Ravan, 1987.

Beinart, William, and Karen Brown. *African Local Knowledge & Livestock Health: Diseases & Treatments in South Africa*. Athens: Ohio University Press, 2013

Beinart, William, and Peter Coates. *Environment and History: The Taming of Nature in the USA and South Africa*. New York: Routledge, 1995.

Beinart, William, and Lotte Hughes. *Environment and Empire*. Oxford: Oxford University Press, 2007.

Beningfield, Jennifer. *The Frightened Land: Land, Landscape, and Politics in South Africa in the Twentieth Century*. New York: Routledge, 2006.

Berman, Bruce, and John Lonsdale. *Unhappy Valley: Conflict in Kenya and Africa, Book One: State and Class*. London: James Currey, 1992.

Blunt, Alison. *Travel, Gender, and Imperialism: Mary Kingsley and West Africa*. New York: Guilford Press, 1994.

Bonner, Philip. *Kings, Commoners, and Concessionaires: The Evolution and Dissolution of the Nineteenth-century Swazi State*. Johannesburg: Ravan, 1983.

Bull, Marjorie. *Abraham de Smidt: Artist and Surveyor-General of the Cape Colony*. Cape Town: Printpak, 1981.

Bundy, Colin. *The Rise and Fall of the South African Peasantry*. 2nd ed. Cape Town: David Philip, 1988.

Burnett, D. Graham. *Masters of All They Surveyed: Exploration, Geography, and a British El Dorado*. Chicago: University of Chicago Press, 2000.

Byrnes, Giselle. *Boundary Markers: Land Surveying and the Colonisation of New Zealand*. Wellington: Bridget William Books, 2001.

Campbell, James T. *Songs of Zion: The African Methodist Episcopal Church in the United States and South Africa*. Oxford: Oxford University Press, 1995.

Carruthers, Jane. *The Kruger National Park: a Social and Political History*. Pietermaritzburg: University of Natal Press, 1995.

Carter, Gwendolen M., Thomas Karis, and Newell M. Stultz. *South Africa's Transkei: The Politics of Domestic Colonialism*. Evanston: Northwestern University Press, 1967.

Carter, Paul. *The Road to Botany Bay*. London: Faber and Faber, 1987.

Carton, Benedict. *Blood From Your Children: The Colonial Origins of Generational Conflict in South Africa*. Charlottesville: University Press of Virginia, 2000.

Cell, John W. *The Highest Stage of White Supremacy: The Origins of Segregation in South Africa and the American South*. Cambridge: Cambridge University Press, 1982.

Changuion, Louis, and Bertus Steenkamp. *Disputed Land: The Historical Development of the South African Land Issue, 1652–2011*. Pretoria: Protea, 2012.

Chanock, Martin. *The Making of South African Legal Culture 1902–1936: Fear, Favour and Prejudice*. Cambridge: Cambridge University Press, 2001.

Christopher, A.J. *The Crown Lands of British South Africa, 1853–1914*. Kingston, ON: Limestone Press, 1984.

——. *The British Empire at Its Zenith*. London: Croom Helm, 1988.

Cohn, Bernard S. *Colonialism and Its Forms of Knowledge: The British in India*. Princeton: Princeton University Press, 1996.

Cooper, Frederick. *Colonialism in Question: Theory, Knowledge, History*. Berkeley: University of California Press, 2005.

Craib, Raymond B. *Cartographic Mexico: A History of State Fixations and Fugitive Landscapes*. Durham: Duke University Press, 2004.

Crais, Clifton C. *White Supremacy and Black Resistance in Pre-Industrial South Africa: The Making of the Colonial Order in the Eastern Cape, 1770–1865*. Cambridge: Cambridge University Press, 1992.

——. *The Politics of Evil: Magic, State Power, and the Political Imagination in South Africa*. Cambridge: Cambridge University Press, 2002.

——. *Poverty, War, and Violence in South Africa*. Cambridge: Cambridge University Press, 2011.

Crush, Jonathan. *The Struggle for Swazi Labour, 1890–1920*. Kingston, ON: McGill-Queen's University Press, 1992.

Davenport, T.R.H., and C.C. Saunders, *South Africa: A Modern History*. 5th ed. New York: St. Martin's, 2000.

De Smidt, Abraham. *A Brief History of the Surveys and Cartography of the Colony of the Cape of Good Hope: Read Before the International Geographical Congress (London, July, 1895)*. Brighton: T.G. Bishop, 1895.

Delius, Peter. *The Land Belongs to Us: The Pedi Polity, the Boers, and the British in the Nineteenth-Century Transvaal.* Johannesburg: Ravan, 1983.

Dening, Greg. *Islands and Beaches: Discourse on a Silent Land: Marquesas 1774–1880.* Chicago: Dorsey, 1980.

Derricourt, Robin. *Prehistoric Man in the Ciskei and Transkei.* Cape Town: Struik, 1977.

Driver, Felix. *Geography Militant: Cultures of Exploration and Empire.* London: Blackwell, 2001.

Dubow, Saul. *A Commonwealth of Knowledge: Science, Sensibility, and White South Africa, 1820–2000.* Oxford: Oxford University Press, 2006.

———. *Racial Segregaion and the Origins of Apartheid in South Africa, 1919–36.* London: Macmillan, 1989.

Duly, L.C. *British Land Policy at the Cape, 1795–1844: A Study of Administrative Procedures in the Empire.* Durham: Duke University Press, 1968.

Duminy, Andrew. *Mapping South Africa.* Johannesburg: Jacana, 2011.

Edney, Matthew. *Mapping an Empire: the Geographical Construction of British India, 1765–1843.* Chicago: University of Chicago Press, 1997.

Elbourne, Elizabeth. *Blood Ground: Colonialism, Missions, and the Contest for Christianity in the Cape Colony and Britain, 1799–1853.* Kingston, ON: McGill-Queen's University Press, 2002.

Etherington, Norman. *The Great Treks: The Transformation of Southern Africa, 1815–1854.* London: Pearson, 2001.

Evans, Ivan. *Bureaucracy and Race: Native Administration in South Africa.* Berkeley: University of California Press, 1997.

Ferreira, O.J.O. *Montanha in Zoutpansberg: 'n Portuguese Handelsending van Inhambane se Besoek aan Schoemansdal, 1855–1856.* Pretoria: Protea, 2002.

Foucault, Michel. *Power/Knowledge: Selected Interviews and Other Writings, 1972–1977.* Edited and translated by Colin Gordon. New York: Pantheon, 1980.

Fox, Adam. *Oral and Literate Culture in England, 1500–1700.* Oxford: Clarendon, 2000.

Fredrickson, George M. *White Supremacy: A Comparative Study in American & South African History.* Oxford: Oxford University Press, 1981.

Gevisser, Mark. *A Legacy of Liberation: Thabo Mbeki and the Future of the South African Dream.* London: Macmillan, 2009.

Greed, Clara. *Surveying Sisters: Women in a Traditional Male Profession.* London: Routledge, 1991.

Guy, Jeff. *Theophilus Shepstone and the Forging of Natal.* Pietermaritzburg: University of KwaZulu-Natal Press, 2013.

Hall, Martin. *The Changing Past: Farmers, Kings, and Traders in Southern Africa, 200–1860.* Cape Town: David Philip, 1987.

Hammond-Tooke, W.D. *Command or Consensus: The Development of Transkeian Local Government.* Cape Town: David Philip, 1975.

Hannah, Matthew G. *Governmentality and the Mastery of Territory in Nineteenth-Century America*. Cambridge: Cambridge University Press, 2000.

Harley, J.B. *The New Nature of Maps: Essays in the History of Cartography*. Edited by Paul Laxton. Baltimore: Johns Hopkins University Press, 2001.

Harries, Patrick. *Butterflies and Barbarians: Swiss Missionaries and Systems of Knowledge in South-East Africa*. Oxford: James Currey, 2007.

Harris, Cole. *Making Native Space: Colonialism, Resistance, and Reserves in British Columbia*. Vancouver: UBC Press, 2002.

Henkel, C.C. *The Native- or Transkeian Territories: The Country between Cape Colony and Natal*. Hamburg: V & D Actien-Gesellschaft, 1903.

Herbst, Jeffrey. *States and Power in Africa: Comparative Lessons in Authority and Control*. Princeton: Princeton University Press, 2000.

Hickman, A.S. *Rhodesia Served the Queen: Rhodesian Forces in the Boer War, 1899–1902*. 2 vols. Salisbury [Harare]: Government Printers, 1970–1975.

Hofmeyr, Isabel. *"We Spend Our Years as a Tale That Is Told": Oral Historical Narrative in a South African Chiefdom*. Johannesburg: Witwatersrand University Press, 1993.

Hoxie, Frederick C. *A Final Promise: The Campaign to Assimilate the Indians, 1880–1920*. New ed. Omaha: University of Nebraska Press, 2001.

Hubbard, Bill (Jr). *American Boundaries: The Nation, the States, and the Rectangular Survey*. Chicago: University of Chicago Press, 2009.

Hughes, David McDermott. *From Enslavement to Environmentalism: Politics on a South African Frontier*. Seattle: University of Washington Press, 2006.

Huigen, Siegfried. *Knowledge and Colonialism: Eighteenth Century Travellers in South Africa*. Leiden: Brill, 2009.

Iliffe, John. *Africans: The History of a Continent*. New ed. Cambridge: Cambridge University Press, 2007.

Jacob, Christian. *The Sovereign Map: Theoretical Approaches in Cartography throughout History*. Edited by Ed Dahl. Translated by Tom Conley. Chicago: University of Chicago Press, 2006.

Jacobs, Nancy. *Environment, Power, and Injustice: A South African History*. Cambridge: Cambridge University Press, 2003.

Jeeves, A.H., and J. Crush, eds. *Black Farms White Labor: The State and Agrarian Change in South Africa, 1910–1950*. Portsmouth, NH: Heinemann, 1997.

Kain, Roger J.P., and Elizabeth Baigent. *The Cadastral Map in the Service of the State*. Chicago: University of Chicago Press, 1992.

Keegan, T.J. *Colonial South Africa and the Origins of the Racial Order*. Cape Town: David Philip, 1996.

——. Keegan, T.J. *Rural Transformations in Industrializing South Africa: The Southern Highveld to 1914*. London: Macmillan, 1987.

Kirkaldy, Alan. *Capturing the Soul: The Vhavenda and the Missionaries, 1870–1900.* Pretoria: Protea, 2005.

Knowles, L.C.A., and C.M. Knowles. *The Economic Development of the British Overseas Empire.* Vol. 3. London: George Routledge & Sons, 1936.

Koeman, C., ed. *Tabvlae geographicae qvibvs colonia bonae spei antiqva depingitvr.* Amsterdam: NVHA Uitgevers Maatschappij, 1952.

Krikler, Jeremy. *Revolution from Above, Rebellion from Below: The Agrarian Transvaal at the Turn of the Century.* Oxford: Clarendon, 1993.

Kumar, Deepak. *Science and the Raj, 1857–1905.* Delhi: Oxford University Press, 1997.

Laband, John. *The Transvaal Rebellion: The First Boer War, 1880–1881.* London: Pearson-Longman, 2005.

Lahiff, Edward. *An Apartheid Oasis? Agriculture and Rural Livelihoods in Venda.* London: Frank Cass, 2000.

Lambert, John. *Betrayed Trust: Africans and the State in Colonial Natal.* Pietermaritzburg: University of Natal Press, 1995.

Landau, Paul. *Popular Politics in the History of South Africa, 1400–1948.* Cambridge: Cambridge University Press, 2011.

Lester, Alan. *From Colonization to Democracy: A New Historical Geography of South Africa.* London: I.B. Tauris, 1996.

———. *Imperial Networks: Creating Identities in Nineteenth-Century South Africa and Britain.* London: Routledge, 2001.

Lewis, Martin W., and Kären E. Wigen, *The Myth of Continents: A Critique of Metageography.* Berkeley: University of California Press, 1997.

Loveland, Ian. *By Due Process of Law? Racial Discrimination and the Right to Vote in South Africa 1855–1960.* Oxford: Hart Publishing, 1999.

Maclennan, Ben. *A Proper Degree of Terror: John Graham and the Cape's Eastern Frontier.* Johannesburg: Ravan, 1986.

Mamdani, Mahmood. *Citizen and Subject: Contemporary Africa and the Legacy of Late Colonialism.* Princeton: Princeton University Press, 1996.

McClendon, Thomas V. *White King, Black Lords: Shepstone and the Colonial State in Natal, South Africa.* Rochester: University of Rochester Press, 2010.

Mignolo, Walter. *The Darker Side of the Renaissance.* 2nd ed. Ann Arbor: University of Michigan Press, 2003.

Mills, M.E. Elton, and M. Wilson. *Keiskammahoek Rural Survey.* Vol. 4, *Land Tenure.* Pietermaritzburg: Shuter and Shooter, 1952.

Möller-Malan, Dorothea. *The Chair of the Ramabulanas.* Cape Town: Central News Agency, 1953.

Morton, Fred. *When Rustling Became an Art: Pilane's Kgatla and the Transvaal Frontier, 1820–1902.* Cape Town: David Philip, 2009.

Nasson, Bill. *The War for South Africa: The Anglo-Boer War, 1899–1902*. Cape Town: Tafelberg, 2009.

Nemutanzhela, Thiathu. *Ploughing Amongst the Stones: The Story of "Betterment" in the Zoutpansberg, 1939–1944*. Johannesburg: Ravan, 1999.

Ntsebeza, Lungisile. *Democracy Compromised: Chiefs and the Politics of the Land in South Africa*. Leiden: Brill, 2004.

Odendaal, André. *The Founders: The Origins of the ANC and the Struggle for Democracy in South Africa*. Johannesburg: Jacana, 2012.

——. *Vukani Bantu!: The Beginnings of Black Protest Politics in South Africa to 1912*. Cape Town: David Philip, 1984.

Otis, D.S. *The Dawes Act and the Allotment of Indian Lands*. Edited by F.P. Prucha. Norman: University of Oklahoma Press, 1973 . First published 1934.

Peires, J.B. *The Dead Will Arise: Nongqawuse and the Great Xhosa Cattle-Killing Movement of 1856–7*. Johannesberg: Ravan, 1989.

——. *The House of Phalo: A History of the Xhosa People in the Days of Their Independence*. Berkeley: University of California Press, 1981.

Penn, Nigel. *The Forgotten Frontier: Colonist & Khoisan on the Cape's Northern Frontier in the Eighteenth Century*. Athens: Ohio University Press, 2005.

Pickles, John. *A History of Spaces: Cartographic Reason, Mapping, and the Geo-coded World*. London: Routledge, 2004.

Pierce, Steven. *Farmers and the State in Colonial Kano: Land Tenure and the Legal Imagination*. Bloomington: Indiana University Press, 2005.

Pikirayi, Innocent. *The Zimbabwe Culture: Origins and Decline of Southern Zambesian States*. Walnut Creek, CA: AltaMira, 2001.

Plaatje, Sol T. *Native Life in South Africa*. Johannesburg: Ravan, 1982. First published 1916.

Pratt, Mary Louise. *Imperial Eyes: Travel Writing and Transculturation*. London: Routledge, 1992.

Price, Richard. *Making Empire: Colonal Encounters and the Creation of Imperial Rule in Nineteenth-Century Africa*. Cambridge: Cambridge University Press, 2008.

Raj, Kapil. *Relocating Modern Science: Circulation and the Construction of Knowledge in South Asia and Europe, 1650–1900*. New York: Palgrave Macmillan, 2007.

Rebert, Paula. *La Gran Línea: Mapping the United States-Mexico Boundary, 1849–1857*. Austin: University of Texas Press, 2001.

Redding, Sean. *Sorcery and Sovereignty: Taxation, Power, and Rebellion in South Africa, 1880–1963*. Athens: Ohio University Press, 2006.

Richards, Thomas. *The Imperial Archive: Knowledge and the Fantasy of Empire*. London: Verso, 1993.

Richings, Gordon. *The Life and Work of Charles Michell*. Simon's Town: Fernwood Press, 2006.

Ross, Robert. *Adam Kok's Griquas: A Study in the Development of Stratification in South Africa*. Cambridge: Cambridge University Press, 1976.

——. *The Borders of Race in Colonial South Africa: The Kat River Settlement, 1829–1856*. Cambridge: Cambridge University Press, 2014.

Rotberg, Robert I. *The Founder*. Oxford: Oxford University Press, 1988.

Ruskin, Steven. *John Herschel's Cape Voyage: Private Science, Public Imagination and the Ambitions of Empire*. Burlington, VT: Ashgate, 2004.

Said, Edward. *Culture and Imperialism*. New York: Vintage Books, 1994.

Scott, James C. *Seeing Like a State: How Certain Schemes to Improve the Human Condition Have Failed*. New Haven: Yale University Press, 1998.

Seed, Patricia. *Ceremonies of Possession in Europe's Conquest of the New World*. Cambridge: Cambridge University Press, 1995.

Shillington, Kevin. *The Colonisation of the Southern Tswana 1870–1900*. Johannesburg: Ravan, 1985.

Simons, Phillida Brooke. *The Life and Work of Charles Bell*. Vlaeberg: Fernwood Press, 1998.

Stapleton, Timothy. *Maqoma: Xhosa Resistance to Colonial Advance*. Johannesburg: Jonathan Ball, 1994.

Stayt, Hugh A. *The Bavenda*. Oxford: Oxford University Press, 1931.

Stefansson, Anders. *Manifest Destiny: American Expansion and the Empire of Right*. New York: Hill & Wang, 1995.

Stone, Jeffrey C. *A Short History of the Cartography of Africa*. Lewiston, ME: Edwin Mellen, 1995.

Storrar, C.D. *The Four Faces of Fourcade*. Cape Town: Maskew Miller, 1990.

Switzer, Les. *Power & Resistance in an African Society: The Ciskei Xhosa and the Making of South Africa*. Madison: University of Wisconsin Press, 1993.

Tempelhoff, J.W.N. *Townspeople of the Soutpansberg: A Centenary History*. Louis Trichardt: Greater Louis Trichardt TLC, 1999.

Theal, G.M. *The History of South Africa*. Vol. 10. London: T.F. Unwin, 1919.

Thornton, John K. *Africa and Africans in the Making of the Atlantic World*. 2nd ed. Cambridge: Cambridge University Press, 1998.

Tilley, Helen. *Africa as a Living Laboratory: Empire, Development, and the Problem of Scientific Knowledge, 1870–1950*. Chicago: University of Chicago Press, 2011.

Tropp, Jacob A. *Natures of Colonial Change: Environmental Relations in the Making of the Transkei*. Athens: Ohio University Press, 2006.

Van Biljon Petrus. *Grensbakens tussen Blank en Swart in Suid-Afrika*. Cape Town: Juta, 1947.

Van Jaarsveld, F.A. *The Afrikaner's Interpretation of South African History*. Cape Town: Simondium, 1964.

Van Onselen, Charles. *The Seed is Mine: The Life of Kas Maine, a South African Sharecropper*. New York: Hill & Wang, 1996.

Van Warmelo, N.J., comp. *Contributions towards Venda History, Religion, and Tribal Ritual*. Pretoria: Government Printer, 1960.

Verran, Helen. *Science and an African Logic*. Chicago: University of Chicago Press, 2001.

Warwick, Peter. *Black People and the South African War 1899–1902*. Cambridge: Cambridge University Press, 1983.

Weaver, John C. *The Great Land Rush and the Making of the Modern World, 1650–1900*. Kingston, ON: McGill-Queen's University Press, 2003.

Welsh, David. *The Roots of Segregation: Native Policy in Colonial Natal*. Cape Town: Oxford University Press, 1971.

Whitaker, D. *Whitaker's Almanack, 1899*. London: J. Whitaker & Sons, 1899.

Williams, J. Michael. *Chieftaincy, the State, and Democracy: Political Legitimacy in Post-Apartheid South Africa*. Bloomington: Indiana University Press, 2010.

Williams, Watkin Wynn. *The Life of General Sir Charles Warren G.C.M.G K.C.B.F.R.S., Colonel Commandant, Royal Engineers*. Oxford: Basil Blackwell, 1941.

Winichakul, Thongchai. *Siam Mapped: A History of the Geo-Body of a Nation*. Honolulu: University of Hawai'i Press, 1994.

Woolmore, William. *The Bushveldt Carbineers and the Pietersburg Light Horse*. McCrae: Slouch Hat, 2002.

Yawitch, Joanne. *Betterment and the Myth of Homeland Agriculture*. Johannesburg: SAIRR, 1981.

Young, Crawford. *The African Colonial State in Comparative Perspective*. New Haven: Yale University Press, 1994.

Zachrisson, Per. *An African Area in Change: Belingwe, 1894–1946*. Gothenburg: Dept of History in Gothenburg, 1978.

Articles, Chapters, and Papers

Adas, Michael P. "From Settler Colony to Global Hegemon: Integrating the Exceptionalist Narrative of the American Experience in World History." *American Historical Review* 106, no. 5 (2001): 1692–1720.

Adler, Michelle. "'Skirting the Edges of Civilization': Two Victorian Women Travelers and 'Colonial Spaces' in South Africa." In *Text, Theory, Space: Land, Literature and History in South Africa and Australia*, edited by K. Darian-Smith, Liz Gunner, and S. Nuttall, 83–98. London: Routledge, 1996.

Anderson, D., and D. Throup. "The Agrarian Economy of Central Province, Kenya, 1918 to 1939." In *The Economies of Africa and Asia in the Inter-War Depression*, edited by Ian Brown, 8–28. New York: Routledge, 1989.

Baker, A.E. "*Historical Notes on Land Surveying and the Surveyor-General's Office (Cape) 1652–1950*." Unpublished manuscript, NGI Library, 1958.

Balogun, O.Y. "The Training of Nigerian Surveyors in the Colonial Era." *Surveying and Mapping* 45, no. 2 (1985): 159–167.

Bank, Andrew. "Losing Faith in the Civilizing Mission: The Premature Decline of Humanitarian Liberalism at the Cape, 1840–60." In *Empire and Others: British Encounters with Indigenous Peoples, 1600–1850*, edited by M. Daunton and R. Halpern, 364–383. Philadelphia: University of Pennsylvania, 1999.

Barker, John. "Where the Missionary Frontier Ran Ahead of Empire." In *Missions and Empire*, edited by Norman Etherington, 86–106. Oxford: Oxford University Press, 2005.

Barnes, Teresa. "Virgin Territory? Travel and Migration by African Women in Twentieth Century South Africa." In *Women in African Colonial Histories*, edited by Jean Allman, Susan Geiger, and Nakanyike Musisi, 164–190. Bloomington: Indiana University Press, 2002.

Bassett, Thomas J. "Introduction: The Land Question and Agricultural Transformation in Sub-Saharan Africa." In *Land in African Agrarian Systems*, edited by Thomas J. Bassett and Donald E. Crummey, 3–31. Madison: University of Wisconsin Press, 1993.

——. "African Influences on European Mapping of Africa in the 19th and Early 20th Centuries." English manuscript version of chapter in *Culture dell'Alterità: il territorio africano e le sue rappresentazioni*, edited by E.C. Moreschi, 359–371. Milan: UNICOPLI, 1998.

——. "Indigenous Mapmaking in Intertropical Africa." In *Cartography in the Traditional Africa, American, Arctic, Australian, and Pacific Societies*, book 3, vol. 2 of *The History of Cartography*, edited by David Woodward and G. Malcolm Lewis, 24–48. Chicago: University of Chicago Press, 1998.

Bassett, Thomas J., and Philip W. Porter, "'From the Best Authorities': The Mountains of Kong in the Cartography of West Africa." *Journal of African History* 32 (1991): 367–413.

Bederman, Sanford H. "The Royal Geographical Society, E.G. Ravenstein, and *A Map of Eastern Equatorial Africa—1877–1883*." *Imago Mundi* 44 (1992): 106–119.

Beinart, William. "Soil Erosion, Conservation and Ideas about Development: A Southern African Exploration, 1900–1960." *Journal of Southern African Studies* 11, no. 1 (1984): 52–83.

Beinart, William, Karen Brown, and Daniel Gilfoyle. "Experts and Expertise in Colonial Africa Reconsidered: Science and the Interpenetration of Knowledge." *African Affairs* 108, no. 432 (2009): 424–425.

Beinart, William, and Peter Delius. "Introduction: Approaches to South African Agrarian History." In *Putting a Plough to the Ground: Accumulation and Disposession in Rural South Africa 1850–1930*, edited by W. Beinart and P. Delius, 1–55. Johannesburg: Ravan, 1986.

Bergh, Johan. "Grondregte in Suid-Afrika: 'n 19de Eeuse Transvaalse Perspektief." *Historia* 40, no. 2 (1995): 39–47.

———. "Die Veranderende Grense van 'Transvaal' 1840–1994." *Historia* 41, no. 2 (1996): 11–17.

———. "Grondverdeeling tussen Blank en Swart in Suid-Afrika: 'n 19de-Eeuse Transvaalse Perspektief." *Genl. J.B.M. Hertzoggedenklesing* XXXIV (2005).

———. "'(To) Reserve to the Native Tribes Such Locations as They May Be Fairly and Equitably Entitled To': The Transvaal Location Commission (1881–1899)." *South African Historical Journal* 54, no. 1 (2005): 1–15.

Bernstein, H. "Land Reform in Southern Africa in World-Historical Perspective." *Review of African Political Economy* 96 (2003): 203–226.

Boeyens, J.C.A. "'Black Ivory': The Indenture System and Slavery in Zoutpansberg." In *Slavery in South Africa: Captive Labor on the Dutch Frontier*, edited by E.A. Eldredge and F. Morton, 187–214. Boulder: Westview Press, 1994.

———. "Die Konflik Tussen die Venda en die Blankes in Transvaal, 1864–1869." *Archives Year Book for South African History* 53, no. 1 (1990).

Bouch, Richard. "Glen Grey before Cecil Rhodes: How a Crisis of Local Colonial Authority Led to the Glen Grey Act of 1894." *Canadian Journal of African Studies* 27, no. 1 (1993): 1–24.

———. "The Mfengu Revisited: The 19th Century Experience of One Mfengu Community through the Eyes of Historians and Contemporaries." *Institute of Commonwealth Studies Collected Seminar Papers: Societies of Southern Africa in the 19th and 20th Centuries* 42 (1992): 81–89.

Braun, Bruce. "Producing Vertical Territory: Geology and Governmentality in Late Victorian Canada." *Ecumene* 7, no. 1 (2000): 7–46.

Braun, L.F. "Spatial Institutionalisation and the Settler State: Survey and Mapping in the Eastern Transvaal, 1852–1905." *South African Historical Journal* 53, no. 1 (2005): 146–178.

———. "The Colonial Archive and Maps of the Western Transkei, 1857–1898." In *Proceedings of the Symposium of the Commission on the History of Cartography in the 19th and 20th Centuries* [2008], edited by E.C. Liebenberg, Peter Collier, and I.J. Demhardt, Chapter 2. Pretoria: ICA, 2009.

———. "Missionary Cartography in Colonial Africa: Cases from South Africa." In *History of Cartography: International Symposium of the ICA Commission, 2010*, edited by E.C. Liebenberg and I.J. Demhardt, 249–272. Berlin: Springer, 2012.

———. "The Returns of the King: The Case of Mphephu and Western Venda, 1899–1904." *Journal of Southern African Studies* 39, no. 2 (2013): 271–291.

Bridges, Roy. "Nineteenth-Century Exploration and Mapping: The Role of the Royal Geographical Society." In *Maps and Mapping of Africa*, edited by P.M. Larby, 9–13. London: SCOLMA/BRICMICS, 1987.

Bundy, Colin. "New Nation, New History? Constructing the Past in Post-apartheid South Africa," in *History Making and Present Day Politics*, edited by Hans Erik Stolten, 73–97. Uppsala: Nordiska Afrikainstitutet, 2007.

Burnett, D. Graham. "Hydrographic Discipline among the Navigators: Charting an 'Empire of Commerce and Science' in the Nineteenth Century Pacific." In *The Imperial Map: Cartography and the Mastery of Empire*, edited by James R. Akerman, 185–259. Chicago: University of Chicago Press, 2009.

Cameron, James M.R. "Agents and Agencies in Geography and Empire: The Case of George Grey." In *Geography and Imperialism 1820–1940*, edited by M. Bell, R. Butlin, and M. Heffernan, 13–35. Manchester: Manchester University Press, 1995.

Campbell, W.A. "The South African Frontier, 1865–1885: A Study in Expansion," *Archives Year Book for South African History* 22 (1965).

Carruthers, Jane. "Friedrich Jeppe: Mapping the Transvaal c.1850–1899." *Journal of Southern African Studies* 29, no. 4 (2003): 955–975.

——. "Cartographical Rivalries: Friedrich Jeppe and the Transvaal." In *Mapping Colonial Conquest: Australia and Southern Africa*, edited by Norman Etherington, 102–122. Crawley: University of Western Australia, 2007.

Chanock, Martin. "Paradigms, Policies, and Property: A Review of the Customary Law of Land Tenure." In *Law in Colonial Africa*, edited by Kristin Mann and Richard Roberts, 61–84. London: James Currey, 1991.

Christopher, A.J. "The European Concept of a Farm in Southern Africa." *Historia* 15, no. 2 (1970): 93–99.

Colson, Elizabeth. "The Impact of the Colonial Period on the Definition of Land Rights." In *Colonialism in Africa 1870–1960*, edited by Victor Turner, 3:193–215. Cambridge: Cambridge University Press, 1971.

Comaroff, John L. "Images of Empire, Contests of Conscience." In *Tensions of Empire: Colonial Cultures in a Bourgeois World*, edited by Frederick Cooper and Ann Stoler, 163–197. Berkeley: University of California, 1997.

Cousins, Ben. "Agrarian Reform and the 'Two Economies': Transforming South Africa's Countryside." In *The Land Question in South Africa: The Challenge of Transformation and Redustribution*, edited by Lungisile Ntsebeza and Ruth Hall, 220–245. Cape Town: HSRC Press, 2007.

——. "More than Socially Embedded: The Distinctive Character of 'Communal Tenure' Regimes and its Implications for Land Policy." *Journal of Agrarian Change* 7, no. 3 (2007): 281–315.

Craib, Raymond B. "The Archive in the Field: Document, Discourse, and Space in Mexico's Agrarian Reform." *Journal of Historical Geography* 36 (2010): 411–420.

——. "Relocating Cartography." *Postcolonial Studies* 12, no. 4 (2009): 481–490.

Crais, Clifton C. "Conquest, State Formation, and the Subaltern Imagination in Rural South Africa." In *The Culture of Power in Southern Africa: Essays on State Formation and the Political Imagination*, edited by Clifton C. Crais, 27–48. Portsmouth, NH: Heinemann, 2003.

———. "Custom and the Politics of Sovereignty in South Africa," *Journal of Social History* 39, no. 3 (2006): 721–740.

———. "The Vacant Land: The Mythology of British Expansion in the Eastern Cape, South Africa." *Journal of Social History* 25, no. 2 (1991): 255–275.

Davenport, T.R.H. "The Cape Liberal Tradition to 1910." In *Democratic Liberalism in South Africa: Its History and Prospect*, edited by Jeffrey Butler, Richard Elphick, and David Welsh, 21–34. Cape Town: David Philip, 1987.

Davey, A.M. "Moodie's Road to Fortune." *Pretoriana* 71 (Apr–Dec 1973): 36–39.

De Beer, F.C. "Determining the Merits of Land Claims: A Challenge for the Anthropologist." *Anthropology Southern Africa* 26, no. 3–4 (2003): 131–142.

De Vaal, J.B. "The Bygone Days of the Soutpansberg: Schoemansdal, the former Zoutpansbergdorp (Soutpansberg Town) (1848–1867)." In *A Cameo From the Past: The Prehistory and Early History of the Kruger National Park*, edited by U. de V. Pienaar, 169–202. Pretoria: Protea, 2013.

———. "Die Rol van João Albasini in die Transvaal Geskiedenis." *Archives Year Book for South African History* 16, no. 1 (1953).

Delius, Peter. "Abel Erasmus: Power and Profit in the Eastern Transvaal." In *Putting a Plough to the Ground: Accumulation and Dispossession in Rural South Africa, 1850–1930*, edited by W. Beinart, P. Delius, and S. Trapido, 176–127. Johannesburg: Ravan, 1986.

———. "The Ndzundza Ndebele: Indenture and the Making of Ethnic Identity, 1883–1914." In *Holding Their Ground: Class, Locality, and Culture in 19th and 20th Century South Africa*, edited by P. Bonner, I. Hofmeyr, D. James, and T. Lodge, 227–258. Johannesburg: Ravan, 1987.

———. "Sebatakgomo and the Zoutpansberg Balemi Association: The ANC, the Communist Party and Rural Organization, 1939–55." *Journal of African History* 34, no. 2 (1993): 293–313.

———. "Contested Terrain: Land Rights and Chiefly Power in Historical Perspective." In *Land, Power, & Custom: Controversies Generated by South Africa's Communal Land Rights Act*, edited by A. Claassens and B. Cousins, 211–237. Athens: Ohio University Press, 2007.

Delius, Peter, and M.H. Schoeman. "Revisiting Bokoni: Populating the Stone Ruins of the Mpumalanga Escarpment." In *Five Hundred Years Rediscovered: Southern African Precedents and Prospects*, edited by Natalie Swanepoel, Amanda Esterhuysen, and Philip Bonner, 135–167. Johannesburg: Witwatersrand University Press, 2008.

Derricourt, Robin. "Early European Travellers in the Ciskei and Transkei." *African Studies* 35, no. 3–4 (1976): 273–291.

——. "Settlement in the Transkei and Ciskei before the Mfecane." In *Beyond the Cape Frontier: Studies in the History of the Transkei and Ciskei*, edited by C.C. Saunders and R. Derricourt, 39–82. London: Longman, 1974.

"Devenish and the M'Pefu War." *Pretoriana* 2, no. 1 (1952): 7–8.

Doucakis, Alkis. "The Origins of Doornfontein and its adjoining farms being the earliest histories of Johannesburg, Bedfordview, Edenvale, Sandton, Alberton and Germiston, 1841–1853." *Historia* 42, no. 2 (1997): 1–32.

——. "'Een uur gans overkruys': The Earliest Form of Land Survey North of the Vaal, 1841–1860s." In *A Century of Land Surveying in the Transvaal, 1903–2003*, edited by D.S. Pound, et al., 66–70. Pretoria: Sereti Press, 2003.

Dreier, Marcel. "Years of Terrible Drought: Surviving the 1895–1897 Supply–Crisis in the Limpopo Area" Limpopo Research Project, University of Basel, 2005. Accessed 28 January 2012. http://pages.unibas.ch/afrika/limpopo/papers/limpopo_pdf/limpopo_dreier.pdf.

Du Plessis, H. "Die Territoriale Organisasie van die Venda." *African Studies* 4, no. 3 (1945): 122–127.

Du Toit, A.E. "The Cape Frontier: A Study of Native Policy with Special Reference to the Years 1847 to 1866." *Archives Year Book for South African History* 17, no. 1 (1954).

Edgecombe, Ruth. "The Glen Grey Act: Local Origins of an Abortive 'Bill for Africa'." In *Studies in Local History: Essays in Honour of Professor Winifred Maxwell*, edited by J.A. Benyon, et al., 89–98. London: Oxford University Press, 1976.

Edney, Matthew. "British Military Education, Mapmaking, and Military 'Map-Mindedness' in the Later Enlightenment." *Cartographic Journal* 31, no. 1 (1994): 14–20.

——. "The Irony of Imperial Mapping." In *The Imperial Map: Cartography and the Mastery of Empire*, edited by James R. Akerman, 11–45. Chicago: University of Chicago Press, 2009.

Edwards, W.M. "Early Land Grants in South Africa," In Colonial No. 70, *Conference of Empire Survey Officers 1931: Report of Proceedings*. London: HMSO, 1932.

Eldredge, E.A. "Delagoa Bay and the Hinterland in the Early Nineteenth Century: Politics, Trade, Slaves, and Slave Raiding." In *Slavery in South Africa: Captive Labor on the Dutch Frontier*, edited by E.A. Eldredge and F. Morton, 127–165. Boulder: Westview Press, 1994.

Elphick, Richard, and V.C. Malherbe. "The Khoisan to 1828." In *The Shaping of South African Society 1652–1840*, edited by R. Elphick and H. Giliomee, 3–65. Middletown, CT: Wesleyan University Press, 1989.

Erlank, Natasha. "Gendering Commonality: African Men and the 1883 Commission on Native Law and Custom." *Journal of Southern African Studies* 29, no. 4 (2003): 937–953.

Etherington, Norman. "The 'Shepstone System' in the Colony of Natal and Beyond the Borders." In *Natal and Zululand from Earliest Times to 1910*, edited by Andrew Duminy and Bill Guest, 170–192. Pietermaritzburg: Shuter and Shooter, 1989.

——. "A False Emptiness: How Historians May Have Been Misled by Early Nineteenth Century Maps of South-eastern Africa." *Imago Mundi* 56, no. 1 (2004): 67–86.

——. "A Tempest in a Teapot? Nineteenth-Century Contests for Land in South Africa's Caledon Valley and the Invention of the *mfecane*." *Journal of African History* 45, no. 2 (2004): 203–219.

——. "Putting Tribes on Maps." In *Mapping Colonial Conquest: Australia and Southern Africa*, edited by Norman Etherington, 79–101. Crawley: University of Western Australia, 2007.

Everingham, Mark, and Crystal Jannecke. "Land Restitution and Democratic Citizenship in South Africa." *Journal of Southern African Studies* 32, no. 3 (2006): 545–562.

Fagan, Eduard. "Roman-Dutch Law in Its South African Historical Context." In *Southern Cross: Civil Law & Common Law in South Africa*, edited by R. Zimmerman and D. Visser, 33–64. Oxford: Oxford University Press, 1996.

Fay, Derick. "Dilemmas of 'Indigenous Tenure' in South Africa: Traditional Authorities and the Constitutional Challenge to the 2004 Communal Land Rights Act." In *Indigenous Knowledge and the Environment in Africa and North America*, edited by David M. Gordon and Shepard Krech III, 287–306. Athens: Ohio University Press, 2012.

Feinberg, Harvey M. "The Natives Land Act of 1913 in South Africa: Politics, Race and Segregation in the Early 20th Century." *International Journal of African Historical Studies* 26, no. 1 (1993): 65–109.

——. "Pre-Apartheid African Land Ownership and the Implication for the Current Restitution Debate in South Africa," *Historia* 40, no. 2 (1995): 48–63.

——. "The 1913 Natives Land Act in South Africa: Politics, Race, & Segregation in the Early 20th Century." *International Journal of African Historical Studies* 26, no. 1 (1996): 65–109.

——. "Protest in South Africa: Prominent Black Leaders' Commentary on the Natives Land Act, 1913–1936." *Historia* 52, no. 2 (2006): 119–144.

Feinberg, Harvey M., and Andre Horn. "South African Territorial Segregation: New Data on African Farm Purchases, 1913–1936." *Journal of African History* 50, no. 1 (2009): 41–60.

Ferreira, O.J.O. "Schoemansdal: Van Voortrekkervoorpos tot Volksfeesterrein." *Contree* 1 (1977): 5–10.

Fisher, R.C. "The Emergence and Education of the Land Surveying Profession 1813–1912." In *History of Surveying and Land Tenure Collected Papers Volume 2: Surveying and Land Tenure at the Cape, 1813–1912*, edited by R.C. Fisher, 39–64. Cape Town: IPLSWC, 2004.

Foucault, M. "Questions on Geography." In *Power/Knowledge: Selected Interviews and Other Writings, 1972–1977*, edited and translated by Colin Gordon, 63–77. New York: Pantheon, 1980.

Frere, H.B.E. "On Systems of Land Tenure among Aboriginal Tribes in South Africa." *Journal of the Anthropological Institute of Great Britain and Ireland* 12 (1883): 258–276.

Giliomee, Herman. "The Eastern Frontier, 1770–1812." In *The Shaping of South African Society, 1652–1840*, edited by R. Elphick and H. Giliomee, 421–471. Middletown, CT: Wesleyan University Press, 1989.

Godlewska, Anne. "Napoleon's Geographers (1797–1815): Imperialists and Soldiers of Modernity." In *Geography and Empire*, edited by Anne Godlewska and Neil Smith, 31–53. Oxford: Blackwell, 1994.

Gray, Christopher. "The Disappearing District? Territorial Transformation in Southern Gabon 1850–1950." In *The Spatial Factor in African History: The Relationship of the Social, Material, and Perceptual*, edited by Allen M. Howard and Richard M. Shain, 221–244. Leiden: Brill, 2005.

Guelke, Leonard. "Land Tenure and Settlement at the Cape." In *History of Surveying and Land Tenure in South Africa Volume 1: Surveying and Land Tenure in the Cape 1652–1812*, edited by C.G.C. Martin and K.J. Friedlaender, 7–34. Cape Town: University of Cape Town, 1984.

——. "Freehold Farmers and Frontier Settlers, 1652–1780." In *The Shaping of South African Society, 1652–1840*, edited by R. Elphick and H. Giliomee, 66–108. Middletown, CT: Wesleyan University Press, 1989.

Hall, Ruth. "Reconciling the Past, Present, and Future: The Parameters and Practices of Land Restitution in South Africa." In *Land, Memory, Reconstruction, and Justice: Perspectives on Land Claims in South Africa*, edited by C. Walker, A. Bohlin, R. Hall, and T. Kepe, 17–40. Athens: University of Ohio Press, 2010.

Hall, Ruth, and Edward Lahiff. "Budgeting for land reform." PLAAS Policy Brief 13 (2004), University of the Western Cape.

Harley, J.B. "Maps, Knowledge, and Power." In *The Iconography of Landscape*, edited by Denis Cosgrove and Stephen Daniels, 277–312. Cambridge: Cambridge University Press, 1988.

Hendricks, Fred, and Lungisile Ntsebeza. "Chiefs and Rural Government in Post-Apartheid South Africa." *African Journal of Political Science* 4, no. 1 (1999): 99–126.

Hirson, Baruch. "Rural Revolt in South Africa 1937–51." *Collected Seminar Papers, Institute of Commonwealth Studies* 21 (1977): 115–132.

Holdich, T.H. "How Are We to Get Maps of Africa?" *Geographical Journal* 18 (1901): 590–601.

Howard, Allen M. "Nodes, Networks, Landscapes, and Regions: Reading the Social History of Tropical Africa 1700s–1920." In *The Spatial Factor in African History: The*

Relationship of the Social, Material, and Perceptual, edited by Allen M. Howard and Richard M. Shain, 21–140. Leiden: Brill, 2005.

Hunt, Charles G. "Some Notes on Indigenous Map-Making in Africa." In *Maps and Africa*, edited by Jeffrey C. Stone, 32–35. Aberdeen: Abderdeen University, 1994.

Jacobs, Margaret D. "Parallel or Intersecting Tracks? The History of the US West and Comparative Settler Colonialism." *Settler Colonial Studies* 4, no. 2 (2014): 155–161.

James, Deborah, Alex Xola Ngonini, and Geoffrey Mphahle Nkadimeng. "(Re) Constituting Class?: Owners, Tenants, and the Politics of Land Reform in Mpumalanga." *Journal of Southern African Studies* 31, no. 4 (2005): 825–844.

——. "Die Transvaal'sche oder Süd-Afrikanische Republik." *Petermanns Geographischen Mittheilungen*, Ergänzungsheft 24 (1868): 1–15.

Jeppe, Friedrich. "Notes on Some of the Physical and Geological Features of the Transvaal, to Accompany His New Map of the Transvaal and Surrounding Territories." *Journal of the Royal Geographical Society of London* 47 (1877): 217–250.

——. "The Zoutpansberg Goldfields in the South African Republic." *Geographical Journal* 2, no. 3 (Sep 1893): 213–237.

Jolly, Pieter. "Interaction between South-Eastern San and Southern Nguni and Sotho Communities, c.1400 to c.1880." *South African Historical Journal* 35, no. 1 (1996): 30–61.

Jones, Adam, and Isabel Voigt. "'Just a First Sketchy Makeshift': German Travellers and their Cartographic Encounters in Africa, 1850–1914." *History in Africa* 39, no. 2 (2012): 9–39.

Keegan, Timothy J. "The Origins of Agrarian Capitalism: A Reply." *Journal of Southern African Studies* 15, no. 4 (1989): 666–684.

Kelso, Clare. "Ideology of Mapping in Apartheid South Africa." *South African Geographical Journal* 81, no. 1 (1999): 15–21.

Kirkaldy, Alan. "The Darkness within the Light: Berlin Missionaries and the Landscape of Vendaland, 1870–1900." *Historia* 48, no. 1 (2003): 169–202.

Kirkaldy, Alan, and Lize Kriel. "Converts and Conservatives: Missionary Representations of African Rulers in the Northern Transvaal, 1870–1900." *Social Sciences & Missions* 18 (2006): 109–144.

Kriel, Lize. "African Reaction to White Penetration: The Hananwa of Blouberg, ca. 1886–1894." *Historia* 45, no. 1 (2000): 57–70.

Krikler, Jeremy. "Social Neurosis and Hysterical Pre-Cognition in South Africa: A Case-Study and Reflections." *Journal of Social History* 28, no. 3 (1995): 491–520.

Lehmann, Karin. "Aboriginal Title, Indigenous Rights, and the Right to Culture." *South African Journal of Human Rights* 20 (2004): 86–118.

Lester, Alan. "Cultural Construction and Spatial Strategy on the Eastern Cape Frontier, 1806-c.1838." *South African Geographical Journal* 78, no. 2 (1996): 98–107.

——. “Introduction: Historical Geographies of Southern Africa.” *Journal of Southern African Studies* 29, no. 3 (2003): 595–613.

——. “Humanitarians and White Settlers in the Nineteenth Century.” In *Missions and Empire*, edited by Norman Etherington, 64–85. Oxford: Oxford University Press, 2005.

Lewis, Jack. “The Rise and Fall of the South African Peasantry: A Critique and Reassessment.” *Journal of Southern African Studies* 11, no. 1 (1984): 1–24.

Lewsen, Phyllis. “Liberals in Politics and Administration, 1936–1948,” In *Democratic Liberalism in South Africa: Its History and Prospect*, edited by Jeffrey Butler, Richard Elphick, and David Welsh, 98–115. Cape Town: David Philip, 1987.

Liebenberg, E.C. “Mapping British South Africa: The Case of G.S.G.S. 2230.” *Imago Mundi* 49 (1997): 129–142.

——. “The Role of the Compilation Map in British South Africa.” *The Globe* 46 (1998): 42–58.

——. “Mapping South Africa in the Mid-19th Century: The Cartography of James Centlivres Chase.” *Historia* 52, no. 2 (2007): 1–18.

——. “‘Providing a Tolerably Correct Map of South Africa’: The Cartography of Henry Hall.” In *Proceedings of the International Symposium of the ICA Working Group on the History of Colonial Cartography in the 19th and 20th Centuries* [2006], edited by P. van der Krogt, E.C. Liebenberg, and I.J. Demhardt, Chapter 8. Pretoria: ICA, 2007.

Liesegang, Gerhard. “New Light on Venda Traditions: Mahumane’s Account of 1730.” *History in Africa* 4 (1977): 163–181.

Maasdorp, G.H. “Correspondence: The Red Line System.” *South African Survey Journal* 1 (1925): 334–335.

Maclennan, Don. “The Stone Cairns of Southern Africa.” *The Digging Stick* 17, no. 1 (2000): 7–10.

Maggs, Tim. “The Mpumalanga Escarpment Settlements: Some Answers, Many Questions.” In *Five Hundred Years Rediscovered: Southern African Precedents and Prospects*, edited by Natalie Swanepoel, Amanda Esterhuysen, and Philip Bonner, 169–181. Johannesburg: Witwatersrand University Press, 2008.

McAllister, Patrick. “Resistance to ‘Betterment’ in the Transkei: A Case Study from Willowvale District.” *Journal of Southern African Studies* 15, no. 2 (1989): 346–368.

McEwan, Cheryl. “‘The Mother of the Peoples’: Geographical Knowledge and the Empowering of Mary Slessor.” In *Geography and Imperialism 1820–1940*, edited by John M. MacKenzie, 125–150. Manchester: Manchester University Press, 1995.

Metzer, Jacob, and Stanley Engerman. “Some Considerations of Ethno-nationality (and Other Distinctions), Property Rights in Land, and Territorial Sovereignty.” In *Land Rights, Ethno-Nationality, and Sovereignty in History*, edited by Jacob Metzer and Stanley L. Engerman, 1–15. London: Routledge, 2004.

Mitchell, Laura J. "Global Context, Local Objects, and Cultural Frontiers: Unsettling South Africa's National History in Four Moves." *Settler Colonial Studies* 4, no. 2 (2014): 162–170.

Möller-Malan, Dorothea. "Die Donker Soutpansberg." *Historia* 2, no. 1 (1957): 25–50; *Historia* 2, no. 2 (1957): 167–183; *Historia* 3, no. 1 (1958): 47–53; *Historia* 3, no. 2 (1958):115–121; *Historia* 3, no. 3 (1958): 185–197; *Historia* 3, no. 4 (1958): 256–266.

Morton, Barry "Servitude, Slave Trading, and Slavery in the Kalahari." In *Slavery in South Africa: Captive Labor on the Dutch Frontier*, ed. E.A. Eldredge and F. Morton, 215–250. Boulder: Westview Press, 1994.

Morton, R.F. "Chiefs and Ethnic Unity in Two Colonial Worlds: The BaKgatla baga Kgafela of the Bechuanaland Protectorate and the Transvaal, 1872–1966." In *Partitioned Africans: Ethnic Relations across Africa's International Boundaries, 1994–1984*, edited by A.J. Asiwaju, 127–153. New York: St. Martin's, 1985.

Motenda, M.M. "History of the Venda and of the Lemba." In *The Copper Miners of Musina and the Early History of the Zoutpansberg*, edited and translated by N.J. van Warmelo, 51–70. Pretoria: Government Printer, 1940.

Moyo, Sam. "Three Decades of Agrarian Reform in Zimbabwe." *Journal of Peasant Studies* 38 (2011): 493–531.

Nell, Dawn. "'For the Public Benefit': Livestock Statistics and Expertise in the Late Nineteenth-Century Cape Colony, 1850–1900." In *Science and Society in Southern Africa*, edited by Saul Dubow, 100–115. Manchester: Manchester University Press, 2000.

Nugent, Paul. "Arbitrary Lines and the People's Minds: A Dissenting View on Colonial Boundaries in West Africa." In *African Boundaries: Barriers, Conduits, and Opportunities*, edited by A.J. Asiwaju and Paul Nugent, 35–67. New York: Pinter, 1996.

Obree, J.G., L.F. Braun, and R.C. Fisher, "Land Policy at the Cape and the Office of the Surveyor-General, 1813–1912." In *History of Surveying and Land Tenure Collected Papers Volume 2: Surveying and Land Tenure at the Cape, 1813–1912*, edited by R.C. Fisher, 11–38. Cape Town: IPLSWC, 2004.

Otto, J.C. "Die Regsgronde van die Grondbesit deur die Boere in Noordost Transvaal," *Historiese Studies* 1, no. 4 (1940): 46–59.

Penn, Nigel. "Mapping the Cape: John Barrow and the First British Occupation of the Colony, 1795–1803." In *Maps and Africa*, edited by Jeffrey C. Stone, 108–127. Aberdeen: University of Aberdeen, 1993.

Phoofolo, Pule. "Zafa! Kwahlwa! Kwasa!: African Responses to the Rinderpest Epizootic in the Transkeian Territories, 1897–8." *Kronos* 30 (2004): 94–117.

Pienaar, U. de V. "Karel Trichardt: Pioneer and Explorer." In *A Cameo from the Past: The Prehistory and Early History of the Kruger National Park*, edited by U. de V. Pienaar, 131–145. Pretoria: Protea, 2013.

Posel, Deborah. "A Mania for Measurement: Statistics and Statecraft in the Transition to Apartheid." In *Science and Society in Southern Africa*, edited by Saul Dubow, 116–142. Manchester: Manchester University Press, 2000.

Potgieter, F.J. "Die Vestiging van die Blanke in Transvaal (1837–1886)." *Archives Year Book for South African History* 21, no. 2 (1958).

Pratt, Mary Louise. "Scratches on the Face of the Country; or, What Mr. Barrow Saw in the Land of the Bushmen." *Critical Inquiry* 12, no. 1 (1985): 119–143.

Rich, Paul. "The Origins of Apartheid Ideology: The Case of Ernest Stubbs and Transvaal Native Administration, c.1902–1932." *African Affairs* 79, no. 315 (1980): 171–194.

Roberts, Richard, and Kristin Mann. "Law in Colonial Africa." In *Law in Colonial Africa*, edited by Kristin Mann and Richard Roberts, 3–58. London: James Currey, 1991.

Robinson, J. "'A Perfect System of Control'? State Power and 'Native Locations' in South Africa." *Environment and Planning D: Society and Space* 8 (1990): 135–162.

Rose-Redwood, Reuben S. "The Surveyor's Model of the World: The Uses and Abuses of History in Introductory Surveying Textbooks." *Cartographica* 39, no. 4 (2004): 45–54.

———. "Indexing the Great Ledger of the Community: Urban House Numbering, City Directories, and the Production of Spatial Legibility." *Journal of Human Geography* 34 (2008): 286–310.

Saunders, C.C. "The Annexation of the Transkeian Territories." *Archives Year Book for South African History* 39 (1976).

———. "Political Processes in the Southern African Frontier Zone." In *The Frontier in History: North America and Southern Africa Compared*, edited by H. Lamar and L. Thompson, 149–71. New Haven: Yale University Press, 1981.

Schaffer, Simon. "Exact Measurement is an English Science." In *The Values of Precision*, edited by M. Norton Wise, 135–172. Princeton: Princeton University Press, 1995.

Schunke, H.C. "Kaffraria und die östlichen Grenz-Distrikte der Kaap-Kolonie," *Petermanns Geographische Mittheilungen* 31 (1885): 161–171, 201–209.

———. "The Transkeian Territories: Their Physical Geography and Ethnology," *Transactions of the South African Philosophical Society* 8, no. 1 (1890–91): 1–11.

Stals, W.A. "Die Kwessie van Naturelle-eiendomsreg op Grond in Transvaal, 1838–1884," *Archives Year Book for South African History* 35, no. 1 (1972).

Stapleton, Timothy. "The Expansion of a Pseudo-Ethnicity on the Eastern Cape: Reconsidering the Fingo 'Exodus' of 1865." *International Journal of African Historical Studies* 29 (1996): 233–250.

———. "'Valuable, Gallant and Faithful Assistants': The Fingo (or Mfengu) as Colonial Military Allies during the Cape-Xhosa Wars, 135–1881." In *Soldiers and Settlers in Africa, 1850–1918*, edited by Stephen Miller, 15–47. Leiden: Brill, 2009.

Stone, Jeffrey C. "Pioneer Geodesy: The Arc of the 30th Meridian in Former Northern Rhodesia." *Cartographic Journal* 13 (1976): 122–128.

Switzer, Les. "The Beginnings of African Protest Journalism at the Cape." In *South Africa's Alternative Press: Voices of Protest and Resistance, 1880–1960*, edited by Les Switzer, 57–82. Cambridge: Cambridge University Press, 1997.

Tempelhoff, J.W.N. "Die Okkupasiestelsel in die Distrik Soutpansberg, 1886–1899." *Archives Year Book for South African History* 60 (1997).

Theron, Bridget. "Theophilus Shepstone and the Transvaal Colony, 1877–1879." *Kleio* 34 (2002): 104–127.

Thompson, Leonard M. "Co-operation and Conflict: The Highveld." In *The Oxford History of South Africa*, edited by Monica Wilson and Leonard M. Thompson, 1: 391–446. Oxford: Oxford University Press, 1971.

Thompson, Leonard M., and Howard Lamar. "Comparative Frontier History." In *The Frontier in History: North America and Southern Africa Compared*, edited by H. Lamar and L. Thompson, 3–13. New Haven: Yale University Press, 1981.

Thompson, R.J., and B.M. Nicholls. "The Glen Grey Act: Forgotten Dimensions on an Old Theme." *South African Journal of Economic History* 8 (1993): 58–70.

Trapido, Stanley. "Reflections on Land, Office, and Wealth in the South African Republic, 1850–1900." In *Economy and Society in Pre-Industrial South Africa*, edited by Shula Marks and Anthony Atmore, 350–368. New York: Longman, 1981.

Tropp, Jacob. "Locust Invasions and Tensions over Environmental and Bodily Health in the Colonial Transkei." In *Indigenous Knowledge and the Environment in Africa and North America*, edited by David M. Gordon and Shepard Krech, 113–128. Athens: Ohio University Press, 2012.

Turner, Frederick Jackson. "The Significance of the Frontier in American History." *Annual Report of the American Historical Association* 4 (1893): 199–227.

Ülgen, Özlem. "Developing the Doctrine of Aboriginal Title in South Africa: Source and Content." *Journal of African Law* 46, no. 2 (2002): 131–154.

Vail, Leroy. "Introduction: Ethnicity in Southern African History." In *The Creation of Tribalism in Southern Africa*, edited by Leroy Vail, 1–19. Berkeley: University of California Press, 1989.

Van den Bergh, Gert. "Voortrekker plaasbesetting op die Transvaalse Hoëveld: 'n Versteurde Beeld." *South African Journal of Surveying and Mapping* 20, no. 7 (1990): 301–311.

Van den Bersselaar Dmitri. "Acknowledging Knowledge: Dissemination and Reception of Expertise in Colonial Africa." *History in Africa* 33 (2006): 389–393.

Van der Merwe, P.J. "Die Matabeles en die Voortrekkers." *Archives Year Book for South African History* 49, no. 2 (1986).

Van der Post, D.J. "Land Law and Registration in Some of the Black Rural Areas of Southern Africa." *Acta Juridica* (1985): 213–240.

Van Jaarsveld, F.A. "Landmeting in die oue dae." *Historiese Studies* 8, no. 1 (1947): 45–53.

——. "Die Veldkornet en sy Aandeel in die Opbou van die Suid-Afrikaanse Republiek tot 1870," *Archives Year Book for South African History* 13 (1950).

Veracini, Lorenzo. "Colonial Genocides: Notes for the Analysis of a Settler Archive." In *Empire, Colony, Genocide: Conquest, Occupation, and Subaltern Resistance in World History*, edited by A. Dirk Moses, 148–161. New York: Berghahn, 2010.

——. "The Imagined Geographies of Settler Colonialism." In *Making Settler Colonial Space: Perspectives on Race, Place and Identity*, edited by Tracey Banivanua Mar and Penelope Edmonds, 179–197. New York: Palgrave Macmillan, 2010.

Vivan, Itala. "Geography, Literature, and the African Territory: Some Observations on the Western Map and the Representation of Territory in the South African Literary Imagination." *Research in African Literatures* 31 (2000): 49–69.

Voigt, Isabel, and Kathrin Fritsch. "Transcultural Aspects of Exploring and Mapping South West Africa between 1850 and 1914." *Journal of Namibian Studies* 9, no. 1 (2011): 61–83.

Wagenaar, E.J.C. "A Forgotten Frontier Zone: Settlements and Reactions in the Stormberg Area between 1820–60." *Archives Year Book for South African History* 45, no. 2 (1984).

Wagner, Roger. "Zoutpansberg: The Dynamics of a Hunting Frontier, 1848–1867." In *Economy and Society in Pre-Industrial South Africa*, edited by Shula Marks and Anthony Atmore, 313–349. New York: Longman, 1981.

Walker, Cherryl. "The Limits to Land Reform: Rethinking 'the Land Question'." *Journal of Southern African Studies* 31, no. 4 (2005): 805–824.

Watts, Michael J. "Idioms of Land and Labor: Producing Politics and Rice in Senegambia." In *Land in African Agrarian Systems*, edited by Thomas J. Bassett and Donald Crummey, 157–193. Madison: University of Wisconsin Press, 1993.

Weaver, John C. "The Dismal Science, Land Reform, and the Cape Boers, 1805–22." *Journal of Imperial and Commonwealth History* 29, no. 3 (2001): 1–32.

Webb, Denver A. "Lords of All They Surveyed? The Royal Engineers, Surveying, Mapping and Development in South Africa's Eastern Cape." *African Historical Review* 45, no. 1 (2013): 22–45.

Webster, Alan. "Unmasking the Fingo: The War of 1835 Revisited." In *The Mfecane Aftermath: Reconstructive Debates in Southern African History*, edited by Carolyn Hamilton, 241–276. Johannesburg: University of Witwatersrand Press, 1995.

Wedepohl, M.W. "Historical Review of Legislation Affecting Surveying and Registration of Land in the Transvaal." *South African Survey Journal* 9, no. 2 (1958): 8–25.

Wilks, Ivor. "On Mentally Mapping Greater Asante: A Study in Time and Motion." *Journal of African History* 33, no. 2 (1992): 175–190.

Williams, Donovan. *UmFundisi: A Biography of Tiyo Soga, 1829–1871*. Lovedale: Lovedale Press, 1978.

Wilson, Francis. "Farming, 1866–1966." In *The Oxford History of South Africa*, edited by Monica Wilson and Leonard M. Thompson, 2: 104–171. Oxford: Oxford University Press, 1971.

Wilson, Monica. "The Growth of Peasant Communities." In *The Oxford History of South Africa*, edited by Monica Wilson and Leonard M. Thompson, 2: 49–103. Oxford: Oxford University Press, 1971.

Woods, Michael. "The Elite Countryside: Shifting Rural Geographies of the Transnational Super-Rich." In *Geographies of the Super-Rich*, edited by Iain Hay, 123–136. Cheltenham: Edward Elgar, 2013.

Wright, John K. "Sonqua, Bosjesmans, Bushmen, and abaThwa: Comments and Queries on Pre-Modern Identification." *South African Historical Journal* 35, no. 2 (1996): 16–29.

———. "Turbulent Times: Political Transformations in the North and East, 1760s–1830s." In *The Cambridge History of South Africa* vol. 1, edited by C. Hamilton, B. Mbenga, and R. Ross, 211–252. Cambridge: Cambridge University Press, 2010.

Yanou, Mike Akomaye. "The 1913 Cut-off Date for Restitution of Dispossessed Land in South Africa: A Critical Appraisal." *Africa Development* (*Afrique et Developpment*) 31, no. 3 (2006): 177–188.

Zakiewicz, Tomasz. "Units of Length Measure and Geodetic Standards at the Cape, 1813–1912." In *The History of Surveying and Land Tenure Collected Papers Volume 2*, edited by R.C. Fisher, 181–209. Cape Town: IPLSWC, 2004.

Zimudzi, Tapiwa. "Power Syndrome: Robert Mugabe and the Land Reform and Governance Crisis in Zimbabwe." *South African Historical Journal* 47 (2002): 213–228.

Theses and Dissertations

Ally, R.T. "The Development of the System of Individual Tenure for Africans, with special reference to the Glen Grey Act, c.1894–1922." Master's thesis, Rhodes University, 1985.

Bouch, Richard. "The Colonization of Queenstown (Eastern Cape) and its Hinterland, 1852–1886." PhD diss., University of London, 1992.

Cilliers, J.H. "Die Administrasie en Benutting van Transvaalsse Kroongrond 1900–1906." D.Litt et Phil diss., UNISA 1978.

Erasmus, D.J. "Re-thinking the Great Trek: A Study of the Nature and Development of the Boer Community in the Ohrigstad/Lydenburg Area, 1845–1877." Master's thesis, Rhodes University, 1995.

Jones, B.M. "The Apportionment, Tenure, Registration, and Survey of Land in Southern Africa and Proposals for the Establishment of a Cadastral System for the Bantu Areas of South Africa." PhD diss., University of Natal, 1964.

Liebenberg, E.C. "Die Topografiese Kartering van Suid-Afrika 1879–1972." Master's thesis, UNISA, 1973

Manona, Cordwell Sizwe. "Captain Matthew Smith Blyth's Work in South Africa, 1869–89." Master's thesis, UNISA, 1973.

Mulaudzi, Maanda. "'U shuma bulasi': Agrarian transformation in the Zoutpansberg District of South Africa, up to 1946." PhD diss., University of Minnesota, 2000.

Mumford, Ian. "Milestones in Nineteenth-Century Lithography." PhD diss., University of Reading, 1999.

Naude, Petrus. "Boerdery in die Suid-Afrikaanse Republiek, 1858–1899." 2 vols. D.Litt. diss., University of Pretoria, 1945.

Nemudzivhadi, M.H. "The Conflict between Mphephu and the South African Republic, 1895–1899." Master's thesis, UNISA, 1977.

Nemudzivhadi, M.H. "The Attempts by Makhado to Revive the Venda Kingdom, 1864–1895." PhD diss., Potchefstroom University for Christian Higher Education, 1998.

Rademeyer, J.I. "Die Oorlog teên Magato (M'Pefu) 1898." Master's thesis, UNISA, 1943.

Ralushai, Victor N.M.N. "Conflicting Accounts of Venda History with Particular Reference to the Role of Mutupo to Social Organisation." PhD diss., Queen's University Belfast, 1977.

Robson, L.G. "The Royal Engineers and Settlement Planning in the Cape Colony, 1806–1872." PhD diss., University of Pretoria, 2011.

Spicer, M.W. "The War of Ngcayecibi, 1877–8." Master's thesis, Rhodes University, 1978.

Stals, W.A. "Die Britse Beleid teenoor en Administrasie van die Swartes in Transvaal, 1877–1881." D.Phil diss., University of Pretoria, 1985.

Theron-Bushell, Bridget. "Puppet on an Imperial String? Owen Lanyon in South Africa, 1875–1881." D.Litt et Phil diss., UNISA, 2002.

Thompson, R.J. "Cecil Rhodes, the Glen Grey Act, and the Labour Question in the Politics of the Cape Colony." Master's thesis, Rhodes University, 1991.

Wagenaar, E.J.C. "A History of the Thembu and Their Relationship with the Cape Colony, 1850–1900." PhD diss., Rhodes University, 1990.

Van Rensburg, J.F.J. "Die Opmeet en Toeken van Grond in die Oranje Vrystaat tot 1902." PhD diss., University of the Free State, 1990.

Internet Publications

Centre for Law and Society, Rural Women's Action Research Programme, University of Cape Town. *Custom Contested: Views & Voices* (blog). http://www.customcontested.co.za/.

Institute for Poverty, Land, and Agrarian Studies. *Another Countryside* (blog). http://www.plaas.org.za/blog/.

Limpopo Tourism and Parks Board. http://www.golimpopo.com/.

Index